By the same Author

Autobiography
THE PUPIL: A Memory of Love (Wolfhound Press 1981)
THE SEALS (1925)
THE CLIMATE OF LOVE (1961)
INGLORIOUS SOLDIER (1968)
THE BRAHMS WALTZ (1970)

Poetry
THE TREMULOUS STRING (1926)
THE BRANCH OF HAWTHORN TREE (1927)
FOR DAWS TO PECK AT (1929)
SEVENTEEN SONNETS (1932)
THE INSUBSTANTIAL PAGEANT (1951)
THE VELVET BOW AND OTHER POEMS (1972)

Literary Criticism
THE MASTERPIECE AND THE MAN OR
YEATS AS I KNEW HIM (1959)

Biography
NETTA (1960)

Travel
SWISS ENCHANTMENT (1950)
AUSTRIA (1953)
WESTERN GERMANY (1955)
THE RHINE AND ITS CASTLES (1957)
IN SEARCH OF WINTER SPORT (1953)

Ballet and Film Ballet
AN INTRUDER AT THE BALLET (1952)
THE RED SHOES BALLET (1948)
TALES OF HOFFMANN (1951)

Anthology
THE LIVING TORCH (A.E.) (1937)

MOUNT IDA

Monk Gibbon

WOLFHOUND PRESS

Published 1983
WOLFHOUND PRESS
68 Mountjoy Square, Dublin 1.

© 1983, 1948 Monk Gibbon

British Library Cataloguing in Publication Data

Gibbon, Monk
    Mount Ida.
    1. Gibbon, Monk — Biography
    2. Authors, Irish — 20th Century — Biography
    I. Title
    821'.912   PR6013.I23

    ISBN 0-905473-99-X

TO

THE KNOWN BELOVED

MOUNT IDA

BEAUTY, goodness, truth, these three,
Found a boy, no shepherd he,
Nor of Priam, nor indeed
To high destiny decreed.

Spake to him, while youth still ran
In the throbbing veins its span,
'Choose between us now and name
Which shall have the foremost claim?'

Long he pondered, since, alas,
Lovely each as other was.
First to one would almost turn,
Straight her neighbour made heart burn.

'Thee. No, thee. No, thee, whose brow
Such clear serenity does show.
Wait! for in her sister's eyes
Still more constant kindness lies.'

Thus did waver, while youth ran
All too swift its measured span;
Until, tiring of the play,
In scorn, they turned from him away.

Now, alone, behold him, he,
Who too faintly loved all three,
Thrice-deserted, envy-green,
Cry, 'Would my choice had beauty been!'

But the Mount Ida of this book is not the Mount Ida of the poem – which has lain long in a drawer unpublished – nor are the goddesses of the poem the goddesses in question now. The rival claims of beauty, truth and goodness, for that matter, are not inconsistent with one another; nor, for the wise, has any conflicting choice necessarily to be made. Indeed like Bottom's purposed prologue to Pyramus and Thisbe it seems that if the poem is printed at all everything in it must be explained to be something else. But to do so here would be a mistake. A book should explain itself. No prologue should be longer than Moon's well-spoken footnote to his part on that same occasion: 'All that I have to say is to tell you that the lanthorn is the moon, I, the man in the moon; this thorn-bush my thorn-bush; and this dog, my dog.'

MOUNT IDA

PART I

WHEN my great-uncle, John Edge, died a number of his possessions came to my father, and when my father died these
passed to me. In a house where nothing had been discarded for
thirty years and where many things had accumulated, the accretions
of sentiment not of one but of several generations, I found much
which was trivial and worthless; but one thing was to give me grave
and genuine pleasure.

It was a stereoscope. More than sixty years before, John Edge had
bought it in Naples from 'Grillet, Photographe du Roi, in the Via
Parthenope.' Of all his possessions, including even his books, and he
had a fine library, it was this perhaps which pleased me most.

I have not yet forgotten the stab of delight which this seventy-year-
old toy gave me. The photographs were on glass against a milky-
white backing which did not interfere with their transparency when
held up to the light. One raised what seemed to be a pair of bin-
oculars to one's eyes, focused them and was miraculously translated.
It was no peep-show at which one gazed. So good were the slides, so
faithful the effect of distance and perspective that there was nothing
to suggest that the panorama was not actually there. If any further
degree of realism had been necessary, it was provided by a small
mirror in the top of the stereoscope. By holding it up to the window
and tilting it one could get any desired effect of light and shade.
One could produce dawn, midday or dusk at will, bathe the slopes
of a mountain in sunlight, or plunge those same slopes into the
greyness of late afternoon, a greyness in which it seemed possible
that at any minute one would see the first flakes of a new fall of
snow darkening the air.

I looked into a lost world. The scene was an orchard in Switzerland in spring facing up a hillside towards a hotel perched on a
rounded eminence at the entrance to a narrow valley. Everywhere
there were indications of the freshness and prodigality of the season.
One looked across the wall of a garden, a wall eaved with tiles, to
the orchard where apple trees were in flower above roughly-turned
earth. Behind and above the orchard rose the pine-covered slopes of
a gorge where a drifting fringe of mist could be seen against the
flank of the mountain. Through the thick leafage of the foreground
one caught a glimpse of a neighbouring roof, some farm or villa

barely visible amongst the trees. The light shone on the leaves, as though after a shower of rain, and one could see between and beyond them each leaf in separate relief and with the transparency and translucency which sunlight gives. One could distinguish between the shimmering leaves of a poplar and the flat shining leaves of what was probably a young beech. Across the top of the wall a spray of mimosa trailed its fernlike softness. In the garden a slender pole carrying a wire stood out with absolute saliency.

What I saw had all the intimacy of the actual, yet those leaves on which I gazed, and on which the light glistened so joyously, had dropped from their stems perhaps seventy years before. The soil under the apple trees in that hillside orchard had been turned again and again. More than sixty winters had come in succession and reproved the exuberance of the spring which gave them birth. To look was to be reminded of the eternal sequence, life for ever giving with one hand and taking with the other. The leaves drop from the trees. The freshness of every spring dies and is again reborn. It is not only man who destroys. If Time is a vandal perpetually sacking the city of human endeavour and levelling it with the dust, Nature herself is a Penelope, for ever unravelling the beautiful web which she herself has made, building up the forms only to destroy them again, almost as soon as created.

What pleased me so much was the thought that with the stereoscope I had not merely conquered space, but had effectively triumphed over the still more relentless enemy, Time. I saw the Boulevard Montmartre in Paris one hot afternoon in summer before the Franco-Prussian War, the shop fronts shaded and throwing their deep black shadows on to the dusty pavement of the street. Six black-coated and top-hatted gentlemen had elected to climb on to the top of a horse-bus, in which one rode inside. Eight other vehicles were in sight, the social rank of each of them unmistakable, despite the fact that the drivers of every one, except the bus, were also wearing top hats. There was the obviously-hired open victoria, with its tired horse, slowly conveying a tourist about the city; the smart cabriolet with the very erect coachman, waiting outside while her ladyship shopped; the staid brougham, respectable but without style, drawn by its white horse; lifting slightly leaden feet, the little pony and cart delivering the laundry, the pony dozing unattended beside the pavement, while a bootblack drowsed against a lamp-post nearby and an almost-crinolined lady eyed him, meditatively, as though in two minds whether to have her shoes cleaned or not.

14

I saw this street in Paris, this sultry moment in a July long past, given its dusty immortality. I saw the Rhine, winding unhurried through low-lying meadows and past high-castled crags. I saw the Matterhorn, still inviolate, three years before Whymper climbed it. I saw the cascade of Griesbach, and the tea-garden beside it, a carafe of water standing upon one of the iron tables set out beneath the trees. I saw the Mauvais Pas de l'Aiguille du Charmoz, at a time when alpenstocks were still fashionable and ladies climbed in skirts.

But of all the views the one that held me longest was one of the water lane at Clarens flowing down its narrow alley between leafy banks, flanked by a paved pathway where tall weeds flourished in profusion. I knew the place myself. I had visited it, and now, somersaulting through time, I saw it at a moment before ever I had gone there. On the far side of the road bridging the stream two chalets, a jumble of successive additions and alterations, so old that seventy odd years can have made little difference to them, basked in the sun. Under their wide eaves hung ropes of onions and a line of washing. It was midsummer. The sunlight threw everything into strong relief, the washing drying on a balcony, the rungs of a ladder against the wall, some wood stacked in a heap. In a strip of garden, separated by a low stone parapet from the stream, onions were growing, their tops already beginning to seed. Looking up the course of the stream one could pick out the separate stalks of grass which sprouted in tufts from the wall, stalks so slender and real that it seemed as though at any minute a wind might stir them. A girl was seated on this low wall, her hands on her lap, while in the shadow nearby, a shadow so deep as to make him at first remain unnoticed, a young man, holding one of those huge straw hats which vine-dressers wear, stood as though silently contemplating her. Whoever had taken the picture had caught them, probably at midday, in one of those moments of brief relaxation, when, even for the labourer, time stands still. They, and the scene in which they figured, seemed part of a serene dream; and the dream was life. As I looked towards them, time fused. This moment, three-quarters of a century before, blended with another eight years back when I had visited the same spot, and when the sun, making its spangled tracery on those very stones, had shone through the leaves on my face as it shone on the face of the vine-dresser now – or, rather, many years ago.

He can have little thought as he stood there by the millrace at mid-day, half in warm sunlight, half in shade, enjoying a momentary lull in the day's work, that this alone of all his actions in life would survive on record. It survived and I contemplated it now on a thin sheet of glass. It was impossible that he could still be living, but if he were, and if I were to seek him out and remind him of the occasion, he would inevitably have long since forgotten it. Only a tithe of human experience escapes reaching immediate limbo. The peasant's life, inarticulate, without scribe or witness, always anonymous, passes soonest of all to the still greater anonymity of death.

And, my thoughts leaving them, I asked myself for how many moments in my own life would I desire a like survival. How much of the sum and total of our days would we wish recorded, so that a stranger, long after, might know that it had been? Change is the law of our being and yet our instinct is for the eternal. The best moments in life are often indefinable, fragile, inexpressibly slight, a compound of mood, condition and time, defying analysis. Some possess almost mystical significance, as, for instance, that moment when, looking at someone we have disliked, we catch an expression of great weariness and fatigue in their face and our heart fills instantly with reverence, with a sense of overwhelming pity, a sudden flooding of goodwill, as though to say, 'You too, poor fellow traveller, find this business of living a hard one.'

Christians and ancients alike knew this moment of pity as a good one, a complete catharsis of the soul. And as well as this there are others equally brief, equally intangible, of the same profound significance, messengers which come, deliver their message, and depart. But it was not of these that I was thinking when I asked myself whether it would be possible to look into the past and to see there, recorded as in a mirror, the exact scene, the precise occasion, without addition or embellishment. It was rather of the visual, the dramatic, of that arrested instant, as in the water lane at Clarens, when the pattern of our life becomes vivid, and seems part of that other pattern which is the changing panorama of Nature. It is strange that men of letters, who are affected as strongly as any one class by this nostalgia for the past, prefer in most cases to mix life with imagination before they record it, taking from it a little of its authenticity before setting it down. Perhaps in the long run a man's imaginations are as real as his deeds; in the case of genius the former outlast the latter, the 'insubstantial pageant' of existence is the first to fade, and Hamlet in a sense outlives his creator. But to certain minds the real, the actual, is imbued with romance, simply because it was the real. To such minds the fact that a thing took place gives it a significance quite unaffected by the fact that now, as part of the past rather than the present, it has scarcely any greater validity than a dream. Once it was real. Even in the quite trivial memoirs of uninteresting people they can detect something which – because the image reflected is from life – fiction lacks.

To be happy is to wish time to stand still. Life slips from us continually, but for a long time we do not realise it. It seems as though it flowed towards us rather than flowed away. This is the real climacteric, when we realise, what youth for some reason has never troubled to heed, that the stream recedes from us as well as approaches. In that moment age casts its first shadow upon the grass. This nostalgia for lost beauty, what is it? We do not come into the world with it, any more than a child knows what homesickness is until the first parting has taken place. But from that moment when, returning to something we had loved, or revisiting something that had given us pleasure, we find it even in the minutest degree changed, less than itself – in that moment we waken to the whole pathos of circumstance. Only the young live in a world that is not consciously slipping from them. Once let us become aware of this ebbing of the very tide which delights us and it is hard not to let it colour even our happiest moments, if we allow them to become reflective. If we were philosophers we would think of beauty as being eternally reborn as well as eternally perishing, of the upthrust of petals not yet unfolded, as well as the fluttering of dead leaves towards the ground; of faces in which a certain grace gives as yet only an inkling of what will presently be, or of limbs to be endowed with swiftness, that have not yet even formed in the womb. But we are not philosophers, or rather we can only philosophise as far as regret, regret for a past that has slipped from us.

We can never completely recreate that past because to do so we should first have to recreate ourselves. Indeed, it is very doubtful if we remember things at all. Rather we remember our emotions about things. If the occasion and scene is recollected it is because it formed a background to our own feelings in respect to them. Joy is a good remembrancer, fear is another. Anything which strikes severely at self-esteem is likely to remain fixed in memory, cut in acid as though on copper plate. I can see myself as a young subaltern in the First World War, standing in a dingy room of the Town Hall of Marquise, being savagely rated by my major for wearing gumboots instead of riding boots on a wet day on convoy duty; and, because of the cruelty of his remarks, occasion and setting are sharply fixed in my mind. Or I am on the Somme, months later, returning with my wagons from a spot where forty men a day are said to be killed, and fear – now that it is behind me – is succeeded by such a keen sense of relief, that the sight of a dead horse lying by the roadside seems only to emphasise the exultation of my mood, and my joy in living. Or I am in Ireland, years before, at my grand-father's country home, kneeling as a child on a wide beach near some sand-dunes, lifting up the warm sand in my palms and allowing it to trickle slowly out through my fingers; and such contentment – such oblivion of all past personal distress and all present contemporaneous world misery – fills my being, such consciousness of the complete benevolence of occasion and place towards me, that I seem almost to be tasting eternal bliss.

The sand-dunes in Wexford, ruined Sailly, the dusty office-room in Normandy are remembered because emotion fixed them in memory. But the greater part of life slips from us, and even the occasions emotion has touched are blurred in recollection, if we have never recorded them. Most men have been in love, but how many of them can remember, other than dimly, what they felt, when they were? And yet of all experiences it is the most salient. Falling in love tells us almost more about ourselves than love itself. It is the moment of apprehension, of recognition, when the soul seems on the point of becoming self-aware. 'In love and beauty if anywhere,'' says Santayana, 'even the common man thinks he has visitations from a better world, approaches to a lost happiness; a happiness never tasted by us in this world, and yet so natural, so expected, that we look for it at every corner, in every new face; we look for it with so much confidence, with so much depth of expectation that we never quite overcome our disappointment that it is not found.'

If we were to salve anything from life it might well be such moments as these. And not merely the moment when we loved deeply, for it is the inclination of many men to keep silent about what touches them so intimately, but the moment when we stood as it were on the threshold of love, when we crossed it for an instant, or when it needed only a slight change of circumstance to have made us enter that transfigured territory. If we re-enter that country we should come as the returned exile rather than as the geographer anxious to chart its territories. The metaphysic of love will puzzle us. When Middleton Murry asks, 'Was it indeed Beauty which called forth Love, or was it Love discovered Beauty? Is it the presence of Love within men's hearts – the awakening of a strange emotion – which tells them that Beauty is there; or is it that they perceive

Beauty and the effect of that perception upon them is to awaken Love?' – we pause, confronted with a philosophic problem of such magnitude that it seems impossible to discuss it without discussing all the ultimates.

But though love belongs to the profundities, though it submits no more patiently to analysis than existence itself, nevertheless it remains a fact, and if we turn back on our lives there are few of us who will not presently encounter it. It is the jest of the comedians. Men jest of whatever lies nearest to their hearts and touches them most seriously, so that in war, as I have seen myself, there is no jest so often on their lips as that of death. In the same way love's sighs, its sleeplessness, the immense importance it attaches to what in other circumstances would be mere triviality, its selfishness, its preoccupation with its own concerns, combined with its universal and carefree goodwill, all these things amuse those who have been, or are afraid they may become, its victims. The Greek poet was right who, invoking God to help him to keep his own wits while writing of the passions of others said, 'For there was never any yet who could wholly escape love, and never shall be any, never so long as beauty shall be, never so long as eyes can see.'

We may deride love, we may regret it, but there can hardly be a man who, looking into the past and being reminded of his own youth, does not at some time feel moved to say, what the Chinese said long ago about it, in one of their proverbs, 'All other pleasures are not worth its pains.'

AFTER the First World War I studied farming and later became a schoolmaster. I did this partly to escape melancholy. If we live with the young we share to some degree in their light-heartedness and we are as indifferent to their sorrows, or rather their griefs seem as trivial to us as ours perhaps to God.

I became a pedagogue, usher in a small boarding-school of about thirty boys. Every time the train takes me to Holyhead on my way to Ireland I catch a glimpse of the scene of my bondage. Looking out of the window, soon after Chester is passed, as we sweep through a succession of those seaside resorts which have made the North Wales coast what it is, I wait for that brief moment when, in a flash, like to a man drowning or merely, as one has told us, falling from his mule in the Pyrenees, his whole life suddenly unrolls before him. I shall see, if I am quick, just enough to make me relive the past. As we thunder through the empty station, with that rhythmic metallic beat of wheels which seems to quicken, or perhaps merely to gain in force, through some echo from the deserted platform, it unfolds for an instant. I may see only the station hotel whose threshold I crossed on a single occasion; or merely get a lightning glimpse of the village street which, since it is set at right angles to the railway line, is gone in the blink of an eyelid; but whatever it is, it will hold just sufficient evanescent familiarity to recreate a brief period in my life, like an empty scent-bottle from which the scent has gone, but which still yields, if the stopper is removed, a faint aroma of its former perfume.

I remember my first arrival in the place. It was autumn. The summer influx of visitors was over and by the fourth week in September the little town, trim, cheerful and clean, straggling outwards from a central core of shops, was already settling back into its winter sleep of respectability and quiet. After the departure of the holiday-makers something of its original simplicity, its virginity, which it must have lost about thirty years before, returned to it in winter. A village had stood in this spot for well over a century, but, except for the church and a few cold-looking stone or slate cottages on the outskirts, everything gave the impression of recent growth, there seemed to be no building of any age, only prosperous shops, neat villas recently sprung up, and pleasant detached houses, sheltered from the road by gardens and shrubberies which cannot have been more than fifteen or twenty years in growing.

Vandeleur,[1] the Headmaster, met me at the station. He was a man of middle height, bearing himself with the careful carriage of those who, halfway through their sixties, have no intention of yielding to age before they must. Without an actual stoop, but with a slight disposition, that of his profession, to poke head and shoulders forward and to thrust his hands behind his back at odd moments, his solitary figure in black coming forward along the platform filled me with a sudden uneasiness as soon as he drew near enough for me to see his face, for it was a face deeply red, almost purple, suffused, with heavy eyes and slightly pendulous underlids, blood-hound's eyes, a face that might have suggested – but quite unjustly – the drunkard's, the face of a man passionate, irascible, who all his

[1] I have changed his name.

life had been fighting against a demon of temper. He was a clergyman but had been schoolmastering for more than forty years. Proudly emblazoned on the title-page of his prospectus were the words: 'A School for the Sons of Gentlemen.' In these words I always saw a hint to those who were doubtful on the score of their gentility to make it their choice and thus clinch the matter finally.

We walked up from the station together, and as we went he told me about the school, how it had moved to its present quarters which had been specially built for it about three years before, and how he had been able to get the architect to embody a number of his own suggestions in the building so that it could be converted at any time into two semi-detached dwelling-places.

'The boys are not back yet. They come to-morrow. You will be teaching English and History to all forms, and other subjects to some of the juniors. You and my son-in-law, who is my right-hand man, share the supervision of games. He and my daughter live beside us. He is reading for his final and so I am trying to spare him as much as possible. My daughter has a small day-school for girls. You will meet them both at tea, and they will be dining with us this evening. My wife is away at the moment, so they come up more often.'

We had come up the main street and out of the town and now, leaving the nucleus of a brand-new garden city on our right, we turned up a short blind road which ran a little way and then stopped, unable to go any further because of the steeply-rising flank of the mountain immediately ahead. I remember my satisfaction at finding that we were outside the town and that, with the exception of the house Vandeleur had built for his married daughter, and one other across the road on the edge of a field in which long rank grass grew until such time as the builder's board should be taken down, we had no neighbours and there was nothing to obstruct our open views. The school itself was a fine building with red-tiled roof, wide eaves, and timbered in Jacobean style. It faced south-west, looking out on the brown copse of undergrowth clothing the lower slopes of the hill which rose immediately on our left, and further afield to country still unspoilt, to the green tumbled hillside with its great quarry at Dyserth, and the scattered group of old cottages beside it. That ridge of hill, at right angles to the sea, almost wild, save for its stone walls, sheep and occasional grey-slated house, was to become a hinterland for me to escape to in days to come, a region where one could still dream without being reminded of one's fellow creatures or of anything except the bleak countryside, the stone walls and grey boulders and the long, straight, frozen ridge turned up by the plough.

'Well, we are nearly there.'

Walking beside me with his brisk but slightly prudent step, my new employer corresponded almost exactly to my conception of an eighteenth-century Tory parson, courtly, dapper, a savourer, I imagined, of the good things of life, but at the same time the conscious representative of Church and State. He had a tendency to direct his gaze towards the ground, and it required an almost imperceptible effort for him to look directly at you. But when he did look at you, from under those lowered brows, his gaze, though a little searching and bloodshot, was friendly enough. It was plain that he wished to put me at my ease, had high hopes of me, those hopes which – despite innumerable disappointments – every headmaster of a private school entertains when a new member of his staff arrives.

'Come along. It is almost tea-time.'

We went through a wooden gate and up some steps to a small porch at the side of the building. I was shown into a hall, furnished with taste and very different from the bleak desolation of so many boys' schools. At tea in the drawing-room I was introduced to his daughter, sallow, black-haired and a little weary-looking; and to his son-in-law, a grave young man, short and stocky, who gave the impression that he was exercising that severe degree of self-control necessary in anyone who is trying to live with his wife's relations. With them was a Miss Winsor, a middle-aged, trim, amusing little governess, lean as a snipe, well trained in her vocation, a newcomer like myself and a colleague, for, though much of her work would be at the girls' school, she taught also in our junior forms and had all her meals with us. She was used to young children, had been teaching for years, but this was her first school post, and she had as many questions to ask as I had. We chattered away. Everyone talked hopefully. All terms begin in this spirit of zest and enthusiasm. It is right that they should. They end with almost equal certainty in a spirit of fatigue, irritability and frayed nerves.

Next day the term began. I had been free in the morning to wander round, to go down the town and purchase a few things for the tiny study which had been held out as an incentive to someone with an interest in literary pursuits. Soon after lunch the first pupils began to arrive. They were new boys and their arrival was as dramatic to them as mine had been to me the previous day. Generally a parent accompanied them, full of those pathetic and apologetic

22

footnotes to personal idiosyncrasy which nearly every parent wishes to make on these occasions, but which the wise, the stern, and the very diffident forbear making. But by six o'clock these early comers had ceased to be lonely oases in the desert of an empty class-room, and were being jostled by a crowd of noisy, cocksure, confident youth, everyone talking together, exchanging their holiday experiences, asking questions, all equally intent on making the best of the *fait accompli*, and not betraying by the flicker of an eyelid that they were the smallest degree homesick. For a number of them this was true; they enjoyed the noise and bustle, they definitely preferred community life; and since these were generally the hardier spirits they set the tone for the rest. Only when I saw some slightly pensive expression, a faint nausea, a mere aloofness, did I know that a boy was either new or that home still had power to exercise its nostalgic sway; and it was towards these boys that I gravitated, glad to think, as I watched a smile slowly mount to their faces, that by a word or two I could make them feel a little less lonely.

I was launched on my new career. I came to it from an existence with hardly any degree of external compulsion, and for that reason I found this most exacting of all routines particularly hard. For a number of years after the war I had lived a life of relative idleness. A grateful Government, grateful to an extremely indifferent soldier, had given me a disability pension and the opportunity of studying farming in the Channel Islands. There I had tasted a life as idyllic as the life one reads of in books. Jersey had altered hardly at all from the time when Victor Hugo lived there; its villas were the same neat one-storied villas which he had known, and their rose-hung verandas must have greeted his eyes with much the same show of blossom as they greeted mine. In some respects, conditions in the island were still feudal, in others almost Biblical. I thrashed mustard with a flail in a field overlooking the blue waters of St. Aubin's Bay. I watched old women in sun-bonnets leading home at the end of the day half a dozen mild-eyed, saffron-coloured cows, with chains round their horns, from the pastures where they had been tethered. And I would be an ingrate if I ever forgot how for three years and more my winter of the spirit was succeeded by a late spring in which all that the war had deprived me of was restored. I had been little more than a boy when I had first put on uniform. My military career had embraced successive stages of enthusiasm, disillusion, and final embitterment. The effect of the war on me had been to make more acute than ever the *Sturm und Drang* period through which in any case I would have been passing. But in Jersey, still pursued by melancholy, but with a wealth of influence to counteract it I forgot political acerbities; bitterness found a solvent in friends, in the company of children, and in scenery as unspoilt as any that Theocritus describes. I tasted happiness such as I had not known since childhood. The war, and my reading at that time, had made me an agnostic, but it seemed to me now that God might well have had a hand in this creation which confronted me, and that in more than one respect it was good.

But even Arcady can betray us. Mine betrayed me. When at last I left Jersey it was in a mood chastened and unhappy and I had been roused into seeing in any routine activity a remedy for that depression which threatens us when our affairs have gone wrong and when we have too much time to think about them. Teaching was to be my salvation, or so I was given to understand.

I had bowed my neck to the yoke. I did not find it easy. The tenor and tempo of my days was changed completely. My farming had only been a sort of pastime resorted to on account of ill-health. I had held the handles of a plough once or twice; I had attended bee-keeping demonstrations by an elderly clergyman; I had groomed the yellow and fawn-coloured Jersey cattle, beautiful as deer, and had seen them led round the show-ring by their proud owners. I had found subjects for more than one poem in the bucolic peace of my surroundings and in contemplating others working. But it had been a case of playing at farming; the farmer to whom I was attached was quite content if he saw me for a small part of each day. I was never anything but a free agent.

But now every instant of my day was accounted for. From the time I rose at 7 a.m. until dinner at 7.30 in the evening there was hardly a moment that I could call my own. If I was not teaching or supervising games or preparation, or taking the boys for a walk, I was expected to be keeping a friendly – or unfriendly – eye upon their activities out of school hours. I lived in a whirl of busy happenings. I was perpetually having questions fired at me, answering them or else asking them myself.

'But why haven't you got a pen?'

'No, I don't think you are in this class.'

'All right. If you say Matron wants you, I suppose you must go.'

An old trout knows the pool, and its whirls and eddies mean nothing to him. But a new post, even to the experienced, until he adapts himself to his environment, is tiring; while to the neophyte it is exhausting. Meals are no respite, for they carry with them as much responsibility, as much need for concentrated attention, as any other time.

'Please, sir, can you tell us——'

'Oh, yes, sir, we want to know——'

'I will, but don't put your elbows on the table——'

If I had been more accustomed to it, I might have found in the regularity and certainty of the routine a certain compensation. The life was pleasant enough in many ways. During the day the school was always lively, bustling and cheerful. Breakfast was an eager babbling of young voices, lunch a heightened version of the same. There was a breathing space of about twenty minutes in the morning when the boys had cocoa, and we gathered in Vandeleur's study, listening to a chorus of voices just outside the door, and drinking a cup of tea before joining the boys in the playground. Afternoon tea in the drawing-room was another brief interlude. Then we sat round the cake-stand, sipped tea out of fine china, ate currant cake, pretending for the moment that we were human beings, but prepared, the instant the minute-hand reached twenty-five minutes past four, to gather up the bundle of exercise books from the chair by the door and beat a hasty retreat. Whatever other complaint could be brought against the life, one could not say that it was static. The question always was, 'What next?' and it was a question to which one could be always absolutely certain there was some answer.

It is true that I was fond of children, had had many child friends in Jersey, and had even written and published character sketches about them. But it is one thing to love children as a kind of spontaneous recreation, while they are still unspoiled by community life, with all their native charm and originality untouched; and another to love them in a school, where they have become herd-conscious, noisy and obtuse, and to love them under these conditions from eight till one, and from two till seven. My work was not so much arduous as endless. I had had no previous experience in teaching; but to read *Æsop's Fables* with seven-year-olds, or Shakespeare with fourteen-year-olds, to follow the course of the arrow until it duly lodges in Harold's eye, or to drown the Duke of Clarence in a butt of Malmsey wine does not unduly tax the intelligence. In addition, I taught Latin to beginners, and arithmetic to children who had a short while since left their cradles. I was well fed, but I had as much freedom as a domestic servant – that is to say, I was free on Thursday afternoons, and on every other Sunday, and if I went out in the evening I was expected to mention the fact to Vandeleur, lest the school should be left without a master.

The grindstone to which I had surrendered my nose was merciless.

'I wonder if you could give these small boys something to do while the others are drilling.'

'Please, sir, we're to ask you for some prep.'

'Matron wants to know——'

'Perhaps you could undertake——?'

I felt overwhelmed. And there was more to it than that. Let the truth be told. I was just a little ashamed of being a schoolmaster at all. I thought of myself rather as a poet, or poet in the making. But no one who desires an assistant master for his school deliberately engages a poet. A schoolmaster is one kind of monomaniac, a writer is another. It is nearly always a mistake for monomaniacs to think that they can co-operate usefully; someone is sure to have the worst of the bargain.

I had been given to understand before ever I came that I would be able to find some time for literary pursuits, and the promise of a study of my own had been taken by me as an earnest of this. The study proved to be a small room sandwiched between the senior boys' play-room and the corridor and main classrooms, and equipped with table, armchair, tiny fireplace and gas-jet – bare, unattractive, but a distinct and welcome haven of refuge to me. From the moment I entered it I felt myself once more my own master. When I shut the door I shut everything out from me – school, colleagues, even the boys playing next door – as though they had ceased to exist. A book and the typescript of some poem, the last number of the Irish literary weekly to which I was an occasional contributor, the fire to which I drew up the battered armchair, and the table at which I sat down to write – none of these had any association or connection with the rest of my day. Vandeleur had been told that I was an expert in English subjects and ardently fond of children. He saw this ardent child-lover and literary expert, who I am sure he had hoped, at the very least, would start a school magazine, escape to his room on every possible occasion for a little peace and quiet. But for this privacy my life would have been almost unbearable. It was this which restored my independence and self-esteem, this and perhaps the sight of some words of mine on the printed page. Only thus could I rehabilitate myself in my own eyes.

Perhaps it was as well that Miss Winsor, the colleague who had arrived with me, new to school teaching, but well trained in her vocation as governess, accustomed to young children and without any great educational heresies, was a contrast to me in every respect. She knew her work and she earned her salary, and it is not certain that I did either. It was strange, but I suppose by mere effervescence and cheek, and perhaps by her detection of a genuine underlying good intention behind all my theories, I won her approval and we were good friends. If I did nothing else, I made her laugh, outwardly, and still more often inwardly. She saw in me a rebel against the conventions. She was one of the subdued trio at dinner each evening. There was a formal courtesy about this meal which I secretly appreciated. It formed the one link between myself and my employer. I had soon discovered that he was quick-tempered and violent. In class his voice was capable of rising to a howl of frenzy. But from 7.30 on the tempo of the school slowed down and Vandeleur became the elderly clergyman rather than the schoolmaster. School topics were abandoned and we deliberately discussed other things. Sometimes we spoke little during the meal, but the atmosphere, if not more genial, was more restful than anything which had preceded it all day. If I seemed to assert myself, I did so cautiously and with extreme politeness, a contrast to the brusque and rebellious attitude I was capable of adopting at other times. Once a week on Sundays Vandeleur's son-in-law and his wife dined with us. On these occasions the decanter of port was taken from the sideboard and circulated. Vandeleur's quiet courtliness at such a moment, a certain old-world urbanity of manner, brought about a metamorphosis – from the man I knew in working hours – as strange as any in Ovid. He abandoned for the moment all 'shop'; he no longer shrieked aloud in frenzies of rage, but chatted in an easy undertone, and if we had only had ideas a little more in common the party would have been a most friendly one. But we had few or none. When the meal was over we would adjourn to his study. There for nearly three-quarters of an hour we sat in uneasy silence, broken only by occasional nervous spurts of conversation. I have no doubt that it was kind of Vandeleur to ask us into his study, after first giving us a glass of port. There was no real obligation for him to do either. It is possible that he was nearly as bored as we were, but I doubt this. For one thing, the old are not so easily bored as the young, and for another it was Vandeleur who chose the topics of conversation and we who responded to them as best we could. We were none of us so scintillating or so well admixed that there was any likelihood of the proceedings ever becoming brilliant, or indeed anything but downright dull.

Dull we were, and dull we proved ourselves to be, sinking ever as the minutes passed into a deeper and deeper slough of dullness. I was impatient by nature, and on the second or third of these occasions – an early one, certainly, for I rather think the practice was afterwards discontinued – I had endured forty minutes of boredom when I rose boldly to my feet, and, murmuring that I had something to do in my room, withdrew. Glued by polite convention to their chairs, the rest remained for another forty minutes. I was surprised when a few days later, referring to the incident, timid little Miss Winsor remarked to me, 'I never admired you so much as I did at that moment.' Surprised in the first instance that she should admire me at all, and surprised, secondly, that she, who had been bred in an iron convention of politeness, and was supposed to be thoroughly enjoying the proceedings, should have approved a breach of tradition and even of good manners.

This picture I draw of myself is unattractive, but it would be wrong to think I was merely the hireling shepherd. To the work I had undertaken I brought all the idealism and enthusiasm, as well as all the inexperience, of the amateur. I had read a little educational theory and had been imbued with the doctrines of sentimental liberalism then very much current. Shelley believed in the perfectibility of man, I in the perfection of childhood. The flower had only to be left to itself to unfold into beauty. Young and intolerant, I had not then realised that to prune the roots or to give support with a trellis is not necessarily an offence against perfection. The pendulum of educational theory had moved almost full swing from the time Vandeleur first began to teach to the time when I came to him as assistant master. The cult of liberty was now at its height. It had even penetrated most nurseries; only the intense conservatism of the boys' preparatory schools had been able to resist it.

How uncongenial the whole of Vandeleur's system was to me can be deduced from a poem which was written within a week or two of my arrival, and sent to a friend. This friend and critic – herself a mother – described it as 'the worst and silliest poem you have ever written,' and she was probably right. But I give it here, since it is such a faithful indication of my mood.

The New Class

Children, I spoil your souls,
I do you wrong,
All God made you to be
Must be undone.

Were you free yesterday?
  Not so then, now.
The joy you feel in life
  You must not show.

Those who were eager once,
  Live that trait down.
Those who smiled much, be wise
  And feign a frown.

You may not speak to me
  Unless I speak.
You must learn now to turn
  That other cheek.

Once you would run with shouts
  Towards each new thing.
Knowledge is new, but know,
  One does not sing.

Time that before was short
  Will now be long
Children, I spoil your souls,
  I do you wrong.

Vandeleur's system cannot have been wholly bad, because the children survived it, were pleasant, friendly, affectionate and well-mannered and probably better off than if left to the caprice of their own will and temperament, breaking windows or defacing walls when they felt like it, as one expert advocated.

What distressed me about my new environment was probably not that I was in a bad school, but that I was in a school at all. At this time I would not have conceded that there were any virtues to be gained from a community life. To me it seemed that school took all the spontaneity out of the young child. I once saw a little boy in class laugh triumphantly over the solution to his sum. He was reproved and it was made plain to him that he must never burst out laughing over a sum again. Such conduct disturbed one's neighbours. If to enter the Kingdom of Heaven was to become like a little child, I argued that Vandeleur and all like him were as busy as possible expatriating those who were already there.

I was harassed, I was tired, I seemed perpetually busy. I detested

Vandeleur's scenes with the children, of which there were many. There was little in my new existence that I could imagine I would ever want to remember, and I would not remember it now had there not at this moment emerged on the scene another character round whom all my memories of the place and people would group themselves like crystals round a centre.

Vandeleur had begun the term at a disadvantage. It almost seemed as though the fates had conspired against him. His wife was away staying with a relative in Switzerland; his son-in-law, his right-hand man, was reading for his exam, and not merely were there two new members of his staff to be initiated into the ways of the school, but a third new member had failed to materialise. We had heard much about this missing colleague, or rather about the difficulties in obtaining from the Ministry of Labour a permit for her entry into the country, for she was a Swiss girl coming to teach French in both schools. I am not sure when she was first mentioned. But once mentioned, she became a perennial topic of conversation. Vandeleur's daughter, short-handed for the same reason, was as loud in her laments as her father. Though busy enough in her own school, she had undertaken the teaching of French in some of our junior forms, and the rest were being accounted for by Miss Winsor. Day after day passed and there was no sign of the absentee. We had almost despaired of her appearance when it was announced one morning at breakfast that the permit had at last been granted; and Miss Winsor was asked to undertake the meeting of 'Mademoiselle' the following Thursday at the railway junction twenty miles away.

Thursday was my free afternoon, and, returning from one of my long rambles, I heard that she had come. That evening at dinner we were joined by a girl with fair, short hair, wearing a plaid dress of brown cloth with a red line. She was not tall, but something lithe and active about her as she followed Vandeleur into the room with an easy independent stride, gave the impression of height. I remember what instantly struck me was that, though autumn was well advanced, and the rest of us had lost whatever tan the summer had given us, she herself was deeply sun-burnt, bronzed like some young Atalanta—not only her face, but her arms, almost to the shoulder. The contrast between the smooth fair hair, the bronzed skin, and the red line of the plaid dress made as it were a pattern, that kind of mental pattern which one can visualise long afterwards.

Real personality is felt instantly. Hitherto we had sat each night, three people round a dinner-table that was typically English, formal, polite, talking in low tones, in a setting that might almost have been lit by candles, and disturbed only by the tinkling serenity of Miss Winsor's laugh. The newcomer, however, could not take on the colour of her surroundings so completely. She was too natural, too relaxed, too little subdued to the existent convention. It was as though a stone had been thrown into standing water. It was not so much that she talked a great deal, for she did not. But all that she said, bearing as it did the hallmark of vital youth, seemed to show a keener sincerity, a livelier appreciation of life than the hushed platitudes which we had been exchanging until now. In the same way that a season without any very radical change can nevertheless announce itself in a single day, so now her advent seemed to mark a new era.

It might be thought that Vandeleur would have been pleased at finding he had been sent someone of vigour and character as well as charm, rather than a nonentity, especially as he was not by any means immune to the attractions of her sex. But from the first there was something hesitant in his acceptance of her. Talking quietly and without any appearance of monopolising the conversation, she yet managed to tell us a good deal about herself. One of her first personal confessions was that she was 'crazy' about all forms of sport. She amused us, and a little shocked Vandeleur, by the degree of camaraderie she appeared to have established with a team of New Zealand Rugby footballers who had travelled up on the train with her from Southampton. Miss Winsor made things no better next day by describing how as their train left the station the All-Blacks had leant from the window, shouting their farewells to her, and promising her a ticket for their next match at Liverpool, if she would come and see them play.

What was troubling Vandeleur was not the project of a visit to Liverpool, which he could ban, and had mentally banned already. It was something nearer his interests and the interests of his school. She had come on the understanding – or rather, it appeared now, the misunderstanding – that she knew no English. As the meal progressed he was horrified to find that, though she talked it brokenly and with a little diffidence, she had quite a good vocabulary. Certain Americanisms crept in from time to time, and once or twice in answer to some question she replied, with a laugh, 'Sure!' At last Vandeleur asked her suavely if it were not the case that she had some American friends. She denied that she knew any Americans, but made the naïve confession – naïve in the circumstances – that within the last two years she had read nearly two hundred books in English.

'Tales of adventure and tales of the Wild West appeal to me greatly. It is probably from these that I have learnt "Sure!" You are not using it often, then?'

'We use it, but not as often as the Americans.'

'I like your English authors, Conrad, Galsworthy, Hardy. I have read too the Irishman, George Birmingham, and been amused by his *Spanish Gold*. All the part about the yacht is so good. Oh, how I have laughed!'

She laughed at the recollection of it now, a friendly, natural laugh, taking us into her confidence and showing a row of very white even teeth. But Vandeleur himself did not laugh. He looked, rather, the picture of a man who has been sold a pup. This is the perennial difficulty of all such situations. Those who cross the Channel to teach French to the young – without a salary – are only too anxious to learn English themselves. Indeed, that is their chief objective in coming. But an impression prevails among their hosts that children are a great deal more likely to talk French if they know that they will not be understood in their own language. Vandeleur had certainly gathered from his wife that the girl whom she had interviewed in Switzerland knew little or no English. It appeared now that he had been misled, and he did not take the trouble to disguise his annoyance. The laws of the country forbade him to pay her anything, but if he had been doing so he might have accused her of taking the post on false pretences. Others lose their employment because of their ignorance; she was in danger of losing hers because she was not ignorant enough.

He need not have worried. In the days which followed she proved herself a most competent instructress, possessed of a natural gift for teaching. Though she had never taught before, she was one of those people who have no difficulty in controlling the young or commanding their interest. She was kept busy between the two schools, and one might see her at any hour of the day leaving the pleasant, timbered house with the steep roof and brown tiles just below the boys' school, and coming along the footpath, her books under her arm, striding with an easy gait like that of a French university student, or running head downwards if she was late. She helped to supervise the girls in the afternoon and played hockey with them, but she took tea with us, and she dined with us in the evening.

Looking across the table at dinner the following night, I thought again how like an Amazon she was, her skin bronzed, her hair fair, her arms deeply sunburnt. She was from Geneva, yet there was something distinctly Nordic in her appearance, and presently I would learn that her mother was a Dane who had married a Swiss. Slim, lithe, active rather than graceful – she seemed to show in every movement she made that her body was the trained servant of her will. Her short hair was combed straight back off her forehead, some of it falling either side of her face, and when she got excited she would push it back with one hand with a gesture masculine rather than feminine in its impatience. In everything she suggested the open air, the sun, the wind, exercise and effort. Turning her head to say good night to one of the boys at the dinner table – for it was the custom for the seniors to come in, pass round the table and shake hands with each of us in turn – her profile reminded me of a Minoan, bronzed, fleet and sun-loving, one of those Cretans about whom she was so anxious to read, consulting me as to some book Sir Arthur Evans had written on the subject, although her dress suggested rather French or Swiss middle-class good taste. It was sleeveless, very dark blue, almost black, and with a narrow decorative red collar which gave it piquancy. Certainly that dress was bought in Switzerland, in Geneva, or perhaps in Lausanne, and her sunburn was the sunburn of the Swiss mountains and the snows, rather than of the Mediterranean, of the Dodecanese or of Crete.

And yet, as I presently discovered, the Mediterranean knew her as well as the mountain heights and snows of her native land. She was only nineteen, but adventures are to the adventurous. A few days later, as I walked down to the football field with a group of boys, one of them remarked to me:

'Did you know, sir? Mademoiselle was in the Olympic Games.'

She was already 'Mademoiselle' to everyone, labelled from the moment she came to the country, in the same way that all her compatriots are labelled.

'No, that's interesting. What did she do? Was she running?'

'No, sir. She sailed, sir.'

'She has some photographs of it and she's going to show them to us.'

Her Olympic status had plainly conferred lustre on her in their eyes. And it did so quite a little in mine too. That evening after class, as she gathered up her books to go down to the girls' school, and I waited in the corridor to take the boys in to tea, I asked her whether what I had heard was true. Yes, it was quite true. She had represented Switzerland in the single-handed sailing class, the only woman competitor among sixteen men.

CMI   33

'Did you win?'

'No, but I came about halfway up the list and managed to beat France.'

'That seems pretty good. I'm sure the Frenchman wasn't pleased to be beaten by a woman?'

'Oh, he took it quite well. He was a good sport.'

It seemed odd that she, a Switzer, should be interested in sailing.

'Living beside the Lake of Geneva, my family has always spent a large part of the summer months on the lake sailing. I have known and loved boats since I was a child.'

'Gong gone! Gong gone!'

The children poured into tea and there was no time to question her further. It is an indication of the tempo of our lives that though in the days which followed I saw her often, any conversation there was between us was on these lines, in odd snatches and at odd moments, in spite of, rather than because of, our common duties. It might have been a week later that I returned rather earlier than usual from a short walk with the boys along the sea front between showers, for the weather had been bad and there had been no football, to find her bent over some corrections in one of the class-rooms, while waiting for tea.

'Well, what was it like down at the sea?'

'Pretty rough. Hardly the weather for sailing!'

'Oh, I am used to all weathers.'

I learnt, now or at some later time, that she and a friend, a French girl, of about her own age, had sailed in a small boat for six winter months in the Mediterranean, keeping at sea nearly the whole time. The Yacht Club of France had formally shown its appreciation of their pluck and endurance.

'We have even been across to Corsica. And for fourteen days in bad weather we have been alone on another small island.'

She told it laughing, as though it hardly deserved to be thought an adventure.

Some days later, when I happened to mention Alain Gerbault, the young Frenchman who had sailed the Atlantic single-handed, I learnt that she knew him.

'I and my friend were at Cannes on our cruising expedition when he was fitting out his boat. We helped him lay in his stores.'

'What is he like?'

'He is all tension. All – what you call it? – nervous energy. He is not a person without nerves – rather with many.'

34

I had read about Gerbault and had admired his indifference not merely to death but to every degree of loneliness and danger. Now I met someone who knew the man himself. It was not surprising that she shone a little by reflected glory, more especially when she herself could lay claim to many of the very qualities which had made his achievement possible. What mystified me was that, having done so much already, she should now be here in an obscure preparatory school teaching French for no salary.

'There is a reason,' she said enigmatically, when I hinted surprise. 'I have a secret purpose of my own.'

Her air of mystification was as it were the seal of her youth, for it is only the young who close their mouths firmly in this fashion, and hint at dark secrets, which they will betray perhaps before the day is over.

What that secret purpose was I would learn presently; but not from her. When it did transpire the reason was at once surprising and simple enough. It was Vandeleur's daughter who betrayed it to me, a day or two later in a moment of irritation.

'The girl has only one ambition; and that is to travel. That is why she is here, to improve her English, so that she may get a post on an English yacht. She is actually reading for a navigation exam – her mate's certificate, or something – in the evenings. It is absurd. Girls cannot do these things.'

Poor Vandeleur! of the three recruits to his staff Fate had given him one with literary aspirations, and another who ardently longed to take her mate's certificate and become a ship's navigator. Each was here with an ulterior motive.

Neither was actually inefficient. Indeed, Mademoiselle was remarkably able; quick, imaginative, yet patient, and the boys liked her from the first. But she was unconventional. It says much that whereas before her arrival I myself seemed all too often guilty in this respect, when she came I paled into complete conventionality beside her. If I had broken some of the traditions of the place, she broke them all with an unconcern which argued either ignorance or a complete indifference. To me she seemed a refreshing antidote to a régime far too formal. She was like a gust of wind blowing through rooms that ordinarily have all their windows shut. She was not deliberately inconsiderate, she was simply spontaneous and entirely natural. If my casual manners savoured sometimes of rudeness, hers did not, but only of a perfectly natural assumption of freedom. For instance, during 'Break' in the morning she would stroll about the garden sunk in thought, preferring this to remaining with her colleagues in the dining-room over a cup of tea; and if Vandeleur, who passed through the garden sometimes on his way to his daughter's house, met her along one of the paths, in her yellow woollen dress with its rolled-up sleeves, he was probably a little surprised at the encounter. Why should she perambulate in solitude when no one else had done so before?

She was eager to learn English and she spoke it quite well with occasional mispronunciations. Convulsed with laughter, she might exclaim, 'I am become incappable of speech!' Sometimes idiom betrayed her, as, for instance, one evening when we had both been asked to make up a four at bridge after Mrs. Vandeleur returned from Switzerland at half-term. Mademoiselle amused us all by complaining, when she was asked why she did not play a certain card, 'How can I do that when I am leading all the time in the strength of the dead?' 'Dummy' in French is 'le mort' and she had been leading up to the strength of the exposed hand, and not, as it might seem, receiving aid from spiritualistic sources. But it was not often that she blundered as badly as this. Rather Vandeleur continued to worry because she knew too much English, convinced that because of this she would not speak enough French to the boys.

Just as this irritated him, so many of my own shortcomings must have irritated him still more. He was not naturally patient and I gave occasion again and again for him to lose the little patience he had. I had refused to impose silence on my youngest pupils, protesting that such a procedure was unnatural. In class the very fact that I was new to my work made it easier for me to enjoy their chatter. But out of school, when it might be thought that I would have been more tolerant of noise, my impulse was to slink away, to escape and hide myself from it. Vandeleur took his classes standing by the blackboard, black-coated and with ruler and chalk in hand. I, who never touched chalk in my life and shivered at the sound of it scraping against the board, would sometimes take mine at the far end of the same room, my feet up on the window-ledge, my back against its frame, spouting ardently from the book in front of me. My volubility and assumption of ease on these occasions was not without a faint trace of malice, because I objected strongly to teaching in a room where two other classes were in progress.

The school was well equipped in most ways, but there was a shortage of classroom space at certain times of the day, generally immediately before and after meals, when the dining-room was not available for teaching. Then two and sometimes three classes might be in progress in the one large double classroom. They were small classes, never more than about ten boys; others would be going on elsewhere, in the boys' playroom or, in the case of senior boys, in the Headmaster's study. The best use was made of the space available. But the fact remained that quite often one found oneself teaching in the same room as two other people, one of whom was generally Vandeleur himself.

Vandeleur's own discipline was extremely strict, creating a quite artificial relationship between teacher and taught. He looked after the boys, liked, when in mellow vein, to see them enjoying themselves, fed them exceedingly well, took care of their health and was certainly capable of showing genuine concern on their behalf. But in class he was violent-tempered; and the repugnant fact remained that boys were beaten, that they were rated violently for stupidity, and that though we masters might shout at them they might not utter a syllable before the raised arm had won a nod of assent from us. All this, though strictly orthodox to Vandeleur's generation, was nauseating to me. One Sunday morning, separated by two doors and a corridor, I nevertheless heard him savagely rulering some victim who, I learnt later, had failed to get his catechism correctly by heart. All his classes were taken with a ruler in hand and there were few lessons when it did not come into vigorous use. This enraged me. My letters home were full of it. I think I must have known very little about the practice of contemporary preparatory schools, for to my family it seemed much less dreadful than it did to me; a rather stern relative, my severe critic at any time, even passing the comment, 'He will never teach if he despises the slim gentleman.' Despise? I regarded it as the abomination of desolation dwelling in the holy of holies.

Mademoiselle had only been a week in the school when with me she was the witness of a rather extraordinary scene.

Though Vandeleur caned boys from time to time, I am probably wrong in suggesting that he used this weapon unduly. In class, however, he had come to depend almost habitually on a few strokes of the ruler to stimulate interest or to reprove misdemeanour. It was second nature to him, and it became almost second nature to the boys to extend a reluctant palm at any moment. But there was one little boy in the school whom I never saw him touch. He was called Andrew. As a pupil he was a trial, because he was casual, absent-minded, and self-assertive. He was an only child and had all the

37

faults of an only child. Plunged for the first time this term into a new environment, he was dazed and puzzled by it and a little aggressive. He was excitable, uncontrolled, a child rather than a schoolboy. To cut him off from his fellows still more, he had not yet got school clothes, but wore a loosely knitted woollen jersey of some bright colour which made him look different from the other boys. His high-pitched voice with its slight Scotch tang was also different and frequently raised, so that I got to know it well. He was impervious to ridicule because, like Adam in his earlier days, he had not yet learnt what it was to feel ashamed. When we went for a walk he would instinctively link his hand in mine. Impatient, foolish, egotistical, he expected everybody to show interest in what he was doing, while conceding the most perfunctory attention to their affairs; but one forgave him all this – or at least I did – when in some flash of spontaneous enthusiasm he revealed the child mind in all its native virtue. He recited beautifully, he loved poetry, he loved drawing, and he loved them for themselves, not for any ulterior or scholastic motive. His delight was infectious, a reminder of one's own in similar circumstances.

He was a day boy, and I imagine that his parents, knowing how excitable and undisciplined he was and that at seven years old a child is seldom the better for being terrified, had stipulated to Vandeleur that he was not to be beaten. For whereas every other offender in the school tasted inevitably the rigour of the ruler, I never saw this small boy, who was far more trying and occasionally equally stupid, actually struck. If Vandeleur had given his word to the parents, he certainly kept it; or if – which would be still more to his credit – having seen that the child was exceptionally highly-strung and might be gravely injured by such treatment, he had voluntarily decided that never under any provocation would he strike him, then by some superhuman effort he managed to keep to his resolution.

On this particular morning I was teaching at the far end of the large classroom while Vandeleur himself was taking the "babies" nearby. I do not know what it was that made him lose his temper so greatly, but suddenly I heard him shout in an infuriated voice at Andrew, 'Come out here. Come out. Now lie on the floor. Lie on the floor.' The child, cowed and terrified by this sudden onslaught, lay down on the floor on his back, at the side of the master's desk. Whereupon Vandeleur, losing his temper more completely than ever, and as though the misunderstanding had been wilful, bellowed at him, 'No, lie on your face. Lie on your face.'

The child turned over and lay on his face, I forget for how long. It is always distressing to see anyone lose self-control completely, and before a roomful of boys it was doubly distressing. There was nothing to be done. Displays of frantic irritation, nearly as bad as this, had taken place often before, and would take place again. But to a new-comer to the profession it was displeasing. I felt that I had witnessed something derogatory to human dignity.

An incident like this was bound to prejudice me. And, continually, in a number of ways I let my disapproval transpire. Once Vandeleur shouted at me in anger, 'You are the most self-opinionated young man I have ever met – always trying to teach me my own job.' The accusation was true. Forty years of schoolmastering are sufficient to try the temper of most men, without encountering at the end of that time a mentor who had not even been born when one began. My easy-going manners must have annoyed him frequently, just as the inelasticity and rigidity of the school arrangements often fretted me. One morning he called me aside quietly and, realising that the offence in this instance was quite unconscious, intimated to me, as kindly and discreetly as possible, that he considered 'Right-ho' the wrong mode of acknowledging, and expressing willingness to carry out, my headmaster's orders. I had not realised till that moment that I was in the habit of addressing him in this fashion, but I was quite willing to subscribe to the tenet that it was unsuitable.

Little by little, however, I began to settle into the routine. Its all too few oases of liberty were the greener and more welcome by con-trast. One of the best moments in the week was, when, having strolled down while the boys were at tea to the local newsagent to fetch my copy of A.E.'s literary weekly, I carried it back under my arm, secure in the knowledge that I was going to enjoy it that even-ing, feet up on the mantelpiece in front of my little fire. To read it was to return for a few hours to another and more congenial world. I would glance at it in the dusk as I walked, or later at my desk when taking preparation with the boys, to see if it contained any contribution of mine, and if it did the quarrels and humiliations of my day were quickly forgotten. In any case, it was read greedily from cover to cover. The sagacity, the serenity of A.E., discussing the hundred and one issues of those crucial times dispelled any personal pettiness. I could not guess then that I was one day to arrange in book form the very passages in the journal which now gave me most pleasure.

It was not a period of poetic activity for me. I was too busy otherwise. Once, inspired by the sight of a child with deep auburn hair, disciplined generally in two business-like plaits, but allowed to flow over her shoulders in splendid prodigality on the one afternoon in the week when she and her companions came up from the girls' school to share in a dancing-class with the boys – it was Thursday and my free afternoon and so I saw them only occasionally – inspired by this twelve-year-old child, her face freckled, her expression honest and alert, who walked with the upright carriage of a young queen, I remembered how performance can fall short of promise and wrote:

> Earth, this child,
> Like a young tree,
> Clean-limbed, very straight,
> Deserves well of thee.
> See to it now that one
> Joined perfectly
> So well begun ends not
> Ungracefully.

Of her youth, though she will never know it, this still lingers, the memory of her as she came to school in the morning among the satchelled pupils, holding herself with all the unconscious and instinctive grace of childhood, as though such pride of carriage were Nature's rather than the individual's; the memory also, as I passed her in the corridor on her way to class, of her bronze-coloured hair unbraided, its texture as fine as silk, flowing in a great wave below her waist, her back straight and her head held high and triumphant as ever. If my wish for her was fulfilled, other eyes will not have been slow to notice her grace as she grew older. But even if denied, Nature will reproduce the pattern elsewhere. The mould is not lost.

Though I believed myself set down in the midst of Philistia, there was one person in the school whose literary interests were nearly as keen as my own. This was the Swiss girl. It was soon evident that she had other interests besides sailing. Sometimes I would find her in the Matron's room in the evening when I went to borrow the daily paper. Miss Thorpe, the Matron, was a business-like person, brusque and outspoken, who ran her own department with very little interference from Vandeleur or anyone else. I do not know whether the boys liked her or not; I imagine that they did, despite her occasional severities. But she certainly had their bodily welfare at heart and was able to control them without nagging, and without too much reference to central authority. From the first, Mademoiselle took to her as being more humorous, less set, less obsessed by school interests than her other colleagues. 'Thorpey' was as English as anyone, but she represented a side of the English that was more human, breezier, less prim and condemnatory than this Swiss girl encountered elsewhere. Occasionally I found them together, chatting amicably, and would remain for a few minutes talking.

One evening Mademoiselle tapped on my study door to return an article on Anatole France which I had lent her. France was one of my favourite authors at this time. The lucidity, the grace, the gentle irony of his style had delighted me with the first book of his I had read. When she knocked at my door to return the essay I was all eagerness to hear her opinion.

'Did you like it?'

She shook her head and made a face.

'I am not such an admirer of Anatole France. The article about him might be good if it was written differently, but it is all too serious. These generalisations are always silly. I hate generalisation' – then she added with a rueful look – 'though I am always philosophising myself.'

She handed me the paper and our talk drifted to other things, other writers. Standing in the open doorway of my room, she answered the questions I had begun to ask her about French poets and French poetry.

She believed that contemporary judgments were nearly always foolish and false.

'Look at Hugo. They thought him the greatest poet of France in the nineteenth century. Now he may survive perhaps, by a few fragments from *Les Châtiments*. But how much else of his poetry will people want to read? The real poets of that age are Verlaine, Rimbaud, Leforgue, of whom practically no one had heard at the time they were writing.'

I liked Hugo, and was distressed to hear him belittled, but since I was much better acquainted with his prose than with his poetry I was not in a position to undertake his defence. I told her what an English writer, George Moore, had said of him, 'If he had written three books of verse instead of twenty-three he would have more chance of being remembered.'

'That is perhaps true.'

' "To reach posterity one must travel light!" '

'Who said that?'

'Anatole France!'

We laughed.

When she spoke of poetry it was with a slow gravity and after a slight pause which came not from ignorance of my language, but as if, having thought out the matter deeply, she was prepared to give a considered judgment. My own acquaintance with Verhaeren, Remy de Gourmont, Samain, de Regnier, Francis Jammes and their contemporaries I owed to two books. One was Amy Lowell's study, *Six Living French Poets*, which had interested me profoundly. The other was that too little known book by Thomas Bodkin, *May It please Your Lordships*, in which the translator's art has been carried to a pitch of perfection very rarely reached. Bodkin's translations are printed side by side with the original poem, a challenge to the severest critics of that art which some people feel must always show traces of its bastard origin. I know no others so consistently good. Throughout the whole book one seems to be reading, in two different languages, separate poems upon an identical theme, born out of the same inspiration, and each equally successful in its own way.

Thanks to these two books, I was not wholly at a disadvantage now. I asked her about Vildrac.

'Yes, I like him.'

'Paul Fort?'

'He also.'

'De Regnier?'

De Regnier she admired intensely.

'I have a book by him with me now, some little "odelettes" which I must lend you.'

I thanked her, though de Regnier at this time was the poet who appealed to me least of his generation. The work of his which I knew seemed to me too purely decorative, affected almost, as though he were striving after the effects of a Watteau or Fragonard in verse.

'Francis Jammes?'

She smiled and shook her head and I gathered that he was a little too tame, too pedestrian.

'What René Bazin is in prose he is in poetry, I suppose you would say?'

She nodded.

'All the same, I like them both' – and my thoughts went back to Jersey and to the dining-room of a country rectory whither I used to go twice a week to read René Bazin's *La Terre qui Meurt* with an old white-haired clergyman, Rector of one of the twelve island parishes. We were simple souls, he and I, lovers of the soil and of those who cultivate it, and no book chosen for a task – and this one was part of my course for an examination – could have been calculated to give us so much mutual pleasure. Brittany was only a little distance away. On a clear day one could see it across twenty miles of intervening blue water; and as we read we seemed to be living and moving among the peasant protagonists of the tale. Always we were loth to tear ourselves away when summoned into the drawing-room for tea by the white-capped old lady, whose at-home day it was, and who had no intention of allowing her husband to prolong the lesson indefinitely.

I was not going to retract my loyalty to Bazin now when a book of his had given me so much pleasure, and I defend both him and Jammes, who had written as good bucolic poetry as exists in his language.

She did not dispute the issue. '*Chacun à son gout.*' The poet who had given her most pleasure was Laforgue, and his work I did not know at all.

It was something to have found another person in the school with kindred interests. At dinner in the evenings conversation was forced to skim the surface of things discreetly; it never touched on literature and the arts. Now I had someone with whom to talk about these things.

'Well, I must go now. I shall be late for my English lesson.'

She placed the paper containing the article I had lent her on my mantelpiece. Since she was *au pair*, it had been arranged that on certain evenings in the week she should read English down at the girls' school with Vandeleur's daughter. To the latter, who had already enough on her hands, it must have been one more burden at the end of the long day. With her olive complexion, jet black hair done in a knob, and huge brown eyes in which I so often saw traces of fatigue, she seemed too well disciplined to complain. Quiet, capable, never fussing, never relaxing completely, there was something a little tragic about this young woman who ran her day-school so efficiently that its troubles, if it had any, were not allowed to reach her father's ears. Indeed, I rarely remember hearing it mentioned, though she would chat about the boys' affairs when she came up to supper. Her pupils seemed happy, alert and bright, and with Miss Winsor and 'Mademoiselle' as her assistants she could count herself well-staffed. But that she had plenty to worry about I learnt presently. She was expecting a baby; she had the anxiety of her husband's exam, and her school was a comparatively recent venture only now getting on its feet. At a time when she might have seemed entitled to be the carefree bride, she was over-weighted with responsibility, and what to my mind made this more, and not less, distressing was the fact that she seemed to accept this role without wish or power to resist it. Into her manner had crept a faint apathy, as though she had stilled the capacity alike for joy and for its opposite. She belonged to that race of Marthas who, though their own capacity for happiness is small, feel a vague sense of grievance against the Marys who have managed to shuffle off the responsibilities to which they themselves remain bound.

The English lesson at the end of the day may have been a trial of patience, but she never showed it. While it was in progress her husband bent over his books. Phlegmatic, of low vitality, with sallow complexion and brown eyes like his wife's, he carried, like her, the virtue of self-control to a pitch that was either super-human or subhuman. His handling of the boys was firm but kindly enough. Occasionally I would hear him rap out an irritated comment to one of them, but for the most part he performed all his duties quietly and efficiently, if in a somewhat impersonal way. It was as a colleague that he showed his especial patience. He was friendly to me, gave me advice upon my work, smiled inwardly a little, I imagine, when I lost my temper, and from the first saw an irreconcilable incompatibility between his father-in-law and myself. 'It is no one's fault,' he said to me once in his peace-loving way. 'Certain temperaments are just completely antithetical to one another. You irritate my father-in-law, and he irritates you, and neither of you are really to blame. You are oil and water. You will never mix.' Though he ran thus far alongside the hare, I suspected him sometimes of hunting with the hounds, but in this I probably did him an injustice. Perhaps nature had made him easy-going and placatory by disposition, the one person in the establishment unlikely to give sudden rein to anger or any other emotion. If so, it was as well, for his position was by no means easy. Only a conciliatory temperament could have hit it off as well as he did with his father-in-law. Vandeleur liked him, saw in him his successor, and there never seemed to be the smallest difference of opinion between them. But that was partly due to the fact that one of the two was resolutely determined not to differ. Whoever else was likely to produce explosions, this quiet, self-contained, patient young man was not.

44

If the lesson was a burden to his wife, it was a joy and a delight to the pupil. They were reading *Henry V* aloud together. Its vigour, its masculinity, its humour must have appealed to the Swiss girl. She herself would have hit it off well with a Fluellen or a Gower. She would even have known what line to take with 'an ancient Pistol.' Besides, it was all part of her plan of campaign, and, if one has a plan of campaign, anything which contributes to its success is necessarily pleasure. Mademoiselle departed down to the girls' school now, obviously eagerly looking forward to her reading.

About a week after this by a happy accident a still greater treat fell to her lot. A travelling company of Shakespearean actors arrived at Rhyl, the big, deserted seaside town along the coast. They had relied, I imagine, largely for their audience on the many surrounding schools. Vandeleur decided to take some of his older pupils. On the day before the performance one of the boys developed a cold, and Mademoiselle, who had not been coming, was offered the spare ticket. That evening she read up the whole play so that she might follow it without difficulty next day on the stage. It was typical of the thoroughness which she brought to all that interested her. We drove over in a charabanc, and, though she showed it less noisily, I imagine that she felt as much zest and excitement as the boys. It was a break in the monotony of our ordinary school life. Actually, the entertainment was rather disappointing. The acting appealed to her, but to me it seemed very poor.

'Did it not seem lifeless to you?' I asked her afterwards.

'Oh no, it was very good,' she said firmly and with conviction, as though that closed the matter, and there could be no further question of its excellence.

On Sunday she accompanied us to church, regarding the extremely lengthy sermon as in the nature of another English lesson. Until her arrival I had sat with the school at the back of the choir and at the very end of the pew against the iron partition of the Lady Chapel. Now she sat there, and I was amused to see her immediately lean her head against the very piece of wall which had formerly supported mine. It was in small disregards of convention such as this that we probably annoyed Vandeleur most. 'Now I can no longer go to sleep,' I whispered to her. I wondered how much of the service she could follow and how far it held her sympathies. The sermon was sometimes as much as three-quarters of an hour long, a severe test of attention. But the man was a good preacher. A sermon upon labour which I approved very heartily she failed to

45

follow, but one, a few Sundays later, of a much more metaphysical nature, aroused in her an unexpected interest.

For metaphysics attracted her. 'I am wondering a lot about life,' was her way of putting it.

Once, after a long talk about literature I said to her, 'Don't you ever write yourself?'

She gave a little shrug of self-disgust. 'Oh yes, I am writing all the time. But it is of no interest to anyone. It is philosophic. Afterwards I am hating it all.'

Hating it all. There were moments when I felt about my new life that I was 'hating it all.' Only to my actual teaching did I seem to bring that spontaneity which made it a joy. If Vandeleur had his theory of education, I, the complete neophyte, had also mine. I believed firmly that only that was valuable which sprang direct from inspiration, and that this held true, whether of a poem or a lesson. Whatever became mechanical or set instantly lost its worth. Everything must spring from the heart. It was a counsel of perfection applied to a highly organised and specialised concern, which had been run for years on completely different lines, and it says much for the system that I was able to disturb it so little—indeed, presently looked like being absorbed by it myself. Vandeleur might have said, 'Yes, you teach by inspiration. You read De la Mare's poetry to my seven-year-olds, and capture their interest by leaping over the countryside in company with his three jolly farmers, or burying pots of blackberry jam for fairies with his old woman. But what will your leaps amount to when you have been teaching like me for forty years? What will happen when you go blackberry-picking for the four hundredth time? Where will your inspiration be then?' I might well have paled before such a question. Fortunately, he did not ask it. Instead, after all our disagreements he was to give me a testimonial in which, despite significant omissions, he could say that I had a great gift for the teaching of English.

I had no experience. I taught by instinct rather than by a particular method. But the children seemed to learn something and to enjoy their classes. Vandeleur did not interfere. Indeed, he showed considerable tolerance. Once he crossed the room to suggest that Shelley's 'Ode to a Skylark' was a somewhat difficult poem for a class of eleven-year-olds to learn by heart. He implied that, even if they did succeed in learning it, they would not understand it. I listened to his point, shook my head and said, 'I don't agree with you.' I relied on the music of the poem, its marked rhythm, and its repetitive effects to keep interest alive. Understanding of the actual lines could come later. Presently he was to hear them declaim it with gusto, the successive similes mounting triumphantly to their lips. They learnt to enjoy the beat of the rhythm if nothing else. And, when they came to the verse –

> 'Yet if we could scorn
> Hate, and pride, and fear;
> If we were things born
> Not to shed a tear,
> I know not how thy joy we ever should come near.' –

the monosyllabic and almost savage pathos of these wonderful lines, if wasted on them, never failed to move me.

It would be wrong to think that Vandeleur and I made no attempt to bridge our difficulties. We did, but they were only spasmodically successful. At once sensitive yet conceited, outspoken yet shy, anxious to please but nevertheless defiant, in the long run I probably made even fewer concessions than did my quick-tempered employer. My time-table fretted me. When Vandeleur halfway through the term asked me to rehearse and produce a school play, I refused on the ground that I had as much as I could do already. He lost his temper and said that he was an old man, but he would do it himself. And he kept his word, coaching the boys in Anstey's *Vice Versa*, and producing it with a certain amount of help from his family, so that I never set eyes on the play until the parents came down for it at the end of the term.

I was embittered, perhaps at times a little unfair. Oil and water assuredly we were. Our very preferences differed. The youngest boy in the school was little Williamson, aged six, a youth of grave precosity and impeccable character. He was completely broken to community life and a striking contrast to the fidgety and bohemian Andrew. He would set out with us on Sunday mornings, wearing a white Eton collar over his tweed suit, rather as though he had been born in one, and walking as solemnly as an alderman to church. His Headmaster adored him; I have seen him beam on the child with real affection, claiming him by his side as we set off. Whereas to me he was an unutterable little prig. I snubbed him on all possible occasions, and it was almost a relief to hear from the older boys that he had evidently sensed my antipathy, and had had the strength of mind to cock snooks at me behind my back in prep. When Vandeleur relaxed and was genial with the boys I thought only with gloomy satisfaction how Gray or Goldsmith had fixed exactly that moment in pedagogy when the tyrant smiles. It did not occur to me that my own lessons, especially with the younger children, must be somewhat of a trial to my employer. I was patient with them, tried to be kindly, and the result was that they all chattered away at the tops of their voices like birds in the parrot house at the Zoo. Then Vandeleur would cross the room and tell them that they must be more quiet. It was this disciplining of the younger forms that I found most difficult. They were not deliberately unruly, but they all wished to talk at once. Their worst exhibition of garrulity was not in class at all, but when, going down to the football field in the afternoon, they all surrounded me at once, and started clamouring to be made captain of a side. Pandemonium reigned. Will it be believed that before I left the school it was my practice to break off a willow switch from the nearby hedge and threaten them with its use – nay, even use it – if they were not more quiet? That time, however, was still a little way off.

The days passed quickly enough. Though I hated Vandeleur's methods, I liked the boys and was beginning to see that in spite of the system – or was it because of it? – something good-natured and invincibly buoyant emerged in character. The most beaten were often the most cheerful; or perhaps one should reverse the premise and say that the most cheerful, being also the most irrepressible, were oftenest in trouble. I would look across the room at dinnertime and see Mademoiselle laughing with animation with some boy who had had a terrible gruelling in class that morning. She looked like a happy schoolboy herself, with her Minoan profile, the nose pointed and reliant, the chin resolute, despite the crease of amusement that lined each cheek. I myself sat at the foot of the adjoining table, 'Chicken' on one side of me, George on the other. George was often in trouble. He was rulered in class and his air of jaunty indifference when he returned from Vandeleur's study after a caning endeared him to me.

'Did it hurt, George?'

He would smile enigmatically as much as to say, 'Life contains these things, you know.' His eyes had not even filled and there was not a trace of that self-pity which brings moisture to most eyes, even when a caning has not been very severe. He was a philosopher in such matters or else a hardened little sinner. Only ten or eleven, he had been at school already for four years. Small for his age, with hard corners, literally as well as metaphorically, his joints were round and knubbly and very bony, and if he had a gentler side he concealed it well. His turned-up nose with its tendency to be bright pink had earned him the nickname of 'Cherry-nose.' But he was as indifferent to these personalities as he was to canings, only acknowledging them by a scornful smile, or, if he thought they emanated from an inferior, by swift recrimination. Having settled comfortably into a junior form, he showed no signs of ever leaving it. Considered 'backward,' he could be sharp enough over his sums, if there was sufficient competition in the class to arouse his interest. He was interested also in literature, and when I had read them *Goblin Market* that morning it had been George who was the most attentive and who, before I began, had given lurid particulars of what he would do to anyone who interrupted indiscreetly or asked unnecessary questions.

He had even literary aspirations which operated under a severe handicap, for his spelling was fantastic. Since he had no idea of phonetics, all he wrote was as unintelligible as the Hittite script. The letters were thrown on to the page in any order that occurred to him. A whole essay full of the advantages and disadvantages of a 'fite' had mystified me completely – they had been allowed a free choice of subject – until towards the end I realised that I was reading a treatise on domestic happiness, and that 'fite' was George's method of spelling 'wife.'

Beside me now at the dinner table I could see his turned-up red nose over his apologetic smile, a smile that might be one of sheer habit, but suggested more often the consciousness that he had been doing something naughty and must appear unconcerned. Opposite him sat 'Chicken,' round-faced, large-eyed, with a big head set on a very slender neck, and slightly Mongolian high cheek bones. Chicken was not yet ten years old, but he had already had three years' experience of school. He and George played question games the entire meal, games in which they had to give in turn the names of a series of things in alphabetical succession. When they had exhausted the towns of the world and the motor cars of two continents, they had a spelling game in which each contributed alternate letters, endeavouring to make their opponent complete a word and so 'lose a life.' A good game and one at which George, probably partly because of his disability, consistently endeavoured to cheat, launching non-existent words on an all too brief career, and being successfully challenged by Chicken, with whom spelling was a strong point. Periodically I was called on to arbitrate.

'No, George. There is no such word as that; there is a French word, but you are not having French words.'

He would accept defeat quite amicably. But at the same time he was a most almighty little boss. If the game was not being played his way, or if he conceived that he had been injured, he would down tools and refuse to play for the rest of the meal.

Leaning across the table, he would take the opportunity to try me with a riddle. 'Sir, if it takes three yards of red petticoat to make a white waistcoat for an elephant, how long will it take a bumble bee with clogs on to walk through the skin of a sausage backwards without disturbing the meat?'

'Quite easy, George.'

'How?'

'By algebra.'

George did not do algebra, but Chicken, who was very bright for his nine and a half years, had already begun. He looked at me reproachfully:

'You couldn't really, could you, sir?'

'No, of course not, Chicken.'

This was the measure of my days. It was all gay enough, better than stewing in the juice of one's own melancholy. But it was fatiguing, an endless strain on attention, and far removed from every secret ambition which I cherished! It was true that there were compensations. The school was comfortable, up-to-date and well-designed, not sordid, ugly and inkstained, as it might easily have been. It had given me a distinctly pleasant shock when I first approached it when it stood, under the long spur of hill, only a few fields below the spot where a great face of rock, like a deserted quarry, opened in the hillside. A high plain, flat as a Tibetan table-land, lay beyond this to the east, but the spur of hill ran inland at right angles to the sea, to tumbled hilly country, the nearest equivalent in North Wales to downland, fields of green grass cropped short by sheep, low stone walls, exposed ploughland, and below, in the shelter of the hill, wild copses of bramble and hazel or, a little further inland, gracious country with meadows and well-grown trees, old stone cottages and an occasional country park. It was pleasant to look towards all this, pleasant too in the evening to climb the hill and, leaning against some grey boulder of rock or a stone enclosure, to look down on the plain below me where the fields and hedges slept shrouded in the slight mists of autumn, or to turn back in the direction from which I had come and see the gilded pathway of light that the moon had opened up across the sea. Sometimes in the evening when I had tired of reading or my fire had burnt low I would look out, notice the lovely, moonlight night, and, getting my coat, walk as far as Meliden, which lay inland at the far end of the ridge of hill sheltering us; and climb the hill above the quarry there, a steep, winding path with many loose stones, ending in a low wall and a small gate that led on to the open downland. Here I would stand, looking at the night and its many stars, or at the houses in the valley below me, or at the moving lights of a train on its way to Chester, where the line ran close to the sea. In such moments of stillness and remoteness, which under modern conditions it is increasingly easier to secure by night than by day, one possesses the world, and for a brief instant ceases to be possessed by it. I was no longer a bondslave. I was free – free mentally and spiritually, in a way that only youth allows us to be. The air was crisp, the stars scintillating, and I would walk home along a path hard and brittle, with the occasional crackle of ice under my feet and feeling that there was not so much to be pitied in my lot after all.

Each day I saw the Swiss girl. She was losing her sunburn, that bronzed glow which, when she first came, made her skin look almost like gold-leaf. The Welsh autumn had begun to take effect. Autumn it was, as I realised when I went for a walk one Thursday afternoon. All the visitors who in summer had taken possession of this place, half seaside village, half residential refuge, had departed, taking with them whatever gaiety they had once hoped to find here. Along the asphalt esplanade yesterday's rain still lay in great pools, but these puddles were a problem to no one, for no one passed along the sea front. An occasional gull, facing the sea, but seemingly indifferent to it, perched on the edge of the raised wall. Far out, beyond a wide grey stretch of sand, the waves could be seen breaking, and from the same direction was blown occasionally the shrill wrangling of other gulls, adding their melancholy cries to the melancholy of the scene. The tide receded far in this part, only a few miles from the spot where the cattle are still supposed to be called home by one who will never again follow them into the byre. Leaving the front, I went down on the beach and ventured a few hundred yards on to that seemingly endless waste of dreary flats, to watch far out a grey sea, choppy, but not lashed to actual fury, breaking in fretful surf in the distance. It seemed impossible to believe that this grey and melancholy expanse, without horizon except for the distant white line of surf, was the same beach across which crowds of children had run joyfully in summer, their costumes adding still further brightness to the already existent colour in Nature. A rusted bucket, maltreated by many tides and now at last half buried, was the symbol of their departure. All was a grey, flat monotone, and though the sea even in its grimmest mood had power to win my admiration and I enjoyed a certain satisfaction in being able to wander with the whole beach to myself, smelling the sea air, or getting a whiff, indescribable but instantly recognisable, from the distant mud flats, yet I was conscious too of the rigour of the afternoon.

As I climbed once more on to the sea front with its deserted shelters and closed pier, I met Mademoiselle. She was free for an hour and she, too, on this forbidding autumn afternoon, had turned to the sea for consolation. She loved it as much as I did, and had even more right to love it, having lived with it and contended with it and submitted to its moods and caprices. It was a consolation to her even now, though how different must be this grey waste of flats – level and monotonous, broken only by the black outline of some wooden piles, driven at intervals into the sand – from the tideless Mediterranean. We met, talked for a few moments and then, almost immediately, separated. There was no suggestion that we should continue our walk together. It was not simply that I was shy, or that such procedure would be just the thing to irritate Vandeleur if by any chance he had met us; it was rather that we preferred our own company. We were both unsociable. We both knew that Nature is best appreciated alone. She looked cold and blue and unhappy, as though this English adventure on which she had built so many hopes were already ending in dismal failure. Even her navigation studies in the night watches, with their promise of ultimate reward, were only enough to maintain her stoicism, but not her gaiety.

Things were not going too well with her. There had been misunderstanding from the first. If Vandeleur resented her knowing so much English, she reproached him for not having told her before she came that she would have to teach in the girls' school as well as the boys. She had heard nothing about this arrangement in Switzerland. There had been recriminations and counter-recriminations. She was not being paid a penny for her work, but her time was almost as fully occupied as it would have been if she had had a salary. And when she was free there was nothing for her to do. She found herself shackled, like one of those goats one meets in an Irish laneway, so hampered with bandages of old rags and sacking that any taste it has for wandering is completely thwarted. From the first it was plain that she resented the restrictions placed upon her liberty. To her the words life and adventure were almost synonymous. She had come to England to widen her experience, and in some measure to enjoy herself, and life at the school was really very dull. True, she had been allowed to join the local ladies' hockey club, and she played with them once or twice a week on a field beside our football ground. But even a match 'away' gave her very little variety, for she would drive to the place in a charabanc, disembark with her ten companions to play against eleven very similar opponents, and then drive back again as soon as it was over. When the match was at home, we would see her arriving on the ground in her green gym tunic, a contrast to the navy blue of the rest of the team. To them she probably seemed unconventional and independent, as typical perhaps of Continental studenthood as they were of their Welsh small-town upbringing. I doubt whether she was sufficiently adaptable to win their approval; none of their interests were hers, none of hers were theirs. Perhaps the solitary in her militated against her making friends. Just as in the lunch interval she would wander round the garden by herself, so now, when the whistle blew for half-time at hockey, she would leave the little group chatting in the middle of the field and come and squat on the touchline, where she could watch my little boys kicking a football. Knees up to her chin, she would sit there for five minutes in moody silence.

To them she may have seemed rude. To me she seemed the one vital personality in a world of commonplace. She had the same effect on Miss Winsor, who loved to discuss her, if only to relate her latest 'gaffe.' Miss Winsor had learnt that her parents really disapproved of her being in England; they thought that she should be at home in Geneva, helping in the family fur business, and they kept her short of funds for this reason. She wanted to travel, she wanted to see the world; but they looked askance at such restlessness. In a sense, she was an adventuress, for it was as though she knew that life held for her just as much as she could wring from it. She did not expect its largesse to drop into her lap. Indeed, it had been somewhat of a surprise to find that one with so many active interests was drawn also towards the world of ideas. There too she seemed eager, questing, as curious to explore the realm of the mind as to explore the real world. In this she was like the Greeks. It was part of a single vital instinct. She allowed neither side of her nature to dominate the other. She wanted to do things, yet she wanted also to understand them. I was older than her and yet she could impress me by her air of maturity. It was as though she would have liked to appear inscrutable. Humorous, gay, passionately in earnest, quietly assured, it was useless to speculate what might lie behind that calm poise. She could show considerable feeling where literature or poetry was concerned, but never by any chance, even faintly, did she indicate a trace of sentiment in her own character. Had she ever been in love? She was nineteen and it was very likely, but there was nothing in her manner to suggest it. She liked men, was not in the least shy with them – indeed, courted their friendship, as in the case of the New Zealanders – but it was a liking wholly without sentimental bias. Of the emotional side of her nature I had no inkling. She was at once as frank and obvious as a schoolgirl – the schoolgirl she had not so long ceased to be – and mysterious, as though her silence and inscrutability might be not *naïveté* at all, but a profound or even painful awareness of life.

Turning away from me now on the esplanade, she sauntered off, her hands thrust deeply in the side pockets of her half-length coat, made from some silvered, rather coarse, short-haired skin, whose origin always puzzled me. The skins seemed pieced together so that the hair lay in contrary directions. It was almost a jacket rather than a coat, reaching barely to her hips, an unattractive garment, and the loose blue tam-o'-shanter which she wore with it was unattractive too. There was nothing of Atalanta about her now as she strolled moodily away, her shoulders hunched, with an almost beaten look.

Two days went by without an opportunity to snatch another few words of conversation with her. When it did come it was on the touchline of the football field of a neighbouring school. Having no hockey herself, she had come with the boys to watch the match, which was within easy walking distance for us all. Vandeleur was there, leaning on his walking stick. His irritability was an extreme trial on these occasions. Age improves none of us. Writers become diffuse, clergymen prosy, schoolmasters irascible. In a profession which places such a strain on patience it is perhaps not surprising. Vandeleur's impatience came out very clearly whenever the school played a soccer match. On these occasions we were almost always beaten, a result explained partly by the fact that our numbers were smaller than those of most of the schools whose teams we met, and still more by this other disadvantage peculiar to ourselves. From the time when they went out on to the field the team knew that they

54

would be subjected by their Headmaster to a running commentary of fiery insult. Vandeleur had dropped into the habit of noticing only their shortcomings, and he would stand on the touchline or walk up and down it in a sort of impotent rage. 'Tackle him, tackle him, don't funk!' But if before the match ever begins it is dinned into one's ears that one is a pitiable coward, one is the less likely to show courage when the actual moment comes. My treatment was the exact opposite. I adopted positive and not negative suggestion. Jumping about like a maniac on the touchline, I urged them on, assuring them that they were winning – an old device, as old as Virgil's boat-crew. I might have been at an Irish rugby international, so great was my excitement. I made myself absurd, but I felt that I was doing so in a good cause. The ball had hardly been kicked off before I was shouting, 'Well played So-and-so, oh *well* played.' Even Mademoiselle seemed a little surprised by my fervour and abandon, so completely did I let myself go.

Football matches were on half-holidays, on a Wednesday or a Saturday. On Sundays, or, rather, on every second Sunday – for I shared the duty with Vandeleur's son-in-law – I would take the boys for a walk in the afternoon. Sometimes too on week-days when the ground was too wet for football a walk would be the only alternative, or even when the field was being used, I might be given half a dozen stragglers who, recovering from colds, were deemed unfit to play. With this remnant, I would set off along the roads or lanes. The garrulous Andrew, if he was with me, would walk beside me and chatter the whole time, and I would listen and even respond to that chatter with one half of my brain, while the other half in all likelihood was pursuing a completely different train of thought.

The Sunday walk with all the senior boys – for Matron took a few of the younger ones for 'a short sharp turn,' which was almost as distasteful to her as it was to them – was a somewhat heavier responsibility. It was difficult to prevent it straggling out at greater and greater intervals into the semblance of a demoralised and defeated army. The fact that I was a quick walker made matters worse. If rain threatened, we might be content with a round which took us to the sea-front and back, returning by way of a large private hotel which lay on the outskirts of the town. But if the rain held off, we might change our minds, and, leaving the town and promenade behind us, strike across springy, flat turf to a region that reminded me of David Copperfield's visit to the Peggotty family at Yarmouth. It was on some such open flats that the upturned boat must have

55

lain. A little further on dunes and hollows broke the level vista and, wandering into them, one would be cut off from the whole world with only a horizon of sea-grass and the sky to look at. Into this desolate region I might lead my band and we would find ourselves jumping dykes on the foreshore or crossing narrow plank bridges below which a stream or cutting ran out to empty itself like some miniature Nile over the flats, half mud, half sand. Here one seemed nearer to Nature and less tied to one's noisy herd, though to forget them even for a minute generally meant some prank that had to be punished or at least severely threatened.

Sometimes, without taking to the road at all we might leave the school, cross the opposite field with its coarse yellow grass which no one cut because it waited only for the builder's desecrating hand, and plunge in single file along the narrow little wood path which led along the foot of the hill. Then, when we came out at Meliden, we would climb that steep hillside road, with loud protests from the lazier members of the party. A sense of exhilaration infected us all when we finally reached the rounded brow of the hill and emerged on to a wide expanse of pasture-land, verging on gorse; green close-cropped grass, sheep-grazed, with low grey stone walls or no walls at all, ground where the boys could play games, run and shout exultantly, or suddenly fling themselves down on a flat rock to gaze out across the expanse of plain below. The time when I liked this place best was on those nights when I came here alone, or on some shining Sunday morning when I was free to climb to it before church.

At such moments I breathed wine. But I could enjoy it too with my herd of young barbarians, who were not by any means wholly blind to the beauty of Nature, even if more interested in their own exploits as they leaped and ran. They were able too to respect my own moods of silence and reverie, and perhaps to take advantage of them, though to give them their due I do not think that this was often the case.

And if they could share in my pleasures, I too in a measure could share in theirs. I liked to dramatise life, could enjoy its small adventures as much as they. One Sunday afternoon, we went towards Dyserth, and, tired of the usual route, I suddenly decided to let them climb the face of the hill immediately above the branch railway line, going up a steep, stony gully which turned out to be a good deal steeper than I had thought. It was more like an old avalanche track than anything else and I was relieved when I had got them all safely up, some on their hands and knees, some pushed from behind. But they were ecstatic about the whole business. 'A gloy walk, sir. The best we've had this term,' using one of those coined expressions which suddenly become current in a school, just as, when a boy blushed at table, they would instantly say, 'Stoke up! Stoke up!' They had enjoyed it so much that I felt my momentary anxiety well repaid.

In ways like this, in my enthusiasm at their matches, when I would shout myself hoarse, and in my attempt never to treat them as mere cyphers, but always as human beings, I atoned in some measure for my deficiencies in other respects – for my reluctance to be with them at every moment of the day, for my self-absorption, and my quite evident craving for occasional escape.

I longed to escape, and could escape to my small study when my work was over, or to my room at the top of the house – two retreats where I always felt safe, to read, to smoke, to forget that I was a slave in Egypt. Down at the other school the Swiss girl, who was as little sociable as I was, must sit with her host and hostess in the evening or else retire to her bedroom, which was probably the alternative generally chosen. She showed little inclination, I imagine, to indulge in small talk or to chat about the day's affairs, and unless it was an evening for reading Shakespeare, would slip away like an anchorite immediately to her own cell.

This was the indirect cause of her first real quarrel with Vandeleur. One Sunday morning she arrived at church fuming, and plainly labouring under a burning sense of injustice. When we had taken our seats she whispered to me that Vandeleur had just told her that she could not have the gas in her room any longer at night. Vandeleur, who was late going to bed himself, and I think an indifferent sleeper – must have looked from his window at midnight and seen the light burning in her room, a contravention of his views both on economy, and also, perhaps, on the amount of sleep necessary to ensure an efficient staff. It had roused all the resentment and pettiness of which he was sometimes capable and made him announce to her that if she burnt the gas so late she could not have it at all. It was tyranny, and tyranny which she had been very quick to resent.

'I will refuse. I am not going to write by candlelight. I am doing some articles for a newspaper and it has nothing to do with him if I choose to work.' And her indignation was only silenced by the entry of the choir and the announcement of the first hymn.

Vandeleur's decree seemed to me fantastic. It was the measure of

57

his irritability with her. I saw it too as the measure of how life was always being made difficult for a writer. I sympathised with her, but my impulse was not to foment her indignation, but to get the matter put right if I could.

'Ask for an oil lamp, if they think that more economical. He can hardly refuse you that. Of course, it is nonsense about the gas——'

I awaited my moment and, when a chance presented itself, spoke to Vandeleur's son-in-law.

'Mademoiselle is distressed at being told she cannot have the gas in her room at night. It is a real hardship for her, as she is doing some work for a Swiss newspaper.'

The peacemaker agreed that something must be done. Later I heard that she had won her point. Vandeleur had conceded that she should be allowed the gas until ten o'clock at night.

Until ten o'clock seemed a concession of the most elementary justice, but to her it was a triumph, and her pleasure in it gave a sudden and refreshing glimpse of the schoolgirl behind that mature and inscrutable young woman who at other times so mystified me.

It might have been as well, however, had she never won this small 'victory,' as she so proudly termed it. It was to leave her with a false sense of security. It was to deceive her, like Napoleon, into the mistaken belief that she could win any victory she liked. Flushed with conquest, she determined to carry the war into the enemy's country.

The General Election which had been occupying everyone's thoughts for some weeks was over. Vandeleur had been one of the leading supporters of the Conservative Party and had gone to a public dinner to celebrate its victory. Miss Winsor, Mademoiselle and I were enjoying the novelty of dining alone. In the course of the meal, Mademoiselle announced to us that she intended asking if she might go away for the week-end.

'We are playing hockey against a ladies' team at Colwyn Bay on Saturday, I am going to ask if I may take a bicycle with me when we go, and stay there for the week-end, or perhaps go on to Llandudno. In that way I will see something of the country.'

'Don't be absurd. He will never let you. He is always saying that you are under his charge and that he is responsible for you. You have no friends to go to. It is waste of time to ask him.'

'Does he expect me never to move from this place? Am I a slave or a prisoner?'

Shaking her head so that her hair fell over her temples and had to be pushed back with one hand, she gave an ironical laugh and proclaimed her resolution. She would ask all the same. Her request was perfectly reasonable. She had no teaching over the week-end. Vandeleur's daughter had already offered to lend her a bicycle.

'I want to go somewhere where there are boats.'

'You have the sea here.'

'Yes, there is the sea, but there is not a single boat. I want to go where I can see boats.'

'He will never let you go.'

Like Pharaoh, he could be depended upon to harden his heart. Of that we were perfectly certain. Together we tried to convince her that there was not the smallest chance of the trip being permitted. Old-fashioned and strait-laced, Vandeleur's ideas on women's freedom were those of the previous century, and it would seem to him utterly unsuitable to let this young girl, a foreigner in a strange land, go alone to Llandudno.

'I have friends in Shrewsbury. Why cannot I go and see them?'

'Ask that, by all means. It is a different matter. He will probably allow you. But as for the week-end, you haven't a hope.'

The life she was leading had begun to get on her nerves. She was bored. She felt herself cribbed, cabined and confined instead of drinking deep new draughts of life's unexpectedness, as she had hoped when she came to us. Her mind seethed with unfulfilled aspiration, and here she was, the humblest cog in the most routine-ridden of machines. From Miss Winsor I had learnt that one of her plans was to get to Canada, to find there the life of adventure she longed for.

She had so many plans it was hard to keep pace with them. One day she had remarked to me casually, 'Do you know Tagore?'

'No, but I know Yeats who is his friend.'

'Tagore has a school of his own in India. I think perhaps that I shall leave here, and go out there.'

She said it in the same way that another person might say, 'I think I shall go shopping in Cheltenham this afternoon.' The world was her oyster and she had every intention of opening it.

Actually she was too changeable, too ardent, too impulsive to exercise any discretion when it came to gaining her point. She scorned tact or pliancy; she was too direct, and perhaps in too great a hurry, to trouble about it. When she tried to be subtle, her efforts only made her appear dishonest in a childish sort of way.

This was to be made abundantly plain within the next few days.

The Llandudno project was never mooted. Something happened which sent her off at a tangent. Next morning I was in Vandeleur's study, talking to him at the beginning of break, when she entered, a letter in her hand. The warm room, the carved furniture and heavy carpet, the shelves lined with books, the desk with its tidy arrangement of papers, all reflected Vandeleur's love of comfort and sense of order. Standing in front of the bright coal fire, his hands joined behind him under his black clerical coat, his head thrust slightly forward, he looked over the top of his gold-rimmed pince-nez to where she stood, leaning against the side of the wooden doorway, rather like some dryad, or like Daphne about to withdraw into the laurel.

'Just one moment, Mademoiselle, I shall be finished with Mr. Gibbon in a minute.'

As I went out I wondered if she had come to ask for her leave.

Break was drawing to a close when she met me in the corridor outside my study and told me in a dramatic whisper that she had just had the most tremendous and cataclysmic row with the Headmaster.

'What happened? Did you ask about Saturday?'

'No, my plans were all changed by a letter that I have had this morning.'

She began to laugh a little hysterically.

'Oh, the things that I have said to him. You do not know what I have said. I lost my temper completely.'

She covered her face with her two hands in mock shame.

'Stop laughing. Tell me exactly what happened. You will have to be quick. Break is nearly over.'

She told her story disjointedly. She had received a letter that morning when she came up to the school, and had impulsively gone straight to Vandeleur with it at break, before thinking out any definite line of action. It was like her to act quickly, but I could hardly congratulate her on her diplomacy in this instance.

What did she want?

Might she go to Oxford for the week-end?

To Oxford?

Yes.

Had she a friend there?

Yes, a friend.

A girl friend?

Yes – a girl friend.

She was not a good liar, being too impatient and lacking in real guile. Indeed, it is possible that she was only betrayed into lying by the swift insistence of Vandeleur's sudden and searching cross-examination, which she had not expected. She had lied instinctively, the very alarm with which the question was shot at her telling her that it would be fatal to say anything else.

What was her friend's name?

The name which she let slip was a foreign one, and a moment later she had admitted that the friend was not a girl friend at all, but an Indian student at the University. It was not quite clear to me whether they had ever even met. But there had been an exchange of letters. Correspondence springs up between students of different nations interested in the same things, and it was probably he who had told her of Tagore's wonderful school in Bengal.

I could picture Vandeleur's consternation. I, who was the victim of mild colour-prejudice myself, was a little shocked. What then must Vandeleur's feelings have been!

Actually, his first response had been to congratulate her on having retracted her lie and elected to tell the truth. She made a face when she told me this, and I gathered that the admission had been involuntary, as impulsive as the rest of her behaviour. It was a little ironic that in her anxiety to observe the proprieties on which we had laid such emphasis the previous evening she had produced a friend so little suited to fulfil the duties of a chaperon. She had seen in the letter, which probably only contained a suggestion that she ought to try and visit the University city before leaving England, a chance to get to Oxford. To Oxford she would go.

But she had blundered irretrievably; the effect on Vandeleur was to leave him under the impression that here was a person ready to shatter every existing convention. While congratulating her on the honesty of second thoughts he had given the most categorical refusal to her request, and his refusal had let loose the whole flood of her resentment against him; all her annoyance at the little restrictions which had irritated her ever since her arrival in the school came to a head and her wrath had boiled over completely.

'Oh, I have been a fool. I said anything. I have been a fool.'

It was plain that even now, only five minutes after the event, she already realised that her attack had been ill-advised. What was the good of telling a man of his age and position what one thought of his school and of the restrictions he placed on the liberty of his staff. One cannot teach an old dog tricks. In the case of the gas she had

had a definite grievance, but on the present occasion she had just launched forth on a general diatribe.

'There is the bell. I must go——'

She fled hastily and as I gathered up my books to go into class I wondered how long it would be before I was betrayed into a similar outburst.

Her luck was out. The avenging furies were already on her track. Her attack upon her employer, though she did not know it, had come at the most inopportune moment possible, when she had most need of his good opinion. Sometimes in life events, not so grave in themselves, will link up serially, with the most fatal consequences, just as a run on one colour in roulette may bring us bad luck, or, as in dreams a mocking surrealist sometimes arranges strange concurrences, the full irony of whose conjunction is only apparent to us when we awake.

That evening when the boys had gone in to tea she tapped on my study door. I came to it and, standing in the doorway, she announced quietly:

'I am leaving. I must go back to Switzerland as soon as it can be arranged.'

'What do you mean?'

The explanation was simple enough. I myself had witnessed the first act of the drama that afternoon at tea in the drawing-room. The school doctor had arrived to see Miss Winsor, who had been taken ill. This had been another occasion for annoyance to Vandeleur, for her classes had had to be arranged. Just before the doctor left Mademoiselle asked if she also might see him.

'I have been ill, and I have just heard from my hospital in Switzerland. They recommend a certain treatment. I think it very drastic. If I cannot have it here, I must go to Liverpool twice a week for it.'

There were ships at Liverpool. Were they in her thoughts, at this moment, I wondered, a compensation for what might be before her?

Vandeleur had not yet recovered from the morning's tornado. When she made her request, he muttered rather ungraciously, 'Yes, if you pay him.'

She had followed him out of the room, and I now learnt the sequel.

'You know that I have told you that I have sailed for six months in the Mediterranean. Well, during that time I have contracted malaria and have also had dysentery. I have been treated for it in Switzerland and thought that I was cured. Now I have had a letter from Geneva giving the result of the last bacteriological examination. It appeared that I am not completely cured. I must have further treatment. I have asked to see the doctor and have asked him whether he could give the inoculations. But Vandeleur says that I must go at once. I must leave the school as soon as it can be arranged about my passport.'

The Swiss doctors had told her that she was not infectious. The local doctor said that there was a risk, though a very slight risk, of contagion. But Vandeleur was furious. He railed at her for daring to come into his school with this filthy disease upon her. It was as though he had discovered a pariah or leper in our midst. Whatever sympathy she might have had from him, if any, had been forfeited by her outburst that morning. Indeed, throughout the whole affair I was not to hear a single expression of sympathy of any sort for the victim herself. Her announcement had created a panic. Vandeleur's daughter was terrified because of her husband, who was delicate. Mademoiselle must leave England the moment matters could be arranged with the Home Office. Moreover, Vandeleur had announced that she must pay her own fare back to Switzerland.

This announcement had been to her the last drop in her cup of bitterness, for she was poor. Every penny was of importance to her, and now the savings she had were to be taken from her to buy a ticket back to Geneva – the last place to which she wanted to go.

She reverted to this grievance next morning when I spoke to her for a few minutes during the interval.

'Why should I be made buy my own ticket? If I am sent home now, I shall never get away again. They will keep me for good. My parents have never wished me to travel. They want me to help in the business. My father has had losses, and is gloomy and misanthropic. My brother writes that there is a shadow over the whole house, everyone is *enervé* and quarrelsome. If once I return I shall never get away again. It is the end of all for me.'

The picture which she drew of her home life was probably exaggeratedly dark, but at nineteen, when even the less enterprising feel sometimes that they would like to shake off the trammels of the familiar and strike out a line for themselves, it was understandable. This was a crushing blow to her. Just at the very moment when she had achieved freedom, it was to be snatched away from her and she was to be sent home in disgrace.

'Well, what can you do?'

'I have friends in London. I can go to them if he will let me.'

63

'But will he let you? Your permit to get into the country was for a particular purpose. It wasn't like a passport.'

There was no time to discuss the matter further. She must go to her class. Though I was the person in the school most in sympathy with her point of view and for that reason had become her confidant, it was astonishing how few opportunities we got of exchanging even half a dozen words. It was this that lent an air almost of conspiracy to all our contacts, for if she had anything to tell me it had to be told quickly and generally in an undertone. Details would be filled in later, by herself, or perhaps from what Miss Winsor had been able to glean of the affair.

Next day was Thursday. After lunch I set forth on my customary walk. From the first, conscious that the more the school work weighed upon me the more I must try to escape from it completely the one afternoon in the week when I was free, I had made a point of this. If it was wet or if I was very tired, I might go off to my bed-room after lunch, throw myself on my bed, sleep, and later write, until the usual time came for me to descend to afternoon tea in the drawing-room. The children from the other school, a round dozen or so, would perhaps be gathering up their possessions before departure after the dancing-class – a pair of dancing slippers, a satchel, a woollen scarf that had been mislaid – and for one moment I might catch a glimpse of the tall, straight child with hair like Melisande's flowing to her waist, whose unconscious grace had inspired my poem. But if the day was at all fine, I tried to get away for the whole afternoon.

The previous week I had got as far as St. Asaph. Mounting the bridge above the railway station, I had stood there gazing at the ice-cold background of Welsh hills in a half-circle against the horizon. It would have been impossible to say why, looking at these low, distant, snow-covered hills against the despairing background of a November afternoon sky should give me such illimitable content, unless it was the deep satisfaction that comes from the contemplation of something remote, detached, self-existent, and utterly without reference to ourselves. And yet, having gazed my fill, I had been glad enough to turn back into the town and find some small obscure café in a side street and sit there experiencing a certain sense of comfort and relaxation as I drank my tea and smoked a cigarette with a feeling of detachment almost equal to that which I had felt on the railway bridge.

To-day I walked over to Rhyl by the wide, flat road that ran within a few hundred yards of the sea, flooded fields on one side, sandy pasture-land, suitable only for sheep, but which would be crowded with the tents and huts of campers in the summer, on the other. Heavy, low clouds, full of rain, drifted in a wet, grey sky, and at times a patch of brightness might appear so that one saw the lighter clouds reflected in the huge puddles on the black road. It was a day typically Welsh, for, though one gets exactly the same day in Ireland, in Scotland and in England, it seemed peculiarly appropriate to the present landscape. Rhyl in winter became the ghost of itself, a forlorn, grey, dissenting Welsh ghost. It seemed impossible that it could ever have witnessed even so much frivolity as a concert party upon its sands. Stripped of all its glories, its roundabouts covered over, its ice-cream parlours boarded up, its shooting galleries closed, it became a city of tall, deserted lodging-houses, with empty rooms and unopened windows, in one of which might linger perhaps a small forgotten notice saying that apartments were to let. The occupants and proprietors had withdrawn from the public gaze into a species of retirement which might almost have been called hibernation, going about their trivial daily business, pious and a little exhausted, until it should once more become time for them to take their toll of Mammon and witness its noisy enjoyments. We were luckier. Less known than this larger and more famous watering place along the coast, we catered for the family holiday rather than for the noisy horde from the great cities, and so probably felt the contrast of the seasons less. My own summer holidays as a child had been sometimes spent in North Wales. To one accustomed to Ireland and its easy-going ways, it had always seemed a place of alert, very clean and business-like efficiency, its people abrupt of speech, in a hurry on week-days, but very careful in their religious observances on Sunday. Welsh Nonconformity, like Swiss Calvinism, goes its way, little affected by the customs of the pleasure-seekers for whom it caters. It is to its credit that this is so. The fat, plethoric individuals, covered with sun-blisters and surrounded by a filthy litter of lunch paper and tinfoil – these neo-pagans who are neither beautiful themselves nor respect beauty, and who spend the Sabbath morning stretched on the beach, their attention concentrated on the salacities of their Sunday newspaper – are not necessarily so much higher in the scale of evolution than their hosts, who remain true to a tradition of generations, and who are thought sanctimonious because they prefer to go to church or chapel on Sunday and sing hymns with their young.

EMI   65

I wandered about Rhyl, cheerless enough in itself but an escape from my usual surroundings, along the deserted esplanade and through streets where even the shops seemed to be sunk in a coma. It came as a surprise to see from a poster on a wooden gateway in one of these completely empty roads that a Welsh choir was giving a concert performance at half-past seven that evening in the Pavilion. Here was a chance to listen to some music. I rang up Vandeleur to know if I might be excused returning to dinner in order to hear them. It gives the measure of the strictness of the régime that though it was my free day I thought this necessary. Vandeleur might be annoyed if, contrary to my custom, I stayed out in the evening. He gave his consent, and, walking back along the empty sea-front, I found a café near the pavilion where I had high tea before going on to the concert. It was over early, a not very inspiring entertainment and I returned later in the evening, the solitary passenger in the yellow bus. When I got back and was walking up from the town the light was still burning in the window of the room I believed to be Mademoiselle's at the girls' school. I noticed it as I went by. Was she studying nautical science? Or was she philosophising over the crushing defeat which had followed her little 'victory,' scribbling her reflections on the uncertainty of all things mortal?

It was curious that it should be she and not I with whom Vandeleur had first definitely quarrelled. What did Vandeleur's son-in-law, stooped over his books now in the lower room, think of this latest upheaval? This delicate-looking, quiet young man, worried not a little by the exam he was taking, had he accepted it, as he accepted almost everything with a little abrupt laugh, or a slow, almost inaudible, sigh of surprise? Our temperaments were leagues apart. He found it easier by nature, and was more bound by every circumstance and obligation, to bow to the inevitable. If the repercussions of Vandeleur's temper tried him, he never showed it, never passed any comment, and never himself at least, in my hearing, came into direct conflict with Vandeleur. At times he seemed to me the irritating incarnation of all that was safe and bourgeois and cautious, just as at times I probably maddened him nearly as much as I did his father-in-law. But if this was so, conciliatory by disposition, he concealed the fact. Only very occasionally, when nettled by some omission or carelessness on my part, did a note of faint reproach creep into his voice. On one of the very few occasions on which we had discussed Mademoiselle together he had summed up his whole verdict on her in a single phrase – 'She is a law to

66

herself.' People who were a law to themselves were obviously asking for trouble. He saw us at loggerheads with our employer, and it must have seemed to him often that we were merely reaping what we had sowed, but he remained silent. Outwardly he was the perfect neutral: his job was to carry on, to be patient, to annoy no one.

I could be patient too. Vandeleur could be patient. That was the irony of the situation. Sometimes when I put my point of view to him he would listen with quite a degree of tolerance, and I on my part would do my best not to rile him. We could both be courteous enough when we chose, but we could both also be extremely rude. A certain native bellicosity on each side made a clash sooner or later inevitable. Some unorthodoxy, some disregard of ritual upon my part, some outburst upon Vandeleur's, the spark would drop into the magazine and the explosion would follow. I was an idealist. I still believed in perfection. I loathed the exhibitionism into which schoolmasters so easily drop, so that even their anger is a sort of stage-show put on for the benefit of the class. The voice rises in a shrieking crescendo of nervous irritation. The thing becomes a habit like a drug, stimulating for a time, only to leave one ultimately more exhausted. Sometimes there is a sort of Indian summer of good-will before the full winter of wrath breaks. But it is a false buoyancy, an unnatural elation, which is misleading even to its possessor. I loathed the mixture of ruthlessness and capricious indulgence when, as it were, the cat plays with the mouse before finally destroying it. To make a butt of the stupid boy, to get into the habit of pillorying him before the class, is too easy and can become a sadistic amusement. Soon one approaches him with an almost malicious subconscious pleasure.

Roibeárd ó Faracháin has fixed this moment in 'School Teacher':

> ' . . . I remember
> rage filling head with hot blood, and (God preserve us!)
> ecstasy sprung from anger – so that a cringing
> fear-stricken boy became a joy spring. . . .
>   Therefore I have run
> Shuddering from the chalk dust. I have shunned
> danger of my debasement.'

'A joy spring?' What more terrible source of glee can be discovered than a child's blundering? One has begun the descent to Avernus. It will end like the clergyman Headmaster of Sir Ian Hamilton's illustrious preparatory school, who had evolved a pleasant system of making the small boy whom he wished to punish stand in his study against the wall with his arms extended on either side at shoulder level. He would sit nearby at his desk, writing, with his back to the boy, but observing his reflection from time to time in the glass of a picture. The moment the elbows sagged he would make an unexpected rush from behind, striking at the victim's funny-bone with a heavy ruler.

I held an easy-going belief, contradicted from time to time in biographies of the great, that you can never teach a boy very much against his will, and that for one boy whom you can frighten out of laziness into industry, there are at least two whom you will frighten out of mere mild stupidity into abysmal depths of sheer terror. It is doubtful whether railing and upbraiding and shouting ever produce a single good result which could not be produced equally well, and even better, by quiet demonstration, supposing that one had the patience to resort to it. Nevertheless, tired pedagogues continue to rail, and there is probably a psychological explanation, even for the preliminary phase of deceptive good humour. If our nerves are badly frayed there is a moment just before the climax when a pseudo-gaiety takes possession of us, when we are still able to be gracious and lively – indeed, almost a little elate, a little fey, like the wooers in the *Odyssey* immediately before disaster overtook them. But it is a vivacity explained by nervous exhaustion, and the storm when it does come is all the more terrible. It was my grievance against the teaching profession that they wore their nerves to shreds in this fashion, from a mistaken sense of duty and then allowed outraged Nature to revenge itself upon the children. How much better if they had been just a little less conscientious and in the issue just a little more calm. 'Gentleness and cheerfulness are the supreme virtues; these come before all morality,' said Stevenson; but what schoolmaster of the old school would ever have endorsed such a sentiment?

I was becoming irritable myself and beginning to forsake my principles. Before I left school I would fall utterly from grace. That is what happens to the sentimentalist. When his perfect world shows itself less perfect than he had hoped, he loses patience and goes to the other extreme. It was Marat, the French revolutionary, who announced early in his career that he could not bear the thought of crushing even an insect on the palm of his hand. Already, even in my first term, I had begun to waver. Taking the little game of football was one of my duties which I relished least; then, if ever, it

seemed to me that natural exuberance should be allowed some outlet. But my leniency in actual fact only resulted in chaos. We would
go down to the playing-field, which was five or six hundred yards
from the school, across the main road, and I would lead the way
with a little crowd of happy enthusiasts hopping and running beside
me. But once there they became shrieking demons. Everyone had a
different plan for the game, everyone spoke at once, everyone wanted
to captain one or other of the sides. Surging round me, they raised
their voices to such a pitch that I could understand none of them.
Even when the game at last began, though it had seemed of such
absorbing importance to them before, they were capable of forsaking
it for some other interest. The playing-field was near the railway
line, and once when I was taking 'little game' Vandeleur appeared
at the very moment that a train went past. All the players deserted
the game and rushed to the embankment to look at the train.
Vandeleur, as punishment, sent two of them to walk round the field
and I was made to feel that my control of the situation had been
inadequate. In the end, as soon as we arrived on the field and the
noise began, I would cut my willow twig from the hedge and vow
such instant vengeance upon the next offender that the mere threat
soon became quite as efficacious as its execution. I had discovered
the secret of peace.

Rome made me a Roman. In my second term I became, in a
measure at least, Vandeleur's disciple, lost all horror of physical
duress, and even adopted the ruler in class. I cannot excuse myself
by saying that this was due to the difficulty of maintaining discipline
in a school where a ruler was the almost universal nostrum; for
actually there were three women on the staff who taught quite
successfully without resorting to any methods of violence. No, it is
far more likely that, as with Vandeleur, it was the result of mere
fatigue and irritability.

Let the full measure of my baseness be told. There was a little boy
in the school named Kenneth, happy, chubby-faced, with pendulous
pink cheeks, which became slightly blue in winter, and a look of
shy caution – rather like a nervous lawyer briefed in a bad cause –
except when a smile lit up his face with the most charming expression. He was Welsh, I think, and perhaps there was something of the
Welshman in his slightly self-deprecatory approach to events and
people. He cannot have been more than eight years old. He had a
brother in the school, a sunny, open-countenanced, red-cheeked boy
of twelve, rather stupid, but painstaking and a trier, and therefore

able, by straining every nerve, to keep himself in Vandeleur's good graces. They were day-boys, and their father, a captain in the Merchant Service, was away a good deal of the time.

It was Kenneth's misfortune that he could not spell. Like George, he had no idea whatever of the science of spelling, or of the admittedly capricious relationships which exist between letters and sounds in the English language. If he went on any method at all – and this is doubtful – I suspect that it was a forlorn and frantic effort to memorise the letters of a word separately, and hope, by some magical or providential intervention when the time came that they would fall into their right order. The results, as may be guessed, were fantastic in the extreme. All words remained a capricious mystery to him, and in investigating them one guess was as good as another, and as likely, or rather as certain, to be wrong. He had become a chronic offender and not only his writing but his reading was held up by this inability to spell.

In an evil moment I was asked to improve Kenneth's spelling. He was handed over to me like a lamb for the sacrifice, and I undertook to give him special instruction four or five mornings a week. We began with the best intentions on both sides. Though there was something a little ingratiating about this child's manner, something that, as we say in Ireland, savoured of the 'sleveen' – small wonder considering the hostility of that well-spelt world in which he found himself – there was also much that was attractive, winning and a little pathetic. He was determined to do better. Like the chronic drunkard who once more turns over a new page of reform with every confidence of success, Kenneth was resolved to learn spelling under my tuition or to die in the attempt.

He did not die: rather it was I, his instructor, who felt that the pains of hell had got hold on me. Of all things which irritate the impatient, stupidity probably irritates them most. By temperament quick themselves, they are maddened into fury by the ineptitude of others, an ineptitude for which there seems no excuse. Is not the thing as clear as daylight? So obvious is it to them that, for this very reason, they suffer far more from the impasse than the victims of their wrath, to whom all is amorphous and vague.

Kenneth was stupid. He had a truly amazing faculty for repeating the same fault an infinite number of times. It would appear inconceivable that he could ever make a particular mistake again, yet make it he would. He was as likely, for example, to put down *woh* – with an unctious consciousness of rectitude – as he was to put down *who*. *Woh* was not a careless slip; it was the outcome of mature consideration. He could not get it right. Soon he grew confused. His world became a kaleidoscopic chaos in which *who* and *woh* spun round in frenzied spirals, out of which vortex, even if he paused to think, he was as likely to pick the wrong spelling as the right.

Under these circumstances it is not perhaps surprising that I lost my temper. I would begin the lesson full of goodwill, full of the milk of human kindness, but on the first appearance of *woh* it was exactly as if the dart or banderilla had been planted firmly in the neck of a bull, in the course of a bull-fight. There could not have been a more dismally repentant picador than the blue-cheeked small boy who had just planted it, but there it was, rankling and spluttering, and inviting me to put down my head and charge.

There were four other darts with coloured streamers attached to them which he used to plant quite as often and as accurately – or should one say inaccurately? – in my shoulder muscles. These were the four words, *now*, *know*, *new* and *knew*. We were always encountering them in our reading and I had been foolish enough to imagine that if he could once surmount this *pons asinorum* – in which after all there were only four planks laid across a relatively narrow stream – we should have conquered in principle, and my pupil would be on the high road to realising what spelling meant. Let him once learn to differentiate between *now*, *know*, *new* and *knew*, with their respective meanings, and victory was ours. The rest would follow easily. But to Kenneth it seemed that he was as likely to walk across the tight rope at Olympia on a first trial, with all London watching, as to achieve this mastery even after a painful concentration of will. Just as the picador steps aside a pace and stands with feet together while he watches the bull flash past, so Kenneth, when he had brought up his work, would stand beside my desk, a little apologetic, a little shamefaced, his fat cheeks symbolic at once of apology and of that insane recrudescence of hope for which there was absolutely no foundation in fact. Each of the four words might ring the changes on its three companions; *now* might become *know*, *new* or *knew*, but it would never by any possible chance be itself. The thing became an obsession with both of us.

I encouraged him. I urged him on. But at the next *now* that should have been *know* I would be thrown off my balance. It was a case of King Charles's head.

'What is it? You must know. I've told you so often. *What* is it?'

He would look at me reproachfully and flounder helplessly.

71

'You'll have to have the ruler. You'll have to have the ruler.'

He would make one last desperate and quite absurd effort to rectify matters.

'Hold out your hand.'

Two great tears would well up in his eyes. He had failed again. The moment of retribution had come.

I would give him perhaps a cut on each hand and he would snivel pathetically. What was so distressing was his complete acquiescence in the necessity for this act. Never had unhappy mortal questioned the justice of Fate's sentence less.

In actual fact, he did improve slowly, less perhaps because of the smarting of his palms than because, in spite of this, he felt dimly that his persecutor had a genuine interest in and affection for him.

'I am getting better, aren't I?' he would ask hopefully. 'I haven't had to have the ruler to-day.'

And without wholly perjuring myself I would reply, 'Yes, you are.'

But on other days he would lapse, his stupidity would assume gargantuan proportions, and, standing beside me, forlorn and dejected, a great tear would gather in the corner of each eye as he saw the inevitable approach of Nemesis; or, if the avenging furies had already played their part, a whole course of tears would trickle slowly down his fat, bluish-pink cheeks.

It is true that the ruler was not my only form of punishment. I might banish him from the room for five minutes, leaving him to stand in the passage until told that he might return. Or I might even send him to Vandeleur to say how badly he was doing. If Vandeleur had been teaching him himself, he would have been irritated to madness; but since in actual fact he had washed his hands of him long ago he was able to be benign. Vandeleur would look at him quite benevolently over the top of his gold pince-nez, pretending to be suitably shocked, but, as he was quite fond of the little boy, nothing dreadful would happen. He would lecture him and send him back to me, only too glad to hand him over once more to my suzerainty. I do not think that Vandeleur liked punishment for its own sake; it had simply become an outlet with him for his own extreme irritability; or else it arose from a mistaken sense of duty. Whether I vented my own impatience upon Kenneth's small extended palm, or whether I genuinely thought it the only means of mobilising his sluggish wits, I cannot say. Corporal punishment may awaken a streak of cruelty in us of which we are quite unaware. That is the conclusive argument against it, except for a few offences, for the bully, and for those who are consistently insolent; or, when all else has failed, as a very rare reminder to the forgetful.

But my treatment of Kenneth can hardly be said to have come under any of these headings. It seems to me now to have been brutal. I know that he was often beaten, but I know too that we were good friends in spite of it, and that I had in some way earned his affection. Though I suspected both him and his elder brother of being just a shade plausible, I cannot believe that his friendliness was wholly feigned or that it was his method, conscious or unconscious, of propitiating his oppressor. There may be something of the spaniel in children, but they are the first to sense real contempt and dislike, and to repay it in kind. Kenneth was genuinely fond of me and I of him. We can be severe and even unkind to a child, and strangely enough they will love us in spite of this, if we have not been wholly tyrants. Linking his arm happily through mine as we went down to the football field, he would hop along gaily beside me chatting as we went. His work improved, and he suddenly became brilliant at sums, able, to my intense satisfaction, to beat John Williamson, the brother of the little prig. We both viewed this surprising turn of events with mutual rejoicing.

I was to receive a touching proof of his regard before I left the school. It happened that a temporary member of the staff, the pretty young wife of a local bank official who had come for one term to take certain classes and help Vandeleur out of a difficulty, was leaving also, and it had been suggested to the children that they should subscribe for a presentation to her. In my case, I need hardly say, no such tax was being made upon their assets. But in some obscure fashion Kenneth felt this to be unjust. I had taught him to spell, and I had been two whole terms at the school living with them, whereas she had only come daily for one. A few days before the end of term he knocked on my door just before going home to his lunch. He had brought me a sixpence as a parting presentation of his own. He explained that it was all he had, and that he was sorry it was not more.

I confess to having been utterly humbled and touched in this moment. Embarrassment seized me at the sight of that slightly apologetic small figure, with the pink cheeks and rather full mouth, making this solitary presentation to me in my own study, unknown to Vandeleur. My first impulse was to refuse to take it. Then I said that I would accept it, but that I would get postcards with it to send to him when I had gone. Later his mother sent me a photograph of him in fancy dress. In this the picador who had pierced my irascible and ill-tempered neck so often with those four unfailing darts, standing aside tearfully and extremely puzzled to watch their effect, appeared as a pierrot, in chequered blouse and pantaloon, with baggy velvet artist's cap, seated on the edge of a table, and smiling as though all our separate offences, his of stupidity, mine of acerbity and harshness – and I count mine the worst – were completely forgotten.

I anticipate. These special grinds in spelling belonged to my second term. At the time of which I write my principles were still humanitarian and my classes had nothing to fear from me. Any suffering I did inflict was upon my employer. There were a dozen different ways in which I maddened him. There was my Shakespeare class. Of all my classes in the week, I liked this one with the senior boys the best. We were reading *The Merchant of Venice*, and it was not so much a class as a dramatic rehearsal. Seated along the window-ledge, my feet up, I shared in the reading. I took the part of Shylock. I liked being Shylock and I was a little proud of my mastery of the Jewish lisp. I had discovered that by bringing my tongue forward in my mouth and by a slight pressure of its tip against my teeth, I could achieve just that thickening of utterance which gave a Hebraic similitude to my speech. Besides, most of my sympathies – like Shakespeare's and Brownings's – were with the Jew. Rolling out my words gutterally and with tremendous sympathy for the under-dog, I would voice the resentment of centuries:

'Hath not a Jew eyes? Hath not a Jew hands, organs, dimensions, senses, affections, passions? Fed with the same food, hurt with the same weapons, subject to the same diseases, healed by the same means, warmed and cooled by the same winter and summer as a Christian is? If you prick us, do we not bleed? If you tickle us, do we not laugh? If you poison us, do we not die? and if you wrong us, shall we not r-revenge? If we are like you in the rest, we will r-resemble you in that.'

I would lash myself into a mood of bitter, reproachful fury in such a speech. The boys were hugely delighted, and, losing their self-consciousness, would let themselves go in their own parts. Or there were Shylock's moments of senile pathos: 'No ill luck stirring but what lights o' my shoulders. No sighs but o' my breathing. No tears but o' my shedding.' These gave an equally splendid opportunity. I enjoyed myself. I forgot where I was. Perhaps there was a touch of defiance about it all too. It was a slightly malicious reminder to

74

Vandeleur of the disadvantages of three forms in the same room. I had suffered so much from having to teach little boys mathematics immediately beside him, while he roared at his classes, that it was a golden opportunity to revenge myself. But, in any case, there is only one rule for reading a play aloud; to forget oneself completely, to become the part utterly, extravagantly, without reserve.

I let myself ago. As soon as Shylock came upon the scene the whole room knew it. Vandeleur might have said with Salanio, 'I never heard a passion so distraught, so strange, outrageous and so variable as the dog Jew did utter.' The strange thing was that he took it remarkably patiently. Perhaps he was amused. Perhaps he thought it good for my class, if not for his. Perhaps he suspected me of trying to draw his fire and for that reason withheld it. Only one day, when the double loss of his ducats and his daughter had made Shylock more than ever vocal, he came across to me quietly and suggested that I should moderate my transports a little.

The suggestion was taken in rather ill part.

'If I read at all, I must read with expression.'

It was a sour rejoinder.

He returned to his high desk. Down at the far end of the room I could see Mademoiselle taking her class, wandering nonchalantly up and down behind her pupils in the last bench, or leaning back against the wall with the palms of her hands pressed against the plaster.

As we went in to lunch Mademoiselle whispered to me:

'Poor Vandeleur. I am feeling sorry for him this morning!'

It was generous of her to feel sorry for him, if she really did, for he was showing himself implacable where she was concerned. He had been down to the Police Station about her papers. He had written to the Home Office. She was to leave the country as soon as it could possibly be arranged. Her project of going to friends in London would receive no support from him. Rather, he would oppose it. I do not know what insults she had hurled at him on that historic occasion when she had lost her temper. But evidently they rankled and made him less disposed than ever to be generous. He had never been sympathetic to her from the first evening of her arrival; in fact, he was definitely antagonistic to her and they certainly had nothing in common. And now, with the discovery that she was suffering from dysentery, any plea that might have been in her favour was probably nullified for him by the recollection of that scene.

All Vandeleur's sympathies were against her, whereas all mine, now that she was under a cloud, rallied to her support. If it is possible to suffer persecution mania on behalf of another person, I had begun to suffer a mild form of it for her. My letters home became eloquent on the subject of her wrongs. Without telling Mademoiselle, I had already written to my step-sister, who had a nursing-home in Cheltenham, to ask if there was any chance of her finding her a post *au pair* and letting her take the course of inoculations there. But it would be useless if Vandeleur exerted his influence with the authorities against the plan.

I waited for a good moment and then, as tactfully as possible, put in a plea for Mademoiselle with Vandeleur's daughter, waylaying her in the garden one morning on her way down to her own school before lunch. Had she realised the full consequences of what they were doing? Could she use her influence with her father at least to mitigate the sentence of banishment? Mademoiselle had friends in the country. If she could be allowed to go to them . . .

But the hope that she might side with her own sex was disappointed. It was plain that this girl, so complete a contrast temperamentally and in every taste and disposition to herself, was never going to find an advocate in her.

'Yes, she is a magnificent teacher I know, but——'

To every argument I advanced the reply was the same. Mademoiselle had been lacking in openness, in frankness, in that supreme, axiomatic, Euclidean virtue of the Anglo-Saxon mind – namely, 'being straight.' She had allowed them to form the impression that she knew hardly any English, she had told a fib about her Oxford friend, and she had come to the school when she had no right to, concealing the fact that she was a sick person.

'You say that she has been unscrupulous. But surely in asking quite openly to see the school doctor she showed that she was not aware of any enormity of her behaviour. Her own doctor had told her that it was all right. She came here under a genuine belief that she was cured. She was quite unconscious that she was doing an unfair thing to the school.'

She listened, but shook her head; my advocacy did not seem to be getting me very far. She agreed that Mademoiselle had talent, ambition and originality, but she was unscrupulous, there was too much about her that was incalculable.

'You will harp on her being unscrupulous. But surely at her age and with her ambition to get on, it is easy to appear unscrupulous.

If you were in her position and with her longing to travel——'

The contingency seemed to her too unlikely to be considered.

'She had much better go back to Switzerland.'

I advanced one last argument.

'If you send her back in disgrace to her family now, it will wreck all her plans, it will affect her whole life. She hates Geneva and she will have to remain there for the rest of her days. Do you really think that better for her?'

She did not know, nor did it seem that she very much cared.

'You are like Pilate washing his hands "vainly but not impertinently." '

She had the grace to smile.

I had failed and I knew it would be utterly useless to think of renewing my pleas. It was almost as though these people, so conventional themselves, of such limited and stable aspirations, derived an unconscious satisfaction from defeating the wild and hopeful schemes of this Bohemian who was foolish enough to demand adventure. Life had tamed them, and it was high time that she allowed herself to be tamed by it too.

We side instinctively always with our own temperament. Mademoiselle with her zest for life, her courage, her aspiration, appealed to me. She was picturesque. Her sins of impulse were forgiven her. Whereas the more prudential virtues of this pale, tired-looking girl, with dark eyes, who turned a deaf ear to my pleading, meant nothing to me, and I saw in her, probably quite unfairly, only a typical example of Galsworthy's 'Island Pharisee.'

But, in any case, what was the justification for all this talk of the Swiss girl not being straight? What did it all boil down to? She might not be straight, but it was characteristic of her that she chose the shortest possible route always between two points. That was just her fault. She rode rough-shod towards her objective. In the son-in-law's charitable phrase, she was 'a law unto herself.'

In fact, it was a little her weakness this, to imagine that if you wanted a thing badly enough you were bound to get it in the end. It made her loftily indifferent to what seemed to her trifles, and it did not always work. Sometimes dejection would seize her. Then it was as though the flame had flickered for an instant in a lamp exposed to an ugly draught. She would hang her head, make a wry mouth and murmur, 'I have been a fool!' The lock was not tossed back, but hung half across her face, and she seemed subdued at last. Even then her dejection appeared almost a pose, so intensely and

77

vividly had she impressed on your consciousness all those opposite qualities of resolution, energy and hope. It was impossible to believe that she could surrender even to momentary despair.

Human character is a strangely complex thing. Different people perceive completely different aspects of it. To Vandeleur and his daughter Mademoiselle had come to seem little more than an adventuress. To Miss Winsor, tittering in mock horror, she was an amusing hoyden, capable of amazing indiscretion, a kind of electric battery to shock the rest of us. To 'Thorpey,' who liked her and was a sound assessor of character, she was a head-strong girl who was foolish enough to imagine that she could jostle her way past difficulties in life. 'She will go her own way,' she would say when Miss Wilson or I spoke of having offered her advice – shaking her head and pursing her mouth as though adding the mental corollary, 'And she will learn her lesson.' In the whole school I was the only one to see the other side of the picture, to appreciate the determination, the grip, the aspiration to succeed, to do something, to be something. She was poor. Since her family disapproved of her travels, she was getting no help from them. I had noticed the almost pathetic reverence with which she could speak of money, as though it were the key which opened all those magic casements on which she had long since fixed her eye. She referred often to her 'small economies,' using the phrase in the French sense of savings achieved, not as the means of thrift, but as its result. She had seen, for instance, a pair of lacrosse boots in a shop window at Chester, whither she had gone with the team to play hockey. It would use up 'some small economies' to get them, but she thought it worth it. Once I happened to mention to her Worth's *Yacht Sailing*, a somewhat expensive volume which I had read when living on the five-ton *Eiderduck* at Bosham with a friend.

'Worth's *Yacht Sailing*? It has cost me a year's economies to buy that book.'

A year's economies. And now Vandeleur's announcement that she must buy her own ticket back to Switzerland had threatened to blow all her 'small economies' sky-high in a single terrible explosion. It was scarcely surprising that she seemed depressed.

To be poor and ambitious is a bad combination. One must exercise one's wits. 'I am making every effort,' was a favourite expression with her and one that threw a considerable light on her character. It was almost laughable the number of irons that she had in the fire. She had written, within the last few months, to Rome, to Norway, to San Francisco, to India, with a view to openings there. She had

78

written to the Hudson Bay Company. She was in correspondence with an old clergyman in Canada. All her schemes, the schemes of youth, eternally hopeful and at the same time eternally discontent, might be chimerical; but at least they were not mere day-dreams; she had tried to put them into effect. No grass was ever allowed to grow under those restless feet. And now, one obstinate old man, with whom she had lost her temper, was in a position to wreck them all. If she returned to Geneva, the doors of the prison-house would close on her for ever. She would become one more Iphigenia sacrificed on the altar of family obligation.

There were times, as I have said, when even her heart seemed to fail. Saturday came. That evening when she came down from Matron, finding the door of my study open, she remained to chat for a few minutes. I detected a note of despondency in her outlook. Twice in the course of conversation she let slip, in her casual way, the admission that she felt that things were not going too well with her. Once she said thoughtfully, 'You think that you are free in life, and then you find that you are not free at all.' A little later, with even greater significance, she remarked, as though to herself, 'Life has been very good to me till now. I wonder if it is going to be as nice in the future.'

She stood alone. She must fight her own battle. That was what she felt. She would listen to advice readily enough, but it was doubtful how much of it she was really willing to take. Like Matron, I had an idea sometimes that she believed a little too firmly in her own instinct. In the final issue she would always play her cards in her own way, imagining that to win one has only to wish to win with sufficient intensity.

All the same, she had better know the point of view of the race with which she was dealing; and, an opportunity presenting itself, I said to her:

'You know, Ulysses would have been a failure in England. No Englishman ever prides himself on being adroit. Get that into your head. They have only one virtue – straightness. Cultivate it, or you will do nothing with them.'

We talked together for a little longer. Then as she was going she abruptly stretched out her hand, gripped mine, as a man would, and said, 'You know, it is nice to find friends where one goes as frank as you are.'

The door closed behind her. Of all her actions that handshake had been most revealing. Another person would have taken offence, would have seen in the implied criticism a deadly insult. She welcomed it. I had given her a hint on the idiosyncrasies of the British. It was meant to be friendly. That was all that mattered.

Years afterwards, reading a book by Victoria Sackville-West, I suddenly recognised her historical prototype. It was Joan of Arc. The Swiss girl had all Joan's gay camaraderie, her anxiety to be accepted by men on equal terms; not to ape masculinity, but rather to forget that any distinction of sex existed. She had chaffed with the New Zealanders, that day when she arrived, in just the same spirit in which Joan must have chaffed with her soldiers, a spirit at once gaily innocent and a little envious. Joan, till she had her armour and her horse, must have envied every Frenchman, and in the same way this girl envied men their privilege of doing a hundred and one things that she herself desired to do before she died. She had no wish to be one of them, she was without a trace of that inferiority complex which makes many women tyrannical to their own sex when they achieve positions of authority; all she asked was to be allowed to meet men equally and show that she was akin to them in spirit. Something maiden, something of the huntress, Artemis, was her protection. I could imagine her laughing at their jokes, incapable of being shocked by them, simply because to her they were children, and amusing children, children whose confidence she was determined to win; and also it was not in her nature to be shocked. She was more likely to shock.

Nearly a week went by. I saw her each day, but there was little opportunity to ask her how matters were going. Wednesday came and, since there was no match and Vandeleur's son-in-law was taking the Junior game, I seized the opportunity to escape to the great dunes beyond the railway line, to where the seagulls were crying above the waste flats of sand. Returning along the shore an hour later, I met Mademoiselle pacing the bit of beach in front of the pavilion. She was sauntering listlessly, her hands thrust deep in the pockets of her short coat, her blue velvet tam-o'-shanter pulled down to one side. The day was bitterly cold. She looked wretched. Her step lacked its easy, nonchalant swing. She was no longer the radiant, self-confident creature with skin the colour of gold-beater's leaf, who had been introduced to us that first night at dinner. Rather she was the typical exile. It was her free afternoon. She had no one to whom she could go. Perhaps it was her own fault, perhaps her aloofness was to blame, but not one of her fellow members of the hockey club had troubled to ask her to their homes. She was friendless in a strange land. We had only time to exchange a few words, for I had to get back to the school. She told me they were still doing their best to send her back to Geneva, and were waiting to hear now from London.

'Do not go until you have seen what the Home Office people say. I will back you up if necessary; after all, you've done nothing indictable.'

I decided to make a last appeal to Vandeleur himself. It needed a little courage to do so. The trouble with the sensitive is that they assert themselves violently or else they do not assert themselves at all. It is quite possible for a sensitive person to alternate between awe and insolence; and that was precisely what had happened to me, in the case of my employer. I could be extremely rude to Vandeleur when I felt my integrity of spirit was threatened; but I much preferred to be at peace with him, shrank from his displays of irritability and was always relieved when we found ourselves on amicable terms. Far from wishing to provoke scenes, I dreaded them.

The last thing I wished to do was to provoke a scene now. But one afternoon, finding myself alone with him at the beginning of tea, I summoned up courage, broached the topic of Mademoiselle and ventured to plead her cause. Did he realise how much it meant to her to leave England after she had been trying so long to come to that country? Would it be possible to avoid this extreme step?

He lost his temper at once.

'Her parents never wanted her to leave home. Her first duty is to them,' was his angry reply.

She had weakened her case considerably by ever telling us this, and it was now used as a weapon against her. My move had been well-meant, but it had been waste of time to make it. I could see that his mind was made up. She had come into the country under a permit to teach *au pair*, and she must go out by the same token. He would do nothing to mitigate the severity of the sentence. There seemed – at least to me – to be a note of almost deliberate vengeance in his insistence. He had no sympathy with her aspirations and ambitions. She was not going to remain in his school a moment longer than was necessary, and when she left his school he was going to do his best to see that she returned to Geneva.

If I could not befriend her in this way, I would in another. Soon after I came to the school, A.E., when he heard where I was teaching, had given me an introduction to John Eglinton, the Irish essayist. He and his wife lived in a little house in one of those quiet side roads which helped to maintain the reputation of the place as a residential centre, and I had visited them several times on Sundays. 'Contrairy John,' as George Moore has called him in *Hail and Farewell* (where his half-length portrait has all that author's customary skill and less than his customary malice), had been for years a librarian in the National Library in Dublin, and the friend of most of the prominent figures in the Irish revival. A writer of distinction himself, he had now retired from his post in the Library and had come to live in this out-of-the-way spot in an alien land. This introduction had meant a lot to me. It was a link with the literary world. We contributed to the same weekly in Dublin, he an occasional essay, I an occasional poem. When I entered his house I passed into another world, the world of books, of authorship. He had married late in life and had one child. His wife, his junior by a number of years, fair-haired, pretty, had the soft brogue of Southern Ireland in contrast to the dry, slightly caustic accents of her husband, who came from the North. I was welcome to come and see them whenever I was free. They had been good friends to me and I had told them something about my difficulties and discontents at the school, a recital to which they had listened sympathetically, though I suspected they felt that I was quite capable of defending myself. Once on a walk John Eglinton had revealed the fact that in early youth he too had been usher at a boys' school for a short time. The Grammar School at Drogheda had been the scene of his activities. 'I was the most miserable little cuss in all Ireland, but then I had not' – he paused, and I saw a slightly mischievous expression dawning on his face – 'I had not, if you'll forgive me saying so, your assurance.' And from one of his customary premonitory chuckles he had burst into good-humoured laughter.

Now that life seemed to be using the Swiss girl harshly, I bethought myself of this couple. John Eglinton was translating a German book and was worried about some technical phrases, chiefly to do with mountaineering, and I suggested that she might be able to help. My concern was less for the translation, which was a wretched affair, according to John, and one in which he was beginning to lose interest, than for her. I arranged that she should go to tea with them on Sunday afternoon. I would take her round there after lunch, but could not remain as I was on duty myself. In the hall of the little house she whipped off her soft cloth hat, pushing back her hair from her forehead with her usual gesture. She preferred to be bare-headed; it suited her. I looked at her now, fair-haired, in the brown plaid dress, seated near the table with one arm resting on it, and talking in her slow, deliberate, almost half-humorous English, and she seemed to me a figure at once striking and slightly pathetic. Striking indeed – her Minoan profile, so questing, eager and untamed; and yet at the same time pathetic, since I knew she was fighting an unequal battle against forces far too strong for her. Her schemes from the first had been too ambitious, too high-flown, and now, thanks to a single blunder, they were all to be laid in the dust, while she settled down to the dull routine her family had always proposed for her.

I was glad I had brought her. Within five minutes she was completely at home. I left her with them seated by the fire, her hands clasped round her knees, laughing at her own verdicts on the English and their ways. When I questioned her that night at dinner, she told me that her help with the book had been negligible; she had done no German since she had left school, and the difficult passages were highly idiomatic. But, according to John Eglinton, when I saw him, she had been a considerable help, and she was to go again to tea with them more than once in the weeks that followed.

For the days went by and there seemed to be almost as much difficulty in getting her out of England as there had been in arranging for her to come. About this time, Mrs. Vandeleur returned from abroad and the tension of the situation perceptibly eased. It was a good thing. There had been thunder in the air too long. Mrs. Vandeleur was tall, spectacled, a little prim in appearance, and distinctly reminiscent of Betsy Trotwood in *David Copperfield*. Outspoken, brusque, with a sense of humour, and, I think, a good heart, she could and often did, snub me, if she thought I deserved it; but she never nursed her wrath, she never cherished malice, and, having been absent for the original quarrel, she was not disposed to take anybody else's account of it now. She was kind to Mademoiselle, refused to look on her as a criminal, accepted her without prejudice, and proceeded to form her own judgment on her character. She never, I imagine, attempted to counter the ruling that had gone forth against her, but that did not make her look askance or reproachfully at her while she remained in the school. In actual fact, the two got on extremely well. The Swiss girl had many qualities – good-humour, outspokenness, gaiety, intelligence – which appealed to the older woman.

With her return we ceased to live in an atmosphere of strained reserve. It was she who introduced an occasional game of bridge in

83

the evenings, which Mademoiselle and I were invited to join. Even Vandeleur seemed to forget that he was the Roman autocrat who had pronounced sentence of banishment, and he and Mademoiselle would behave as though quite cordial relations existed between them.

Half-term Saturday came and the boys gave a party to which the girls were invited from the lower school. There were fire-works on the playing-field, followed by games and a wonderful spread. Vandeleur, in his black silk clerical waistcoat, an inch or two of gold watch-chain showing, entered into the fun most fully, joining in many of the games himself, his red face wreathed in smiles. Everyone was friendly. Mademoiselle, her cares forgotten for the moment, was in her element. In a game of Oranges and Lemons, during the final tug-of-war, the boy immediately behind her, who had been holding her round the waist, in the throes of this desperate struggle, lost his hold of all but her accordion-pleated skirt. Suddenly the stitching gave way. The navy blue skirt ripped out to the full width of its many pleats and fell about her ankles, causing a sensation and general merriment, in which Vandeleur was the first to join. She stood there in her dark silk petticoat, gathering up the fallen skirt and laughing at the mishap as heartily as anyone. Only slightly embarrassed, but not in the least angry with the offender, who was all remorse, she slipped away and reappeared quickly in another dress.

She could enjoy a children's party, but she was intolerant of any social contact which seemed unreal. The following Sunday evening the mother of one of the boys came to supper. After supper we all went into the drawing-room to talk. The visitor was a well-read woman who had travelled; but her manner had, as well as a slightly irritating archness, that glib volubility which we associate with people who, not very intellectual themselves, nevertheless like to live on the edge of intellectual movements, and pride themselves on their ability to discuss them. The talk turned on books and, though I usually sat silent at these gatherings, to-night it interested me and I argued furiously and pontificated with all the assurance of youth. This evidently roused the visitor, and she indulged in a certain amount of raillery, some of it witty, some of it rather stupid, at my expense.

Mademoiselle was silent. She was wearing a pale green and yellow printed silk blouse, with narrow brown fur trimmings, a more feminine touch than was usual with her. She was never carelessly or indifferently dressed, but at the same time she gave the impression that clothes were mere incidentals and should never be allowed to become a major preoccupation. But to-night there was something decorative about her, her fair hair and the blouse, with its chintz effect, forming a patterned study in brown and yellow rather like a painting by Gauguin.

She sat leaning forward, her chin on her hand; and as the visitor became more volatile she seemed to become moodier and more mystified. Ordinarily she could laugh readily enough. One would see the very even white teeth flash for an instant and her cheeks would crease in a genial grin. She had plenty of humour herself. She could tell a story well and with a rather roguish gusto, and she was an excellent mimic. But this kind of light badinage was new to her. She could not understand flippancy as a pose, especially when serious subjects were being discussed.

When the guest had gone and we had said good night to Vandeleur, she, I and Miss Winsor lingered for a few minutes in the corridor talking.

Suddenly she said with devastating simplicity,

'Is that woman really silly? Or is she only pretending to be?'

'Pretending to be. Some people have a horror of being thought to take things seriously.'

It was an aspect of the English character which she had not encountered before and she did not approve it. She shrugged her shoulders. How boring to go out of one's way to be stupid.

A boy's cap and blazer were hanging on a peg nearby. Suddenly she donned the blazer, pulled the cap over one eye, stuck an unlit cigarette drooping into one corner of her mouth and said to Miss Winsor, 'I'm going up to make Thorpey laugh!' The Gauguin painting had vanished, and she looked like a Phil May drawing of a Fifth Form schoolboy. Primitive as it might be, this was more her idea of humour than the rather empty persiflage to which we had been listening.

Just as the visitor had mystified her, so she herself remained a mystery to me. She was mysterious. She never put all her cards on the table – perhaps because there was such a tremendous pack of them. One heard of things indirectly. She let things slip. Often her utterances were Delphic and vague. It was as if she wanted to appear inscrutable. Or was it simply the fact that she was a foreigner? She was my junior by several years and yet, in some ways – such is the difference between Continental education and our own, which

85

seems to prolong adolescence deliberately – she made me feel immature. The circumstances of her life had perhaps given her a deceptive air of experience – deceptive, for at the same time there was something extremely simple and wholly unsophisticated about her, an impression of great directness which one associates more properly with children. She was without guile or subtlety in the sense of striking a pose or playing a part. She would have scorned subterfuge. Rather she had gained the reputation of being unscrupulous because of the very directness with which she saw her objective and moved insistently towards it.

The effect of all this was to make me shy where she was concerned, and a little on my guard. I must have seemed to her a rather stilted, dogmatic young man who only let himself go when he read Shakespeare. My bourgeois bias would come down always on the side of prudence, urging her to be less impulsive, giving her good advice. I admired her courage, I admired her independence. I even envied them. I did not believe in her many schemes. Their very multiplicity seemed to cancel them out one against the other, and make them all unlikely. But at the same time I was determined to help her if I could. I made myself her advocate, on principle, because I liked her, and because she symbolised just the very virtues which Vandeleur's world refused to admit were virtues at all. Bourgeois caution can accompany a marked sympathy for, not bohemian standards, but bohemian ideals. It seemed to me monstrous that anyone as young, as vital and as determined, as she was, should be laid on the shelf at her age; and on a Calvinistic Genevan shelf, the full horror of which she had been able to convey to me in half a dozen phrases.

My letters home continued to be full of her, so much so that they were beginning to cause a certain uneasiness to my family. I had offered to Mademoiselle to get my father, who had been a schoolfellow of Wilfrid Grenfell the explorer and knew him well, to write to him in Labrador and see whether he could offer her any kind of a post in his hospital settlement there. She had jumped at the suggestion, and it was only now, in proof, as it were, of her claim to be a suitable person for such a life that she produced some newspaper cuttings about the six months' cruise which she and her girl friend had made in the Mediterranean. There I read of the *intrépidité et modestie* of these two young women and of the recognition it had received from fellow yachtsmen. One night at dinner Mrs. Vandeleur happened to mention a great gale on the Lake of Geneva a year or two before which had blown down one whole wall of a relative's chalet. Mademoiselle said quietly, 'I have a little silver box presented to me by the Yacht Club of Geneva at that time. I was out in my small boat on the lake when the sudden gale came on and I was the only yacht not to run for shelter and to weather it without damage.' She laughed as she added: 'All their masts were snapping!'

This was typical. Her exploits only transpired in this fashion, indirectly and after a time. One charge her detractors could never bring against her was that she boasted. And these casual allusions, these chance revelations were all part of her mystery. One formed a conception of her character, and then something might contradict it or throw doubt on it, or reveal a completely different facet. In the few weeks I had known her, she had undergone more than one metamorphosis in my mind. I had seen her first as an Amazon, self-confident and triumphant; next as a fellow rebel; next as a martyr fallen a little from her former self-assurance. But never at any time had I left that I knew more than a fraction of the whole.

I was to have a further illustration of this a day or two later. Vandeleur announced on November 11th that the school would attend the usual Armistice Day service down at the cenotaph. It was an out-of-door service held in the churchyard of the cold-looking grey church, which stood halfway down the main street, a little back from the roadway. The boys and the staff marched down to the church in a body, together with a small party of girls from the lower school, which Mademoiselle had joined at her own request. We formed a little group of forty or fifty in the crowd round the war memorial in the churchyard. I had been told that there was to be singing in Welsh, and looked forward to it. That at least would be beautiful. I had not worn my war service medals, nor did I ever on these occasions; I would have felt a fraud. I had too little sense of having been either the efficient or the happy warrior. Armistice Day to me meant only dumb regret and resentment and its ceremonial saddened me. To one nourished on the war poetry of Siegfried Sassoon, it was a painful reminder of all the infinite waste and folly which war entails. Mingled with very real gratitude that my own life had been spared was the thought of that friend and contemporary at Oxford, full of far greater intellectual promise than I ever possessed, who had been one of those to die.

The day was raw and cold. I stood there amongst the little group of schoolboys wearing their poppies in a mood of almost sullen melancholy. Suddenly I looked across and noticed the Swiss girl, cold, wretched-looking, a little piece of grey fur wound about her throat, standing in the smaller but corresponding group near us. Her eyes had filled up with tears, and in the face of this neutral, who had been a child at the time of the war, who had no friends involved, no relatives killed, I saw that aspect of universal pity, of sorrow, of tenderness which my own embittered heart failed to feel.

To detect such sensitiveness in her gave me a slight sense of surprise. The foreigner had put me to shame. It was as though she had had a vision of all hopeful and up-standing youth, broken, mutilated, blotted out; of all those tired men, grey-visaged, such as I had seen one evening at Souchez waiting to go up to the advance trenches at dusk, the acceptance of death in their faces. It was not that I had thought of her as unfeeling, it was simply that she had always seemed a person who would be unlikely to show emotion; here was a further proof of how little I knew her.

The following day was Thursday, and John Eglinton had suggested that he should accompany me on my weekly walk, and had invited me back to tea afterwards. I called for him at his house, and we set off along the main road which came from Rhyl, heading towards the confused tumble of hills which lay a mile or two inland between us and Chester. Here was scenery with plenty of variety, which I had explored once or twice already. The road bore away to the left, holding inland, mounting the hill and leaving a line of gigantic sand-dunes below it to the north. Along the brow of the hill four miles off straggled one little hamlet, a group of grey-slated houses and labourers' cottages with a single tea-garden, an eyrie to which few people ever climbed unless their road led through it. There were no other villages in sight, and few houses; instead, steep grass slopes, bramble thickets and patches of gorse sloping down to that gradually widening strip of land between the foot of the hills and the seashore, in which lay the sheltered fields of some farm or country estate.

We set off at a steady pace. 'Contrairy John' was a good walker, unhurried, just as in his conversation there was no trace of undue haste, so that when he made a remark it was always fully flavoured, 'like a nut or an apple,' as Synge has put it. He had plenty of reminiscences of literary Dublin and it was amusing to pump him. He could draw a thumbnail sketch of James Joyce in a peaked yachting cap and dirty white canvas shoes, calling for him on the steps of the National Library and accompanying him back through the streets of Dublin, waving gay salutations to his less respectable friends. Or he could describe his quarrel with A.E. during the time of the Black and Tans, a breach since healed. He was one of the four people in the world, I imagine, who could say that he had quarrelled with A.E. John was from the North, a strong supporter of the Union, who had never found anything particularly shameful in the label 'imperialist.' When the bad times came he refused to modify the convictions of a lifetime in a hurry. They had quarrelled on top of a tram, and A.E. had become so indignant with what John was saying that he had got down off the tram and left him. I could see that tremendous gesture, the brown-bearded figure descending slowly the steps of the tram like Zeus from Olympus, to await another tram to take him to the city, or to continue his way on foot down the Rathmines Road.

A.E. was our theme as we set out this afternoon. John Eglinton was a little inclined to pooh-pooh some aspects of the seer.

'But even Moore has spoken respectfully of A.E. the visionary.'

'Moore is an artist, and everything that serves the purpose of his art——'

Eglinton himself had served it. I thought of Moore's description of him in the great trilogy, 'this gnarled, lovable little man, like a twisted thorn tree.' He had remained friends with Moore after nearly all his other Irish friends had quarrelled with him. He was his literary consultant, one of the several men whom Moore hoped at one time or another would become his biographer; and periodically Moore would descend upon him, to spend a week in lodgings nearby, and pass the days chatting or going for walks with his friend. It was a friendship of opposites, the one dry, caustic, disparaging, the other voluble, quick-tempered and violent. I had found John Eglinton's bookcase full of first editions of Moore, presentation copies with dedications in the author's hand, and it had been thrilling to me, who saw in Moore the last great stylist in English prose, to take down these books and handle them. In the copy of the first volume of *A Storyteller's Holiday* Moore had written, 'To my friend M——,[1] who may not' – the word 'may' had been crossed out and the word 'will' substituted – 'who will not approve much that is in this book.'

John was generous about lending his books. As soon as I had seemed to him a trustworthy person, he had allowed me to take away whatever I liked. He had lent me *Impressions and Opinions*, the book of literary essays which for some reason its author had not seen fit to reprint. To me it seemed to contain some of the best criticism Moore had ever written. Here I had found the famous description

[1] John Eglinton was his pseudonym.

of Verlaine, the essay on Turgeniev, as well as excellent essays on Rimbaud and Laforgue. Knowing that Mademoiselle was interested in these three poets, I had passed on the book to her with a request that she should not keep it too long. The very next night she had brought it back to me, having read nearly the whole. The long study of Balzac had particularly interested her, and we had agreed that it was excellent. I realised then how easily she read English, for she had appreciated the graduated irony of the essay upon Zola, from the description of the first meeting – the disciple nervous and conscious that he has five minutes in which to show that he is not a fool – to the savage attack with which the essay closes.

I told Eglinton this now.

'What is going to happen to her?'

'I don't know. The whole business seems to hang fire. I don't think there is any chance of her being allowed to go to London.'

It was ressuring to learn from him that he and his wife had liked her. She had told them her troubles, told them of her proposed visit to Oxford, which they were disposed to view a good deal less seriously than Vandeleur, dismissing it as a piece of indiscreet impulsiveness. She had told them too of her plans. Obviously, to them all her schemes and projects were chimerical, but at the same time they sympathised with her and felt that she was being badly treated.

We had left the hills to press on for another three or four miles along the coast to a district of huge sand-dunes, where the seabirds cried above our heads and a gust of wind sent the blown sand stinging against our faces. The light was already beginning to fade when we returned over the summit of the rather bleak plateau to dip down into the outskirts of the town by one of the steep paths that wound zigzag down the side of the hill.

That evening when I left the house I took with me Moore's anthology, *Pure Poetry*. In his Preface to this book, he formulates the scarcely tenable theory that the best poetry is never subjective, never sicklied o'er with the pale cast of individual thought, but always external, visual, objective, universal. A strange theory and a strange anthology, omitting all Keats except some trifle about an old gipsy, and lucky in the fact that Sappho, Catullus and Horace are not English and therefore have not to be publicly ostracised. The dogma is absurd, but Moore's beautiful certitude is infectious, proving once again that it is the faithful that matter, even more than what the faithful believe.

Next afternoon, instead of Contrairy John as my fellow pedestrian,

I had half a dozen chattering juniors, who were off the games list because of colds. We set out on the walk past the brickworks – brickworks where nothing ever seemed to be happening, but where bricks presumably were made. Crossing the railway bridge over the local branch line, and avoiding the town, we headed for open country, intending to do a round that would bring us back by the station, a walk that we had once or twice done before. It lay through narrow side roads and lanes by fields where cows grazed rather moodily in the November mist, or waited reflectively in the trampled quagmire by the field gate for the dairy-man to come and fetch them. Towards the end of the round one passed an occasional garden, its tall, clipped privet screening whatever lay beyond, before coming out on the sea road and returning by the town. There had been a good deal of rain lately and, after we had left the main road, about a quarter of a mile further on, we found that the road was completely flooded. A great sheet of water barred our progress. I was besieged with shrill offers to wade through and see how deep it was, but this seemed hardly a wise procedure for recent convalescents. Back we turned and all the way home there was a babble about this great adventure *manqué*, each maintaining valiantly that he could have got through had I let him.

But back in my own room, free for twenty minutes until the after-noon tea gong should go, I forgot these babblings and thought again of Moore's theory of poetry. Poetry should be about things and not thoughts. Was Moore at least partly right? Was there a danger in all cerebral and over-subjective verse? Did my own poems come too often under this condemnation, and would a slight inoculation with Moore's serum do my Muse good?

Coming up the main street that evening after dark, I stopped in front of a fishmonger and poulterer's to admire the way in which the man had arranged his fish, not just on the slabs of marble and ice, but laid out on pieces of bracken. It was an original arrangement and very effective; the sloping marble shelf, the green bracken, fresh, with its jagged edges and pointed fronds, and the pieces of fish, red-speckled plaice, or others white and shining, glistening as though straight from the sea. In the background on a table were two chrysanthemum plants, the petals of their flowers the colour of autumn leaves, while on the opposite wall hung a pheasant and a hare. On it all was thrown a strong artificial light, not only from the shop itself, but from a street lamp outside. It made a surprising and delightful picture, patterned, original. I stood there thinking what an excellent arrangement it was and how it would make a very good poem in the French manner, deliberate, calm, detailed, impersonal. I was still gazing at it when the man came from the back of the shop to know what he could do for me. 'Nothing, thank you. I am only admiring the arrangement of your fish,' and I moved away a little sadly, for not even the first line of the poem had been born. But already, even in that little space of time, imagination had begun to toy with the reflection that sea and earth shared in this harvest, that the two elements had contributed equally to it, man's hand bringing them together, and that this might make an effective conclusion to my poem. An idea, a thought – the very thing I was trying to escape, subjectivity lying in wait for me even here at the fishmonger's, although my mind told me – with a little help from Moore – that ideas in literature are ephemeral, only things are eternal.

Moore had quoted in the Preface to his book what he considered the perfect example of the objective poem, a sonnet of Gautier's, greatly approved by Balzac:

'*Moi je suis la tulipe: une fleur de la Hollande.*'

(A tulip's subjectivity, one might say, but Moore had overlooked that.) It was indeed a beautiful poem, calm, limpid, unperturbed. And, wishing to hear those slow and deliberate cadences read aloud by someone whose French was better than my own, I said to Mademoiselle next day, 'Will you do something for me? Read a French poem aloud. I want to get the rhythm and pace of it.'

'Very well. I will try.'

'When you have finished with your class to-night at six?'

The boys went off to their supper. Vandeleur was in the corridor, putting out the gas, when I asked her into my room and gave her the book.

'Mademoiselle is going to read me something in French, if she may.'

Leaning against the side of my door, she took the book and after a preliminary glance through it read the sonnet to me slowly and thoughtfully. Gautier's poem was a lovely piece of work, austere, flawless, and she read it with the gravity it deserved. Standing there, book in hand, a transverse lock of hair across her forehead, she continued to turn the pages of the anthology when she had finished, and it struck me, not for the first time, that I was lucky to have someone in the school whose interest in literature was as ardent and as genuine as my own.

One of my earliest and greatest dissatisfactions with the educational outlook was that it appeared to view everything, even poetry, with an ulterior motive. A poem was merely something for a child to learn by heart. But to me a poem was enormously important, simply because it was a poem, not because it might presently form part of the mental pabulum of the young. I remember writing to the friend (who had so outspokenly condemned 'The New Class') to thank for the gift of the Manxman T. E. Browne's poems, and saying of his eight lines about the blackbird, 'One such poem would justify a man's life.' Nowadays, even to me, such a verdict seems a little rhetorical. But I meant it then in sober earnest. Youth's values are absolute. To me the creation of a few perfect lines, the crystallisation of experience into even the briefest lyric, provided it was flawless, was a better showing than many men could make at the end of a long life. Gautier was a Romantic himself, but it was only a short step from his work to that of the Parnassians, and the Parnassians brought us to Rimbaud and Laforgue. Seized with a sudden confidence in her sincerity and good faith, I said to her:

'If you like, I will show you some of my own poems. A number of them are prose-poems and very simple. They are appearing shortly in one of the English reviews, the *Fortnightly*, but they have not yet been published as a book.'

'Yes, I would like to see them.'

She said it in that cool, detached voice which she seemed to reserve for anything that touched herself or another person closely.

'You might even translate some of them for me.'

'Perhaps. I would like to see them.'

I gave her the poems and she read one or two of them aloud, slowly, reflectively in a very different manner from my own. When I read aloud I was inclined to pitch the whole tone of a poem on one particular note, as though that were the key to its music, but she varied her voice, giving each verse its separate expression, making each phrase speak for itself. When she read of Breton peasants in Jersey, the peasants spoke more simply and with greater *naïveté* than the rest of the poem, even the tone of her voice changed, and only when they had finished speaking did it become grave and deliberate again. I was not sure that my lyric could bear this dramatisation, but it was interesting to see the experiment made.

'Yes, I would like to take the poems and look at them.'

We had remained talking till nearly dinner-time, both of us still standing.

'A friend of mine, Bodkin, a great authority on art, has made some lovely translations of certain modern French poems. The book is in Cheltenham among some things that I have left with my sister, but I have got leave to go and see my doctor there before my next medical board, and I will get it for you then.'

'When do you go to Cheltenham?'

'On Friday.'

'And return?'

'On Monday.'

'Oh, I shall be gone by then.'

She laughed for the first time with a note not so much of self-pity as of reproach against Fate, then stooped, with her hair fallen over her face to gather up her papers and put them in the portfolio which she carried everywhere with her. She had abandoned the struggle. She was reconciled to going. There was no more talk of refusal. She was only waiting for permission from the Home Office to leave the country. Pride had come to her aid. The Swiss are a proud race and her family had written to say that she was not to remain a moment longer than was necessary in a country where she was not wanted.

That night in the course of discussion she had mentioned four translations by a French poet of inscriptions for the gates of a Chinese city. She thought them extremely fine and had promised to read them aloud to me. But next evening, when I had gone back to my study after dinner, Vandeleur knocked at my door and, appearing in the doorway, announced with a certain degree of diffidence that he could not allow Mademoiselle to come to my room any longer in the way she had been doing. Pulling at the black silk ribbon of his pince-nez, he seemed anxious to put the matter tactfully, but before long he annoyed me by using the expression, 'all the time.'

'She doesn't come all the time. She has only been once or twice. At the very outside, she has not been half a dozen times.'

I could have added that most of the visits had only been of a few minutes' duration; that she had never once sat down on a chair in the small study.

'Well, it doesn't do. I am afraid I must forbid it.'

Did he imagine that because we discussed poetry together we must presently become sentimental, that he would be forced to witness a flirtation under his very nose? Hardly. One of us was shy, the other matter-of-fact; it did not need much penetration to see that it was a little outside both our dispositions. Did he fear gossip among the maids? Whatever his objections, they seemed to me absurd and insulting. I regarded this interference as one more pinprick, one more idiotic restriction, a prudish precaution, which he chose to take for no real reason at all except that it would annoy us.

'Mademoiselle is helping me with some work. Her knowledge of French makes all the difference. She was to read some things to me to-night. If I can't see her here, where can I see her? Can she read to me in Matron's room?'

He reflected a minute and then said:

'Yes, if Matron is there.'

We must have a chaperon who would see that poetry did not lead us astray.

I went up to Matron's room, where I found them both and explained the situation. Thorpey and I were good friends, but she had no wish for her room to be made the scene of a literary conversazione. She made this clear at once. We were given a time limit, after that I must go. She wanted to read the paper.

Mademoiselle produced the material I had given her the night before, together with a note-book of her own with a cardboard cover, and plentifully interleaved with typescripts and manuscripts. It was her commonplace book and it was plain from the variety of handwriting therein that she had been filling it for a number of years.

'I have brought my copies of the Chinese translations. You will find them here. I do not know whether you can read them. And I have brought your own poems also. I have read them all. I have been reading till very late at night, by candle.'

She translated one of the inscriptions into English for me, and gave me the book.

Matron reappeared for a minute. 'Hurry up, you two,' and she went off to give a boy a light to take to the bathroom.

'You had better go now. Matron doesn't like you being here. I have written on a bit of paper about the poems.'

How anxiously when we are young we await the verdict of our friends on those rare occasions when we either read to them or show them our verses! It is true that we write poetry first for ourselves, and that the joy of actually completing the poem to our own satisfaction is the first and chief reward of composition. But the matter cannot be allowed to rest there. We ask criticism, we seek advice, but all that we really want is approval, the seal of reassurance, of an external opinion. Sometimes we dare not even put the matter to the test and prefer after all that half-loaf of our own personal pleasure in the poem, leavened though it is by doubt, to the risk of losing it altogether by inviting a second verdict. I had written little during the war, but in the Channel Islands I had begun to write again. Friends there had shown interest in my work, and when I returned to Ireland other friends and critics there had encouraged me. My poems were beginning to be published; they could not be wholly worthless. And yet I had shown them to this Swiss girl with almost the old failing of heart, the same sense of diffidence, the same dread of disappointment, and that thirst for even the mildest form of praise which one knew in one's teens.

I went down to my room, taking with me her commonplace book and the bundle of poems which she had given me. She had scribbled untidily and in haste on a page torn from a note-book – deletions of some previous jottings figuring upside down in the very middle of what she had to say – her opinion of my poems. Her struggles with a foreign tongue showed more clearly in this attempt to give a literary verdict than it did in the ordinary conversation of daily life.

I read:

'I like nearly all the poetries, and I translated the proses I found with the less difficult words. I don't care for the long proses, nor for the last (separate leaves) philosophical proses: you haven't mastered them now, they are not standing in a whole complete unity like your love songs, and they are annoying. ("Paradox" is an exception because there is more love than philosophy.) It seems to me "The Last Thing" is nicely said, but very common of idea: I met it often till now, I can't tell where. All the things with the shy girl for subject or in the background are splendid. I like "The Northern Town," it is a good objective one. Of course it is silly to write like that, what I like, in generalities; I should need to speak about each page separately. (Better not, the old man is crazy.) I am extremely astonished to see how *greatly simply* you can write, thinking how pompously you are speaking. Translating was extremely difficult to keep the shortness of expression.'

There is no compliment which pleases us so much as that which reaches us with a sting in its tail, as though the latter were really the proof of its sincerity. The words 'greatly simply' were doubly underlined on the slip of paper. If it was a shock to learn that I spoke pompously – in literary disputes, in my sage exchange of political wisdom with Vandeleur, in the ordinary course of daily life – nevertheless, the blow was softened for me by these two underlined words, with their evidence of genuine approval. I could interpret them as I chose, greatly simply, meaning merely very simply; or greatly simply, in the sense that simplicity, as one of the literary virtues, can seem great. I might wince for a moment under the imputation that I was wordy in conversation, but it was immaterial if she could praise, as she had praised, the restraint and directness of my poems. There I had achieved my aim. There I had sown with the hand and not with the whole sack.

The manuscripts had only been in her possession for twenty-four hours, but she had translated two of the prose poems already. She had chosen them, as she had said, not necessarily because she liked them best, but because she found them easiest to translate. For the first time I looked on my thoughts in another language. It was a flattering experience. My muse stood before me in foreign habiliments and with the vanity of youth I was delighted.

As I read I felt a shock of surprise. These were still my poems; the emotion was mine, the original pulse of the heart was mine. But just as parents can feel pride when, for some reason or other, they see their children differently dressed and therefore in an entirely new perspective, or as a stranger might see them, taking pleasure in the novelty of that impression, so now I enjoyed a dual privilege, that of being at once the author of the poem and its curious reader.

I ran up again to Matron's room to catch my translator before she left, to congratulate her upon her work, thank her for it, praise her for her frankness and at the same time tease her a little for having been outspoken.

'So I am talking pompously, am I? Well, it is better to know it.'
She looked a little puzzled.

'I am worried about my English and what I have said. It was so hard to find the words I wanted, and I am thinking all the time, "Is that right?" I know what I wish to say, but not the words, and I am in a great hurry. You are amused then by the way I have put it?'

She expressed her approval of the poems once more, quietly, without effusion, her words carrying the weight of conviction. In her role of critic she had always a touch of quiet assurance. It used to amuse me at other times, but it was highly flattering to vanity now. She repeated what she had said in her note:

'All the poems about your shy girl are splendid. In the philosophic ones you have not found yourself yet.'

'Don't you write at all yourself?'

'Oh yes, but they are nothing.' Then with a laugh she added, 'Philosophic pieces – the very thing I do not like in others!'

I asked her would she translate some more of the poems for me.

'Yes, when I have time. You see, I have not really the time or quiet to do it properly when I am here.'

I had not yet read the French poems which she had lent me, and I was going to find them difficult without her help. I said to her:

'What are you doing to-morrow, Thursday – are you free at all?'

'Yes, for a little in the afternoon.'

'Well, will you come and have tea with me somewhere in the town? We can talk about the poems then.'

'Yes – and we will meet Vandeleur and Thorpey and everyone.' And she made a face.

'What matter if we do? It is his own fault; he's just a silly old man.'

For the first time it was she who was on the side of prudence and I who was impetuous and urgent. Like her, I foresaw the likelihood that we would encounter some colleague and that surprised eyebrows would be raised; but why should we not go and have tea together if we wished? I urged her to come.

'Meet me at the Post Office at a quarter past three. We can go to some tea-shop and get a table to ourselves. They won't be crowded at that hour and we won't be disturbed.'

'All right. But I shall have to be back for a class at five o'clock.'

'That will give us plenty of time. I will bring your papers with me.'

She said good night. Down at the girls' school she had embarked on a new labour, the translation of a book on hockey for some Swiss friend who was coming to play a series of matches in France. She must get back to it now. She was indefatigable. I gathered that it was she who had founded their club in Geneva in the first instance.

I returned to my room. She had given me a whole bundle of material, some loose, some in the cardboard-covered commonplace book which dated back to her childhood. In these jottings and notes, in these extracts and compilations, I seemed to get a glimpse of her real self. This was the workshop in which her ambitions and aspirations had been forged. These were the thoughts, moods, and conceptions to which her mind had responded, the mental luggage which she had felt inclined to carry with her as she went forward in life. She was only nineteen. The earlier poems must have been copied in when she was quite a child, and her handwriting still unformed. Some of them had small coloured pictures cut out and pasted at their head. Later came Verhaeren, Maeterlinck, Baudelaire,

Stevenson and Kipling. She had copied out the whole of de Regnier's long poem, 'Le Vase.' It occupied four pages or more. No one who had not a real love of literature would have gone to all this trouble.

Whatever she liked best had gone into this collection. All that I read had in one way or another helped to make her. Scribbled on the back of a photograph of a yacht in full sail stuck in amongst the other papers I found an extract from a book which I myself had lent her only a few days before. It was from Moore's essay on Degas: the words which Moore puts dramatically into the mouth of the latter's dæmon as to the attitude that he should bring to life:

'Expend not your strength in vain struggling in the elusive world, which tempts you out of yourself; success and failure lie within and not without you; know yourself and seek to bring yourself into harmony with the Will from which you cannot escape, but to which you may bring yourself into obedience and so obtain peace.'

The passage was written in her hasty, yet at the same time curiously precise and characteristic handwriting on the back of the first thing that had come to hand. It seemed to tell me more about her than any previous action or word. I felt as though I had drawn the curtain for a moment on her inmost mind. This was the clue to a self that the world never saw. In the beginning I had thought of her merely as an athlete, someone full of energy and vitality. Presently she had revealed other and literary interests. But I had never suspected a contemplative. She seemed to have too many external interests for that, to be too much the extrovert. When she said that her own writings were in the nature of *choses philosophiques*, I had been a little scornful, amused by this philosopher not yet twenty, who spoke with guarded yet airy confidence of these things, and who combined philosophic contemplation with so many active pursuits. But now I felt a little ashamed. No one would have scribbled down those words taken from an unlikely context who was not at least philosophically inclined. Just as I had to a certain extent 'shown my hand' by letting her read my poems, so in this collection of extracts, gathered over a period of ten years, she had admitted me to the partial intimacy of her brain and heart. And instead of finding sophistication, assurance, limitless and unscrupulous devotion to self-interest, which was all that Vandeleur saw, I found ardour, simplicity, all the ingenuousness and unspeakable pathos of youth, full, as it is, of hope and vague longing, of tenderness and dread, of faith in life, and of faith most of all in itself and its own destiny. I seemed to see the child, the schoolgirl, the young woman,

99

happy enough in her environment of Swiss bourgeois respectability, but reaching out continually towards wider horizons or to gather strange flowers in more remote fields of the mind. My heart warmed towards her in a way it had never done before, in something the same way that our hearts warm with pity when we contemplate, retrospectively, our own youth, its enthusiasms and its aspirations, so many of them unfulfilled, so many of them, in the issue, different from the way we planned them.

There is an instant in most friendships, of which we may not be conscious at all, and seldom are conscious, when, from being a matter of mere mutuality, of shared tastes, of a kindred spirit in many things, sympathy suddenly awakens in us for the person as a whole, and we accept them, not because of our points of agreement, but rather in spite of any points of disagreement which still remain. It is only a step, perhaps, to that next stage when faults will seem virtues. I was lonely. I had left Jersey unhappy. The very poems which Mademoiselle praised were a reminder to me of what distress love can cause us. And now, although I was not in the least degree sentimentally attracted to her, nevertheless she had begun to take hold of my imagination, and I saw her at last no longer as a sequence of contradictory aspects in which the superficial strangeness of foreign nationality played so large a part, but as a human entity like myself.

I looked forward to our meeting on Thursday. But we were not to have tea together after all. The project came to nothing. She had not known, or she had forgotten, that she was wanted for a hockey match against a neighbouring ladies' team. In one way it was as well, for the following day was the one on which I was to go to Cheltenham, and I had a good deal to arrange before I left. After all, despite her assertion to the contrary, she would probably still be there when I returned. We could go then.

It was Friday morning, the dawning of my week-end of freedom, and I celebrated the occasion by getting sacked. I had been taking a class of very small boys for arithmetic at a table in the dining-room. It was unfortunate that Vandeleur should be teaching Greek to some seniors at another table only a yard or two away across the room. My pupils were not rowdy or deliberately undisciplined. I was not conscious that they were making any particular noise. I had taught them to be keen and take an interest in their achievement, and as each seven-year-old finished his sum – they were seated on either side of the table and I at its head – there would be cries of

'I've finished, sir,' 'Do come to me, sir,' 'I've finished,' 'Is it right?'

'Be quiet. I can only attend to one of you at a time. I will come in a minute.'

The babble continued, or there would be silence for a few moments and then it would be resumed. Enthusiasm ran high, and, according to my theories, it was right that it should; the 'babies' were only showing a legitimate interest in their work.

But Vandeleur nearby must have been suffering from steadily increasing irritation at their exuberance. Suddenly he crossed the room and to my surprise snapped out:

'When the interval comes, Mr. Gibbon, you will take your class out and march them round the playground.'

I flushed slowly red. I saw myself the laughing-stock of the whole school, marching at the head of my little band of desperadoes, the eldest of whom was not more than eight, while the rest of the boys stopped kicking their football about to watch us. I said nothing. Vandeleur returned to the two senior boys he was teaching, and, more conscious of our neighbours than we had been before, I lowered my voice, and my class of little boys moderated their transports. Till now we had all been blissfully unaware of causing offence.

The bell for break went and I said to the boys, 'Sit where you are until I know what Mr. Vandeleur wants done with you.'

They remained sitting, while Vandeleur for a few more minutes continued to expound Greek verbs. Sensitive, and very conscious of my *amour propre*, I had no intention of doing what he demanded. When Vandeleur still made no move, I went across to him and asked quietly:

'What do you want me to do with these boys?'

'Take them out and march them round the playground.'

'I am sorry, but I can't do that.'

'Those are my orders.'

'Well, I am afraid I must refuse to carry them out.'

I still spoke quietly, but at the same time I felt a savage resentment, for I believed that he was deliberately trying to humiliate me by a punishment which would reflect even more on me than on the class.

His face flushed a deeper purple than usual, but he did not reply in a hurry. He got up, gathered his books, and moved towards the door, away from the boys who had heard all that was said.

At the door he paused, looking at me as though he hoped for a moment I would change my mind.

'That's what I want done.'

'I'm sorry. I came here as a schoolmaster, not a drill sergeant.'

He signed to me to follow him into his study.

In the study he turned and said, 'I have been schoolmastering a great many years and you are the first man I have ever had who has refused to do what I told him.'

'I am sorry, but you could not expect me to keep discipline among the older boys if you make me look absurd in front of the whole school.'

I had no intention of yielding. Once the opening move had been made, all my latent pugnacity had come to my aid and I had ceased to feel embarrassed.

'All right. You can go. I can't have you on my staff if you refuse to obey me.'

'Very well. I will go. But at the end of next term. I am entitled to a full half-term's notice.'

He burst out angrily, 'You are the most self-opinionated young man I have ever met.' He crossed the room and came back. 'Always trying to teach me my own job.'

'Not at all. Whenever you have pointed anything out to me, I have tried to see it from your point of view. If I obeyed you now I should only be making myself ridiculous.'

'Very well. If you won't do it, I shall have to do it myself.'

I left the study. He went out into the playground, stood in the centre, and watched the small boys march round in a circle in solemn procession. Was this all he had intended me to do? It is possible that the whole row had arisen out of a misunderstanding, and that I had jumped to the false conclusion that I was to participate in the punishment drill myself, whereas he had only meant me to see his wishes enforced. Since I was still angry, I was more inclined to think that he had modified the programme to save his own face, knowing that the sight of their Headmaster marching at the head of the rebellious little band would have been too much even for his well-disciplined school.

I finished my cocoa and returned to the dining-room, where I found the Swiss girl alone. 'I have just had a tremendous row with Vandeleur. I am leaving at the end of next term. It's just as well. I could never have stuck it.' She looked at me in a puzzled, almost stupid way, as if she did not understand, but said nothing. There was no time to give her details. The bell for class had already gone.

'Well, goodbye, and good luck. I expect you'll still be here when

I come back. You have my address in Ireland, haven't you? My father has written to Grenfell. I hope something comes of it.'

I had said goodbye to her, but I was to spend another three-quarters of an hour in her company. When I took my Shakespeare class, she was at the other end of the room, standing in front of the double cupboard, leaning back against the ledge with her hands behind her, as the children wrote something for her. Once or twice she looked towards me, the same look of perplexity in her face, as though still wondering what sort of a fantastic world she was living in, in which row followed cataclysmic row.

I had mystified her, just as she had so often mystified me. Perhaps my hurried words had not made the affair plain. It would have to wait for explanation now. I looked across the classroom at her. She was the one indeterminable factor in the hideous certainty of school routine, a reminder that life could exist and did exist on other terms besides those of the textbook, the broken pen, the desk, and the blackboard on which Vandeleur was demonstrating some problem in careful chalk. Her coming had saved me from suffocation. She had thrown open a window on the outer world. Her very stance now, easy, loose-limbed, informal, showed that she had all the instincts of the free. Misfortune had overtaken her, not because she was timid, but because she had been foolish enough to imagine that one should dare all. She puzzled me. I could not answer the simplest questions in relation to her character. I did not know, for example, whether it was self-confidence and assurance that caused her to make mistakes, or whether most of her mistakes were mistakes of sheer impulse. Ardent, gay, indiscreet, secretive, ambitious, restless, independent, she had seemed to me a mass of contradictions, to be treated with distinct reserve. She was still an enigma, but she was less of an enigma. Within the last week my attitude towards her had undergone a marked modification. I had shed some of my distrust of her. Hitherto she had been merely the courageous and startling protagonist in a play I had been witnessing. I had dramatised her, just as she perhaps a little dramatised herself. But now admiration for certain heroic qualities of spirit had begun to subdue my disapproval of her impetuosity, and at the same time literature had drawn us together. We had exchanged confidences. Reserved as both of us were, we had revealed to one another something of what lay behind the mask.

Vildrac has a poem in which two people, in whom interest in one another is perhaps awakening, plan to watch carefully at their next meeting for signs of that awakened interest to see whether the surmise was justified or not. But they are unlucky; circumstances are against them; when the time comes the most trivial interventions arise, in a whole series, one after another; enough to turn the scale and convince them that they were quite mistaken.

> Nothing at all, said she,
> But fantasy.
> Nothing at all, said he,
> But my vain hope.

Had I reached or was I reaching that first stage in Vildrac's poem? I would have laughed the suggestion out of court if it had been made to me. I would have said that sentiment had not so much as loomed on the horizon for either of us, that I was not even mildly *épris*, and I would have pointed out that the contention could hardly be sustained in view of the fact that I was doing my best to exile the lady to Labrador.

All this would have been true. And yet the fact that my gaze wandered from time to time now to the far end of the classroom, where she was standing, and that it was a satisfaction almost to think that I had joined her in disgrace – as though we had each of us struck a blow in the same good cause, which was the liberty and integrity of the individual, as against the stranglehold of the institution – this alone leant faint support to the theory, a theory which I would have repudiated angrily if anyone had advanced it.

And – though I was ignorant of it of course myself, for the last thing in my thoughts would have been to assess such evidence – other indications might have been taken to illustrate the same contention. For when I had slipped away from my class early, retrieved my case from the small study and made my way to the station to await the Irish mail from Holyhead, my escape into freedom for the first time for many weeks meant less to me than I had expected, and even to a certain degree, seemed inopportune. I had bidden Mademoiselle goodbye without any emotion beyond the pious hope that something would come of my Grenfell scheme for her. But now I regretted that I was leaving her just at the very moment when she seemed to think that things were at last going to move, and – we are egoists – at the moment when I had discovered in her a translator for my poems.

And from the moment I found myself in the train and throughout the succeeding two days of my absence, though it would not be true to say that she was continually in my thoughts, it would be true to say that my thoughts continually reverted to her. I had no sooner arrived in Cheltenham than I asked my sister where I would find the brown Army kitbag which I had left in her charge. And when it had been located and the key produced, I searched eagerly for the volume of Bodkin's translations and sighed with relief when I found it where I had hoped it would be. I had my own copy, signed by Bodkin, safely at home; but this second copy, picked up on the Dublin quays, had been deliberately put aside to await a suitable owner. And now I had found one. The very poem she had been at such pains to copy out at length in her own hand – de Regnier's 'Vase' – was printed here opposite its excellent rendering in English. She would approve it. And what fun it would be to read to her Bodkin's version of Baudelaire's 'furious angel'; or '*Il va neiger*,' by Francis Jammes; or those two quatrains of Rimbaud, almost perfect in either language, and certainly not a shadow less perfect in their English transposition.

'In the blue summer evenings I shall pass
Dreaming down pleasant pathways at my ease
By the sharp corn or through the tender grass,
And, bathing my bare forehead in the breeze,

I shall not talk, I shall not think at all,
Letting my soul by infinite love be swayed,
Wayfaring far afield at Nature's call,
Happy as though I walked beside a maid.'

Those last two lines seemed almost more in keeping with the mood of the poem than the French:

Et j'irai loin, bien loin comme un bohemien
Par la Nature – heureux comme avec une femme.

as though a translation could sometimes by some rare fortune go one better than its original. I looked forward to sharing my enthusiasm with someone so capable of understanding it.

And next morning in Cheltenham, strolling along the familiar 'prom' and admiring, not for the first time, the fountain with its drooping willows, whose green curtain of light tracery was such a joy to the eye in spring, creating the mood of the country in the very heart of the town, it was not long before I succumbed to the temptation to cross the street and enter a bookshop. Masefield had just published *Sard Harker* and the cunning bookseller had no difficulty in persuading me that it was a good opportunity to acquire a first edition. But no sooner had I bought the book than it struck me that it was just such a tale of extravagant adventure, full of such things as nightmare encounters with serpents swinging from trees in the tropical forests of South America, as would delight Mademoiselle; and so a second copy was purchased and papered separately, and I left the shop pleased to think that I had found for her another farewell present of just the kind that would appeal to her.

Yes, she was in my mind. Even I could not have denied that. All the time I thought, 'I hope she is there when I get back. She must be. She said she would be gone, but after all, the affair of the permit has dragged on now for weeks; it is hardly likely to be settled in three days, especially over a week-end.' And when Sunday had come and gone, and I had said goodbye to my sister and to my friends, as the train carried me back to North Wales my mind reverted with an almost involuntary movement to the same theme.

Would she be at school when I returned? Unless the letter had come by the first post on Saturday, it would arrive too late for her to do anything over the week-end. Besides, the Home Office had been dilatory for so long. Why should it change its nature in the twinkling of an eye? On this dilatoriness I built all my hopes. I debated the question repeatedly, weighing all the possibilities, and each time reason brought in the satisfactory verdict that the odds were all against her departure. I imagined the pleasure it would be to show her 'May It please Your Lordships,' to get her to read the poems aloud, and to discuss the two versions with her. I thought too of how much we both could learn from that reading, I of the cadences of French verse, she of the art of the translator.

All the same, it was curious how interest steadily heightened as we drew nearer the moment when the matter would be decided definitely. She was more than ever in my thoughts when at half-past three I got out of the train. Coming up from the station, I thought to myself, 'In a few minutes I shall know for certain.' Opposite the girls' school I looked up at the window of the room which I supposed was hers. It was open. So I was right. She had not departed yet. But the room might not be hers after all. Or they might only be airing it. In the field behind their gymnasium some girls were playing net-ball. I looked to see if she was there. Sometimes she played with them. She was not, and I reminded myself quickly that it was her custom often to go for a solitary walk up the hill behind the house.

At any rate I should know by tea-time. It was nearly four o'clock. There was not long to wait. The boys came back from their game, but I did not like to say to them what I was longing to say, 'Is Mademoiselle still here?' I was afraid that they might detect an underlying anxiety in my tone of voice. Had Miss Winsor been there I should have known very quickly, but she was once more on the sick list. The gong went. Opening the drawing-room door, I thought, 'Shall I see her now or not?' But she was not there. Still, she was often late for tea. No one mentioned her. I seemed fated by circumstance to be kept on tenterhooks. It is the irony of such situations that though it is we who inflict them on ourselves they nevertheless appear to be inflicted on us. Even inanimate objects seemed in the plot. Suddenly it occurred to me to count the tea-cups. Mr. and Mrs. Vandeleur, their son-in-law and daughter, and myself. Five people. Five cups. There were only enough to go round. That settled it. She had gone. But the very minute in which I reached this decision Mrs. Vandeleur exclaimed, 'Oh, we're a cup short. How stupid!' My heart leaped up. The bell was rung, the cup fetched. I thought, 'She will be here any minute. She will run up the steps as she so often does, and enter the room, smiling and apologetic.' But I had miscalculated. At that moment Matron came down. I had forgotten Matron. She bustled in, brusque and cheerful, chatting about every school topic except the one most in my thoughts.

So she must have gone. But hope springs eternal. There were afternoons when Mademoiselle never came to tea at all. It may seem foolish that I did not ask the direct question which would have instantly resolved all my doubts. But the very fact that nothing was said made me suspect a deliberate conspiracy of silence. These people must know that I was curious, and they were deriving a malicious pleasure from the fact, waiting to see how soon curiosity would get the better of discretion. Very well, then, I would disappoint them. I would meet silence with silence. I too would appear indifferent. If I were to ask, they would watch me to see how I took their answer. I had been her champion. They knew I liked her. Often when we are most anxious to appear casual we are least successful. I could not say how well or badly I might come through this ordeal. No, not by the flicker of an eyelid would I show that the matter was of any interest to me.

I never stopped to think that if she had gone it would be ancient history by now, and it might never occur to them to mention it. Whereas if she had not gone there was still less reason for their speaking of her. I was too proud to ask the Vandeleurs. I was too shy to ask the boys. And so my suspense continued. In class after tea, Mrs. Vandeleur came in and I heard some allusion to French preparation. That clinched it. She *had* gone. It was a relief from uncertainty, a relief from what had been uncommonly like suspense. But even then I was not certain. Perhaps I had heard wrong. The boys would surely have said something to me by now. And coming up from posting a letter at six o'clock while the boys were at tea someone went into the school about twenty yards in front of me. A shadow was thrown on the glass screen of the door. It was Mademoiselle's shadow – something about the head which was unmistakable, its poise, the slight thrust forward when she walked. It was about the time she came up each evening. She would have gone up to Matron's room. So she was here after all. Dinner would settle it definitely. It was funny to have been sure that she was gone and now to find that she had not gone at all. Would I tell her so when we met or might it argue too great a preoccupation with her movements?

The second gong sounded. I went across from my room and glanced quickly round the dinner table. The fourth place was laid. She was here; and I thought suddenly of that night when she arrived from Switzerland to take her place at this table for the first time, bronzed and eager as she smiled, exultant in the excitement of encountering a new land. But the meal began without her and continued without any reference to her name. She and I were often late, but we were hardly as late as this. She could not be coming. But why then the vacant place? What had been the object in laying it?

It must have been the stupidity of a servant. About three-quarters way through the meal Vandeleur was called away from the table to the telephone. It was now or never. Mrs. Vandeleur had not been one of Mademoiselle's opponents. She was a more sympathetic person and I felt that I could endure better the scrutiny of her gaze. I took my courage in my hands and said quietly and as casually as possible, 'Mademoiselle has gone, then?' 'Yes, Mademoiselle has gone.' Had she been waiting for this question ever since I returned? 'She went on Saturday. Oh yes, and she left a book for you. I must give it to you. I am sure I don't want it. Rather silly it seemed to me. At least the stories are very trivial, like children's stories. The two I read were children's stories.'

It was a typical Betsy Trotwood remark. 'I'm sure I don't want it.' Why should anyone suppose that she would want it, and why in any case had she waited to mention it till now? In an instant she fell with the swiftness of Lucifer from that minor eminence to which I had exalted her. She was one of the arch-conspirators and I had only played into her hands. She had no right to sneer at the book; it was a gift; to belittle someone else's gift was unforgivable. It showed just that limitation of insight which had annoyed me in Vandeleur and his daughter. If Mademoiselle wanted to leave me a souvenir and had searched hurriedly through her possessions to find one, the impulse had been wholly generous, and I at least appreciated it.

That the book seemed childish was hardly surprising, for it was a children's book. I asked her for it next evening in the drawing-room and she produced it, a book bound in faded mustard-coloured boards, with a picture of a velvet-coated little boy with a watering-can, of the sort, bordering on caricature, which children love, inlaid in black and white in the centre of its cover. It contained a number of tales and a number of similar illustrations, quaint and rather clever. She may have left it for me because she knew that I was interested in children and wrote about them, or because she thought that it might prove useful to me in my classes. But it is more likely that she simply wanted to leave me some memento and it was the first thing that offered. It caused me a slight twinge of conscience, for I had sometimes thought of Mademoiselle as sophisticated or, as the English say, 'deep.' No parting gift could have been more simple-minded, more impulsive, more naïve; only someone entirely natural could have done such a thing. It must have been one of the first books that its owner possessed. It had been printed in Lausanne some fifteen or sixteen years before, and I found on one corner of the title page – in ink already a little faded – her name, the date and the one word 'Noël.' So it had been a Christmas gift to her once in Switzerland – that Switzerland to which she had been so ignominiously driven back.

They had won their point and she had lost hers. They had succeeded in banishing her from the country to which she had come in such high hope. I thought of Vandeleur's indignant 'Her parents never wanted her to leave home. Her first duty is to them.' Was it unconscious malice that had made him so unhelpful, or did he really think that he was doing the right thing in saving her from the life of adventure that she had sought so avidly? Whatever his motive, the result was the same. He had pronounced sentence, and he had been in a position to see it enforced.

Mademoiselle vanished from the scene. In a school, where so

many forces converge, and where the work is shared by a number of people, no one is ever indispensable, or rather individuals can vacate even key positions and the withdrawal of their influence is not noticed for a time; the machine continues to run under its own impetus. And if this is true after years of service, it is still truer of the mere bird of passage, who disappears and is forgotten almost instantly. The term continued. The boys came down to breakfast in the mornings chattering gaily. Vandeleur lost his temper, palms smarted, spelling remained a mystery to Kenneth, and in short life proceeded very much as before. I never once heard Mademoiselle's name mentioned by the boys. I never mentioned it myself. Someone else taught French; that was all.

She was gone. I regretted her. But one person at least of those near to me viewed her departure with a certain relief. It was my father. He had what has come to be known as a complex upon the subject of foreigners. Years before his faith in human nature had received a severe shock. To his surprise, to everyone's surprise, perhaps even to her own, the German *Fräulein* employed to teach his younger sister had burst into a sudden transport of tears on hearing of his engagement to my mother. She wept, she sobbed, declaring that her heart was broken; and though the young, black-bearded curate had never been known to cast a glance in her direction, she allowed it to be generally inferred that her affections had been trifled with. Thenceforward there was implanted in my father's heart such a horror of all things continental that he never fully recovered from it.

My letters to him had been full of the Swiss girl, championing her cause, fulminating against her oppressors, insisting that he should press forward the negotiations with Grenfell. Perhaps my susceptibility, of which he was not unaware, added to his anxiety. From time to time he let drop a carefully-worded hint about the incalculable nature of the foreigner. Did he see me wrecked on some reef of unrequited passion? Or merely annexed quietly and without fuss? The bogy of all this foreboding would have laughed, had she known herself the cause of it. She had other fish to fry, bigger and better fish: the Canadian scheme, for example, those *choses philosophiques* which sometimes occupied her pen, the infinite horizon of her dreams and hopes. Breaking hearts was not in her scheme of things. But my father could hardly be expected to know this, and so his letters continued to drop discreet and guarded warnings.

And yet he had reason to be grateful to her had he but known it.

It had always been his wish that I should travel. As a young man he himself had been to Italy, Egypt, Palestine and Syria, and it was his dictum that a man should travel before marriage, for, once married, he will have little chance. But, apart from France, during the war, and repeated visits to the Channel Islands later, my own wanderings had been very parochial. But now – perhaps unconsciously – the example of this girl who, without influence, without privilege, almost without friends, challenged life so vigorously, had left its mark on me. If she could do all this, what was I doing wasting my time in sheltered backwaters? Tartarin might yet shoot lions in Algiers. I sat down and wrote to a scholastic agency asking them to inform me only of posts abroad. I had the comfortable sense of being committed to adventure. Was it Mademoiselle who had made me see that even the drudgery of teaching could be turned to account? Youth does not analyse its own motives too profoundly, and if it was she who had shamed me out of my lethargy I was probably quite unaware of it. One day in the school playground a telegram was handed to me offering me a post in Switzerland for the following autumn. I had four months of freedom before me and I decided to use them. I went to Paris. There I lived for a few shillings a day in a cheap hotel near the Gare de l'Est, in a bandbox of a room wedged between a staircase and a water-closet and overlooking an eighty-foot drop into a courtyard little larger than a funnel, sweltering for six summer weeks, listening towards 2 a.m. to the tooting of every taxi in Paris, until a veritable heat wave drove me to Touraine. From Touraine I made my way to Normandy, from Normandy to Jersey, from Jersey back to Dublin, then presently to Roundstone in Connemara.

Before September was out I was on my way to Château d'Œx, and had slept my first night across the Swiss frontier beneath a wooden roof on the lakeside at Clarens. Did I remember, next morning, looking at those icy, clear waters in which every grey or pale green stone at the lake's edge is revealed as if through the lens of a reading glass, that it was not so many miles down the lake that the sudden squall had caught the Swiss girl and that she had ridden it out even though masts snapped and everyone else in sight had run for shelter? Probably not. The present was too insistent, too filled with pleasurable sensation, to be linked deliberately with the past. In that green valley in the Canton de Vaud to which I had mounted from the lakeside, and where I listened for the first time to the sound of cowbells as the herds descended from the summer pastures, and saw the cherry trees against the grassy hillside flame into crimson splendour as October waned, I may sometimes have thought of her. I had sent her the books and she had thanked me for them. Occasionally we exchanged letters at considerable intervals of time.

And I was to see her before the winter was out. Heralding her arrival by a postcard received only the same morning, she appeared suddenly in Château d'Œx the following March. She had come up the four hours' journey by train from Geneva to visit a friend in the village. The snow was still on the ground, and she had brought her skis with her. Though I had no class at the school immediately after lunch, I had a private lesson with two pupils at a chalet up the valley, whom I had been persuaded to take for an hour twice a week. I suggested that she should come with me on my way there, she on skis, I hauling a luge behind me. It was more than a year since I had seen her. I had the sense, that we get sometimes in a dream, that I was encountering a friend who has suddenly been transformed into a stranger. We set off. Shyness descended upon us both. Perhaps I was a little ashamed that I could offer her no entertainment at the school, and that my own time seemed to be so full that day, but she had given me no notice. Whatever the reason, neither of us seemed to feel completely at ease. It was not like her to be shy, and her laugh, when she did laugh, refuted that suggestion. All the same she was different. She had undergone some kind of sea-change. Perhaps living at home with her family had transformed her. Then she had been a little more than herself. Now, subdued by the frictions of home life, she seemed a little less. I remember the dominant thought in my mind as I looked at her was, 'But you are really only a child.' She might be sixteen at most. She was wearing a navy-blue serge dress, braided round the skirt, the dress of a Swiss schoolgirl – a schoolgirl of ten years back, for that matter. Only a very few of the Swiss still skied in skirts, and before long they too would have surrendered to the new fashion. Where was the defiant Amazon who had been so much in my thoughts eighteen months before? Where was the assured young woman who had stormed at Vandeleur in his own study, who had almost shocked me by her complete independence; who, as she stood in my doorway listening to me reading aloud always made me feel a little naïve, a little juvenile? She had gone, vanished. She was no legend. Others had known her beside myself. But now she seemed to have been a mere figment of my imagination. And in her place a rather silent schoolgirl slid along on her skis beside me on my way to the Latin lesson.

Finding we had more time than we thought, we climbed up the track alongside a stream in one of the gorges, in order to run down quickly back as far as the road. She led the descent. She was, I knew, an expert on skis, but certainly no one ever seemed less braggart or more unconcernedly and accidentally accomplished in the art. She was like those children whom one sees in Switzerland emerge from school, jump on their 'planks,' and clatter away over the snow to the top of the nearest hill. I can see her even now when we had reached the bottom, leaning forward on her ski sticks, unassuming and a little taciturn, looking down at me whimsically, still prostrate on my luge.

The sun shone, a cat basked on the woodpile against the front of a chalet. The trodden snow of the roadway caught the light, and on the great banks at the side of the road snow crystals glistened. Immediately behind the village, rising sheer like a dizzy and gigantic wall to challenge heaven, ran the long ridge which shut us in on one side, precipitous pasture-lands in summer, their green slopes a contrast to the toothed and rocky crags which faced them across the valley, but transformed now into one huge white precipice. In the clear air and against a background of cerulean blue, it towered above us, while from the summit of its single wedge-shaped battlement, known as the Cathedral, a flurry of snow blew continually like the smoke from a volcano. Sometimes down those steep flanks, scarred with a few ravines, avalanches would thunder with a noise like that of distant guns; but at the head of the valley on the slopes of the isolated, humbler Laitemair, pines sweetened the sunlit air with their scent.

I should have said to her as we stood there, 'Look, I owe all this to you, or partly to you. I might never have seen it if you had not crossed my path. It was your energy which roused me out of my torpor. At the very moment when you were so distressed about your own Odyssey you were launching me upon mine.' I should have said, 'If it is possible for the dæmon of one person to affect the dæmon of another, yours certainly affected mine. From the day we first met, the one implanted in the other a little of its restlessness, a mere trifle, a modicum, a pale reflection. But even that, like the grain of mustard seed of the Bible, could bring forth mountains.'

I should have said it. But I did not. Instead, there was only an uneasy silence.

She came with me as far as the chalet and we said goodbye there.

Her friend, she told me, would be waiting for her. I had a vague feeling of guilt, of treating her ungenerously, inhospitably, but she had arrived casually, almost unannounced, and I had had no time to rearrange my day. Even our farewells seemed infected with a slight constraint. Perhaps it was no more than a sense of wonder at finding ourselves strangers when we had seemed to know each other so well.

I had come abroad. She had returned home. All her plans had come to nothing. All her ambitions had been laid in the dust. 'Expend not your strength in vain struggling in the illusive world. . . .' Was she able, I wondered, to comfort herself with such stoic consolation now that she needed it most? It is strange how a mere phrase can seem to evoke a whole mode of life for us, though really we know nothing about it. She had told me very little about her home, and yet I seemed to see the life to which she had returned. Once, quoting a remark in a letter from her brother, who advised her to remain away at all costs, she had given me a glimpse of the inextinguishable boredom and melancholy awaiting her: the father misanthropic, the family-business fallen on evil days, money losses bringing the spectre of poverty nearer on the horizon. Had she exaggerated? She was one of those to whom I imagined any house would be uncongenial. It was plain at any rate that she viewed the mere thought of return as nothing short of a nightmare. She would be trapped. She would never get away again.

Her horror of the prospect had not been able to save her from it. I remembered now how, soon after she had left North Wales, I had gone round to see John Eglinton and his wife, to return some books and to tell them that she was gone. They were sorry that she had failed to win her point and remain in England, but they seemed to think that it might all be for the best in the end; her schemes had been too grandiose. I told them that I feared the Labrador one had come to nothing; that we had perhaps over-emphasised the adventurousness of her disposition, and that, though Grenfell himself seemed sympathetic, the lady in charge of the settlement, to whom he had referred the matter, was afraid that she might find their winters dull! John shook his head sceptically when I expressed the hope that she would yet find the adventures she was seeking. His own life had been passed in tranquil waters, a life circumscribed by a daily routine, until retirement brought a routine of its own. He was not disposed to encourage wild aspirations. I forget his exact words, but they were to this effect: 'Young women have wished to see the world before now and have had to shelve their ambitions. She will settle down like the rest. She will go home and be tamed, as life tames us all.'

B UT he was wrong. She was to give the lie to him and to all others who had doubted. Neither Vandeleur nor her own family, however much they might wish it, could deflect her from her destiny. Within a few months I heard from her that she had gone as cook on board an English yacht. Later still she rejoined her girl friend to sail to the Levant, to camp on small islands in the Ægean, and excavate relics of that Cretan civilisation which had so interested her. Some years afterwards, in the course of my own wanderings in the Mediterranean, I came periodically upon her tracks. Once in Mitylene, looking down at the boats tied up to the ring-bolts in the quayside, I happened to mention her name, only to learn that, six months before, her tiny yacht had been tied to that very slipway, and that her courage and independence were still a source of wonder and interest to the inhabitants. But this was not all. She was to go to Russia, explore some of its least-visited provinces and write a book on her experiences. She would return a second time to visit Turkestan. 'For nine months she journeyed mostly on camels and horseback through countries with temperatures varying from the two extremes of heat and cold, from the mountain of Tien-shan in North-west Mongolia to Kazalinsk near the shores of Lake Aral. Her route took her through the desert of Kizil Kum and the steppes of the Kirghiz Kazeks, land of the eagle-hunters; she mixed with the crowds in the bazaars of Tashkent and Karahol and took the road to Samarkand.' From Turkestan, standing on the summit of the Ak Ogouz Pass, she looked enviously down into 'the closed province,' the forbidden territory of China. Crossing the world, and, approaching from the east what she had first seen from the west, she entered Sinkiang after all. Journeying with a single companion from Pekin to Cashmere, she would skirt Tibet, travel through desert valleys at an altitude of four thousand feet, watching the wild asses gallop past in single file, eating the flesh of antelope, living on *tsamba*, parched barley mixed with tea made from melted snow. Leaving civilisation behind her, she would discover in regions utterly remote and marked on the map as unexplored a calm joy, a serenity which civilisation had never been able to give her. She could say, 'perseverance even in nothing more than a desire has magical virtues.' Her star, which had seemed so near eclipse when I knew her, was really only beginning to show upon the horizon. In a word, she would take her place, as Sir Denison Ross has said, 'among the great travellers of the world.' For the name written in that child's fairy tale given me after my return from Cheltenham, though it was unknown then, has since become known to many: it was the name of Ella Maillart.

PART II

I REMEMBER in Rome, not the Forum, nor the Esquiline Hill nor the Baths of Diocletian, so much as a terrace overlooking the city near the Garibaldi Statue, where I used to walk sometimes by myself, and some hovels at the back of Janiculum, incredibly dilapidated and flimsy, that sheltered against a great embankment, once part of the wall of the city or of some fortification. It is strange that when I think of the Eternal City it should be not of the splendours of the Vatican, or of mornings spent prowling among the ruins, of the Temple of the Vestals, or the Museum on the Capitol and the Dying Gaul, all of them vivid enough in recollection, but none of them quite so likely to recur as that high terrace where it pleased me to walk alone and those hovels huddled against the wall. This is not to say that the rest of Rome had no interest for me, but rather that memory, utterly capricious in this as in other things, chooses out these two places, without sentimental association or any definite reason for the choice, bringing them to mind before it brings back anything more picturesque or of nearer personal significance.

I came to Rome from Switzerland. After two years I had abandoned teaching, having saved enough money to turn my thoughts South, with an eye fixed hopefully on Palestine and Greece. Already I had crossed the Simplon twice and had wandered as far as Sicily, but these were only short excursions, preludes to the grand tour now to be embarked on with a friend. We were to go from place to place, so long as funds lasted, living in a town until we tired of it, choosing our itinerary by impulse rather than according to any fixed plan, and with no more definite objective than that suggested by an invitation to Jerusalem.

The friend was Alister Mathews. One cold afternoon in Château d'Œx I noticed, crossing the square, a youth wrapped in a long black cloak, not unlike the cloaks worn by some of the Swiss themselves. In this case it savoured a little of affectation, for the owner was English and it is unlike the English abroad to draw attention to themselves other than by the loudness of their voices. Careless in dress myself, prejudice rallied instinctively against anything so studied as this cloak. It was still early autumn, my first autumn in Switzerland. The blood-red leaves of the cherry trees against their background of steep green, those meadows cut twice in the year, the last time in October, and as verdant then as they were in June; the tinkle of cowbells as the cattle descended into the valley after the three months spent in the higher pastures; the cries of the herdsmen as they urged the cattle down the hill; the steely, jagged edge of the Alps against their background of azure sky; the wooden chalets with stupendous overhanging eaves and carved inscriptions, committing the building to the care of Dieu le Seigneur – all these delighted by their novelty. But the black cloak failed to delight merely because it was worn by a compatriot.

And yet, as I was to discover presently, the cloak was only a symbol, a gesture of defiance to an age which regards every departure from the stereotyped as a crime. I had encountered Don Quixote at eighteen. This tall slight figure, fragile, a little inclined to stoop, concealed a spirit ardent and indomitable, and the mannerisms, though they might irritate, were not pose or affectation so much as a determination to exclude the banal world and live as far as possible in that other world in which poets delighted. Standing between two eras, one on the verge of death, the other as yet unborn, Mathews turned without hesitation to the past where he felt more sure of finding beauty.

It was a little time before I knew him well enough to appreciate this. When we met, his school days were still only a few months distant. He had come to Château d'Œx to study languages and to mark time before choosing a career. He had been at Winchester and had its traditional courtesy of manner, but he had cut no great figure there. Precluded from popular success and yet with an individuality strong enough to wish to make itself felt, he had taken refuge in the unaccustomed, the rare, in anything which would differentiate him from the herd which he hated. He had a passion for the seventeenth and eighteenth centuries, a passion which found expression in the collecting of little leather-bound volumes about witchcraft or equally out-of-the-way subjects, treasures which he handled with a reverence that it seemed to me they scarcely deserved. He even took snuff in imitation of the age he so much revered. Feeling in his pocket, he would produce a little silver box, tap it, and offer it to you with an air of faint hope that you might be a person of discrimination like himself, though there was a million-to-one chance against it. Then, when you refused, he would take a pinch himself and replace the box in his pocket with the satisfaction of a duty performed.

Eccentricity as flagrant as this prejudiced one against him, but he himself was so gentle, so far from being assertive that one forgave it. It was the sort of gesture, relatively harmless and before long to be abandoned, that one might expect from this strange-looking youth, the last of the Romantics, the nose the most dominant feature of the face, prominent, curved like the prow of a galley, the skin stretched taut across the bridge making it always white at that point, the mouth small and lacking in character, hinting – what was perhaps true – that only sheer force of personality saved it from weakness.

He had come to the most expensive, the gayest, and at the same time the most homely of the various finishing establishments in Château d'Œx. All who went to the Chalet du Vallon looked back on it ever afterwards as a second home. Mrs. Kitchin, the wife of the Englishman who owned it, had a genius for creating the spirit of a family out of the most heterogeneous material. She would take eight or nine young people of different ages and sex, and in a few weeks they would all give the impression of having grown up together. The chalet radiated friendliness, and the glow of warmth from that household reached others like myself who were not its inmates at all.

One moonlight night in November I descended the steep hill from the École Anglaise to take part in their fortnightly play-reading there, to which a number of outsiders were always invited. The play that night was *Hassan*. When the reading was over, I saw the ghost-like Mathews – he had been Selim, and had read him gently and gravely as if he were indeed the Fountain Ghost of the last scene, a gravity partly shyness, partly deliberate earnestness of manner – leaning against the mantelpiece after the rest who shared his life at the chalet, laughing at his idiosyncrasies and yet liking him in spite of them, had flocked chattering into the low-ceilinged hall for lemonade and sandwiches. Then and often later, until assurance made him outgrow it, an overwhelming shyness seemed to silence him, giving him the effect of a shade from another world, hanging about the outskirts of this group of noisy youth. When he made a remark he made it solemnly, impressively, almost in a whisper, as though he hoped by this very stealthy quiescence to achieve what he could not achieve by self-assertion. And because what he said was generally to the point and charged with considerable feeling, it was like a pebble thrown suddenly into a pond over which a cloud of midges have been hovering.

Of all who had delighted in the music of Flecker's words that night, his pleasure had probably gone deepest. We remained by the fire talking. My original aversion had soon become tolerance; and now tolerance became liking, as I realised how grave and genuine his joy in poetry was. He told me about the printing press which he had acquired while still at school, encouraged by a master there, who was himself a printer of books. His only solace during those years of humiliation had been this hobby of his, leading in course of time to the printing of several small booklets, among them a selection of songs from *The Beggar's Opera*.

'It is the smallest hand-press in England. I need new type for it, really. The type I have is worn, and there are not enough capitals. When I have printed one page I have to distribute the type in order to print the next.'

Moving to a bookshelf behind the sofa, he groped among some papers and produced a small pink-covered booklet with a picture of a lady in eighteenth-century costume decorating the cover.

'*The Parlour of Beauty*. What does that mean?'

'It is a collection of eighteenth-century toilet hints which I found in a rather rare book at home. No one seems to know anything about it. Even the British Museum has not got a copy.'

The hints seemed quaint, but not very important, and it was more interesting, more flattering, at least, to learn that he had been lent a copy of the *Fortnightly* in which Courteney had been printing a number of my prose poems, and that he had liked them well enough to copy them out by hand.

'I am glad you like them. Some day you can make a book out of them for your press.'

It was said jestingly, but he was not the person to forget the jest. Months later, having seen little of each other in the interval, he reminded me of my remark. It was the beginning of our collaboration. Only a few people in life definitely influence the course of our destiny so that if we had never met them the channel which the stream subsequently followed must inevitably have been different. Mathews was such a one in my case and I perhaps in his. He was to print my first volume of poems, standing for ten hours a day in front of his little hand-press in Hampshire, and he was to publish both it and my second. Then, having launched our timid but twofold assault upon Parnassus, he was to fan the faint spark of wanderlust which Ella Maillart had kindled, and we were to set forth on our travels together. Before we ever met he had decided on his vocation. He wished to be a dealer in rare books and, as prelude to this, to study languages and above all to travel. He had abandoned any intention he may ever have possessed – never much – of going to Oxford; and, almost alone among his friends, I did not urge him to go to the University, though he might have discovered there that one can be unhappy at school and yet spread one's wings in that quieter and more urbane climate. But his heart was set against it from the beginning. A twinge of conscience suggests to me that I may not have been entirely disinterested in my advice; that, though I had no part in despatching him to Denmark, to Dresden, to Munich, it was for my sake and to publish my second book (across the title page of which I would write in his copy, *'Poète sans éditeur est poisson sans chef'*) that he presently went to Paris, to live in a tiny narrow-fronted hotel in the Rue Gît-le-Cœur and argue with artists and printers, and eat meals in a humble restaurant, paid for with coupons from a book of tickets. But my weight had only been thrown into a scale already tilted, and if, in publishing the book, he had fried my fish for me, he was soon to make use of me to fry his own. His parents had only consented to the grand tour because he had found a companion to accompany him. Actually, I believe that he would have preferred to travel alone. My resources were more slender than his, and when it was a question of how far afield we should go this hampered him a little. Besides, he had the instinct of the born traveller, who rejoices so much in novelty of impression, in the absence of all continuity, that even a friend is an encumbrance. Bacon says that when we go abroad we should avoid our fellow nationals at all costs, a dictum Mathews would have subscribed to with his whole heart. He was willing to endure loneliness, fatigue and discomfort if by doing so he could capture the last drops of sweetness from modes of life already on the point of vanishing. Long before we joined forces, he had formed a taste for solitary wandering, and when at last I was forced to return home and to leave him in Greece, it was almost with a sigh of relief that he set forth in a rowing-boat from Salonika for the monasteries and solitude of Mount Athos. I had been fortunate in having him as travelling-companion for so long. He had lured me further afield than I would ever have ventured myself; he had made light of all possible dangers and actual hardships on the way. At each stage of our journey, when we were on the point of leaving, he had crushed into his suitcase whatever overflowed from mine and he had helped me in a hundred other different ways. Timidity, dislike of discomfort, a little of Tartarin in my composition would have driven me often to the more obvious haunts if Mathews had not been there to lead me up side streets and down alleys until we ended in some lodging more picturesque than pretentious. Nominally, I might be his cicerone, but in actual fact he was my interpreter and dragoman. His custom when we arrived anywhere for the night was to ask the seediest individual in sight where would be a good place to put up, emphasising the fact that we were students and on a tour. I admired the instinct which made him, the child of rich parents, brought up in comfort, prefer the stark, the humble, the simple, just because, at these levels, life is more varied and more real. Extraordinarily fastidious, unnecessarily so in some things, he was yet heroic in others. He told me once how, travelling third-class in Italy, an old tramp, filthy beyond words, and wearing the strangest assortment of miscellaneous rags, had got into the train and occupied the seat opposite him. They entered into conversation and Mathews presently offered him a pinch of snuff. It was accepted. Then the old man, groping amongst his tatters, at last produced a flask of Chianti, uncorked it, took a long swill and passed it across. 'You refused, of course?' 'No. I didn't want to hurt his feelings, but, without letting him see, I wiped the top of the bottle as much as I could with my hand.' A note of apology had crept into his voice at the confession of even this slight breach of the laws of courtesy.

It is typical that our year's travel together began by my remaining in Switzerland with friends until the first snows had fallen while he set forth on foot across the Simplon to walk down into Italy. From Rome he wrote to tell me that he had managed to get rooms in a convent. He was not a Catholic; any religious bias he had at this time lay rather in the direction of theosophy, of Yoga and the sacred books of the East. Friends in Dresden, however, had told him of a German sisterhood in the Borgo Santo Spirito who took pilgrims, and this had fired his imagination. On arrival in Rome he had gone to them and, though he made no claim to be of their persuasion, something guileless in his manner, something unworldly, and perhaps the fact that he knew their language, had won the hearts of the nuns and they had agreed to take him, and his friend, when he should arrive.

It was characteristic of him to have chosen this hostel in preference to any hotel. His letter conveying this news reached me in Florence, where I was lingering, pleased with the vast Florentine palace, now a pension, with its wide marble staircase and huge, lofty rooms to which I returned after mornings of solitary delight spent wandering through the streets and picture-galleries. His letter though full of the peace and homeliness of his new surroundings warned me not to expect too much. But now as the train carried me slowly southward towards Rome, further and further from the Pension Annelina, the discomforts of third-class travel seemed to be preparing me for austerity. I began to reflect that any refuge would be welcome. Long before the journey was over I had wearied of the hard wooden seats, the crowded railway carriage, the frantic entries and flurried departures – separated by periods of temporary suspension of anxiety during which the occupants of the carriage relaxed, loosened their clothing, went to sleep, or else produced packages of food and ate – which is how the poor must travel. Once in an adjoining compartment a child of seven or eight broke into frantic, hysterical crying because her mother had left her for a few moments. The father, a handsome man with wild, pale-grey eyes, seized her in a frenzy of irritation, as though bereft of his senses, and flung her two or three times against the seat, only desisting to look at me with a sullen, puzzled expression when I cried out from the doorway in bad French that I would hand him over to a gendarme when we got to Rome if he did not stop. '*Il ne faut pas faire cela.*' The child wistful and lovely, with the same pale-grey eyes as her father, continued to cry. For a moment I had glanced into the pit of those two so-different hells – the hell of those who are weary, irritable and on edge, unable to control themselves any longer, and the hell of little children whose security and peace some wholly-imagined catastrophe threatens.

At last, gliding through some smokey brick embankments and a final tunnel, the train drew alongside the platform of the Stazione Centrale, to belch its miscellaneous content into the very heart of Rome. It was a relief to see Mathews at the end of the platform, his familiar brown hat showing above the heads of the crowd as his glance searched the ranks of the emerging passengers. He looked well. It was now two years since we first met and in those two years he had matured considerably, shedding a good deal of his frailty as well as many of his foibles.

'I'll take the rucksack. Can you manage your suitcase? A tram will take us quite near where we are going, only we'll have to change once.'

The tram lurched through the streets of Rome. We changed at the Victor Emmanuele, and as we went on our way he again warned me not to expect too much.

'It's very bare, very simple, you know. We're just beside the

Piazza San Pietro, only two minutes' walk from the Vatican. Your room isn't bad. It's got three beds in it, but you'll have it to yourself. The food is simple, but there is plenty of it. '

I forget where we left the tram, or along what route we made our way to the Suore dell' Addolorata. The convent was the last building in the Borgo Santo Spirito, only a few hundred yards from St. Peter's. I remember an open archway and a long flight of steps – taken three at a time on other occasions when we were unladen and late for meals – from which we turned sharp left into a tiny blind alley with cobbled paving, above the level of the street. This was the only access to the hostel, which seemed tucked away in a corner, aloof from the world, its maroon-coloured door with tiny knocker and white bell remote from all sound or stir, although the rooms at the back overlooked the Street of the Holy Spirit, which while not a main thoroughfare could be noisy enough at times. When I opened my window at night I looked out on to the extreme end of Bellini's Colonnade, its huge pillars, four deep, lit up by a lamp in the street below, and the great mass above them topped by the solitary figure of some saint.

We carried our burdens up the low steps. The place at first sight looked gloomy enough. Mathews rang the bell. After a little while there was a fumbling of chains and the door opened and partially revealed an elderly nun. When she saw who we were she removed the chain to admit us. Tired by my journey, the hostel struck me as cold and cheerless, and Mathews seemed to sense my disapproval. We were taken into a little reception-room scarcely larger than a cupboard, to be interviewed by the Mother Superior. Then the nun who had admitted us led the way up the narrow stairs to the room which I was to occupy. It was large, intended actually for three pilgrims, with a light framework of brass rods below the ceiling across which cotton curtains could be drawn to ensure privacy. But I was the only occupant now and the curtains were drawn back. Mathews had a room downstairs, on the side furthest from the street, smaller, darker, looking out on the cobbled paving where hardly a footstep ever passed, and, though quieter, much less attractive than my own. It lay at the end of a passage, below ground level, with bars to its window; damp and horrible it seemed to me, but he clung to it fondly and was distressed a day or two later when he had to vacate it temporarily in favour of another pilgrim, and come and share mine. So deeply were the instincts of the solitary rooted in him. We were both solitaries; that was the secret of our friendship. Love

126

has been spoken of as an *égoisme à deux*; our friendship was a *solitude à deux*. Nothing pleased us so much as to be sometimes alone; to stretch out on our beds; to read a book and to forget the world. That was bliss; to withdraw a little from life in order to appreciate all the more keenly the sensations it offered. Those who are never alone scarcely know what is happening to them in the turmoil which surrounds them. Downstairs in his dungeon Mathews would read until the mood seized him to go out and explore the streets of Rome or to make his way to the library and change his book. If I wanted him I would descend, knock on his door and in nine cases out of ten he would come to it book in hand. Sometimes he brewed tea there on a small spirit stove, pouring it into a tumbler for me and drinking from the aluminium saucepan himself, a little concerned lest the nuns should hear the hissing of the stove and reproach us with being potential incendiaries. He had no table in his room, and if he wished to write must join me in mine, larger, airier, a little stark, flagged with red tiles and furnished with extreme simplicity – a table, three low beds, three chairs and three washstands, each with its jug and basin of enamelled tin.

In a few days I had grown to love the serenity and quiet of the place as much as Mathews did. I hated to live in a city, but here I found myself in a peaceful backwater, out of all turbulence of the current, the business of Rome sweeping by only a few yards away, yet not touching us at all. The hostel no longer appeared comfortless, only restful and a little austere, and on wet days the tea brewed on the small stove in Mathews' room helped to dispel the gloom. It was early December and Rome was getting a good deal of rain. At night it became suddenly quiet, the noise and traffic died away and people no longer seemed to concern themselves with the centre of Christendom.

I grew even to like the bare room with its tiles and its feeling of space and simplicity. There were no pictures on the wall, only a Crucifix, and a little Madonna with a black face, under a glass case, a relic, we decided, of great age. On the wall of the passage outside were two pictures depicting different death-beds. In one, tailed demons and monsters awaited their wretched and terror-stricken victim. In the other – edifying contrast – the devil was being driven off vanquished, and priests and angels surrounded the bedside of the dying man.

It was a little difficult to connect these crude and savage allegories with the gentle presence of the nuns themselves. We saw only three or four of them all the time we were there. Their quarters lay to the right of ours in a different part of the building. They would appear, attend to our wants and then vanish again as silently as they had come. They came through a double baize-covered doorway through which we never passed save on a single occasion. It was impossible to say whether their community was a large one or a small one, but I imagine that it was small. They belonged to an order known in Germany as the Grey Sisters and they suggested the peasant life of the Black Forest, rather than the city of their adoption with its activity and its intrigues. It was as though a few square roods of Northern Europe had been transplanted here. Mathews was delighted by the atmosphere in which he found himself; it gave him an opportunity to air his German and he felt among friends. The nuns too liked him. He had won their good opinion from the first. They would have been shocked probably if they had known that he read Boccaccio in his room on the ground floor, that he had a liking for what one might call eighteenth-century Pompadourism; and, as well, was deeply infected with the heresy of Origen. But he possessed other characteristics more deserving of their approbation; they discerned, with that infallible sixth sense of spiritual direction, something else which was fresh, unspoilt, virginal; a native innocence, a helplessness, some indefinable quality of youth, which commended him to these good women. One cannot ape virtue, but, in so great or so little measure as one possesses it, it will infallibly suggest itself.

The nuns whom we saw were always the same. There was Schwester Edouarda with a humorous face, narrowing small eyes and sunken mouth, who looked after the rooms upstairs. She must have been over seventy. Her whole demeanour suggested kindly old age, homely sanctification and grace. She never hurried, moving slowly and quietly as though she were already in heaven. She had a disconcerting habit of making sudden appearances when one least expected them, to empty a basin, to bring water, or to tidy the chaos which we had created. After breakfast she would appear suddenly and silently in the room and begin cleaning my shoes. Conversation was impossible between us, for she had no English and I no German. The morning after my arrival, when I wished to shave, I reiterated a number of times 'Hot wasser, hot wasser!' but it was beyond her comprehension, and at last, with a baffled expression, she went to fetch Mathews from his room downstairs to interpret. Then the kindly old face, framed in its headdress as by a white shield, lit up in an amused smile and she went away to fetch it.

Once, Mathews told me he returned to find her kneeling by my bedside, having just made the bed.

'Monk, you are prayed for. There is still hope for you, for her prayers must assuredly be heard in Heaven.'

I have no doubt that the nuns prayed for us, and that they did for every pilgrim in the hostel. But whether this were so or not, something of the serenity of those dedicated lives seemed to penetrate our own, so that though we remained completely outside them, living in a world of different mental outlook and of wholly different circumstance, the sense of sanctity was felt by us all the time. I smile now when I hear people – generally the young – attacking what they think is the idleness and uselessness of the religious community. It was we who were idle, not the nuns. Their day began at three o'clock in the morning, when they rose for prayer in the chapel and ended at nine at night. And though it was never hurried, holding its course quietly like the calm stretch of a river which flows between firm banks, it indicated a continual concentration of will and purpose, directed towards a single end.

The nuns wore flowing grey dresses, a blue apron and a blue coif. Occasionally on the stairs, washing them down or cleaning the stair rods of the worn carpet, we would see young girls wearing a different uniform. They had little hoods and a sort of wide cape or grey tippet around their shoulders and they looked the typical German peasant girl. The moment they saw us their eyes were downcast immediately with an almost involuntary swiftness, as though it were a part of their nature to do so. These were the novices. They had not yet fully renounced the world and they were in no humour to dally with it. They bent over their scrubbing, making us feel, as we passed them, the slight embarrassment of an intruder. The nuns were not afraid to look us in the face. Schwester Wunibalda, who saw about our food, was younger than Schwester Edouarda. It was our amusement to try to make her laugh, and laugh she sometimes did, gaily enough.

It was Schwester Wunibalda who brought the fruit and wine to the table before the meal began, and who, later, placed the dishes on a side-table; but it was Markharoff who served them. Markharoff was a theological student attached to the hostel, who received his board and lodging in return for certain duties performed. He was from Persia, a Chaldean by birth, and had studied in Constantinople, Vienna and now in Rome. Presently his studies would be finished, he would become a priest and would return to some remote corner of

Persia, where his work awaited him. He was only twenty, but he looked much older. His long black cassock just touched the ground and he moved about the room quietly, like the future priest, yet with a friendly air, an air almost of stealthy gaiety. He was our master of ceremonies at meals, he saw that the dishes were passed, and collected our plates when we had finished eating, moving to the side-table to fetch the next. The two decanters of red Frascati wine, placed on the table before the meal began, were passed round by him and he filled everyone's glass. Occasionally, when this was done, he would allow himself a centimetre or so at the bottom of his own, filling it up with water. More rarely still he would drink half a glass undiluted. He never looked after his own wants till he was quite sure all ours were supplied. But when the meal was over, and the rest of the guests had withdrawn, he liked to push away the plates, and, resting his elbows on the table, talk with Mathews and myself.

I remember the meal, my first evening in the convent, and the impression it made on me. The room in which we ate was quite a small one, directly below the big bedroom. It was panelled in wood and a little dark, its only furniture the two tables flanked by benches and the side-table from which the food was served. It seemed forbidding and a little gloomy; its extreme bareness, the momentary silence before the meal, and the way in which the food was placed upon the table – abruptly, without any previous warning, as though eating were a concession to our lower nature, not to be greatly stressed or proclaimed – all contributed to this effect. But the impression was misleading and was to disappear before long; the food, as Mathews had said, was good and there was plenty of it, the wine was cheap but the real Frascati, and in time I grew almost to like the darkly-panelled room and its plain benches, as we lingered over the table, elbows spread, and talked, after the food had gone.

Mathews' friendliness had already broken down any barrier of shyness between himself and Markharoff. Markharoff knew no English, but he was almost equally fluent in German, French and Latin. That night the conversation was almost entirely in German. Later, as a concession to me and to save my friend the labour of continual interpretation, we would resort largely to French, but we had not yet thought of doing this, and I was at a distinct disadvantage. I must listen to an animated babble which was completely incomprehensible to me. Mathews accused me of sitting glum at table, looking just like someone who loathes classical music and who has been dragged to a symphony concert against his will. He liked

130

his simile, but to me it seemed singularly inapt. These guttural '*Achs*' and torrential spates of verbiage, ending in peals of happy laughter, would hardly bear the comparison. An uglier succession of sounds could not be imagined. Laughter always irritates us when we do not understand a language. We can forgive everything else but that. Indeed, it is often a comfort to sit in a foreign restaurant comprehending not one word of the murmur around us, a murmur or continuous clatter as impotent to interrupt the trend of our thoughts as the splashing of water in a fountain. But laughter annoys because it arouses our curiosity. 'What are you laughing at?' And then the joke has to be taken to pieces, translated, its idiom interpreted, until at last it arrives, a forlorn ghost of itself, with scarcely sufficient humour left in it to save it from complete humiliation.

It was so, many times that night, and Mathews grew tired of interpreting for me what was in large measure merely the spontaneous gaiety of himself and his companion. Markharoff's imitation of an old Swiss pilgrim, speaking dialect, was lost on me. Tired by my journey, there seemed very little to laugh at.

I was glad enough when Mathews presently led the way upstairs. I had come to Rome with my mind made up to persuade him to move on to Naples next day. We had a fair amount of time at our disposal, but it was not unlimited, and there seemed little point staying on in a place that we had already seen. I had been in Rome twice before, and he had had several weeks now in which to get to know it. It seemed waste of time to linger. 'We will go to Naples. There we can get a boat to Egypt. Your scheme of walking across Sicily is not a good one. It is the wrong time of year. The moment to see Sicily is early spring.' We spent our first evening arguing, he smoking his pipe, which was gradually taking the place of the much-cherished snuff-box; I, though I had not smoked for months, lighting cigarette after cigarette. Perhaps our vehemence died away in tobacco smoke, or perhaps, throwing open the window of the room, I caught a glimpse of the colonnade of St. Peter's in the moonlight and thought, 'You are here now. You have a chance of tasting a quite different life in completely novel surroundings. There must be much, quite as beautiful as this, in almost every corner of Rome, waiting to be seen. Do not be a fool.' At any rate, the question was shelved and Mathews gained his point by no longer appearing to urge it. Certainly by next morning it was assumed that we were remaining at least for several days.

We were in Rome, but we had nothing of the painstaking spirit of the tourist who checks off each item of interest and is not satisfied until he has completed his programme. All our plans were casual. I am ashamed when I think with how little seriousness or scholarship we regarded our privilege. Rome was our playground, in which it was pleasant to stumble upon antiquity, but it would soon have become tedious if we had felt under any obligation to collect churches or to differentiate schools of painting. The past was of importance to us only in so far as it formed a part of our own present. It interested us as much to watch a woman combing her child's hair in the sunny doorway of some tenement as to come upon a commemorative tablet.

And almost at once this emphasis upon the humanities received a strengthened impulse from another source.

Next morning, over our coffee at breakfast, Mathews said, 'I have asked Elisabeth to meet us for tea this afternoon. At Gargiulo's. At four. I take it you will come?'

Ever since I had known him Mathews had been in love with someone. But not always with the same person. As the last of the Romantics, this was only to be expected: there is no need to reproach him with it. Goethe says, 'The first propensities to love in an uncorrupted youth take altogether a spiritual direction. Nature seems to desire that one sex may by the senses perceive goodness and beauty in the other,' and Mathews' love was of this sort. Once in a moment of expansion he confessed to me that while still a schoolboy, and after months of silent adoration, he had proposed to a girl a year or two older than himself. She had received his proposal in a spirit of levity, and he still blushed with shame whenever he thought of it. He had proposed to no one since, but he had been in love a number of times. If his susceptibility made him unhappy, he had at least the consolation of knowing that much of his joy and inspiration sprang from the same source. '*Il faut s'approfondir dans de beaux rêves*' was a favourite quotation with him. Had he been unperceptive of beauty in young girls he would have been less perceptive of it in the world around him. They might cause him exquisite anguish, but it was they also who stabbed his soul into perceiving the light and shade, the colour and warmth of life and it was from them perhaps that he drew the glow in which other and quite different impressions were warmed as in a crucible.

To give him his due, he had been faithful now for close on two years to the image of the same Dulcinea, a seventeen-year-old damsel whom he had met at the Chalet du Vallon. She had made merciless fun of his idiosyncrasies when they were fellow pupils there, but now, back in her native Gloucestershire, she wrote to him from time to time. Her theme was always the same, hunting and dogs, subjects in which he was not really very interested – though at Winchester his book-plate had included a gun, a dog, a falcon and a fishing-rod, as well as a pile of books – but in which he was able to profess a slight revival of interest for her sake. For some time now this young woman, scornful and a tease, but with fine brown eyes and a sense of humour, had held paramount place in his thoughts. But there had been other minor devotions, both earlier and subsequent, which occasionally occupied them, the former tinged with faint sentimental regret, the latter kindling for a moment those brief fires of expectancy by which love, when it has nothing else to do, keeps itself alive.

Of all such the girl whom he now mentioned stood in a unique position. He had met her my first winter in Switzerland, when the star of Dulcinea had not yet risen on the horizon, and, as we were then barely acquainted, I only heard of her months after she had ceased to trouble his heart acutely. I had gone to Sicily for Christmas, and Mathews was spending his holidays at the Hotel Rosat in Château d'Œx. She was staying in the same hotel, young, very beautiful, a paragon of her kind. Mathews had fallen deeply in love, in love to the point of unhappiness. I was surprised at the emphasis which he afterwards placed on his misery at that time. He was, he explained, only one of many. Wherever she went people paid her this homage. She must almost have grown used to it now. Mathews had survived the experience, and in the result his life had been enriched by a friendship on which he came to place great value. She was a breaker of hearts, but in this instance at least a mender of them too. Nothing argues intelligence in a woman so much as the ability to keep a man's friendship after she has rejected his affection. His wounds were already healed, by the time he knew me well enough to speak of them, and, having once mentioned her, he talked of her often. A letter from her was a distinct event in his life, to be mentioned with pride, though since he had made Dulcinea's acquaintance it had ceased to have any sentimental significance. I formed the impression – the composite total of many references – of a personality vivid and compelling, of an intelligence shrewder and more subtle than any of his other friends, of a nature adventurous and restless like his own, and of a beauty – on this he always laid great stress – that had been fatal to many.

Then, for a time, Elisabeth, a wanderer like himself, passed out of the picture. But they were to be cast ashore again upon the same beach. When he went to Dresden he learnt from a mutual friend that she had preceded him there. Both went to the police-station to enquire for the other's address, and failing to find it met quite by accident on the stairs of a concert-hall that same afternoon. She had become engaged to a young German in Munich whose parents opposed the match. Versailles was still only a few years distant, conditions in Germany were severe, and they did not welcome the idea of a daughter-in-law from the race that had defeated them. In Dresden Mathews saw her often. They had much in common; together they went to museums, to concerts and to art galleries. He took tea with her, listening enviously to her command of German, for she had been talking the language longer than he and was much more skilled in it. It used to amuse me that whenever I praised his German he would remark how much better Elisabeth's was. His admiration remained undiminished. Though the barbed arrows of the god no longer had power to torment him, he was not ashamed to bear their scars.

In Paris, busy with *The Branch of Hawthorn Tree*, which was nearly ready for publication, he heard that her engagement had been broken off. The book had been printed, and rows of work-girls, experts in the art of *pochoir*, were now busy stencilling Le Doux's decorations. During the final stages of the work he had nursed me through mumps in my tiny room in the Rue Gît-le-Cœur, and in a few days would be in quarantine himself. Preferring, if he was to succumb, to do so amongst the mountains rather than in a dingy bed-and-breakfast hotel by the Seine, he decided to go to Switzerland, and announced that he would stop on his way at Lausanne to see Elisabeth and her mother, who were staying there.

'But you are in quarantine. You can't go and see them while you are still in quarantine.'

'I have written and told them so, and she says that it does not matter,' and he set off, travelling third-class by night in order that he might be in Lausanne next morning and spend the day with them.

It was then that he learnt that she and her mother were going to winter in Rome, information perhaps not altogether without influence upon his own plans.

When, having followed him to Château d'Œx, I asked after them, he replied:

'You may meet them. They will very likely be in Rome when we

134

are there. Elisabeth is different, shyer, much more nervous. It's changed her – this business of the broken engagement.'

The friends of our friends, even if unknown to us, are always interesting if only because by their continual recurrence in conversation they form part of a landscape or background surmised yet never seen. Travelling back that first evening across the streets of Rome and listening to Mathew's news, I had asked presently: 'And what of Elisabeth?'

'They were out when I first called. Elisabeth wants to learn Italian, ánd is living with a countess, widow of a famous scholar. Her mother has gone to a pension near the Pincian Gardens. I have seen quite a lot of them since I arrived.'

The prospect intrigued me. It was as though I had long been hearing of Helen, and now shipped to Troy with the latest draft of men, was soon to see her walking upon the walls. Mathews must have detected a little more than passing curiosity in my enquiry, or rather in my manner, as I made it, for, when at breakfast he announced the arrangement that we should all meet for tea, he smiled quizzically, as though it were unlikely I should refuse his invitation.

'. . . I take it you will come?'

'Yes, I should like to.'

'We will all have to meet at Gargiulo's. I am lunching at the Russells. He is Ambassador to the Holy See. My father knows them. A few days ago I went to the Embassy to leave cards. I was wearing my oldest clothes and my rucksack, and an indignant flunkey nearly shooed me down the marble steps and through the ornamental wrought-iron gateway. I had great difficulty in getting him to take my cards. But now I have been asked to lunch and I shall have to wear my best suit.'

'Where is this place where we are all to meet?'

'You know the Piazza di Spagna? Near the English Library. You say you used to go there when you were last in Rome. Well, Gargiulo's is the tea-room just a little further along. Be there at four o'clock. We will all meet in the porch, just by the doorway. No, I have a better idea. I will meet you in the English Library at a quarter to four; you can be looking at books while waiting. Then we can go on together.'

But next morning, thinking that his luncheon party might be over earlier than he expected, and that he would be left with time hanging on his hands, he decided that he could return to the convent for me and that I was to await him there. He arrived soon after three, and, if he had not become interested in some review cuttings which I had brought with me from Florence which praised highly his production of the book, we might have been in time for our appointment.

As it was, we were late. Missing one tram, we had to wait some time for another, and when we reached the Piazza di Spagna it was already after four. Mathews dashed up the steps of Gargiulo's and pushed open the swing doors.

She was sitting just inside the doorway, in one of those shallow alcoves, back from the room in which the tea tables were set. I was impressed by the fact that she accepted our lateness philosophically. She neither reproached us nor seemed to wish to hear our apologies; it was as though she considered a few contemplative moments there as good a way of spending the time as any other, and at once I placed her amongst those women who find friendship with men easy, because they neither exact any special treatment for themselves nor feel obliged to concede it.

She was wearing a narrow toque edged with fur, which, since it concealed her forehead, left one really without knowledge of the true symmetry of her face. I noticed, what Mathews had said I would, a resemblance to a young girl in Ireland, whom I had watched grow up, through a lovely childhood, until a time came when I saw many render a homage which I had been rendering for years, and could cry in whole-hearted admiration, 'Now you are in your shining days.' When Mathews came to Dublin and met the latter, he exclaimed, 'But she is like Elisabeth,' the highest praise he had in his power to confer in those days. Likeness there was; yet it was difficult to say wherein the resemblance lay, for this girl had little of the animation, little of the careless youthful defiance which the other possessed. It was only in the line of the mouth, a line at once proud and tender, that I could detect any definite resemblance or be reminded of a face that had dominated my imagination for years.

I had gone in a mood of some curiosity. I had heard much of this paragon. As Naaman expected the prophet of the Lord to come forth, stand before him and work some great marvel, so had I expected a personality so arresting that one would feel it almost oppressively. But instead of Helen, abroad upon the walls of Troy, making all turn, instead of that intense individuality which Mathews had led one to expect, there had come to tea with us a girl who at first spoke little, silent and less sophisticated than I had envisaged.

She was neither shy nor assured, not indeed the glittering creature I had anticipated, not radiant, nor triumphant, nor a trampler upon men's hearts. Rather she seemed like someone waiting to hear something, but not in the least anxious to make her own personality felt. She left it to us to talk; she was content to watch, to listen, occasionally to comment. It was almost as though she was deliberately passive. Perhaps she realised that her praises had been sung so often in my ears that she was now on trial; as though she stood for the first time in rivalry with her reflected image, or like a person beside his own portrait who wonders whether the onlooker will be disappointed.

I was as little inclined to talk myself. Mathews was in the position of a circus proprietor whose lions will not jump through their hoops. We were his two closest friends, and it was as if by this very fact he had unintentionally put each of us on our guard against the other. Now we had met; the prosaic reality stood in the shadow of whatever radiant creatures his fervent imagination had created when speaking of us.

He ordered tea, and, shouldering the burden of conversation himself, he began to entertain us with a description of his luncheon party.

'The very flunkey who waved me away three days ago was the one who had to stand behind my chair, filling my glass and bringing me a fresh roll. There was a touch of the *Arabian Nights* about it, as though I had suddenly been translated to the palace by the Caliph's special orders. There were three of them in brown livery and white shirts, standing like statues around the table until they were wanted. I enjoyed their attentions all the more because of their past coldness.'

'Tell us about your fellow guests.'

'There was a man with memories of Berlin in 1910 – persistent memories which were always cropping up, no matter what turn the conversation took; a Russian lady who used to be at the Court of St. Petersburg, and another ambassador and his wife. The gentleman with memories remembered the wife in the days of puffed sleeves – in Berlin, of course. She took me in her car as far as the Piazza di Spagna on my way back.'

'And after moving in these exalted circles you propose to foot it through Sicily and stay in humble *trattoria*!'

He liked his host and hostess and had enjoyed himself. For two hours he had returned to the atmosphere of an English home. And he was pleased that into the wide range of conversation he had been able to introduce the topic of fine printing.

Turning to Elisabeth, he said:

'I have not told you. A.E. has reviewed Monk's poems and says that he "is indeed fortunate in his publisher and in the artist who has decorated its pages." He thinks it is the most beautifully printed volume of the season. What do you think of that?'

He groped in his pocket for the review which I had shown him earlier in the afternoon. She knew the book, and had been one of the first to whom he had brought it, and, though it was expensive, had insisted on buying her own copy.

'I agree that some of the decorations are charming. But I hate others. They seem too sophisticated for the poems.'

The tea things were pushed aside and we began to smoke. Our shyness had worn off. The sense of constraint vanished. For an hour and more we remained talking around the table in the shallow alcove by the window, discussing some of those multitudinous interests which we all three shared, the fashionable tea-shop and its other clients coming and going as remote from us as though they did not exist.

Presently the orchestra began to play. Talk languished and Alister went over to the leader to ask him for a tune which he and Elisabeth had heard together in Dresden. He came back saying that they had not got it, but had promised to play it if we returned next day.

'But Monk expects to be in Naples to-morrow!'

The music stopped and the players began to put away their instruments. We resumed our talk. I discovered that I knew one of Elisabeth's schoolfellows. I was surprised to hear her say that she herself was not among the blue-stockings, for her interests now appeared, both from our conversation and from all that Mathews had told me, to be cultural if not actually intellectual – art, music, books, provided she were free to range where she herself liked. She began talking of her life in Paris and of some incident which threatened a friendship she had made, concluding her story by saying:

'No, she was not angry. She said that I was *une jeune fille sérieuse*.'

Glad to have found someone not ashamed to own to serious tastes, I looked at her intently across the table and said challengingly:

'And are you *sérieuse*?'

She seemed surprised, shocked, flabbergasted and a little amused. Then, blushing slightly, said:

'But that is a question one simply doesn't ask!'

Mathews' eyes twinkled, but he said nothing. Serious-minded? Of serious tastes? There could be no harm in that. I had asked the question in all innocence of heart, having grown weary of people to whom flippancy was a duty, and wondering whether she would have had the courage to reply, 'Yes.' But it was plain my ignorance of idiomatic French had led me astray. It was better to say no more.

We had been at Gargiulo's close on two hours, and it was nearly time for her Italian lesson at six. It was deluging rain, and we stood waiting for our tram in the Piazza di Spagna, near the flower-stalls at the foot of the wide flight of steps to the church, stalls blazing with variegated colour – dyed flowers we were told later – half hidden now by the many dripping umbrellas. At last a tram came and we took it, going as far as the Via Ovidio so that we might walk back with Elisabeth to the block of flats where, we assured her, the Italian Contessa would be waiting for her, book in hand. There we said good night and hurried away along the flooded streets, Mathews showing me how by a succession of short cuts the Tiber was reached, and how, once there, the Castel S. Angelo made it easy to find the way back to the convent.

Only when we had walked a little way did I say to him, 'And what is *sérieuse* that one may not ask a person if they are it?'

'Its meaning varies in different contexts. In this instance it meant virtuous, chaste.'

Then, overcome by the recollection of my guileless expression, and Elisabeth's, of slightly reproachful amazement, he burst out laughing, saying that I would be the death of him, that I no sooner met a girl than I looked at her gravely, like Savonarola, or insolently like Casanova, and asked, 'And are you chaste?'

A joke of this sort, at the expense of the ingenuous in another person, is always dear to its possessor, and it was several days before he was willing to abandon it, his eyes narrowing in a delighted twinkle every time anything was said to remind him of the incident. He was anxious to hear my opinion of his paragon, and a little disappointed that I would not acknowledge her, with the single exception of Dulcinea, to be the non-pareil of her sex. All that he could extract from me was a reluctant admission that I had noticed the likeness he had mentioned. But this did not satisfy him. He was distressed that I would not praise outright, and it amused me to find him almost as importunate as Browning when he cried:

> 'Nay, but you who do not love her,
> Is she not pure gold, my mistress?'

Presently he took refuge in the assertion that if I had known her when he first met her two years before I would have been wax in her hands. 'You should have seen her then. She was like an exultant flame.' 'I might have been. I cannot say. A contention of this kind, since it concerns the past, cannot be disputed.' Whatever the reason, her silence, her passivity that afternoon had been a little exceptional. Weeks later, discussing her with him, and happening to mention that my first impression had been of someone almost subdued, he gave a laugh and said, 'Yes, but I haven't often seen her like that.'

Supper at the convent was at seven. We hurried now, not because we should be late, but because the rain still fell in a steady stream out of the dark abysm of night, into which even the great arc-lamps in the street threw their rays for only a few feet.

Raindrops laced these patches of luminosity and pattered about our feet, and the few people we passed seemed like ourselves eager to escape out of the downpour. It was no more variable weather than one would expect for that time of year and fortunately the down-pours were usually after dark. I would hear loud splashing on the flags in front of St. Peter's and, going to my window, would see the rain descending in an almost solid sheet transversely across the pillars of the colonnade. An hour later it might be fine. At last the Santo Spirito was reached. The alley was more sheltered, but the long flight of steps seemed of penitential length, and we were glad when the hostel door closed behind us.

We removed our dripping coats and went to our rooms. There was time to go upstairs, to pour a stream of chilly water from the jug into an enamelled basin and wash our hands before going down to supper. During our whole stay there were never more than four or five other pilgrims in the hostel besides ourselves. At the second table facing us sat a mother and father and their daughter, who con-versed in low undertones if they spoke at all, and who never got beyond the stiff little inclination of the head and the '*Guten Abend*' as they came to or departed from meals. At our own table was Mark-haroff and a young German, who looked as though he might be a student or perhaps an artisan. He had an honest face, clear blue eyes, and a magnificent forehead, square and open; a fine type, but silent and reserved, hardly ever taking part in the conversation at meals and then only by some brief remark. He was growing a beard, a chin beard only, his cheeks remaining shaved, and this gave him the look of a Dürer engraving. This beard held the interest, and excited the envy of Mathews who resolved that we should grow beards also as soon as we were fairly started on our travels.

When Markharoff joined us at table the meal assumed its polyglot character, and I found it almost as trying as the previous evening. There were endless references to two German girls who had been in the hostel, and who used to sing folk-songs after supper in the evening. 'If only the Schürholzes had not gone. You have no idea how good they were. It was exquisite in its way – just perfect of its kind!' – after which it was small consolation to be told that they had left for Naples at two o'clock on the afternoon of the very day I arrived.

At last I slipped away, leaving Mathews to his gurgles, his delighted thigh-slappings, and all the other manifestations of warmhearted but slightly Teutonic emphasis. I went upstairs, drew back my curtain and looked out on the night. The heavy drops of rain no longer slanted across the great fluted lamp-lit pillars. It was raining softly, as though at any moment it might stop. There seemed a promise of better weather, in another hour one might in all likelihood glimpse a star between high, drifting clouds.

Next morning I awoke to find Mathews standing beside my bed, dressed and impatient. The sun was already gilding the pillars on the far side of the Piazza, and I remembered that I had pledged myself to go to Lake Nemi with him if the day were fine. It was fine and our train left in less than an hour. Leaving me to dress in haste, he went to find one of the nuns to ask her for bread and cheese to take with us on our expedition. I found him in the refectory poring over an ancient Baedeker while at the same time he absent-mindedly buttered his rolls and drank his coffee. On occasions like this he was at his best, an unshakable optimism convincing him that everything is possible for those who dare. He was the Don Quixote of our partnership, ready to charge the first windmill encountered, whereas I was Sancho Panza, full of peasant caution and timidity, seeing all the obstacles, and only willing afterwards to admit the rewards.

'Listen. We have two choices. We can either train to Albano, climb to Nemi, and walk down to Frascati; or we can train to Frascati and make it our starting point. Which is it to be?'

'Either, provided we are in time to catch the train.'

It did not look as though we should be. The tram taking us to the Piazza di Venezia proceeded at so slow a pace that we were afraid to continue in it. Leaping out, we hailed a taxi which drove us furiously to the station, but arrived nevertheless three minutes after the train had gone. Disconsolate, we were preparing to return to the convent when someone told us that there was a tram leaving for Albano in forty minutes. It was already there drawn up beside the station, and, getting into it, we produced the books we had brought and read quietly for the next half-hour. One other passenger had climbed aboard, a peasant woman returning with her basket from early marketing, and eventually the tram moved off, beginning a leisurely progress to Albano, so leisurely that it was a full hour before we arrived.

'We must get out here. This tram goes no further. I believe we have missed our connection and will be stuck in this hole for the day.'

We got out and started down the street. Almost immediately another tram overhauled us, going in our direction. Running alongside, risking life and limb, we managed with great difficulty to hurl our rucksacks on to the platform, and ourselves after them, boarding the vehicle like trapeze artists, for this tram was as speedy as the other had been slow, racketing on its way, completely empty, yet with contemptuous disregard for any prospective passenger.

It took us to Genzano, one of the two villages above Lake Nemi. His guide-book told Mathews that the women of Genzano were remarkable for their beauty, but it is a mistake to depend upon a Baedeker forty years old, bought from a book-barrow beside the Seine. We saw only a couple of old crones and one squint-eyed girl, besides a woman in a doorway whose condition might imply that she had found favour in someone's eyes, but who seemed to us as little qualified to sustain the reputation of the village as the others. Making our way through a sea of mud along a filthy alley between dirty-looking cottages, and past the vine-trellised fence of a garden, we reached a point at last where the view opened out. The Lake of Nemi lay directly below us, deep, oval, a jewel in its high, woodland setting, like some hidden and enchanted sanctuary, looking, despite the sunlight, as though it must contain many another secret besides the sunken galley of Caligula. All day high storm-clouds were to hurry across a clear sky, covering the sun for an instant, but never for long. And as the clouds passed, the mood of the lake seemed to change; a little lake, at once friendly and mysterious, friendly when the sun rested on it, mysterious because of the chestnut trees which descended steeply on all sides to its very edge. Here the 'Kings of the Wood,' fugitives from justice, who seized the priesthood by murder and held it until they in turn should be slain, exercised their uneasy sovereignty; here Diana had been worshipped; and here, centuries after men had ceased to worship her, Turner had come to paint 'The Golden Bough,' a wise thing to do, because, though her worship had ceased, the woods in which the goddess once hunted remained; whereas in another fifty years an artist may come and find neither goddess, nor woods, nor Golden Bough, all having had to give way to some trellised structure of steel and iron, gibbeted against a background of waste, in order that men a hundred miles away may heat their bath-water or suck the dust from their carpets. One more sacrifice will have been offered to the only god in whom men still firmly believe, the great god Mammon. Solitude is the bread of the soul, solitude and beauty; but since we no longer believe in the soul there is no need to provide sustenance for it, and comfort must come first – comfort, which the Syrian poet Kahlil Gibran describes as 'that stealthy thing that enters the house a guest, and then becomes a host, and then a master.'

No such thoughts, however, distressed me or filled my head as we skirted Lake Nemi that day, climbing up the dried bed of a stream over brown sandstone, the roots of the chestnut trees six or seven feet high above our heads, where the falling soil had left them denuded. Making our way towards the head of the lake, we came at last out of the shelter of the wood into a small, exposed field swept by a strong wind, and stood looking right down the lake full into the sunlight. It was at its loveliest. The little villages of Nemi and Genzano, facing each other from a height across the intervening stretch of water, were merely picturesque details in a spot that seemed consecrated to silence. Behind us lay Monte Caro. Baedeker warned us that it was impossible to find one's way through the woods to its summit without a guide. But we determined to make the attempt, plunging into the forest again where we had left it. Autumn had stripped the trees of their leaves, but once we were in the wood the mountain top which had stood out stark at a distance could no longer be seen and it became harder and harder to place it correctly. We had nothing to guide us but a narrow track and our own sense of direction. These soon misled us. We held too far to the right, and it was a relief to meet some woodcutters and ask them the way. But the directions they gave us were vague; they were more concerned in demanding a cigarette; and when I had searched my pockets in vain a look of disappointment came into their faces as though Destiny had played them too cruel a trick in bringing strangers to that point and then cheating them of their hopes. The path which they pointed out led still more to the right and presently we heard what we thought were axes and pressed forward to find some men digging a road in the soft red-brown earth. The fact that we were without tobacco made us chary of questioning them; one group of chagrined countenances had been enough, and, leaving them, we plunged once more through the trees and over chestnut leaves piled more than a foot deep till we found a track which led us quickly to the summit of Monte Caro.

Mathews, informative as ever, announced that we were three thousand feet above sea-level, as high in fact as Château d'Œx. Perhaps it is the long, slow train-climb into the Vosges and the still steeper winding ascent, doubling and redoubling upon itself, immediately behind Montreux, that makes the latter seem so high. At any rate, it was hard to believe that we had climbed to the same height now in a few hours. From where we stood we could see for the first time the Sabine Mountains, olive grey, the picturesque barrenness of their stony flanks caught in the light and looking almost like snow; while behind them, with clear-cut edges, towering into heaven to an immense height rose gigantic cloud castles, white and pale grey. Turning a little, we looked across the flat campagna to Rome, a little patch of white sand poured out upon the ground, only a single building of all its many thousands identifiable, the dome of the great cathedral.

I threw myself down on the ground, stretching full-length, and allowed thought to drift over the landscape as lazily and complacently as a white cloud in a clear sky.

Mathews was once more consulting his Baedeker.

'What are you looking for?'

He was identifying an enclosure of blocks of moss-covered stone a little way down the hillside. It had once been a garden, he explained, and the dismal-looking building in the centre, on the point of falling into ruin, plastered over now and distempered a faded pink, had been a monastery and was now an inn.

'Don't be too sure. Your Baedeker is fifty years old, and it may have undergone another metamorphosis in the meantime.'

'Before the monastery was built the ruins of the temple of Jupiter stood here. It was only in the eighteenth century that an English cardinal had the last of them pulled down.'

'First a temple, then a monastery, and now an inn. It is symbolic. Once men gave the loveliest of their sites to the gods, but if a place is beautiful to-day it is more likely to be dedicated to a luxury hotel.'

And while Mathews replaced the guide-book in his rucksack and went down the green slope to investigate the so-called inn, I mused on an age which has thrown out the child, wonder, with the bathwater, superstition. I was sorry that the Cardinal had felt it laid upon him to banish the last traces of Jove, but at least the temple had been replaced by a monastery. It seemed to me that there would be little hope for mankind until they once more consecrated, as they used to, the most beautiful sites that Nature gives them to God. All that was best and most eloquent in civilisation, as well as much that was absurd, foolish and cruel, had its origin in religion, religion in which two elements always are at work, the false eternally betraying the true, the true re-establishing itself, again and again, on the ruins of the false. Mankind, I told myself, can neither live without religion, nor keep it sane and beautiful for long. The children of darkness are forever plotting against the children of light, from within the citadel quite as often as from without. The fanatics, the pharisees destroy from within, the scoffers from outside. But civilisations collapse soon without that essential reverence for absolute values which religion expresses. When men cease to be conscious of their need for spirituality the vacuum makes itself felt. First the gods cease to be real; then all that they stood for ceases to be real also. Rome had discovered this in the days of her decadence. 'Men live,' I thought, 'on the accumulated faith of the past as well as its accumulated self-discipline. Overthrow these and nothing seems missing at first, a few sexual taboos, a little of the prejudice of a Cato, a few rhapsodical impulses, comprehensible, we are told, only in the light of folk-lore – these have gone by the board. But something has gone as well, the mortar which held society together, the integrity of the individual soul; then the rats come out of their holes and begin burrowing under the foundations and there is nothing to withstand them.'

Presently Mathews returned, saying that his nineteenth-century Pausanias, the most informative man of his generation, had not lied and that the first words that greeted him over the doorway, daubed roughly on a piece of wood, were 'Pensione Ristorante.'

'I came round the corner of the house and heard the most beautiful voice singing. It came from a grated window on the ground floor – the window of the kitchen, as a matter of fact.'

It was plain that his blood had quickened expectantly.

'It was a heavy grating and I could see nothing inside. In the flash between hearing the singing and waiting for someone to answer my knock, I had made up a whole romance, deciding that the singer came from Genzano, that the son of the house had gone down and had seen her there and brought her back as his bride. Baedeker would be vindicated after all.'

'And was he?'

'She came to the door finishing the last bars of her song and was as ugly a piece as ever I've set eyes on.'

He looked as though he were uncertain whether to be amused or disconsolate.

'She says that we can have some orange-white Frascati wine if we like to pay five liras a litre for it.'

He had returned to consult me as to whether such an extravagance was justifiable. We decided that it was not. We ate our lunch lying on the grass, overlooking the Alban lake as well as Lake Nemi. The convent had given us bread and butter and fruit, and nearly half a pound each of the cheese of the country, very mild and pleasant-tasting. As we lunched an Alsatian bitch, with huge udders, drew near, looking exactly like the Capitoline wolf; and we threw her our cheese rinds, which she was glad enough to eat: largesse from the bounty of the nuns.

When lunch was eaten we turned our backs on Lake Nemi and walked down to Rocca di Papa, covering in twenty minutes ground that would have taken us close on two hours to ascend. Rocca di Papa was the poorest village I had yet seen in Italy; my mind had to travel as far as my own country to parallel it. It clung to the side of the hill and a little wood descended to its outskirts. It was washing-day and clothes flapped in all the fields around, right up to the edge of this brown copse. A huge yellow quilt was spread over a bush to dry, completely obliterating it. On the top of the rock, dominating this huddle of cottages and giving its name to it, were some ruins and a cross made out of two disused tramlines lashed together with a piece of wire. In the lee of the great rock, hedged-in by a low, circular palisade of faggots, was a cluster of strange-looking edifices, mud huts thatched on sides and roof with broom, pitiable dwelling-places for winter; but they pleased Mathews because they reminded him of an engraving he had treasured as a boy, an illustration of Cook's *Voyages* showing the huts of the South Sea islanders.

We clambered down through someone's garden into a steep, cobbled alley which zigzagged down the hill between incredibly dirty and poor houses for another fifty yards or so. In the streets countless children were playing. Men passed us riding little mules, often with a bundle of hay or a load of faggots laid across the wooden saddle in front of them.

'What do you want to do now? We could visit Tusculum before returning to Frascati. But we should have to descend into the valley first and then climb again.'

Tusculum – the site of Cicero's villa – and the terraces on which he had walked with his daughter Tullia, awaited us. The word evoked for me as keen a memory of youth as the sight of the broom-thatched hovels had done for Mathews. One day when I was still quite young my father had put into my hands Forsythe's *Life of Cicero*, a book beautifully bound in green morocco and embossed with gold, which he had won as a prize at his university. For days afterwards Rome seemed almost as real to me as the home in which I moved. Cicero became my hero, not because of the thunders of his wrath against Cataline, which wearied me a little, but because of his passionate indictment of the Roman, who used his position as proconsul in Sicily in order to plunder the province. Perhaps I had already enough of the collector in me to be made furious by the thought of a man who might first dine with you and then lay claim to the treasures of art you had shown him. I grew to love Cicero for his indignation in so good a cause, and later, when in Shakespeare I came upon the lines:

'While Cicero
Looks with such fiery and such ferret eyes'

they affected me almost as though someone had offered a personal affront to a friend.

A friend he was, thanks to my father who had the gift of infecting me with his own enthusiasms. Of all the descriptions in Forsythe's book, the most moving and the most vivid in memory was that of Cicero's death. When the news of Philippi reached him, a great weariness seized him which made him refuse at first to seek safety in flight. Yielding at last to the entreaties of his attendants, he set forth in a litter. I remember how I followed each stage of that pursuit with the intense partisanship which makes us hope – absurdly – up to the last minute to alter an event two millennia old. It moved me, this thought of a man, not natively heroic, nor by temperament tranquil, or indifferent in the face of danger, meeting death heroically as the only fitting and appropriate mode. And now, when Mathews mentioned Tusculum, I could see again the whole scene on the road, the slaves dazed and dismayed, overtaken by Mark Antony's emissaries, the old man stretching out his head, from the litter, on its thin and scrawny neck, resolute that he would make an end with dignity, telling his pursuers to strike, as strike they did.

We halted for a moment on the outskirts of Rocca di Papa to debate whether we should turn aside to Tusculum or not. But the afternoon was far advanced. We had had our fill of walking. Even if we chose the direct route to Frascati, there were still several miles more before us. Frascati it must be. Rocca di Papa could have had no school, for as we went down the road crowds of children were returning up the hill to the village. They eyed us curiously. Some of them mocked our quick pace by crying out in Italian the equivalent of the soldier's 'Left, Right! Left, Right!' Two small boys stopped us to ask for a light for a cigarette, which, unlike the woodcutters, they were in a position to produce. A couple of men in uniform, wearing olive-green cloaks, passed us on horseback; a mule came by laden with freshly-cut grass and yellow flowers, its grey head just emerging from between the great masses of verdure which projected either side. Some older girls passed us singing and one of them ventured a shy '*Bon soir.*' We were foreigners, but it pleased Mathews to think our nationality was no more definitely established than that.

The sun still rested upon some cypress trees outside a great gateway as we entered Frascati, but a minute later it had gone and with its departure came the reminder that it was winter and late afternoon. There would be no time to visit the villas Falconieri and Aldobrondini, which we had hoped to do. A tram, we were told, left at five o'clock and we must catch it. To my horror, Mathews proceeded to refresh himself with water from a public fountain and then to purchase from a local pastry-cook what he described as a 'Scotch bun,' a mixture of nuts, currants, pastry and plum pudding, eating it with more relish than its looks deserved.

The tram started. The evening grew quickly dark. Ahead the lights of Rome twinkled; behind us those of Frascati. The wind had dropped and in the evening sky an ebony cloud hanging over the campagna drifted away and suddenly revealed the full moon. Tired, footsore, sweaty after our exercise, our hair wild and our shirts open at the neck, we looked what we were, vagabonds in a foreign land, but happy ones. It had been a good day. We were in a mood of self-congratulation. But, contrary to all precedent, Mathews admitted to one slight regret. The convent had no bath. When we returned we must face the chill austerity of tin basins and cold water.

Markharoff opened the door to us when we got back. Like Mathews, I had soon discovered much that was lovable in the swarthy theological student. Though he looked a brigand, there was a delightful innocence about Markharoff, the innocence not of ignorance, but of sheer goodness of heart. One could not live in his company for long without knowing that. He had the gentleness of a girl, he might be a girl in some ways, there was something girlish about his spirit of mischievousness, and the sudden little giggle which he gave at times, or the trick of casting down his eyes and looking deliberately demure; but in many ways his outlook was considerably more mature than our own. Outwardly he was an unattractive seminarist, dark-cheeked, darker than ever at the end of four days before one of his periodic shaves, with a slightly Hittite nose and loose-lipped mouth. His features were Jewish. He looked more like a Frenchman of Jewish origin than a Persian. Once when we began to discuss race at supper, he smiled and murmured, '*Moi? Je suis Sémitique*' an observation we both of us felt to be true. His eyes, huge brown eyes – the eyes of a deer – were the most striking feature of his face, eyes immeasurably sad except that they did not allow themselves for a moment to admit sadness or to indulge in the luxury of self-pity. Instead, they would fill with sudden gaiety or an expression of gentle mockery and whenever they did so, whenever they lit up for an instant in sly malice or sudden, spontaneous mirth, the rest of the face was forgotten, the hooked nose, the coarse lips, the black chin, and one received the impression instead of something gay and in its nature lovely. Markharoff was very poor. We heard little about his family except that they spoke French in his home. He was now trying with the aid of Mathews to learn English, a difficult proceeding, for his day began at cockcrow and it was not easy to arrange a time for the lessons when his theological studies and his duties in the hostel left him so little time for other pursuits. Those studies began at an incredibly early hour, and yet he was our doorkeeper at night, our servitor at meals and the general intermediary between ourselves and the nuns. Entirely guileless, and yet at the same time shrewd and hard-working, life for him was a stern enough business. He was only twenty, but he looked older than his twenty years. It is possible that in the training for the priesthood intellectual discipline is so severe and the régime of life so far removed from indolence that even the soldier is not more hardened in the sense of having to shed self-indulgence and the foibles of adolescence. But whereas the soldier is often brutalised, the future priest is not. Markharoff kept his innocence; his manner was whimsical and winning and he could be the most charming of companions. While he was with us, it was as though he had fled from what was severe and harsh in life and took refuge for a few moments in the playful.

As he placed the chain across the door behind us now, he muttered

'*Venez vite*,' for we were chronic offenders where punctuality for meals was concerned.

The expedition to Nemi had tired us. Next day it was pleasant enough to idle away the morning in Rome, to visit the bookshops, to decide which of three circulating libraries I should patronise, and then, having secured a book, to accompany Mathews to the Forum, there to wander along separate paths, each pursuing his own line of reflection. Mathews announced that he would pay Elisabeth a visit after lunch, and it was understood that I should accompany him. She would probably be at home. He often did this, resting after lunch and going about half-past two, for the midday meal in the contessa's flat was a considerably later affair than ours at the hostel. He enjoyed these visits; they would exchange books, German chiefly, that being the language in which each was most interested at the moment, would talk and sometimes if it were a Sunday would go to a concert together. To-day he would bring me with him.

But at lunch I suddenly announced that I was not coming after all.

'I have plenty to do. I shall stay here and read Lanciani – I know nothing really about the antiquity of Rome.'

He seemed a little disappointed, but accepted my decision, and made no attempt to urge me. He would go alone, as was his custom. It was chance that made him halt at the door of my room just before he started and say once more, 'Aren't you coming? You might as well.' And it was chance, or a dull page in the book I was reading, that made me put it down, abandon my previous decision, and go with him.

On so frail a thread does destiny hang. Indeed, in this instance it hung on one still frailer.

For we were late, it was past the time when he usually called. We walked by the river, hurrying, and when we reached the Via Caro, meeting the porter on the threshold of the building, a disagreeable old man who disliked being asked to operate the lift, we availed ourselves of his unwilling services. He opened the lift door for us with an ill grace. Mathews had been telling me about him as we came along. He was suspected of blackmailing the landlord of the flats and his tenants. The whole building disliked him and on one occasion had actually succeeded in persuading him to go. They subscribed ten pounds as a farewell present. He had accepted the ten pounds and then, changing his mind, had decided to stay on.

One never knew in a story of this kind how much Mathews'

romantic imagination had embroidered the facts. But, looking at the red-faced old ruffian now and listening to his surly mutterings, it seemed that it might well be true.

As we went up someone passed us descending one of the long flights of marble stairs. The wire-netting screening the lift-shaft made it difficult to see. Was it some unsuspected eagerness on my part, or mere dislike of being disappointed, having come so far, or was it chance, once more, that made me say quickly to my companion,

'That was probably Elisabeth.'

Mathews stopped the lift at the next landing, jumped out, and leaned over the balustrade. Then he called down to the figure below. I had been right. It was Elisabeth. She was on her way to see her mother at the pensione and to bring her back to tea with the contessa.

'But I've plenty of time. I can come back for a bit if you like. Tea is not until five.'

She returned to us and together we mounted two more flights of stairs. The contessa's flat was at the top of the building. Elisabeth had forgotten her key and rang the bell. The Italian maid who opened the door smiled at us broadly, perhaps in surprise at the English girl's sudden reappearance, perhaps because she knew Mathews well from previous visits. The big room into which she ushered us was low-ceilinged, but well lit from two windows right in the angle of the wall which overlooked the intersection of the Via Caro and another street far below. It was a pleasant room, furnished in a rather massive style, but with plenty of evidence of the good taste of its owner. The contessa was the widow of a well-known Italian savant, who had been the close friend of the philosopher Croce, and she had known everyone in the intellectual world of that generation. Since his death, partly for economic reasons, partly for companionship, she was in the habit of taking an occasional paying guest, and if desired she would help them in their study of Italian. In this way Elisabeth had come to be here.

The round table in the centre of the room was just being cleared of the last relics of a late lunch; while the maid busied herself with the crumbs, we went over to a smaller table by the window. Mathews produced the book which he had brought to return to her and began to ask about another of which she had told him, a collection of modern folk tales or fables, little stories about animals in a vein half humorous, half satiric.

'I doubt if you will care for it. The humour is very German. I will get them if you like.'

She left the room. She had been wearing her coat and the narrow toque till this moment. When she returned she had discarded them, and in a flash I realised that what Mathews had told me was true; the scales dropped from my eyes: I experienced that sudden over-turning of all former estimate and evaluation which, when it concerns the deeper orientations of the soul, we term 'conversion.'

The Greeks showed extraordinary insight into the human mind when they allotted to the gods their different functions. Bowra tells us that Aphrodite was not entirely or primarily the goddess of love. Physical desire and passion strictly belonged to Eros. Aphrodite's sphere was wider and somewhat different. 'She is more the goddess of beauty than of desire for it. She is the goddess of flowers and of the smiling sea. Her power lies in the enchantment which she throws over visible things. But since the greatest of all enchantments is to be found in the beauty of the human form, the goddess who gives it must also be responsible, even if indirectly, for the spell which it lays over those who see it. In her own way Aphrodite stands for an absolute value, for the magic light which falls at times on life and makes it seem so desirable that men are almost driven to madness. Therefore the Greeks regarded the gift of Aphrodite as a form of madness, and thought her girdle contained those arts of enticement "which steal away even the wits of the wise." Just as Artemis stood for the remote ideal of innocence, so Aphrodite stood for the sudden unexpected moments of entrancing beauty which occur in the visible world and seduce those who see them into a state far removed from their ordinary experience.'

The most subtle definitions of modern psychology take us no further than this, even if we regard it as myth or parable. Indeed, they do not take us as far. If Bowra is right, if this indeed represents the feeling of the Greeks in the matter, their verdict on those complex emotions which assail the human heart, then the best description of my frame of mind at this instant, better than any analysis, however clever, is simply to say that Aphrodite laid her spell on me then.

'Here they are. I will read you a bit out of the one about the crocodile. I know you won't like it.'

She opened the book. Hitherto, having only seen her out of doors, I had not really seen her at all. Discarding her hat had transformed her. Bareheaded, she was a different person. Her forehead had magnificent breadth, and the fair hair brushed back either side of it added to the impression of width and gave the face a dignity and high seriousness which was not there before. Blue eyes, clear and reliant, looked out from beneath that calm brow, and, together with the proud and tender mouth, made human what might otherwise have seemed too near the perfection of the sculptor's art. This was not the girl whom we had met that afternoon at Gargiulo's, who had seemed so silent, but someone else, altogether different, with pale, burnished hair and the assurance of a goddess.

Certain people find it hard to be in the presence of beauty and disguise – or for that matter, even wish to disguise – their pleasure in it, their wonder and astonishment. It is only when the heart loses its innocence that we are afraid to reveal this delight, lest something of the beast creep in to mar it. From the moment of her re-entry into the room I know that I looked at her with such frank admiration that it must have been evident, not merely to her, but to Mathews.

Women have a sixth sense which tells them instantly when they are approved; and it may have been this or, more likely, the need to be beside Mathews if she was to show him the illustrations in the book, which made her move from where she had been sitting to a place immediately opposite me. I could look at her now to my heart's content as she stooped over the book, showing him the drawings, smiling at them or quoting some phrase in the text which amused her.

Though I knew nothing of the language the two were speaking, though the jests in the fables were generally too ponderous, too elaborate to be translated, I sat there, happy enough to be allowed to watch them and dismayed only that the book was so slim.

But the last pages had not been reached when the contessa returned from her walk and came into the room to greet Mathews and be introduced to me. Plump and dark, she was a little woman with a placid, kind face, full of contented serenity; both in appearance and dress she suggested an elderly German *Frau*, rather than what she actually was, the descendant of an ancient and distinguished Italian family. Her knowledge of English, she assured us, was slight, yet she seemed to understand it and speak it quite well. She told me that she had been reading my poems, which Elisabeth had lent her, that she liked them and they had the added merit for a foreigner that they were written simply.

'That is something to be grateful for in my case.'

She insisted that we must stay to tea. Two other visitors were coming. Elisabeth's mother and a Canadian lady, married to an

Italian and mother of a son brilliantly clever, an archæologist, who was at work at present on a book on the Roman Campagna.

'I do not think that the son is coming. But the mother herself is a most intelligent woman, and you would like her: you must certainly meet.'

We looked at each other in dismay. No invitation could have been more welcome, but unfortunately we were not in a position to accept it. Only that morning, going into the office of the American Express Company to cash a traveller's cheque, I had seen, confronting me over the counter, a face that I knew. It was that of Gordon Tibbetts who a year previously had nearly brought mine and Mathews' existence, as well as his own, to an abrupt termination. He had come up to Château d'Œx from Montreux, where he was then working for his firm, to see the final of the Swiss ski championship. My friend Kelly had introduced us and this utterly reckless young man had soon become a member of our circle, joining in all our expeditions. The evening on which the championship concluded, roaming through the village with its banners and evergreen decorations still hung from side to side above the snow-trodden roadway, he had suggested that we should hire a bobsleigh and amuse ourselves with it down the steep village street. This was a pastime in which the Swiss themselves sometimes indulged in the evenings. Bobsleighing upon a road is dangerous at any time; but if you are unacquainted with the technique of the bobsleigh it is one of the less evident forms of lunacy. Though we were all keen skiers and had 'luged' on many occasions, neither Gordon nor any of the party had ever been on a bobsleigh before. He took the wheel himself. Chivalry and a knowledge that, though he was without fear, he was also without prudence, demanded that I should place myself next to him, a buffer state in case such were needed; then came three girls who were with us and finally Mathews, who had been placed in charge of the two grappling-hooks at the back of the bob which acted as brakes. The sport appealed to us even more than we expected and presently, having descended the village street a number of times to loud cries of 'Gare!' we decided it was worth while moving on to the next hamlet about a mile down the valley and getting the benefit of a long, steep stretch of road which at one point crossed the river. Our first attempt to 'shoot' the bridge was almost successful, but not quite, and we determined to make the attempt again. It was nine o'clock and though we no longer had the street lamps to guide us, the moon, in her first quarter, together with the light reflected from the snow, showed up the road and the fields either side distinctly enough. The snow crunched and creaked under our feet as we climbed the hill dragging the bob behind us.

'No braking this time.'

'Mathews, you are not to brake unless we tell you to.'

Mathews assured us that he would not brake without orders. Alas! it is a postulate of bobsleighing that if you are rounding a corner sharply the brake on the outside of the sleigh should be raised so that the hook grips the snow and prevents the sleigh side-slipping. But none of us knew this. We descended the hill at a good speed amid murmurs of approval and swung round the corner. But at this point the sleigh suddenly became unmanageable. Tibbetts spun the wheel round madly, but the ship refused to answer to her tiller. The front runners were at right angles to the rest of the sleigh, which' had got into a complete skid. Mathews, true to his role of Casabianca, did not brake. Indeed, there was no time to brake. If we had skidded ten yards earlier we should have collided with a stone wall. Five yards further on, one side of a farm building awaited us. As it was, we hit the thick post of a more than usually solid fence between the two, and broke it clean across, where it entered the ground. The steering wheel was driven into Tibbetts' stomach with such force that its iron shaft snapped in two. I raised my leg, some-what in the fashion of a cup final footballer or a can-can dancer, and received the impact of the fence on a part where fortunately there are few bones to be broken: we disentangled ourselves from the wreckage of the bob and agreed that Providence had let us off lightly.

Providence had done so, but the owner of the bobsleigh did not. Tibbetts returned to Montreux the poorer by his sixth share of the damage. He did not complain: nor had he complained of, or even been willing to admit, any personal injury or inconvenience at the time of the accident. Twenty odd years of recklessness had taught him – or had it? – that you must be willing to pay for your impru-dence. Impecunious, without family ties, good-looking and charm-ing, I often thought that if he were to achieve a serene old age he needed a wife, and that the sooner some American girl with plenty of money took him in hand before he killed himself the better.

This was the young man who from behind the grille where foreign currency was changed had greeted me this morning. It was like meeting a long-lost friend when least expected, and Mathews and I had been glad to accept his invitation to tea at Babington's at four.

We could not break faith with Gordon, but someone made the intelligent suggestion that we could go and have tea with him and then return to the contessa's tea, which was not until five, a plan that met with everyone's approval.

It was nearly four already. We had been at the flat longer than we realised. Elisabeth must go and fetch her mother, who would be wondering what had happened to her. I must find a dentist, for I had broken a tooth at Nemi the day before and was anxious to have it stopped before we began our wanderings proper. Mathews could go direct to Babington's and tell Gordon that I was coming.

We took a hurried and temporary farewell of our hostess and set off. Elisabeth came with us. Her way lay in the same direction as ours and she had promised to show me how to get to a dentist she knew, with whom I could make an appointment. In the Piazza di Spagna we parted from Mathews. Passing under the windows of the house in which Keats died, and ignoring the adjurations of the holders of the flower-stalls nearby to pause and admire their wares, we went up the long, wide flight of steps that leads to the terrace in front of the church, and, turning back, looked down on Rome.

Rome at dusk is a city of silhouettes, almost every public building black and sharpened against the rose and crimson of sunset. There is the dome of St. Peter's, the angel with his drawn sword on the Castel S. Angelo, the huge obelisk in the Piazza del Popolo; and – quite as picturesque as obelisk and triumphal arch, indeed often more picturesque – the solitary cypresses, the spreading umbrella pines, thrown into relief against the heavens when dusk comes, each with its background of flushed sky darkening with them, as they themselves darken into the velvet blackness of night.

But at four o'clock the process of silhouette had only begun. We looked down on a city of gold and saffron, of orange and tawny, splashed by the occasional crimson of a building that for some reason scorned the almost universal colour. A man interrupted the train of our thoughts offering us postcards for sale, but we shook our heads at him, and turned aside for a moment to enter the church, a church which as it turned out had nothing to offer the idle curiosity of the sightseer, seeming rather to invite our prayers. Coming out again, we continued up the Via degli Artisti, past the huge wrought-iron ornamental gates of someone's garden till we reached the corner.

'I will leave you here. I am quite near my mother's pension now. The dentist is along there. You turn at that lamp and it is the third building that you come to. He is on the ground floor. He is always busy, so you will have to make an appointment. Even then he will keep you waiting a long time when you go. Goodbye until five o'clock.'

Until five o'clock. The words would have had little significance for me if she had spoken them to me a day or two before when we first met. But something had happened to me since I left the hostel earlier in the afternoon. I seemed the same. I have no doubt that I looked the same. The change in me was imponderable, could not be subjected to any analysis or test. It belonged to that same sphere of the irrational to which poetry, song or the effect of music upon us belong. It was simply this – that when she said, 'Until five o'clock,' my heart seemed to give a leap as though it would cry out, 'O fortunate! Even the impatience which beauty induces in us can bear a separation so brief!'

I went along the street as directed. The dentist had gone home, but a hall-porter versed in many languages, having tried me with a few, was at length able to understand my errand and to explain to me that if I liked to come back early enough in the morning I would be sure to find my man free, even though I had no appointment. I returned to Babington's. The tea-shop was full of English visitors. It was a favourite meeting-place. Mathews had not yet explained to Gordon that we must leave early, but this suited our friend well enough, for he himself had an appointment. He ordered tea and we began to speak of Switzerland, of our last meeting, of mutual friends, of the accident with the bobsleigh, and the pluck shown by the girls who were with us on that occasion. Our chatter merged with the general babble of voices, above which we would hear from time to time that predominating contralto note which indicates that the Anglo-Saxon feels completely at home. At five to five we slipped away, sprang on to a tram outside which swung us with its customary violence round the Piazza del Popolo and let us down presently only a few yards from our destination.

We were only a minute or two late. They were just seating themselves about the table as we arrived. I was introduced to Elisabeth's mother, and to the other guest, a determined-looking lady in black, wearing pince-nez, and whose slightly American intonation, together with an Italian name, might have puzzled us if it had not been explained beforehand. Signora Bagnani was a woman with a mind of her own; highly intelligent, when the conversation allowed the fact to be revealed. Her talk tended to revert continually to her son, with whom she assured us we would have much in common. She would like us to meet him. What day would suit us? Would Sunday do? The contessa poured out tea and handed round tiny sandwiches of ham placed between slices of saffron bun. Something benign and restful about this little lady set one instantly at ease. All tea-party talk tends to be fatuous, especially when the tea party is composed of strangers, but the contessa seemed to expect that we should converse easily and naturally, without banalities and without attempted brilliance; and since she herself set the example and since Rome – topic enough for many teas – was the subject, the matter went well enough. I know that I enjoyed the conversation. But if it had been the most foolish in the world I would still have enjoyed it, for like the thrice-blessed of Sappho's poem, I counted it good fortune to be there at all.

She had changed into a black dress and her hair, partly by contrast, partly because the room was now lamplit, seemed more like a gold plaque than ever. The heart when it surrenders surrenders completely. It is like those heretics who, becoming converted, cannot do enough to prove their orthodoxy. As I sat opposite her now the other people in the room seemed not entirely irrelevant, but incidental; useful and agreeable agents of destiny, but at the same time mere lay figures in a scene in which she was the living subject.

Though the talk was of Rome, of books, of music, of places that each of us had known, throughout it all there remained one remark which was never spoken and which yet seemed continually on my lips, axiomatic to all else that was said, the remark: 'You are lovely and I know it.' That was the tacit admission whenever my gaze rested upon her and perhaps even whenever it met hers. I never paused to ask myself whether such open appreciation were welcome or unwelcome, still less whether it were wise. Indeed, it is just barely possible that what I suspect of having been so evident was not so at all, for romantic love has this in common with madness that it projects its own interpretation upon every circumstance. But in any case I did not mind. The broad forehead, the sweep of that fair hair, gleaming like treasure from Mycenæ, the blue, intent, clear eyes, the warm colouring of the curved cheek lit partly by the glow from the shaded lamps, but still more by some inner glow and radiation from within – these were my excuse and my vindication. They exacted that instinctive and ungrudging homage which we render almost in spite of ourselves. Chateaubriand speaks of 'beauty, that serious trifle,' but makes his *amende* almost in the same breath, adding that 'it remains when all the rest has passed away.' I conceded now only what seemed to be her due. Admiration, though it may be one step in the direction of love, differs from it in this, that it is disinterested, does not have to stop to question its own worth, and is the free tribute of a heart that expects nothing in return.

I must have looked at her with the same wondering attention which she had seen many times already. A few years earlier she might have merely surmised my admiration in the way that youth, sometimes anxiously and hopefully, sometimes in a spirit of mocking indifference, suspects its conquests. But in her case such states of naïve uncertainty cannot have lasted long. Long before this, long before her engagement to the young German, she must have learnt to recognise infallibly in the other sex all the symptoms of awakened interest. Had my admiration been half as frank as it was, she must nevertheless have guessed it.

And, as I have said already, in the instant in which she is approved a woman becomes by so much more herself. Thenceforward everything which she does, every movement she makes, seems governed by some inner harmony or rhythm akin to the inspiration which gives sureness to poet or musician. When we are inspired we cannot make a mistake; the right word, the right phrase suggests itself inevitably. And in the same way, when she is admired, woman seems to respond to some inner law of her being which makes every gesture, every look, every phrase and intonation, lovely and inevitable, as inevitable and poignant as that moment of pause, that arrested single note in a nocturne of Chopin.

Signora Bagnani was still pressing us to visit her and to make the acquaintance of her son the archæologist. She was more certain than ever that we would be congenial spirits. Furthermore, she had discovered that she knew relations of my mother in Montreal. A connection of the Canadian Merediths was here in Rome and one of her best friends, and, if we would only name a day, she would arrange that meeting also.

Her insistence, though kindly-meant, was a little embarrassing. Our days in Rome were numbered and a tea party threatened to be a waste of valuable time. Again she suggested Sunday. Again I excused myself, this time on the ground that there was a concert that afternoon to which Mathews and I had thought of going. And almost in the same breath I turned to Elisabeth and said, 'Will you come with us?' But this, it appears, was just the thing. Signora Bagnani had been given tickets for that very concert. She would be there.

What was easier than for us to meet after the concert and return to tea with her. And, turning to Elisabeth she said, 'You will come too?'

Instantly the affair assumed an entirely different complexion. This good-natured woman whose importunity a minute before almost annoyed me now took on the aspect of a *deus ex machina* able to straighten out all difficulties. I became as eager to approve her suggestions as before I had been reluctant. Elisabeth said that she would come, the concert promised to be a good one; and there remained only the slight problem of picking out a comparative stranger in a crowded hall, a problem that would have to solve itself when the day came.

We left the house and walked back to the Borgo Santo Spirito. It was about seven o'clock in the evening. We walked through the gardens at the back of the Piazza Cavour and along the riverside. Looking over the parapet one saw not the muddy yellow Tiber of the daytime but a darker, shadowy and more mysterious stream, moving sluggishly and with huge slow eddies, between its high-walled banks. The pathway glistened from the rain which had recently fallen and in some places the water lay in such sheets that we had to step off on to the road to avoid them. Looming up like a gigantic pill-box, we saw the Castel S. Angelo crowned with its dramatic winged angel brandishing his sword. I could never see that huge mass of brick, the most instantly recognisable of all Rome's many saliencies, without thinking, not of Hadrian, who built it, but of Benvenuto Cellini, who has described for us how he escaped from it, and of the Cenci who were imprisoned there. Just beyond the San Angelo, under a bridge named after one of the Popes, the pharos on the Janiculum cast in rotation on to the water the reflection of its green and orange and crimson lights from the hillside above. By daytime the small pharos gleamed snow white on Janiculum, a landmark in its way. It had been placed there after the war as a war memorial by the Italians of South America, and at night the colours which it reflected in the tawny waters were the national colours. They appeared on the dark slowly-moving surface under the archway like globes of magic fruit put there by fairy hands or like the misleading signals of an Ariel to lure mariners to their doom.

We walked slowly. The street lights along the pathway duplicated themselves in the Tiber and behind the bend of the river beyond the bridge a few very clear stars had risen above the dome of St. Peter in an open patch of sky. I talked little and my disinclination to talk must have struck Mathews, who was usually the more silent of the two. He was sensitive enough to the moods of a companion, but even if he had been singularly without perception he must have noticed that a change had occurred·since that moment earlier in the afternoon when I had been so reluctant to accompany him. He had listened to me urging the project of the concert on Sunday afternoon with fervour or at least with importunity, and this also cannot have passed unnoticed. My *volte-face* was in a sense his vindication. So much had he boasted – 'boast' is scarcely the word for that form of innocent rhapsody – that my failure to be more impressed by his friend when we did meet had been a disappointment to him. And now, when he had ceased to expect it, his judgment was suddenly vindicated and he found it a little hard to prevent a note of triumph from creeping into his voice.

'Do you know I think that you are already a little in love with her? I almost believe I prejudiced you against her deliberately, praising her, but saying that she would not appeal to you, because I wanted to see how completely you would refute my words.'

'And now you are sorry because I do?'

'No, I won't say that.'

The suggestion that he had foreseen and staged this dramatic recantation was, of course, absurd, but he chuckled over it happily and was persuaded that it was true. It pleased him to think that he had played a Machiavellian role. Our plan of leaving for Naples on Saturday had already gone by the board, foundered in an instant, as he put it, 'on the reefs of the lady's beauty.'

The return to the convent was like the return to another world. After the warmth and comfort of the Contessa's large room, with its elaborate furnishing, the stark simplicity of the hostel struck one anew. That sensation of cold loneliness which the place had given me on the afternoon of my arrival, the dark passages, the scrubbed wooden stairs lit only by the faint 'glim' burning in a little dish of oil in front of a religious picture, the floor of the bedroom with its great stone tiles, all these impressed themselves once more on consciousness, even though I had grown to accept and almost to like them. The Byronic gloom of Mathews' cell on the ground floor would have depressed me unutterably, but I was spared that, save on those occasions when I descended to drink tea with him. That very morning he had had to leave it. He had abandoned his miniature prison with extreme regret, for though most people would have considered the prospect through a barred window of a brick wall three feet away a doubtful privilege, he had rejoiced in it, had loved to have his possessions spread round him and had appreciated the opportunity it afforded of taking an occasional pinch of snuff without being laughed at. Flinging his books and possessions anyhow into a couple of suitcases, he had carried them upstairs and taken over one of the two empty beds in my room.

Though he vacated his cell with ill grace, he bore no ill will to his supplanter. He had ceded it to an elderly German lady, who came, we were told, often to the convent. It was Markharoff who had tapped at his door that morning and told him that the new arrival was unable to sleep on the noisier side of the building, and for that reason would he change his room? It was from him too that we had learnt that she was a princess of the House of Mecklenburg, fallen on evil days because of the German revolution and suffering something remarkably like poverty. Small, fragile-looking, with white hair, she had the reputation of being very devout, but that did not prevent her being an amusing companion and excellent company at meals. We both liked her, and she and Mathews chatted away with great animation and, moreover, were willing to abandon German for my sake and to speak English.

When I first came to the convent it puzzled me that Markharoff, every time he offered Mathews a dish at meals, would add in a gentle undertone, 'Sagesse!' I imagined that it was a formula, some phrase or convention of etiquette which I had never come across before, but which was accounted good manners here. Presently, however, it transpired that it was a nickname, the nickname which he and the two German girls, who sang folk-songs in the evenings, had given Alister before I arrived in the hostel. Perhaps they considered it suited to his tall, dreamy aloofness and the sudden, kindly beam of the eyes above his rather schoolboyish smile.

'*Encore un peu de vin* – Sagesse?'

When I had grown to know and like Markharoff, I pretended to be a little jealous that my friend should have a nickname and I none and urged him to give me one too. After an abortive attempt at calling me 'Justice' in French, which failed completely, Markharoff fell back on 'Princesse,' pronounced as the French pronounce it, 'prah-n-cess.' There was no reason for this except that I had been accustomed at meals to sit opposite the little old lady with white hair, and when she left there was nothing to prevent my inheriting her title. 'Princesse' accordingly I became.

But his real reason was probably a Lewis Carroll childish delight in the purely absurd and because the two words rhymed, or rather possessed assonance.

'*Des pommes de terre* – Sagesse?'

And then, passing a dish to me with the same gentle deprecatory air,

'*Un peu de viande* – Princesse?'

Sagesse and Princesse we remained to the day of our departure. He used the names always with great gravity, casting down his eyes demurely in a spirit of playful mockery. Mock seriousness was a favourite trick with him, and mild buffoonery, though in actual fact his character was one of considerable earnestness.

Our days in Rome were approaching a pattern. In the mornings we explored, or, as the saying is, pottered about; in the afternoons a succession of tea-parties claimed us. I had brought with me from Alan Coltart, an artist friend in Château d'Œx, an introduction to a woman artist living in the British School at Rome. She had invited us to take tea with her at five, but subsequent to our acceptance of this invitation Elisabeth's mother had suggested that we should join her and the contessa and Elisabeth at the Embassy Tea-rooms earlier in the afternoon, a dual engagement which, like that of the previous day, seemed quite feasible. That morning I had gone again to the dentist and had wandered later into the Pincian Gardens nearby. I took with me a book which Elisabeth had recommended and which I had got without difficulty from the English Library. It was the life of Chopin by Guy de Pourtalès, one of those biographies which, like Maurois' famous book on Shelley, is more concerned with the emotions than with the acts and achievements of their subject. I read seated on the flat top of the terrace balustrade, my back against the wall and my knees drawn up, for there did not seem to be any chairs in the gardens, at least none nearby. Immediately below me, a small enclosed garden laid out after the Dutch fashion clung to the side of the hill, while below that again lay Rome. Chopin's youth, its extreme sensibility, his gentleness, his extravagant romanticism, the exquisite anguish which love was able to inflict upon him, as well as the old-fashioned and mannered politeness of his time, all reminded me of Mathews, and I wondered whether when Elisabeth recommended me the book this had been in her mind. Mathews himself came into the Pincian Gardens later in the morning while I was still there, saw me from a distance and with his instinct of the solitary avoided me. 'I did not like the site you had chosen,' he explained to me at lunch. 'Besides, you were reading.' He had been to buy the tickets for the concert on Sunday, had come back through the gardens and, like me, finding the day a mild one, had taken up a position above a small oval lake with a fountain playing in the middle of it and had read Lanciani on the Roman Campagna. He was delighted with his morning, describing to me the small girl of three who with her nurse occupied one of the seats nearby, the child continually asking the nurse for words to copy and then writing each of them laboriously and with great skill into her book. 'Before I left there must have been half an exercise book full of *Mon-tag-na's* and *Ti amo's*. You have never seen such industry. Nothing could distract her from the path of knowledge. She is due some day for literary fame.' Later two Italian students had come by and he had watched them running races round the pond while their two girl-friends held their books for them. They had been as formal as Germans about heel-clicking and hand-shaking when it came to saying goodbye, and all this little drama had interested him, dividing his attention with his book. Life was a pageant and a pageant which it was amusing to watch. All his zest for it showed itself on these occasions and when he came to describe them afterwards.

'Do you mean to say you have taken only a morning to read the Chopin?'

'I have still a few pages to finish. It is quite a short book. I will read them now after lunch, and then I can take the book back to the Library when we go this afternoon. I am going to get Cotterill's *Greece*. That will take longer.'

I was at the Library in plenty of time. From there it was only a short distance to the Trinità de' Monti and the Embassy Tea-rooms. The contessa had brought an Italian friend with her and it was as though yesterday's tea party had been re-staged with a single change in the caste. It seemed only a few minutes before it was time to rise and murmur our apologies, explaining that our engagement at the British School must be kept.

'Sunday, then,' Mathews said. 'The concert is at four. I got the tickets for it this morning. We will call for you in plenty of time. We may see you in the morning, earlier, if you decide to come to the Terme Museum.'

Elisabeth nodded her head in assent.

'And if we are very lonely after lunch to-morrow we may chance our hand and come and see you. But you are not to wait in for us.'

The postscript was mine. It had been made on the spur of the moment, and since my friend was accustomed to pay these post-prandial visits it did not seem an overbold suggestion.

But Mathews was indignant. As we went down the steps to catch our tram to the British School he lectured me.

'You are absolutely in love with her. The last thing you have any right to be. Not content with seeing her the day after to-morrow at the concert, you urge her to come with us to the Terme Museum that morning. And then, since even that seems too far off, you say that if we are lonely we will go and see her to-morrow. If we are lonely! Really, Monk, you make me smile. A week ago you wanted nothing so much as your own company. Now you are lonely—lonely simply because you have made friends.'

We climbed on to a tram and he continued his tirade, which, though half in jest, had just a tinge of real irritation in it as well.

'You sit next her. You tell her how much more lovely she looks without a hat. You praise her to her face in the same way that you might praise a poem. And you announce that if you are lonely you must go and see her.'

'I said that if *we* were lonely.'

'Four days ago you grumbled that you knew Rome already and did not wish to waste your time here. Now you discover that you hardly know Rome at all. It will take you weeks to touch even the fringe of its antiquities.'

He burst out laughing. He was indignant. But his indignation was less real than his amusement. Even if it had been more real, I could have afforded to ignore it. For in reply to the suggestion I had thrown out so casually, Elisabeth had said, 'Yes, I shall wait in for you until half-past three. If you have not come by then, I shall know that you are not coming.' So easily, so casually almost, do things arrange themselves if we only allow them to do so.

In a large, high-ceilinged studio we took our second tea. Vast white-washed walls, an open fire-place, in which a wood fire burned, and a divan, all suggested the surroundings of the artist, but there were no pictures on the wall to need discreet appraisement and, instead, our hostess, a cheerful, alert woman of thirty-five with a pleasant, frank manner, occupied us with the description of the island from which she had just returned, an island unknown to tourists, reached from some small obscure port near Pisa, so remote and so lovely that it was with difficulty that she had forced herself to return to Rome.

'You must go there one day yourselves – an island truly unspoilt.'

We vowed that we would. We are all delighted when we discover a place of this sort, so delighted that we announce the find to every friend; and in this way – for each man kills the thing he loves – every solitude is made populous. We agreed now that the worst that could befall a beautiful site was to be visited by any lovers of beauty. They will blurt out their secret as surely as the barber blabbed the secret of Midas' ears to the rushes, and if enough people begin to talk, someone will whisper presently that there is money to be made. One island, Guernsey, has preserved its coastal scenery by passing a law forbidding anyone to build within a mile of its bays; and perhaps others in time will follow this example, before the enterprising have turned their lascivious glances upon them, and allowed their thoughts to stray in the direction of rape.

Conversation passed to other things. Presently our hostess began to talk about my poems, saying, in her direct fashion, 'You write as you speak,' a remark which made Mathews burst out laughing and exclaim, 'Yes, but not quite so prolifically.'

'His Muse is a strong, silent woman. She opens her mouth all too seldom. Whereas he – well, you've heard him for yourself!'

'Irishmen find it easy to talk.'

'But not so easy to write a poem?'

'No. You remember what Yeats says

'A line will take us hours maybe;
Yet if it does not seem a moment's thought
Our stitching and unstitching has been naught.'

We had enjoyed our visit, but, as was always happening, we were late reaching the convent for supper. Once again we were reduced to running up the broad flight of steps under the archway. Once again the bell was rung, we heard a fumbling of chains and the door was partly opened to reveal Markharoff. As soon as he saw who we were, he opened it wider, saying admonishingly, 'Venez vite.' Chronic offenders where punctuality was concerned, this was not the first occasion we had arrived on the steps ten minutes after the time supper was supposed to begin.

At supper the Princess entertained us with her account of something she had witnessed that morning on her walk. She had been in the street above Trajan's Forum. Suddenly she had been astonished to see men with sacks and great leather gauntlets leaping down into the Forum. They had gone down to collect the cats. The Forum, like other of Rome's oldest parts, fills with all the stray cats of the city. They go there and remain there like the Greek prisoners of war in the latomia at Syracuse; and just as the proud Sicilian ladies would walk outside the gates of the city in the evening and, leaning on the arms of their slaves and with perfume held to their nostrils, gaze down into the quarries, so now the citizens of Rome, as they pass along the street above, pause for a moment and look down on the cats. There are hundreds of them of every size, shape and colour. How they first descended is a mystery, but having once arrived they remain, imprisoned by the steep sides of the sunk Forum. On fine days they can be seen sunning themselves on the ruins of the monuments. They occupy the whole place as if it were their own. But though the sun reaches the spot and warms the stones there is a shortage of food. They are dependent upon whatever charity Olympus chooses to extend from the street above. And Olympus is forgetful. The thing has become a scandal for the strongest cats turn cannibal and eat the others. The Princess assured us that she had seen the men grabbing the cats and putting them into the sacks. They had been careful, however, to sort out the fat from the lean, and when we enquired why this was so, it was explained to us that the former would be eaten presently by the poorer people of Rome.

Mathews was incredulous. People did not eat cats. The idea was loathly. It was for their pelts and not their plumpness that the finer specimens had been selected. The contessa's maid, however, when we retailed the story next afternoon at the flat, endorsed it. It was correct. She herself had eaten cat. True, she did not know that she was doing so, but was under the impression that she was partaking of some particularly tender rabbit.

After lunch Mathews had not even bothered to enquire if I was lonely. It was assumed that we were going. The contessa was out when we arrived, and Elisabeth, who looked tired, seemed glad that we had come. We had only been in the room a few minutes when Naples was mentioned, and she said:

'When are you going?'

'We don't know. We never do. We have no plans. Probably early next week. It is always a business uprooting. *Partir c'est mourir un peu!*'

There had flashed into my mind the words which my friend Kelly had used when he said goodbye to me a few weeks before in Château d'Œx.

She repeated the words after me in a low voice, as though they were already familiar to her.

'Partir c'est mourir un peu.'

'Do you know the phrase? I had never heard it till the other day. Apparently it is quite well known.'

'It is from a poem, "Rondel de l'Adieu," by a man called Edmond Haraucourt. I think he's still alive. I can show you the whole poem if you like. I have it in my commonplace book.'

She left the room and returned a minute later with a notebook covered in black American cloth into which she was in the habit of copying whatever pleased her. She read us the poem aloud, but it was disappointing:

> *'Partir c'est mourir un peu*
> *C'est mourir à ce qu'on aime,*
> *On laisse un peu de soi-même*
> *En toute heure et dans tout lieu. . . .'*

But these and the lines which followed them added nothing to that one phrase, which had already said all; a phrase as poignant almost as the Latin *Lachrimæ rerum*.

'The truth is no poem was needed. We were better off without it. Those five words are a poem in themselves.'

'I rather agree.'

'How different it sounds in English. "To go away is to die a little." It is untranslatable. No other language could ever say it so well.'

'Read us some more from your book.'

She did so; but many of the extracts were in German and, like the fables on a former occasion, they set us bickering. They were indignant that I was not more appreciative and that I clamoured for clearer exposition.

'But the point? The point?'

'It is impossible. You have just said yourself that French is often untranslatable. Then why not German?'

'Quite so. French is untranslatable because it is so keen, so incisive, so pungent, so brief. But all this is ponderous, elephantine, Jumbo balanced with enormous effort on one foot on a tub.'

I was on my hobby-horse again.

'That is only because you do not know the language. You have no idea how joyous and childlike the Germans are.'

'Alister tells me the same, but he can never produce documentary proof.'

We wrangled, but without taking it seriously. The two linguists had me at a disadvantage. If the extract was in French, she read so fast that I could not follow. Alister's eyes twinkled roguishly, for he knew that this was so, but I was content enough to be watching that fair head stooped over the book, and to be listening to her voice, as she turned the pages impatiently searching for something new.

'Monk has a notebook in which he jots things down too. But it is a good deal smaller than yours. He carries it around in his pocket.'

They made me produce it. It was a tiny note-book, bought in Denmark a few months before, with a picture of a black poodle sitting on its haunches in the middle of the yellow cover.

'Read us some of your discoveries.'

Her face lit up when the first thing which it disgorged was Goethe's fine phrase: 'Nothing is more terrible than ignorance with spurs on.'

But succeeding items convinced her that my note-book held a little too much of the moralist.

'All yours have a purpose. In every one there is something improving, the motive to teach. Mine have no motive; they are there simply because they please me.'

I might have pleaded that my note-book was too small for anything except brevities and that therefore it lent itself to the aphorism, but the charge in the main seemed true.

'I suppose you are right. But is this "improving," when Amiel says, "Look twice if what you want is a just conception. Look once if what you want is a sense of beauty"?'

She smiled, and said, 'I subscribe to that.'

Turning over the pages, I came to a dictum of Confucius: 'I have not seen one who loves virtue as he loves beauty.'

She smiled again and said, 'Yes, I subscribe to that too.'

Mathews, who was beginning to tire a little of the recital, enquired about a head in marble which a peasant sculptor had been doing of her, when she was in Munich. Telling us that it was finished and that she had a photograph of it, she went to fetch it.

'It is at my uncle's house in London, and will be exhibited later.'

But either the photograph failed to do justice to the marble or the head itself was a failure, we were both agreed on that; and when she showed us a photograph of another version in clay which was never finished, we infinitely preferred it.

It was after four o'clock and time we were going. I had an engagement to meet an American professor and his son, fellow pensionnaires at the Annalina in Florence, who had since come to Rome; Elisabeth

169

must do some Christmas shopping; Alister was returning to the convent. We descended the many flights of stairs with him and then took the tram together to the Piazza di Spagna. There we parted. When I returned to the convent after seeing my friends, I found Mathews lying on his bed reading. He looked at me critically for a moment and then said:

'Well, and are you as much enslaved as ever?'

I remained silent. I realised that behind his raillery was a certain anxiety, almost a certain self-reproach as though events were taking a turn which he had not quite anticipated. That I was a little enslaved we were both agreed. The previous day, coming down the steps from the Trinità de' Monti at five o'clock, with an evening sky all pinks and greens outlining the buildings of the city, I had cried, 'She is magnificent – *elle est magnifique.*' And Mathews knew that it was not of the city, but of the girl from whom we had just parted that I spoke.

If beauty is the solvent which transmutes life, discovering in it that minor significance for which we have all the time been looking; still more if it frees speech for us, there is some excuse for awaiting its advent breathlessly, and going out eagerly to meet it. It is too rare an event in our lives ever to become a commonplace. It is the lifting of the veil, the troubling of the waters.

In my journal at this time I pleaded on behalf of all that which stabs consciousness into acute awareness. It seemed to me that to be always careful, never to allow personality to take any risk, was the part of the coward. To feel nothing, lest, presently, one should feel pain. And I compared the philosophic spirit, the acquired calm of an Epictetus or an Aurelius, with the passion of Lear crying out over the corpse of Cordelia. In the one case serene acceptation of the worst; the same spirit – or was it pride? – which made Goethe remark, when he heard of the death of his only son, a drunkard and a failure, 'I am aware that I engendered a mortal son': in the other, despair. And yet what was it that made one at times prefer the passionate intensity of the crazy old king? I ask myself the same question now, and I give an answer which I might not have been able to give then. We prefer Lear because he is nearer our common humanity and because his despair springs from those deep sources of human impulse which are still instinctive. He wakes echoes in our own hearts. He is a puppet in a pageant in which we ourselves are also puppets. Whereas to appreciate Aurelius we must already be partly Aurelius ourselves. We must have risen a step in the scale.

In the great moments of life, I wrote, the intensity of passion, as with Lear, relieves us from the need of being logical. 'It is the same with love.' And perhaps all that had gone before was but the excuse for this remark. Beauty, love, vision – the three were interrelated, so that to predicate one was to predicate the other two as well. And since beauty and vision were without reproach, ends in themselves even for the philosophically-minded, perhaps there was excuse also for love. Had I read then and did I remember that Plotinus, the purest-minded of all the mystics, makes three men potential candidates for the higher vision – the Metaphysician, the Musician, the Lover? Though he is placed lowest in the scale, the lover is included in this high company, for he holds for a moment within his grasp the insight which may raise him to the contemplation of pure being. I had learnt long before this that beauty can hurt as well as delight us. The more ardent our temperament, the more susceptible to impressions, the sooner do we discover that joy can stab almost as keenly as anguish and that extreme sensibility carries with it certain penalties of its own.

> He who loves beauty wisely
> Loves her least touch;
> She can scourge him with arrows
> Who loves too much;
> Who turns aside, who lingers,
> Who leaves the throng,
> She can scourge him with scorpions
> Who loves too long.

But there seemed no danger of my loving too long in the present instance or even, I would probably have said, of my loving at all. I admired. I admired extravagantly, but that was a different matter. Why should one not admire? In the phrase which I was always hearing as a child I might be playing with fire, but I played with it, or so I told myself, with safety. I had every reason to think that present circumstances held no danger for either of us. Elisabeth's heart was still in Munich. Mathews had told me that, and he believed that there was still a possibility of a reconciliation. She had been deeply in love with her young German. It was only his family who at long last, after months of effort, had succeeded in breaking their engagement.

And there was a personal reason of even greater force. Two years before, in the narrow Corso Umberto of Taormina in Sicily, I had met the girl who, some deep prompting instantly convinced me, would one day be my wife. She was travelling with her parents and her brothers. As she turned from the shop windows into which she had been looking to be introduced to me, I saw dark hair, high cheek-bones, hazel, very honest eyes, with great breadth between them, and a curved, sensitively-shaped mouth; and heard a voice, musical and with great clearness and sincerity of intonation – such a voice as might have won Lear's praise of Cordelia's. Intuition, obscure and inexplicable, something more than susceptibility on this occasion, made me feel that the encounter held far greater significance for me than any to which the actual moment entitled it. And in the week that followed, meeting often in that steep little hillside town, Ætna's triangle of pure snow towering far above the blue waters of the strait, and the promontory of Naxos with its crowded orange groves, floating upon the sea's surface far below like a ship at anchor, I had had six days in which to have this first instinct of the heart confirmed. We had listened together in the tiny, crowded garden of von Gloeden, an old German baron in exile, to the thin, eager sound of reed pipes played by some Sicilian boy from the hills, and I had seen my companion's eyes fill with sudden emotion at that music – gay, impersonal, spontaneous, spilt on the air like bird-song, linked to the earth as the trees and the grasses are, and bubbling up as carefree, as though the world had had no single trouble or distress to disquiet it since the shepherds of Theocritus had piped, two thousand years before, perhaps in that very spot.

Such music, such moments shared, such a gesture of immortal happiness had made what was surmise before seem certainty, and such certainty the two years which followed had only strengthened. Though I might not be engaged in the official sense, I regarded myself as an engaged man. This was known to Mathews; it was known also to Elisabeth, for he had told her. This was the loyalty at which my friend had hinted, a loyalty openly confessed and already conditionally ratified, awaiting only my return from my travels to announce it to the world.

It will be asked how, when this was so, I could allow myself even that mild extravagance of homage elsewhere, which at once amused and distressed Mathews? But the answer has already been given. Beauty was its own justification, its own excuse for wonder and awe. To those for whom emotion and principle never come into conflict, either because their principles are too strong or their emotions too well guarded, it will seem that I deliberately abandoned myself to a passing fancy while flattering myself that I still remained loyal to a fixed one. But I told myself there was no question of that fundamental loyalty being affected. I remembered too that I had never made any secret to anyone of my susceptibility.

I may have wondered sometimes whether it was quite fair to admire anyone so openly, when my admiration could lead to nothing. But here again my mind was ready with its excuse. I told myself in the first place that there was no risk of my admiration being misunderstood. I had not to deal with a child, someone whose feelings might be easily and deeply wounded. In that case I might have much to reproach myself with. But this girl was twenty-two. According to Mathews, she was used to admiration, she had had nothing else for years. And as though this explanation was not quite enough in itself, I added another and much more subtle reason. I reminded myself that she was unhappy, that the broken engagement to one who was more accustomed to break hearts than to have her own broken had made a deep impression on her. It was probably all to the good that she should find herself a subject of admiration once more, even though she knew – as undoubtedly she did – that the incense burned before her shrine was quite ephemeral. Indeed, it was plain that her own mother and the Contessa encouraged our visits, pleased that she had found two cavaliers to take her about and to break the monotony of her days.

Mathews might ask whether I was as much enslaved as ever, but I brushed the question aside as facetious and gave no answer. If my position was ambiguous, that was my own affair.

Sunday dawned bright and clear; the day seemed to invite one out of doors. I left the convent early, resolved to visit the Forum and the museum on the Capitol before going on to the Terme. Mathews, urged to come with me, refused. 'No. I have a headache. I will stay here and read, and join you both later. It is quite a small museum, so that it will be easy to find you. *Au revoir*. Do not think too much of the fair one, but give your whole attention to the wonders of antiquity and to beauty in marble. It is safer.' He added that he had thought her 'very *lebhaft* yesterday,' but since I did not know what *lebhaft* was, his remark was wasted on me. I left him, with vague agreement as to the hour when we should meet. It was a lovely morning, like one of those that in late January sometimes prophesy spring. Something in the freshness of the morning infected my own spirit. I trod the cobble-stones of the Borgo Santo Spirito with elation – that very elation which I sometimes grudged Mathews

– the elation of being alone, of looking at every passer-by as though he were a figure in a picture, or a character in a romance, existing only for my distraction and amusement; the elation of seeing the pageant of life unroll and feeling oneself the privileged spectator. Through the half-opened door of some poor *trattoria* I would see the stout figure of a woman spreading a white table-cloth and placing the decanter of wine on it, and her slow, deliberate movements had the same effect on me as a Dutch interior in a picture-gallery. While I waited by the river for the tram to take me to the centre of the town, a child ran gaily past and it seemed to me that for a minute I shared its joy; and when, at last, the tardy tram pulled up beside me and I had jumped on board, I looked at the sleepy conductor when he took my fare with a patronising benevolence, as though he had been entrusted with a walking-on part in a play in which I myself played the lead.

Though admission was free on Sunday, the Forum was deserted; it was too early for many visitors. I stood on the site of the palace of the Cæsars, overlooking the immense medley of excavated ruins below, the three pillars and the fragment of pediment of the temple of Castor and Pollux standing out from the surrounding confusion like three lines of Sappho, articulate over the centuries. It was pleasant to look down on the almost empty space below, and to evoke the Rome I had known, or rather imagined, as a child, ever since the day when my father had first put into my hands a tiny, blue-bound history of the Republic. There is a tide in the imaginative life of the child, as in the affairs of men, which it is dangerous to miss, and this tide my father judged exactly. The eagle drops the hare in mid-air so that its young may swoop for it, and my father may have shared the enthusiasms of his own youth with me in order to make them mine. Did he in the seclusion of his study sometimes dip secretly into that little blue volume, so that at-breakfast next day Brutus or Cato might seem almost a family friend? Or had it been bred into him for life as a schoolboy? If he had not talked about Cataline over his bacon and eggs almost in the same way that another parent might have referred to some contemporary sensation, if he had not praised Gracchus or condemned Sulla quite as vigorously as he approved Carson or abused Lloyd George, the Romans would have remained strangers to me. And now, as I descended into the Forum and moved from one ruin to another, reconstructing as much of its past significance as my knowledge of archæology allowed, I realised that any interest it possessed for me I owed to him.

I had time to wander for more than an hour before going up the long flight of very wide and shallow steps to the Capitoline Museum. It was not yet eleven o'clock. I could hear the church bells of Rome ringing, but in the museum itself they were stilled, and the only sound was that of my own or another's footsteps on the tiled floor. A museum at any time, but most of all on a Sunday morning, has a little of the atmosphere of a temple, a temple of the humanities where man pays homage to the achievements of the transcendent element in himself. I stopped only long enough to visit some of the antique heads which I loved so well and to pause for a minute before 'The Dying Gaul.'

A little before midday I made my way to the Terme. It was a small museum. There were few people there and it was easy to find Mathews, who had arrived five minutes before.

'Is Elisabeth here?'

'If she is, she will be in one of the rooms where the sculptures are.'

We found her upstairs, the sole occupant of the gallery. She greeted us casually, without effusion, as though preoccupied with other things. She was looking at the Venus Anadyomene of Cyrene, which, she and Mathews maintained, reminded them strongly of her younger sister, still at school in Switzerland. She was another beauty, according to Mathews, and an object of keenest affection to Elisabeth who insisted that she possessed all the graces and gifts which she herself lacked, and an equilibrium which she envied. Nothing was too great praise for this sister, and one had only to mention her by name for Elisabeth's whole expression to soften.

We passed from one room to another, silent for the most part, inclined to separate rather than to keep together, only calling to our companions when we found something which we felt needed comment.

'Look at this Roman girl. She must be about fifteen. Look at the way her hair is wisped forward in curls in front of her ears. It's the latest fashion now. Solomon was right. There is nothing new under the sun.'

Only when we had seen everything which interested us did conversation stray into other channels. Mathews amused Elisabeth now by telling her how the chaos in our room was beginning to cause distress to the good nuns.

'Monk is the untidiest devil on earth. I am nearly as bad. The whole room is littered with our belongings – books, clothes, writing materials, everything. Schwester Edouarda was apparently so worried

175

by all the mess and the muddle that she fished in my suitcase this morning till she rooted out a copy of *The Times*. This she opened out and laid in sheets over our heaps of socks, shoes, letters and books on the bed. I don't know whether it is meant as a gentle reproof or because she can't cope with the chaos and feels that all she can do is to conceal it. Anyhow, everything is now veiled in the decent obscurity of neatly-spread newspaper.'

'The room is large enough, but there is so little actual furniture. We have to treat the spare bed as though it were a sort of extra table or even a hanging wardrobe.'

'I can't understand your staying in a convent at all. If you were Roman Catholics, now, it would be different.'

'It is so that Alister may speak his beloved German. You forget that the nuns are German.'

She began to tell us about a friend of hers in France called Antoinette, who had been given a year by her parents in which to get married.

'If she is not married by the spring of next year they say she must enter a convent. Isn't it monstrous? The poor girl has no wish to enter a convent, but she is getting on, and if she does not find a husband she must. Her family are adamant.'

'Is that how things are done? Surely they can't force her if she has no vocation?'

'She will be made to discover one. In France there is no disgrace equal to that of being an old maid. Well, I am glad I am English. At least I won't have to enter a convent.'

Mathews courteously assured her that, were she French a hundred times over, she would be spared such a step. They embarked on a fantastic story, which each had heard from a different source, of a beautiful novice being bricked up into the wall of a church in Spain for some offence against discipline, while a casual visitor remained the passive spectator of this iniquity. Elisabeth believed it because she had a horror of religious orders. Alister would have liked to believe it, not because he was in the least anti-clerical, but because such incidents added a little colour to life. Of the three, I alone was frankly sceptical.

We descended the steps of the museum still arguing the point.

'The nuns are arranging for Monk to attend a public audience of the Pope. They did the same for me soon after I got here. They know that we are heretics, but I suppose for that very reason we must seem all the more in need of grace.'

176

At no time since our arrival in the convent had the nuns asked us directly if we were Protestants, but they must have known from the first that we were. They had been a little reluctant to accept Alister as a guest when he first came to them, but he had persuaded them, partly by his very importunity, partly by the reference he was able to give from his German friend. In taking us they displayed a generous tolerance. The other guests, even if they were not making an actual pilgrimage, were closely identified with religion; they were Catholics of a devout type like the Princess, who used it as her *pied-à-terre* in Rome. But we on the contrary had no specific religious pretensions. We might speak of ourselves as 'pilgrims,' and say that we were going presently to Jerusalem, but it was not suggested for a moment that ours was a pilgrimage in the full meaning of the word. We were travellers of the most ordinary and least exalted kind, and our only credentials were the frankness and enthusiasm of youth. The nuns never made any attempt to influence our religion, unless by this offer to obtain a card of admission for a Papal audience, an opportunity which Mathews had embraced gladly, since it was just such a ceremony as appealed to him. When I arrived he had informed me that they would make the same arrangement for me.

Only on reconsidering all the circumstances do I begin to suspect my friend of a little harmless guile in this matter. He had his own motives for fostering our reputation as pilgrims, and in fairness to him I must add that, when we arrived in the Holy Land, he did not forget his friends of the Borgo Santo Spirito, sending them rosaries which had been laid on the stones of the Holy Sepulchre, and even a sugared Easter egg with a sacred text inscribed thereon. He was not so ingenuous that he did not realise that a visit to the Vatican was one way of pleasing the nuns. It is possible, even, that by coming to the hostel at all I stood committed to this step, and that, like Richelieu and his handling of Louis XIV, he was able to convince me that I was taking voluntarily a course to which he had really pledged me before ever I arrived.

But it was curious that he who had fostered the affair from the beginning, as soon as it was all arranged, should begin to twit me for having accepted. It was so now as we came down the steps of the museum.

'Monk is only going to the Vatican because he has the highest respect for the present Pope as an Alpine climber. Someone has told him that before becoming a prisoner in Rome he ascended many peaks and even slept a night alone on Monte Rosa, higher than any man ever slept in Europe before. When he kneels to kiss the ring it will be in homage to the spirit of gallant and intrepid human courage, not in acceptance of any claims to infallibility. But now Monk is assailed by tremors of conscience, strange doubts have come over him that the man he is going to see isn't the right one, the one that was a climber in his youth. That would be a serious matter. If the Pope has never been near Monte Rosa, if he has never been on a mountain at all——'

I did not grudge Mathews his little joke. It had a slender foundation in fact. It was indeed Achilles Ratti whom I was going to see, but no one at the Suore dell' Addollorata seemed aware of his mountaineering exploits as a young priest, and I had begun to wonder whether what I had heard was true. But it surprised me that Elisabeth should disapprove the visit as strongly as she did. It was as though I had suddenly announced that I was about to offer sacrifice to Baal, or to bow the knee in the house of Rimmon.

'There, you see for yourself how Elisabeth has taken it. None of your Protestant friends will ever speak to you again. You say that you will acquire kudos in the eyes of various acquaintances in Connemara, like the blind man at Roundstone, who was so delighted when he heard that you had seen "the burning mountain"; but that is not the point, Monk, that is not the point.'

It was not the point. The real point, indeed the only point, was Mathews' whimsical smile of huge delight as he rallied me for doing what he had so tactfully plotted that I should do.

Elisabeth parted from us in the square. We returned to the convent for lunch. As we went I voiced my surprise at the line she had taken over the projected audience.

'I did not expect her to be interested in the news: but I had not expected her to be shocked. I might have been telling one of the most Low Church of my friends that I was on the point of conversion to Rome.'

Mathews, however, had an explanation.

'She has had a wholly secular upbringing and so she hasn't much sympathy with any religion. She has had to fend for herself, with a little help from her school, a little from the Ethical Church in London, a little from the occasional preachers she has heard.'

'I suppose she regards the Roman Church as being a repository of all the superstitions.'

'Yes, probably.'

'Kipling has said that individuals look at each other across seas of misunderstanding; still more do institutions. But Roman Catholicism is not all pomp and ceremony, not all ritual and gaudy decoration. Could anything be simpler and more austere than our surroundings here? My few days with the Suore dell' Adollorata have convinced me that there is less tinsel and more holiness in Catholicism than I expected. Not even my Protestant blood can find fault with the one tiny picture which hangs in our room or with the plain crucifix halfway down the stairs. It is all as stark and simple as a country church in Ireland.'

At half-past three we were back at the Via Lucrezio Caro calling for Elisabeth to take her to the concert. It was at the Augusteo and not far away. We could walk there, she said. Crossing the river, we soon became confused by the number of small streets on the far side and were just beginning to fear that we would be late after all when Mathews caught sight of a crowd flocking towards a point a little distance ahead and cried out that we were saved. Our seats were in the balcony, and this occasioned further delay, for, searching for the right door by which to reach them, we had to retrace our steps a couple of times. But once in them and gazing down into the auditorium below, almost the first person we sighted was Signora Bagnani and beside her a rather good-looking young man with a heavy, dark moustache who was doubtless her son.

'Good! We know where they are. Now all we have to do is to get to them when the concert is over. That doesn't look as though it would be very easy.'

The concert hall was crowded. Our seats were at the extreme edge of the curved balcony looking down on the orchestra. Elisabeth sat between us, so that unless we turned to compare impressions I had no excuse to look at her. She had removed her hat and the music would have been a matter of complete indifference to me had we been differently placed. As it was, it seemed to drag endlessly on and the notes on the programme only served to confuse me. Less in the mood perhaps for music than my companions, I found the Schumann Symphony tedious and very long. Zaudouai was conducting, and a number of his own works figured in the programme; and, once embarked on his own compositions, he gave encore after encore. Finally, the concert ended in a terrific din, with Berlioz's *Romeo and Juliet*, the basses blaring forth as though it were the trump of doom, delighting the audience and rousing them to an even greater pitch of enthusiasm than they had reached already.

179

It was long after six o'clock. The crowd moved slowly out. We signalled to our hostess to wait for us by one of the side doors, while we made our way down to her. Outside in the street there were no taxis to be had and we had to walk to the Piazza da Spagna before finding one. The driver was told to drive quickly. Bagnani himself had gone on to apologise to their other guest for our being so late. Signora Bagnani was too cultivated to inveigh against the prolixity of composers or the vanity of conductors, but plainly she was distressed at the turn things had taken. To save time, we were taken up quickly by a lift which served the adjoining flat, and conducted through some empty rooms by a maid who led the way holding a candle, till we found ourselves in the Bagnani's own beautiful and luxuriously furnished apartment.

Elderly, tall and courteous, with a little white moustache and a slight stoop, the Canadian connection whom I had been asked to meet had remained unperturbed by our failure to appear. It was strange to find myself discussing a number of people whose names I had often heard on the lips of my mother and stepsisters but whom I had never met. Two of my stepsisters had once spent a winter in Canada and had returned to delight us as children with the gift of tiny live terrapins and the sight of real Red Indian moccasins and snow-shoes. Tea had been brought as soon as we arrived, belated but welcome. A firework show was being given somewhere in the city. We heard the noise of rockets and went to the window to watch, drawing back the curtains and looking out on great showers of variously-coloured stars falling as though from a fountain over some buildings in the distance.

'You say that you are going to Greece. I have one piece of advice to give you. In the villages, when you go to bed, tie the sleeves of your pyjamas tightly at the wrists with string. And have a silk scarf which you can wind around your neck. It is your only chance of protection. Even then your hands will get bitten.'

We thanked Bagnani for his solicitude on our behalf. He had been in Greece on several occasions studying and making excavations. Fortunately, the country was to give the lie to its reputation in this respect, perhaps because the warm weather had not yet come when we were there. Mr. Allen, who had waited so long for us, took his leave almost immediately and Bagnani led me into his study to show me his very fine library of Greek and Roman literature, books on the ancients, and archæological works. Proofs were lying on the huge carved mahogany desk in the centre of the room, for he was at work on an English translation of some Italian book, as well as his own on the Roman Campagna. I looked enviously at these shelves filled with a wealth of literary and technical interest. It was the library of a scholar in which one could have browsed contentedly for weeks.

'I see you have the Greek anthology. I want to know more about the metres and rhythms its poets employed. My own Greek is not good enough. It never got further than the *Alcestis* at school and a little of the Greek Testament. Read me one of Meleager's epigrams. It will give me some idea. Surely the Greek language was too dental and labial to be as musical as for example modern Italian, where the five vowels seem like a scale on which the language achieves almost every conceivable musical cadence?'

'I will read it to you, but pronouncing it as one pronounces modern Greek, a way which I believe is much nearer the original than that which used to be adopted by the scholars.'

He did so, but the poem was too short to give a very clear idea whether he was right or not, and it was reserved for a future occasion to vindicate him completely.

We returned to the drawing-room. People interested in ideas tend, when they meet for the first time, to talk too much, and to range over a wider variety of topic than they ordinarily would, as though they could not establish contact too quickly with another mind. This, perhaps, explained our garrulity now. Someone complained that Inge had referred to the Empire of the Cæsars as a military despotism, and Bagnani, probably not uninfluenced by the trend of contemporary politics in Italy, began at once to inveigh against the looseness of terminology in historical writings.

'In philosophy if a term is used you know exactly what is meant. If I speak of Idealism the word conveys to you what I wish to convey. We are both agreed as to what Idealism is.' (Were we? Catching Mathews' eye, I raised a slightly sceptical eyebrow. I was not so sure.) 'But if I speak of a military despotism neither you nor I nor anyone knows precisely what is meant. Was the rule of the Cæsars a despotism? The individual probably had more liberty then than he ever had under the republic. There was a Constitution, and no Constitution could have been more strictly respected. What is a military despotism, anyway?'

He hurled the question at us as though he would hold us strictly accountable for our answer.

It was left for me to reply.

'All government is based ultimately on force. We know that. But where force is very obviously to the forefront, where the real sanction which everybody knows and recognises is the will of the legionaries, then I suppose it is fair enough to talk of a military despotism. Constitutional government is where the individual of his own free will cedes a certain amount of his liberty to others, submitting voluntarily to authority for his own good. Even here a government in the extreme instance stands or falls by the force which it can command in an emergency. But that is different from allowing one part of the community – namely, its soldiers – to dictate to the rest. . . .'

The talk passed to other things. In a few minutes we were embarked upon a spate of discussion, a great deal more interesting to ourselves than to our companions. Each had discovered in the other a metaphysician and when metaphysicians meet silence is the last thing to be expected. Bagnani spoke well, though he gave the impression not so much of parading his knowledge as of cramming as much erudition into his talk at any given point as it could hold. Obviously he was a real scholar and widely read, but his conversation had a rather dogmatic note, the manner of a cross-examining counsel, which frightened his audience, who felt that he had complete command of the facts whereas they had not. His inclination to rant, I discovered later, was partly nervousness and partly perhaps the effect of living alone with a strong-minded mother; a defence against dictatorship from the quarter where one was most loved. Self-assertion is not always egoism; occasionally it is self-protection, a protest against the danger that our personality may be swamped. His mother did not parade her brains, but it was easy to see that she had them, and, with them, great strength of character as well as enormous pride and interest in her son. Plainly, it pleased her to see him hot in argument now, crossing swords with us all, and whenever we hinted that it was time to go she reassured us, indifferent apparently to the hour of their evening meal. She herself was to cross swords presently with Mathews and Elisabeth upon the subject of the German nation. She disliked Germans, and the two Tedeschi, as we called them, instantly took up arms on their behalf, defending them vigorously. Hitherto Alister had been content to sit back in his chair listening and venturing an occasional thoughtful observation, but now his voice was raised with the rest.

The evening was boring Elisabeth. She was not interested in the presentation of abstract ideas. Art interested her because it was something personal and emotional and could be made a part of oneself. Poetry and music interested her for the same reason. But metaphysics or philosophy made no appeal to her, for all theory was anathema. For two hours she had listened to little else while we ranted on, giving our views on Platonism, on Greek pronunciation, on anthropology, and on a dozen other issues; and, just as earlier in the afternoon Schumann's symphony had bored me, so had she grown more and more wearied by this torrent of abstractions. To discuss Germans was permissible, because Germans were people, living men and women, individuals whom one had met; but to discuss the German race, or the Germanic ideal, would have roused in her an instant scorn, whereas to Bagnani and myself – theorists both of us – it would have been the sounding of the trumpet in the ears of the war-horse.

At last we rose to go. It was insisted that we must dine with them before we left Rome and that, if possible, the son should take us in his Fiat for a day in the Campagna. We went down the wide marble staircase, leaving the flat this time by its own door, and we were no sooner outside in the street and the great carved door closed behind us than Elisabeth exclaimed, as though to the witnessing vault of night far above our heads:

'Well, I'm more sure than ever that I shall marry a stupid man!'

Mathews had liked Bagnani well enough.

'Of course, he is frightfully didactic. I am Sir Oracle, and when I ope my mouth——'

'If only he would not shoot his questions at you, point-blank questions to which you have no answer.'

We were all three tired. It was far too late to expect food when we returned to the convent, and the part of Rome in which we found ourselves, a residential quarter where the well-to-do lived, did not simplify the problem of getting something to eat. No small shop lurked round the corner like the small shops into which Mathews and I had dived so often on autumn evenings in Paris near the Rue Gît-le-Coeur. At last, after walking a long way, we discovered a café, but the best that it could provide was coffee and a little plum-cake, served at a marble table with every reminder that it was Sunday evening and that everyone with any sense was indoors in their own home. We ate almost in silence. I had had all the talk I wished, the others more than they wanted. We must see Elisabeth home before returning. It was a quarter-past nine. We discovered the outer door of the flats just being closed by the disagreeable porter, a scoundrel if there ever was one, I thought, as he eyed us now with surly suspicion.

Our companion bid us good night and we set out hurriedly.

'I thought Elisabeth was *fairly* irritated,' Mathews commented when we had gone a little way.

'Yes, but why?'

'All that theorising bored her. She got more and more furious with you two. You simply wouldn't stop.'

'I could see something was wrong.'

Markharoff admitted us when we returned. He told us that Schwester Wunibalda had waited for some time after her usual bedtime to give us food. Finally, she had gone, since it did not seem we were coming.

Next morning Mathews announced that he was going to have a bath at the public baths in Rome.

I thought at first that he was jesting.

'Are you crazy?'

'Not at all. We cannot have one here. What do you expect me to do? Besides, the place is perfectly clean; it's in the Corso.'

I had inherited, not only my mother's zest for life and her susceptibility to impressions, but some of her fastidiousness as well, if it can be termed fastidiousness to prefer having no bath at all to having one in a public bath-house; and this was to inconvenience us more than once on our travels. Mathews would dive into shops and purchase food from which I recoiled in horror. As a child I had been taught to dread infection and, though such a complex may be useful to us sometimes, it is not without its disadvantages. There was no bath in the convent and no more hot water arrived in the mornings than served us for shaving. But better far the painful contortions of basin-bathing in cold water than to share a bathroom, however clean, with any Italian who chose to enter off the streets of Rome. When Mathews announced his intention of bathing with the general public my instinctive reaction was:

'You are mad!'

'Nonsense, Monk, nonsense. The place is perfectly clean.'

He departed in good spirits, promising to tell me all about it when he returned. An entry in his journal duly recorded the incident: 'I had a fine public bath to-day at. a bath establishment on the Corso. . . .' After the bath, feeling greatly refreshed, he made his way to the Vatican Museum to look once more at the gems of fourteenth-century religious art. When he returned at lunch the bath was already forgotten and he announced that he had written a poem.

'Good. What is it about? Read it to me.'

'It is about the nuns here.'

It was the first occasion I had known him break into verse. Taking a slip of paper from his pocket he began to read.

'Of the Sisters of the Sorrowful Mother in Rome.

'These with pale hands and innocent holy faces
Singing quiet hymns to Mary in starry places,
Comfort these also, still in the world's ways,
Knowing but half the beauty of their dim-cloistered days.'

He meant it. Indeed, it might be said that we both meant it. With that innocent hypocrisy of which youth is often guilty, since it likes to possess opposites, we found the world's ways, in the more harmless sense of the term, quite amusing, and would have been loath to leave them; while at the same time we could sentimentalise over and almost envy the serenity of those lives which had rejected the world. The nuns had converted us, if not to their faith, then to their goodness. It was becoming a more and more illuminating experience to live in a convent and to find simplicity and sanctity in a mode of life that we had been taught to distrust. The nuns had brought with them from their northern birthplace the quiet, the peace, the docility of peasant women and they had added to this atmosphere of a Bavarian farmhouse the benign calm of sanctified usefulness and a tolerance and detachment which influenced us far more than if they had made any well-intentioned efforts to do so.

Staying at the convent and taking solitary rambles as I did, I was beginning to get the taste of Rome. The young, enviable in so many respects, are not least enviable in this, that their imagination is largely carefree, that it can brood upon the human scene without having to identify itself too closely with any one aspect of it, feeling no personal responsibility in the matter and desiring none. Its business is still to 'stand and stare.' And since the essential of content-ment for some natures is contemplation, this very detachment from life is the most certain means to its enjoyment. In such moments we seem a part of the silent landscape which we confront. We are at once the dreamer and a part of the dream. Places have moods and they impose themselves on us in the degree that we are receptive, but their moods are not dependent on ours: at least we imagine that if there were no human spectator at all the mood of the place would still remain, self-contemplative, part of the planetary consciousness, part of the 'world-dream.' The lonely, the out-of-the-way exercises a brooding fascination over us. Just as the faintly-pink distempered wall of a farmhouse by moonlight had, years before, delighted me again and again in my evening walks in Jersey, so that the scene seemed one deliberately planned – like a picture – by some invisible hand to give pleasure, even though only to a single beholder, so now in Rome I discovered nooks and backwaters capable of giving an almost equally keen stab of delight. The coloured lights thrown successively, with a brief interval between each, on to the waters of the Tiber beneath the archway continued to draw my attention whenever I passed in the evening. Often at dusk crossing the bridge near the Castel Sant Angelo I would look over the parapet to the high ground beyond and to the little 'lighthouse' near the summit gleaming like a white pillar, against its background of dark trees. And presently the first shaft of light, a deep red, would flash out into the darkness of the December evening.

It must have been the pleasure this toy – for toy in a sense it was, although it commemorated the courageous dead – gave me, that led me one afternoon to go in search of the pharos and try to see it at closer quarters. A tram took me the greater part of the way, climbing steeply through suburbs, shabbily genteel, such as one sees in both Rome and Paris, where the houses seem half asleep, drugged and dusty and silent, and looking as though no foot ever crossed their threshold from day to day. The war memorial was less accessible than I had imagined and, abandoning my search for it, or perhaps still engaged on the quest, I entered some public gardens and found myself on the terrace where the bronze statue of Garibaldi stands, a beautiful statue, on horseback, the old man in a tasselled cap gazing out across the city he had claimed, his hands resting lightly on the reins of the patient horse and an expression at once intent, brooding, serene in his far-seeing eyes. It had been a happy inspiration to place the statue there, on Janiculum, overlooking the city and its multitudinous buildings, and yet in a spot so quiet that for a quarter of an hour or more I paced alone along the box-edged pathways, undisturbed by any sound whatever except the distant protest of a child at some command of its nursemaid. Influenced perhaps by the serenity of that bronze figure, I remained there for some time, pacing meditatively along the paths and returning to the terrace again and again to gaze out over the magnificent panorama far below.

The afternoon closed slowly in; a gentle melancholy invaded the air. When I left the terrace the light was failing – the gardens shut early in winter – and, turning up a narrow roadway opposite the gates, I found myself in what was almost country. Some sodden fields lay to one side of the road, skirted by a few bare trees and a district worker's garden plot smelling of dank soil and cabbage stalks; on the other side, across some waste ground, lying a little back from the road, ran a huge embankment, part of the wall of the city or of some century-old fortification, and between two great buttresses of this wall had sprung up one of the strangest and most pathetic settlements imaginable. About seven or eight shacks, built out of pieces of packing-cases and waste iron, wood refuse and even old sacking, huddled together in a travesty of community life. It was mid-winter and each one of these frail structures looked as though it would tumble down if a finger touched it. Some of the occupants had burrowed into the great bank which supported the wall, constructing as it were small caves, supplementary shelters, if not for themselves, then for their possessions. Disused, indescribably sordid, depressing, the very ground they occupied had the appearance of a refuse dump. All was dingy, flimsy and incredibly cold; a tinker's caravan was luxury by comparison. And yet in these hutches families were being reared and old people were ending their days; fantastic as it might seem, each was a home and a habitation.

I retraced my steps to Janiculum, chastened a little by the sight of such poverty. No one passed me. The gates of the garden had been shut. Garibaldi upon horseback brooded over the city, emblem of dreams come true. Outside the gate children, full of ardent project, played in the fading light, while upon both alike, upon the living children and the bronze horseman descended the darkness of evening, making them seem part of the same spectacle, the same pageant which the mind contemplated, but from a distance, and in which it found infinite solace and calm.

There is a world of difference, I know, between such voluntary solitude as I enjoyed then – pseudo-solitude one might call it – and real loneliness in the heart of a great city. I had only to return to the Borgo Santo Spirito to find myself among friends. Over the supper table in the dark little dining-room, Markharoff passing the dishes with half-whimsical, half-deferential air, would twit Mathews with his strange beliefs. He suspected Sagesse of being a Buddhist on the strength of the latter's preoccupation with theosophy, a hint of which must have reached him; and he was inclined to be scornful on the subject of Buddha 'and his three wives.' He never referred to

Buddha that he did not refer also to these three wives, and it was useless to protest and say that the sage had only had one wife, and indeed had left her when he began his religious mission. If he liked a joke, Markharoff clung to it as fondly as I do myself, and he continued to refer to Buddha and his three wives with such gentle insistence that in the end he almost convinced us that he was better informed than we were and had access to sources of information not available to us. It is just possible that he was making a genuine mistake, having confused Buddha with Mahomet, who allowed his followers as many as four wives at one time. But it is more probable that he was simply pulling our legs.

This delight in the absurd and slightly nonsensical was a mask which it amused him to adopt, but which was never intended to hide, and never did hide for an instant, his real and deep earnestness. Conversation at our table was now, for my sake, almost altogether in French. Sometimes he would be drawn into a theological discussion and would reveal the firmness of his faith, tempered by considerable tolerance, as well as awareness that there might be errors and abuses even in the bosom of Mother Church. Intrigues and rivalries, quarrels among high dignitaries distressed him, and then he would suddenly mutter as though reassuring himself, 'It was the same when St. Francis was here.' He was no bigot. He believed that Mathews could go to Heaven, and Protestants too for that matter, a concession which to anyone reared in Ireland – though I dare say most Irish priests, if pressed, would make it – seemed immense. One evening talk turned on the doctrine of eternal punishment. Markharoff began to draw theological diagrams on the table-cloth for me with the point of a fork.

'On peut exprimer par une formule. A chacun Dieu donne "grace suffisante". '

He looked at me with his great brown eyes, laying enormous emphasis on the two words, grace suffisante.

'Eh bien, regardez. L'homme, grace suffisante, il s'agit – ciel. L'homme, grace suffisante, il ne s'agit pas – enfer.'

There was the equation. Take it or leave it. It was not God's fault if one chose to leave it. So simply could be justified the ways of the Almighty to man, even on this matter of a punishment which seemed disproportionate to any conceivable crime.

'Mais vous avez dit que la grace est suffisante,' I interrupted.

'Oui, mais il ne s'agit pas.'

It was no use arguing. He repeated, 'il ne s'agit pas.' I had not apprehended the distinction, vital to his point, between grace *sufficing*, available if one chose to make use of it, and grace sufficient – grace ample in itself without further obligation on the recipient – which was the meaning I read into 'suffisante.' And so I saw his argument as an attempt to acquit God by asserting that He had provided every man with a free passport to Heaven, while all the time He had really subsequently invalidated it and refused a visa.

We enjoyed these talks with Markharoff. On those rare occasions when we were in good time for meals we would come to table equipped with a book, but the moment Markharoff appeared the books were laid aside. We read much. Sometimes I would pay a visit to the library in the morning, and, taking out a volume which did not require too lengthy a consideration, would return for another the same evening. I enjoyed these visits to the bookshops, and part of my day was often spent there. There were three English libraries in Rome and each of them at some time had enjoyed our patronage. Of the three, Warner's was undoubtedly the best. Piale's English library, into which Mathews had been lured by mistake before getting his bearings in Rome, was antediluvian. All its books were covered in stiff red calico and belonged to the period when Baron Tauchnitz was just beginning to make himself useful. Brown's, owned by a masterly-looking English lady, was better, but contained many books which might well have been given to Piale. Warner's in the Piazza di Spagna, run by a young American, assisted by a good-looking Russian youth, who spoke English excellently, was more up to date than either of the other two. Its two square windows, with picturesquely leaded panes, looked out on one corner of the square, and it was reached, not from the front, but by a door in the side of an archway. Its books were almost all new and excellently chosen.

It was Elisabeth who had told us of it, and, going one morning into the tiny triangular division at the far end, tucked away with an amazing regard for economy of space, and devoted to books on Greece and Rome, as well as a section in modern foreign languages, I discovered her searching amongst the latter. It was a surprise and a most agreeable one.

'What am I going to take? With so many you never know how to choose. I want something in French. I think I shall get *Père Goriot*. I have just brought back *La Vie Prodigieuse de Balzac. Une Vie Prodigieuse* indeed. What a man!'

Turning the pages of *Père Goriot*, she discovered a portrait of its author as frontispiece and showed it to me with evident approval.

189

'Fat, greasy and unshaven, and you manage to like him?'

'That didn't matter. He was Balzac.'

In all three of us, I think, and not merely in Alister, there was a hint of that native of La Mancha who had made the contents of his library the starting point of his adventures, the course whence he drew inspiration and strength for the determination to insist on a romantic conception of life. We shared a common enthusiasm – that enthusiasm which makes books quite as important an element in life as events. When we met, it seemed to us as natural to ask one another 'What are you reading now?' as 'What are you doing?'

'What have you discovered?' she said to me now.

'A book that I can read in a few hours. A critical study of the three Sitwells. But I want to decide now on something that I can snatch quickly when I come back this evening.'

She moved along the shelves with the predatory air of the book-lover who has no time to waste on rubbish, her hand ready to reach out whenever she saw something that might interest her. In the section devoted to books on painting, she pointed to a translation of Rodin's *L'Art* and exclaimed,

'Magnificent. One of the best books ever written.'

'Good. I can get it this evening when I return my other.'

'The English translation, I am told, is very bad. If you like, I will lend you my own copy in French. It is fully illustrated too. But you must promise faithfully to return it.'

'I will. Is the French hard?'

'No, it is very straightforward. If you can read any French at all, you can read it.'

At that moment my eye caught sight of a book of which I had seen only one copy ever before, my own. It was Bliss Carman's *Sappho* which, despite its inclusion in 'The King's Classics,' has passed almost out of the cognisance of the booksellers. Bliss Carman was a Canadian, and a stepsister had brought it back with her from Canada, together with the moccasins and terrapins. As soon as it came into the house, my elder sister made the book her own, sharing it with me as one shares the most treasured of possessions, for we were at an age when the fire and passion of these brief poems, delicate and lovely as the cameo embossed on the cover, was like the sudden revelation of a world suspected but hitherto unknown. They had the added enchantment that they evoked Greece. One seemed to breathe the very air of the islands, in that halcyon age before ever Athens had asserted her dominion. Bliss Carman had taken the fragments, a line perhaps, sometimes even only a single word, and like a sculptor given an arm, a hand, a finger and asked to reconstruct the statue from which it came, so had he imagined the whole poem which Sappho made, and then by some *tour de force* essayed to write it. For years I was envious that my sister should have established squatter's rights over the book, and one day when, like Herod, she was in the mood to promise me half her kingdom – I was going to the war, I think – I demanded and was given it. Her name remained upon the title page, but she added mine above it.

'What Rodin's book means to you, this means to me.'

I put it into Elisabeth's hands and left her for a few minutes while I groped amongst the other poets on one of the lower shelves in the library. I could have repeated by heart the poems which she was reading, or at least many of them.

> 'Cyprus, Paphos, or Panormus
> May detain thee with their splendour
> Of oblations on thine altars,
> O imperial Aphrodite.
>
> Yet do thou regard, with pity
> For a nameless child of passion,
> This small unfrequented valley
> By the sea, O sea-born mother.'

'Yes, they are lovely, very lovely.'

We were in no hurry. It amused us to browse along the shelves comparing our impressions of books that we had both read.

'Hullo. Stephens' *Crock of Gold*. You've read that, of course?'

'No.'

'You must read it some day.'

She agreed that this would be the next book she got from the library.

At last we were ready to leave. For some days now Mathews had been troubled with a cough, and I had promised to try to get him something for it.

'What are you doing now? I have to go and get some cough lozenges for Alister. If you have nothing better to do, will you come with me?'

She would come, and she knew a chemist where we could get them. We crossed the Piazza and turned down a street past the Ministero Degli Affari Esteri whither I had gone one day to see an Italian *attaché* whom I had met with his Danish wife in Assens the summer before. Nearby was the chemist's. English throat lozenges were a fantastic price, the Italian variety looked unpleasing; but Alister's bark must be stopped and we decided in favour of the former. Leaving the shop, we walked up the Corso, crossed back over the river and began walking along beside it. We had been discussing Rodin and his opinion that there is as much beauty to be seen to-day as there ever was in Greece, if we had eyes to see it.

Suddenly I said to her, 'You've had lots of admiration in your time. It must be interesting to be beautiful and to watch the impact of beauty on different people, the response they make under the same stimulus.'

'It isn't interesting. No one admires you for what you really are, only for what they think you are. What they are admiring is their idea of you, never your real self.'

She spoke a little bitterly, as though beauty were a mask, a gift which really defeated its own purpose, meant to reveal the soul, but actually standing between the soul and its apprehension by another. It is the eternal complaint of woman, this complaint that she is never loved for herself, but only for her attributes, and perhaps there is some measure of justification in it for, to give them their due, women themselves are willing to love where there are no outward attractions – a Balzac, for instance. But it was a complaint new to me then, and for the first time I saw that beauty has its own tragedy. To have the emphasis laid always upon the outward – to be approached by everyone in a spirit of selfish wonderment, as though one were a figure in a museum or an ornament on a mantel-shelf, cannot remain agreeable for very long to any but shallow minds. With adolescence it is different. Standing on the threshold of life, uncertain of oneself, all approval brings pleasure. The time has not yet come when it seems less pleasing that eyes should turn and heads swing round to follow with a glance which is at once appreciative and a little insulting – impersonal appraisement, or else the greed, and hungry look, of those who regard beauty as their prey. Such a time is still far off. Youth has its rights, and to blossom under admiration is one of its prerogatives. The sap rises in the twig, the branch buds; the cheeks of the young flush, at a hint, at a mere surmise that they are approved.

> Now at this season Love, who's wise,
> Knowing his time must surely come,
> Sets in her face a signal sweet
> Denied to some.

If she was fair before, she'll now
Suddenly into beauty spring.
If she was young, he'll add to that
Another thing.

All her shy grace will seem to spring
Out of an eagerness within
And in her cheeks the colour mount –
To warm her skin.

Never before or after quite
Will she be as she is to-day;
Love, who is wise, has seen to that,
To have his way.

Denied to some? I thought of La Ballerina. She was one of
Markharoff's jests; indeed, she was his arch-jest; one more ebullition
of that spirit of gentle mockery when, with eyes cast demurely down
and hands clasped together over his tunic, he would make us wonder
for an instant whether he was being serious or not. On these occasions
he tried not to betray even by a flicker of an eyelid his real mood.
He would be gay; then at his gayest he would become suddenly
decorous, either to puzzle us or because he thought that he ought
to, and it was almost impossible to know the precise moment when
irony ended and seriousness began. Sometimes, however, the spirit
of mockery would get completely the better of him and he would
give an imitation of La Ballerina. Linking his hands together over
his head, he would stand, feet well apart, and strike absurd and
extravagant poses. As stiff as a rod, he yet in some way managed to
convey, in absurd caricature, the effect of the ballet. In his long
black cassock, he would swing first to one side and then to the other,
holding out his hands imploringly one moment, coquettishly the
next. And then, suddenly dropping his arms, he would smile for one
lightning instant and become as demure as before.

We would laugh. And yet the Ballerina was really not comedy at
all, but tragedy. She was the idiot daughter of the German couple
who sat at the second long table by themselves. The old man was
grey-haired, with a rather fine head, not unlike Ruskin's, and
bearded, although his cheeks were shaved. He walked deliberately,
bowed with grave politeness when he came into the room, and talked
little. The mother was delicate, kept to her bedroom a good deal and
never appeared at the evening meal, leaving father and daughter

to dine alone. She must have been pretty in her youth and she still kept the remnants of her good looks, together with a slightly affected graciousness.

La Ballerina was short and stocky, built somewhat after the fashion of a sawdust doll whose joints are stiff and will not bend properly. She was inclined to be stout and she moved stiffly and jerkily in a sort of parody of the rather heavy walk of her father. She wore her hair in two short pigtails hanging over her shoulders and had a wide mouth and a snub, turned-up nose. Her eyes, very small, with pink lids, were the tiny eyes of the imbecile, which, when they look at you, do not seem to focus quite perfectly. Indeed, in this very pink and rather blank face there was always the puzzled and pathetic expression of the soul over which life passes in a certain sense as a dream.

When she followed her father into the room she would bow to us with a grotesque smirk and repeat '*Guten Abend*,' which he had just uttered. She wore a pinafore over her dress, and it was only necessary for her to turn her head towards you to see at once that she was not as other girls. Sometimes after he had left the room she would return timorously to fill the glass of wine which he had forgotten to take with him. This unfortunate girl was nineteen. She looked fifteen and it was impossible to think of her as any older. Sometimes I would look critically at her parents, trying to account for the misfortune of their daughter, but there was nothing in either of them to explain it. We learnt that they wished to get her into a convent so that when they died she would be cared for.

It was Markharoff who told us that she had confided in him that at one time she used to dance and had even had lessons in that accomplishment. From this was born the fantastic story of La Ballerina and of dancing practice in her room in the mornings; from it, too, all Markharoff's extravagant pantomime. Despite his gentleness in every other respect, there was something slightly brutal in his attitude to this unfortunate girl, an almost cruel mockery, as though he were visiting on her some buried and quite unconscious antagonism to her whole sex. His mimicry made me roar with laughter; to see him solemnly pirouetting about the room, his hands joined above his head, was a sight for the gods. And yet I felt it was just a shade cruel. His sense of fun had run amok. Of the three of us, I, being a little older, was probably the only one conscious of pathos as well as comedy. One afternoon in Rome, on the far side of the Tunnel from the Piazza di Spagna, I caught sight of the unfortunate Ballerina. She was clinging in close pursuit to her mother, who was advancing behind the father to catch a tram. La Ballerina followed, hugging an umbrella, wearing an ill-fitting knitted coat and a curious-shaped, knitted cap. The cap was pulled down almost over her eyes, but from under it her hair escaped, plastered down on either side of her forehead, before forming into the two short plaits. In her blank face was a look of dogged pursuit, of blind, helpless direction towards the object nearest in view, of puzzled and ridiculous determination, mixed with all the pathos of helplessness, as though she knew no more now than at any time what exactly life was doing to her.

La Ballerina symbolised all that was grotesque, pathetic, unfinished. Into her small eyes, peering at life with a mixture of suspicion and alarm, there would come suddenly – what was almost more pathetic – a look of sudden deliberate graciousness, when the corners of her mouth would turn up in a smile. We are all unfinished, all grotesque, all in varying degree pathetic, judged by any standard of perfection; and it is perhaps this simple fact, realised with all the intensity of the saint, that allows him to love even the leper, or that made Wordsworth always refer to idiots as 'God's children.' If, on the stage of life, 'the best in this kind' are truly 'but shadows,' then the least, the most humble – seen with the passionate impartiality of sainthood – is not so far removed from them.

I myself had too much of the pagan in me to look at La Ballerina without faint uneasiness. She was as it were the parody of her sex, a living reminder at every meal that beauty is the exception rather than the rule. If we love and appreciate beauty, it is only too easy for us to shrink from ugliness, and my journal at this time was full of dissertations upon the inspirational value to us of what is lovely. All else, I wrote, was unreal by comparison, 'cloudy, murky, without any vital signification.' I argued that it was scarcely to be wondered at that we should await eagerly 'the miracle which made the scales drop from our eyes.'

I did not say what the miracle was, but it is not hard to guess. The miracle was beauty, and as I walked back from the library with Elisabeth now it surprised me to hear her deprecate the very gift that seemed to me as precious as any that life could give. I could understand how very little admiration of beauty might seem really disinterested; behind it, always, there might seem to be lurking something predatory, something possessive. But to be told that beauty was an impediment, that it threw dust in the eyes even of the idealists, making them turn from the real self to pursue a phantasy of their own creation – that was illuminating.

'Yes, I suppose you are right. I had not thought of it in that way before.'

We left the river and I accompanied her as far as the flat and said goodbye to her there. When I returned to the convent Mathews was a little envious when he heard with whom my morning had been spent.

'It is just your luck. How do you manage these things?'

He had had a disappointment that morning. A flat packet had arrived from Dulcinea in Gloucestershire. He had torn it open, felt cardboard within and exclaimed joyously, 'It is a photograph!' It was a photograph indeed, but not the one he had expected. Five fat spaniel puppies had been persuaded to pose for the camera of a professional, and it was the resultant calendar which had been sent to him as a Christmas gift. The moment was tragic, but it had been impossible to avoid laughing at his crestfallen face.

But though she mocked him in this fashion – intentionally or unintentionally – the damsel in the Cotswolds to whom spaniels and horses meant more than books still held first place in his affections. At the same time, it did not altogether please him to see me burning incense at a shrine where he himself had once worshipped with so much ardour. There were moments when he was a little nettled by it. His concern was not solely for himself. When it seemed to him that I was most in danger of complete subjugation, he would look at me disapprovingly and ask, 'How much of this will you confess when you return to England?' 'All, of course.' 'All, and be forgiven?' 'I hope so.' 'Then why not confess it now?' 'Because the whole thing might take on a quite exaggerated complexion.'

He could see the force of this. He laughed, but he believed me. I believed myself. But there were moments also when he felt that I trespassed on his rights. He would remind me that I had only known Elisabeth a week, whereas she had been his friend for two years. He was still her confidant. To him she would tell her worries and distresses, her anxiety about the post in London which had been offered her and her family's reluctance that she should accept it. He enjoyed such *tête-à-têtes*. On one occasion he remarked plaintively to me, 'When you came into the room the atmosphere altered at once.' He remained to her what he had always been, an amusing, faithful, charming and, in his own way, quite unique friend. Sometimes his voice would be upraised to me in praise of her. 'She is the unhooded falcon. For two years now I have known her, in Paris, in Munich, in Dresden, in Switzerland, in Italy, and all the time she has been free. Now she must come down to the falconer's lure, be tamed, and work in London of all places. And part of my life goes with her.' A moment later he added reflectively, 'I too have winged through many heavens.' At other times he would be still more vocal in her praises. 'She is incredibly lovely with her hat off. When she laughs and turns her head a little and looks at you searchingly, with her elbow resting on the table and her hand against her forehead. Do you know what her hair reminds me of? Of Yeats's line, "Men thrashed corn at midnight by a tress, a little stolen tress." '

Mathews and I would never have gravitated towards one another had there not been this streak of the romantic in us both. It was this which made him forgive me, even when he felt most disposed to be jealous. He would chuckle suddenly and forget that he resented the interloper. The truth was he wished to live in a Mozartian world. He hated the blatancy, the vulgarity and the emptiness of a civilisation which has first derided and exiled all genuine emotion, and then made the attempt to live on mere sensation. The feeling that it was a paramount duty to escape at all costs the sterility of cynicism and that paraded repudiation of all the deeper well-springs of feeling made Mathews avoid the beaten track, made him prefer the poor to the rich and the eccentric to the conventional, made him stay at out-of-the-way places and cultivate unlikely people. But the surest way of all to escape it was to fall in love oneself, or to watch others fall in love. Then the world of Mozart, the world of Schubert at last became real. He was like an exile repatriated to his native land, viewing everything with delight, because it had never at any time been far from his thoughts.

He must have known that Elisabeth at this time was constantly in my own thoughts, and that it pleased me to talk to him about her. As far as that went, she was a welcome subject with us both.

That night he said to me:

'I am glad that you realise how beautiful she is. I knew you would. Two years ago in Château d'Œx, you have no idea of the anguish she caused me. She was even lovelier then,' and he began to compare her and a certain Marianne Langreuter, whose name I had never heard till that moment. 'Marianne Langreuter was perhaps more amazingly and strikingly beautiful, but I feel Elisabeth is more human. And yet it was just that ultra-human beauty that I worshipped in Marianne Langreuter. Elisabeth's beauty is possible.

Marianne's was hardly so.' It was after this flight of homage that he went on to add hastily, in the fashion of one who has forgotten his 'Ora pro nobis': 'All the same, Jean remains the real love, the ideal, *die Gesehnte*.'

I went to the window, drew the curtains and looked out. Rome was lovely on such a night. The moon had risen and cast its serene light over everything, rising in an absolutely clear heaven, rain-washed from any cloud. I saw one of those skies that we had been having lately when, after perhaps a day of rain showers, the wind suddenly drops, and the air becomes still. Moonlight steeped all. In that serene and pale light, the city seemed to sleep, a ghostly replica of itself, touched by some enchanter's wand. The smooth pillars of Bellini's colonnade cast shadows black as night, but the Piazza itself, the dome of St. Peter's, and the shining roofs of buildings nearby were bathed in a milky whiteness. A memorable night, so lovely that we planned to visit the ruins of the Colosseum later in the evening, after our supper; a resolution never kept, for when the time came and we looked out, the sky had altered, banks of light, mottled cloud had spread themselves everywhere over it, and the moon was but the pale ghost of what she had been, a shade from another world, glimpsed occasionally through a rainbow-tinted veil.

The day of the Papal audience came. A nun led us across the square of St. Peter's and handed us over to an attendant at a door of the Vatican. Two other guests from the hostel accompanied me. The young Bavarian who sat on a bench facing us at meals had put on his best suit. A handkerchief with a border to it emerged from his breast-pocket as well as his fountain-pen. With his blue eyes, square forehead and splendidly honest face he looked like one of those peasant artisans of Oberammergau who abandon their work for a time to take part in the Passion Play. The third member of the party was a retired German actress, fat and kindly, who had come to the convent a few days before. I was amused to find that even the Pope cannot dictate to a woman what she shall wear. On the back of the card of admittance had been depicted a melancholy female in deep mourning, the skirt of her dress touching the ground, its sleeves tied tightly at the wrists in the fashion that Bagnani had recommended to us for Greece. This was the type of costume prescribed, and to which the actress, who normally wore a bright green jersey and short tweed skirt, had almost conformed. But in the audience itself I was to notice dresses which were not black at all but pale grey, sleeves very nearly diaphanous, and skirts which whispered, if they did not shout, defiance at the Pope's Chamberlain and his regulations.

Entering the Vatican, we were led down numerous corridors till we came to the foot of the Scala Regia, and, passing the two Swiss halberdiers in the bright uniform of mauve and yellow which Michelangelo is supposed to have designed, we went up the long flight of marble stairs, beneath the pillared arch with its trumpeting angels, following in the wake of other arrivals, till we came to the lofty, massive double doors through which the crowd were flocking. We waited a long time in the great hall of audience. Nearly two hundred people, marshalled in a continuous line round the walls of the vast room, stood talking to one another in undertones or fingering the rosaries and religious emblems which they had brought with them in the hope that the Pope would bless them. I had time to study my fellow pilgrims. Near me, but at right angles, their backs to the adjoining wall, stood three youths of sixteen in the walking-dress of the German student, fawn wind-jackets, flannel shirts with coloured woollen ties, bright tie-pins, and saffron-coloured shorts. That evening, with Mathews to interpret, I learnt from the Bavarian that they were *Wandervögel* who had walked all the way to Rome from Munich. It had taken them forty-six days to come, stopping sometimes on the way to earn money for their expenses. But even without his knowledge I could see, as they waited with hands clasped one across the other, that the occasion, of significance to us all, was of very special significance to them. My attention was drawn not so much by the expression of rapture and excitement on the faces of two of the boys, as by that of dumb docility on the face of the third. He was the tallest of the three and very plain, the eyebrows arched high above the small eyes, the nose snub and with tightened nostrils, the mouth pursed. He looked like the swineherd of some fairy story, doomed to be the butt of readier wits; he might have been the hero of one of Hans Andersen's tales, or even Hans Andersen himself in his ungainly and unhappy youth.

The audience was for a certain hour, but the hour came, passed and still nothing happened. It might have seemed that there was some hitch in the proceedings, only that the ushers remained so calm, shaking their heads when questioned, unable to give any reason for the delay, but not greatly concerned by it. But at last even they became restive. The private audiences which preceded the public one were evidently taking a great deal longer than expected. More minutes passed and still the Pope did not come. Suddenly there was a stir. The ushers motioned us to kneel down. Something was about to happen. Across the room, in a group of white-robed children accompanied by their nurses or governesses, a child in a yellow dress, her brown locks fallen about her face, hugged herself with excitement and laughed happily. The small boys beside her showed a greater reserve. They were solemn and overawed.

A door was flung open at the far end of the audience chamber and, still conversing with those who had formed the last of his private audiences that day, the Holy Father entered. Kneeling with the rest, I felt awed, impressed and at the same time a little disturbed, wondering at this last minute, when it was already too late, whether I should have come, and what I should do when the hand with the ring upon it was extended to me. Should I kiss it? Was it an act of hypocrisy to be kneeling at all? Did it imply an allegiance which I did not feel, and if so, would it not make matters worse if I were to kiss the ring? But I need not have concerned myself. No one was obliged to kiss the ring. The Pope had kept us waiting so long that he was not in the mood to delay us any longer. He swept quickly round the room, in a lightning progress, extending his hand as he went. I bowed my head as he came to me and the next instant he was gone. Those who wished could seize the hand as it passed and kiss the ring, but they must be quick. There was no time to dally, no time to produce a rosary or medal to be blessed. Only when he came to the three students who had walked from Munich did the Pope pause instantly in his swift progress. Stopping opposite them, he spoke to them, asking them questions in their own language and waiting for them to reply. The eyes of the kneeling boys were fixed on his, conscious of the honour that was being paid them. Then he raised his hand. Into the face of the dullard, into his little eyes, leaped for a second an expression of ineffable hope. For a moment it seemed to him that the Pope's hand was about to rest upon his head. It was succeeded as quickly by one of slight chagrin. The hand which had been raised rested not on his, but on the head of one of his companions. For an instant I saw in the countenance of this gawky, moon-faced lad a look of dumb inarticulate pathos, a look instantly effaced as something unworthy, as though the vision of Paradise had been offered him only to be snatched away. And in that upturned face, at once stupid and sublime, there seemed symbolised all the devotion, all the reverence, all the blind loyalty, all the hope and all the disappointment of which poor humanity is capable.

The Pope gave his blessing and then resumed his swift progress round the room. Only once again did he pause, and that was when he came to the two groups of children with their attendants near the door. With them also he conversed for a few moments. In all that crowd of ardent and eager devotees, it was the youths who had come on foot, and the children, who seemed to him the most deserving of attention; and this action of his – spontaneous, instinctive almost – was a reminder that Christianity, despite all its divisions and quarrels, has certain universal features; the humble, the young, the helpless, the undefended being held to be as important as – nay, more important than – any in its eyes.

I had seen the Pope. I had seen the man whose lot it was to love millions of souls as I perhaps loved a few. Christian love remains a mystery save to the mystic and to the saint. We find it hard to conceive of love save in terms of individuals or to envisage a tide of benevolence going forth to encircle the world. When Sister Edouarda knelt at the bedside in our room it was not simply for us, not simply for those beneath the hostel roof that she prayed, but for humanity – humanity, that distressing aggregate which most of us find it so hard to tolerate, much more to love. And in just this fashion must the Pope pray too. The wide face, the eyes set well apart behind their gold spectacles, the firm mouth that I had watched as he spoke to the boys, were indeed the face and eyes of the man who had made the first Italian traverse of Monte Rosa from Macugnana to Zermatt, who had slept a night in the snow, and who would never see the mountains again, having left them for this voluntary prison.[1] With the weight of the world's cares upon his shoulders, did he ever regret them, did he ever long for them once more? The same tenacity which had made him a good mountaineer was to make him a few years later cling to life in the face of grave odds, through months of illness; celebrate his eightieth birthday in the way he wished, despite all caveats from his physicians; and survive, to speak his mind out plainly on European affairs; at a time and in circumstances when other men might have been glad to shuffle off this mortal coil and be gone. Had I kissed his ring I should have had nothing to reproach myself with or to regret. More than once, indeed many times in the ten years that followed, Pius XI was to voice the conscience of Christianity, courageously and unmistakeably, which is quite as important as – if not even more important than – to voice its dogmas.

The audience was over. It had lasted a minute or two in all.

[1] It was still a year or two before the Concordat.

While I had been at the Vatican, Alister and Markharoff, seated on one of the benches in the hostel dining-room, had been discussing the problems and shortcomings of Mother Church. Mathews epitomised the conversation for me later in the day, making me wonder whether his German or Markharoff's French could have led to misunderstanding, or whether Mathews could not resist the temptation to heighten his effects. There was an element of melo-drama in most of the stories. A whole political party in France had been outlawed, and the paper which was its mouthpiece placed on the Index. Notwithstanding this, a certain French cardinal had con-tinued reading and even admiring it. In a private interview with the Pope, a few days before, he had remained obstinate. He had even reproached the Pope with showing undue favour to precisely similar opinions in Italy, and demanded why? What was sauce for the French goose should be sauce also for the Italian gander.

' "*Ce n'est pas votre affaire*," answered the Pope; whereupon the angry Cardinal overthrew the chair on which he had been sitting, flung it from him across the room, and left without crossing himself or genuflecting. He has been excommunicated, but in the papers one reads that he has wished to enter a monastery.'

His eyes glistened with excitement, as he retailed the story with evident relish.

'But, Alister, if the interview was a private one how does anyone know what happened at it? And the chair——?'

'They could have found the overturned chair afterwards.'

Obviously, he thought it ungenerous of me to question the picturesqueness of his version. That Markharoff worried about scandals which penetrated even to the Vatican, I knew, for he had alluded to them in our talks at supper.

The Princess had left. She had gone to Capri and Mathews had returned immediately and with every manifestation of joy to his subterranean prison. Thither he would invite me in the afternoons to join him once more for a four o'clock cup of tea. I had excited his deepest scorn one day in the room upstairs because, being left in charge of the boiling kettle at a moment when he had been called out of the room on some errand, I had neglected to infuse the tea and had excused myself by saying that I did not know if there was any tea in the small silver infuser which he had deposited carefully upon the table.

'Couldn't you even look?'

'Well, I suppose I could have done.'

He snorted indignantly.

I was left once more in solitary occupation of the big room and, to tell the truth, had my own reasons for being just as glad as he was. I was beginning to find the Yoga cleansing-breath a little trying in the mornings. Mathews was not only interested in theosophy, but he had purchased a series of excellent books, unconnected with the movement, by a writer who veiled his identity under the pseudonym 'Ramacharaka.' They embraced the various kinds of Yoga, Bhakti Yoga, Raja Yoga and so forth; and the one which I had read myself, *Fourteen Lessons in Yogi Philosophy*, had seemed to me well-written and to contain a great deal of wisdom. The volume, however, which was Mathews' especial favourite at that moment was the one which appealed to me least, for it tended to encourage the valetudinarian rather than the philosopher. It was the one on 'Hatha Yoga,' the Yoga of health and physical well-being. Here Mathews had discovered a number of practices and principles which, properly used, he assured me would result in great physical prowess and increased mental vigour. Yoga could achieve anything. It could even achieve, he explained, a reversal of the whole digestive process or the passing of a cloth – but I have no wish to dwell on its achievements in these directions, which were only interesting because they showed that Nature is not the complete automaton that we think her.

In the very forefront of all the Hatha Yoga teachings were the breathing exercises. There were a number of different kinds of these, but all alike must be begun and ended by the Yoga cleansing-breath. Leaping out of bed in the mornings, I would see the tall and rather bony figure of my friend getting ready for this ordeal. Ordeal it was, but the ordeal was really mine rather than his. For the cleansing-breath consisted in the ejection of all air from the lungs in a series of short sharp puffs. It must be done through the nostrils and was not unlike a person blowing his nose repeatedly without a handkerchief to aid him. Alternatively, it might be compared to a snake in a moment of irritation, or a rheumy goat, trying to clear its air passages in the corner of a hay-barn, where the dust-laden atmosphere is distressing it. This comparison is perhaps the best of the three, for the whole object of the cleansing-breath was to clear the air passages before settling down to the real business of breathing rhythmically, which, I may add, was a great deal less objectionable both to hear and to witness.

Morning after morning I had had to listen to the cleansing-breath and had expressed my opinion of it in no uncertain terms. Mathews would only smile indulgently, brush my objections aside with a light hand, or say that my own physical contortions were just as painful – to watch. But now he had departed, taking with him the cleansing-breath and also his cough, which racked him considerably, and which was beginning to worry us by its persistence. I had the big room to myself. I would no longer return to find him sitting on his bed, patching the elbow of an old coat, a task which had occupied him for nearly an hour, or triumphantly brandishing a small paper-covered copy of *Faust* which he had picked up in a German bookshop that day.

On the same say that the Princess left, the two German girls, about whom I had heard so much, returned from Naples to spend one night in the hostel before continuing on their way to Cologne. Sister Edouarda knocked on the door and summoned Alister to tell him the good news. He ran downstairs and I could hear great laughter and effusion of greetings. I had heard much about the two cousins, of their jollity and cheerfulness and of how the whole room would remain sitting on at table after the evening meal until nearly ten o'clock, while these girls laughed and entertained them. Mathews' eyes lit up whenever he mentioned these evenings. 'We are to tell them when we go to Naples and they will meet us there.' But we had not gone to Naples, we had lingered on in Rome, and now, instead, they had returned to us.

The sounds of laughter and cordiality floated up the stairs. Mathews called to me and I went down to the little waiting-room, beside the refectory, with its single narrow window, its horse-hair sofa, its clock, and the visitors' book which we had signed when we arrived.

He introduced us.

'It is the Schurholzes, Monk. They are here for one night and you must certainly hear them sing.'

He had always spoken of them as girls, but in actual fact they would neither of them see thirty again. Tall, with a very wide mouth and prominent teeth, showing perpetually because she was continually laughing, one of the two cousins formed a strong contrast to the other, who was smaller and better-looking, with auburn hair and the rather freckled complexion which goes with very fair eyelashes. Short, energetic-looking and with tremendous animation, she was describing the day of their visit by steamer to Capri when I entered the room. She told us she had already made the day's adventures the subject of a four-page poem in mock heroic couplets, which she would read to Alister later. The sea had been rough, there had been extreme difficulty in getting into the Blue Grotto, and finally when they had made the attempt a great wave caught them just as they were inside, and overturned the boat. She, an Englishman, and the island boatman, its only occupants, were all three thrown into the water and had to swim round patiently until a second boat which was already in the grotto came to their rescue. Because of the heavy sea running outside, the entrance admitted less light than usual, and in the darkness the Englishman was missed for a time. Not knowing that there was ledge of rock on to which he could climb, he continued to swim round and round. Finally, all three were rescued, the boat righted, and they returned to the steamer, to be landed at the Grande Marina, where she had gone to bed at the hotel while her dripping clothes were dried.

'My clothes were not properly dry when we had to start back to Naples. And I have not even a cold to show for it. The Englishman complimented me upon my courage and he has invited me to accompany him to Africa.'

It was all treated as a tremendous joke, and I could not help feeling that if a boat must capsize in the Blue Grotto it had chosen the right kind of passenger on whom to make the experiment. Nothing could quench such exuberant resilience.

Alister had made a mistake. They were not staying at the hostel after all. Their train for Cologne left so early in the morning that they must take their things to the station now and stop at a hotel nearby. They would return, however, and sup at the convent.

'What a shame that we are going out. Now you will not hear them sing,' Mathews exclaimed in a tone of the deepest dejection, for we were pledged to dine at the Bagnanis and had to be there at half-past seven. Markharoff was equally loud in his expressions of regret. An evening in their company, he assured me, was something not to be missed.

But I was not to miss this pleasure after all. As soon as they learnt of our difficulty, they said that they would return to the hostel at six and sing for us then. At about twenty past six we heard their voices downstairs and joined them and Markharoff in the little dining-room. But first of all the poem must be read. This was done with great animation by the author herself; while her companion, who knew no English, kept up a running commentary in German, punctuated with laughter and clapping of hands, playing the part of foil to so much talent almost too effusively. All this elaborate pantomime, so far from helping to give me some idea of the course of the narrative, only made it harder to follow than ever. And while the lady continued to applaud delightedly, and Alister sat by smiling gravely, my mind returned to the story that 'See-You-Later' had told us of these two cousins. 'See-You-Later' was a German-American nurse from a hospital in New York who had been a short while in the hostel, a good enough sort, but a little flighty and arch. We had given her this nickname from her habit of flinging the phrase at you in her best – and therefore all the more incongruous – Yankee, as she frisked out of the room after some absurd attempt to flirt with Markharoff. She told us one evening something of the tragedy of the life of this woman whom I now heard reading. She had made an unhappy marriage, and, like Mrs. Alving in Ibsen's *Ghosts*, had left her husband almost immediately. She had divorced him, but in the eyes of her Church she was still married and now, eight years later, she was trying to obtain an annulment of her marriage from the Vatican. She and her companion lived in Cologne and ran a home for fallen girls. It was hard to relate all this to the exuberant, almost forced, air of gaiety which – perhaps it was the language difficulty once more – was beginning to get on my nerves. And then, just as the poem had grown to seem almost interminable, it suddenly ended, the poet was congratulated by us all and someone said:

'And now will you sing?'

Her whole manner instantly changed. She got up, and with the simplicity of a child bidden to do some task, she stood at the end of the table, folded her hands and began to sing in a clear contralto, limpid and unerring as a thrush singing in a garden at evening. The first note was the foretaste and assurance of all that followed. I had now the explanation of Alister's and Markharoff's enthusiasm. In an age when all talent is tapped, canalised and exploited almost as soon as it makes its appearance, it is a rarity to meet perfection of art in the amateur; and yet the amateur – in the sense in which many of the Elizabethan poets were amateurs – is able to bring an intimacy and spontaneity into art which the professional must often envy. It was so now. We listened to a voice lyrical, authentic, without the slightest trace of self-consciousness. The experience was comparable to the keenest delight that any concert-hall could give. Four people were its privileged audience, and in just the same prodigal fashion in which this woman, we had been told, gave her life to the unfortunates in Cologne, so she seemed now to share her talent with us, oblivious of the quality of her gift.

She sang first a German song to the air Hahn wrote for Verlaine's *L'heure exquise* and which Alma Gluck has sung so exquisitely. I knew the music already, lovely as all Hahn's settings of Verlaine are, elusive, wistful yet full of passion and feeling. No other composer has ever been so closely allied to his poet as Hahn is to Verlaine, unless it be Le Fleming when he sets Blake or William Barnes. Music and words seem born in the same instant, the one the necessary corollary of the other. After Hahn came the *Ave Maria* of Schubert, then *Kennst du das Land, Heilige Nacht* and, finally, the lullaby, *Guten Abend, Guten Nacht*. All that she sang was sung without effort. The voice seemed only part of some other and more spiritual entity behind it, which was breaking through into sound. It was the soul become articulate. I listened with an ever-increasing reverence and admiration. Until now this woman had seemed to me pleasant but a little noisy, one of those people who are perpetually talking and, who easily become fatiguing, a feminine Mark Tapley who conceives it her duty to whistle cheerfully, or at least to laugh, upon every occasion. But now my whole opinion of her changed. No one could sing in this particular fashion whose heart was not clean, joyous and courageous.

It was long after seven o'clock. Schwester Wunibalda was waiting to bring in the supper. But we could not tear ourselves away. We kept pleading for just one more. Markharoff added his entreaties to ours, seated on the corner of the bench, his knees draped in his cassock and an expression of deep, serene joy in his sad brown eyes. 'Did I not tell you so?' he whispered to me in French. We should be late at the Bagnani's. That could not be helped. At last we tore ourselves away, thanked them for our entertainment, wished them *bon voyage*, for we should not see them again, and, dashing across the square, flung ourselves on to a tram which appeared at that most opportune moment. Elisabeth was waiting for us; she had only to put on her coat and we reached the Bagnani's flat just as a clock was striking the half-hour.

An evening different from any we had had for some time awaited us. We had changed into dark suits, the nearest thing to evening-dress that our travelling wardrobes offered. Elisabeth, the fur collar of her coat turned up and a light scarf over her head, led the way up the marble stairs and we followed, framing apologies with which to meet our hostess. But Signora Bagnani waved them aside, assuring us we were not really late. A minute or two later we were at the dinner-table, enjoying a succession of courses and wine of a curious flavour, slightly alien to our palate, but not so alien that our glasses must not be kept continually filled. Conversation never flagged; with such an experienced hostess and so many interests in common, it was unlikely that it should. Bagnani had discarded a good deal of the pedant; he appeared more human and made us feel altogether at ease. He had overcome his initial shyness, and no longer talked in the assertive, high-pitched voice which had irritated us on the previous occasion; but one could see from the flutter of his hands and his general manner that he was still nervous, and for a moment I wondered whether he too had fallen under the spell of Elisabeth. It was possible; on the other hand, his excitement seemed intellectual rather than emotional.

When the meal was over we went into the library, and he produced cigarettes from Cyprus, which he pressed upon us continually, encouraging me to smoke more than I had done for days. I had been made to promise, when we were last there, to read some of my own poems when we came again, and had agreed on the one condition that Bagnani in return should read aloud to us in Greek. The bargain had seemed worth making at the time, but faced with it now I began to regret it. A copy of my book was produced and when I had read several poems from it, Alister asked whether I could not remember one of the prose-poems which he had printed on his handpress.

'Say them "The Earth Lover," Monk.'

'*All their words are only foolishness. Whom shall I believe? For all are certain, yet all cannot be right. They tell me that I shall drink wine with the immortals in heaven; they tell me that I shall wander a shade amongst other shades in the sunless country of the dead; they tell me that I shall sleep eternally. But I know only that I have loved the gorse on the hill, and the small sheltered bay, and the coming of summer, and autumn, and the blue stillness of the sky on starry nights, and quietness, and the conversation of friends, and the soft kisses of children; and for all these let him that gave them bear witness that I was not ungrateful.*'

'I like that.'

'Can you remember another?'

'I think so. Have you any choice?'

' "Of one who has beauty." '

'*What have they given you, they who give all, wise thoughts to one man, sorrow to another, to a third a heart that no sad thought can enter? Have they given you these things; or have they given you others like them, safe, and secure, and in a quiet place? Or have they given you a gift that all hearts leap to tell of — for hearts are foolish?*'

The prose-poems led to a discussion on poetry and on the nature of rhyme and cadence. Bagnani refused to read to us from the *Anthology*, remarking, 'No, I feel more like Sophocles.' Going to his bookshelves, he took down one of the plays, found what he wanted and began to read. He read magnificently, getting better and better as he became more worked up by the passion of what he read. It might be Greek to us, figuratively as well as literally, but that did not matter; we could realise the heartrending, tragic grandeur of which the language was capable, its pathos and force. When he had read us as much as he wished of these dialogues between messenger and attendant, these terrific choruses, the talk turned to the Latin poets and he began to recite from them. Horace and Catullus were as familiar to him in memory as Yeats to us, and I began to congratulate myself on my bargain after all and on having an interpreter whom one could question on the different effects achievable in different languages.

'Sapphics could never be as effective in Latin as in Greek. I will read you some Sapphics by a modern Italian poet.'

He went to the adjoining room, fetched the book and read them, but to me it seemed that Swinburne had done far better in English.

'The Italian has treated the metre with too great freedom.'

'What of Italian prose?'

'Machiavelli has never been beaten.'

He read us a passage from *The Prince* which sounded to my ears forceful, business-like writing, but hardly musical. A poem of Carducci followed. Then someone mentioned Dante.

'Read us from Dante.'

He read us with exquisite tenderness the encounter with the ghosts of Paolo and Francesca. He read slowly, stopping every now and then to comment.

'Wonderful how Dante makes even the omnipotent unalterable law of God suspended, arrested for a moment by this power of love!'

I asked myself whether my two fellow guests were enjoying the evening as much as I was. Mathews seemed to be; he told us that Rendall at Winchester was the only other man who had ever made Greek live for him in the same way. Someone mentioned the German language. Bagnani or his mother deprecated its art and achievement and instantly an apple of discord had been thrown into the party which it took a little time to forget.

Mathews sat near the bookcase, behind Elisabeth, who was on the far side of Bagnani and directly opposite me. She was wearing a pale dress, cream or very light fawn, one of those dresses which can pass as evening-dress or not, as one wishes. Her beauty never seemed to depend upon clothes. She had the characteristic in common with Ella Maillart of being not actually indifferent to clothes, but steadfastly averse to becoming their slave. They were incidental, whereas character and personality were fundamental. She was beautifully dressed now, but one did not notice that, seeing only the extraordinary beauty of face, of carriage, of expression. There was something triumphant about her whole demeanour this evening. Perhaps the aureole of gold hair, perhaps the wonderful colouring with its faint suffusion beneath the transparent skin, perhaps the firm moulding of the different features, of the curved cheek, of the chin, made her seem more goddess and less girl. Certain it was that if the homage of the ear at this moment was Bagnani's, the homage of the eye was hers. Here was something perfectly achieved. My glance had only to rest on her for a moment for her to seem the living poem, fit to take her place beside every utterance, however lovely, from the past.

She professed herself quite out of her depth. We might talk. She was content to listen. Alister from his corner ventured a shrewd remark from time to time. Elisabeth remained silent. Her detestation of all theory, of all abstract generalisation, seemed to prevent her from taking part in the discussion. Once when Bagnani, who had been reciting Catullus for us for some time, embarked on another poem, she said quickly, 'That's not Catullus. That's Horace' – alone of the three to recognise instantly the change. But this solitary remark was the sole indication that she was as well qualified as any of us, to appreciate the entertainment that was being offered.

Talk passed to the subject of religion. Bagnani himself was a Catholic, but not his mother. As a controversialist, he showed himself astute. In two minutes we had got down to differences in outlook, fundamental and not superficial. There had been no skirmishing about the outposts. Revelation, verbal inspiration, a growing tradition entrusted specifically to a certain body of men – you either accepted these things or you did not. Both Mathews and I had sympathies with mysticism, he with Eastern, I with neo-Platonic, and I would have liked to contend now that the real Church is the one Inge has written of, the invisible one, the body of elect in all sects, the 'soul of the Church,' as Lunn, a Catholic himself, has put it to me. But across the small table on which the coffee cups still tarried, floated scraps of conversation between Elisabeth and Signora Bagnani, and in my anxiety to catch these and at the same time not to lose the threads of my discussion with the son, it seemed to me that I might be conceding ground that I had no right to concede. I could hear Elisabeth say, 'What I can't understand is at what point we began to have souls – when the soul was born,' and it was tempting to interpose and tell her that Plotinus thought of all matter as ensouled in some degree; even a stone was ensouled, until you arrived at last at nothingness, which was matter absolute and impermeable. All life is placed in an ascending scale according to how far it is capable of receiving the rays of Divine Soul, and permitting them to penetrate – that Soul from which all went forth and to which all will presently return.

From religion talk passed to war. Elisabeth had the rationalists' detestation of war; it was the supreme wastage, the final folly; and indeed, to all who see human existence as a brief individual adventure ending in complete annihilation, war is the very essence of the tragic in human life. Curiously enough, men without faith in a future life seem to find it as easy to die for abstract and national ideals as the believer, casting existence away with gallant indifference or almost scornfully, giving their one irreplaceable possession as though it were a trifle which was never of very much significance from the beginning. Many have no choice in the matter, but others are informed by a deliberate stoicism and gallantry, voluntary agents, but motived by forces and influences vaster than themselves, just as Homer made the gods responsible for most that took place upon the plains of Troy. Bagnani, but for a quite different reason, defended war. It was 'part of the game,' and if indeed 'man has eternity,' an amusing enough part. It still brought out many fine qualities. Biologically, it was no longer justifiable, for it meant the survival of the least fit, but, even admitting this, it was better than racial deterioration from luxury or sheer boredom. Elisabeth would have none of this. I saw her face light up with the fervour of moral enthusiasm; here was something absolute, definite, quite decided in her mind. To me war had been hateful largely because, as I had known it, it became soon not merely the defacer of all that was beautiful, but the greatest hypocrite, the supreme liar, the inconceivably base and petty and hysterical exploiter of men's enthusiasms through propaganda, the cause for which any lie was justifiable. It distorted men's minds by making them hate, not merely real enormities and abuses – of which there are always plenty – but manufactured ones, deliberately furnished in the salaried service of newspaper or cause. Such propaganda generally overreaches itself, and ends by driving youth's sympathies where they need never have been.

The symposium ended on war. It was after midnight. When we had seen Elisabeth home, we hurried back through the empty streets, to be stopped for a minute and questioned by a patrol of Fascisti as we neared the Borgo Santo Spirito. Markharoff unbolted the door for us, pale, his eyes heavy with sleep, the book he had been reading on the sofa still in his hand; and, more silent than usual, fastened the chain behind us and motioned us up to bed.

We felt a little ashamed at having kept him waiting so long, seeing him so obviously weary now. We knew that he must be up at cockcrow and at work on his studies. But no word of censure or reproach passed his lips. If he felt any, he showed it only by his silence. Infinitely good-natured, it would have been unlike him to complain. When we were late for meals, as we so often were, his quick '*Venez vite*' was his only comment, and now as we slipped apologetically past him his quite evident fatigue touched our conscience more than if he had spoken.

For some days now Mathews had been distressed by Schwester Edouarda's silence. 'She has not said a word to me all day.' He was convinced he had offended her in some way. Perhaps her Christian forbearance was at last exhausted by his extraordinary untidiness. His relief was intense when Markharoff explained the true reason. 'In Advent the sisters may not speak unnecessarily, and the Schwester Oberein holds all their letters for them until Christmas.'

The nuns rose at 4.30 a.m. each day, he told us, for prayer, meditation, and examination of conscience. 'Do you examine your conscience?' he added, fixing me with those brown eyes of his, so completely guileless, though I am not sure that their intense seriousness did not veil irony on this occasion. Appearing as they did, silently from time to time through the baize-covered doorway to attend to their guests, the good sisters were still vested with a slight air of mystery for me. We could only converse by signs. I remembered the shock and the sense of relief I experienced when I first heard Schwester Wunibalda laugh, as she brought in our supper on my second night, and gradually I had come to feel more at ease in their company. A day or two before we left Mathews informed me that we were invited by them to some service connected with the Christmas season. Passing through the mysterious doorway early one morning for the first and only time, we were conducted up a very narrow staircase and into a tiny chapel no larger than a fair-sized room. I knelt beside my Buddhistically-disposed friend while the nuns prayed in front of us at an altar decorated in blue, fresh as a child's dream, and we added our prayers to theirs. Presently we all rose and a hymn was sung in German, to a tune familiar to me. At that moment the sanctity of our surroundings, the simple piety of our companions, enveloped us, and we both, I think, felt proud that they had counted us worthy to pray beside them.

Our stay at the Suore dell' Addollorata had almost drawn to a close. Already my arrival from Florence that early December afternoon on the platform of the Stazione Nazionale, exclaiming, 'Naples, the day after to-morrow!' seemed so far off as to belong to a different world; for it is our moods, our states of consciousness, that measure time for us and not the ticking of a clock. For days I had been inventing fresh excuses to remain, or so at least it seemed to Mathews, who took a puckish delight in exposing them for the pitiable pretences that they were. It had become almost a game between us.

'I have discovered a magnificent collection of the Loeb Classics at Warner's,' I would say to him. 'There is enough reading there to last me weeks.'

'But your library subscription ends to-morrow. It is not worth your while renewing it for another whole fortnight.'

'I cannot go to Naples to-morrow. I have no Italian money. I have only Swiss and English notes.'

'There is no difficulty about that. I can lend you the forty lire for your ticket.'

Neither of us took these controversies seriously. And dinner at the Bagnani's had provided us with a pretext for remaining another three days. Bagnani had agreed to his mother's suggestion that he should take us for a day's motoring in the Campagna. The expedition would be to the district of Tibur, that Tibur of which Horace wrote to his friend Furcus Aristius, 'Do you know a happier or more beautiful place than Tibur, where the winters are mild, and where the zephyrs moderate the warmth of summer days?' Nine times, we are told, he mentions it, nearly always with a caressing epithet. 'It is green Tibur, dew-fed Tibur, Tibur never arid, leisurely Tibur, breezy Tibur, Tibur sloping to the sun.'

It had been difficult to fix a date. Bagnani could not manage the next day, so it was settled that we should remain over Wednesday.

213

'Where will you take them?'

'To Tivoli and then on to the site of Horace's Sabine farm.'

Once again I had hesitated until it was plain that Elisabeth was being included in the invitation, then given the suggestion my cordial and complete approval.

'But you don't want me,' she had said. 'Three men are enough. I am sure that you will be far happier by yourselves.'

We had all assured her that this was very far from being the case.

On Wednesday morning we met outside Bagnani's flat at nine o'clock. He was already waiting for us beside his big open Fiat, smoking a cigarette and calling to the maid to be quick with the sandwiches. We had struck a glorious day between two very wet ones; rain overnight had only freshened everything and the sun shone from an absolutely clear sky. We drove out through the untidy suburbs of Rome and headed across the Campagna, amusing Bagnani by telling him how the porter at the contessa's flat had sworn at us when we tried to come down in the lift, after calling for Elisabeth, saying we would break the machine which was meant only for ascending.

'Even when you want to go up he often won't open the lift door until you give him a tip.'

Elisabeth had taken off her hat and was sitting in front beside Bagnani, who drove, like Jehu, furiously. As we neared Tivoli, huge sulphur clouds from the streams joined with the mists sucked up from the plains and obscured everything. We had been watching the Apennines with delight, the more distant of them covered by snow, and we felt indignant that not only they but the sun which had been illuminating them should be blotted out by these rolling banks of mist. As we climbed the hill to Tivoli, looking back at Hadrian's Villa in the trees below, we emerged into sunlight again. Bagnani suggested we should avoid the Villa d'Este, known to us all already, but should pay a brief visit to the waterfall and the little round temple of the Sybil above it. 'You must see the waterfall from below; it looks best from there.' We drove straight through the town and left the car in an open archway beside a bridge. But the view of the falls from below was disappointing and only urged us to try from above. We climbed back up the road to the falls proper, passing the little temple of the Sybil, clinging to the very side of the hill above the gorge. The river, we were told, had been diverted from its old bed after a terrible flood had swept away half the town. It now flowed through an artificial tunnel nearly two hundred yards long

214

before emerging at the top of the fall. One could enter the tunnel and, daring one's friends to follow, walk along a narrow ledge to note the terrific pace at which the water moved, a heavy brick thrown in being swept along the surface for several yards before sinking. We descended to a third viewpoint which allowed us to see the water as it emerged from the tunnel.

'What a place to commit suicide!'

It was Elisabeth who said it.

'A quick death and a dramatic one, to be hurled along the swirling torrent like a stone from a sling, unconscious before you reached the bottom.'

'I'm not so sure. It looks to me as though the water strikes a rock there about forty feet down.'

It was hard to judge, so great was the volume of water coming over. I went and stood at the extreme end of the path, on a ledge near dripping shrubs. The fall of the water seemed almost continuous until it pitched into the basin far below to surge again in clouds of vaporous spray. The noise was deafening. I stood wondering if it were possible to detect in the drifts of spray a sequence or pattern which might reappear every few minutes. The quantity of water coming over at any moment seemed the same, its destiny by right should be no different, but the vapour rose in forms too vague and shadowy to be really distinguishable. Tiring of this amusement, I looked up at the fall itself, thinking that, if one watched for long enough that incessant drop of the water surging down the cliff, the effect would be hypnotic. When I turned round my friends had gone, but presently Mathews returned asking if I found the place conducive to poetic meditation.

'We have been waiting for you nearly ten minutes.'

I followed him back and we descended by even steeper paths to the Pool of the Sirens, a depressing spot, deprived now of almost all water, so that one hoped for their own sakes its occupants had deserted it long ago. The same was true of the Cascade of Neptune, a wild chasm nearly two hundred feet deep, once romantic but now reduced to a sorry trickle, jackdaws flying from side to side of the gorge, with an untidy tangle of undergrowth clinging to its precipitous flanks. Climbing once more, by a path up the far side of the gorge, we returned to the car, coming suddenly from deep shadow into sunlight, so that the morning infected us with its cheerfulness and we went on our way gaily.

We had turned our backs on Rome. A green marsh lay immediately

215

below us on our right; beyond that the hills rose on either side. Presently we passed the remnants of the old aqueduct, not mounted on columns, as in the Campagna, but at ground level, its weathered red brick contrasting favourably with the modern counterpart on the opposite side of the road, a tubular concrete eyesore which time had not yet had the chance to mellow. From time to time the car swerved as we met mules heavily laden with great bundles of brush-wood, or we would swing across the road to avoid one of the huge country carts in which three animals, of different species and size – a mule, a horse and an ox perhaps – pulled in unison, harnessed abreast. Our course followed that of the river, and passing through Castel Modana and Vicovaro I began to think that even without any archæological objective it had been worth while coming for the drive alone. Bagnani drove quickly, almost recklessly, talking continuously over his shoulder to us in the back of the car.

'Horace's so-called "villa" at Tivoli is spurious, but the Sabine farm to which I am taking you is almost certainly authentic. Tradition has assigned it to Horace for centuries, but it was only about fifteen years ago, and after much wrangling among the archæologists, that they excavated. All the familiar landmarks of the neighbourhood are there unchanged, only their names are altered, Vicovaro instead of Varra, Bradella instead of Mandella, Licenzia instead of Digentia. You can look from it across to Rocca Giovanna on the site of the ruined temple of Vacuna, and the scene is the one that Horace himself loved. The hillside is probably more fertile now than when the poet wrote, "Even the sloes and ruddy cornels bear their fruit more abundantly here than elsewhere." Cornels and sloes may have given way to olives and figs, just as walnuts and chestnuts have replaced Horace's oaks and ilex, but his description still holds good: wherever the hill is uncultivated it is still overrun with brambles and fragrant with herbs.' He began to chant actual lines from the poet vindicating the site, at the same time driving with such a casual air that pleasure in his conversation was qualified a little by dread that he would overturn the car.

The road curved continually among the hills, further and further into the country and away from practically all signs of life. At last, emerging into a more sunlit valley surrounded by huge cone-shaped brown mountains, we saw on a small hill, clinging untidily to the cliff's very edge, a crazy-looking little town, a mere part of that brown countryside, inanimate as the rest of the valley. Stopping short of it about a mile, we got out of the car near a green mound capped by trees, Bagnani leading the way up a slippery, muddy path between rows of chestnuts to a tiny wood beyond which, on a raised plateau, lay the site of the villa. A guardian in a peaked cap came from a miserable little shack nearby to show us the ruins, walls of about two and a half feet high of diamond-shaped stones set in mortar clearly indicating the position of the different rooms, the whole villa about the size of the average English country house. The man got down on his knees and started scraping away the heap of gravel and yellow sand which had been spread over a floor mosaic to protect it, then, fetching some bottles of water, he poured them out to make the colours show up better. It was the floor of a bedroom, very well preserved, the mosaic patterned to show where the bed should stand, and, giving only half my attention to the babble of archæological terms which reached my ears – *frigidarium*, *piscina* and the rest – I watched some hens taking a dust-bath under a thyme-bush nearby. The view Horace had known and loved seemed more interesting than the thresholds on which he had stood; a delightful view, intimate, peaceful, one on which a poet might look for days without tiring. Three children were driving a few sheep up the hill, throwing stones to direct them, and I began to think that the real tragedy, more distressing than the fact that Horace's walls had been pulled down to make contribution first to a bathing establishment and then to a Christian Church, was the fact that no flourishing farm existed any longer in this spot. The place was fresh, cool and lovely, a little breeze blew through it from end to end, between the hill on one side and the tree-covered mound on the other. The ground sloped gently away in front of the wood; a low hill, with three green fields stretched across it, lay to the left of the road, while beyond it a larger hill, cultivated and considerably less brown than its neighbours, rose by easy stages out of the plain.

'Imagine it in summer,' Bagnani was saying, while the three little girls, who had tired of their herding, jumped in and out of the excavated site of the bath nearby, 'far from the dust and heat of Rome, house-parties to enliven the quiet, the five small outlying farms to be seen to, the slaves to be given their orders for the day, an ode composed to Maecenas.' I was willing enough to imagine it in summer. But there was no need to go so far in search of one, or to bring the spectre of imperial Rome into the picture; any summer would do – last summer, next summer, so long as the hill threw its welcome shade over the little valley, the stream ran on, the chestnuts flourished and flowers studded the marshy grass.

217

We left the site and drove on, up a wild road rising steeply, with a sharp bend every thirty or forty yards, rock on one side, a sheer drop on the other, barren yet friendly hills all around. Suddenly, as we came over a final crest, Mathews uttered a sharp exclamation of delight. The line of the Apennines lay before us, their snowy summits almost Alpine in their effect. We could see for mile upon mile in the clear air. Above the mountains there drifted white, billowy clouds and an occasional dove-grey one. Bagnani stopped the car so that we might see better, and in Mathews' face I saw such an expression of intense delight that it was plain that for him this was the great moment of the day.

We were hard by Orvieto, and it was decided we should lunch there. Though the day was warm enough for an out-of-door meal, thirst sent us to the only inn in the place in search of something to drink with our sandwiches. The Trattoria Amici, primitive in the extreme and with exactly the same smell as an Irish country store, opened on to a courtyard where pigeons dozed on the window-ledges, and mothers sat sunning themselves on the doorsteps with babies in their laps. Little boys gathered round the unexpected novelty of a motor-car, in such numbers that it looked as though they were taking it by storm. We went inside and to the cleanest of white table-cloths were brought bread and cheese and yellow Frascati wine; and we ate with the appetite of adventure.

But it seemed almost a crime to be indoors and eating. I slipped out presently, and turned down a crazily-cobbled side street so that I might get a better view of the superb snow-fields edging the horizon. Lone, remote, their white solitude of winter contrasting strangely with the summer warmth of the day, the mountains edged the horizon; and I seemed, standing there, to share in their peace and their remoteness. If mortal man has any pleasures akin to the pleasure of the immortal gods he must surely have it in such moments of serene contemplation, when, for the very briefest span, he seems to have made that 'flight of the alone to the alone,' and when, indifferent to all other considerations, he looks on creation with delight, and without misgiving. I forgot my friends. I forgot the girl whose presence with us that day had been my chief reason for coming. The past slipped from my mind; I ceased to worry about the future, aware only of those calm, snow-covered slopes, far-off, un-troubled of man, like a picture on which the gods might daily gaze, finding each day fresh reason to approve it.

'Where have you been? We were looking for you.'

Bagnani was not sparing himself. Few people could have shown us so much of the country in the time at our disposal, and his programme was not yet completed. We paid the inn and drove on through wild country where little rough-coated, grey cattle, long-horned and with soft long hair, grazed in green fields. Presently the road dipped steeply, curving under a great rock-face until the plain was almost reached, only to begin the ascent immediately again. I heard the names Poggia Moiana, Fara, Fabra, Sabina, but names mean nothing on such occasions. I know that we climbed another hill, that the car was left in a courtyard, and that, following Bagnani, we came suddenly out on a terrace, a fifty-foot drop at our feet, and a most magnificent view of the whole Campagna stretched before us. Monte Soracte lay to our right, looking like a less-toothed Dent du Midi without its snows. We could see the Dome of St. Peter's. We could even get a glimpse of a little shimmering strip of the Mediterranean, fifty miles distant.

It was Elisabeth who noticed it first. She had enjoyed the day as much as any of us, but the sun was beginning to set over Rome, the air had turned chill, and she was glad to get back in the car and know that we were now heading for Rome. The sun was full on the windscreen, which made driving difficult. Bagnani, tired by the endless bends of the mountain road, drove faster now that we were on a straight one. A little foal trotting along the road turned suddenly as we tried to get past it, lurched into us and limped away, having struck its shoulder against the mudguard. A look of mingled distress and indignation came into Elisabeth's face, and, seeing it, Bagnani exclaimed, 'Oh, did I hit it?' Lamps were twinkling in the blue-green mistiness of early dusk as we passed the cloaked *octroi*-keeper and a moment or two later we were inside the town walls. We drove to the Bagnani's flat. He pressed us to come up and have tea. It was about half-past five and it was pleasant to find ourselves in the warm room, to drink many cups of tea, to smoke, to look at his etchings, his book of eighteenth-century engravings and some excellent drawings in coloured chalk by a friend, and to find before long that the symposium of a few days before had recommenced.

Outside Ireland, outside Dublin itself, I have never met anyone else who was so willing to range over the whole conversational field as Bagnani. He talked with the ardour of a man genuinely interested in ideas, not solely as intellectual playthings but as the stuff of life itself. Fond of paradox, perhaps a little too fond – contending, for instance, that the most dramatic and stirring and living incidents in ancient drama were not acted at all but merely described by messengers who crossed the scene, our modern craving for sensation and actual depiction putting us really further from and not nearer to the event; contending too that Buddhism was a poor religion compared with Christianity, because it was possible to be the perfect Buddhist, whereas the ideals of Christianity are unattainable and therefore a perpetual incentive.

Suddenly the conversation took, as it always does on these occasions, a more metaphysical twist. Bagnani was inveighing once more against all looseness of definition.

'One must have definition. Can you speak of "dog," for example, without using a definition? In science if one uses an expression one knows exactly what it means. But in philosophy it may mean anything. Everyone gives to a term the particular meaning that suits them. Zoology is certain of its definitions. An ignorant man seeing a Pekinese, a St. Bernard and a Shetland pony would say, "Three different species of animal," but zoology has defined two of them as the same. And if this is true of a word like "dog," how much more necessary is it in the case of an abstract term like "love." What is love? What do we mean when we speak of love? Could you get half a dozen people in the world to agree what exactly they meant by love? No. Each one gives the word the meaning which suits him.'

He flung the question at us challengingly in his high-pitched voice, and I wondered once more whether he was falling in love and if this was the metaphysician's initial and highly characteristic gambit in a game which had yet to be played. At the word 'love,' launched at us with his customary defiance, everyone's attention suddenly quickened. Till now – as he admitted to me later – Mathews had felt as though he were 'wandering in a fog.' Occasional rifts of light came through, but that was all. He could apprehend detail but not the general *suite d'idées*. But this latest challenge was intelligible to anyone. How indeed should one define love? Was it desire, affection, appreciation, wonder, or what? Looking at Elisabeth, the light falling on her face from a lamp immediately above her head, it seemed to me that if we were to discuss the subject at all the moment was well chosen. Only the abrupt way in which Bagnani had introduced the topic, with even more than his usual intensity, surprised me. I argued that wherever love was present there must be genuine benevolence of intention, an outgoing of goodwill. This was the one ingredient every definition must

220

include. Bagnani himself raged against all definitions alike, attacking each in turn. In the end a dictionary was actually fetched to see if it could give us any help, but it only proved that even the lexicographers could not agree.

It was getting late. We must be going. There could be no question now of our leaving Rome next day as we had planned. We had talked away the two hours when we should have been packing. Mathews agreed that this was so, and for my part I had never seriously thought that we were going. We would remain in Rome one more day. But even that did not permit us lingering now. Elisabeth would be late for dinner if we stayed much longer. The day had tired her. She had sat listening to the conversation, silent most of the time, taking no part in it. She would talk freely with Mathews and myself, but, perhaps because he dealt in abstractions, Bagnani always seemed to silence her.

We went down to the hall. The maid had called Bagnani to the telephone as we came out on the stairs and as we waited for him to return Elisabeth said suddenly:

'I can't understand you people who talk and talk, trying to put names to things, when names are quite unnecessary. Either you love or you don't love, but if you do love it is something you are quite certain about, it doesn't need words to decide it for you.'

Love was something one knew and felt and there was nothing more to be said. My heart told me she was right, and yet I was willing to argue the point. Bagnani, having returned to bid us goodbye and wish us a pleasant time on our travels, said to Elisabeth, 'Well, you are here for another week. I hope we shall see more of each other,' a remark that caused me a slight stab of envy, to think that his would be the privilege which we no longer possessed. She was to dine with them again. As we walked away, I defended the theorists. Ideas, imaginations, abstractions were not to be despised. Most of life, as we knew it, was based on ideas, someone's ideas.

'All thought filters down eventually to the mob and finds expression in life. One can trace an idea through its many stages from the philosophic treatise where it first originated to the magazine-story in which it finds itself in ten years' time. Even a writer like Joyce, even Bergson reaches the man in the street eventually. Thought is like water continually seeking new levels at which to percolate.'

But my argument did not affect her contempt for the spate of metaphysical reasoning to which she had just been listening.

'Words! Words! It all seems so unnecessary.'

'Haven't you discovered that most of us have courage enough to talk, but not to live?'

'Yes, but it's wrong. One ought to live.'

And then with an emphasis almost petulant, she added:

'We live more in one action than in a million words.'

The tram stopped beside us and we climbed in. It had been a wonderful day and Mathews admitted frankly that he was glad that our departure had been postponed. He was still straining at the leash but a day such as we had just had was worth having for itself.

We left Elisabeth at her door and walked back to the convent. Once again we were late. Once again we were obliged to run up the broad flight of steps under the archway. The bell was rung, the chain rattled and the door opened a few inches to reveal Markharoff. He must have been growing tired of seeing us arriving, breathless and hatless, on the steps ten minutes after the time supper should have begun, but this occasion would be very nearly the last.

'*Venez vite.*'

We washed and hurried down to the little dining-room. But the meal was spoilt for Mathews when halfway through it, Schwester Wunibalda appeared and presented him with a washing-bill of colossal proportions. The *blanchisseuse* was waiting outside the door, and he felt obliged to pay it without a murmur, for had he not seen his week's laundry return the day before and was it not at this moment in his room? He looked down the list of items, however, with a jaundiced eye.

'Four lira for washing a pair of pyjamas. Surely that is a little excessive; four lira, nearly elevenpence?'

Markharoff seized the opportunity for a little badinage.

'*C'est une blanchisseuse très distinguée.*'

It was that which gave her the right, it appeared, to charge such prices. And when we asked why she was so distinguished the reply was that she had a diploma and painted hair.

Though she lived in this street, '*Sie ist sehr klassisch.*'

Very classical. A classical laundress: whoever heard of such a thing? Markharoff smiled demurely at his little joke and suddenly I burst into delighted laughter, for it had just dawned on me that the washing-bill must be mine. It was not Mathews' at all. No wonder he was finding it a little difficult to identify the different items.

'You have paid for my laundry. How generous you are. You are always doing these impulsive things. I quite agree with you that some of the charges are excessive; four lira for a pair of pyjamas is absurd; but what does it matter when one has a friend——?'

A look of mortification and then of relief came into his face, mortification at the thought of having to dun me for the money for days, relief because the mystery had been cleared up. But soon he brightened, and, leaning his elbows on the table, began to tell a story of a German girl who had been kissed by starlight. She confessed to her priest. But the priest referred her to his superior, who in turn said, 'This is a heavier sin than I can deal with. I must refer you to God the Father.'

'And——?'

'God the Father said, "My child, that was what I made stars for!" '

Mathews' eyes twinkled as he told us. He was twenty, young for his age and shy. It was extremely doubtful if he had ever kissed anyone by starlight himself, indeed it was altogether unlikely that he had. But that did not prevent him from regarding benevolently those who had, or from taking a vicarious pleasure in romance. Just as he had viewed my own sudden susceptibility with a certain indulgence, so could he imagine the Almighty viewing indulgently the kisses of youth.

Next morning at breakfast he announced that he was going to the post office to ask them to forward his letters to Taormina. We would take the boat from Naples and go straight to Sicily.

'Then you must go to Taormina alone.'

'But why?'

'It is too soon to go to Sicily straight from here. And in any case when we do go, I shall let you visit Taormina alone.'

There was nothing he would have liked better. To tell the truth, this modern Marco Polo, despite his gift for friendship, and though he had been genuinely pleased to see me when I came to Rome, valued solitude so highly, or rather valued the novelty and freshness of impressions among strangers, so much, that his ideal travelling companion would have been one who on all occasions insisted on going in the opposite direction, meeting periodically merely to compare notes. The irony of the situation, however, lay in the fact that since I was the elder of the two, and since Mathews had only been allowed to travel because I happened to be travelling, I had, as it were, the casting vote on these occasions.

'You can go to Taormina if you like, but you must go alone. If you get ill there your mother will blame me.' I could not forbear smiling. 'Though you may not realise it, I am supposed to be your guardian angel. But for me you would never have been allowed to launch yourself across Europe. You are a little too volatile. I am the steadying influence in your life.'

He smiled and the subject was temporarily shelved. We were leaving Rome in twenty-four hours' time and our destination was still undetermined. Eventually, I persuaded him to come to Naples. We could decide there what our next move would be, whether to Palermo, by boat, to walk round Sicily with rucksacks; or to Syracuse and, thence, direct to Egypt.

It was our last day in Rome. La Ballerina had celebrated her birthday a few days before and it was mine to-day. The weather was chilly. In the Campagna the previous afternoon we had all three suddenly had the feeling of being in England. It may have been, as Mathews said, the starlings in great mobs against the sunset, or one or two stretches of oak wood and fields that were like the English countryside; but Elisabeth's explanation had been that it was because she felt cold for the first time for years.

The difficult issue of our next move having been decided, Mathews announced that he was going to say goodbye to Elisabeth.

'You remember that we told her we would go this morning.'

He began to talk of her, saying that in a week's time he would have known her two years.

'It was two days before Christmas when I met her. At a dance at the Rosat. During those two years she and I have been free of at least half a dozen countries: we could go where we chose. That is the right sort of life. And now she must go back to London and to a post. Do you realise that she leaves Rome in five days' time to go to Lausanne and from there to England? London is to be the grave of her two years of freedom.'

I had not realised it. What I had realised, and realised keenly enough, was that I left Rome myself next day. It was the separation, not what was happening to us subsequently.

'You go and see her now, Alister. I will change my book at the library first. I have time to take one out now and return it again this evening. I will follow you to the flat.'

He seemed to think this a good idea. When I joined them they were still discussing a letter that had come from England the night before, which disquieted Elisabeth, for it implied that her work there might not begin for several months. We told her our own plans, Naples for the moment, then Egypt or Sicily.

I reminded her of her offer to lend me Rodin's book.

'Yes, but you must promise faithfully to return it. I think that it is almost my favourite book.'

In all friendships when we are, at once, a little afraid that they may grow to more, but still more fearful lest a link so slight should break completely, the mind, like those lovers in Vildrac's poem, instinctively seeks out some excuse, some pretext which will prevent this happening. A piece of information promised by letter, a book borrowed which must presently be returned, any excuse is good enough so long as the door which we would leave slightly ajar is not finally closed.

And yet I knew that this door was closing, that there were a number of excellent reasons why it should close, and that though I might write to her from Egypt or Syria, to return her book, sanity would have been re-established by then. I would have forgotten, a little, that reverence and wonder with which I looked at her now, that instinctive, momentary homage which Rodin says the soul must always render to *la Beauté*, if it is capable of perceiving it at all.

I knew this, but, suddenly for a moment grown indiscreet and hearing her say that their plans to return to Lausanne remained unchanged and that they would be leaving Rome the following week, I remarked:

'You know it is a crime to leave this part of the world without seeing Naples. You and your mother should come there now. You may never get another chance.'

She shook her head. It was impossible. It was true that she ought to see Naples. But her mother hated new places, hated moving. It had taken weeks of persuasion to make her come from Lausanne to Rome and now she was returning at the first opportunity. If she must be abroad she preferred Switzerland. Nothing would persuade her to undertake a further excursion.

We rose to go. Elisabeth came with us to the door of the flat to say goodbye. In the hall, shaking hands with her, I said:

'You have added tremendously to the pleasure of our stay in Rome.'

The phrase was laughable in its inadequacy. Had my eyes ever hinted to her the extent of the debt? If Mathews were to be believed, they must have done so many times.

'Goodbye. Take care of the Rodin. You are bound by the most solemn vows not to lose it and to return it to me. It is written very simply. That is partly the beauty of it. And all he says has the entire conviction of his heart behind it.'

'Goodbye, Elisabeth. Good luck.'

Mathews was shaking her warmly by the hand. This was the last occasion on which he would see his unhooded falcon free and untamed.

We went down the interminable marble stairs to the street below, a wide street which looked deserted and unfriendly now that we took our leave of it for the last time, its gutter littered with scraps of dirty paper. Gloom had fallen upon us as soon as we left the flat. It was a day of rain and greyness. Back in the convent we read and wrote letters, Mathews muttering to himself in German, phrases whose significance were lost upon me, except that I understood them to indicate that he felt wretched.

That afternoon I took him with me to the shacks at the back of the Janiculum. They had haunted me since the day I first saw them. Perhaps the fact that it was my birthday made me think it would be kind to buy some trifles and take them to the children there. Mathews agreed at once. It had been raining hard all the morning. About three, when the rain had become a mere drizzle, we sallied forth, buying toys, chocolate and apples in some of the humble little shops near the Borgo Santo Spirito, little local shops full of not one but a hundred commodities. Mathews haggled lengthily, and unsuccessfully, when it seemed to him that the price had been increased fourfold for our benefit. A tram took us to the Janiculum and we made our way through muddy lanes to the road outside the walls; the evening was getting dark, mists mounting from the valley below and a vast melancholy over everything. There was the place fully as desolate as I had pictured it, with the smell of rotting cabbage stalks and wood-ash hanging about it. The sight of such squalor distressed Matthews as much as it had distressed me, and from a passer-by we learnt that the huts had been placed there by people who could find no housing in the city; something would be done for them eventually, but for the present they must stay here. Every city hides its sores, and Rome hid these. But, because they possessed a pathetic intimacy, because they still insisted on the necessity of the home, of the family, of the individual, because they looked out on a line of trees which would presently turn green and on fields where plants would grow, they were, to me at least, a little less terrible, terrible as they were, than the noisy, impersonal misery of great cities, where money is made, but where the souls of men are forced to starve.

Lights were already shining through the chinks and crevices of some of the huts. I had no Italian, Mathews very little. It had failed him when he attempted to tell the shopkeeper that he was an exorbitant rascal. But it was easy now to show what we had brought, to murmur that they were for the *bambini* – '*Per tutti i bambini. Buon Natale!*' – and to leave the adults to make the division amongst the children themselves. We gave our gifts to three mothers outside one of the shacks. Their faces lit up with pathetic delight and with surprise at this strange visitation. The oldest and most neatly-dressed of the three gave us a tired smile, revealing the many gaps in her broken teeth, while a younger woman poured out a stream of profuse thanks, of which we could understand only the general intention. Thrusting the packages into their hands, the tin motor-cars which might not survive the morrow, the sweets, the apples, we smiled, bade them goodbye, and, embarrassed by their gratitude for so little, turned and walked swiftly away. Skirting the wall for a few hundred yards we came to the gate of the gardens, passed it and made our way to where the tram-lines from the Piazza Venezia terminated.

The tram took us back to the city. Mathews was silent. It surprised me that he should be showing so much gloom over a departure for which he had been pleading for days. We called for our letters at the Poste Restante, went to a little German travel agency nearby and bought two third-class tickets to Naples and then made our way to Warner's. There we browsed for a time. Then we separated.

'I shall go on to Piali's. I want to take a book with me to Naples. I can post it back to the library from there.'

Bidding me abruptly goodbye, he departed to do this and then to return to the convent and finish his packing. I continued reading in the library, loath to tear myself away from the last collection of books in my own language that I was likely to see for some time. The library was deserted. Only the assistant remained. I continued to range along its shelves. Suddenly I looked at the library clock. It was ten minutes to seven. I must hurry. I would take no book to Naples. It might only be lost. I put the book I had been reading back on the shelves and hurried out. The weather had become worse still, and I was glad to jump on to the running-board of a passing tram and find shelter inside. I felt cold, tired, a little melancholy. Looking out as we passed the Via Ovidio, I could see the block of flats visible in spite of the driving rain, and thought to myself, '*Partir c'est mourir un peu.*'

Yes, it was true. To go away was to die a little, to die in some small degree.

SUPPER was just beginning. I ran up to my room, washed my hands and descended in haste to the dining-room. For a few minutes we ate in silence. Then Mathews said quietly,

'I have something exciting to tell you.'

For the first time I noticed, as it were retrospectively, that there had been an air of mystery about him, ever since I had joined him at table.

'Oh, what is it?'

'Elisabeth and her mother have been here.'

He laughed when he saw the expression upon my face. Connoisseur in sensation as he was, I had not disappointed him. I looked dumbfounded.

'Yes, they were sorry to miss you. They waited for a time, but you were so late. Elisabeth is coming with us to Naples to-morrow.'

There are only a few moments in life when things happen not so much logically, in the ordinary sense of the word, as logically in the sense of the fairy tale, that is to say, evolved not by any normal sequence of events, but by romantic necessity, so that, though we feel the appropriateness, we feel also an intense surprise and wonder. From the time when we read our first fairy tale in which, contrary to all probability, everything happens precisely at the right moment when for it to happen any other way would be completely fatal – from that time onward, we go through life hoping, on occasion, that exactly the same thing will happen to us, that the Gordian knot will be cut at the last minute and that something utterly consistent by this fairy-tale standard, but completely unlikely by any other, will happen to us. But it never does. Long ago I had abandoned all such hopes. Long ago I had ceased to believe in any last-minute interference with the natural sequence of events. And now to the hardened unbeliever the miracle had occurred.

With teasing deliberation, Mathews began to tell how after leaving me he had browsed in Piali's Library, choosing Loti's *Madame Chrysanthème* to take to Naples, and how, shortly after his return, Markharoff had knocked on his door. '*Es sind zwei Engländerinnen die mit Ihnen sprechen wollen*' ('Two English ladies want to speak to you').

'I came downstairs wondering for a minute if it was some joke, but there in the priest's room, seated on the sofa along the wall,

228

were Elisabeth and her mother – think of it, Monk, Elisabeth in a convent, and she hates them!'

He resumed eating as though this were the moment when dramatic exigency demanded a pause.

'Hurry up. Tell me more.'

He was not to be denied the joys of recital. He refused to hurry.

'I sat down between them on the sofa. They seemed shy, as if they didn't quite know where to begin. It had been the Contessa's idea. She said it was very foolish of Elisabeth not to go to Naples while she had the chance: it was perfectly *convenable* knowing us and' – he smiled as though not quite decided yet which of us should regard himself as chaperon – 'Elisabeth's mother would see this. What was rather sweet was that Elisabeth herself worried that we mightn't like it, that it would upset our plans. Of course, I told them that this was absurd, as we hadn't any. Then they said that you might object; it was unfortunate that you weren't here.'

'What did you say to that?'

He smiled more broadly than ever.

'I told them that it was a contingency which need not be considered. I was certain you would be delighted.'

Was he inventing it all? It was impossible to think so. No, it was true; the inconceivable had happened.

'She insists that we are to change nothing for her. We are still to travel third-class and she will come with us. Elisabeth, who is used to *trains-de-luxe*! We are to pick her up in the taxi to-morrow and when we get to Naples she is to telephone her address to her mother. We have only three days. She must be back in Rome on Sunday. You barely missed them, but supper was ready and they had a taxi waiting at the steps.'

He finished his story and looked at me triumphantly, like a showman who has brought off a difficult legerdemain. Though we irritated one another often, though our idiosyncrasies sometimes clashed, and though we quarrelled occasionally, it was in moments such as these, when he crushed the last drop of innocent enthusiasm and lyrical fervour out of life's experiences, that I liked Mathews best. Then he seemed to embody and express, not only his own youth, but also, by sympathy and identification of outlook, a portion of my own.

It was necessary I should go and pack or I would not be ready.

'Oh, I have one other funny thing to tell you,' he called after me as I reached the door.

'In the moment between their departure and supper, when I had gone back to my room, Markharoff again knocked at my door. When I opened it, he was there with the mad girl.'

He meant La Ballerina. 'She made a little bob, and solemnly presented me with a Christmas card from the family Kaulbach, with all their good wishes. Of course, I made a polite speech in my best German, and told her what joy it gave me to receive it, and asked her specially to thank her lady mother.'

The mother had been poorly for several days and we had not seen her. La Ballerina had had to celebrate her birthday in her absence. It was characteristic of the cordiality and friendliness which Mathews' genial boyish manner – rooted in genuine goodwill – inspired everywhere he went that this family, with whom he had exchanged only the customary greetings at meals, should now send him a card for Christmas.

'And then?'

'And then? She blinked, gave that extraordinary smirk she does, and went away.'

La Ballerina presenting the Christmas card of her family at the doorway of Alister's cell. The incident formed no pictorial image in my mind, though it might well have done so. Instead, I saw only Elisabeth and her mother sitting side by side on the horsehair sofa in the priest's room, explaining their advent and apologising for it. Mathews teased me, threatened to relate fully at a future date the mood and manner in which I had received his tidings; then he departed to his own room to pack.

In his journal he was to write that night:

'I told him quietly . . . he became outrageously happy.'

NEXT morning, when we left, the nuns, though it was still Advent, came to see us off and sped us on our way with friendly speeches. Even the Mother Superior, whom we very rarely saw, was there to bid us goodbye. Warm-hearted German phrases echoed in Mathews' ears and pleased him, and he kept replying to them with the same cordiality. He was full of promises that when he got to Jerusalem he would remember to send them something, rosary or medallion, which had been laid upon the Holy Tomb. As for

Markharoff, he shook hands with us so warmly and his brown, melancholy eyes lit up with such good will that it was plain he felt that he was losing friends.

At a quarter past six he had tapped on Mathews' door. By eight o'clock we had breakfasted and were ready to leave. The sun was full on the dome of St. Peter's, the morning air almost frosty. Carrying our suitcases and bulging rucksacks, we descended the wide steps into the Borgo Santo Spirito to summon a taxi which, as soon as we had entered it, seemed to become infected with a spirit of wild capriciousness, attempting first to charge a tram, and continuing to lurch and swerve violently on every possible occasion, as though wishing to remind us of the uncertainty of all things mortal.

Elisabeth was already standing on the steps with the contessa's maid. The latter helped her into the taxi, gave us her suitcase, then burst into laughter, as though this were the fitting climax to the many visits the two strange *Inglesi* had paid to the house. An elopement *à trois*. She was still laughing and waving to us as we turned the corner.

I remember the journey to Naples much as one remembers some dream, in which, in the midst of the chaos of event, the mind suddenly pauses, arrested by a sense of beauty, or by something which seems of enormous emotional significance at the time, so that when one wakes, it alone seems of importance. The station was crowded. It was one of those trains not for the rich alone, but for all who can or must travel. While my companions went to purchase a third ticket I fought my way along the corridor looking for seats. But there were none for late arrivals. In every carriage not-over-clean humanity was already in possession, surrounded by its packages, sighing with relief, and spitting on the floor with great vehemence, satisfied at having successfully staked a claim. I began to despair. Near the top of the train, however, three sleepy Italian porters, evidently off night-duty, had stretched out, and now made room with a good grace. One of them, a fat, laughing, genial fellow, made some joke; his companions told him to be silent. They allowed me to take possession of a corner seat by the window and two others, and on these I spread my impedimenta, sighed with as much relief as any other passenger, but forbore to spit. When Elisabeth and Mathews joined me they declared that it was one of the oldest carriages they had ever seen, even for Italy, but agreed that in the circumstances their courier had done as well as could be expected.

The train was late starting. Eventually we moved slowly out, past the dingy backyards, the high tenement buildings – an open window midway revealing for a moment every secret of some sordid room – and the blank walls and sooty hoardings which confront the traveller who enters or leaves any great city by rail. Presently came the tiny and forlorn gardens of back streets, and after them the straggling suburbs. At last we were out in the open country. It was still early. The roads were empty – so empty that it was a surprise to see a team of white oxen on their way to work.

Elisabeth sat beside me in the corner, Mathews on the opposite seat. He was in good form, slapping his gloved hands together, obviously in the mood when one must laugh for sheer joy, even though there may be nothing specific to laugh at. Just as the nostrils of a horse dilate with excitement, so he seemed to sniff the air now. It was for just such a day as this that he had shaken the dust of England off his feet, postponed any thought of a university career, and taken to the road with the rather reluctant consent of his parents.

Presently talk slackened, and while with enormous deliberation the train climbed into the heart of the mountains, we closed our eyes, imagining that we might sleep. But it was useless. I leant across to ask Mathews for a book, and, groping in his bulging rucksack, he produced *Madame Chrysanthème*. I opened it and, seeing Elisabeth lean forward to catch a glimpse of the page, I offered it to her.

'No, of course not. We can share it for that matter.'

It is this moment, salient as the memories surviving sleep, which emerges most clearly from the jumbled impressions of the journey. I taste again its sudden, still serenity. Now for the first time – one more step on the path which leads to actual love – I ceased to admire impersonally, in the way in which one admires a statue or a scene, and I felt, without recognising fully the significance of the change, a sudden reverence, no longer merely for the outward form, but for the individual. Was it that she herself had dropped the mask? Was it that she revealed an aspect of herself hitherto hardly suspected, at once more gentle and serene than any that I had yet glimpsed? She seemed younger, less assured, more like the day of our first meeting at Gargiulo's, which I had almost forgotten.

We read together from the same book. I sat by her shoulder, and whichever reached the end of the page first turned to see if the other were finished. I was the slower reader of the two, but I hurried now, reading quickly that I might have the pleasure of watching her reading, and might meet her eyes when, presently, they were raised in question to mine. She read gravely, not impatiently. The curve of her flushed cheek, the broad forehead, the downcast eyes casting an almost imperceptible shadow from their lowered lashes, and the tenderness of the half-amused mouth, all made me feel that for the first time I saw her as she truly was, no longer the bronze and silver-haired goddess, Athene or Diana, but some Greek maiden from the islands, from some seaport or village in the hills, a creature of living flesh and blood.

As we read Mathews watched us with amused benevolence. If he grudged us anything, it was not his book, but the looks which we exchanged, when our eyes happened to meet. Outside, as the train moved slowly forward, stopping from time to time at some wayside station, we could see a line of distant mountains, their summits covered in sunlit snow. But it was Loti's world which really held our attention, a world of sampans and of sailors, of tiny Japanese gardens on the hills, and of lights up the mountainside at dusk.

At midday we made our way down the train to the second-class restaurant-car, elbowing our way past the crowded carriages, each with its own atmosphere, fœtid, or acrid with the smell of cheap tobacco. We fell over the feet of those who preferred to eat their food in the corridor, over children, over suitcases, but were allowed to pass everywhere amicably and without resentment. One man was playing a Jew's harp, others were singing. In the dining-car we settled ourselves in a luxury which seemed plutocratic after the scenes we had just left, and prepared to enjoy the meal. It was to cost us twenty lire each, nearly enough for a whole day's residence in the convent, but it seemed well worth it, as the waiter brought *hors d'œuvres*, spaghetti, *côte de veau* and presently cheese and much fruit. The train was passing through a country of hills and olive groves, with an occasional palm tree, premonitory of the south. When we returned to our carriage we found that a huge nun, her face covered with warts, had possessed herself of Elisabeth's seat by the window. With an easy graciousness, she offered us the remainder of the space which had been ours. The porters had long since got out and in their places were now some artisans and a train-sick girl who was travelling with the nun, her eyes tightly closed, her head against the partition.

They looked at us with a certain amount of interest. We began to discuss our plans. All at once there seemed to be a tacit agreement that we should not stay in Naples. The weather was too fine to remain in a town. We must go somewhere nearby on the gulf. The first thing to do was to persuade Elisabeth that she need not return until Monday. For her to go back, as she had originally intended, the day after to-morrow, would give us no time to go anywhere. It was characteristic of the spirit in which the whole expedition moved that not once were the more orthodox baits of the tourist – Pompeii, Herculaneum, the hotel on Vesuvius – even so much as mentioned. We preferred to go where we could look on a world of living beauty, in which real people moved, and – if antiquity must be brought into it at all – not the antiquity of stones, but of the very scenes which Virgil had loved. I had been to Capri already once, and for this reason did not greatly favour it now. Ischia might be beautiful, but it was a little uncertain what accommodation would await us there, and if this was true of Ischia it was still more true of Procida and the other small islands. Though we had the feeling of fleeing from civilisation and our friends, we did not wish to flee too far. Finally, after much discussion, Sorrento, opposite to Capri and on the extreme tip of the southern arm of the gulf, was mentioned. It promised many of the advantages of the islands without itself being one.

'The boats call there on their way to Capri. We can go by boat.'

It had more than this to recommend it. The two German girls who had returned to the Convent had been loud in its praises. They had given Mathews the name of their hotel – the Hôtel de la Sirene – and the very fact that we knew of a prospective lodging was another argument in Sorrento's favour, for to arrive late in the evening, and to be at the mercy of every hotel tout, was just what we most wished to avoid. Only two things were necessary, to find out whether we could reach Sorrento that night, and for Elisabeth to wire her mother that she would not be back till Monday.

'Consult your Baedeker, Alister. Tell us about the Hôtel Sirene.'

He knew that I was poking fun at him; nevertheless, he turned its tattered pages and produced the information that (in 1874 or there-abouts) the Sirene and the Tasso nearby were the favourite hotels in Sorrento. ' "They are the oldest established and lie close together. Both are kept by the brothers Garguilo and are on the extreme edge of the cliff overhanging the bay. Charges are high and are the same in fact as the best hotels in Naples." Now are you satisfied?'

'Not altogether, unless the charges have come down in the meanwhile.'

'If the worst comes to the worst, we can take the train from Castellamare and drive on from there. But let's discover first if there is a boat.'

234

One of the men in the carriage, a mechanic in black gaiters, produced a thumbed *orario* from his pocket and we gathered round him to consult it. But our combined efforts to interpret it only ended in a general shrugging of shoulders and shaking of heads. Either it did not contain the information needed or it refused to yield it up. It was simpler to leap out of the train on to the platform at Naples and ask.

'When is the next boat to Sorrento?'

'There is one in half an hour's time.'

We drove straight to the smaller harbour. The little coastal steamer which had taken me to Capri eighteen months before was moored alongside the quay. It had been crowded then, for it was Easter and the time of tourists, but to-day there was scarcely a soul on board. An elderly English couple walked up and down the almost empty deck, and an old woman with a coloured handkerchief over her head came up to us in the hope of selling newspapers. From our seats on the boat we looked down on a host of fishing vessels, their nets piled in a great heap level with the gunwales. Behind us, like a defiant buttress thrust out into the sea, against which the waves could weary themselves, lay the Castello del Ovo, while up the hillside, towards its castled summit, rose Naples itself, with its fine parks and gardens, its gleaming villas, its lines of multi-coloured washing strung from window to window across narrow alleys, its innumerable streets teeming with life – a city of noise and clamour, of church bells, street-singers and shouting children, a city of memories of past glory and elegance, past bloodshed and disaster.

Five minutes before the boat was due to leave the passengers began to arrive. The emptiness of the deck had been misleading; we had reckoned without the Italian temperament. They came hurrying along the quay, umbrellas under their arms, carrying their purchases in big handkerchiefs tied at the four corners. No crates of live fowls, no great baskets of fresh green vegetables such as had accompanied me at Easter, but instead almost every conceivable shape and size of uncouth bundle clasped frantically by its owner. The steamer blew a blast on its siren, everyone began running, but this was only a piece of terrorism on the part of the Captain, who knew his clientele. What was more disconcerting was to find at the last minute that tickets were not to be bought on board, but must be purchased at the foot of the long pier.

'You must go and get them, Monk. It is your mistake.'

'Yes, and when I return I will find that you have sailed without me.'

Mathews smiled, but Elisabeth volunteered to come with me as proof that there was no plot to abandon me in Naples.

We hurried down the pier, laughing as we went. From the moment we had picked her up in the taxi she had proved herself the most accommodating of fellow travellers, a romantic like ourselves. She might have been one of those mediæval characters, disguised as a page, who accompanied their menfolk in adventure and shared their hardships without complaint. In the train the feeling, perhaps, that she had thrust herself upon us had made her passive – passive and a little silent; as though she were effacing herself deliberately. But there was no need for any such note of apology. Rather, she seemed our destined companion from the start.

We returned with the tickets. The steamer blew two more blasts to round up the most tardy of the late-comers. As the boat moved out the town opened up to view on the hill, revealing clearly the parts that had been hidden before. The air was a little cold – colder than it had been in Rome. Without any wind to speak of, there seemed nevertheless to be some strange kind of ground-swell at work, noticeable in the harbour even where the water appeared absolutely calm, and making the little steamer roll with a persistent deliberation the moment she was outside.

We sat on deck, green, turbulent waves, but without crests, rising and falling all the time beneath the ship, taking her with them. Vesuvius lay straight in front of us. Against the faint blue of the sky its outline rose very distinct in the clear, almost frosty, air of the December afternoon. Halfway up the sunlight rested on and kindled the trees in the brown wood on its flank and caught the white walls of the hotel. From the coned summit of the mountain a huge cloud of smoke billowed up, white at first, but more brown over the country towards Vietri, whither the breeze slowly carried it. Scanning the low-lying stretch of coast between Vesuvius and the sea, we strove to pick out the exact position of Pompeii, difficult to discern behind the many white villas along the foreshore, though we must have been moving over almost the very spot where the Elder Pliny's boat was, when scientific curiosity prompted him to draw nearer the fatal coast. The Gulf was at its loveliest. No view even in summer could have been more beautiful than the one we saw. The sun shone; the sky was a pale azure, the green, rapidly-moving sea rose and fell beneath our bows with a continually swelling motion. Once a fishing vessel passed us, moving swiftly, thanks rather to the tide than to the breeze then blowing, and we admired the brilliant hue of her orange topsail. Baiae lay behind us, and Procida, and the islands nearby, the promontory running out from the land seeming deceptively to join them. The mountain on Ischia rose out of the sea like some great pyramid which time has defaced, large, black and jagged. As the light gradually paled so its dark outline would take on a more sinister aspect, aloof, remote, almost apocalyptic, tossing its head to the sky, the least tractable of all the islands in the Gulf.

Crossing the bay, the steamer coasted along its southern shore. The first port of call was a mere cove under the crags, a rocky beach of piled-up stones, holding on the narrowest and most grudging tenure the little it had been able to snatch from the sea. From the stone slipway, black as the cliff which towered above it, boats were putting hastily out. The steamer dropped anchor and waited for them. A few peasants and fisherfolk, who had left that morning to shop in Naples, watched their purchases dropped into the bobbing row-boats and then descended themselves. A goat was lowered over the side, bleating plaintively. A fisherman who had come in the vain hope of a tourist rowed his empty boat away disconsolately, shouting some insult as he went, but his words were drowned by the noise of the chain as the anchor was hauled in. Standing out from the shore once more, we saw, behind the high cliff, unsuspected hitherto, deep curving valleys, covered with olive trees, running far back into the hills. As we skirted the coast the panorama unfolded like a scene in a theatre. It was grand opera scenery, checking the breath by its beauty, the colours changing with the changing light. A fisherman's hut, its walls a medley of soft pinks and greens and tawny browns, hung on the edge of the cliff; summer villas, perched in precipitate places, overlooked the whole expanse of the bay to distant Ischia; a tiny chapel, its walls a lovely pink like those of the fisherman's hut, balanced perilously on a crag.

Still hugging the cliffs and keeping well inshore, the steamer rounded a number of small headlands, which masked what lay immediately beyond. As we came into the lee of each we lost the sunlight for a while, the water became a deeper green, the air colder, and something, perhaps the melancholy of winter, infected our mood. But a moment later we would be reprieved. Once we emerged from behind one of these headlands to find the sun immediately above the saddle of Capri; for a minute or two our course lay directly on to the island, and we advanced along a shaft of light cast across the water directly on to the bow of the steamer. It was as if we moved to some millennial landfall. We could still see behind us the long, sloping line of Vesuvius, rhythmic and lovely, rising gradually until it joined the equally rhythmic and seemingly equally solid cloud of white smoke which coiled slowly upwards into the sky. The moment was imperishable; memory could never turn traitor and take it from us. As the sun dipped behind Capri the smoke became tinged with pink, a few clouds on the horizon, grey and opalescent hitherto, took on edges of pink also, the water at the shore's edge, which had been like melted sapphires, deepened now, and the light, as it often does at this moment of sunset, achieved a magic clarity, endorsing every object with a strange saliency.

The breeze which had been negligible was freshening, the sea became more troubled, the air definitely chill. We began to wonder how soon Sorrento would be reached. It was strange how with the departure of the sunlight the landscape underwent a metamorphosis; the colours that had delighted a moment before faded. The cliffs we were passing now were of dark-brown-coloured rock, gashed with red and cleft by huge chasms. Great caves, with portals as straight as a Corinthian column, and hanging lintels of jagged rock, added a note of savagery to the scene. On a spur of land right under the cliff, so near that they seemed only a few yards from us, were three or four large villas, cold, dark, tenantless at this time of year, spelling nothing but sadness in the shadow of late afternoon.

When the last of the headlands had been rounded, we came in sight of Sorrento itself, and the long line of buildings straggling along the top of the cliff. Their shuttered windows looked blindly down; their walls of sickly red and rain-washed yellows, and the flaking paint of their woodwork repelled us, and only emphasised the melancholy which we already felt. The dominant impression was one of gloom. Clusters of dark greenery clung to the fretted rock; here and there steep flights of steps, cut into the cliff, led to the dismal pathos of some tiny terraced garden, a garden which must wait another four months before the foot of any visitor would enter it, or any hand rest upon its rusty balustrade.

It is true that we were approaching from the poorer and less fashionable end of the town. As we drew nearer the harbour the hotels increased in size and importance, and a face appeared suddenly at an unshuttered window. A number of boats rowed out to meet us, the hopes of the owners of most of them to be disappointed, for Capri seemed the destination of nearly everyone left on board.

Once more the chain of the anchor rattled noisily, once more a chorus of voices shouted in rivalry. It was our turn now to move ourselves and our belongings hastily to the deck below. It did not seem at all too soon; we were chilled by the two hours spent on deck, and the boats bobbing in the swell below us presaged the end of a voyage that was becoming tedious.

'Listen, Alister. You must ask for our rooms in German. The Teutons are thriftier than the English and the hotels do not dare to charge them so much.'

'All right. But you must keep quiet, then.'

A barefooted fisherman swarming up a rope on to the deck claimed us as his, and kept us against all-comers. We climbed down a ladder into his boat and he asked where we wished to go.

'To the Sirene. We shall try it first, at any rate.'

But the moment La Sirene was mentioned half a dozen voices cried out that we were in the wrong boat; the Sirene had its own boatman. Our man, however, remained firmly insistent; he would take us wherever we wished to go; and, watching his gnarled toes pressed against the floorboards, we admired the vigour with which he rowed us the few hundred yards to shore.

Dipping a trailing hand in the water, Mathews cried, 'Do you know, the sea is lukewarm!'

It was, but we ourselves were cold enough. As we neared the pier, our oarsman called out that we were for the Sirene, and immediately a tall, broad figure, wearing a brown braided coat tightly buttoned, and a peaked cap with the ribbon of the Sirene encircling it, came forward to claim us. He was one of the few hotel porters who had troubled to meet the evening boat. His bland expression, small eyes, and tiny fair moustache gave him a Teutonic cast of countenance. Perhaps because of this – later we were to discover he was a Russian refugee versed in half a dozen languages – or because I had already let slip a phrase in my native tongue, our plan of masquerading as needy Germans collapsed immediately, and to our discomfiture he addressed us unhesitatingly in English. The fact that our linguistic ruse had failed, gave us the air of guilty children. At the end of the wooden landing-stage two officers of local Customs examined the baggage, but, thanks to the moral support of our uniformed guide, it was less than five minutes before we had transferred ourselves and our kit to a tiny skiff alongside, in which a boatman waited. Standing up in the stern as he directed operations – there was scarcely room for him to sit even had he wished – our commissionaire had a slightly Napoleonic air, at once majestic and a little ridiculous. He had taken charge of the situation. Presently he remarked:

'You will need one double and one single room.'

Struck then by the ambiguity of our ménage, we glanced at one another and all three burst out laughing.

'No, no. Three rooms!'

The man seemed to think he had blundered and offered us a clumsy apology.

Our journey had lasted nine hours. Looking up at the cliff which rose sheer above us for a hundred feet or more we saw the Hôtel Sirene, its name blazoned in white paint on the rock-face below the terrace. It was obviously a hotel of the first order. If we had not been so tired our instinct would have been to beat an immediate retreat. But we owed it to our companion not to prolong our wanderings and, in any case, it is doubtful if we could have faced the look of surprise, disgust and outraged majesty on the face of our escort had we taken it into our heads to turn back.

The boat rowed in under the cliff to a tiny jetty close to a number of wooden bathing-boxes, and, jumping out, the Commissionaire told us that a lift would take us up through the rock to the hotel above. We followed him down a dark and dripping tunnel cut in the solid cliff to the entrance of the lift. The door was shut, chains were set in motion and we began to ascend.

We emerged in a garden. Orange trees, shrubs and ornamental bushes, lit partly by an arc-light at the top of some steps, and partly by the cone-like flame of Sorrento's war memorial shining from its pedestal of stone, gave an impression slightly exotic and at the same time instantaneously peaceful and serene. Had he been unlashed from the mast and allowed by his fellow mariners to make his way ashore, Ulysses himself could hardly have felt more relief than we felt now, brushing against the dark, flat, shining leaves of the orange trees as we went through the garden to the door that had been opened for us. There was no need to hurry. I stooped under the weight of my heavy rucksack to read a quotation from Virgil cut in the face of the rock. Mathews went ahead to negotiate. He related afterwards how, on hearing the charges, he had spread his hands in genuine horror, and had obtained for us, by this spontaneous gesture of dismay, a very slight reduction in terms. There was a little diffi-culty about our rooms. Till the following morning there would be none vacant overlooking the bay.

'You and I must share one, Monk; it's annoying, but a double room is cheaper, that's one good thing. All the rooms seem gigantic. Wait till you see ours; you could billet a regiment in it.'

He slipped off his rucksack with relief, and watched it and his valise carried upstairs.

'In a sense, we are lucky. After the Suore dell' Addollarata it is highway robbery, but it is not really dear as hotels go. To be pluto-cratic for a change will be good fun.'

In phrases like these he excused his extravagance. It was one of the delights of travelling with him that though for the sake of seeing life he was willing to take vows of poverty, he could enjoy the occasion when these vows were relaxed.

Our room was indeed enormous. Painted butterflies fluttered insouciantly on the high ceiling; the large dressing-table was elaborately carved; our feet, accustomed to stone flags and bare boards, sank soundlessly in the heavy pile of expensive carpets.

'What a room, Monk! I can't even move across it without seeing myself in several mirrors.'

He was back in his Louis XV world, a world of chandeliers, gilt mirrors and damask hangings, the world he had loved as a boy. His courtly manners found their natural setting in this environment. He was no longer the Tedesco student with his haversack, he was once more the youth who, in addition to a pile of volumes, had put hawk, rod and gun on his first book-plate.

True to his Yoga principles, however, of drinking large quantities of water before each meal, he rang for the chambermaid now, and asked in his best Italian for '*Acqua calda, ed acqua a bere.*' 'All r-right,' she replied jauntily, and disappeared, to despatch presently an elderly waiter in a tail coat, who presented a croft of water to him on a silver tray. As soon as the door had closed again, this disciple of Indian asceticism burst into delighted laughter, feeling the incon-gruity between what had just happened and his own travel-stained appearance, with the contents of his rucksack strewn untidily on the floor around him.

Washed and groomed, we went down to dinner. Yesterday at this very hour, returning to the Borgo Santo Spirito, such an adventure would have seemed so far removed from the realm of reality as to be absurd, yet now, twenty-four hours later, by a sequence which seemed natural enough in retrospect, it was taking place.

The dinner was excellent, and we ate greedily, forgetting how only a few days before we had been loud in praise of the simplicity of convent fare. The hotel combined the feeling of a leisured Italian country villa with a very considerable degree of comfort. Modernised skilfully, it had kept its graciousness, its links with an earlier period when donkeys were in demand for a day's expedition into the hills, and the railway did not even extend to Castellamare. It, and the other hotel across the garden, were now the property of an Englishman who seldom came there except in the spring. The manager was an exceedingly handsome young Viennese, well-groomed, alert, intelligent, a man of such completely natural charm that one could not meet him on the stairs without wishing to exchange a few words with him. He was married to a good-looking young Italian, with glossy, black hair, quiet and composed, but equally friendly in her way.

When the meal was over we went, not to the great drawing-room, but to a little salon we had discovered halfway up the stairs, where no one came but ourselves. To our delight a fire was burning there; we had not seen one for weeks. The addition of Elisabeth to the party, the comfort and quiet of the hotel, the fire crackling and glowing, gave to our first night away from Rome, which Mathews and I had expected to be so lonely, almost the intimacy of home.

We sat over the fire, Mathews still chuckling over the chance which had brought us to these surroundings. Elisabeth denied that she was tired after the journey, and it was suggested presently that she should read aloud to us. Loti's book was fetched and in a voice very clear and flexible, with just that varying intonation which brings the written word to life, she began to read. It was a book wholly appropriate to our mood, romantic, idyllic. I looked at my friend clasping his knees at the far side of the fire, and it seemed that he radiated goodwill, as though he were saying, 'It is for this that friendship exists.' To read aloud, to share one's moods and emotions with companions capable of appreciating what we appreciate, to rest and relax, to be young – yes, that alone in itself – surely that was to be happy?

And yet to be romantic is invariably, sooner or later, to be a little sad, and to be young is to feel oneself at moments strangely old. Loti's adumbrations on the subject of marriage had turned the talk in that direction.

'The best, indeed the only reason for marrying is that one is in love.'

I looked at Elisabeth, surprised that she did not qualify her statement in any way.

'To marry with that as the sole reason is not enough. One needs something more. Affection. A sense of assured affinity.'

Mathews pondered the point:

'A sense of assured affinity is only one aspect of love, Monk. Love to me is rather' – he paused for an instant – 'a state of ecstatic suspense.'

Ecstatic suspense. Though seven years separated us in age, I was still young enough to appreciate that he had given the ideal definition of love in youth. To be always on the brink of the illimitable, with the tremor of uncertain hope in one's heart, that was to be in love and to know at once its anguish and its joy.

'Yes. All the same, the Japanese marriage of Loti was a flimsy, artificial, coloured-paper affair. Love has stronger elements in it than that; devotion, loyalty, shared sorrows, as well as shared delights.'

No one seemed disposed to contravert this, but prompted by some link in the conversation we began to lament the fact that we were growing old.

'Monk admits that he is bitterly envious of my youth, Elisabeth. If he does or says anything with a touch of malice in it, he ascribes it to unconscious jealousy on his part.'

'Alister is right. A Faustian jealousy seizes one and finds expression in some sneer or jibe, or in a mere domination of will.'

Mathews looked pained.

'You are a little unfair to yourself. Anyone who analyses his own motives closely generally is. All the same, I don't see how eight years can make so much difference. But I know what you mean. Do you know, I myself often feel old. When I look back to my arrival in Switzerland——'

This was too much. Elisabeth, who was twenty-two, had spoken as though she were falling into the sere and yellow leaf, but when Mathews, who would only attain his majority some months later in a mountain-village in Greece, spoke also in this strain, the absurdity of the conversation dawned on us, and we burst out laughing.

The wood fire had died down. It was time to go to bed.

'Think, Monk. You will wake up in the morning and see butterflies flitting in the cerulean blue above your head.'

'Yes, and I have only to cross the corridor to look out on the whole Gulf of Naples.'

The whole Gulf. Heavy curtains hung across the window of the room, but, drawing them aside, we opened a glass door and went out on to the tiny iron balcony. The breeze had dropped since dusk, and the air was mild enough. The night rose above us with its myriad of stars. All round the bay could be seen a number of lights, near and distinct, or distant and uncertain. We could hear the hushed lapping of the waves far below, and looking down the sheer face of the cliff we saw a coiling eddy of black water where some lamp near the water's edge cast its light for a few feet into the darkness. Tact, an impulse of generosity, or mere chance, made Mathews leave us for a moment alone. Standing beside Elisabeth on the balcony, I said quietly:

'Give me a kiss.'

In all adventures of the heart there comes a time when one must either go forwards or turn back. To see things in the germ, as Laotze says, is wisdom. To stop them in the germ may be common sense. But if one has not stopped them – what then? I had made no secret of my admiration, and to stand there, now, in silence, and by starlight, seemed the part of a laggard. What had God made the starlight for? Conscience, forgetting that mine had been the original gambit – 'You should see Naples' – stilled itself with the equivocation that all that was happening since we had left Rome was none of my doing; it was Fate's. As such it should be accepted gladly and gratefully. I told myself there could be no misunderstanding on either side, and since this was so, it would be foolish not to take those few kisses which the logic of event offered, and which even loyalty itself could scarcely grudge.

She shook her head gravely, as though my suggestion were a piece of folly which from the start it had been tacitly agreed should be ruled out. I heard her say very quietly, 'No,' and conscience had enough vitality left to make me feel a faint sense of relief. Indeed, 'No' seemed as good an answer as 'Yes.' A philanderer would have become more urgent, pressing his point, instigating manœuvre and counter-manœuvre. But the only kiss which is worth having is the kiss given freely and eagerly, the unabashed kiss of affection, or the candid and passionate kiss of love. To steal such kisses is impossible, and all others are but the mimicry of puppets aping emotions which they do not feel.

Mathews rejoined us, saying that we would catch cold if we remained outside any longer. We would decide to-morrow what we should do, when we saw what kind of a day it was. Perhaps an expedition to Capri, perhaps one along the coast. If Capri, then we must be up early, for the boat left soon after ten. It was still undecided whether we should return to the Sirene or not; we could settle that when the morning came.

But when we woke next morning, the point had been already settled. Alister had leaped out of bed at seven, wakened probably by the early departure of some visitors. He felt responsible, on occasions like this, for seeing that everything ran according to schedule. If we were going to Capri, he must call Elisabeth; and, going down the passage, he had knocked on the wrong door, and been roundly cursed by the occupant of the room, an Englishman, for his pains. Hearing his voice raised loud in apology on the landing, Elisabeth had come to her door, telling him that she had been sick in the night. The cold and fatigue of the journey must have upset her. There could be no question of an expedition for her that day.

Mathews returned to me lamenting this piece of bad luck. I slipped across the corridor to look out from the window of a room just vacated by some visitor. There was the Gulf. In the half-light of dawn the outline of the opposite shore showed dimly. The sea was choppy; the day had a threatening air. A siren sounded. It was the steamer returning from Capri on its way to Naples. The waiting boats rocked even more than they had done the night before. Down on the beach a long line of people were hauling in a circular fishing net whose corks floated on the surface of the water. The catch would go on the steamer, to be sold that day in Naples. Girls strained at the rope as well as men, bare-footed, their sleeves rolled back to the elbow, brightly coloured handkerchiefs on their heads. In the grey morning light these fisher-folk, far below me on the beach, looked like figures in a dream.

Mathews joined me. He was full of sympathy for the invalid, but a little concerned as to how the day should now be spent. We agreed that it was well we had come to the Sirene instead of going in search of cheaper lodgings; to be ill in some dingy *trattoria* would have been dreadful. When we had breakfasted we went up to Elisabeth's room. She smiled ruefully, a little sardonically at us.

'Well, I knew that I should spoil the expedition.'

We assured her that she was completely wrong if she thought that. It had been worth coming for yesterday alone, though we reproached ourselves for not having moved sooner from the upper deck of the boat. It was foolish also to have gone out on the balcony and lingered there without our coats. It was our fault that she had caught this chill.

'The maid has promised to move me across the corridor later in the morning to a room where I can look out on the bay. I am going to try and get some sleep before that. Now, remember you are not to alter any of your plans on my account.'

'They are to move us to a room above the cliff too. That was the agreement last night if we stayed. Several people went away this morning.'

I told her that Mathews could not make up his mind whether to go to Capri or not.

'Go, of course, both of you. I shall be perfectly all right and when you come back in the evening you can tell me all about it.'

'There is no question of Monk coming. He has been there already. He spent ten days there. I doubt if I shall go. The weather——'

The day, which had been only tolerably fine when we first looked out, had clouded up considerably and rain threatened.

'Wait half an hour and then see. You will know better then. You say that the boat doesn't go until ten.'

'We have brought you some illustrated papers, a thermometer, aspirin. Is there anything else you want? If you have a chill, you had much better stay where you are. You have plenty of books?'

'Yes, plenty. Alister brought me some. I don't think I have a temperature. When I have had some sleep I shall be all right. I am a fraud. I don't deserve all this attention.'

She smiled at the solicitude of her two cavaliers, and the maid coming into the room at that moment smiled at us too, cheerfully, a little archly, as though she found herself cast for a part in *Cosí Fan Tutti* or *The Barber of Seville*.

We went down to the *grande salle*. Mathews produced his book; I fetched my journal and began to write down notes of the journey from Naples – scenery may seem ineffaceable in memory at the time, but it is as evanescent as mist unless we take the trouble to record it. I thought of Curzon's reply, when someone had asked him the secret of travel: 'Read about it before. Think about it at the time. Write about it afterwards,' and then he had added, what in certain moods would have seemed to Mathews the heart of the whole matter – 'Above all, travel alone!'

From time to time we looked towards the window. A scud of rain had swept across the bay, but now the sky cleared and it looked as though it might be fine. Alister decided to go. He fetched his rucksack from his room, collected a sandwich lunch from the waiter and professed himself grateful for my offer to see him off. Together we made our way through the garden, the lift plunged us down its damp and drafty shaft through the solid rock and we emerged on the quay, a chilly spot now with no other passengers in sight and scarcely a *concierge* from any of the hotels, for this was a steamer on which visitors were unlikely to arrive. I watched the tall figure of my friend, knapsack on back, climb into one of the little bobbing boats to be rowed out to the steamer, envying him his trip very little this particular day with the wind blowing and the sea rough. Then the lift took me once more to the top of the cliff and I made my way through the garden to the road.

The morning was mine to spend as I chose. I would go for a walk. I turned and followed the tramline through the town till it ended, strolling along in a mood at once idle, happy and aimless, feeling that freedom from all responsibility which is the joy of the traveller. In a mood of this sort we view life with so much detachment that it almost seems to prove Buddha's point, that liberation from any personal wish is the secret of happiness. Is it that we are freed from all desire, or is it that our desires are limitless, and yet are momentarily satisfied when we identify ourselves for an instant with what in all probability we will never see again? Everything which we enjoy then, we enjoy disinterestedly; existence has neither past nor future, and, when we turn away, time will stand still at the point at which we left it for evermore. Even in childhood I had discovered that a house, a window shafted with sunlight, or the spangled shade of some vast beech tree thrown upon the grass of a lawn, would become, imaginatively, so completely mine – in the instant that I drove past it in my grandmother's carriage – that I could live a whole lifetime there before the horses' heads were once more turned towards home.

The shops amused me with their gay handkerchiefs and shawls, their great dolls dressed in the costume of the district, and their other souvenirs tricked out to catch the eye of visitors. But the shops soon ended. A little further on two grey stone tablets, cut in a rock by the roadside, offered to the attention of the passer-by a poem by Tasso, together with a translation into English so vile that it was impossible to understand its meaning. The self-confident linguist had been unfortunate all round. There was a misprint as well. 'Look it at sea.' Evidently a proof-reader was necessary, even when one's words were being cut in stone.

The road curved continually under high faces of rock, and after about twenty minutes' walking I found myself at the Capo di

Sorrento. Above the road a long, pleasant building, white-washed and looking straight across the bay at the high mountains immediately behind Sorrento, proclaimed itself to be the Pension Miramare. Curiosity and the thought that I might one day return to the district made me mount the flight of steps from the road; and the pleasant-faced woman who appeared on the veranda to answer my questions told me that she was Danish – she spoke English well, as nearly all Danes do – and that she had been there several years. She had no guests now, but later in the season there would be plenty.

'The Russian novelist Gorki lives in that villa across the road. You can just see its roof below there, amongst the olive trees. No doubt you have heard of him.'

So Maxim Gorki lived here, amongst the palms and the olive groves, reluctant to return to his native land, where they had named a town after him.

'His lungs——'

She gave me a postcard of the view from her porch to remind me of the place, told me how to reach the Roman ruins which were right on the sea's edge; and, crossing the road, I wondered whether I should see Gorki's pale face and sunken black eyes, familiar from photographs, as I skirted his villa. The narrow lane, however, lay between high walls; two dogs ran barking along the top, and presently I emerged on to a slope of land strewn with grey rocks, which ran down to meet the sea. The Roman villa had been built on its extreme tip; like those at Baiae it seemed to have one foot in ocean, one on earth. The square blocks of its foundation – vast rooms built almost on the water's edge – huge mortared arches, a causeway that might have been part of a bath or a tunnel, battered by centuries of storm, still held their own. It was a stupendous site to have chosen. Whereas younger ruins are often dank and melancholy, ivy-strangled, and seem to carry with them an evil heritage from the past, these, after two thousand years, were clean and sweet, swept by the wind and washed by the waves, reflecting still the mind of their owner and suggesting the sunny weather when builders had first brought white stones to that place. The breeze blew in my face, bracing and salt; I could see one small fishing boat running before it with a single sail. Behind Sorrento, a mélange of many-coloured walls perched on the very edge of the cliff, rose the mountains, first a line of low brown mountains scarred with rock, then a line of higher ones beyond, whose summits, touching the clouds, looked grey.

I had no regrets for Capri. A shower broke over the sea, but it missed the promontory, so that the sunlight shafted down upon the villa, and on the half-submerged platform of white calciferous rock glimpsed in the water below. The sea was deep blue, troubled with white crests, and changing under the influence of the drifting clouds now to indigo, now to a deep shade of green. The waves broke quickly over the rocks, carrying their spray almost to the place where I was lying. Only when I had grown cold did I move away to continue my walk round the promontory. But a wall had to be climbed, an orange grove crossed and several dogs driven off before I came out once more on a narrow headland path, slippery and a little dangerous, which brought me presently within sight of a fishing village, and of Capri, five or six miles off, rising like some great monster out of the sea. The main road was near at hand, and I turned back along it well satisfied with all I had seen.

It was almost lunch-time when I got back. I had enjoyed my walk. Running upstairs, I washed hastily, for a bell had already sounded. I returned along the passage and knocked at Elisabeth's door. There was no answer. Of course, they had moved her to a different room across the passage. I tried the door opposite and knocked again.

'Yes. Come in.'

She was sitting up in bed, propped against two pillows, the coverlet strewn with the books and papers we had brought her earlier in the day.

She smiled when she saw me.

'How are you now?'

'Quite all right. I tell you there is nothing the matter with me. I was just tired. And perhaps I caught some kind of chill.'

'Alister has gone. He will have had a rather rough trip. I am going down to lunch. I will come and talk to you afterwards, if I may. What are you having?'

'The maid is getting me something. I really only want fruit, but she insists on my having more than that. She is really rather charming. I could not have any one kinder, or more vivacious and amusing to look after me. The manager's wife has been to see me too. She brought me more papers.'

I went down to lunch reassured and in a mood of elation, partly the effect of my walk, but partly also the outcome of having reached a resolution, though what it was that I had resolved I myself could hardly have said. There were only half a dozen other guests lunching, and they maintained the reserve of the night before. I spoke to no one, no one except the waiter spoke to me. From the table where I sat by the window I could see the crests of the waves rising one behind the other, like the tree tops of a miniature pine forest. There was undoubtedly much more wind now than when we woke this morning, or than when Mathews started on his trip. But I need not pity him; he was a good sailor.

When I finished I went up to Elisabeth's room to find her smoothing back her hair from off her temples with a little ivory comb, rather like a child that wishes to make itself tidy. It seemed absurd that someone who looked so young should have been lamenting her lost youth only the evening before. She was wearing a pink dressing jacket, wide-sleeved and edged with fur. Her hair, now brushed to one side as if held by a slide, though no slide held it, gave her again the appearance of a sea-nymph or dryad, and once again, as on the previous day in the train, it seemed to me that I had been admiring a stranger hitherto, and that I was only now beginning to know her as she truly was.

I crossed the room, sat down on the bed beside her, and said:

'Give me the kiss you refused me last night.'

She looked at me with eyes half-reproachful, half-tender, as though she had expected this moment and yet in a sense regretted it.

'Is that fair to your girl?'

'She will forgive me.'

'Will you tell her?'

'Of course. One can't lie where love is concerned. One must tell everything.'

'When will you tell her?'

'When I return. It would be cruel and foolish to tell her now. She will forgive me when I am back.'

'That is one way of seeing it.'

She turned her head and with one of those gestures of extreme simplicity which we remember long afterwards, gave me her mouth to kiss. It was as though the tenderness of which I had scarcely suspected her till the previous day proved itself now, in the warmth of those lips offered me, lips half-opened as though she were about to speak, and then suddenly silent.

I had no regret. I had broken faith with the absent, but it seemed a small crime in my eyes. If it is possible to speak of kisses at once chaste and passionate those were the kisses that I now gave. Like Daudet's shepherd in the Pyrenees, pointing to the wheeling arch of night, and describing the constellations to his master's daughter, who has been benighted and whose adored head rests sleepily against his shoulder, so no dark thought crossed my mind now. Love there was between us, but love of a strange kind, unspoken, without protestation, only admitted when our eyes met; a love without past or future, without expectation or hope. And yet it filled me with a sense of triumph. I sat and talked to her; praised her as I had done so often, but more openly; laid my cheek close to hers and breathed the very faint scent of eau-de-Cologne which seemed to come from her hair. Once she put her arms about my neck and with a gesture of infinite tenderness, a gesture at once voluntary and lovely, as though she would prove it was not solely to my importunity she yielded, drew me to her for a moment, kissing me of her own accord. The next instant her arms were withdrawn. It was I who gave, she who received my kisses, she who surrendered her mouth to mine.

The room to which they had moved her was a vast one, light and airy, with a radiator by the window, and a fire, which they had lit for her, burning in the grate. A vast mirror six feet high, and almost as broad, reflected, as though it were a wall fresco, the view of the gulf outside with a boat crossing it, a view so much in the convention of Neapolitan art that it was a little difficult to believe it actually existed. Crossing to the great window, I looked out. Yes, there was the sailing-boat, tacking up slowly against the wind. The afternoon had turned out indifferently fine. Occasionally the sun would come out, and then the water of the bay would turn from a sombre grey to a vivid pale green, flecked with white, but the day remained unsympathetic. What was happening to Alister? How was he faring?

'Look up at your ceiling. It is strewn with the whole galaxy of Heaven.'

Instead of the butterflies which had amused Mathews so much in our room the night before groups of painted stars of gold and silver had been scattered at random in a firmament that was not solely the Almighty's handiwork.

'I know. I have been admiring them. Especially the cluster over by the window. The gold are the fixed stars, the silver are the planets. Only there seem too many to be the planets.'

Someone knocked at the door. It was Madame, the black-haired wife of the charming Viennese, come to enquire for the invalid. She remained talking for a little while; perhaps she felt she had some responsibility towards this girl, for when I suggested another walk she encouraged me at once in the idea, saying that there were a number of interesting ones, all within easy reach. Her husband would help me. He was called and between them they explained how I could climb the hill at the back of the town and get an excellent view from the monastery near the top.

A steep little path almost opposite the hotel took me presently through the yard of a farm where a heavily-built girl in straw slippers showed me the paved track I was seeking. High walls either side of the alley way shut out the view, but, stepping into a field where vines were growing, I could look back on the orange groves rising up the low hills on the far side of the town, and see how the rain from the heavy showers that morning was still lying in the shallow trenches dug around the vines. Crossing an orchard, I drew near the monastery. It was an untidy collection of pink-washed buildings, including a theological seminary and a charity school for younger boys. Let haphazardly into a wall at one side of the path were a number of small glazed tiles, crudely designed. One could recognise Elijah being fed by the ravens, Daniel in the lions' den, and St. Francis with the birds. On the far side of the orchard an open doorway drew me for a moment into a low-roofed stable where some grey and fawn-coloured cattle, none of them too well fed, were slowly chewing the cud. I passed the chapel gates and continued round the side of a white building till I came upon a group of little boys playing a game. They looked cold, unhappy and uncared-for. In an angle of two walls sods had been heaped up and a crib made; toy animals were gathered in an enclosure outside a little cave, while in the cave itself a tiny Madonna was dangling from a string noose around her neck. Evidently imagination had been unable to conceive of any other way of keeping her upright. Some older boys, less numb with cold, less unhappy-looking, worked assiduously in a field nearby; others played a game of bowls with great wooden balls on the uneven playground. A grubby-looking theological student, dark and unshaven, passed me, trailing his cassock over his arm; an abbé in a wide hat crossed the playground. It seemed to me that I had seldom seen such a windswept, cheerless and uninviting spot; even the little crib with its strangled Madonna appeared only an ironical commentary on the Christmas season, though in the eyes of the children it must appear a thing of beauty, the one liberating touch in a scene of depression.

As I went down the hill I saw that the boat from Capri was coming across. The smoke from its funnel blew out in a long line behind it. If I hurried, I would be in time to meet my friend.

Mathews, burnt a deep brick-red from the wind rather than the sun, had a graphic account to give of his day. The steamer had stopped at the Grande Marina, and then gone along the cliffs to the Blue Grotto. But it was doubtful if anyone could get into the grotto with the sea that was running.

'There were half a dozen boats waiting a little way out from the cliff. Five of us decided to go, but only two people were allowed in each boat, and I found myself odd man out. My boatman didn't like that, and kept shouting up to the deck for another passenger. At last a handsome young Italian, with patent leather boots and white spats and an elegant black coat – a commercial traveller, I suspect, for I had noticed him on deck with his shiny leather bag – came gingerly and quiveringly down the ladder, to join me in my cockle-shell. He didn't want to come, but I and the boatman persuaded him. It was exciting, Monk, our little fleet bobbing up and down like corks on the water. I asked the boatman if he remembered the Tedesca whose boat had capsized one day last week. Oh yes, he remembered her well. "It was very rough that day. *Molto brutto*. It was very rough to-day also." You know the entrance to the grotto is only three or four yards wide so that the boats can't row?'

'Yes. The boatman pulls you through by a chain along the roof of the channel.'

'Exactly. But you went on a calm day. To-day whenever there was a big wave the whole entrance filled completely. We had to wait a quarter of an hour before we could even make the attempt. Then the first boat dashed in. But a wave caught it when it was halfway and for several seconds we saw nothing but foaming water and heard an awful thud as the wood struck the rock. Our own boatman drew his breath despairingly.'

'It's their own fault. Sooner than lose their money on a bad day the boatmen take these risks.'

'They only get ten lira and whatever tip you give them. Anyway, when he saw what happened to the first boat, *Monsieur le Commis-Voyageur* said he must return to the steamer immediately. The boatman didn't like that at all. He clasped his hands begging the man to stay. "*Prego, caro signor.*" In a few minutes our boat would be able to go in. Honestly, you would have laughed if you had seen it. The commercial traveller insisting that he must go back and the man imploring him to stay. In the end he took him back to the steamer and then returned with me. After ten minutes' more waiting we got through. I had to lie flat on the bottom of the boat, and only got an earful of water and my knees wet.'

He paused to adjust the strap of his rucksack over his shoulder before we entered the lift.

'And what did you think of the grotto?'

'Superb. It is as though there were blue lamps everywhere under the water – that is, at the entrance end where the light is strongest.'

'You probably had less light than we had. I was there in April. Did a boy swim round in the water looking like a silver fish?'

'No.'

'A youth of about sixteen did when I was there. And then he climbed out and stood on a rock with his knees still in the water and sang "*O Sole Mio*" in a voice as good as Caruso's. A magnificent voice. I suppose it was really the echo that made it seem so.'

'I envy you that, but you can hardly expect anyone to do that sort of thing in December. Anyway, the real problem now was would we be able to get out. The sea was getting rougher all the time, and I had visions of being stuck there for twenty-four hours or more. Between waves the air was sucked through the channel with a sort of hissing noise and when the wave came, even though it was outside, it sent in showers of spray. I lay on the boards of the boat for ten minutes while my man held the end of the chain waiting for a favourable moment to try and get through. At last we managed it. But our alarms weren't over. As we came out I heard the steamer hooting and when I got to my feet there she was moving away. Awful panic. She must have got tired waiting for us. However, it was all right. She had drifted away from us downwind despite the fact that she had her anchor out, and was now coming back. "*Adesso molto monete per me*" was the first thing my boatman said when we got out. My mackintosh was pretty wet, but they assured me on board I was the driest of the whole party.'

He told his story with gusto, deriving enjoyment even from his sousing.

The lift had taken us up, and he continued his recital in our room, pausing to peel himself an orange, for he was thirsty and had had no tea.

'And Elisabeth, how is she?'

'Better. She says you are to go in and tell her about your day. She is in the next room now.'

They had moved us also across the corridor into a huger room than ever, with three big windows overlooking the gulf. Mathews finished a second orange, washed vigorously, gulped down three glasses of cold water with the air of an epicure, and, tucking the copy of *Madame Chrysanthème* under his arm, followed me next door. There he resumed his account of the day's adventures. He went on to tell how he had gone in search of the pair of cord-soled sandals I had asked him to get. On the way he had seen something rather charming. An old man in a long ragged cloak, and a boy, had laid their hats down in front of a shrine by the path's edge. Then the old man blew up a little bagpipe and the boy played on his flute and sang. 'The flute had a lovely note. It was as though it were all done in honour of the Virgin and not any passer-by.'

I was reminded of Anatole France's juggler, playing his tricks before the altar, but Mathews did not know the story.

He had then climbed to the Tiberio, and dropping stones over the low parapet of wall that tops the great face of cliff from which the victims of Tiberius are said to have been thrown, had watched them take their full ten seconds to reach the sea.

'When I was there eighteen months ago a young priest could not bring himself to look over at all. He said it brought him too near eternity.'

'I should have thought it was his business to live as near eternity as possible. He holds ground-rents in the place.'

An old woman had taken Mathews through her cottage to look at the Roman lighthouse, and he had lunched among fragrant bushes overlooking the sea, not far from the sanctuary chapel and the bronze Virgin on her marble pillar.

'It was glorious. From where I lay I could see both sides of the island at once, and, across the water, a glimpse of the coast of Calabria under the flat umbrella-top of a huge pine. The boat did not leave until four, and on the way back I walked about the deck and talked with a middle-aged Dutch couple who were returning to Naples.'

He had finished telling his adventures and produced Loti, and we began to read aloud. I sat by the side of the bed on a low chair, and when it came to Alister's turn to read my hand reached up to find Elisabeth's and rest on it under the coverlet, to hold it in mine even when she began to read again. In that slight action Mathews read all. It was not that I had supplanted him, but in that instant it was made plain to him that I was on terms which his shyness, if nothing else, had debarred all along. He would pass no comment. He would accept the fact with his customary generosity. Not a hint would pass his lips that the turn things had taken caused him surprise, much less resentment. He refused to distress either of his friends by seeming to disapprove. But in his journal he was to write a little bitterly: 'I cannot help being jealous. I am so very much "third person" when I am with them. Until he knew my friend he despised her and now he has fallen head over heels in love. Rather amusing. . . .'

We went down to dinner. He was hungry after his long day, but I ate quickly and in a mood of silent abstraction, and when the dessert was brought I rose.

'I am going up to Elisabeth now. I said we would go after dinner. Finish your fruit. There is no hurry. Come when you are ready, not before.'

He looked at me instantly, smiled thoughtfully and a little quizzically, as though I had stressed the words quite sufficiently for my meaning to be plain, and said:

'Very good. I will come later when I am ready.'

I went up to her room. She had finished eating, but the tray still rested upon her knees. Just as I was about to push it away the maid entered and claimed it. When the door closed, seated on the side of her bed, it seemed natural for me to lean over, draw her towards me and kiss her mouth. The sleeve of her jacket had fallen back to the elbow. I saw the narrow ivory bangle high up on her arm, slipped my own arm round her, caught her fingers and kissed them too. She had turned her face away on the pillow. To lean over, find her lips again and kiss that half-averted mouth was but the prelude to many more kisses, the prelude to love-making, gentler, less insistent than the love-making of passion. Even when I drew her to me and stooped over to kiss, not the bare shoulder from which the jacket had slipped, but the inner arm above the ivory slave bangle; even then it was not so much the kiss of sensuality as the kiss of tenderness. By nature I might be sensuous, and not merely sensuous, but sensual; but I had had no experience of the further implications of love-making, I was to remain chaste till I married, and for this reason, if for no other, it was easier for me to be content now with kisses. In any case, there is a moment, even for the most sensual natures, when beauty overwhelms us in its own right, when we pause before it silent and awed, and when, consumed with a sense only of tenderness, the voice of desire is stilled. Lifting her face to mine, I was reminded more than ever of her prototype in Ireland, whose image had leaped into mind when I first saw her. There was the same flowerlike expression, the same mute half-reproach in the limpid eyes, the same softened corners to blur the edges of the mouth.

Consideration on the part of Alister made him linger over his dessert. When he had finished the meal he went upstairs and, instead of coming to us, began to write his journal in the adjoining room. From there the low tones of our voices could reach him.

Once she said to me:

'Will you regret this afterwards?'

'Never. There is something a little base about all such regrets. Only the coward indulges in them. If one regrets such things at all one should regret them before they ever happen.'

'Do you?'

'No.'

She turned her head and allowed me to kiss her again, offering her lips with that simplicity which children, and those who love at least a little, possess.

Suddenly she laughed.

'I am thinking of what the Contessa said to me, *"Rien qu'un sentiment guerit un sentiment."* '

'Do you think it is true?'

'Yes, a little.'

Even disappointment in love had its own prophylactic, a hair of the dog that bit you. Here was the straw for conscience to clutch at. She had been miserably unhappy these past months. I knew that. If this helped to efface her unhappiness, if it helped to push the past into the limbo of the forgotten – well, so much the better, I was by that much the less to blame in my own eyes.

Mathews had left us together for a long time; separated only by the door which linked our big room with the other, he could hear our voices, a low murmur, or draw his own conclusions from the significance of our silence. Now he joined us, his eyes twinkling, but not unkindly, and, sitting down, began to add to the saga of his voyage a few details that he had forgotten.

Presently he looked at his watch. It was ten o'clock: we had both had an active day, and Elisabeth had had little sleep the night before. Saying good night to her, we returned to our room, where Mathews resumed work on his journal. I was tired. Unable to sleep unless a room is in darkness, I picked up a book and sat reading on the sofa until he should be ready. Still he wrote. Still his hand continued to travel over the page. Everything of the day's adventures must be set down. My own journal was a thing of fits and starts, dependent often upon mood or awaiting inspiration. His was a sacred obligation. Suddenly I lost my temper completely. I told him I disliked sharing a room quite as much as he did. It was not my fault if we had to do so. I told him that I was weary, that I had been waiting for half an hour already, and that he seemed to be prolonging the agony merely to annoy me. My outburst surprised him; he had never seen me show such irritability before. Getting up quietly, he closed the book, pocketed his pen and began to prepare for bed.

Next morning we looked out from our window and saw that the day did not intend to be kind. There was a driving wind and even an occasional flurry of snow across the bay. Presently quite large flakes began to fall. How fortunate that the two German girls should have told us of this place, where we could be so comfortable and where the weather was less able to daunt us.

Elisabeth was much better. She would get up for lunch. She suggested that meanwhile we should read poetry together in her room. Her tastes were ours. We had chosen the right sort of travel companion. Without anything of the pedant, without any pretensions to being the intellectual, she nevertheless brought to books that intensity of emotional sympathy which is more important than erudition.

'You are sure to have something we can read, Alister. You seem to have a small travelling library between you. No wonder your suitcases are the despair of porters.'

He went away and returned with a pocket anthology of Irish verse and another book.

'Let us each choose in turn and read a poem aloud.'

Mathews chose 'The man whom sorrow named his friend.' He read in a low, earnest voice as though it were almost *lése-majesté* to attempt to read his favourite poet aloud.

Then he passed the book to me.

'Listen, Elisabeth. You hate war. I am going to read you the finest anti-war poem ever written, more impassioned than anything any great poet has ever achieved on the same theme.'

> 'While going the road to Sweet Athy
> Hurroo! Hurroo!
> While going the road to Sweet Athy
> Hurroo! Hurroo!
> While going the road to Sweet Athy
> A stick in my hand and a drop in my eye
> A doleful damsel I heard cry,
>   'Och, Johnny I hardly knew ye!'
>
> With drums and guns and guns and drums,
>   The enemy nearly slew ye,
>   My darling dear, you look so queer,
>   Och, Johnny, I hardly knew ye!

'Where are your eyes that looked so mild?
Hurroo! Hurroo!
Where are your eyes that looked so mild?
Hurroo! Hurroo!
Where are your eyes that looked so mild?
When my poor heart you first beguiled?
Why did you run from me and the child?
    Och, Johnny I hardly knew ye!

With drums and guns and guns and drums
    The enemy nearly slew ye,
      My darling dear, you look so queer,
    Och, Johnny, I hardly knew ye!

'Where are the legs with which you run?
Hurroo! Hurroo!
Where are the legs with which you run?
Hurroo! Hurroo!
Where are the legs with which you run?
When you went to carry a gun?
Indeed, your dancing days are done,
    Och, Johnny, I hardly knew ye!

With drums and guns and guns and drums
    The enemy nearly slew ye,
      My darling dear, you look so queer,
    Och, Johnny, I hardly knew ye! . . .'

Elisabeth stopped me:
'What are you reading us?'
'An anonymous ballad, the work of some hedge-poet, hawked about the streets and lanes of Ireland before ever it found its way into a book, satire fierce because it is really tender.'

    'It grieved my heart to see you sail,
    Hurroo! Hurroo!
    It grieved my heart to see you sail,
    Hurroo! Hurroo!
    It grieved my heart to see you sail,
    Though from my heart you took leg bail –
    Like a cod you're doubled up head and tail,
      Och, Johnny, I hardly knew ye!

With drums and guns and guns and drums
 The enemy nearly slew ye,
  My darling dear, you look so queer,
  Och, Johnny, I hardly knew ye!

'You haven't an arm and you haven't a leg,
Hurroo! Hurroo!
You haven't an arm and you haven't a leg,
Hurroo! Hurroo!
You haven't an arm and you haven't a leg,
You're an eyeless, noseless, chickenless egg;
You'll have to be put in a bowl to beg;
  Och, Johnny, I hardly knew ye!

With drums and guns and guns and drums
 The enemy nearly slew ye,
  My darling dear, you look so queer,
  Och, Johnny, I hardly knew ye! . . .'

They interrupted again to ask if I could give them no idea even of its date.

'I don't know. There is a touch of the Uncle Toby period about the refrain "Hurroo! Hurroo!" I should think that it was early eighteenth century rather than the Napoleonic wars.'

I read on. The different inflexions of voice – polite surprise, irony, expostulation, mockery, reproach, scarcely-veiled despair – which were possible in turn in the reiterated, 'Och, Johnny, I hardly knew ye'; the typically Irish mixture of sardonic humour and almost savage pity; phrases as near the tragic as anything short of tragedy can be, made the ballad a wonderful one to read aloud and I enjoyed reading it.

'I'm happy for to see you home,
Hurroo! Hurroo!
I'm happy for to see you home,
Hurroo! Hurroo!
I'm happy for to see you home
All from the island of Sulloon
So low in flesh, so high in bone
  Och, Johnny, I hardly knew ye!

With drums and guns and guns and drums
 The enemy nearly slew ye,
  My darling dear, you look so queer,
  Och, Johnny, I hardly knew ye!

'But sad as it is to see you so
Hurroo! Hurroo!
But sad as it is to see you so
Hurroo! Hurroo!
But sad as it is to see you so
And to think of you now as an object of woe
Your Peggy'll still keep you on as her beau,
  Och, Johnny, I hardly knew ye!

With drums and guns and guns and drums
  The enemy nearly slew ye,
  My darling dear, you look so queer,
  Och, Johnny, I hardly knew ye!'

'Do you agree with my verdict?'
'Yes, we agree.'
'War seen for what it really is.'
'Read us another ballad.'

I read them 'Riding with O'Hanlon.' Presently Mathews went to his room and fetched a little paper-covered *Faust* and, in a language more musical to their ears than to mine, they began to read it aloud in turn to each other.

He saw me as his supplanter. He could write of me as 'that old poacher', regretting his own shyness, which, though it made life as he admitted, 'in some ways the more exquisite,' placed him at a disadvantage. But I had not really supplanted him in the sense of affecting in any way his own friendship. Elisabeth's whole attitude made it plain that nothing was changed between them; he was still her good comrade, all the more valued because he was too large-hearted to appear jealous. He might regret the limitations his shyness imposed on him, he might make a wry face at the thought of being, as he put it, so much 'third person' when he was with us, but had shown that he was too loyal to us both to display resentment. All the romantic in him rallied to make him step aside, benevolently neutral, if secretly a little envious: for the next best to being in love oneself was to watch others in love. And he believed that we were. Once, in my room, murmuring something about my having 'won her heart', he added defiantly, 'All the same, she remains a high and indescribably beautiful ideal to me.' She did. Nothing that had happened could make him forget his own ecstasies and despairs of two years before when he had first known her; and nothing that could happen would alter the solid basis of friendship since then which had come to exist between them. Though he might envy me, his position was in some ways really more secure than that fragile edifice which my own passionate admiration had built up in so short a time.

They looked as though in complete rapport now. Their voices declaimed their beloved German phrases, and after a time I picked up a book lying on the bed and began to turn its pages. Like the joy of finding a coin in a purse which one has believed to be emptied, I came suddenly now upon a poem of Yeats which was new to me. I had been reading him since I was fourteen, for my father bought each book as it appeared, from the private press of the poet's sisters, and I imagined I knew everything he had written. But I did not know this.

> 'Never give all the heart, for love
> Will hardly seem worth thinking of
> To passionate women if it seem
> Certain, and they never dream
> That it fades out from kiss to kiss;
> For everything that's lovely is
> But a brief, dreamy, kind delight.
> O never give the heart outright,
> For they, for all smooth lips can say,
> Have given their hearts up to the play.
> And who could play it well enough
> If deaf and dumb and blind with love?
> He that made this knows all the cost,
> For he gave all his heart and lost.'

It was a discovery. My first impulse was to cry out, 'Listen to this. I have just found it. Isn't it splendid.' But for some reason, hardly formulated even to myself, I did not tell them of it. Like all that touches us most deeply in literature, these bitter yet lovely cadences seemed too personal, and too intimate a delight to be shared. If I read the poem it would only start an endless debate, one that could never be decided. Was it true? Was the whole secret of loving not to love too much? That every woman was a coquette at heart, that love was a game to be played, not that she might win, but merely that she might have the excitement of wondering whether it was possible to win, ran altogether counter to my own conception of it. I refused to see love as dissimulation. Never! But the anguish of Yeats's lines gave me a brief glimpse into the heart which, because it has not dissimulated, because it has surrendered completely and unconditionally, wonders with forlorn bitterness whether it would not have been better to have disguised the real depths of its feeling, and to have played a part from the first.

It was getting late. Elisabeth said she must dress; she had only stayed in bed because the morning was so unattractive. Mathews and I decided that there was just time to run down to the harbour before lunch; the day was grey and cheerless, the snowstorm that had swept across the bay for five minutes earlier in the morning had left its trace on the hills and orange groves, while on the heights behind, the ridges stood out white and wintry. We walked smartly, descending by the narrow zigzag road which led down past cliff-face and veils of hanging vegetation to the tiny Marina below. It was Sunday. The road was deserted except for a solitary fisherman returning from making his boat more secure. When we reached the beach at the foot of the cliff winter seemed to strike us with fresh force. In the shade the air was still colder, but there was something bracing about the sea's impatience as it slapped angrily against the rocks, and in defiance of it we began to climb out along the partly-flooded slip, seeing how far we could go safely without getting wet. A gale was blowing; we delighted in the strong smell of the seaweed in our nostrils and the sting of the salt water on our cheeks. Wind and spray added to the feeling of exhilaration and defiance, and, as though evoked in memory by sheer contrast, Mathews began to tell me of his first school in Dorset, and of how its master had had a pool blasted in a huge ledge on a stretch of rocky coast where the boys went twice a week to bathe and bask for long hours in the sunshine. I could see Mathews as he described himself stealing away with a book to some lonely rock's edge, and reading there while his companions shouted to one another, clambering about among the pools, or throwing stones into the sun-irradiated waters, whilst, almost imperceptibly, gently swelling, the tide rose until it should cover the ledge altogether.

The recollection gave him little pleasure, for he had been a timid and solitary schoolboy, 'a white blackbird'; whereas now he could slap his hands together, gazing out with delight over the turbulent water and rejoicing in that sense of freedom for which he had longed so often. He was emancipated. He had left the past behind, the moody boredoms and despairs of his schooldays, and he stood on the threshold of the adventurous future.

The sky was heavy with grey clouds and threatened more snow.

The fishing-boats were all drawn up high on the stony beach. We hastened back up the road, refreshed by our brief encounter with the gale, but glad enough to find ourselves back in the sheltered garden of the hotel. The Russian exile in his military frockcoat, clicked his heels together when he saw us, and greeted us with a salute and a restrained smile. He seemed at once to enjoy and to be bored by his present life, performing his duties always with great punctiliousness, but rather in the spirit of one who plays a part, yet desires to play it well, like an adult pretending to be a child.

Elisabeth met us in the lobby. We sat down to lunch in the great dining-room with its elaborate frescoes, its doors with painted landscapes, its wreaths and cornices and high ceiling – the one in our yet larger bedroom had disclosed chubby cupids flying towards one another through a cloudy empyrean – and we congratulated ourselves on being once more united, for, though our visit was almost over, this was the first time Elisabeth had joined us at table. Birds of passage as we were, we had no sense of being hurried. Time is what we make of it, and the forty-odd hours we had been there already were dyed for us all with a deep significance. Moving in that egocentric world which all those who are in love inhabit, I measured it by my own impressions and emotions; and, since these were so crucial, it seemed to stretch limitlessly into an indefinite past. All that had gone before was prehistoric; all that had happened since was prolonged in time.

There were only one or two guests in the room beside ourselves. Their hushed talk reached us at our table, but made no impression, and our own tones, as always when a hotel is almost empty, were lowered in consideration for them.

When the meal was over we withdrew to the little room where a fire had been lit, and drawing up the low velvet-covered chairs towards the blaze we debated what we should do.

'Alister must produce some more literature for us.'

'All right. But what?'

'Another anthology.'

He went away and returned presently with Bridges' *Spirit of Man*.

'It has prose extracts as well as poems, but they are all given anonymously. If you want to know the author of any particular passage you must turn to the end of the book to find out.'

Elisabeth suggested that we should play a game which she had once played before.

'Each of us will choose an extract and the other two must guess by the style whose they think it is.'

'Monk will win, I know.'

'I'm not so sure. But, anyway, begin; you can read first.'

Mathews' choice was too easy. 'But when the soul giveth heed with her proper faculty, she is at once away and off into that other world of Purity, Eternity, Immortality, and things unchanging; and finding there her kindred——' He was allowed to read no further.

'Plato!' we cried with one accord.

Hoping to dupe us, he followed this immediately with 'Have we not found then a narrow path which promises to lead us and our argument to the conclusion that while we are in the body, and while the soul is contaminated with its evils, our desire will never be thoroughly satisfied; and our desire, we say, is of the Truth.'

'Plato again! He stamps his mind upon every sentence.'

But other stylists were less hall-marked. Some little-known lines of Tennyson defeated us. I was caught out by St. Augustine. Pascal was given credit for, '*Dieu est présent dans la nature, mais la nature n'est pas Dieu: il y a une nature en Dieu, mais ce n'est pas Dieu même,*' which was really the reflection of that prince of doubters, Amiel.

When Elisabeth's turn came, she said, 'Here is one you will both know:

> 'Nothing is here for tears, nothing to wail
> Or knock the breast, no weakness, no contempt,
> Dispraise, or blame, nothing but well and fair
> And what may quiet us in death so noble.'

Though we both knew it, or thought we did, I ascribed it to the closing scene of Shelley's 'Cenci,' to which it seemed akin in mood; Mathews made a present of it to Shakespeare; a bad blunder in each case, for it was the close of *Samson Agonistes*.

The extract which was to puzzle us most, however, was couched in terms of simple piety. It also was Elisabeth's discovery.

'Ask God for gladness. Be glad like children, like the birds of heaven. And let not the sin of men dismay you in your doings: fear not lest it choke your work and hinder its accomplishment. Say not, Sin is powerful, Ungodliness is powerful, bad Conventionalism is powerful: while we are solitary and powerless: the world will choke us and will frustrate the good work. Away with such despondency, my children. . . . On this earth we truly wander and are as it were lost; so that were it not for the glorious figure of Christ

265

before us we should perish utterly. . . . Much on earth is hidden from us, but there is given us in recompense the secret conviction of our living bond with another world, a celestial and loftier world; and the very roots of our thoughts and sensations are not here but there, in other worlds. And that is why the philosophers say that on earth it is impossible to know the essence of things.'

'George Herbert?'

'No.'

'Jeremy Taylor?'

'No.'

'Donne?'

'No.'

'Newman?'

'No.'

'One of the saints?'

'No.'

'We give it up.'

'Are you sure?'

'Yes I am afraid so.'

'It is the novelist, Dostoievsky.'

The game amused us. The book passed from hand to hand. In less than twenty-four hours we would have separated, Elisabeth would be on her way back to Rome, and Mathews and I searching for cheap lodgings in Naples. But just as the Suore dell' Addollorata, which we had left only two days before, seemed already to belong to another life, so to-morrow seemed immeasurably remote, an eventuality which need not be reckoned with yet.

It was still blowing hard, but the sky had lightened somewhat. Perhaps we should go out. Coats were fetched and arm-in-arm we stepped out into what Mathews called a piping gale. Uncertain, drifting clouds predicted the coming thaw. The snow-crested mountains not so far distant and the orange groves, with an occasional tree on which the fruit shone bright and yellow, seemed a contradiction in terms, exhilarating, strange. We walked in the direction in which I had gone alone the previous day. The road was empty; more snow had fallen during the morning than we realised, though the cloak which had covered Vesuvius had already receded a little. Mathews decided to go as far as the ruins of the Roman Villa, but it was too cold for Elisabeth to stay out so long after being indoors all the previous day, and she and I returned to the hotel together.

More wood had been placed on the fire in the *petit salon*, and, drawing up our chairs, we sat in the failing light while she told me of her two years in Germany, and of the bitterness of the people there, the bitterness of a defeated nation. She began to speak of her dissatisfaction with her own life, at having achieved so little despite all the advantages which had fallen to her lot. While others worked, changed the face of things, she stood by indifferent – no, not indifferent, but uncommitted.

Mathews found us in the semi-darkness and joined us by the fire. He had returned from his walk exultant. 'Grand weather, healthy weather. I remember nothing like it since my walk across the Simplon!' He had seen no one after he left us except three wild men with guns, followed by a couple of mongrel dogs.

He sank into one of the low wicker chairs, his knees folded almost to his chin.

'Elisabeth is discouraged. She says that she has done nothing with her life, only lived. She has never justified her existence. She thinks it is only the doers who count.'

Mathews was inclined to take the line which I had already taken, that to be something – we might have added especially if it was to be beautiful – was quite as important in its way as action.

'Even the saints stress the significance of "becoming". A fretful busy-ness isn't everything. That is one of the cardinal errors of our civilisation. We only feel justified when we are interfering, but the greatest things, the most significant, are happening all the time without any stir at all. Look at Alister. He is following the path of Yogi endeavour. He puffs and snuffles in the most horrible fashion every morning and evening. But something will come of it in the end; you may be sure of that. He will become something, even if he does nothing.'

The words were spoken more than half in earnest, but she was the last person likely to derive consolation from them; for, as she had told us often before, she had no feeling for the mystical. Mathews' interest in the occult did not even amuse her; it bored her. Life was something practical. She felt herself one of its failures, caring more for sensation, for the emotions which it could give, than for achievement. It was her own fault if now she saw the emptiness of it and was her own harshest judge.

'I wish I could think of the lines in which Yeats vindicates beauty for its own sake. They might comfort you. Surely to be a woman is an art in itself? Our lives are continually influencing other lives in ways that we know nothing of.'

She gave a slight, self-deprecating shrug of the shoulders as though no implied compliment could comfort her since she knew the truth.

She was a mystery to me. She remained a mystery to Mathews even after two years' acquaintance. If my love had gone a little further, if it had not halted at that initial stage of delight in what was lovely, I might by now have understood her better. For in love there are certain clearly-defined stages, and we can recognise them for ourselves. In the beginning to see the person loved, to be in their presence, is enough, and seems to us the very height of good fortune; to meet them again after even the briefest absence has all the thrill and delight of novelty. This is love's childhood, its golden age, when we are nearer than we shall ever be again to the mood of poetry, moving on an enchanted hillside like the protagonists in a Greek fable. It is succeeded by, or rather to it is presently added, a second stage when love is not only a lyrical delight in what is visual, but a feeling of devotion and reverence to personality itself. Indeed, for many love begins here and has had no precedent mist of enchantment. Once this stage is reached everything about the person loved is of importance to us. Their thoughts are ours, their joys, their sorrows. Incapable of detaching ourselves in mind from them, we experience that mood of inquietude, anxiety and restless solicitude, which the poet knew when he cried that a hundred dangers –

'Threaten the head that I love.'

But my love had not reached this stage.

Looking at her now in front of the fire, her face partly in shadow and partly in the glow of the burning logs, I knew that she was beautiful, but this was almost the sum total of my knowledge about her. It was as though I had said, 'We go through life looking for those rare instants of poetry which it vouchsafes us. You are one of them. Why not tell you so? Why not exchange those few kisses which fate seems to have given us, and which we would be foolish not to accept?'; and as though she had looked at me and then, after a moment's hesitation, said, 'You also? Then so be it. Will you be different from the others, I wonder?'

The fire died down, but our talk continued. We seemed like the friends of Boccaccio who fled from Florence, from a plague-stricken world to a place where, for a few hours, they could live romance as well as read it. Next morning we were to leave. We should have been

268

there three nights and less than three days in all, for we must leave at the crack of dawn, but we should have experienced something unforgettable. After dinner we went up to the larger room overhead, for the fire in the little salon had gone out. There we read Loti aloud for the last time. It had become almost a ceremony: so much so that if I were to read the book again now I think it likely that I would find – who knows? – that it was Sorrento and the fireside at the Sirene that it evoked for me, and not Japan at all.

Mathews had already asked for our bills. They had been brought, had appalled us for an instant, and then, as speedily, been forgotten. Had it been worth it? We laughed both of us at the absurdity of even asking such a question.

He woke me at six-thirty. We must pack. We had left all that for the morning, wishing to keep till the last minute the sense of leisure and luxury, but now it was necessary to hurry. I packed meticulously but slowly, and soon Mathews was offering to cram the overflow into my rucksack for me. By eight o'clock, having taken a cordial fare-well of our host and his wife, we were running out of the gate and down the road towards the tramline for Castellamare, accompanied by two baize-aproned porters, with our luggage slung on wide leather straps across their shoulders. A slight frost that crackled underfoot at this early hour, and an absolutely clear sky, promised well for the day. We were leaving when we should really be arriving. But at the terminus we found no tram. Had it gone? Had Mathews got the times wrong? The porters were inclined to think that we had missed it, and a number of carriage-drivers approached offering to take us to Castellamare. We rejected their offers, someone saying that there would be another tram in half an hour's time, but they continued to hover nearby, like birds disappointed of their prey, hopeful that something might presently make us change our minds. However, we were destined neither to be driven by them to Castellamare nor, for that matter, to go there at all that day. Conflicting rumours presently resolved themselves into one persistent rumour that there had been a bad landslide on the road, which was completely blocked, and that we would be cut off from Castellamare for at least twenty-four hours. When this had been confirmed by a telephone call from the tourist office nearby, even the persistent drivers ceased to solicit us. How then to return? The morning boat had already gone at half-past seven; there would be no boat now until five o'clock in the afternoon. We looked at each other in mingled dismay and amusement. The porters, shouldering our luggage once more, started to carry it back to the hotel, while we followed, a little shamefaced, a little confused, wondering what our next move was to be.

But we had forgotten the Viennese. From the moment of our arrival he and his Sorrentine wife had been fairy godparents to us. Certain people, partly from natural charm, partly from a genuine goodwill towards their fellow creatures, stand out from among their fellows. This man was one of them. He and his wife were at once all sympathy. They understood, they accepted, they reassured; it was almost as though they had expected something like this to happen. What could be more natural than to have one's luggage carried away from the hotel door one minute and carried back the next? Since our whole visit from the moment of our arrival had been just a shade fantastic, this was a fitting climax to it. After five minutes' conversation with them, we began to see the thing not as a disaster at all, but as a blessing. Nothing could be simpler. We would stay there again that night. He would send a telegram to Elisabeth's mother if she would write it out for him. And since the day was such a glorious one he had a suggestion to make. We should take a little carriage and drive in the opposite direction to Amalfi. It would be the pleasantest expedition imaginable, the place itself was interesting and we would get a magnificent view of the coast to the south as we went.

Mathews was all enthusiasm. Elisabeth was worried, for she had already altered her plans once in agreeing to remain over until Monday. But there seemed nothing else to be done. To go by the evening boat would mean that she could not reach Rome until after midnight. She sat down to write the telegram, and Mathews, glancing at me, rubbed his hands together with delight, like a schoolboy who has been successful in some prank. The three men were delighted, the two women, more dubious at first, had now accepted the solution as the only one possible in the circumstances.

The tall *concierge* was sent to look for a little carriage. He returned with an open vehicle, double-hooded, to which two rather scraggy horses were harnessed, driven by an extremely ancient Jehu. 'The horses are old, the driver is older, but the chariot itself is oldest,' was Mathews' verdict as he inspected it. It was almost a museum piece. A boat-like body hung on leathers above four high wheels; cushions, which had once been dark blue, had faded to a nondescript grey; the two hoods folded back were of cracked black leather. The driver, a tiny man, white-haired, sallow, more than a little shaky on his legs, climbed down to stand beside his horses, whip in hand. He was asked how much he wanted to take us to Amalfi and back. 'A hundred and twenty-five lire,' was his reply. It was as much as a day's complete pension at the Sirene for us, but Amalfi was thirty-five kilometres away across the mountains and it seemed worth it. We closed with him, feeling that one could not drive about the country, even in a vehicle of the pre-Garibaldian era, for nothing.

We got our coats, Mathews' rucksack, another rug, and climbed in. The driver mounted the box, our host and his wife waved their hands gaily to us, and we drove off, swinging out of the gate with as much style as the two long-tailed, rather scraggy Rosinantes could manage. But almost immediately we had come to a halt in the large open square in Sorrento. 'Go on,' we shouted to the driver. He took no notice. 'Go on,' we shouted again. Still he remained motionless on the box, as though completely indifferent to our protests. Mathews began to abuse him in mingled French and Italian – we had not paid to be driven to Amalfi only to be stranded outside a yard gateway in Sorrento. The old man indicated that he was waiting for something. Presently a boy came running out with two nose-bags for the horses, and a small armful of hay. So that was it. Of course, horses must be fed; and the provender was safely stowed away under the driver's feet. Off we rolled again with a tremendous clatter along the flagged street, but we had only gone a few hundred yards when the carriage pulled up sharply once again. This time the driver climbed slowly down from his seat, and, ignoring us as completely as he had done on the previous occasion, ambled forward to the horses' heads. What was happening now? While we waited, we talked, and chaffed one another at the slowness of our progress. We had reached the outskirts of Sorrento. A woman leaned out of a window above us, and proceeded to shake a quilt directly over our heads. Presently the driver picked up his horse's foot, removed a stone from it, and climbed back on to the box without a word, as though on this occasion his silence had been vindicated.

The road led back first towards Meta, behind which the mountains rose, lovely and austere. It was only six days before Christmas, there had been ice on the road down in Sorrento, and a sprinkling of white hoar frost under the orange trees; and as we climbed past the groves now great ruts graven into the stone caught the wheels of the *carozza* and dragged it one side or the other. Above our heads the sky was a cerulean blue and presently the warmth of the sun would begin to make itself felt. Till then there was a frosty tang in the air, and when the road entered, as it often did, a cutting between the rock we felt the sharpness of winter. I sat opposite my companions with my back to the horses, looking across the gulf below us, to Vesuvius in the north, still smoking, with snow once more upon its lower slopes. As we drew near the top of the col the road turned and twisted. At one point the foundation had slipped – men were even now working upon it – and we passed, strange sight, a steam-roller upside down on its back, a wooden barrier protecting the breach through which it had fallen.

The superb promise of the day reconciled us to the cold each time we entered a cutting. The other two suggested that I should join them on the opposite seat. There was room really for three abreast, and it would be warmer for us all. 'Presently; when we get over the col. Then I will have the view in front of me as we come down.' 'But why not now?' I changed. I sat between them and my hands met Elisabeth's under the rug. Mathews' eyes twinkled benevolently when we asked each other presently with an innocent air, 'Are your hands cold?' 'No, are yours?' We teased him. 'Alister, this is one of the great moments of your life. Your heart's wish is fulfilled. You are back in the eighteenth century, a grand seigneur, rolling over the roads of Italy in your private carriage. Doesn't he look the very part with his high silk scarf like a stock, and his aquiline nose, and his arm resting negligently on the side of the carriage?' 'I not only look the part; I feel it,' he assured us, smiling back at us joyously.

And I could well agree with him. I shared his delight. Now for the first time for years I travelled again in a civilised fashion. When cars were not yet so fashionable in Southern Ireland as to make a victoria or wagonette ridiculous, I had been accustoned to loll at ease in the great bucket-shaped seat beside the coachman, in my grandfather's wagonette, which he had designed for my grand-mother, so that she might sit in comfort beside him when he drove himself. We would make our slow and dreamy progress between hedges heavy with the scent of honeysuckle and wild roses, a means of transport so unperturbed, so leisurely, fostering so successfully a taste for meditation and idle contemplation that it may be said to have influenced my whole life. It was a paradox to me in those days that the coachman should always walk the horses down a hill and trot them up it; this seemed contrary to good sense and con-sideration for animals, until one day he explained that Nanky-Poo, the off chestnut, was not too sound on his front legs and could not be trusted to trot down hills. Thence forward I awaited with greater equanimity the moment when the grating brake would be released and we would sweep up the next steep incline. The big wagonette was replaced by a car, but I never forsook my allegiance to it; and now, as we climbed slowly from Sorrento, though the road was rough and the *carozza* lurched violently, I was reminded of those days. The horses were not inclined to hurry, and indeed their driver behaved as if he felt they would need nursing before the day finished, but to the three occupants of the carriage no minor discomfort could interfere with the fact that the day was theirs, life and youth were theirs, and Time himself even seemed to have halted his caravan for their especial benefit.

We came over the col and entered the warm south. We had found summer. The road had only to descend a mile or so and then we would follow it for nearly fifteen miles along the coast to Amalfi, a road blasted out of the living rock, generally a hundred feet or so above the sea. We looked towards that sea now. It lay sapphire-blue under a blue sky and was of a calmness indescribable. A little way out from the shore were the three islands of the Syrens, their dark outlines floating on that blue water like beasts asleep. They lay enchanted in the stillness, as on that day perhaps when the men of Ulysses had rowed swiftly by them, indifferent to the singing that they could not hear.

The brakes of the *carozza* scraped, and the *carozza* itself creaked and groaned as we wound to and fro, descending to where the road began to skirt the sea, while the vast expanse of ocean visible to us narrowed gradually as we dropped in height. The sunlight shimmered golden in a great shaft of light running towards the horizon for miles across the sea; and the eye and mind followed that light-flooded highway which seemed to reach out to infinity, an infinity containing not only the past and the future but all of the present which we would preserve, cling to and make permanently ours.

Below us, separated from one another by high buttresses of rock, were tiny bays, inviolate except to a boat; bays in which wavelets of green water broke presently in froth on the margin of beaches only a few yards wide. Sometimes the pale green of the sea turned a dark mauve over beds of seaweed, and the shining bottom of silver sand was lost. Above us goats scrambled among the rocks, and we caught our breath at the first sight of the pink-flushed, snow-capped mountains behind Paestum. As we passed a cottage a little girl darted out and ran for a quarter of a mile behind the carriage. We threw her an orange, only to regret our generosity for she evidently had hoped for money and did not bother to thank us for it. We were extremely hungry ourselves. The hotel had provided us with a sandwich lunch, and we decided to eat it now and have another meal when we got to Amalfi. I moved back to my former place, and Elisabeth, her feet wrapped in a rug on the seat beside me, searched the depths of Mathews' rucksack and proceeded to dispense the provender found there. As she did so we rolled into Positano – Positano, very little more than halfway to Amalfi. Streetless, except for the road on which we drove, the houses clinging higgledy-piggledy to the hillside, it had an Oriental look about it, two towers which might have belonged to mosques adding to this Eastern effect.

The drive was proving longer than we had expected. Our feet were cold, and presently I put mine on the seat beside Mathews, where his elbow rested on them. His were beside me, covered with the rucksack. We told stories. An Italian some years before had fallen in love with a friend of Elisabeth's in Rome. He proposed and was refused. The next day he came to her door, opened it, and shot himself on the threshold before her eyes.

'A very inconsiderate thing to do. The meanest kind of revenge. Anyway, suicide is the act of a coward.'

'The Romans didn't think so. "And then what's great, what's noble, we'll do it after the high Roman fashion, and make death proud to take us." '

'They believed in it if they thought it was the only way to avoid dishonour. Even then it was probably largely a matter of racial pride. It takes a still greater man to endure humiliation.'

'The Latins have a fine sense of the dramatic in these things. There was another man who shot himself in the Borghese in front of Canova's statue of Napoleon's sister Pauline.'

'Had he fallen in love with her, or with it?'

'I think with her. She was in Rome at the time.'

'Well, it showed some consideration at least to choose the statue.'

I did not tell them, for I had not heard it at the time, about the the very young Italian cavalry officer who many years before had fallen in love with an Irish girl in Rome, a relative of Winifred Letts the writer, who told me the story. He, too, proposed and he, too, was refused. Years later she received from Italy a photograph of

Pius the Ninth. Across it was written the four words, 'You made me Pope.'

One man shoots himself, another enters the Church and presently becomes its head. We are creatures of destiny, but it is we ourselves who decide what that destiny shall be.

The carriage threw us violently from side to side, as it swung to avoid great holes in the road. Mathews said, it was like being in a ship at sea. We had lapsed once more into silence. My two companions accused me of being *pensif*.

'Why do you expect me always to look cheerful?' and I told them how once at Christmas in a pension in Switzerland a little girl of six in whom I took an interest, fixing me with a curious eye one day at lunch, had amused her mother by nicknaming me *triste homme*, a nickname that secretly won my admiration for her perspicacity. She must have surprised me in a mood of abstraction or in some unguarded moment and seen there an expression which the rest of the pension, who thought me all cheerfulness and gaiety, never saw. Thenceforward I was always *triste homme* to her, for, having once given me the name, she was not going to have it contradicted.

I could have told them now that one of the joys of the horse-drawn vehicle is that it lends itself to being *pensif*.

'Look at him. He's completely *kaput*.'

'What is *kaput*? You know I don't understand German.'

'Everyone knows what *kaput* is, even if they don't know another word in the language.'

A barefooted man, seated by the roadside, jumped to his feet as we went past, signalling to ask for a lift. The driver shouted something, whipped up his horses and drove on. But we insisted that he must stop, and when the man, seeing that we had changed our intention, began to run after us, we called to him that he might have a ride on the box. He climbed up, smiling gratefully at us, and triumphantly at the driver, as he took his place beside him; whereupon the latter became very sulky, angry that his decision should have been overruled. Perhaps he was thinking of his horses and of the distance that would have to be covered before they saw the stable that night. But it had been worth while giving the man a ride, if only to see the welcome accorded his homecoming a few kilometres further on. His home was by the roadside, and the whole family rushed out, waving and shouting, to receive him. If ever there was joy in a man's face it was in his then as they crowded round him, jubilant and elate.

The drive seemed to have lasted an interminable time. We were on the last stage of it now. The road had become even more dramatic; jagged peaks of rock rose out of the sea, and through natural arches one could glimpse the deep blue water with the sunlight glistening upon it. A steep, unbroken line of rock overhung the road on the land side, while the many breaches in the low wall on the other seemed to invite our *carozza* to take one last colossal swerve, more serious than any that had preceded it, and hurtle us into the sea far below. Tunnels occurred with ever greater frequency and we realised the stupendous task which had confronted the engineers who made the road. Through these tunnels we caught recurring glimpses of a castle on the jutting promontory on the further side of Amalfi, but not of the town itself, which was separated from us by a succession of curves in the road, each of them skirting a small bay, and which lay tucked away behind a final fold of rock. When at last we drew near to it, it was to plunge into a longer tunnel than ever; then, suddenly, when we had almost ceased to believe that our drive could ever have an ending, we found ourselves back in the sunlight with the glistening white walls of the Cappuccini monastery looking down from their airy perch immediately above us.

I had been to Amalfi once before, and had stayed for a few nights at the monastery, which now for the second time in its long history had been converted into an hotel. It had been amusing to sleep in the narrow confines of a monk's cell, to rise early next morning and climb to Ravello, and see there Wagner's haven of retirement and the very furniture that must have greeted him on his periodic returns; or to wander presently by chance into what is perhaps the loveliest and most dramatically situated garden in the world, and learn with surprise that these dizzy terraces, skirted by seas of mauve iris blossom, were the property of an absent English nobleman. I remembered my descent to Amalfi in the evening. The town that had glimmered vaguely in the dusk then, with an occasional light showing in some window, was bright now with blazing white and vivid colour. Though shrunk from its former importance, it basked contentedly in the sunshine, forgetful of the days when it had been the peer of Venice and Gaeta, its code the maritime law of the whole Mediterranean. In the little harbour below, swinging at their moorings, or drawn up on the narrow strip of beach, the fishing-boats seemed to ignore the wide expanse of deep blue sea that confronted them; while behind them, mixture of beauty and squalor, rose the town itself, a fantastic jumble of white and yellow buildings, many of them ancient, all of them dirty, clambering, with the exception of those planted securely along the quay, up the hillside, until the mountain beetling above them forbade any further foothold. Narrow, terraced vineyards and lemon groves occupied every inch of ground on which man had not built.

We stopped at the Cappuccini – that was inevitable. Outside the entrance to the tunnel, where the steep flight of steps to the terrace begins, a livid and disgusting homunculus, writhing about on two stumps and brandishing his two abnormally short arms, which ended abruptly without any wrists in three shapeless fingers, tried to awaken the pity of two hundred Americans, streaming down the steps on their way back to a fleet of cars that awaited them in the road. They were part of a pleasure-cruise, ashore for the day, doing one of their periodic land excursions. Some of them, reminiscent of Romans in their slave-borne litters, were being carried in cushioned seats, slung between poles, up the several hundred steps to the Cappuccini, steps formidable to anyone, but most of all to age, corpulence or infirmity. Our equipage, dilapidated, shabby, the tired horses stretching out their necks after the long journey, formed a strange contrast to the string of absolutely uniform and highly-polished Fiat cars drawn up by the roadside. In a few minutes, after a little shouting and talk, each traveller had been shepherded to his allotted place and the whole fleet of cars moved off and disappeared as if by magic.

Mathews had been bargaining with the hotel porter over the matter of a second lunch. Evidently they had come to some agreement, for the man took the rucksack and, slinging it over his shoulder, he proceeded to lead the way up the endless steps. We climbed behind him, breathless long before we reached the terrace at the top. The long, low, white, cheerful-looking building, built into the face of the rock which towers above it, looks out over the bay, and down on the town almost at its feet. The German manageress explained that we must wait a few minutes while our lunch was being prepared. We walked out along the terrace bordered by a steep orange grove, passing through the double line of great white pillars which formed a pergola for roses, to climb presently to a little viewpoint – Belle Vue it was called – in the wood above.[1] On a platform jutting over the rocks below, a stone table had been set, and seats,

[1] No one can ever mount to that little viewpoint again and look down from there on what we saw, for a year or two later a tremendous landslide swept away wood, terrace and orange grove in one mighty wave of destruction.

and from there, as though one were in the crow's-nest of a ship, we could gaze over the untroubled waters below, catch a glimpse of the cliff face of Ravello, and even imagine that we saw the faint outlines of the great temples at Paestum in the plain.

We were stiff, a little tired after our four hours' drive, entranced by the beauty of what we saw, but already, especially Elisabeth, concerned at the thought of the length of time it would take us to return. We went down to the Cappuccini, admired its mementoes of great men – Longfellow's photograph, Gladstone's autograph – and found our way along the vaulted, white-washed passage, hung with pictures of considerable merit by artists who found this the easiest way of paying their bill, to the dining-room where, in company with a few other late-comers, we found lunch awaiting us. Mathews had the air of a Napoleon who has reached Moscow safely, but is a little apprehensive about the return. Once at table, we discovered we were all of us less hungry than we had imagined. We hurried through the meal, called for our coffee, and soon were hastening down the steps once more to the road. But the *carozza* and its elderly driver had vanished. He had been given an advance of five lire to get himself something to eat, and making our way – it was only a matter of a few hundred yards – into the town, we found him, and the *carozza*, in the square, where a group of other horse-vehicles were waiting for hire. Here I just missed being the victim of an unpleasant contretemps. Our own horses were shaking their nosebags aloft, in a last vain hope of finding something in them. As I made towards them, a pace or two in front of my companions, a scraggy and vicious-looking chestnut from a neighbouring vehicle, its ears laid back, the whites of its eyes showing, its teeth bared, rushed forward from behind to bite me. I heard Alister and Elisabeth cry out to warn me; and, making the rejoinder I had learnt in an Army depot, where one passes continually through horse-lines of newly-arrived and uncertain-tempered animals, I had just time now to strike the creature across the nose with the edge of my open hand before it could seize my arm. Our driver was solemnly dusting our carriage with a feather brush in almost ostentatious preparation for our return. He had bought himself a small cigar and was smoking it with much satisfaction. Thin, frail, old, a little battered, dependent on his two sorry nags for his livelihood, there was something more than a trifle pathetic about this display of magnificence, following a five-lire advance of dues. Of all jetsam in life, left high and dry by the receding tide of time, perhaps the most pitiful, and at the same time the most gentle, the most invested with human dignity, is the jarvey, the cab- or hansom-driver. He is now almost extinct, but, despite every misfortune, despite every stroke of poverty, he has gone down fighting, ignoring all degradations, all humiliations on the part of those who would scorn him; keeping his dignity as though the mere comradeship of his horse placed him a step above any man who bows his head in idolatry to a machine.

It was three o'clock. In a little over an hour and a half it would be dark. The sun had taken on a more wintry aspect, and we decided that it would be better to have the hood up from the beginning. So the two hoods on either side were opened and, with a little difficulty, fastened together in the centre with a bolt that dropped across into a slot. One side window allowed itself to be raised, but the other defied all our efforts and had to be left open; while it was only the ingenuity of Mathews that persuaded the small window behind the driver's seat to function. We stopped at the Cappuccini to collect our rucksack and other impedimenta. The *carozza* had become a closed coach – or at least partially closed – and we did not altogether appreciate the change. It is true we had been dreading the cold of the return journey and we had found a remedy against this. But with the pale winter sunlight still outside, and the view curtailed, it seemed strange to be driving along the road, shut in, obliged to crane our necks if there was anything which we particularly wanted to keep in view. We had lost a little of the *Stimmung* of the morning, – '*abattus* by our lunch' was Elisabeth's explanation – but the prospect of nearly four hours' driving, with darkness long before they were completed, was probably the real one. The carriage swerved as violently as it had done when we were coming, and the low parapet at the side of the road seemed more than ever to invite disaster. Mathews lamented that he could not 'take the ribbons' and drive himself. 'Why don't you?' we exclaimed with one accord, so eagerly, that our motive, which was quite disinterested, was misunderstood, and he burst out laughing. All the same he would do it, if the driver would let him; and, tapping on the window, we signalled to the latter to pull up. He did so and Mathews got out, climbed on the box and took the reins. With his high scarf, his belted coat, and heavy leather gloves he looked more than ever the slightly cold hero of an eighteenth-century romance. Though he had not driven for several years, he had had practice enough in Hampshire as a boy, and we felt safe in his hands. I slipped my arm round Elisabeth, drew her towards me, and kissed her lips for the first time that day; stolen kisses, and the day itself stolen, stolen when we had least expected it. It was as though Fate, of its own accord, had added this postscript of the Amalfi expedition to our adventures.

Mathews may have thought that he had sacrificed himself for our benefit, but he was to enjoy it, and to give us a good deal of distraction as well. He had only been driving a few minutes when the door of the carriage burst suddenly open and began to scrape against the rock-face at the side of the road. We struggled to close it, but it was impossible; we shouted, but in vain; the noise of the lurching vehicle was too great for us to be heard, and the two figures on the box continued completely abstracted from us and from the contemplation of anything except the road ahead of them. Ceasing to shout, I made one more tremendous effort, and, as the carriage drew slightly away from the wall of rock, succeeded in pulling-to the door, which had threatened at any moment to be torn off its hinges. A few kilometres further on we struck the tail of a coal-cart, and were pursued by an angry carter, who, however, failed to prove that any damage had been done. The halt gave us an opportunity to tell Mathews of the previous misadventure.

It was cold outside, especially for one's feet, but the position on the box had its compensations. It was drawing near the time of sunset; the sea was pooled in gold; the sun hung on the horizon, bright red; while, in the sky above, where drifted great reefs of light grey clouds, flushed with crimson or with edges brightly gilded, the pale green and saffron lake of evening offered a less tangible, but even more lovely, ocean than earth.

And still Mathews drove. We closed our eyes, dozed, tried to sleep a little. Elisabeth had turned up the fur collar of her coat, leaning her head against the opposite corner of the swaying carriage. Each time that I opened my eyes I saw through the open window the sunlight still lingering on the water below. The light was beginning to go; it would be dusk, full dusk, before we reached Positano. Alister must be frozen upon the box, but he remained there, driving slowly but well; the horses were not capable of very much, he explained later; with another pair he would have made a better showing. Then rather abruptly the carriage pulled up and we heard shouting and a dispute. We had been passing a small *trattoria* by the roadside and the old man, although Mathews held the reins, had shouted to his horses to stop. They did so, and, calling out in a frail voice '*Vino!*' the driver prepared to get down. We could hear

Mathews shouting to him, 'No, no, no,' and see him holding the old fellow by his belt and coat-tails as he tried to get off the box. I leaped out, and, convinced that he had already fortified himself sufficiently at Amalfi, began to add my protests to my friend's. Elisabeth was afraid that he was drunk already, 'He will drive us all over the cliff into the sea.' We assured her this was not so yet, but if we once began stopping at every *trattoria*, it soon would be. Awed by our combined onslaught, the old man began to make excuses, saying that he only wanted some string to tie the harness. The owner of the inn came out with a glass of wine and a bit of thin rope, with which they would have pretended to mend the harness as prelude to drinking, had we allowed it. But Mathews was adamant and, refusing to listen to the innkeeper's plea that it was cold, he whipped up the horses and drove on. That glass, whatever it might hold, would not reach the lips for which it had been intended, and, as we drove away, we heard the landlord still calling pleadingly, '*Fa freddo, bisogna bere*' ('It is cold, you must drink').

Every moment the sunset colours had become lovelier over the sea, and over the islands of the Syrens. But now they faded. It was growing definitely dark. At last Mathews rejoined us inside, slapping his hands and stamping his feet to get them warm, and retailing with much gusto his version of the incident on the box. Our spirits, which had seemed to sink on leaving Amalfi, revived; we agreed that we no longer cared how long the return journey took; rough and stony as the road was, we had grown used to the motion of the carriage, and indeed liked it. Mathews announced that he was beginning to thaw. The thought of the old man on the box outside distressed us, but it was better that he should be cold than that he should be drunk. We sat three abreast, our feet up on the opposite seat. Mathews, searching his rucksack, produced figs and apples to cheer us, and suggested that we should sing. He and Elisabeth sang German nursery rhymes which I did not know; presently I would sing Negro spirituals; we whistled Rimsky Korsakov's lovely and wistful 'Chanson Hindoue,' and Elisabeth harvested from memory as much as she could of a Chopin nocturne.

Positano lay ahead of us, round the next curve of the bay, across the next cleft in the coast. It was almost dark by the time we reached it, and the white houses glimmering up the hillside made it seem even more beautiful to Elisabeth than Amalfi. We were only halfway but time had ceased to count for us; we were resigned to seeing it stretch out towards ultimate arrival in a dim and unvisualised future.

Elisabeth began telling of her childhood in South Africa, of the freedom which for years her mother allowed her. 'She knows me; if I were not free——' The implication was that by giving her complete freedom her mother had achieved what she could never have achieved by restraint.

'Tell us about your school.'

She began to describe the large co-educational school to which she had gone at the end of the war. Its founder was a great idealist and her chief complaint against it seemed to be that it was too rational a preparation for an irrational world.

'We were left with a feeling of superiority, as though we had been inoculated against all the follies to which less fortunate mortals are subject when they go out into the world.'

'Which, of course, you had been!'

I said it mischievously and in the semi-darkness of the carriage I saw such light as there was falling aslant her face as she smiled, and that slow smile, as I watched it, gave me as much pleasure as any caress. There were times when I asked myself whether I ought not to be a little deaf to her charm, as Ulysses was deaf to the voices of the Syrens on those very islands which we were passing now, whether I had not as much need of rope and masthead or of wax-filled ears. Something suspicious in my nature, or in the nature of my whole sex, had sowed from time to time an occasional and quickly-uprooted seed of doubt. Now, not for the first time, I began to wonder about her character. Was it her fault that she had broken so many hearts? She was not a flirt in the accepted sense of the word. She was without any of the tricks of the coquette. She seemed to think relatively little of clothes or appearance; she scorned make-up. With none of the affectations or mannerisms of those who deliberately, or lightheartedly, debase the currency of love until it is valueless, she was more dangerous than any flirt, for the simple reason that she despised flirtation. She was not indifferent to admiration, far from it; but it must be in the gold currency of love on the man's part. That was what it amounted to. She had come into the world capable of appreciating the full significance of the moment in which one loves or is loved. As one can discover the exquisite and wistful melancholy of a particular type of music, and the experience of it can, for ever after, translate us instantly and gladly to another world, so, perhaps, had she discovered love.

She wanted to live poetry as well as to read it, and there was nothing artificial or simulated about this wish. To be loved was wonderful; it was to watch the poem come to life. Even in the matter of friendship, friendship with the other sex probably meant more to her than friendship with her own. For just as there are men who turn instinctively to women for friendship, not because they are lacking in masculinity, but rather because women are more sensitive where art and similar interests are concerned, so Elisabeth seemed to prefer men as her friends because she had more in common with them. It was more natural for her to be driving along the road from Positano now with us than if she had done so with two women friends. We, her cavaliers, gave her the kind of conversation she liked, of books, of people, of music, and, moreover, that adulation and appreciation which made the adventure romantic.

She was telling us now how she had been sent by her uncle to a grinder in London.

'He wished me to have special coaching in Latin. I used to go twice a week. The coach to whom I was sent was thirty-five. I was sixteen. He used to kiss me. When the time came for each lesson I would say to myself, "I won't go. I won't." But always I went. In the end.'

'And always he used to kiss you?'

'Yes. Always it ended the same way.'

I could see the whole scene, the dull November afternoon, the dusty, untidy room, with its old-fashioned furniture, the mantelpiece with its leaning copies of Livy and Tacitus, and this man who had been the first to kiss the flower-like face which had been lifted, a moment before, to mine. I knew the type exactly, or it seemed to me that I did; bored with drudgery, too 'emancipated' to be troubled much with principles, a sceptic, the makings of an inebriate, fuddled and repellent, in whom all that was natural and wholesome would have long since perished in the fusty atmosphere of a scholarship tarnished and a little salacious. And as I thought of it, hate filled my heart. Who was this blackguard who had committed such a trespass against her youth at the moment when, in Synge's phrase, 'She was just going up to the boundaries that are set to childhood'?

'Why didn't you tell your uncle?'

'I was afraid to. There would only have been a most terrible row. The man would have got into trouble and I would have felt myself responsible.'

It was strange to think that what she was describing had happened only five years before and yet she spoke of it almost as though it belonged to another life. From that day what had been her attitude towards my sex? How many others had followed that first offender? Sometimes in a chance phrase she implied that she had seen through that humbug, 'man', long ago; as when she informed me that it was never very long before married men told you that their wives did not understand them. In such a remark she might seem sophisticated and even cynical; but I told myself that she could not be really sophisticated or she would never have formed and retained her friendship with Alister – Alister, who was shy, romantic, inarticulate, lamenting to me his shyness, and at the same time admitting that it was that same shyness which had given him the most 'exquisite moments' of the last two years. Was it really that she perceived, with the instinct of a woman to whom love is never a trifle, that it is only by people like Alister, by the born romantic, or by foreigners, that one can be loved as one wants to be loved, by the boy who is all heart, though he knows nothing of passion, or by the man who is all passion, but understands a woman's heart, for it is of the stuff of Mathews that lovers are made?

As we rolled forward slowly over the rough road, my thoughts, which had been translated vividly and far afield to something remote and quite unknown by her story, which had distressed me and made me so indignant (uselessly, for it is always useless to reproach the past), returned gradually to the present and it seemed to me idle to trouble any more about something I could never know – namely, its whole effect upon her character – and wiser merely to be grateful for the present. To be happy even for a day, that was an achievement. The drive, memorable in itself, had been made a hundredfold more memorable by its circumstance. Even Mathews, in addition to his own enjoyment, seemed to feel a second and vicarious pleasure in ours.

Elisabeth complained of the cold. We wrapped the rug around her more closely. It had become quite dark, and we could scarcely see one another's faces. The old man got down and began to fumble with the side-lamps, trying to light the candles in them. But his hands were so cold that at first he could not strike a match. At last he did so and we drove on, the smell from the hot, japanned surface of the lamp, as the candles burnt up, reaching us through the open window. The old fellow drove well, faster than Mathews, knowing the road and his horses. Once when a cart drawn by several horses pulled into the side of the road to let us go by its lamp, fixed low, cast a gigantic shadow of our own vehicle on to the rock face which we were passing – like a grotesque silhouette illustration to a fairy tale – and we laughed at the fantastic, long-bodied coach that we saw, rolling on its way with wheels almost higher than its roof.

We were no longer tired, and the pace, which had seemed so slow when we first set out that morning, by now seemed the natural one. It was colder than ever. A wave of pity for the old man sitting on the box, with his stooped shoulders and frozen hands, swept over us, a little too sentimental to be real. Mathews suggested that he should get out and drive again. We refused to allow him.

'But nothing will warm him now, short of putting him inside the coach with a rug.' Carried away by his sense of the absurd, he urged that this was the proper course to follow.

'One of us must drive. He can sit in the coach, and the other two must walk either side as guards of honour. In this way we can return to Sorrento, in becoming fashion, and not with a crime on our conscience.' Pity for the old man was forgotten in the fantasy of such a return.

At last we came over the col and saw below us the lights around the Gulf, the lights of Naples, where we had expected to sleep that morning. There was still a considerable distance to go, but once having crossed the mountain we had the sense of having already arrived. As we neared the spot where the steam-roller lay wheels uppermost, we looked out of the window a little apprehensively, but we passed it safely in the darkness without knowing. The lights of Meta gleamed ahead, and presently we found ourselves back on the paved road which led to Sorrento. The two long-tailed horses plucked up heart as the old driver suddenly whipped them up and we clattered into Sorrento in style. He had chosen the nearer road to the hotel, but for some reason a barrier had been placed across it with a warning lantern tied to it, and we learnt that it was closed. None of us had the heart to make the old fellow turn back and drive round. Standing there in the light of the carriage candles beside his sweating and steaming horses, he looked a pathetic figure, bare-headed, white-haired, his eyes watering with the cold. We told him that we would walk the rest of the way. It would only take us ten minutes. The horses had done enough already. We paid him his fare and gave him a tip with which he seemed satisfied, then, groping in the bottom of the carriage, we recovered our rucksack and the great heavy rug which had been lent us by the hotel. Linking arms, we ran down the road, glad to be back at last, but triumphant after our adventure. We passed the tablet to Tasso, its lettering clear under the light of a nearby lamp, we passed the cone-shaped beacon of the war memorial, and as we came running under the arched entrance to the garden of the Sirene, we saw the Russian *concierge* waiting by the marble steps ready to take the carriage rug from us and to enquire discreetly whether we had enjoyed our day.

Assuredly we had enjoyed it. We had driven more than forty miles since setting out that morning; we were hungry, stiff, a little tired, but our exultation was self-evident. It seemed reflected in the face of our friendly host when we recounted to him the experiences of the day. We might have been his relatives or close personal friends judging by the pleasure he took in the success of our expedition. At dinner he came across to us, clapped his hands together, and laughing, at once mischievously and a little guiltily, remarked, 'I must say something to you. At eleven came a man to say there were no trams or vehicles because they thought there *might* be a landslide; the road was open all day, but nothing was allowed there because they were afraid of an accident.' So the landslide which had kept us here another day was mythical. It had served its purpose well, it had shown us Amalfi and Positano and the islands of the Syrens, and, having done this, it had proved itself the baseless fabric of a dream, leaving a great deal less débris to clear up than if it had been real.

Dinner, the remains of the bottle of Capri wine we had ordered for lunch the day before, talk and elation over the day's adventures made us forget our fatigue. But when the meal was finished the discovery that two other guests had taken possession of the wood fire in the little salon where we had hoped to stretch our limbs drove us upstairs. Elisabeth was more tired than she had admitted. She would go to bed and presently we would read together as we had done each evening. Back in our own room, our journals were produced and we began to jot down notes of the day. When we joined her I continued to write at a table by the window while Mathews, when it was suggested by Elisabeth that it was his business to entertain her, looked at her dumbly, almost as though he had become shy in our company, until she proposed that they should read a French book together. It was inconceivable that I should threaten his friendship, which had long preceded mine, but indirectly I had affected it. Watching us together this last week had brought him vivid memories of the time when he had once worshipped vainly at the same shrine, and, though he prided himself a little that he had lived to survive love and enjoy friendship, he could not wholly forget that it was with his friend that I had fallen in love, overshadowing him in her thoughts, for these few days. Nevertheless, he had accepted his position of 'third person' with admirable generosity, ceasing even to make his accustomed jokes at my expense. Perhaps our Louis Quatorze setting, which continued to delight him, with its cherubed ceilings, huge chandeliers and intimate atmosphere of the boudoir, reconciled him to an eventuality which he could not have foreseen; and, like a French abbé in one of the eighteenth-century tales which he so much enjoyed, he took pleasure in being the discreet companion, someone who could at once admire beauty and help to enliven its conversation.

Feet up on the far bed, he read now in his slightly throaty, meticulous voice, whenever his turn came; while I wrote furiously at the table nearby.

'Alister, you croak. Elisabeth reads French aloud much better than you do. She gives the words their natural music. The moment you take the book from her I notice the difference.'

He admitted the indictment, while she defended him just as she had defended me when he laughed at my mispronunciations.

My pen had run out of ink and I went next door to look for some, forgetting that I had packed it that morning and that our luggage was still downstairs in the hall. When I returned they were talking with more intimacy than I had seen since we came to Sorrento. Mathews was relating how when he went to Dresden his father had given him an introduction to ex-King Ferdinand of Bulgaria, who was a fellow ornithologist; and how, when he visited him, the old gentleman had taken him into a room where there were a number of great cages full of tiny birds, and, waving a taper-fingered hand in their direction, had said, 'These are my only subjects now.' Dresden had many memories. I could hear them capping one another's recollections of what had happened there a year before. 'Oh and do you remember——?' Yes, and then we——' Afterwards in our room Mathews admitted that these few moments alone with her had been for him the high-water mark of the evening, a reassurance that nothing could shake their friendship. His loyalty and devotion to her remained what they had always been. Only that morning before breakfast he had said to me, 'You have no idea, Monk, she is the kindest-hearted creature,' and he began quoting instances of her kindness, which had transpired unconsciously in casual conversation: her goodness to a girl in Lausanne, betrayed by an unhappy love affair; her care for a mad girl in München; her concern for a child crying overhead in an hotel where she was staying. It interested me to see how even he, who had known her so long, could discover new and unsuspected facets of her character. I too had reason to wonder at its diversity. Was it that she enjoyed mystifying us a little, leaving us with the feeling that she was even more complex than we had imagined? Sometimes, perhaps from an impulse, which we all have, to impress, she would say things that implied a wealth of cynical experience; yet I could not be sure that it was not I who read into them this interpretation. It seemed to me, perhaps because he had suffered so deeply when he was in love with her himself, that Mathews was less puzzled than I by this contradictory side, this spirit of mischief and mockery, the expression of a mood that seemed to say that she had seen through man in all his types and variations long ago; and that, though he had often admitted to me a streak of hardness in her – less so now since she, who had broken so many hearts, had suffered the same fate herself – he deliberately ignored all that might remind him of such a side, accepting her contradictions without question; while I, who had known her a so much shorter time, continued to puzzle over them.

There was the story she had told us of the Frenchman, husband of her friend in Paris, who had fallen in love with her. She had been fond of this man. Indeed, she said he was the only man who had ever completely understood her. Presently he wrote proposing that they should elope together. 'And what did you do?' She gave a little laugh. 'I sent the letter to his wife.' To my somewhat naïve and unsuspecting mind, this ruthlessness towards a man for whom she admitted she had cared seemed an act of the basest treachery – treachery to love, even if loyalty to the woman who was first her friend. I did not realise that an offer of elopement from a married man is often a little less than a compliment, for he may have no intention whatever of making a final break with his wife. 'What happened?' 'There was a tremendous row. All the relatives blamed me, saying that it was my fault. In the end a priest was called in and he succeeded at last in calming everyone down.' 'And what did the wife say?' 'She said I was *une jeune fille bien honnête*.'

'*Honnête*' perhaps, but a little less than generous. That Frenchman, sophisticated, mature, object almost of my jealousy, how had he felt when she turned the tables on him so unexpectedly? That the list of her victims was long I knew from Mathews. Was there some strange streak in her whereby, though she loved the homage of men, she despised man himself? Just as the philanderer sees in almost every woman, of any pretension to charm, the opportunity for new experience, so did she see in every man a chance to study that strange, inept and foolish species?

It was waste of time to ask such questions. Even the least complex personality does not reveal itself to a stranger in a few days – in a few meetings. But, in her case, what arrested attention as much as anything was the fact that she never seemed anxious to establish a flattering legend and to bask in its sunshine, but rather to denigrate personality and present it in an unfavourable light. It was an impulse akin, perhaps, to the mood which had prompted her to cry to me that afternoon in Rome, 'No one admires you for what you really are, only for what they think you are.' Yet, looking at her now, as she talked to Mathews, their animation hushed for fear of disturbing me, I felt that all speculation was idle and unworthy, that no one, for instance, could be more pleasantly frank than she was at this instant; and I realised afresh, what I had felt before so often, that it was her ardour and interest in life which made her the perfect companion.

After a while Mathews said good night to us, and went away next door to continue his own writing in greater quiet. The huge room seemed still when he was gone. I closed my note-book, went over to the bed, sat down on the end of it and curled my feet up under me. I was glad to talk, so glad that to have lighted a cigarette, as I generally did, would have been an irrelevance. We talked as those do for whom almost any topic is significant, because it may chance to disclose a little more of the personality of the individual in whom they are interested. My doubts about her vanished; indeed, they had never existed except as a ghostly threat to the happiness of understanding her. And how lovely she was, her head against the huge white pillow, her hair pushed back off her forehead, in her eyes an expression at once dreamy and intent. My hand no longer sought hers; instead, I was content to look at her, realising once again that beauty is sacred and that those who enjoy its contemplation stand on holy ground. An overwhelming sense of reverence seized me, a vast sense of privilege. They know nothing of love who do not know its moments of humility. Nothing could ever rob me of or make me regret these past three days. They were imperishable, lovely, altogether unexpected. I would get up from where I sat, in a few minutes now, and kiss her good night. That in itself was a strange miracle. Who could have foreseen it a few days ago? And how many kisses had she given me that first afternoon, when, raising her face to mine, I had seen there the look of her prototype, the young girl in

Ireland? It was as though boyhood in its ardour had glimpsed one aspect of Plato's ideal beauty, something absolute and immortal, valid in that other world of eternal values, so that it was rather a recognition than a fresh encounter to meet it now. I seemed to have found something that my youth had lost and had been in search of ever since, without expectation, without hope of finding.

I got up, kissed her good night, and she accepted the kiss, as she had accepted so many others, not turning her head away until I should find her mouth, but offering her lips to mine with the frank surrender of a child. To attempt to recapture such moments, to speak of them at all, is, in a measure, to give them their death sentence; for the heart will carry something for years in safety which, like the contents of kings' tombs, falls to a little dust when overtaken by the light of day or the indiscretion of speech. I remember that a faint aromatic sweetness – from her hair, from the forearm on which my hand had rested as I drew her towards me – still clung to my own hand when I returned to the next room, and that, so great is the evocative power of all such things, it was sufficient almost to make her presence still seem real.

Our departure next morning was more dignified than its rehearsal the previous day. The greater part of our packing had been already done, and it was only a matter now of gathering up the oddments. Once more we bid our genial Austrian and his wife goodbye, once more we betook ourselves to the terminus to sit this time for the best part of half an hour in an empty tram. The postbags from the different hamlets around were being sorted on the ground immediately in front. No one showed any sign of haste or immediate departure. The tram seemed utterly indifferent to any commitments the official timetable might have made for it, and our feet grew colder and colder, while our tempers frayed.

'We must have something to read. Alister, could you possibly ferret something out of your baggage – the Irish book, if you know where it is?'

A little reluctantly Mathews fetched his rucksack and began to grope.

'I've found it – you can read to us, Monk.'

It was the same small blue anthology which had given us so much pleasure already. It was strange how this book with its Irish melancholy of wet skies and grey clouds of loneliness and broken hearts had been our mental companion for three days, so that we seemed at once in Ireland and in Italy. Only those who love books deeply can enjoy this ubiquity of spirit.

He passed the book to me, and I began to read:

'It is late last night the dog was speaking of you,
The snipe was speaking of you in her deep marsh;
It is you are the lonely bird throughout the woods,
And that you may be without a mate until you find me.'

'What have you chosen this time?'
' "Donall Oge." A translation from the Gaelic by Lady Gregory.'

'You promised and you said a lie to me,
That you would be before me where the sheep are flocked.
I gave a whistle and three hundred cries to you,
And I found nothing but a bleating lamb.

'You promised me a thing that was hard for you,
A ship of gold under a silver mast,
Twelve towns and a market in all of them,
And a fine white court by the side of the sea:

'You promised me a thing that is not possible,
That you would give me gloves of the skin of a fish,
That you would give me shoes of the skin of a bird,
And a suit of the dearest silk in Ireland.

'My mother said to me not to be talking with you,
To-day or to-morrow or on the Sunday
It was a bad time she took for telling me that,
It was shutting the door after the house was robbed.

'You have taken the east from me, you have taken the west from me.
You have taken what is before me, and what is behind me;
You have taken the moon, you have taken the sun from me,
And my fear is great you have taken God from me.'

'I wish you had read that the other day, then I could have copied it into my black book.'

'It is not too late now,' Mathews said.

Elisabeth began to search in her bag for a piece of paper on which she could write.

'Give me the paper; I'll make you a copy. It won't take a minute.

Now, Alister, read, but not too fast, and when my hand gets tired you can write and I'll read.'

But we had no sooner discovered a reason for remaining stationary than the tram decided it was high time to be in motion.

'Hurry, it is going to start. They are gathering up the mail bags.'

It was true; the tram was on the point of moving. But our haste was unnecessary. It would take us an hour and a quarter, as we discovered presently, to reach Castellamare, and during that time we would have numerous lengthy waits at wayside halts to complete the transcription. More mail bags, more discussion, more sorting of letters, more officials leaving the door open that our feet might become quite numb. Even Mathews failed to find compensations, grumbling that the day was as grey and melancholy as England's worst. The road was an unromantic version of the one we had traversed the previous afternoon – like it, cut under a precipice of rock, but lacking variety or dramatic interest. At Castellamare, where the tramlines ended we transferred to the train. The station was dirty and untidy and full of people. Running up and down the platform to get warm before returning to the crowded third-class carriage into which we had somehow managed to push ourselves and our luggage, we became detached from Mathews, who had gone to ask the price of some fruit. Elisabeth, in one of her puckish humours, thought it a good joke, but it distressed me to think that he might be looking for us. Eventually, having found him at the far end of the platform, we all three squeezed into the carriage, and the train started off, crawling at a snail's pace. The view failed to interest us. Looking out of the window, we saw a changed Vesuvius, shrunk, of ignoble appearance, like the flat little cone into which children play their tiddly-winks. Its slopes were streaked with melting snow, and from the summit a little weary smoke rose to a dead sky. It was an anticlimax to the beauty we had gazed at as we sailed from Naples four days before. Surrendering to our environment, we forgot that we had come from a hotel with tritons on the glass panels of its doors, and landscapes in the corners of its ceilings, and we peeled oranges unashamedly into our laps, and ate them, complaining all the while of our boredom. At last the train crept slowly into the dingy suburbs of the southern side of Naples and we found ourselves, heavily laden with luggage, elbowing our way along the platform to a taxi.

Our friend in the bank in Rome had given us the address of a pension in the Via Parthenope. We drove there, for the train to

Rome was not until five that evening, and we must get rid of our own luggage and then show Elisabeth something of Naples. The taxi pulled up on the harbour front outside a shabby-looking three-story building. I volunteered to go in and inspect the lodging. An untidy woman, professing herself unable to deal with the situation, made me mount many flights of stairs to a room on the top floor, where in a wide bed, under rumpled bedclothes, though it was now twelve o'clock noon, a fat man with curly black hair was still lying. I enquired his pension terms per day. 'Forty lire.' 'Impossible. That is too much.' 'How much you give?' Tentatively I murmured something about twenty-five. 'Done.' It was said so eagerly I had no doubt that if I had mentioned a figure considerably less he would have closed with that also, and somehow or other have made the proposition pay. It was Naples' method of doing business. Mathews would drink a glass of local Chartreuse in a shop, enquire the price of a bottle and be told 'Thirty lire.' 'Too much.' 'How much you give for it?' 'Fifteen.' 'Take it.' But the method defeats its own object, for, suspecting that he should have said eight instead of fifteen, Mathews would end by not buying the bottle at all. In the same way now, the sudden reduction in his terms made me disinclined to become the pensionnaire of the gentleman in the bed, still more so when I had seen his rooms. I returned to the taxi shaking my head. 'Dirty and unattractive. I certainly don't want to go there.' 'Try the house next door. It was there the German girls stayed on their way back from Capri.' The neighbouring pension was dingy enough also, though it had a better dining-room. Its proprietor, grey-haired, tie-less, in his shirt sleeves, told me that lunch if we stayed would be ten lire, and full pension forty-five a day. An exception to the species, he did not seem inclined to bargain. I returned to the car. But while I had been inside, the hotel porter of another pension, one of those individuals who, wearing a peaked cap and armed with a number of printed cards, perambulate the streets touting for custom, had noticed the waiting taxi, and had approached Alister and Elisabeth and given them the address of a new German pension near the electric station. A babble of voices greeted me in four languages, the representative of the Hotel Pension Novela, the chauffeur, and the two occupants of the taxi all having chosen a different one in which to negotiate. It was the chauffeur who eventually established that what the man said was true. The pension was not far, almost on the sea-front, and near the station from which Elisabeth must go that evening; if nothing else, it would be a convenient place at which to lunch and leave our luggage, while we continued the search elsewhere. The hotel porter jumped on to the step of the taxi and, holding on by the door-handle, he directed our driver to the Novela.

It was a modest building, considerably less imposing than its picture on the card had led us to believe. Mathews, sent in to negotiate, remained a long time, and returned at last to say that he did not like it. Nor did we, very much, when we entered. The brand-new, shoddy furniture was banal in the extreme, though it had the advantage of being clean. The truth was that we had been demoralised by our four days of luxury and the sooner we got back to cheapness the better, or our resources would never get us as far as Palestine. The day discouraged us, making decision difficult. I was for finding out if there was a boat for Egypt and sailing that night. Naples, that on a sunny day rises up the hillside from the harbour like a pack of multi-coloured cards thrown down in gay confusion, appeared now as grey and dismal as any northern port. Why should we stay when it really had nothing to offer us? But to take boat for Egypt at such short notice was impossible; it was a wish rather than a serious suggestion. Alister proposed that we should unload our luggage at the pension while he would go to Vomero to look at the convent recommended by the Grey Sisters in Rome. Elisabeth and I would lunch presently at the Novela, and meet him later at the Museum; then we could decide definitely where we would stay. I could see that he himself had no desire to go anywhere other than the convent. Vomero was the suburb immediately above Naples, reached by tram and funicular, not very convenient for sight-seeing; but already I was filled with such a loathing for cheap lodgings, it seemed quite likely this plan would be the best. Mathews explained to the German manager, a weedy, pale, consumptive-looking fellow, that two of us would return to lunch in about fifty minutes, and that we would decide later about rooms. He departed with an air of buoyant resolution. We saw him spring on to a tram, wave to us and disappear inside.

The sights of Naples lay a little heavily upon our conscience, and, deciding there was time before lunch to visit the famous aquarium, we took a tram which left us near the Public Gardens. As we walked along the Via Carracciolo, before turning into the Gardens, we talked of indifferent things, discussing Alister's chances of success, or commenting on the intense cold and wintry bleakness of the day.

Bleak indeed it was, and my own mood seemed to take its colour from the weather. It was as though for four days I had been living in a dream, one of those enchanted dreams which the taker of hashish is supposed to enjoy, in which everything is roseate and one has only to reach out a finger to be conscious of illimitable power; but was now plunged back suddenly into the cold external world.

'*Triste homme?*'

'Yes, that's right. *Triste homme.*'

She who had been so dispirited when we reached Castellamare seemed now by one of her sudden reversals of humour to be almost elate, whereas my own spirits had sunk to zero. She mocked me gently for my melancholy, yet admitted that, though she had said nothing at the time, she herself had been in the depths of depression on the Sunday, two days before. Our moods are incomprehensible, or, rather, like the Blue Nile and its sources, they may have their origin in a hinterland so distant that it is easier to accept them and not to ask ourselves how they arise. But my mood now was easy enough to explain. I was tired. The emotional strain of the last few days had begun to tell; my mind had been stretched to tension point, keyed to a pitch of sensitivity, when like a crab that has lost its shell we are hurt by the merest trifle. One such pin-prick had wounded me only a few minutes before. When we got into the taxi at the station it had seemed to me that Elisabeth had deliberately placed herself away from me, and with Mathews between us, and this action, possibly quite unconscious on her part, was at once construed, in my present tension of nerves, as a deliberate attempt to put me in my place, to remind me that it was just as easy for her to be indifferent as to be kind. I had winced under the imagined rebuff, and it had continued to rankle, opening up a complete terrain of mistrust upon my part.

For men are strange creatures, indignant if they are repelled, yet horrified at the thought of being courted. Honour demands that they should always deem themselves the pursuer, always think that they have retained the initiative. I remembered now an incident at Sorrento on the afternoon when Mathews had gone to Capri. We had been silent for a minute or two, and then Elisabeth, apropos of nothing that had gone before in our conversation, but almost as though she felt prompted at this juncture to confess to something lying upon conscience, had said quietly:

'You know I did a rotten thing once. I deliberately tried to make someone love me.'

It flashed across my mind that she spoke of me; and instantly, and instinctively, pride recoiled from the suggestion. I winced, and asked in a tone so icy as to freeze any further confidences, 'Oh, and am I your victim?' And she, seeing perhaps that I was annoyed, had replied quickly, 'Oh, no, it was a long time ago and I was very young at the time,' leaving me wondering, as I gazed out of the window at the bay with its white horses, whether I had been mistaken after all.

Yet the conviction persisted that my surmise had been right. What else could her remark mean, emerging out of complete irrelevance? Why should anyone trouble to admit that they had tried to attract love when they were young? It was no crime. Every girl in her senses would do the same. She had been about to take the blame for our friendship on her shoulders, to admit that she had said to herself when we first met in Rome, 'I could make him love me, if I liked, and I do like.' But my reaction was not to ask if this were so, and, perhaps, to learn from her lips that she cared for me. I had accepted the half-loaf of ephemeral love, and I was content to do so. More would have distressed me. The word love had never been spoken between us. Instead of showing the apprehension of the real lover towards anything that threatens misunderstanding, or that touches the happiness of a personality that has become inestimably precious to him; instead of welcoming an opportunity to learn what her feeling towards me really was, I had silenced her by the wounded pride of my tone. And this had been deliberate; for any admission that she had wished to make me love her would have opened up the whole question of whether her attempt had been successful (did I love her in the fullest sense of the word, as a person, or did I only love her in the same way, but to a heightened degree, that one loves everything that is beautiful?) and that was a question which I had not even troubled to debate in my own thoughts.

And so, though her confession may have sprung from something gentle in her nature, an impulse of genuine regret, and not something hard and triumphant at all, I ignored it, for if, even for a moment, I had treated it as such, all silences would have been overthrown between us and we should have been confronted with a situation which I at least refused to envisage.

And just as this incident had remained a disturbing factor in consciousness, and when forgotten would suddenly return for no reason at all, so now her action in the taxi, which may have been quite unconscious, took on the aspect of caprice, becoming a point of focus for all my previous speculations as to the true nature of her character.

The rain dripped from the ilex trees along the pathway as we walked towards the aquarium. The gardens which ordinarily would have been full of pedestrians and playing children, were now, at lunch time, completely deserted, and when we came round a corner upon an old man sweeping leaves it was with a sense of surprise as though we had expected to find no other human beings there beside ourselves. As we walked away from him I said to her:

'It is a funny thing, but I know less of you now than I did in Rome.'

'Really. Why?'

'I suppose I have seen more sides of you since then. Certainly you are more puzzling to me now.'

'Perhaps so.'

'Whereas you know all about me.'

'Yes, I think that is true.'

She seemed satisfied that this should be so, as though it were woman's prerogative to remain inscrutable. But my remark was a foolish one, for women love to feel their power, yet they despise a little those who allow them to do so. All that she had said the previous day, of men in general, and of certain men in particular, had left me with the feeling that she regarded them as at once her enemies and her slaves, that they were capable of inspiring in her, at least sometimes, a certain contempt. Since our drive to Amalfi she had made me realise that I touched only the fringe of her character; that what had once seemed relatively simple and idyllic was actually far less simple than I had supposed. And all these thoughts which, as they moved through my mind like far-off, sullen flashes of lightning before storm, brought me no nearer a solution, renewed themselves now, troubling me, until I pushed them from me.

We had reached the aquarium.

'Here we are.'

It was a rather gloomy little building standing in the middle of a grove of ilex trees and skirted by a hedge of laurel.

'I can't say that it looks very attractive.'

'You must wait till you are inside. Then you will think you are in fairyland.'

We paid our money and entered. I remembered how, when I had come here on my travels two years before, this vision of a marine world had opened up vistas of enchanted territory, beauty that I had never suspected, so that, discouraged by the thought of the increasing ugliness of earth due to its usurpation by man – a thought always with me – I had wondered whether one day we might be forced to go beneath the sea in search of beauty, to 'call a new world into existence to redress the balance of the old ' But now flippancy took the place of fantasy and philosophic day-dreams and, amused by these underwater panoramas, each tank with its background of painted scenery and its foreground of living and moving wonder, we discussed in which we should choose to spend our lives if we were forced to do so. One of them suggested a scene in Ceylon; brightly-hued anemones emphasised its Oriental note, while thick-stalked yellow plants waved their heavy foliage like so many date-palms.

'That's rather pleasant, don't you think – quite gay, in fact. But I don't like the far dark corner; what's happening there?'

'It's deliberately darkened for some creature that hates the light.'

'Oh look, how lovely. You can see right through them.'

She was pointing to a shoal of tiny rainbow-tinted fish with bars across their flanks which had swum suddenly to the centre of the tank, and then darted as fleetly away. The larger fish that had disturbed them continued his casual cruise with piscine insouciance.

Awed a little by the glimmering twilight of this submarine world into which the light filtered from above, we moved in the half darkness of the great hall to where miracles of fragile delicacy floated in a sea-green setting. Venus's girdle, the frailest thing in Nature, hung suspended in the water, or floated with easy grace like a long, silvery ribbon, gleaming sometimes with violet lights, or, in the darker portions of the tank, shining with an orange phosphorescence. An electric discharge seemed to shimmer from end to end through this fragile creature, in steady recurrence, as though a tremor of emotion had passed through it, or as though it were sending out a message in code. A pair of angel-fish, camouflaged by their brilliant hues against the gaily-coloured coral, moved always one behind the other, the distance between them never varying. We paused presently in front of a tank in which great encrusted amphorae of the Roman era lay on the sea floor, and huge eels – delicacies in the banquets at Baiae – cruised amongst them.

'Look at the head of that fellow poking out of a pot.'

Nearby, among many-shaped and multi-coloured fish, tiny sea-horses swam demurely, with amusing precision and dignity, like illustrations to a fairy tale. An octopus in a tank to himself, hideous, bulbous-nosed, grotesque, was lured with difficulty to the front by placing our hands flat against the glass. Hideous little eyes squinted at us from the centre of the bloated mass, while thick, waving tentacles stretched greedily in all directions or adhered, with their series of graded white suckers, to the glass between us, and we amused ourselves by studying what we imagined was his expression of enraged frustration. It brought to mind the scene in the cave in Hugo's *Toilers of the Sea*, when, struggling all the time to draw his knife, the man wrestles, like Laöcoon, against the terrible enemy which has drawn him under water.

Presently we crossed to the far side of the aquarium to a shallow open trough in which an electric ray dragged out its existence, giving shocks to any visitor with courage enough to put a hand down through the water and grasp it firmly. I had done so before, and I did so again now, as did Elisabeth. It was perhaps characteristic of both of us that, having had our thrill, we should forthwith sentimentalise over the miseries of its existence; a poor life, even for a fish, entertaining idle humanity and listening – if a fish can listen – to their squawks of fear and excitement as the shock shot up the arm to the elbow, and they hastily let go. But the world is full of poor lives; the mummer's is not by any means the worst. Better this, perhaps, than the fishmonger's slab; just as the life of a clown in some little wayside circus, with the wind flapping the draughty tent at night, as autumn advances, may seem better to him than the threatened embrace of icy Mother Earth.

Making their tour of the big hall were an American couple whom we had seen on the Capri boat four days before, the woman amusing us when, camera in hand, she had called in shrill desperation to the man, 'I can't get you *and* Vesuvius.' Life, we had agreed, was like that: it was impossible to have everything at once.

The visit to the aquarium had made us almost gay. We left it and walked back along the Via Carracciolo. Few people were about. The day was one to discourage tourists and it was the hour of most people's midday meal. A man passed us, pushing a hand-barrow, shoulders stooped forward in desperate energy, like some Sisyphus returned to modern life. A fisherman made his way to the little harbour of boats. A cyclist, sending up jets like spouting fountains from the pools of water in the road, sped by quickly, intent on his destination, wherever that might be. The leaves of the bays and laurels and of the tall ilex trees in the garden bordering the Corso glistened with tiny drops of moisture as though they had broken into a sweat. A grey mist held everything in its grip.

The secrets of the heart are like the secrets which children share, meaningless to the rest of the world. Something happened now so slight in itself, so trivial, but of such shattering import that it seems foolish to attempt to convey it.

We had walked a little way. It is possible that a phrase of mine, something I had said, created the occasion. A feigned jocularity may have made her think me indifferent to the idea of our parting. But if so her revenge was terrible and effective. Suddenly she made a remark at which the whole fabric of my world seemed to totter on its base and then fall. It is strange that from the instant she uttered them I could never remember her actual words, only their general significance and their effect upon me. That I can remember as vividly as anything in life. It was as though Circe had touched me with her wand, uttering at the same time words of insult and contemptuous dismissal.

If we are sentimental, we prefer that an idyll should remain an idyll, even in memory, and not be dethroned suddenly and savagely at the very moment when it still means most to us. Her remark was shattering because it struck at self-esteem. It was as though she said, 'You flatter yourself if you think that this has meant much to me.' It seemed to belittle everything that had taken place between us, casting into the gutter all those memories which I had thought to hold sacred and lovely. I was convinced that she had meant to wound, wishing to convey to me that I was small game to one of her experience, a gentle Don Juan, less possessive, less aggressive than most, knowing very little in fact of the passions and jealousies of my sex.

All this by implication in a single phrase! And, as she said it, the sea broke in a great sheet of spray over the wall further along the Corso, and a taxi passing at that moment splashed us with its mud.

I had one instant reaction to her words, not to let her know by a sign, by a flicker of an eyelash, that they had wounded me. I felt as though I had been struck in the pit of the stomach. I experienced the same sensation of sickening emptiness. Yet all the time pride kept saying to me, 'There are only another three or four hours before you bid her goodbye. Do not let her see that you have winced. She must never know that she has wounded you perhaps even more effectively than she meant.'

It is possible that I misunderstood her completely, that she had intended no unkindness and that I misconstrued what she said. Or, again, she may have struck this blow deliberately, to end with the clean incision of finality an episode that had only arisen on the absolute understanding that it should be ephemeral. She may have wished deliberately to give our friendship the *coup de grâce* which she felt decency demanded, allowing sentiment no chance, ruling out all regrets, all backward glances, all that might tempt to renewal.

But my impression was not this; rather it was that she meant to be unkind, that she meant to wound, that she wished perhaps to make one last discovery in relation to my character, the discovery of how I would react under the lash. The strain which all emotion imposes on us can play strange tricks with consciousness. But it is a little difficult, even allowing for heightened sensitiveness and stretched nerves, to believe that a blow whose effect lasted for years could have been wholly imaginary. It is quite possible – in love everything is possible – but it is unlikely. And yet that is what this blow did. It numbed me, it made me reluctant even to revert in thought to the occasion. All these years I have had an opportunity of putting the matter to the test, of testing whether her words were meant unkindly or not. But I have not taken it. This in itself is significant. I dreaded a still more severe wound to self-esteem. For, hard on the remark which hurt me and, as though arising out of whatever train of thought was in her mind at the time, she said:

'Do you know the stories of Albert Samain?'

'I know his poems, but not the stories.'

'You must read them. One especially. Hyalis. It is about a little faun. Hyalis. Will you remember that?'

'Yes.'

Once again mind leaped to its own swift and maybe erroneous conclusion. I was the faun, the goat-footed satyr, harmless and a little naïve. Was it imagination or did she seem to imply that in that story I would find the clue to much, to myself perhaps, to our idyll – that same idyll which she had a moment before traduced with a word of scorn? I know that I reasoned instantly that here was the key to her earlier and cryptic utterance and that I had only to use it for all to be made clear. But I did not use it for that very reason. For years the book did not come my way. Then one day it was put into my hands. I read the other three tales. But I did not read Hyalis. It contained – it might contain – the key to too great a mystery. If I read it I should know. I preferred ignorance. I do not know now. Would it prove to be completely irrelevant, throwing no light on the occasion at all? Would it strike at the heart, reopening an old wound? Or would it fill me with self-reproach for having misunderstood her so completely? I cannot say. But it is evidence, if nothing else, of how deeply the blow had struck home, that for fourteen years I preferred uncertainty and deliberately abstained from putting the matter to the test. Some day curiosity may get the better of me and I shall read Samain's tale.

We walked to the corner where the tram had dropped us half an hour earlier and awaited one in which to return. At last we heard it reeling and rattling along in the distance. It came into sight, stopped, took us on board, and lurched off once more. Two o'clock had struck before we found ourselves back at the Pension Novela, and then began a dismal wait in the new and uncomfortable wicker-work chairs of the pretentious little sitting-room until our lunch should be ready. I remember how, true to my resolution of showing by no sign that I was even aware that she had tried to hurt me – as, I began to feel, she had hurt so many others, treating them like pawns whose moves and dispositions she herself decided – I rallied her about our tardy gesture to antiquity, which we had left to the last minute, not even troubling to turn aside to see Pompeii. Only a little time remained, only a few hours, to keep up a pretence, to put a brave face on it, like a boxer who has been badly shaken, but whose whole aim is not to let his opponent know this, counting the seconds until the gong shall sound. We would go to the Museum. I would show her what I knew she would appreciate, the finest antique heads in the world, than which Greek and Roman art have nothing better of their kind to offer: the colossal head of Cæsar with the wide brow and unpierced eyeballs, dominating by their very expression of sightless detachment; the Euripides looking out from under bent brows, with deeply-gazing eyes; the Seneca, with sagging mouth, sunken cheeks and matted, untidy hair, baffled, bedraggled, yet almost heroic.

'I always look at the Seneca and wonder whether the sculptor meant to convey that he was unvanquished, unconquerable, despite every humiliation, or whether his intention was really unkind, as though to say, "See to what a pass too much thinking and too little moral courage can bring a man."'

'I seem to know it. I must have seen reproductions of it somewhere.'

'It is despair. Despair incarnate, the despair of wisdom impotent against stupidity, of goodness helpless against evil. Perhaps it is the despair of failure; perhaps he compromised too much.'

She would approve the Seneca, but she would like still better the Greek marbles. She would find in them something that the Roman bronze, for all its realism, lacked, dignity, profundity, detachment. They plumb the human spirit to its very depths. They carry us beyond aspect to those soul-stresses which account for aspect, every physical trait leading us to contemplate some spiritual counterpart, so that we no longer read in marble, but in the book of life. The serene gravity of the Euripides, the locks receding from the high forehead, but falling long on either side of the face, the firm line of the mouth half hidden by the hair on the upper lip, all suggest that, though this head, like the Homer, may be an ideal conception, it is at the same time the very type and symbol of certain human qualities.

'There are four or five versions of the Euripides, obviously from a common origin, differing only in detail or finish. I have seen others in the Glyptotek in Copenhagen. But there is one in the Museum here that is by far the best. Perhaps it really is the original. It says completely what all the others are trying to say.'

It was nearly three. Lunch had been slow in coming, and we dawdled over it because of its very dullness. Then Elisabeth, a rare occurrence for her, had chosen to take out a cigarette and smoke it slowly.

'Are you ready?'

'Yes.'

'We haven't much time to spare.'

The Metro took us across Naples with several waits and changes and, running up the steps of the Museum, we explained to the porter that when a tall young Inglese arrived he was to be told that we were there and would meet him if he waited for us at the entrance. It was a shock to learn that the Museum closed at a quarter past four. It seemed scarcely worth Mathews' while to pay twelve lire for the few minutes which would be his, and, if the man were intelligent, he would have no difficulty in recognising him. Our own visit would be hurried enough; we must see everything in the next half-hour.

Passing quickly into the first room, I began to search for the heads that we had talked of. The Cæsar was easily found, three or four times life size, the crisp hair receding slightly from the forehead, the mouth parted with an expression almost of amusement, the brow unfurrowed, only two great lines either side of the mouth showing that events leave their imprint even upon the strong.

'Hurry. The Greek heads are further on. But I want to show you the Seneca first. I can't imagine a greater contrast. Through here.'

The green bronze has turned almost black, the head is tilted to one side, as though in anguish or to escape a blow, the eyeballs are

303

pierced, white with black pupils, and in them is an expression, not of fear, but of actual terror, of agony, of abandonment. From a little distance it might almost be the portrait of a man howling.

'He looks beaten.'

'The apotheosis of pedagogy. See what it was to have been tutor to Nero.'

'Show me the Homer.'

We moved along the gallery to where it stood solitary, on a round pillar with a square base. Words failed before the nobility of that conception. Man's hand has never cut so deeply in marble the lineaments of the soul. Homer is an old man, the sightless eyes are sunken far in the head, with that expression of complete submission which only the blind know. The cheeks are sunk too, the hair flat, bound with a fillet and clustering at the side of the temples in curls. The beard also is in tight curls. On that brow, deeply furrowed vertically and horizontally, every line that sorrow or strain can make seems to have been graven, and the patient mouth, drooping, almost querulous, with the querulousness of those who are very old, seems about to utter some sublime phrase and then to falter. And yet – who but the Greeks could have done this – the whole effect is not failure, not complaint, certainly not complaint, but rather serenity, acceptance by old age of the terms on which we hold life, age which has seen all, endured all, and learned to leave to the gods the final verdict on mortal affairs. The last virtue is submission, and the last word is not ours. Those sightless eyeballs have seen man's strength, the grace of youth, and woman's calm, unswerving fortitude, and they are content with that – content now till death close them.

She remained silent in front of the pedestal and her silence seemed to me more eloquent than any words.

It was an anticlimax to press on into the other rooms, to pause before the Pompeian banker, with its expression of brutal cunning, the mouth pulled down at one side in a slobber, a great mole or carbuncle on the left side of his chin; the crooked nose, the wrinkled skin below the eyes, the huge flapping ears, all testifying to the candour of the sculptor, and the phallic footnote on the pillar in imitation of a Hermes, offering its strange commentary on contemporary Roman taste.

We had delayed so long over the masterpieces that there was time only to glance at the exhibits from Pompeii in the rooms upstairs, at the prunes and blackened egg shells, fishbones and flower seeds, at

the moulds for pastry and the cake of raisins, all of them two thous-
and years old. We passed quickly from one case to another, stopping
only for a moment before the dark-eyed conception of Sappho by
some Pompeian hack artist, and the mosaic Cave Canem with the
barking dog, which I remembered so well as a child in a reproduc-
tion which my father had brought back from Naples, a jaunty, lively
dog, tail up and yapping loudly.

'It hung in the hall and I never looked at it that I did not feel it
was about to bite me.'

All the time, as I led the way, I talked to her with a sense of
relief that there was so much to interest us, so much to help me hide
my thoughts. To put a gallant face on it, that was all that mattered.
Was she used to those whom she subjected, presently, when she had
tired of them, crying for mercy? I should never cry. To seem indifferent, elate, unconcerned, even as she seemed herself – that was
the task.

A strange-looking, shabby individual in a coat with a fur collar,
wearing his hat and carrying a walking-stick, was following us
around the gallery shutting the windows as he went. Nothing less
like an official could be imagined, and it was some time before it
dawned on us that he was one, and that he was giving us a delicate
hint that we should not be welcome one moment after the quarter-
hour had struck. We came down the great marble staircase, shooed
out of the last few rooms, in one of which Breughel's masterpiece,
his Seven Blind Men, had held us for an instant, and discovered
Mathews reading a book under one of the pillars. He was surprised
to see us so soon.

'They told you, didn't they, the Museum closes early to-day?'

'Yes, and I've been reading here.'

He was full of his expedition to Vomero, describing it to us as
we made our way back to the Metro. He had discovered the
convent of the Grey Sisters of Santa Elisabetta, and it was a haven
of refuge of which even I would approve. The funicular took
you almost there; then it was only a few hundred yards from the
station.

'There is snow still lying in the gardens up at Vomero, mushy
and a bit melancholy. But the convent itself is delightful. It is the
last house in a road which is a cul-de-sac. We could not be quieter.
The Schwester-oberin showed me two rooms when I told her where
we had stayed in Rome; and then she gave me lunch, a splendid
lunch, soup with yolk of egg in it, an omelette and *petits pois*, two

German meat-balls with mashed potatoes, and then nuts, apples and tangerines *ad lib*. And all that for eight lire.'

He rattled on, telling me that the nuns were kindness itself, a little more assured in manner, more human, more mundane than those in Rome.

'You see, they go out into Naples and nurse. The hostel is run partly for people out of employment – Germans, of course; governesses and people like that. The nuns rustle about in long draperies, with a grey veil hanging down, and a different coif from the ones in Rome, smaller, more like a round half disc. The convent is rather palatial. It has white marble stairs. The building is a comparatively new one. Perhaps it was some wealthy person's villa before.'

'So you propose to take the veil again? I did not know one was allowed to do so twice,' Elisabeth said.

'I do not see why he wants to stay in Naples at all. If there is a boat to Egypt to-night why don't we take it?'

To get away, to uproot ourselves, even to travel steerage to Alexandria, as we had always agreed to do, seemed at that moment better than to linger in a place with so many memories. But it would be selfishness to drag him away unless he were willing to come. This was not his second visit, as it was mine.

'Well, what did you settle?'

'Nothing. I did not like to do so without first consulting you. I left the question open. I told them if we were coming we would try and arrive not too late to-night.'

'It will end by our going there.'

We had reached the Metro, only to find that there was a twenty minutes' wait before the next train. Sitting on the windy platform, we amused ourselves exchanging our passports and criticising the respective likenesses they contained. There was an air of forced gaiety over all we said or did, which supported us and yet deceived no one. We were shades in some underworld, who had left the light of the sun the previous day and knew it. Once I apologised for having dawdled so long over my lunch, thus shortening our time at the Museum.

'Oh, but I was just as much to blame as you. I smoked.'

Our eyes met, and for a brief instant – as though the clock of time had been put back – there seemed recreated between us the old kindness; and I experienced a sense of immeasurable comfort, which was only momentary.

All was bustle and stir at the big station when we reached it. It was the new electrified line to Rome, almost halving the time of the journey, and still a novelty and a pride to all Italians. We accompanied Elisabeth along the train to look for an empty carriage. I found one at last and, putting her in a corner seat, had just time to stoop quickly and kiss her twice when Mathews, coming along the corridor behind, saw us, and paused tactfully to adjust the snake-skin belt round his raincoat before joining us.

'Elisabeth will need a supplementary ticket for the *rapide*,' he announced. 'I will get that if you will go and fetch her case from the pension. There is plenty of time.'

It was a matter of only a minute to run down the road and find the pension, but on my return I re-entered the station by different stairs and arrived on the platform in doubt as to which end of the train I had reached. Setting off in the wrong direction, I walked down its length only to encounter the American friends whom I had first met in Florence, a charming professor of literature at one of the universities, and his sixteen-year-old son. We had seen them only the day before at Amalfi for a moment, on the steps of the Cappuccini.

I retraced my steps.

'Elisabeth, my American friends are down the train if you would sooner travel with them.'

Already her carriage had filled up. There was a man in each corner. Yes, she would like to, and, going down the train, I handed her over to her escort, who were shy but friendly, and insisted on vacating the window seat in her favour. But now Mathews, who was purchasing her ticket, would not find her when he returned to the first carriage, and, going in search of him, I was in time to intercept him as he made his way up the platform.

The signal had been given for all not travelling to leave the train. We stood on the platform, craning our necks to look up at the high corridor window to which Elisabeth had come, then gazing along the length of the train, or at its great wheels and couplings. It was about to start. We shouted goodbye. But it was a false alarm. Nothing happened and we resumed our talk, full of the banalities which such occasions foster.

'The newspapers all say that there has been a great storm at Naples. My mother will be frantic.'

'Put all the blame on us.'

'Say we insisted.'

'That won't make any difference. She will *me laver la tête* all the same.'

For the second time horns were sounded and officials shouted. It really was going now. The train moved slowly out of the station. She stood at the window looking back at us. Now it was gone. We turned away. Everything which had happened since we had left Rome four days before seemed to have happened in the flash of a dream, and, just as in dreams the content of the dream seems immeasurably great in comparison to the brevity of the time which has elapsed, so now the gulf which separated Rome and Naples seemed almost to contain years.

For the fourth time we returned to the dismal and uninspiring precincts of the Novela, to collect our own suitcases, to load ourselves up with them like beasts of burden, a stuffed rucksack across the shoulders, a heavy suitcase in each hand, and to carry them with frequent rests as far as the cloakroom of the Metro. There we deposited them and made our way quickly across the town to Cook's to see if any letters awaited us. Mathews had been abusive of Naples by day. He had not yet seen that confusion of red, yellow, brown and white buildings in the sunlight on one of those days when the smoke from the cone of Vesuvius, mounting up in a great coil in the still air, falls over on its side by the sheer weight of its own mass. But it was more beautiful, he maintained, than Rome by night. We walked along the sea-front. The multitudinous lights up the hill, the huge circle of lights, too, showing in the velvet darkness across the water and continuing right round the bay, outlining it, so that one could surmise every town and village, the water-front itself with the black mass of the Castello del Ovo rising from where the waves lapped against its bastions – all this delighted him; and, now that he had found a resting-place which he approved, he seemed glad that we were to remain.

But even his enthusiasm was scarcely proof against the fatigues of the day. The mail at Cook's, when we got there, was disappointingly small. There was only a letter for me and a postcard for him.

'Nothing from Markharoff? I hope we haven't offended him.'

It had been a problem when leaving the Borgo Santo Spirito to know how to express our gratitude for all the Chaldean's kindness and our penitence for the amount of trouble we had given him. We know that he was badly off; there must be books that he would like to buy, and finally we had decided to leave a fifty-lire note for him on the table in the priests' room, together with a written message expressing a little of our gratitude.

It was some days yet before we would receive a letter from him, and, when it came, it would puzzle us.

Markharoff wrote: '*Illustre Sagesse, très touché de votre bonté, charité, persévérance et de votre moralité altruiste, j'ai l'honneur de vous accuser d'avoir commis une violation très (grave) de la loi morale, religieuse et sociale en me laissant sur la table une lettre renfermant 50 lires italiennes. Si je ne vous ai pas écrit c'est que j'avais tellement honte. Comment un garçon de 21 ans, pauvre (naturellement, pas spirituellement) laisse pour moi une si grande somme d'argent — je ne pouvais pas même concevoir. C'est cause de cela est un grand crime devant la loi sociale (à cause de votre pauvreté). Je vous remercie de toutes les graces, que vous m'avez accordées par votre présence corporelle et individuelle, par votre bel esprit et surtout par votre disposition surnaturelle et exceptionelle par rapport aux autres. Je vous souhaite à l'occasion des fêtes passées, présentes et futures tout ce qui peut contribuer à votre propre satisfaction. . . .*'

Was he hurt by our gift, was he laughing at us, or was it not irony at all but genuine gratitude together with his customary delight in extravagant language, which made him write in such a strain? It was hard to say. We had an uneasy sense of having blundered, of having patronised where patronage was unforgivable, or else of having left Markharoff under the impression that we were even poorer than we were.

We felt that our visit to Cook's had hardly been worth it. By the time we had returned to the Metro station, resumed our burdens and waited on the draughty platform, Mathews' spirits had sunk to almost as low an ebb as my own. He had rejected my contention that it was possible to do the whole journey by tram and was full of apologies when later I was proved right. He looked pinched and cold, and the cough which had continued to worry him in Sorrento was more insistent than ever.

'If you like, I will open my suitcase and look for some chocolate for you.'

He seemed grateful.

The Metro, when at last it came, took us to Monte Santo and from there we were faced with a walk of several hundred yards to the foot of the funicular. Once more we cursed the bulkiness of our luggage. The man at the barrier had amused us by lifting a package in either hand and estimating their weight by guesswork before charging, but what that weight was we knew well enough now, as we staggered along towards the funicular steps. There we waited with the crowd returning from their day's work, watching the cable revolve as the little car slowly descended. Crushed at last into one of the narrow carriages, our impedimenta made us cordially

309

disliked. People stumbled over the suitcases and were unable to stand in comfort because of our rucksacks, which dug into their backs. Tired-eyed and resentful, returning from shop and office, they looked at us with silent irritation. No longer Inglesi milords, driving the coast-road in our chaise, or lounging at ease beneath lofty ceilings on which gilded butterflies conducted their eternal revels, we had become a part, and an unpopular part, of that hurried, sweating herd which flows through the streets of Naples each evening at dusk.

At last the slowly-rising car drew level with the tiers of steps in Vomero Station. We bundled out. Mathews, hastening in spite of his load, led the way with confidence, as though he had memorised every inch of it earlier in the day. It was strangely quiet up here after the crowded carriages and the heat and bustle of the platform. Already the air felt different in this suburb, up on a hill, apart and yet only a few hundred yards from the city. Below us the multitudinous lights of Naples seemed as impersonal and remote as the Milky Way. Ahead of us appeared to be waste land and ruined buildings, but suddenly we stopped by a white porch with high steps, and setting down his load Mathews rang the bell.

'*Nous sommes arrivés*,' he said with relief.

We had arrived, and, the moment the door opened, the smiling graciousness of the middle-aged nun who came to it made us feel pilgrims once more, and welcome. Like a boat that has been storm-tossed but that has made harbour, like prodigals who had forgotten sanctity but had returned home, we followed her up the stairs, past the small light burning in front of an image beneath which artificial flowers clustered in a vase, to the rooms which my friend had seen earlier in the day. We had come to a hostel, homely, joyous, almost maternal in its solicitude for our welfare. The tiled room, clean, with its electric light and warm stove, where we ate our supper, and to which came presently the sister who had cooked it to look on us almost as curios, was itself a welcome.

But next morning lying in bed in my room, with the sun shining on the snow still heaped in the corners and crevices of the small square platform outside, the clear sky showing above, I experienced all the acute anguish which I had felt on the Via Carracciolo the previous afternoon. It is said that the revenges of Aphrodite are always terrible. Perhaps I had exposed myself to such revenge by pretending to be the votary of that goddess when I was not in a position to sustain the role. If so, I was now reaping my reward. Mathews visited me and found me turning over the pages of Rodin's book, the book which Elisabeth had lent me, my one remaining link with her, so full of moving and penetrating reflections on *la beauté*. He looked at me quizzically as though he understood the cause of my melancholy, nor did I say anything that might enlighten him. But I was suffering, not the pangs of love parted – a separation which he seemed to think had grieved Elisabeth as well as me – but rather of love disillusioned. Three or four drops of subtle poison, poured into my ear as into the ear of Hamlet's sleeping father, had had power in an instant to overthrow my world. The blow still sickened me. I smiled at his friendly raillery, but there was death in my heart, only my sense of irony was amused that he should be so ignorant of its true cause. It was laughable, but it was tragic.

I had said that nothing could ever rob me of or make me forget these last few days, and now she herself had robbed me of them. Is it that love of any sort puts us on a rack? I remembered with what scorn, holding that reason should always be supreme in its control of our lives, I had thought of men who shot themselves when they discovered their wives unfaithful to them; cowards, unable to adjust themselves to the blows of Fate. But now, in a much lesser degree, I seemed to experience the same sickening and paralysing sensation, as though something axiomatic to my whole confidence in life had in the twinkling of an eye been proved false. I had been given a sudden glimpse of an aspect of the human heart I had never encountered before. The basis of trust on which my whole conception of life was founded had been shaken. It was incomprehensible to me that one could wish to hurt someone for whom one had once felt affection, or say a thing from a mere desire to see how another person would react under the rebuff. Between friends – still more between those who loved – I had imagined it to be impossible that things could be other than exactly what they seemed. I told myself that it was not wholly true that I was a philanderer to be given no more than the deserts of a philanderer; for the admiration, reverence and affection I had offered had been whole-hearted and real, and what wounded me now was to suspect that I had had something less in return.

Being a poor psychologist and perhaps sentimental in my whole outlook on love, it never occurred to me that it was possible for any-one to love, and, at the same time, and almost in the same breath, to be cruel. I was obsessed with this idea of basic treachery. Love was something of absolute validity. Either it existed or it did not exist, but, if it did exist, it was incompatible with unkindness. And it was this treachery to something that had seemed completely valid, that struck at the very core of human understanding, opening up vistas of horror, in which all that one had thought genuine might perhaps turn out to be sham. It overwhelmed like a nightmare. Out of that pit ascended horrible shapes, types of unexpected treachery and falseness, that gibbered at me, hinting that even in what lies nearest the heart we may find ourselves one day deceived.

I was conscious only of my own wound. Egoists are like that, insensitive where others are concerned, hypersensitive themselves. I never attempted to see things from a woman's point of view, or to ask whether, though I insisted upon the true coin of real affection myself, I might not have appeared to be offering spurious or false coin in exchange. I did not raise the question, but, if I had, I would – confidently though perhaps mistakenly – have replied that it was not so.

And if it is asked, what cause had I to reproach her when, never once, had I implied by the slightest phrase that she was even of transitory importance to me, yet could be so wounded when she appeared to slight an affection not even hinted, much less declared, then I must explain, once more, that to have spoken, to have thought even, in terms of lasting affection would have been to my mind the cardinal disloyalty. So long as I did not do this, so long as the position was absolutely defined, not merely for one of us, but for both, so long were we safe. But – and here lay the source of all my anguish – within these limits, it had seemed to me possible – and our eyes had often implied as much when they met – to entertain love, travelling, as it were, incognito, and to cherish an emotion perfectly genuine despite all the strictures that hedged it about. I saw our few days together as brief, irresponsible but real; and it was the suggestion that they were not real at all, that I had been gulled, and was merely the clumsy and rather ingenuous quarry of a highly-experienced huntress that filled me with a sense of such burning chagrin that pride had been my only aid.

IT was the coldest winter for more than a quarter of a century. All over Europe men shivered. In Rome at night the thermometer dropped to four degrees below zero, while in Switzerland readings as low as thirty degrees were recorded. Naples had had its first snow for twenty years. But in the convent of the Grey Sisters at Vomero the rigours of the winter were held at arm's length. I would receive my breakfast on a tray in the mornings, and then be left free to read or write, or to copy into my commonplace book reflections from Rodin. Mathews, whose cough had become a bark, found himself fussed over by the kindly nuns. They gave him a hot-water bottle at night and hot lemon drinks when he was going to bed. They were equally solicitous upon the subject of our food. Distressed because they considered we did not eat enough, they would hold over our heads the dreadful threat, 'To-morrow will be Friday,' as though the prospect of rice and tomato sauce, omelette and Brat Kartoffeln, cheese, fruit, nuts, with red wine, followed by a dessert of little mandarin oranges, fresh from Sicily, still with a leaf or two attached to their stalks, must be sufficiently appalling in its stark austerity to frighten us into eating more to-day.

In the afternoons we would explore Naples and its environs, some-times together, more often separately, indulging our solitary tastes and returning about six to the convent to warm ourselves over the stove until the evening meal should be served. While we waited we would talk of our day's experiences. Mathews would describe how he had seen two men with bagpipes playing to a little crowd at a street corner. Later, continuing his walk between high stone walls, he had come upon a great archway, and looked through it into a mouldering courtyard, where, under a huge willow tree, a group of girls were drawing water from a pump, while a little boy scrambled up a ruinous stone stairway, and a cloud of white doves rose into the air about his head. I would tell of my own walks in by-streets and suburbs, of how I had met with a fourteen-year-old beauty, hand-some as only an Italian of that age can be, but with an amazing voice, a voice like a man shouting at a mule. Or perhaps I had pushed open a glass door from which sounds of extreme desolation reached me, and, coming upon two little children, had attempted to comfort them with a few soldi, to find that young though they were they knew money when they saw it. They were not like the three-year-old discovered in a barber's shop a few doors down, crowded with children awaiting their turn. She was nursing a baby as though her years already demanded that she should make herself useful; but though responsibility weighed heavily upon her, a coin meant nothing to her. Once on these walks I trespassed through an open gate on to a terrace high above the town, and standing by the wall of someone's vineyard I looked across to Castellamare, past where the long slope of Vesuvius ended and the flat land beyond, to the Capo di Sorrento and all that country which held so many memories for me.

One evening Mathews returned from Cook's with a letter from Elisabeth. She had written to her 'two chaperons' a joint letter from Rome, thanking them for four days she would not easily forget. She had asked: 'Do the Santa Elisabettas look after you better than the plain Elisabetta did? Do they mend your socks for you?' And she had added: '*triste homme*, I have just finished reading *The Crock of Gold* – it's lovely – I am awfully glad you introduced us. Some of it has already been written into the black book.' But her letter, wholly friendly and kindly as it was, had not been able to dispel the impression of that moment on the sea-front at Naples, and when we came to its concluding sentence, '*les meilleurs salutations du fond du mon sale petit cœur noir,*' Mathews wondered why I smiled so grimly.

It was ironic how all my suspicions of her found reinforcement in things which she herself had said; her story of the Frenchman, for instance, and the letter sent to his wife; and now this phrase in her own letter. Yet I had only to turn to her markings of Rodin's book to discover there, by their shrewd insight and feeling, a wholly different side to her character, just as I had only to discuss her with Mathews – which I did from time to time, but oh, so cautiously – to be reminded by him of her good nature, her thoughtfulness, and her new-found gentleness in dealing with other people. I know that I liked to talk of her, trying to derive comfort from the past, from that moment when, lifting her face to mine, she had placed her arms with such tenderness about my neck. Surely then she had loved? A little? Surely too when she defended me for having cut short her visit to the Museum it was in a spirit of goodwill? If I thought of Sorrento at all – but I preferred to think of Rome, when the heart still had nothing to trouble its serene and tranquil joy – it was in the mood of Keats' knight, before he wakened on his cold hillside.

> 'I made a garland for her head,
> And bracelets too and fragrant zone,
> She looked at me as she did love,
> And made sweet moan.'

I might cry as he did:

> 'She found me roots of relish sweet
> And honey wild and manna dew;
> And sure in language strange she said,
> "I love thee true." '

But had she ever said it? Or had I myself said it for that matter? With the easy logic of my sex, it seemed to me that I had – that to whatever else I had been disloyal, I had not turned traitor to love by one act, one word, one thought that was not sincere. And it was because of this that her own seeming betrayal was so bitter. I was so convinced of this betrayal that I never questioned it, but rather sought consolation in attempting her defence, in telling myself that she owed nothing to my sex, least of all faith, that she had assessed them rightly, that all that had happened in her life was the justification of her scorn for us.

Coming into my room one morning, Mathews found me scribbling on a sheet of paper.

'What is it?'

'A poem.'

'You have given it no title.'

' "Coquette." "Circe in the making." I don't know. I shall decide later.'

'May I read it?'

'Yes, if you like.'

He read it carefully and then gave it back.

'I don't wholly understand it. It's a little obscure, not like your other poems. What were you thinking of when you wrote it?'

'Of Elisabeth, and that man who taught her Latin when she was sixteen.'

'Oh, I see. I doubt if it would mean much to the ordinary reader. I prefer you when you are simpler.'

I agreed with his verdict, but I had written the poem which I had wished to write. If we have loved and then suffered a shock or disillusion, we grasp all too eagerly at anything which may rehabilitate the loved image in our heart. Like those flowers in Alpine pastures which in April, forcing their way through the caked ice and blackened patches of snow, and, ignoring completely the fact that winter has ever fallen upon them, insist only that spring shall be remembered, so had I, out of bitterness, out of sharp disillusion – by casting back to our time in Rome, to something rooted in an earlier season of happiness, and by seeking reasons for any unkindness which she might have shown – succeeded, not in forgetting, but rather in excusing that icy chill which had once so shocked me, and had recreated the spring of the heart. I was no longer Elisabeth's accuser. She stood acquitted, in a measure at least, in my thoughts.

315

I had become her advocate, and the lines which Mathews found so incomprehensible were these:

> Is it your fault because,
> Even while still a child,
> All would swing round and look,
> Waking a spirit wild;
> Presently one more bold,
> Ignorant how much hung
> On that betrayal slight,
> Took toll of lips still young;
> Afterwards many more,
> Greedy of beauty all,
> Trying to shake the bough
> So that the fruit would fall;
> Until, in time, you learned
> Too well how men are made,
> Knowing the line to take
> Before the snare was laid?
> Now you revenge yourself,
> Taking of all the toll
> That one, more thoughtless, took
> Once, of your lovely soul.

PART III

Snow is nature's wand of enchantment. As a child I thought of snow as a wet flake, vague and drifting, fluttering slowly down to vanish presently as a point of moisture against the window pane. And though these wet flakes might cohere, might even remain long enough to form a strangely stealthy covering to the gravel pathway, or to be crushed into an instantly adhesive snowball or snowman, I still knew practically nothing about snow. I was still ignorant of its magic. Not until I had spent two years in Switzerland, the second ending in one of those exceptional winters when the snow comes early in October and remains, quite low down, sun-blazoned by day, but preserved by the hardest of spring frosts each night, until almost May, did I begin to feel about snow as other men come to feel about the sea, to whom every tide, every changing aspect of the surface of that vast expanse, is of interest. As varied, quite as subject to mood and sudden change, seen against a patterned landscape which gives it infinite diversity, snow is responsible, next to spring, for the most miraculous, the most enchanting, of all the transformation scenes to which the seasons treat us. From the moment when the first flakes, multiplying rapidly, appear, black against the monotone of pale grey sky, falling ceaselessly, as though they were the souls of all those who had been or would ever be, drawn by some immutable law from the furthest corners of the universe, dropping in endless succession towards matter, which would embrace them – from that moment the miracle becomes possible. It is possible, but it is not assured. The snow may lie for a few hours on the ground and along the branches of the trees, a blanket so heavy that they droop and even break under its weight, but this wet, clogging substance, still so evidently the near relative of rain, is snow only in the elementary sense, lowest of all in the hierarchy of potential beauty. It has yet to be transformed and to transform. And this may never happen. A sudden rise in the temperature and with a dull thud the blanketing mass slips from the branch to the ground, and, almost before it reaches it, begins to dissolve into a forlorn and murky slush, to lie there a little longer and then become a slow trickle of water down the hillside between the firs.

For the first twenty-four or even thirty-six hours of its existence, snow is not snow at all in the complete sense. It has a whole series of rebirths before it; and for these it is dependent upon frost. Frost is the magician that will change its nature, that will rearrange the crystals along the slender boughs of a cherry tree in a delicate tracery – like the airy imagination of some worker in glass – so graceful that even in spring the blossom itself is not more lovely. Frost will take whole fields of wet, clogging flakes and transform them in a single night to powder snow, crisp, almost brittle, of the substance of dry salt, through which the points of the ski cut with a rustling sound, a slight hiss, as it falls back either side like the double wave made by the prow of a ship. Frost will attach crystal to crystal, bending the particles, rearranging their pattern, in defiance of gravitation, until a huge cornice, massive as the architrave of a temple, overhangs the eave of a chalet. Thanks to frost, when we step out into the night air, the snow will creak under our boots like the sound of creaking leather, and the icy ruts in the roadway crunch under our footsteps. And if the frost continues, if the thermometer drops sufficiently low, we may even see, as I have seen, the moonlight falling with a bluish tint out of the vast night sky upon huge crystals as large as pennies, part of a high feather-bed bank of snow along the vanished margin of some tiny stream, and, stretching out a ski stick to touch them, may hear them fall with a tinkling sound like the chink of fairy coins.

This Arcady to which snow translates us is not the one about which the poets wrote, but it is no less lovely. And as the Goths once invaded Greece so have the Barbarians invaded this other Arcady and overrun it. Stamped and beaten to a pounded consistency never intended by Nature, trodden till not a single ridge appears on its surface, snow has become for many merely the playground across which they glide and reglide all day. Within a few hours of a fresh fall, whole mountainsides surrender to this fate. Ski races, which in deep snow were a test of a man's initiative as well as his courage, must now take place over a beaten uniformity, because to hold them in virgin snow would make the pace slower, or would give an advantage to anyone who could run in a predecessor's tracks. A regiment of soldiers has been known to turn out during a championship to trample the course into what is officially known as 'hard snow.' Modern life is like that, a *reductio ad absurdum*, in the interests of the majority, but often to the ultimate loss of all. For the initiate, the real lover of snow, it is doubtful if these trampled wastes deserve the name of snow at all. Rather he thinks of fences almost buried beneath a crystalline structure which it would seem desecration to touch; of sloping fields cut perhaps by the single track of some lone runner; of the winter stillness of snow-covered summer pasture land, reached after an hour's climb, when, with a sense of surprise, he suddenly hears the twitter of a bird from the fringe of a neighbouring wood. Or he thinks of still loftier heights, those vast snowfields, remote, inaccessible, virginal, on which the sun rests all day in burnished splendour, and lingers on, after the valley has passed into shade and the air grown suddenly chill, favouring them with the last rose-tinted caress of evening just as it favoured them with the first faint flush of dawn.

Twice in my life I have been lucky enough to enjoy a mode of existence which was on the point of vanishing. I went to the Channel Islands immediately after the First World War, when life there was still static, differing very little from what it had been a century previously. In the ten years which followed, Jersey was to change more than in the hundred that had gone before. The island became the happy hunting ground of tax-dodgers, and their wealth did its best to turn a community of farmers, of modestly-incomed retired civil servants, and feudal seigneurs, most of them as poor as church mice, into a suburban Eden in which the farmer counted hardly at all. In the same way a few years later I knew Switzerland in what Arnold Lunn himself has admitted was the golden age of winter sports. Snow was its own justification then, a means to an end, but still reverenced. Memory surrenders to me scene after scene of that metamorphosed landscape. I recall how, arrested by its beauty, I was filled with sudden ecstasy, or stood gazing at it in quiet, contemplative bliss. I remember how nightly in January I used to pace a high narrow pathway near the school in Château d'Œx filled with a sense of peace, a mood of mingled elation and serenity such as most men might envy. No one else came there, and I looked across the valley to where the rising moon outlined the toothed summits of Rüblihorn and Gummfluh and the Rocher du Midi. The mountains upreared their crests to heaven against the depthless night sky, in a cold, austere beauty, lonely, remote and utterly indifferent to the twinkling lights of the village at their feet. Only the black shadow of a hay chalet above the path was a reminder of the fellowship of man. Or I remember how I crossed the River Sarine late one afternoon to reach the protected northern slopes away from the village, and how, in that stillness of the pine woods, deterred a little from any great recklessness by the recent tale of a solitary skier smothered in the snow only a few yards from his hotel, I stood exultant at the top of a little slope, breathing in the keen, slightly resin-scented air before pointing my skis downhill. I think of ascending the Hahnanmoos, from Adelboden, alone, early one morning, climbing the lower part of the valley in icy mist and finding, when I reached the col and ate my lunch, that a jacket of very thin ice had formed between the outer shell and the inner envelope of my hard-boiled egg and that the meat in my sandwiches had frozen stiff as a piece of board. Wind-slab had formed on the far side of the col, treacherous stuff, easy to break through on skis, and highly dangerous; but at last I came to the first pines in the wood and the first glimpse of Lenk in the valley far below, and at that moment the sun, which had hitherto been so coy, broke through the mist, and presently the pine needles began to smell, and in the warmth of that sun a light steam, like incense, ascended from the boughs of the trees.

I think of the Ulmer Hütte in the Arlberg, sole indication of man and his existence, in a limitless white world; an expanse of snow so vast, so lofty and at the same time so friendly in its dazzling serenity, that it was as though one had withdrawn to a monastery of the spirit, designed by Nature herself as an escape from human affairs. Steep slopes, that threatened avalanches, mounted to a jagged black ridge to the left of the hut, while others, steep enough but not sheer, flowed out in all directions, rolling, undulating, inviting, from the narrow plateau of safety in that high place. I remember how, having climbed to the hut and eaten my lunch there, intoxicated by that white expanse under the midday sun, I scorned the easier line of descent and plunged down a steep pitch in the wake of some experts, cutting a line through untracked snow to run out exultant at the bottom. I learned later that the people I had chosen to follow were racers, training for the Arlberg-Kandahar. I had committed myself to a route of increasing difficulty and I had eventually to abandon it and to look for an alternative, joining myself to two Hungarian students, to see a nasty small avalanche come down only a few yards from our leading track, and to find myself at last when the light had almost gone, tired and considerably relieved, stretched out on a window bench in the Hospice of St. Christophe, drinking hot coffee and resting aching limbs.

Or I think of Kühtai – Kühtai also in Austria – and at once memory, stabbed by an even keener spur than that of snow, leaps into life and offers not one but a whole succession of pictures.

WE went from Innsbruck to Selrain by bus. I remember how we descended from the high carriage at Innsbruck, glad to have finished the longest stage of our journey, but thanks to third-class sleepers on the train, less tired than most of those who travelled with us. There remained, however, two further stages. A motor bus would take us through Kematin to Gries in the Selrain Valley. There we would begin a three hours' climb by sledge to Kühtai itself.

I was travelling again with Mathews. It was no grand tour this time, but only a brief excursion. It was seven years since we travelled together, seven years since we had been fellow pilgrims in the hostel at Vomero above Naples. That tour had been a success. From Naples we had gone to Sicily to explore like vagabonds the lonelier parts of that island. We had picked fruit in its orange groves and stayed at the humblest of lodgings. Presently we had taken ship at Syracuse and travelled steerage to Alexandria, to wander about the bazaars of Cairo, sniffing perfumes from little phials, or to visit the museum and gaze wonderstruck at the marvels of Tutankhamen's tomb. From Egypt we had gone on to Palestine and spent a month in Jerusalem. From there we had turned north to Tabka on the Sea of Galilee. Waking early one morning in the guest-house on the lakeside, run by a solitary monk who seemed to relish his independence, I had wandered forth alone, to find myself where the seven streams enter the lake, spellbound by the freshness and beauty and stillness of the morning; the grass lush and green, the lake of Galilee a glistening jewel where a few birds splashed in the sunlight; a spot so holy with the natural holiness of dawn, as well as by association, that every traditional site in the sacred city seemed meaningless by comparison. We had gone from Tabka to Damascus across the mountain road under Hermon, fellow passengers in a car with three Arabs and a sheep; from Damascus to Baalbek; from Baalbek to Beyrout. Spring had found us in Cyprus and presently in Greece; there once more we had shouldered our rucksacks and gone from village to village. In Athens we had parted, I to return home, Mathews to continue wandering – to visit Mount Athos, to call upon the reigning monarch of Bulgaria, to whom he had an introduction, and to write me letters about his travels from time to time. His Wanderlust was as strongly upon him as ever. In the years that followed he was to spend the greater part of his time abroad, reappearing in England from time to time, but eager always to get away again, to travel, to escape, to safeguard that independence of spirit which he valued as his most precious possession.

It is said that in seven years we undergo a complete physiological metamorphosis, every molecule in our body changing and not one remaining the same. Like the old woman in the nursery rhyme whose petticoats were cut round about her knees, we might be justified in exclaiming, 'Lawks-a-mussy on me, this is none of I!' And while this is happening to our bodies, what changes have taken place in the psyche itself? Seven years had certainly changed both Mathews and me. They had first created, then threatened to widen, then once more begun to narrow a breach between us. The gulf which divided us was an ideological one. The fault may have been mine. Perhaps I had begun to show something of the mental and moral tyrant, the irritation of a man who, seeing his younger friend sowing his doctrinaire wild oats, would like to cut the process short. But whereas my own had been the impassioned wild oats of political resentment, in which love of Ireland, pacifism and vague social dissatisfaction had all commingled – to no very great effect, if the truth be told – the wild oats of Mathews were of a different sort. They were esoteric, occult, mystical wild oats. He had been drawn into one of those movements where the longings and aspirations of the soul towards esoteric enlightment are offered a rich banquet. It is the fate of such movements to attract, as well as the genuine disciple, every crank and faddist who desires a new and exclusive gospel. I watched my friend facing the most difficult of his post-adolescent years, aided only by the somewhat vague aphorisms of a Buddhistic Monist and fortified by a diet of chopped roots and nuts. Though I shared fully his respect for all who attempt to plumb the mysteries of consciousness, or destiny, the sight of Mathews trying to save himself by carrots and Yoga-breathing irritated me beyond measure. To float on a sea of wordy generalisations and be forbidden on principle to swim, seemed to me the surest way to drown.

Indeed the path of enlightenment that my friend had chosen appeared to me a spurious one. For there are two kinds of mysticism. There is the mysticism which cries with the Greek poet, 'All the ways of life are full of Zeus,' or with the nineteenth-century Hindu sage, Rama Krishna, 'You see many stars at night in the sky, but find them not when the sun rises; can you say that there are no stars in the heaven of day? So, O man! because you behold not God in the days of your ignorance, say not that there is no God.' Such a mysticism is behind all religion. Its whole aim is to penetrate the nature of being, and to surrender to the will of the Ultimate. It is not necessarily vague; indeed its approach to phenomena may be strictly scientific – an attempt to discover the spiritual laws which are the counterpart of those in the natural world.

But as well as this primary mysticism – which for the most part goes its lonely way, leaving each with the obligation to work out his own salvation, slowly and painfully, no step of the way conceded until the initiate himself has deserved it, so that knowledge ultimately depends on vision, and vision upon an authentic direction of will – as well as this genuine kind there is another more questionable sort. Here all depends upon membership of a movement, of subscription to a dogma, even if it be only the dogma that all dogmas are indefensible.

But those who seek salvation in a movement will find little there which does not exist in some measure already in themselves. As the snail carries its house upon its back, so men take with them, even into a new religion, their foibles and failings. Only a genuine reorientation of being will permit us to escape our dispositions. Faults of character, strangely disguised, are often the first to accompany us into the new fold.

I had no fault to find with Mathews' Messiah, Krishnamurti, personally. Indeed, I had joined the Order of the Star myself, for a short time, but had never been able to make up my mind to attend any of the camps, before, presently, the teacher himself, boldly rejecting messiahship, disbanded the movement. It had been not Krishnaji but his followers – whom he himself once described as 'short-haired women and long-haired men' – that I distrusted. I was jealous of their influence over my friend. He had been brought into contact with a number of people, idealistic but at the same time flattering themselves that they stood above herd-morality. They were emancipated and eccentric, with fads and fancies kindred to or different from his own; persons who might think lightly of adultery and yet be horrified at the idea of eating an egg. Mathews practised the austerities of his sect. He had become a rigid vegetarian and had given up smoking. I could respect him for living up to his principles, but I should have liked to know better where they were leading him. That he hoped for something from these rigours was evident, but what exactly he hoped for was a little less plain. To me his austerities all seemed to be directed towards placating – or

325

perhaps developing – the ever-insistent ego, while leaving the rest of the world at a despised distance.

Mathews and I had drifted further and further apart. It had come to this. We could not be in each other's company long without wrangling, and only rigid self-control on both sides avoided a real quarrel.[1]

Perhaps I was the aggressor. We met seldom, but when we did I instantly attacked his views with the vehemence almost of a missionary who has strayed into a Hindu temple and been deeply shocked by what he sees there. Mathews would defend himself, at first smilingly expostulative, but presently nettled. 'I assure you, you are wrong, Monk. . . .' But was I wrong? If the tendency of my mind was to harden, to crystallise, to condemn, his own tendency was to 'drift into a penumbra.' He had not the vaguest idea himself where he was heading; all was indefinite, wordy, moving in a cloud cuckooland of vague expectation towards some unspecified Nirvana.

My attitude to him was perhaps lacking in sympathy and understanding. But to me he seemed to be drifting towards disaster. The young women who crossed his path in the course of these theosophic meanderings I suspected of being unprincipled, heartless, full of vague and dangerous theories, and as unhappy as he was himself. He was not likely to find salvation in them; rather the reverse. He appeared in fact to be standing on the brink of one of those mental hells from which we can only escape if all the forces of health, sanity, friendship, self-forgetfulness and hard work rally to our aid.

I had stood once on the brink of such a hell myself and been saved from it only by departure to Jersey, by the good friends I found there, by fields, by children, by acceptance, by submission. But Mathews had nothing of this sort to help him. Once I went to see him in Paris for a couple of nights on my way back from a trip abroad. I found him living in a stable-yard off a thronged street in one of the lesser-known and shabbier districts. A row of horse boxes had been converted with the aid of a little whitewash into an equal number of 'studios.' A narrow gallery, rather like those platforms one sees in a

[1] A poem written at this time, 'Estrangement,' gives a good idea how matters stood between us. Before leaving Switzerland, on the eve of our tour, a very early fall of snow had given us the opportunity of setting out one morning from Château d'Œx, where the valley was still green, and climbing, at times thigh-deep in snow, the slopes of La Lécherette, in order to cross the col to L'Etivaz. The poem refers retrospectively to this, and to other incidents later in the tour itself.

mouse's cage, projected from the back wall, for nearly half the depth of the apartment, and was reached by a ladder; and on this platform a camp bedstead and a straw pallet indicated that it was to be regarded as a bedroom. Mathews made up a bed for me on the ground floor and at a deal table regaled me three times daily with a bowl of chopped vegetables, raw carrots and parsnips, and some cheese and tea. I do not think he knew another soul among the artists, sculptors, students and eccentrics who inhabited the courtyard and who were practically never seen, either remaining indoors always in their separate cells, except to draw water occasionally from a tap in the courtyard, or else leaving them so early in the morning and returning to them so late at night that they never crossed our path. Mathews' spirits were at their lowest ebb.

It would have been striking the defenceless to have even hinted criticism at that moment. Instead, I took him to tea on Sunday afternoon with the artists Jan and Cora Gordon, whom I had met recently in Dorset, and in their genial company and in a studio considerably less comfortless, his frozen spirits were to thaw a little. They saw much of him in the weeks that followed, realising in what a desperate and agonised frame of mind he was, unhappy and alone. Excess of misery drove him presently back to England, where a doctor shook his head, deprecated his physical condition and spoke of nerves, and the pangs of prolonged adolescence.

But it was not the doctor's prescriptions so much as work and cheerful companionship and an interest in life that were to effect his salvation. Soon after this he was lucky enough to find a niche at the very school to whose history we had listened that day on the drive from Amalfi; and there, perpetually busy, his skill in languages as well as his knowledge of printing put to full use, teased, but heartily liked by his colleagues, and working under a man of remarkable character and influence, he began to find his old self, to brood less and to enjoy the bustle of life more. His universe was no longer egocentric; he was overworked, but he was happy, whereas in Paris, with no work at all, he had almost wearied of life.

Now that he was in England we saw more of each other. Soon our friendship began to emerge from the clouds which had threatened it, and to recover its old accord. Once more I could admire the zest which he brought to things, his charm and good humour. Once more I could admire his astonishing efficiency when he liked to apply himself to the practical. Indeed, it was amusing to notice how his new friends, so far from regarding him as a gloomy introvert, treated him as a model of business-like reliability, and when it came to travelling made him the courier and manager of their expeditions.

I saw this one Christmas when I travelled out to Austria with him when he was in charge of such a party. Mathews was as much their cicerone as he had once been mine. I would have liked to accompany him to Zürs, where they were going, but I had made my plans too late. All Alister had been able to do for me was to find me quarters at St. Anton in a pension where I understood I would be joining English friends of his own. But this was a misunderstanding. There were no English-speaking guests when I arrived, and there was no room in the actual pension itself. Instead I found myself sleeping in a chalet nearby belonging to a friendly, bearded little man, Gomperz, son of the famous nineteenth-century classical scholar. Even with Gomperz's kindness the holiday had been a lonely one. I remember it chiefly because it was the means of introducing me later to Kühtai. Next year I did not go abroad, and the following one Mathews, who had tired of being forced into a sociability with which his mood was not really in accord, pledged to festivities that often bored him, wrote to tell me that he had tactfully disentangled himself from the school party, and suggested that we might take our holiday together. He proposed Obergurgl or Vent in the Oetzthal; for Switzerland was still hugging the gold standard and therefore out of the question. But when I wrote to Gomperz to sound him on these resorts, I learnt that they were at their best in spring, that January was too early for them and that the wind blew off the glacier with a severity that could daunt even a skier's heart. 'I suggest you go to Kühtai instead,' he replied. 'It is over six thousand feet high, but it is sheltered from the north wind and indeed from every wind, being a sort of cup in the mountains. There is no village, only the Alpengasthof. If the *gasthof* is full, you could probably get rooms at the Dortmünder Hut nearby, recently built and generally crowded with Germans, but probably empty now, since they have placed a ban on foreign travel. You can tell them at the Alpengasthof that I sent you, if you like.'

I forwarded Gomperz's letter to Mathews. He wrote about rooms immediately, and presently I heard that he had secured us a double room in the annexe of the *gasthof*, all that was available and, as he explained to me, he was lucky to get even that, for it was late to try for accommodation anywhere. Boxing Day found us on the deck of the Channel steamer, that chill, inevitable prelude to days of sunshine, and at Dieppe we entered a train which was to take us to

Paris to catch the night express for Innsbruck. Next morning Gomperz came to greet us on the platform at St. Anton, when we halted there for a few minutes, and to hand over to me my ski-ing kit which for two years had been left in Austrian care. His world was to fall into ruins within a few years, for, though everyone liked this gentle, good-natured little man, he would be racially distasteful to the Nazis, and his career of usefulness in St. Anton, like that of Hannes Schneider – suspected of being politically unsound – would be cut short by them. But that morning the cloud was still no larger than a man's hand on the horizon, and Gomperz greeted us cheerfully. He promised us good snow conditions and was pleased when Mathews whipped out his camera and photographed him on the station platform just before the train moved off. A couple of hours later and we were in Innsbruck and at our rail journey's end.

But only our rail journey's. We had still to drive by motor bus to Gries and begin the long climb to Kühtai from there. It was this last part of the trip to which Mathews looked forward with the keenest ardour. The fact that we would be beginning it late in the afternoon with darkness and night closing in on us, so far from being a deterrent, only seemed to whet his appetite. His foresight in the matter of third-class sleeping berths paid him; for, if he had not slept soundly from the suburbs of Paris until near Zurich, he would have been less disposed to entertain the emotions of a true romantic now.

We had less than half an hour in Innsbruck. Its streets looked cold and unsympathetic on this grey December afternoon. Only a few blackened heaps of snow on the pavement's edge afforded a dingy reminder of the purpose of our visit. It was an hour and a quarter's drive on to Gries, delayed a little by halts to deliver the mail-bag at each village through which we passed, and to disembark some *Frau*, laden with the products of her morning's shopping. I remember nothing of the drive except a great curve in the road when we swept swiftly round a corner to begin a long slow ascent through a pine wood, the resinous scent of its trees an earnest that the mountains were not far off.

I remember, however, clearly, the scene of sudden, confused activity at Gries when we descended outside the post-house restaurant, and when, leaving their luggage to be unloaded from the top of the bus, the bus passengers, several of whose faces were familiar from the train journey the previous night, crowded into the restaurant to drink hot coffee, before beginning their long climb.

It was here that Mathews' forethought stood him in good stead.

He had written to the Alpengasthof, days previously, to order a sledge to be at Gries, and now he took possession of one of the two sent down by Scheiber, the manager, to meet us, the second being reserved for the transport of luggage. It was an extravagance, but it was an extravagance which those who had elected to walk the whole distance, seemed, now, to wish they had committed.

For Mathews it might be said to have been almost a necessity, for it afforded him a complete justification for wearing his sheepskin coat. Seven years before we had each of us bought one of these coats in Jerusalem. Long – reaching almost to the ankles, made out of skins sewn together and rather roughly finished, the fleece within turned back to form collar, cuffs and very wide lapels, the sight of these coats displayed in the bazaar had filled us with instant envy. It was sufficient to see a British Government official attending service in the Anglican cathedral in one to convince us that even our own families could in time be made to accept them. It is true that to don one was to be transformed into something between a Tibetan merchant and a Russian prince, and that Mathews, by adding to his the purchase of a round black astrakhan cap, made himself look more than ever like a crony of Peter the Great. But there was nothing in this metamorphosis which was distasteful to him. Rather he enjoyed it and, if its use had not been handicapped by climatic considerations, the sheepskin coat might even have become the rival in his affections of the once famous cloak.

Mine I decided to send home from Jerusalem as a gift to my father. It would make him a most suitable motoring coat. The parcel was made up, sealed, registered and despatched. But that good man, probably of all Dublin clerics the least concerned about his clothes had, notwithstanding this indifference to the sartorial, refused to wear it. The soft, pristine whiteness of the sheepskins may have seemed to him too much like appearing in the shriven garments of the saved. He did not wear it and, finding he did not wear it when I returned from abroad, I took back my gift. But I found it as hard myself to put it into use. In the house, on a cold day, writing in a room without a fire, if offered an alternative to a dressing-gown, but further than this I never got. Mathews showing a courageous disregard for the appropriate moment, resolutely forced his into use, wearing it whenever he went abroad, and even managing to get it so dirty in trains that it had to be sent to the cleaners. But actually – and he would have admitted this himself – it only became really serviceable on an occasion such as the long sleigh journey up to Zurs. Then indeed he could feel that the purchase had been anything but a foolish one, but at other times he must have felt less sure.

It had been a mild surprise to me, when we met at the barrier at Victoria Station for the start of our journey, to find him already wearing it. The skins had grown slightly sooty once more, and his prow-like nose emerged like the beak of some strange bird above the curled lamb's wool. Standing on the platform by the carriage door he produced a rather exotic effect, an effect less noticeable, however, among the devotees of winter sport than it would have been elsewhere. But at Gries I was glad enough to un-pack my own coat from the rucksack where it lay hidden and to be helped into it by my friend. It was after four o'clock. We were told that other sledges would come down later in the evening to bring up the rest of the luggage. Those who were walking had already set off. We climbed into the sleigh and started after them.

The evening was closing in; it was already almost dusk. Only the reflection from the snow made it lighter than it would otherwise have been. We had several thousand feet to climb. Down here at Gries the snow was only a few centimetres deep. On the track it had become worn in more than one place, so that the steel runners of the sleigh, instead of running smoothly, would grate suddenly on gravel and small stones and bring the vehicle nearly to a halt.

Indeed, I soon discovered that for a variety of reasons my share in the price of the sleigh was going to be largely wasted. These rough patches when the animal was dragging almost a dead weight over the ground, and, later still, steep pitches of road which, though covered with an adequate amount of snow, rose often at a cruel angle, soon had the mule that was pulling the vehicle tired out. In the gloom of dusk I could see great clouds of steam rising from its sweating flanks. In the circumstances, whenever the hill steepened, I preferred to get out and walk. Mathews, his round astrakhan cap suggesting the steppes of Tartary, remained seated in the sleigh, refusing to believe that an animal performing what, for it, was a daily function, could be suffering unduly.

But even if I had not been stirred to compassion by the sight of the straining animal and its throbbing flanks when we paused at the top of some steep rise to allow it to draw breath, my sleigh ride would in any case have been interrupted. We had passed through one tiny village, the steeple of its church looming dimly up against a back-ground of pine trees, and were ascending a long steep stretch that

331

led out of that particular level of the valley. At the top of this ascent, where the track scrambled tortuously over the brow of the hill, was a cluster of wooden buildings, a rough, rather poor-looking farm and its cattle sheds. Out of one of these, or perhaps out of the chalet itself – for we could see the dim flicker of a candle through the aperture of a half-shuttered window – came a youth, English, very polite, speaking in the hushed tones of one who has a favour to ask. He belonged to the party who had set off ahead of us walking.

'I am very sorry, but we have a girl here with us who has collapsed. I wonder if you could help us.'

'Certainly. She can have my seat in the sleigh.'

In the dim light of the farm interior, surrounded by goats and by the farmer's children, who were breathing whatever infection was being sent forth on the warm, hay-scented air, I found them administering brandy to the sufferer. I had no difficulty in identifying her. In fact, even before I paused in the half-open doorway I was already aware who she must be.

A rooted antipathy to colds, combined with an unfortunate predisposition when I do get them to get them violently, had long ago made me highly observant of their symptoms and conscious of their mere adjacency. In the corridor of the train leaving Paris I had noticed almost instantly an English girl, flushed and with every indication of a feverish cold at its most acute stage upon her, and had thought to myself: 'That is the sort of young person who fills Swiss hotels with influenza at this time of year and spoils fifty other holidays as well as her own. It is grossly inconsiderate of her to come.' Sauntering up and down the platform before we left Paris, bareheaded, her face crimson, a woollen scarf wound loosely round her neck, she reminded me of the worst moments in my own catarrhal history, and, though she was pretty, filled me with a sense of keen resentment. I could only congratulate myself that I was not doomed to travel cooped up all night with her, one of eight people in the same ill-ventilated compartment. At Innsbruck, however, she had reappeared. By some malicious destiny, for there were a hundred other places in Austria to which she might have been going, it had been decreed that she should be continuing her journey with us. There were three buses going from Innsbruck to Gries, but Fate, I need hardly say, arranged that she should climb into mine and sit a couple of seats behind me. Noisy, smothered in cold, typical of agreeable English youth at its worst – that is to say, when it forgets that it is in a foreign land and is a little too inclined to display the insensitivity, if not the arrogance, of a ruling caste – she seemed at the same time to be the life and soul of her party. I had to listen to their comments upon her appearance as they discussed whether she had a temperature or not. I could hear their voices raised in shrill debate upon this point. 'Look at Peggy now. I'm sure she has a temperature.' 'I'm sure she has.' 'She's so red.' 'Yes, she's so red.'

It was true; red she was, lobster-red, a menace to herself and everyone else, yet repudiating indignantly the suggestion that she should remain at Gries for the night. At Gries it had been a relief to lose touch with her, but, as I went into the restaurant for coffee, the last words I heard were the vain pleas of her friends, supplicating hre, unsuccessfully, to change out of the light brown shoes she was wearing before beginning her four hours' climb in the snow.

Entering the shed doorway, I had known instinctly whom it was I should see. Irony decreed that I, the only person probably on the whole journey who had felt savage resentment at her inconsideration, should urge her now, with a heart secretly still full of censure, to accept my seat in the sleigh, and not merely do this, but, despite the fact that I felt in any case she was bound to die of pneumonia, should press on her the very coat I was wearing, the rug I had over my knees and even the pair of ski gloves which I had donned over my others when we left Gries. The only hint of disapproval that escaped me was in the tartness of my remark, 'People in the state you are in have no right to travel.'

She was too wretched to notice it, and too young in any case to feel guilty. Neither she nor her friends had reached an age when such things seem criminal, but they were profuse in their apologies for inconveniencing us. They thanked the farmer and, leaving his children doomed to a germ that was in London only yesterday, took their places behind the sleigh and we set off.

I had behaved chivalrously. Indeed, there was a touch of almost Elizabethan gallantry in the promptness with which I had responded to the young man's appeal, insisting that the girl should have my seat in the sleigh and not Mathews'. The latter had not even troubled to offer his, nor had he had time to do so. But I am far from claiming any credit for my act. The truth is that I much preferred the ardours of a walk to the close proximity to the invalid which a seat in the sleigh entailed. I must not be a hypocrite. I will admit that, had Mathews offered his seat, there would probably have ensued a scene almost French in the vehemence of its rival protestations of politeness, and the thing might have ended in fisticuffs. Fortunately, however, he did not. He appeared very comfortable where he was and the thin leather shoes he was wearing were much less suited to the road than my snow boots. The same reluctance to dismount which had kept him where he was on the hills, kept him there now, and I admired the rather icy cordiality – the aloof graciousness of a Russian prince – with which he permitted the girl to be tucked into the rugs beside him.

It was almost dark. The sleigh moved off, accompanied by a body-guard of five or six people leaning on ski-sticks walking behind it. We had started before the other sleigh, but in the delay occasioned by changing passengers it had passed us and I could hear the bell on the harness of the mule in front receding slowly further and further into the distance. The valley appeared to have widened; we were on a higher level and a fair expanse of snow seemed to lie either side of the track; the ascent was less steep, but all trace of human habitations had ceased and we no longer saw the flickering light of an occasional chalet or of some stable where a farmer milked his cows. Mathews, always courteous, sat straight up, venturing an occasional enquiry for the comfort of his new companion, who, if she had been noisy only an hour ago, was silent enough now. Never-theless, he seemed a little aloof spiritually from her, his gloved hands folded in his lap on the rug in front of him and an expression on his face as though he were wondering how soon he would have to abandon his own seat to another maiden in distress.

I left the party and began to walk on ahead of the sleigh. We were climbing higher and higher, through a succession of mountain gorges, steep-sided, starless. Periodically the route lost its steepness and we walked for a time on the flat, the floor of some valley in the ascend-ing series. In the darkness, and with a wider expanse of level snow on either side, the track had become a good deal harder to distin-guish. Occasional upright posts marked the route, but it was difficult to see these until one was quite near them. Night muffled every sound in a stillness that was almost uncanny. One walked as if in a dream. Every possible grandeur and immensity in the scene around was shut out as though by a wall. I remembered now that visitors were recommended not to leave Gries unless they could make Kühtai by daylight. It would be easy to get lost. With the sleigh and its driver to accompany us, there was no danger of this now, but, walking ahead until the bells on the harness became inaudible, it seemed to me that I might be in some Arctic waste rather than the mountains, so silent had all around me become.

Once I blundered off the track into deeper snow and could only find my way back by stamping cautiously till I felt trodden snow under my feet again. The next time this happened I waited for the tinkle of the sleigh-bells behind me before resuming soundings for the lost track. Periodically, when I thought that I had got too far ahead, I leant forward on my ski-sticks, resting, and waited for the remainder of the party to come up. Then impatience would send me ahead once more.

It was a three and a half hours' walk even for the fairly active, but I had lost the sense of time and was content to plod quietly ahead, without any feeling of fatigue and equally without any expectation of ultimate arrival. Once, when we were climbing steeply again, some skiers passed us, running down in the darkness to Gries – a risky proceeding – and as they sped by they shouted a word of encouragement to us in German.

At last we finished climbing and appeared to be moving along the level or, if anything, downhill. Though I did not know it, we were now crossing the col, a narrow saddle with rounded heights either side of it, which were invisible in the darkness, and still higher peaks behind them. Kühtai lay a little below us, this side of the head of a long, wooded gorge that ran down to Oetz, a gorge used in summer as the quickest approach, but considered unsafe, because of avalanches, in winter. Hence the journey on to Innsbruck, instead of leaving the train at Stams, and the long, slow climb from the direction of Selrain and Gries.

A big wooden hay-barn was the first indication that we were returning to human habitation, and then, coming over a hillock in the track and round a curve, we saw the lights of the Alpengasthof below us in the dark. They were about a quarter of a mile ahead. The track sloped steeply down and, for the first time in the whole journey, the mule no longer needed to strain at the sleigh, but was forced to trot smartly ahead in order to avoid being overrun by it.

It is strange that our most vivid recollections are often not of places that we have known well, that were familiar to us for months or even years, but rather of places that we visited for a few days or perhaps only for a few hours. It is part of the general fastidiousness of memory that it prefers the freshness of original impressions to a familiarity which has staled. Megouliana in the Peloponnese remains with me, although I stayed there only for two days. And in the same way I know that this high mountain retreat which I approached now, in a country which has since been swept from the political map

335

and subsequently restored to it, is indelibly engraved upon memory, and I suspect that this may be so because I remained there quite a short time, and also because circumstance endowed it with just those emotional attributes on which the mind seizes with eagerness. What we recollect is not so much the place or the thing, as how the place or the thing affected us. Perhaps the only real history is the history of the soul, and we recall everything by its emotional significance for us – a bright day, an exultant morning, a profound and moving sunset, these remain ours simply because they are a part of that history. We are at the mercy of mood. Of all that life pours into our lap only a little seems worth keeping permanently, and this because we made it a portion of ourselves.

It was after eight o'clock when we arrived. Our arrival can have differed very little from the arrival of travellers in winter at this very place six hundred years before. For what was now the *gasthof* had been an imperial hunting lodge then, and though visitors in January can have been few, it is possible that an occasional intrepid Hapsburg came even in midwinter, for whom a bear-hunt or the destruction of wolves was of more interest than the festivities of Vienna. They can have climbed no more slowly in the darkness from Gries than we did, and our sleighs halted now outside the identical stone walls and great-eaved porch where theirs had then. For it was not the least attraction of this spot that, apart from giving one an initial feeling of having fled the world and being cut off from it in complete and lofty isolation, everything contributed to link the past and the present and to make one feel that a complete cleavage with history – which its new role might have led one to expect – had by some good fortune been avoided.

By some good fortune. For the survival was accidental even more than intentional. What mattered was not so much the deliberate retention of certain archaic features, like the 'princely chamber' upstairs which the Emperor Maximilian had occupied, but rather in little trivial details which to the observant hinted a continuity of life that no change of function in the building, no invasion of the modern spirit had yet been able to alter. For instance, when we had stamped our way up a shallow flight of stone steps in the passage-way between *gasthof* and stable and had knocked off (against the iron balustrade of the wooden porch) a portion of the snow collected on our boots, we entered a wide, flagged corridor that ran the length of the building, and which in its vastness and impressiveness might have been the setting for one of the novels of Scott. There were couples in ski-ing clothes playing ping-pong at the near end of this huge hall, but they did not create a great sense of incongruity, and a minute later a peasant entered carrying the evening milk in pails hung from a wooden frame on his shoulders, his nailed boots sounding on the flags and his black-bearded face a replica of the faces of his forebears in the Middle Ages. He had come from the stable, which was just across from the porch, separated from it by a few yards, and reached by a passage through the snow. There was something symbolic and satisfactory in the proximity of this stable. Here was continuity, centuries of slow-munching beasts in the quiet darkness of long winter nights. Just as the heaped-up shavings on the floor of the carpenter's workshop, where one went to get one's skis waxed, symbolised something that was constant and eternal, not something that should be bundled out of sight in favour of chromium-plated efficiency, so the stable, the peasant bringing in the milk, and a host of other details, slight in themselves, served to remind one that the world is not wholly a world of cosmopolitan pleasure-seekers, but of simple and homely people as well.

It had been one of the attractions of the Alpengasthof that its prospectus boasted openly that it possessed 'neither jazz-band nor cocktail bar,' but that instead it offered sport, sunshine, good snow, fresh air, good beer, native wine and good cooking. 'They dance in Kühtai,' said the little brochure which Gomperz had sent me, 'but they dance in ski clothes.' In every one of its seven claims it was to vindicate itself presently, fully and completely. Only in one case had we to wait a few days for proof, and that was sunshine. We could test the last of the seven almost immediately, for they were serving dinner at the very moment we arrived. The maid took us to our room in the annexe about twenty yards away, a small wooden chalet recently built, its lower story a single long dormitory fitted with bunks like a youth hostel, the upper one a series of separate rooms, each with a glass door opening on to a sun balcony. Mathews and I were to share one of these. We washed hastily, then found our way back, a little cautiously in the darkness, down a steep slope of snow to the main building.

When the hunting-lodge had become an hotel no structural changes had been made in it, except that a huge wooden dining-hall had been built out at the back. It had the appearance rather of an extended porch, and windows ran its entire length. Here in two adjoining rooms, separated by a glass partition, meals were served at a number of small tables. Round these same tables, when the meal had been cleared away, groups of people would remain to talk or read; or the tables would be pushed back to the walls to make room for dancing. Here too at midday, when the sun emerged from its twenty-minute retirement behind the peak of a mountain, one could throw open a window and, sniffing the frosted air, which entered together with the sunlight, decide whether the action needed or did not need an apology to one's fellow lunchers.

There was a predominance of Austrian guests in the hotel just now; later there would be an English invasion, and they would take possession of the place with an easy assurance and self-assertion which the Continental visitor lacks. The group of young people walking behind the sleigh in the darkness to-night, and we ourselves, were the fore-runners of this invasion. Mathews, true to his Baconian principles, would regret it. The raucous laughter of the more exuberant Anglo-Saxon grated upon his nerves. He disapproved the insularity of his race, and would have fully endorsed Lunn's condemnation of the youth he noticed in the train whose whole expression changed when he looked down and discovered that the girl, on whose foot he had trodden in his haste to reach his ski-sticks, and to whom he was about to apologise, was only Swiss and not English. One should not malign the English, for they are a great people and, with liberalism rampant, have become almost too fond of maligning themselves, but in this particular respect – the manners of their gilded youth abroad – they expose themselves to censure. To be noisy, exhilarated, and at the same time to eye the native of a country as though he hardly existed, is one way of showing oneself ill-bred.

We sat down to dinner. Looking across the table at me, Mathews' eyes twinkled in the fashion of former days. It was doubtless a satisfaction to him that of the voices around us the majority spoke German. If I wanted to ask the simplest question, I was dependent upon his aid. Once more my sloth, or my inability to study a language intelligently and to take enjoyment in its idiom, placed me completely at his mercy. It is true that I was still a student of French. Of the books which I had brought with me to Kühtai, four were in that language, an anthology of the work of Paul Fort, *Le Blé qui Lève*, by Réné Bazin, and two volumes of de Régnier's poetry, picked up in a Copenhagen bookshop for a few kroner the summer before, and added at the last minute to my travelling library now, with the idea that Mathews would be an aid to their appreciation.

He was my interpreter to-night and a cordial one at that, his geniality a mixture of gratitude and elation – gratitude for my having found this place, remote beyond his wildest dreams, elation at its being so much in accord with his own tastes. So too, when, having dined, we returned to the annexe and found ourselves in a small, exceedingly narrow room, with two beds placed tandem-wise between door and window, he instantly conceded to me the right of choice, and raised no objection when I elected to sleep in the bed by the window. By choosing this, I was in a position to prevent Mathews opening so much of the window at night that we would discover our sponges frozen solid in the morning. Conversely, I could prevent him shutting it completely, in which case I, in the bed nearest the radiator, would have stifled. Lastly, and perhaps of greatest importance in my eyes, when I woke in the morning I could, if I wished, reverse my bedclothes, according to habit, putting my pillow at the far end of the bed, and remain there reading as long as I liked with the light over my shoulder on the page of my book.

My bloodless victory had given me these three considerable advantages. We had both come well-equipped with literature. Coming up from Gries, the mules had strained and sweated under the weight of our valises, and the weight of our valises had been largely the weight of the books in them. As well as the French books, I had brought the Latin treatises of Cato and Varro upon agriculture in the Loeb library; Santayana's *Three Philosophic Poets*, *Lucretius*, *Dante and Goethe*, and a complete treatise on Greek literature and religion, *The Makers of Hellas*. Mathews would supplement these if necessary. For to read quietly in the morning in bed while he continued sleeping – we were of different habit, he remaining over at the *gasthof* till nearly midnight, writing or reading, or listening to the conversation around him, I retiring to my room almost as soon as dinner was over – was part of the holiday I had promised myself; and my mornings were always pleasantly occupied if I chose to delay the moment when I would cross the snow to the *gasthof* and demand my breakfast.

And in actual fact this was how many of them began. For the first five days of our stay we did not see the sun once. The sky was clouded completely and it snowed nearly the whole time. To come down to the *gasthof* at midday for lunch and see the snow blowing in little eddies round the wide wooden eaves of the great stone building, or to return there at four, with the flakes still whirling down out of an impenetrable greyness overhead, increased the sense of isolation that one had already; and yet this sense of isolation was

339

in one way comforting, as though emphasising the remoteness and the self-sufficiency of the place and the fact that it held the whole world at arm's length. It must have known many such days in winter. Occasionally, we were told, it would be cut off completely from the valley below for as much as a week at a time. No food, no letters, no visitors could reach it. But this group of eaved roofs, including the steep pent-roof of a tiny adjoining chapel, engulfed in a white waste between hidden mountains, adapting themselves to the forces of Nature, which they understood, rather than attempting to contest them, gave such an impression of solidity, of permanence, that, so far from inspiring loneliness or apprehension, they reassured one by appearing part of a more static order.

It is true that until one had seen the place in sunlight – the speared peaks of the mountains rising all round against a sapphire sky – one had seen only half the picture. The other half was even more characteristic. But for sunlight we had to wait nearly a week.

The morning after our arrival, Mathews – fresh after his sleigh ride, so I taunted him – was out on his skis, but I was content to go over my equipment, restored to me at St. Anton by Gomperz; to wax my skis elaborately, a ritual every skier enjoys; and, discovering that the leather of the boots which had stood me in such good stead for years in Switzerland was perished, to purchase a new pair in 'the shop' in the great corridor of the *gasthof*. The shop was a tiny glass-fronted booth, something between a kiosk and a cupboard, where a slightly deaf girl dispensed stamps and cigarettes, ski-wax and sunburn-cream at certain fixed times, generally after meals, muddling her change to her own disadvantage in the polyglot confusion around her.

It was a piece of good fortune to find a pair that fitted me, as they had only a few.

'Alister, my boots were rotten. After all, I've had them ten years and they weren't new when I got them. I've bought another pair in the hotel.'

'Good, Monk.'

'What did you do this morning?'

'Went to one of the classes.'

Of the seventy or eighty guests in the hotel, probably less than one-third were really expert skiers. These might be recognised, if in no other way, by the fact that they were very seldom to be seen in the hotel for lunch. They left early in the morning and returned late in the afternoon, and a rucksack always accompanied them on their expeditions. A few were English, but the greater number were Austrian. Some were students, slept in the dormitory at the annexe, and produced their own food from a rucksack there, so that one only saw them in the *gasthof* itself if they brought a friend down in the evening to drink beer. These were the best skiers of all. They had skied since childhood, and one admired their intense devotion to the sport as well as envied them their skill. Even their evenings were devoted to a careful waxing of their skis, to make possible a still earlier start next morning.

But the experts were a minority and the *gasthof* had its own very well-organised ski-ing school for the less experienced. In this way a guest was saved from lethargy and indecision. His day was planned for him if he liked to avail himself of the plan. At ten o'clock every morning, we discovered, a bell rang in the hotel to announce that the morning session was starting. The classes lasted till midday, and again at half-past two the school reassembled for another two hours of instruction. It was the same system which had proved so successful at St. Anton and made it world-famous. One could attend or not as one chose. If the morning session had been too exhausting, the afternoon one could be ignored. There is something in human nature which appreciates an orderly routine and a not too exacting discipline imposed from without. If nothing else, it obviates the making of endless decisions. Even those who are solitary by nature find a satisfaction in responding to a collective effort which lifts from them the burden of making up their minds.

Mathews had had his mind made up for him that morning and had enjoyed himself. This was evident when he returned at midday.

'Are you going to join?'

'I don't think so.'

'The classes are free. It doesn't cost anything.'

'I know, but even so——'

At St. Anton the régime had been so rigid that a pupil might be kept practising stem-bogens on the same slope for the greater part of his holiday. It was part of a set policy of preventing beginners from venturing on mountains too steep for them. But this endless rehearsing looked so monotonous that I had avoided the classes altogether. Too impatient to practise assiduously, I preferred to potter alone. I remained, even after a number of seasons' experience, an erratic and only moderately competent skier. It is true that a combination of recklessness and cunning had allowed me, early in my ski-ing career, to win a small cup for racing, my first time on a mountain. But this had only been a flash in the pan, and my ski-ing, begun with such promise, had continued less gloriously, so that now after seven or eight years it might be said of it that it was less daring and very little more accomplished. I skied with the disadvantage of a steel splint upon a knee dislocated originally at hockey, but this incommoded me very little. The plain truth was that I had from the start been too much enamoured of the joys of the Schüss ever to take the trouble to acquire complete mastery of the turns. When I reflected now that I had once lived for two whole years in the Alps, shame overtook me that I had not made better use of my opportunities. I had been the prodigal skier, never in the mood to spend time acquiring a technique, but an hour was coming, was indeed bound to come, when with less love of falling I would begin to realise my folly and to taste the husks.

It had not yet come, however, and it is extremely unlikely that I would have gone to the classes now, if I had not chanced to see the pupils of one of them on my second morning, practising straight running on a steep slope with a good run out. Envy at the sight of that rushing descent moved me to join them. This was something I could do. And, having once joined, pride and a spirit of emulation kept me there. It is easier to practise a difficult turn over and over again in company rather than alone, for in company one is spurred by the success or given fresh heart by the failure of one's compeers. When we met in the annexe before lunch Mathews remarked:

'I see you've changed your mind.'

'Yes, in Rome one may as well be a Roman.'

'What's Hans like?'

'Quite a good sort.'

There were three classes, one for beginners, one for those who showed some mastery of the turns, and a third for skiers of experience. I had begun in the middle class under the instruction of Hans, who, in a white peaked cap and leaning on his very long leather-handled ski-sticks, would shout tactful encouragement from the top of a small eminence to his pupils. But two days later I was promoted to the class above. This was taken by Trio, another university student, tall, gay, handsome, with a face terribly slashed by duelling scars. I was flattered by my quick promotion to his charge from that of the solid, quiet, slow-moving Hans, a good skier and an excellent instructor; but it was more amusing to be with Trio, with his gaiety, his buffoonery, and his magnificent daring on skis. All the instructors were Austrian university students, probably unpaid, but receiving a holiday in return for their services. Trio, debonair, carefree, self-indifferent, was the gayest and most untrammelled of the three. There was a streak of recklessness about him, with his wry smile and laughing expression, a streak of recklessness and a tiny streak of mischief as well. It would have been a mistake to entrust him with the beginners whom even the mild admonitions of Hans might have discouraged. But he was a success in the position he held. The top class was the 'touring class,' but since it was snowing most of the day, and fresh snow on slopes of any steepness is highly dangerous until it has settled, tours were debarred, and instead we hardened our muscles on the practice slopes. Trio never bullied his pupils, but he would mock them gently into attempting something difficult, and if that failed he would demonstrate it with such perfect ease himself that one was tempted to imitate him. I could cultivate my taste for the straight Schüss now with his full approval, knowing that he looked forward with glee to the moment when, nearing the end of the slope, one would have first to crash across an icy path and then to negotiate in heavy snow a series of abrupt undulations in the ground. It was a test at once of muscle, imagination, and will. When Trio had watched almost his entire class one after another come to separate grief, he would jump quickly round on his skis, descend the hill at breakneck speed, and rejoin us. Forming in single file, we would remount the hill slowly behind him to repeat the ordeal. Again and again he encouraged us, having toiled painfully up the slope, to launch ourselves once more down it, inviting disaster at the bottom. Again and again we did so with varying emotions, fear, resolution, exultation. So the morning continued. Finally, returning with his own class in single file behind him, Hans with his white peaked cap, would pass us on the path below, and, seeing our predicament, would taunt Trio in German, voicing the very suspicion I had just voiced a moment before in an undertone to Mathews, '*Sie sind Sadist.*' Whereat Trio would grin.

For Mathews was also a member of this class. I found him there when I arrived. His ski-ing was better than mine, a little safer, a shade more assured, his turns more dependable and his falls fewer. As stylists there was little to chose between us. Mathews' hooked back, his rucksack standing out upon it like a hunchback's hump, as he headed forward into the falling snow-flakes, was very little preferable to my own ugly crouch, hands and wrists pushed forward, centre of gravity as low as possible, in an attempt to hold my speed as well as to minimise the dangerous effects of a fall. When I had

343

begun ski-ing ten years before there were still men and women in the world who skied like demi-gods, or like some species of poised and lovely bird. It was the golden age of ski-ing. It was not merely permissible but it was customary to ski upright. I remember Rose Steger – not an expert by any means – and how she used to descend the slopes at Château d'Œx, straight as a die, head thrown back triumphantly, her arms close to her side, the clenched hands grasping the ski-sticks held a little behind her hips. She moved over the snow like some exultant figure of Olympian kinship to whom the inevitable fall at the bottom of the hill meant nothing. So must the gods ski, if they ski at all, ignoring all theories as to the centre of gravity and the safety of the Arlberg crouch.

In ten years, international rivalry changed ski-ing from an art to a science and all romance departed from it. In those early days it had been beautiful to watch as well as thrilling. I was in Château d'Œx when the Swiss Championship was held there. The course was a very severe one. I had climbed to a point on La Lécherette where I could see the competitors come over the rise for their first downward rush after mounting from l'Etivaz. As they came over it they were confronted by a steep pitch of considerable difficulty, hemmed in on either side by pine woods, so that all manœuvering must take place in a narrow glade. Man after man, seeing it, straddled his ski-sticks and rode them to the bottom, for stick-riding at that time was still permitted. Only a few, scorning such tactics, took it straight, depending upon a lightning turn at high speed to save them when the pace became too great to hold. 'Schmidt Peter' was one of these. He was from Adelboden, a guide, Peter Schmidt, – or 'Schmidt Pater,' as everyone called him. He appeared suddenly over the rise to swoop down like some creature winged not at the shoulders but, like the god Mercury, at his feet, passing like a flash within a yard of the chalet wall near which I was standing, and saved from crashing into it by a perfect Christie only a second before. Broad-shouldered, upright, leaning away from the slope rather than towards it, his head and shoulders thrown back defiantly, his hands, from which the ski-sticks hung by their leather thongs over the flexed wrists, extended slightly in front and to either side of him, balancing him, in a fashion now hardly ever seen, but lovely and graceful to watch as a young girl poised for a jump, who stretches out her fingers in airy anticipation at the leap before her, so he shot past us, easily, effortlessly, as though he floated over the ground, the muscles stiffening to resolution only in the moment of need. The slightest miscalculation, a fraction of an inch and he must have crashed into the chalet wall. But at the right moment the foot was thrust forward, the shoulders thrown back still more, and the bird swooped, the skier changed his direction, swerved, and was off on an opposite diagonal of flight. It was the apotheosis of ski-ing, a valedictory gesture to all that was poetical and triumphant in the art. Compared to him, the stick-riders were like some species of grotesque and displeasing gnome, who had emerged from concealment in a mountain cavern to frighten us with their clumsy efforts.

It was effortless, it was splendid, but, apparently, it was not *la guerre*. For when later I descended to the winning flags to enquire the result of the race, praising 'Schmidt Pater's' style and magnificent nerve, I learnt that his gallant gesture had helped to defeat him, that the stick-riders had reached the easier part of the course not half so fatigued as he. He had skied triumphantly, but they had won the race. And within a year or two all such ski-ing had vanished. The crouchers had won. Ugliness had prevailed. Stick-riding was forbidden, but the crouch became the only position for racing. Of course, the erect position is more dangerous. If a man skis like a beetle, he will fall like a beetle too, whereas if he skis as the Swiss did in the early days of racing, his fall – if he does fall – will be like the fall of Lucifer from Heaven. Our values have altered. We are no longer interested in the poetry of things. Instead we have a pinchbeck interest in times, in split seconds, in records, as though the only romance left to us were the romance of clocks and cog-wheels. But the Greeks, who originated sport, saw in it poetry and beauty as well as rivalry, and so it became for them an inspiring ceremonial, an expression of gratitude to the gods for strength and loveliness, a theme for poet and sculptor, as well as a mere contest of muscle and skill.

It is easier to praise the upright position in ski-ing than to be its exponent. No one seeing either Mathews or myself on skis would have mistaken us for demi-gods. We had long since, when the descent was steep, begun to crouch like the rest of the world, thinking more of our own safety than of the poetry of motion: 'Bend the knees. Lower! Lower!' I would mutter to myself, thrusting my arms forward to keep my balance, consoled, as the pace grew faster and faster, with the thought that if I fell in this almost sitting position I was less likely to break a limb. And Mathews' tall form, with its stoop forward from the shoulders, would, as the angle of the hill steepened, make much the same concessions to frail nature.

345

From ten o'clock on, each morning, the *gasthof* was deserted. Every guest, the novices included, was out of doors discovering the thrill of ski-ing. The girl to whom I had given my seat in the sleigh was one of the most ardent of these devotees. She had not died of pneumonia after all. Rather, to my intense surprise, I had seen her out on the slopes the very next morning. Disapproval of her conduct still prejudiced me against her. It was a day or two before I could bring myself to speak to her. Then, finding myself near her in a ski class, I said:

'Young woman, you have great powers of recuperation!'

'Oh, nothing ever kills me.'

'Don't be too sure. That is an illusion from which we all sooner or later awaken.'

She had not yet learned to crouch. She skied upright, and when she fell she fell with the violence of a tree which crashes to its destruction. Soon she would learn better. She would be converted like the rest of us.

For nearly a week it had continued to snow. We had not seen either sun or sky since we arrived. If it was not actually snowing, low grey clouds obscured the whole firmament and hid the higher peaks of the mountains.

That same day after lunch Mathews announced,

'Trio is going to take us for a run this afternoon.'

'Oh, how did you hear that?'

'He told me when I went down to the carpenter's shop about my bindings.'

'He must be sick of seeing us on the practice slopes.'

'Yes. That's probably it. We are to bring skins.'

We paraded at half-past two. About eight of the class elected to come. Two others wished to accompany us, but Trio rejected them, deciding that they might find the run too difficult. They were sent off to join Hans, and to refresh their memory of stemming. We could picture how their afternoon would be spent, 'Lower. Lower. Touch the right ankle' – and the pupil, in six cases out of ten, despairing of touching the right ankle and alarmed by his increasing pace, would stiffen, straighten up, career a little way down the hill out of control, and presently sit down. Hans had seen it happen a thousand times and did not mind, but it enraged Trio. He was an amazing fellow, as indifferent to his own comfort as he was suspected by Hans of being indifferent to the sufferings of his pupils. He had not even brought gloves this afternoon, and he looked rather like some gaunt, mocking, very youthful Mephistopheles, beardless and with cheeks slightly tinged with blue.

We lined up in front of him.

It was not snowing, but the day was grey and unfriendly.

'Where are we going?' I asked Mathews.

'The Wiesenberg. What everyone calls the Plum-pudding.'

The Plum-pudding lay to one side of the sleigh-track, just at the point where it came over the col and dipped down on to Kühtai. We had heard it mentioned often enough, but as yet, thanks to the weather, we had never seen it. Nor were we to see it this afternoon. We halted by the hay chalet to put on our skins, then began climbing a very steep pitch on the right, through masses of heavy snow which covered what seemed to be numerous small shrubs, like frauchan bushes. Trio made the track, a tiring business under such conditions. With his long legs and long stride, he forged ahead, thrusting forward rhythmically into the heavy snow. We had barely reached the top of the rise and come out, a little breathless, on a more gentle gradient, when fog closed suddenly in on us, and we could not see more than a few yards ahead. In the greyness of the late December afternoon visibility had been poor enough before, but at least we had been able to see the black forms of the trees across the valley and the huge eaved roof of the *gasthof* below. But now all landmarks disappeared. We went forward into a white, cotton-wool blankness, into which we passed rather as a man passes into a different state of consciousness under an anæsthetic. The fog had come up in a moment. Though we were climbing in single file less than a yard apart, and in danger of committing the unforgiveable sin of the beginner who treads on his predecessor's skis, nevertheless it was impossible for us ever to see our leader and hard enough, if one delayed for a moment to adjust a ski-binding, to pick up the man immediately in front. It would have been utterly unlike Trio to turn back. Nor did he do so. We pressed steadily on. We advanced into nothingness. The world seemed to drop from us. We might have been spirits moving in the formless void before the creation of the planets. Sometimes the slope steepened and our sealskins, which for a time had been unnecessary, once more came into use. Then it would flatten out again, allowing us to quicken pace once more.

I remembered now all the stories I had read of the dangers of ski-ing on a mountain in fog. In fog one loses the sense of direction completely. One can plunge over a precipice guilelessly and in naïve confidence. Though the gradient up which we had just come was perfectly safe in itself, being rounded and without any sheer declivities, it was nevertheless steep enough to account for the most abrupt precipices on another side of the mountain. Supposing in our descent we wandered too far to the left and went over one of these, or started an avalanche?

These and other apprehensions, equally agreeable, occupied my mind. Mathews, on the contrary, was enjoying himself hugely. In certain respects he had infinitely more temerity than I. He never suffered anxiety from the thought of possible dangers. His imagination never ran away with him. The red lines traced on the maps to mark places where there was a risk of avalanches left him unmoved – indeed, only amused him – whereas they stirred all my latent apprehensiveness, and made me experience, if not the horrors of actual suffocation, at least an anticipatory tremor or two. It is a mistake to have too lively a power of visualisation. As we climbed now I recalled all the descriptions of avalanches I had read, and I thought of the advice which experts offer as to how one should act in the emergency. I remembered their warning that unless one can undo one's ski-straps in time, and remove one's skis, there is little or no chance of being saved; of how, even then, it is essential to try at all costs to keep the head up, swimming with the arms in the moving snow much as a man swims in water, until that moment when, the avalanche having slowed down, one finds onself crushed in by the tightly packed snow with a pressure that is almost intolerable. If at that moment one's head is still above the snow then one is saved, or, if one can even move an arm sufficiently to make some sort of an air channel to the surface, one may be found in a few hours' time and dug out. But to be flung forward with one's skis on is almost certain death, unless by some good fortune the point of a ski-stick or the tip of a ski betrays one's position to the rescue-party in time.

The worst terrors are nearly always the terrors of the imagination. In an emergency, if, to use Sir Toby's expression, we have enough blood in our liver to clog the foot of a flea, we rise to the occasion and are spurred, alike by fear and by a sense of human dignity, to play the man. But a feeling of *noblesse oblige* is less effective against a mere apprehension. It is incompetent to deal with something that has not yet happened. Instead, we are left to exercise ceaseless vigilance against a contingency that may never arise. I had prepared myself often in imagination for that moment when I would stoop down to unbuckle my ski-straps. I had fixed it vividly in consciousness

348

by a series of mental rehearsals. It looked as though I might be glad of these rehearsals now.

Something in my expression as we made one of our periodic halts to take breath must have betrayed my mood, and Mathews smilingly twitted me on my anxiety.

'Monk, you will never see home again.'

'How much further does the wretched Trio expect us to go? It's late enough as it is.'

'You don't expect us to turn back, do you?'

'How does he hope to find our way when we can't see three yards in front of us?'

'*En avant, mon brave.*'

We resumed our climb. I could hear Mathews joking with Trio in German as the latter moved forward once more, and I gathered that he was telling him that one member of his party at least considered that he was leading us to our destruction.

We climbed for another quarter of an hour. The ascent suddenly became steeper and we began to mount between rocks and huge boulders covered with snow. The final twenty yards was so steep that our sealskins could not keep their grip and our skis began to slip back.

This last scramble brought us out by a large rock on what appeared to be, so far as one could judge in the dense fog, a tiny plateau on the summit of the mountain. This was our objective. From here we were to start down. Trio gave the order to take our sealskins off. It was bitterly cold. In unfastening mine and in my hurry to do the thing quickly, I barked my knuckles against the rock, and this trivial discomfiture only seemed symbolic of our plight, one more manifestation of the disapproval of fortune. The light layer of snow along the top of our skis could be knocked off by tapping the side of the ski with one's stick, but the tiny patches of ice along the ski edges themselves, where moisture had frozen hard between sealskin and ski, had to be chiselled off with the steel point of the stick. If left, the snow would be sure to ball on them on the way down and would make running impossible.

It was too cold and there was no time to wax these places now. One scraped the ice off with the tip of the ski-stick as best one could. We could see absolutely nothing around us. A white cloud enveloped us as though we had been received up into heaven. Mathews grinned at me. He knew that my apprehensiveness generally spoilt such adventures for me. I might rise to the emergency, I did rise to it, but

349

I was incapable of really enjoying it; whereas for him a spice of danger gave the thing zest. He volunteered to run last so that if anyone got a really bad fall he could, in ski-ing parlance, 'pick up the pieces.'

We made the descent in about twenty minutes. It had taken nearly an hour and a half to climb. Had not one of the party, an Australian, courageous but without a great deal of experience, fallen badly, taking a terrific header into the snow and barking his nose, we should have taken even less. Trio led the way and I followed, running swiftly in his tracks and without falling at all on the earlier part of the descent. Periodically we would halt, and wait for the others to come up. They would emerge out of the mist one by one like wraiths, or like the dancers in some symbolic ballet of the snow, only to recall us to reality, the moment they pulled up beside us, by a jest or by their exultant laughter. As we got lower the fog became less dense and we could see more of our surroundings. By the time we had reached the top of the final descent the valley was clearly visible below us, and the straight line of the black wooden fence dividing it. The big snowfall had been late coming this year; normally the fence would be completely covered by now. To the left was the dark outline of the *gasthof* in its waste of snow, one light already showing in the building. Though the most difficult part of the run was still before us, and though I was to fall heavily at least half a dozen times in negotiating it – for the small bushes, only partly buried, did not make ski-ing easy – yet the sense of relief at seeing the fence, the wooden hay-barn, the *gasthof* itself, in the rapidly dimming light made this last part of the expedition more enjoyable to me than the earlier, when I had been running well.

And yet my fears throughout had been entirely imaginary. For when the fine weather came and I could see a little more of the Wiesenberg, I realised that even if we had lost our way no harm could possibly have befallen us. The run must have been so familiar to Trio that the thickest fog could hardly have misled him. But even had it done so, we should still have run no more risk than children who slide down a rick into a thick bed of loose straw. The rounded sides of the Plum-pudding held no precipices at any point and we could have hurled ourselves over its side wherever we wished.

Back once more in our own room, changing our clothes before going over to the main building, I grew a little ashamed of my apprehensions and even attempted to excuse them.

'Every man has his own brand of timidity. You are nervous on a horse, Mathews. I've noticed it. Well, I am nervous on a mountain. That is all the difference between us.'

His jesting at my expense on the run had rankled and I wanted to put him in his place. Falstaff's magnificently cynical defence of cowardice was what I really needed to meet the occasion, but unfortunately it was not to hand. 'Honour pricks me on. Yea, but how if honour prick me off when I come on? How then? Can honour set to a leg? No. Or an arm? No. Or take away the grief of a wound? No. Honour hath no skill in surgery then? No. What is honour? A word. What is that word, honour? Air. A trim reckoning! Who hath it? He that died o' Wednesday. Doth he feel it? No. Doth he hear it? No. Is it insensible then? Yea, to the dead.' Such cogent eloquence was beyond me, but I did the best I could in my own humbler line. Was it an offence, I asked him, to dislike the notion of slow suffocation in the snow? Avalanches did happen, and they happened generally to people who were foolish enough not to worry about them. Was there anything wrong in wanting to see home again? Was nostalgia a crime?

'Don't you ever feel lonely on *your* solitary travels? I suppose not, or you would have given them up long ago, Mungo Park!'

'You are quite wrong, Monk. Often I feel terribly lonely.'

I was surprised to hear him say that he could feel terribly lonely. But it was quite plain that he spoke the truth. His thirst for novelty might win against the dread of loneliness, but the loneliness was there all the same, and he was capable, he assured me, of thinking of his home as wistfully as ever I thought of mine; on Mount Athos, in some humble *trattoria* in Italy, or back street in Lisbon, he had tasted to the full the bitterness of the exile. He made this confession so gently and so frankly, that all my wrath was turned away, and I regretted having called him Mungo Park or twitted him with being an indifferent horseman.

He left me now to go over to the *gasthof* for tea. Afternoon tea, or rather an afternoon cup of chocolate or coffee, for that was our preference, was an extra on the bill, a temptation to which Mathews succumbed regularly, but which I resisted as often as possible. Occasionally I accompanied him over to the *gasthof* and we would sit talking afterwards in the little Austrian room. It was here that he had all his meals, with students and ski-instructors and casual visitors who came for a single meal. We no longer fed together. We had not quarrelled, but we had disagreed – without any rancour on either side – as to where we should eat. With the arrival of another large contingent of our fellow countrymen, the front rooms had become too breezy and British for Mathews. I also really preferred the sound of foreign voices, since it is much less easy to be distracted by what one cannot understand. But the two front rooms had one compensation which in my eyes outweighed their disadvantages. At midday, when it was fine, it was possible to fling open a window and eat in the direct rays of the sun, whereas in the little room at the back no sun entered. A half-forgotten fragrance of cigar smoke hung about the air; this also prejudiced it in my eyes. It was not possible for us to compromise: the midday meal in one place and the others elsewhere would have been confusing for the waitresses. Each preserved his independence of action. After a little mild wrangling in which neither side would give way, Mathews went off to the room at the back and I remained where I was. He sat at a table by himself in the extreme corner. A book propped against his glass took the place of any conversational advantages which it would have been within my poor power to offer. From time to time he would lay it down, to exchange a phrase with some neighbouring table. It was here that I sometimes joined him for chocolate in the late afternoon. The tiny room was dark, but picturesque. As one came through the passage from the main corridor it was exactly opposite the pantry. Panelled in wood, it was known as 'The Peasant Room,' and both it and 'The Princely Chamber' overhead were used to emphasise the traditions of the building. In the corner nearest the door was a huge wood-burning stove, covered in white tiles rather like the stoves to be seen in Russia. Occasionally an Englishman would come here to write a letter, or to play a game of chess with a friend; but for the most part it remained not only Austrian in character but in occupation.

Two days later it ceased snowing. The clouds broke up. The sun shone. Instead of the muffled greyness in which, for nearly a week, we had been condemned to live and move, instead of the constant veil of snowflakes which had hung between us and our surroundings, we woke to a clear sky. In the sharp, frosty morning air the dark, serrated edges of the peaks stood out against the saffron background of dawn. For the first time we could realise where we were – in a world of our own – a white mountain fastness which sparkled and glistened like a child's dream. If the exhilaration of that keen air in our lungs had not in itself been enough to elate us the scene around must surely have shamed us into wonder. The rounded form of the Wiesenberg was one huge field of white, unsullied snow, except where pines, in solitary grace or in small groups of two or three, dotted its northern slopes. Rising to severe and jagged peaks the flanks of the mountains proper glistened in the sunlight, mantled with untrodden snow, save where stark ribs of rock showed where the snow had been unable to lie. At the head of the wooded descent to Oetz the sun struck a pyramid-shaped peak, making great patches of dark shadow on its face where the concave rocks overhung, or where a precipice fell sheer away. A hundred small details – the half-emergent wooden fence along the borders of some frozen and completely hidden stream, the posts driven in the ground to mark the course of the sleigh-track, a flank of rock, the wadded outline of a shrub, and still more the signs of human activity round the *gasthof* itself, a snow-shovel, a stack of logs, a sleigh propped against the wall – all combined to give a sense of intimacy to the landscape and to save one from feeling overwhelmed by its majestic grandeur.

'Just look at that view!'

'Yes, just look at it!'

'What are you going to do this morning, Alister?'

'Read in the sun. I feel lazy.'

'I think I shall potter.'

At least half our day was spent out of doors. It was a good moment when at ten o'clock in the morning, the air still cold enough to form tiny icicles in the nostrils with each intake of breath, one clattered off up the icy path in pursuit of the rest of the class. The main practice grounds were on the opposite side of the *gasthof* to the slopes where Trio had tested us so severely. They were reached by the same path down which the sleighs came each evening from Gries. The learners assembled outside the *gasthof* and followed the instructor to whatever knoll or slope he considered suited to their proficiency. There, one below the other, at right angles to the hill, they would form a sort of moving escalator, side-stepping slowly up the hill until each pupil reached the head of the line, when it became his turn to come out in front and attempt whatever manœuvre was being taught. He would start off diffidently or in high hope, zig-zagging down, making use of the turns they were practising; but before long he would probably get out of control, career madly away, overrun the mark and end up far beyond where he had intended. It reminded me of those days when I had watched recruit officers galloping off the parade ground on recalcitrant mounts. Of course, there was an alternative to being run away with by one's skis. This was simply to sit down. But even this demanded courage.

Whichever solution was chosen, the pupil would eventually come to a halt and would then start working his way back to the class, to rejoin it as quickly as he could, and to begin the process of side-stepping up the hill all over again.

If one was late for class in the morning, one hurried off up the path to join it wherever it was already practising. I was often late: hastening along, I would presently get out of breath, would pause, prop my haunches against the handles of my ski-sticks behind me, to avoid slipping down the hill, and stand there contemplating the crowded slopes. I had a pleasant sense these days that I was being virtuous, that I was at last attempting to put some kind of polish on my ski-ing, and that the fruits of this reformation were already beginning to show. At the same time the best moment of the morning for me was at the very end of the class when we were taken through deep untrodden powder-snow to a fence at the top of a very steep field above the path and told to launch ourselves down. Trio would start us from a point so sheer that, incapable of the jump turn, the only thing one could do was to edge oneself round till the skis pointed downhill, holding back the while against the slope by pressing one's stomach on the handles of the extended ski-sticks until the whole weight of the body rested on them. Then, after a few seconds' pause to contemplate the line intended and to gather courage, one removed the sticks and slipped swiftly away, crashing presently across the obstacle of the hard-trodden, ice-bound path, and gadarening for nearly half a mile over the practice slopes, past timid learners, till one came to the floor of the valley.

One reached the bottom with eyes filled with tears, but with a heart elate. It was the conclusion of the class so far as Trio was concerned, but very often, if instruction had ended early, and if there was time before lunch, Mathews and I would remount for a second trip, less perilous than the first, thanks to the departure of the classes, with whom there was no danger of colliding, but equally thrilling. 'Once more, Alister?' 'Yes, once more.' And we would turn back and start the climb again, ten minutes of arduous climbing for the sake of a descent that cannot have lasted more than a minute at most.

Other mornings we might spend this interval before lunch basking in the sun on the wooden balcony of the annexe, resting after the exertions of the lesson. It was here too that I returned immediately after lunch, to lie in a deck chair in the sun, to read and, in all likelihood, presently to doze. Sometimes I neglected the summons to the afternoon ski-class, listened to them assembling on the path below and setting forth, and then turned again to my book. At least another hour of sunshine was mine if I chose to remain, and I could then get my skis and amuse myself on them alone until dusk. Mathews, even more solitary by inclination than I, was the last person to protest at such abstention. There were days when he would go to the class while I remained behind; others when he remained and I went. Even if we had not seen each other all afternoon we would meet in the evening before dinner; he would come across from the *gasthof* to tell me of some student with whom he had been discussing ski-ing, or I would return to the annexe to find him reading upon his bed in the rather inadequate light from the red-shaded electric lamp.

Reading was not the least of the pleasures that our life in this place offered. I read much myself. I read Bazin. I read Santayana on his three poets. Goethe, whom I appreciated as man, as questing spirit, rather than as philosopher, fared badly in this last role. His interpreter made him seem vague and woolly in comparison with the Latin poet or the Italian. Perhaps Santayana over-emphasised the welter of ideas, hardly a cosmos, rather a chaos, a sort of gigantic enveloping fog of cerebration in which the poet moved, much as we had moved that afternoon upon the Wiesenberg. Goethe is simple when he is lyrical, or when there comes out in him a streak of rather childish playfulness, as in certain passages in Faust. But in his philosophic prose his style is never that of the Greeks whom he admired so much. It is never that simplification of outlook and statement, which, for the Hellene, was the last step which profound thought must take.

And laying Santayana down, I would tell myself, 'Goethe is as like Plato or Sophocles as baroque art is like Pheidias and no more. His talent is lyrical, personal, interpretative rather than philosophic. His philosophy is only part of the landscape of his mind, interesting as such but of no real significance. Shakespeare can put more actual philosophy into a single line than Goethe into many pages.'

An unfair verdict, perhaps, and in any case one has no right to pass judgment on a poet whom one cannot read in the original. But since Santayana had made him one of his three philosophic poets he must be judged as such. To Mathews, returning to rid himself of his ski-boots or to change into another coat for dinner, I might throw out an insult or two, in the hope that he would rise up and defend the Teutonic mind. But his arrival was more likely a reminder that my ski-boots were not yet greased for the morning, and, springing up, I would forget Santayana and Goethe alike in the task of greasing them. Then we would grope our way down the staircase and across to the *gasthof* for dinner, to light, to warmth, to good food, and to the sound of quiet voices murmuring in different tongues around us.

It was a happy existence. And at the end of each day there was sleep. I was glad enough to go across to my room after dinner, to read for a time and presently to put out the light. Plato denied the title of 'true pleasure' to anything which was merely passive. The pleasures of the wise he says are pure and true, all others are a shadow only. Though he concedes that 'nothing is pleasanter than health,' he will not allow even it a place in the first order, since it is a pleasure only recognisable in rest, by cessation or in absence. The true pleasures of the soul are of a higher sort. For this reason he must also have rejected sleep, as pleasure of mere cessation. And yet it would be possible to argue that sleep is something more than this. Esoteric writers hint as much. If we are to believe them, it is a veil hung between the waking self and its immortal counterpart. In it we sink back upon ourselves. They would say that it held quite as large a measure of our true being as full consciousness. And it is strange that in sleep men do solve their problems and resolve their doubts. The brain awakes and discovers its solution furnished. Sleep has untied the Gordian knot. It is possible to go still further, and, scaling the dizzy and dangerous heights of metaphysic, to say that in sleep the human mind perhaps follows – from afar – the analogy of the Universal Mind, in that act of self-contemplation from which radiates all, which conserves, withdraws into itself, returns to its centre, before blossoming again in action. Sleep is an aspect in miniature of a universal process, that process of which the seasons are only another example; conservation, withdrawal, retreat; and then presently the reawakening of latent energy, arousal, the breathing out, the going forth which is life.

One need not go as far as this in order to vindicate sleep. It is its own justification. Even as a child I looked forward to sleep and saw no privilege in its postponement. And now at Kühtai, after the day's activity of mind or body, it seemed a blessing to be accepted without delay or hesitation. Often it was long before ten o'clock when I would reach for the switch and plunge the narrow room into darkness. Mathews' return about midnight disturbed me little, no more than the few times I would wake, in any case, in the course of the night. The window was open, but if neither the Austrian *duvet*, that most elusive of all forms of bedclothes, nor the sheepskin coat laid across it to keep it in place, slipped from their position, one remained unaffected by the cold even on the frostiest night. That the nights were cold and the frosts hard could be seen by the huge cornice of snow frozen to the eaves, over the door of the *gasthof*, in the morning, and by the great icicles hanging from the sides of the roof which we noticed when we breakfasted, icicles which had to be knocked down with a long pole as soon as the sun rose, lest they should drop on to the head of some passer-by later in the day.

Into this quiet and untroubled existence of serene activity of mind and of still more joyous activity of body another element was now to come, and it was to come quite by chance.

One evening on the lower slopes, when most of the other skiers had already returned to the *gasthof*, I found myself prolonging as late as possible the moment of my own departure. The evening was drawing in. The slopes were deserted by all except a few last stragglers whose enthusiasm had kept them here after the classes had gone. It was still quite light, but the time was approaching when it would suddenly become impossible to judge with any accuracy the precise gradient of the slope, or even to decide whether it was up or down. Then ski-ing becomes a matter of faith. The fact that I had come out late encouraged me to linger. Climbing to the fence above the path, I ran down swiftly, for at this time of day the snow, touched by the approach of the night frost, becomes perceptibly faster. The exhilaration of the descent – and I had allowed my skis to carry me over the last rise to the furthest point possible, a sort of cup or hollow out of sight of the practice slopes – prompted me to repeat the experience. I turned back and began to climb again.

I had only retraced my way a few yards when I noticed two girls ski-ing nearby. They were practising without an instructor and seemed to have come here in order to learn in solitude and to avoid the curious stares of the more expert.

One of the two was a short, insignificant-looking person with glasses, very intent upon the business in hand. I should not have noticed her at all if it had not been for her companion, who was taller and wearing a primrose-yellow jacket, made of oiled silk, like a yachtsman's jacket, except that the sleeves were wider and puffed at the shoulder. It was this vivid splash of colour against the white snow which first drew my attenton to her, but having once looked in that direction my gaze was instantly arrested for a different reason.

357

In that brief instant of time which it takes to tell us that a face is lovely, I was aware not only of this but also of a strange and striking resemblance to the face which had had so much of the admiration of my callow boyhood in Ireland. So startling was this impression that for a moment I actually believed that chance had brought to this place that phœnix of my youth, whom I had known when she was not only loveliest but least conscious of it. I had never heard of her going abroad at Christmas, but in these days, when so many did go abroad, it was not beyond the bounds of possibility that she should have come here with her husband. I reminded myself that of the few Englishmen in the *gasthof* when I arrived one had been Jacques, an acquaintance; and this coincidence seemed almost to argue in favour of another, even less likely, one.

I looked towards her dumbfounded. I remained leaning on my ski-sticks and watching the yellow jacket from a distance, until reason asserted itself and assured me that my surmise could not be right. Even then doubt lingered. Would she presently raise arched eyebrows in surprise and suddenly call my name?

I deceived myself. I imagined that the past had come to meet me, whereas in actual fact I had gone of my own volition to meet the past. Propped against my sticks, I appeared to be resting long after there was any valid excuse for me to rest. Presently a few words in what seemed to me a foreign language reached my ears as the friend betook herself to a hump of ground a little way off and began very slowly to stem down it. The girl in the yellow jacket remained. By the cautiousness and uncertainty of her manner she was obviously a complete beginner. Though the long black ski-trousers, the business-like white ribbed stockings, together with the coloured ski-sock just visible over the top of her boot, might give her the appearance of an adept, such an impression was belied by every movement she made. She was about to come down that last drop of the practice slope into a cup-shaped hollow, which, though only a few yards in depth, was still sheer enough to add its excitement to the run. I admired her resolution, but at the same time it seemed to me a little foolhardy. She had pushed herself very carefully with her sticks to its extreme brink. Then at the last minute courage failed, she changed her mind and turned to remount the crest. But this was even more fatal than a descent might have been. Her skis slipped back and, instead of coming down in the orthodox style, as she had intended, it looked as if she might do so backwards, had not her progress been very speedily interrupted by a fall.

It was one of those falls when it seems impossible that the victim should ever get sufficiently disentangled to rise again. I went across, not to assist her, for it is almost impossible for another person still on skis to be anything but a hindrance upon such occasions, but to offer discreet advice. Stopping a little above her on the slope, I looked down at her with as much seriousness as tact and the occasion demanded. It is useless in a fall on a slope of any steepness to try to get up until the skis are at right angles to the face of the slope, otherwise they will inevitably slip back, and the victim, before he has even got safely on his feet, will fall once more. The first thing to do, therefore, is to disentagle one's skis, roll over, and get them parallel with the base of the hill. After that one may try to rise. I had imagined that I had heard her speaking French with her friend a moment before, and it was in clumsy French that I addressed her now.

'*Mettez-vous à côté.*'

Had Mathews been there I would probably have seen him smile. I was very vague myself as to whether the words bore the significance intended. '*Mettez-vous à côté.*' What *did* it mean? 'Put yourself on one side'? 'Efface yourself'?

She was lying helpless where she had fallen and looked up at me smiling, amused at her plight. It had begun to snow very slightly. In the snow the complexion attains a transparency which nothing else can give it. Warm with exercise, it glows translucently in contrast to the few flakes of snow which may have gathered on eyebrows or forehead. The face at which I looked down might have been the face of Aurora, and the vivid yellow coat suggested the fields of daffodil across which the goddess moves at dawn. Against the grey monotony of the snow all round us it seemed a symbol of spring. In colouring, in expression, in a certain candid and detached openness of gaze, in clearness of skin and health of complexion, she was a living reminder of that other. I saw now not so much an actual likeness in feature as an astonishing resemblance in type.

If we have ever admired a particular face, we will always be quick to recognise and approve any resemblance to it. There may be only some distant, almost indefinable, kinship, but the eye will instantly appraise it. Indeed, so slender can these links be that it is almost as though what commanded admiration in the first instance was an abstraction, not a face, but a quality, or an idea; so that our delight in beauty is really our delight in seeing this quality given perfect visual expression. We love, but what we love is really the prototype laid up in heaven. And we have only to rediscover this same quality in another face for it to command our immediate allegiance. One could argue on these lines; making love as it were a general bias, or trend of temperament; or one might argue that what one loves is always the particular, and that having lost it the search is one that will continue long afterwards. In every face that we meet we will seek for that vanished flame; and merely to think that we have found it will excite us in a measure that no other discovery could do. Of the two theories the first seems to me the truer, but either would take a whole treatise to justify.

I know that so strong was the resemblance now that, had I voiced my secret thoughts, I should have told her to be in no hurry to move, to remain where she was, since she had recreated for me something that I had thought was lost. But my directions had been followed and she had succeeded in getting her skis downhill. She got up. The black cap or ear-protector which she was wearing gave her forehead a lovely rounded effect, besides adding a certain business-like touch to her costume. For though this might be her first after-noon on skis she was entitled to look the part. As I turned away – if I stayed any longer I should be staring – she was already on her feet. She called after me in English, though with a slightly foreign accent, 'Thank you.'

I climbed slowly back to the fence above the path for my final run. In the fading light it was increasingly difficult to make the quick adaptations necessary for a change in speed or a sudden dip in the ground, but there was still enough light to save me from actual disaster.

As I ran down I wondered whether I would see the two neophytes again. It was not so long since I had left them. But when I plunged swiftly over the lip of the hollow where I had stood a few minutes before, to skid for several yards in an open Christie on the slightly crusted level snow at the bottom, they had already gone. I looked around and saw them in the distance, returning over the snow towards the *gasthof*. My first feeling was one of fierce resentment against the friend whose face I had hardly taken the trouble to notice. She was to blame for this retreat – an officious busybody, an interfering duenna who had conceived it her duty to hurry away from strangers: or alternatively she became in my imagination a slothful gourmand for whom the call of the afternoon cup of choco-late had proved too strong. If telepathy can prevail between complete strangers the mild-mannered and bespectacled friend retreating in the distance must have wondered at this moment what black shadow it was which had suddenly and for no reason crossed her mind. I told myself that, but for her, I might have spoken to the stranger again, I might have found out her nationality, even her name.

I remained where I stood for another five minutes watching through a curtain of drifting snow-flakes a party of people, half a mile away, coming slowly down the gorge on the far side of the stream. They followed one another in single file. I noticed how at the mouth of the gorge, from which they were just emerging, the rocks at first rose sheerly, but that above these precipitous rock-faces the snow lay thick on slopes steep as a penthouse roof, from which it threatened to avalanche at any minute; and I admired the prudence with which, separated from one another by a few yards, they moved slowly, and with apparent indifference, though, of course, at this time of day the danger of the mass becoming detached was much less. I wondered whether my own apprehensive and excitable temperament would have been equal to the test. I stood there musing after they had left the gorge and while they crossed, with every appearance of weariness, the level stretch that still lay between them and the *gasthof*.

It was still snowing gently. Against the grey sky the falling flakes of snow appeared black and not white. They fell steadily, imperturbably, spinning round, but never deviating from their downward trend, with that ceaseless continuity which of all phenomena in Nature makes them most suggest perpetual motion. The eye, hypnotised by them, loses power to contemplate anything else, and the mind, equally hypnotised, seems at last to have discovered a formula through which it can escape at will from the torment of thought.

When I did move from where I stood it was to walk slowly back to the *gasthof*. I left my skis in the great stone basement beneath the building and made my way up the steep little path to the annexe. The sound of low voices came from the room downstairs where tired skiers, students here for a few days, were removing their boots and groping in rucksacks for the food which they had brought with them. In the doorway of the building, Anna, the stocky peasant maid, who looked after the chalet, met me, carrying some jugs of water – Anna, whose age must be about thirty, and whose mild eyes were so wonderfully expressive of motherly goodwill that when she smiled at us it seemed always to be the frank smile with which one greets children.

She smiled now and made way for me to pass. I went upstairs. Mathews was reading on his bed. The room was so small that if one read anywhere it must be there. The two beds, the wooden wardrobe built out from the wall between them, the large plaster chimney on the opposite side of the room, which, coming up from the dormitory below, provided us with welcome extra warmth and an opportunity of drying our clothes, the radiator, two washstands, a small table folding out from the wall on a hinge – by the time all these had been fitted in there was barely room for a small stool and a single wooden chair.

I took off my boots, stuffed them with pieces of newspaper which took the place of trees, removed the steel splint from my knee and changed my coat. Mathews continued to read.

'I saw a rather beautiful girl on the snow this afternoon.'

'Oh, where did you see her?'

'At the bottom of the practice slopes.'

'Is she staying at the *gasthof*?'

'I don't know. I suppose so.'

'What was she like?'

At the mention of the yellow jacket, he said that he also had seen her.

'Yes, she is beautiful.'

Then he added:

'But remember that everyone looks beautiful when it is snowing.'

Did he think that this note of warning was necessary, warranted by some inflexion in my voice when I spoke? I cannot say. He continued reading for some minutes longer. Then, looking at his watch and suddenly discovering that it was long past his usual hour for afternoon tea, he leaped from his bed and prepared to depart.

'Are you coming?'

'No, not to-day.'

Mathews departed across the snow, leaving me to read. He had lent me a few days before a book peculiarly calculated to emphasise my present mood. It was a translation of a novel by a foreign writer who was new to me. In the pages of this book I had found something that we expect normally from poetry rather than from prose, an evocation of all the mingled anguish and exaltation which youth experiences when, becoming acutely aware of beauty of the individual, it becomes, at the same time and by the same tremendous upsurge of creative energy, equally aware of the sum total of the beauty in Nature, and of all that is at once tragic and lovely and wistful in dawn or dusk or waning afternoon. A *tour de force* of lyricism, it told me something I already knew, and had known since childhood. Anatole France says somewhere that the human race might have been spared some of its worst pangs if the poets had not invented love for it; it is by reading about the complaint that we succumb to it. But is this the case? Quite young children are a good deal more susceptible than we imagine. Long before I was ten I knew what it was to wish passionately to see a particular face. This could hardly be laid at the door of the poets I had then read. We come into the world equipped to love without any aid from the poets. It is merely that they pile fuel upon a fire which already exists. What I read now, the description of the delight in appearance, comparable to, but transcending, the delight that a spray of cherry blossom, or the slow, rhythmic and patterned outrush of a wave up a sandy beach can give us, found an instant correspondence in my mood. Some might say that I had taken my cue from the book – that, as Anatole France suggested, I contracted love from its pages. But it would be truer perhaps to say that it influenced me indirectly, by waking recollection, in the same way that a person who had travelled in Spain or Portugal, hearing a stranger talking of these countries, might be so stirred as to cry out, 'Shall I never see Cordoba again?' No book at that instant could have been a more forceful reminder of that inalienable and exquisite heritage which was ours in youth, if we cared to accept it, and had not tarnished our imagination. Every page gave back to me, as from the clear depths of a mirror, all the minutiæ, all the details, all the associations of an emotion which I had felt in the past, and which, at this moment, I was strongly disposed to feel once more.

I continued reading. I looked forward to the moment when I would go across to the *gasthof* at dinner-time and see again a face that had seemed to me lovely in the snow. And yet I postponed it, for the very reason that I looked forward to it. Making my book the excuse, I reflected, perhaps only half-consciously, that every minute I delayed made it only the more certain that she would be already there when I arrived. Like a man who has come into a legacy that is entirely unexpected – in this case merely the legacy of looking upon what I intensely admired – I refused to show any undue haste in claiming it. I invested present impatience, deliberately, as a premium against the risk of any temporary future disappointment. Temporary only, because I felt absolutely safe. No one ever left Kühtai in the evening or indeed later than two o'clock in the afternoon. It was impossible therefore that someone whom I had seen as recently as five o'clock could since have gone.

At last I put down my book, got my snow-boots and departed. But when I entered the dining-room she was not there. Nor did she come later. I looked at every face with that mixture of tense expectation and assumed indifference which is emotion's attempt to conceal its secret, not simply from others, but from itself. I knew that in the instant of seeing her I would experience again that surprised wonder and delight, that curious sense of liberation which accompanies our escape from a purely logical world into a world where emotion is its own justification. Before beauty the heart turns aside from logic, from expediency, from prudence, as one might turn from an unjust tyrant, and cries defiantly, 'I appeal unto Cæsar.' And the reply comes – weighted, it may be, with tremendous destiny – 'Thou hast appealed unto Cæsar. Unto Cæsar shalt thou go.'

I do not say that I was ready to make any such imprudent and extravagant appeal now to a court other than the court of reason. But in any case I was saved making it.

She did not come. Neither in the room where I sat myself, nor in the adjoining one, clearly visible through the glass partition, nor in the little Austrian room where Mathews, 'gone native,' was eating and reading at the same time, was there anyone who in the least resembled her. I told myself that she and her friend, newcomers to the snow, were probably tired after their journey and would dine late. Until the very end of the meal, and after, I continued to anticipate their arrival. I could almost feel that sudden relief of mind and contemptuous amusement at ever having doubted, which would be mine when they did come. As each late-comer entered I expected disappointment to vanish. But the meal finished, and she had not appeared. She had gone to bed. She was dining in her room. Whatever the reason, it was plain she would not come now and I must wait until morning for a moment which I had been foolish enough to count as already mine.

But morning did not vouchsafe it either. She was not at breakfast. That was not surprising, for it was a meal which guests took when they felt so disposed. But she was not with any of the ski-classes, when they paraded; nor was she on the snow-slopes later in the morning. The yellow wind-jacket would have been easily seen; but even supposing she had not chosen to wear it, it was a simple matter to pick out any newcomer. At lunch I expected confidently to see her, but I was disappointed again. The day passed. Into my head there entered a fantastic explanation that so far from seeming casual that evening on the snow I must have betrayed so much surprised admiration in a single look – that admiration, almost insulting in its smouldering intensity of the Latin races, who have no hesitation in letting a woman see that they consider her *molto bella* – that the duenna had fled with her forthwith. It was absurd, but what else was I to think? Since the Oetzthal gorge was closed, we were on the route to nowhere, and could in no circumstance be used as a stepping-stone. To come to Kühtai on the evening of one day, merely to leave it early on the morning of the next, seemed completely senseless. And yet, unless I had become subject suddenly to hallucinations, or unless the two people whom I had seen had both succumbed to illness and were keeping to their room, this appeared to be what had happened. Either they had done this, or – even more astonishing – they had come in the afternoon and had left again at nightfall on the same day.

At lunch next day I looked up suddenly and saw through the glass partition someone in the adjoining room wearing a black ear-cap similar to the one the girl in the yellow jacket had worn. When she turned, her forehead in profile – since the cap gave it the same contour – reminded me of the one I had seen, but the hair was darker and the face had none of that grace which, since it combines perfection of line with gentleness of expression, softens into beauty, and which was what I remembered. This was the face of a woman of thirty, hard and assured. I was at a loss to know how I could have been so profoundly stirred only two days before by what moved me so little now. But I remembered Mathews' words, 'Everyone looks beautiful in the snow,' and, since no other solution offered, I accepted this one. I accepted it with some slight chastening of heart, ashamed for two reasons, ashamed in the first instance to have shown myself so susceptible to impressions, and ashamed then to have found those impressions so transitory.

And, since I felt that I had emphasised the whole incident unduly, not only to myself but in an unguarded moment to my friend, I began to jest about it with him. It was a jest against myself, but one of those jests that we undertake in secret self-defence. The girl had vanished. She had never existed, except as a myth of my own creation.

'She is as elusive as your Everest climber, Alister.'

A few afternoons before, he had returned to the annexe in some excitement with a rumour that there was a man staying in the *gasthof*, or at least expected there, who had 'climbed Mount Everest'.

'But I thought that no one had climbed it?'

'When I say climb I only mean that he has been on two of the expeditions – partly climbed it.'

Curiosity had been roused at the thought of this prodigy in our midst, and from then on we had scanned the faces of our fellow guests eagerly, hoping to discover in one of them the indubitable lineaments of Himalayan prowess. But the hotel seemed only full of nonentities. No one knew anything of the individual in question. No one confirmed the rumour. It was impossible even to discover how it had started. Someone, coming from somewhere else, had told someone——

In the same way the incident in the snow was beginning to seem to me a myth. Just as the mountaineer had refused to materialise, so the girl whom I had seen in the snow seemed to have melted into thin air. Like Mrs. Harris, there was 'no sich person'.

'I shall look for her no more; she's vanished like your mountaineer. I'm beginning to doubt whether either of them ever existed.'

But coming from the *gasthof* after the evening meal, standing on the path for a moment to look at the effect of the curious little stub-ended chapel, silhouetted. against the night sky, I forgot my jest, repudiated it, and wondered once more at the mystery of that dis-appearance, musing on the part chance plays in our lives. It was long since I had experienced such an instant response to the stimulus of beauty, and I had certainly not planned it, for if I had been in search of a pretty face there were plenty in the *gasthof* already. Cold and a little melancholy, I sought warmth in the great underground stable nearby. Often in the evening, wishing to be alone, or having come out to breathe the clear, frosted night air, I would slip into this stable with a slight feeling of guilt as though I were a trespasser, yet remembering the similar pleasure it used to give me in Switzerland to stand in the doorway of some warm byre and watch the beasts – prisoners for the whole winter except when the farmer took them for an occasional walk on a fine day through the snow – munching in the dim, acrid-smelling semi-darkness. The stable at Kühtai was a huge one, the snow heaped up outside against its strong stone walls helping to keep it warm. A pathway, slippery with ice, led through the snow to the low doorway almost immediately opposite the porch of the *gasthof*. It could be reached too by wooden steps down from the hay-barn and the carpenter's shop overhead, and what made it seem underground was partly the banked-up snow all round, and partly this fact that its foundations had been cut back into the hill, so that the barn above it was on a different ground-level and could be reached from the far side without climbing.

I knew where to grope in the darkness to find the switch that would suddenly flash a light, dusty and cobweb-obscured at its source, upon this vast catacomb. The beasts had been given their hay, bedded down and left for the night. The stable seemed like a great vaulted cavern, a subterranean pound, shared by a number of different creatures in a mood of tolerant amity, each accepting its neighbour, whatever that neighbour might be. Night, warmth, shelter from the cold outside united them in an unspoken fellowship, just as men exhausted by fighting and drawn together in a common misery will show kindness to an enemy. Along one wall stood the cows, eight or nine of them, a couple lying down, chewing the cud, the rest still pulling at the hay from between the wooden bars of an alley that ran at the back of their stalls. Not far off were three or four goats, pretty-looking creatures like deer, nibbling busily at their provender. They looked round at me, as I passed, with shy curiosity, differing in this from their neighbours who, munching steadily the whole time, never condescended to show awareness of an intruder. Along a low partition wall three sleepy-looking hens, brown as partridges, perched informally, loth to be disturbed at this hour. In one corner were the pigs, in another a wooden enclosure, across which a tiny calf staggered on uncertain legs when it saw me, under the impression that it was to be fed again. The two fingers extended to be slobbered over by its shining muzzle, and rasped by the rough tongue, were a poor substitute for the pail of milk it had expected.

I made my tour of the place slowly, unhurried, a vicarious sharer in that quiet contentment. The heavy-smelling leather harness hanging across a bar, a pronged fork thrust in a heap of hay, the cobwebs on the huge heavy beams, were all a part of an immemorial setting. One of the mules stamped a foot on the stone paving, breaking that half-silence in which the other beasts munched and meditated. A pig grunted, a chain rattled, a hen murmured a sleepy protest. But none of these sounds disturbed – rather, they seemed to confirm – the serenity of the moment. It was *pax bestiarum*, the peace of the beasts; humble, perhaps, but reassuring; comforting; instinct with all the sense of warmth and service, and even love, on the part of the creature, so that it seemed a good thing to work in a stable, even perhaps to be born in a stable.

I visited each corner, looked at each beast. Then I emerged once more into the night. It was splendid as a pageant for kings. Above the indistinct glimmering of the snowfields rose the black outline of the mountain peaks, while above the peaks again rose the multitudinous stars, the whole spangled arch of heaven, lovely, distant, overwhelming, and yet as consoling in its sheer magnificence as the perfumed, hay-scented darkness which I had just left. The sight shamed me with a sense of my own unworthiness, my inability to hold it, to make it a part of myself, to live in its contemplation. But although it shamed me, when I remembered how ephemeral such moments of awe are in our lives, nevertheless I was uplifted by it while it lasted. I seemed to possess the heavens, to be part, as in truth I was, of some immortal procession, the full grandeur of which had only dawned on me now.

I returned to the annexe. I was in bed, but not asleep, when Mathews came in. We did not speak. But next morning when he heard me stir he said,

'Monk, we are fools. I have solved the mystery. That girl must be down at the hut.'

'What hut?'

'The Dortmünder.'

Though I saw it every day against its background of dark pines, I had forgotten the existence of the Dortmünder Hütte. When Gomperz had written to me from St. Anton, he had mentioned it at the end of his letter. 'If the *gasthof* is full, you could probably get rooms at the Dortmünder Hütte nearby.'

It was only about six or seven hundred yards away from the *gasthof*. But it was on the side away from the usual practice slopes, the side where Trio had first taken us to practise the Schüss. And now for nearly a week we seemed to have had no occasion to go there.

'Wouldn't we have seen her again if she were so near?'

'Not necessarily. The people down there don't come up here a lot.'

'Yes, you are probably right. Why didn't I think of it before?'

The explanation was so simple that it was amazing it had not occurred to either of us sooner. But when we are puzzled it is always the obvious which we overlook, just as a man searching for his spectacle-case never dreams that he may be carrying it with his book in his hand. It was quite true to say that no one in their senses would ever come to Kühtai at this time of year and leave it the same night or early next morning. But it is a mistake to draw conclusions too quickly. When I had seen the two figures retreating over the snow it was in the direction of the *gasthof*, but the direction of the *gasthof* was also the direction of the Dortmünder Hütte.

It stood at the very head of the valley, looking across to the trees, at the entrance to the Langenthal gorge, little more than half a mile away, but in a direction we never went. Perhaps because it was inconspicuous against its background of trees I had forgotten its existence. Though called a hut, it was really an extremely well-built and solid three-story chalet, not so very much smaller than the *gasthof* itself.

I had gathered from Gomperz's letter that it had been built by the ski-clubs of Austria as a centre for ski-ing activities, but that political disturbances and the decision of the German Government that their nationals should 'winter-sport' in their own country had rendered it almost deserted.

Once Mathews had suggested his theory, I seized on it as almost certainly right. I proposed to him that we should cut our ski-class that afternoon and put the matter to the test.

'If she is at the Dortmünder and if we go down there this afternoon and ski on those slopes nearby we are fairly certain to see her.'

'All right.'

Curiosity, but still more good nature made him agree.

We set out after lunch. It was still early afternoon. Between *gasthof* and Hütte a small path led across half a mile of uneven ground, crossing a tiny stream on its way. We had gone halfway, and I, who was a little ahead of my friend, had reached a gap in the heavy wooden fence – broken by the snows of past winters, and already almost covered by the snows of this – and was about to cross the cleft in the ground where the stream ran, when Mathews called to me from the path behind:

'You need go no further.'

'Why?'

'You are wasting your time.'

I returned to the spot where he was standing. He looked at me with a good-natured but slightly ironical smile, and then said:

'I have just seen the yellow wind-jacket.'

'Where?'

I looked towards the slope on our right to which he pointed, but could only see a few dark figures practising with a guide a little way off.

'I see no one.'

'She must be below the ridge of the hill. I am certain I saw her a moment ago. It would be impossible to mistake that jacket.'

He was right. We left the path and with as casual an air as possible began to mount the ground on our right. Before we had gone many yards, I saw her. Her friend was on the hill with the guide receiving instruction, but she herself had her back turned to us and was ski-ing rather cautiously down a slight slope in the opposite direction. A cleft in the ground, part of the same dyke down which the stream ran, had hidden her until now.

So she was not a myth after all. She was real. I felt a sense of relief, like a man reassured of his sanity when he has begun to doubt it. I was vindicated, and the presence of this instructor with them, whom I did not know by sight, proved that they were staying at the Dortmünder. What was to be done next? We stood at the top of the ridge debating the point. Mathews was for going across to them now and ski-ing nearby. If I really wished to make their acquaintance, it was, he assured me, the only way. But this course did not commend itself to me. I was seized with a sudden shyness. Such a move seemed too crude, too obvious, especially as an individual lesson and not a class was in progress. We had climbed the ridge with all too little evident purpose. To ski down to them now was almost the equivalent of accosting them. For though on the other side of the *gasthof* a certain number of people were nearly always practising, here, in the direction of the Dortmünder, the slopes were generally deserted. What might have seemed accident in the one place would appear intrusion in the other.

'No, Mathews. Come away. It is the girl right enough. We will see her some other time. Don't stare at her now.'

My anxiety not to seem the intruder might appear to do me credit. But actually the reverse was the case, for it was the anxiety, not of good manners, but of dread of taking a false step. I wished to speak to her, but I did not wish to risk prejudicing myself in her eyes. Had I viewed it all as casually as Mathews, caring little for the issue, I might have carried it off with a good grace. But because it meant much to me I dared not risk it.

Leaning on our ski-sticks, we faced them across the slope, looking down as though about to descend. But now we abandoned our intention. Having stood there a little while, we turned, climbed up the slope at the back, rejoined the upper path and returned presently to the hotel.

I had satisfied myself at least that she was real. And the very difficulty experienced in establishing her existence had strengthened her hold over my imagination. To have met her again immediately, to have chatted with her, laughed with her friends, perhaps even have become a little bored, might have been the surest way to cure my preoccupation. Instead of which I had had several days in which to think about her and wonder what had become of her.

'Alister, we must get to know them. It will be quite easy. We will go down to the Dortmünder some evening and drink beer there. They are sure to be in the hut at that time and it will be comparatively easy to get to know them.'

He agreed. But at the same time he showed an extraordinary reluctance to put the plan into action. Every time it was propounded he countered with some objection. It may have been merely native obstinacy; a dislike of being used as a cat's-paw. Or else, having detected a note slightly too urgent in my advocacy of the plan, he had decided that the whole matter would be better dropped. In any case, he was not to be moved. For two evenings he refused to leave the *gasthof*, excusing himself with a variety of reasons. It was too cold. It was not the evening to sally forth. The snow which had fallen earlier in the evening was still soft and untrodden. He had no snow-boots, whereas I had. We must have a hard frost, so that the path would be frozen and crisp underfoot when we went. Finally, he made the outrageous stipulation that there must be stars.

'But, heavens, man, she may be gone before there are stars. They all say that it is going to snow for weeks, and in that case stars are an impossibility. It is not my fault that you have come out without snow-boots. You can wear your ski-boots, or, if you insist on wearing shoes I will walk in front and you can plant your feet in my footsteps.'

He might have replied that he did not propose to play page to my Wenceslas. But he did not trouble to reply at all. Instead, he reached for his book.

Forced to laugh in spite of myself, my annoyance with him should have warned me. I felt something not very far from real resentment that he should refuse to come except on his own terms. Reading the book he had lent me had re-awakened in me a mood of lyrical awareness and I had surrendered to it. It was irony or else extreme stupidity that made him ask why I did not go alone. It infuriated me. He must know perfectly well that it would be hard enough even with his support to pay a visit to the Dortmünder and not disclose too obviously and fatally its real intention, the fact that I had come not for the sake of its beer, but for the pleasure of looking at one of the guests.

That evening, about half an hour before dinner, going into the crowded pantry opposite the Austrian room in search of stamps I found another intruder there, rating the maid in a high-pitched voice, at once plaintive and dictatorial. The owner of the voice was a little man with a grey moustache and a fresh complexion. His ski-clothes were old-fashioned. Tight fawn mackintosh trousers wound themselves round his legs. I gathered that he had walked all the way up from Oetz by the route supposed to be closed in winter and was now complaining of the delay in furnishing him with hot water. He reminded me a little of George Moore in one of his more petulant moments. His type of windjacket, and still more the furled mackintosh trousers, were antediluvian and incongruous in these days when winter sports fashions had become gaudy. The maid made some excuse for the delay, and he walked away with a curiously short step which seemed to hitch his already abbreviated trousers higher and higher as he went.

Next morning, one of the first across to the dining-room, I found the newcomer already breakfasting at a small table beside my own, and in a tone meant to be kindly, but possibly a shade patronising, remarked:

'I hope you're not tired after your long walk yesterday?'

His pink face flushed, he looked at me like an indignant prawn, and replied that he was not at all tired. I seemed to have dropped a brick. A moment later an opportunity for revenge presented itself and he took it. I had enquired about Obergurgl, the place from which he had just come. What were the conditions there? Would I be likely to enjoy it?

A note of irritation came into his high-pitched voice as he shot back at me a series of questions:

'Well, what do you want? It depends on you. Do you want peaks? Do you want glaciers? Do you want to get to the tops of mountains?'

It was quite plain from the scorn of his voice that he thought that I was the very last person likely to want any of these things. Indeed, he pronounced each word with such biting sarcasm that I began to wonder myself whether I did want them. I supposed not, now that I came to think of it.

Intuition told me that I had blundered badly, and I regretted my well-meaning enquiry. After breakfast I repeated the incident to Mathews.

'Alister, something tells me that that is the man who has climbed Everest.'

'Nonsense, Monk. Impossible. Quite impossible.'

But nothing is impossible. The insignificant pedestrian was indeed the hero for whom we had been scanning the horizon so anxiously. Middle-aged, shy, full of impatient brusquerie, which he was presently to belie when I knew him better, he must have been amused as well as touched a little on the raw by my tender solicitude for his supposed fatigue after a four-hour stroll up from Oetz. I could not have chosen a worse subject for my sympathy.

Two days went by. The yellow jacket had never appeared again on the slope where I had originally seen it. It was almost as though the spot were being deliberately avoided. I began to wonder whether our voices on that later occasion, when Mathews and I had debated whether to join the skiers, had not carried too clearly across the snow in the open air, and I asked myself whether in speaking English we had not made an unwarrantable assumption that our words would be unintelligible to foreign ears. Had I branded myself as a cad from the start? Or was it simply that the Dortmünder instructors preferred to take their pupils near the hut itself?

One morning I went towards the lower valley and, returning along the path, saw her ski-ing again near the spot where Mathews had rediscovered her. A guide was giving instruction and the voices which came to me seemed as though they might be German. Certainly they were not French. I had paused on the path to speak first to some children whom I knew, and who were returning from an instruction run. Then, meeting Jacques, back from a long tour after a night spent in a cabin on the mountains, I remained talking to him. I was foolish enough to be pleased at the thought that she could see that I had friends in the place, and that I was not some doubtful and prowling *caballero*, anxious to strike up an acquaintance with her merely to relieve the boredom of my loneliness.

She may have seen us talking, but it brought me no nearer to knowing her.

And yet, in the end, the thing achieved itself with a naturalness and simplicity which might have made me wonder why I had ever worried. A particularly strenuous class next morning sent me to my room after lunch to read for a while and then to sleep like a log for more than an hour. When I awoke it was already half-past three. The classes had scattered. It was too late to join them. Often they ended the afternoon session with a miniature tour. I went out on the veranda and looked across the snow. There, in the very place where I had first seen it, was the yellow jacket, ski-ing once more. I put on my boots, got my skis, climbed the path, ran down to them, and, stopping nearby, said smiling:

'*Alors*, you don't fall quite so much to-day?'

'No, not so much.'

Mathews had gone out earlier in the afternoon, having been asked by two schoolboys who were staying in the annexe to show them a particular run. About half an hour later he descended upon us, his rucksack swinging from his shoulders as he pulled up sharply by the fence. In the intervals of going our separate ways, in my case to *schuss*, in theirs to practise cautiously, I had talked quite a little to both the owner of the yellow jacket and her companion; and now, friendly and with his usual charm and courtesy of manner, Mathews seemed to assume from the first that we were all acquainted. We learnt that they were Dutch, and staying at the Dortmünder because there were no rooms vacant at the Alpengasthof the night they arrived. Their English was good, if a little hesitant, and presently we found ourselves giving them hints on ski-ing, which they were glad enough to accept. It was their first season in the snow. A party of five of them had come together. As they talked to us, and still more when they left us to return to the Dortmünder, I experienced a sense at once of relief and of quiet exultation. During the whole time we were together I had looked at her, not with that frank admiration which I felt, but with the casual glance of one who meets a stranger, or, rather, in this instance, of a man who fears to betray his feelings. And now, when she had gone, I told myself, not that she was as lovely as I had at first thought her, nor that she was less lovely, but simply that I had achieved that great and unexpected privilege of being able, when we next met, to speak to her.

Falling in love is marked for all men by just such milestones.

Mathews and I retraced our steps to the annexe after the two girls had gone. I was happy in a carefree fashion. He must have seen that. He did not enquire how the thing had been done; instead, he accepted the accomplished fact. He did not even remind me that the emergence of the stars was now no longer necessary. Some instinct of tact, the feeling that it was no longer something to joke about, made him keep silent.

'Are you going to have chocolate?'

'Yes, but I'll change first. The side of my knee gets painful if I leave the steel splint on too long.'

'What about de Régnier?'

'I'll bring him.'

He was reading the poems with me, a few at a time, each afternoon, or in the morning before we came across to breakfast, and I was a convert already to the Frenchman, whose classical austerity of diction as well as love of classical themes never for an instant allow one to forget that he is French. De Régnier suggests not so much antiquity itself as some Louis Quatorze setting in which, because antiquity is loved, one keeps coming continually on a medallion, a garden statue, an imitation temple – something to remind one of the Greek and Roman world.

The poems lent themselves to declamation. Their slow measured cadences move to their culmination with that unhurried grace which is so characteristic of a certain type of French poetry. The nearest thing in English is Gray's 'Elegy,' where there is the same feeling of steady, cumulative, inevitable force, like a river which flows on its way with certainty and floods even the surrounding fields, while seeming scarcely to move. In 'Le Miroir des Heures' and 'La Sandale Aillé' there were poems in which the poet seemed to use verse with as great ease as other men use prose. Here were phrases as graceful as the image on a carved gem; others seemed burdened with as great a weight of implication as the expression in a woman's passion-dimmed eyes; others would translate us to the Levant and in a sentence, a word, would recreate for us our own wanderings there. 'Le jour décroît. Stamboul s'éloigne!' 'Dans le bazar bruyant, mystérieux et sombre.'

> Quand je ferme les yeux, o souvenir, je vois
> Une cour de mosquée où le pigeon roucoule
> Et, sur le pavé blanc que bigarre la foule
> L'ombre d'un dôme rond et de minarets droits.

It was for the sake of just such a picture, of just such pictures, that Mathews had abandoned all thought of a university career, had embarked on discomforts that only fell short of being lousy, and had tasted extreme loneliness in strange lands. De Régnier had been my discovery, but in introducing him to Mathews I seemed to be only introducing Mathews to himself, so akin were they in spirit in certain respects. Sometimes it seemed to me that my friend had all the qualifications, all the perceptions and sensations of a poet, and that he lacked merely the one gift of speech. His eye, always alert, always perceptive, could detect in the midst of discomfort whatever was novel, picturesque and quaint. Once or twice he had read aloud a few phrases from his journal and I realised that it contained enough poetic ore, precious metal drawn from casual encounter, to last a writer for months. He lacked only the skill of the craftsman to beat the gold into shape. Two years or so before he had given up keeping the famous journal, which had maintained a continued existence from his early schooldays at Winchester for more than ten years. His period of desolation had put him out of conceit with life, and having once abandoned it he had never resumed it.

But I had only to listen to him reading the poems aloud in the mornings to know how near in mood he was to poetry. There it lay, the whole secret of our friendship, the mere fact that he was someone who loved poetry and who took it seriously. Not merely the poetry of books, but the wordless poetry of life itself. '*Le jour décroît. Stamboul s'éloigne!*' I had disliked him when we met first. I had thought him precious, until one day it had dawned on me that of all my acquaintances he was the one most likely to make sacrifices for art. He was of the elect. He lived for those occasional perceptions which lift one out of the commonplace and make life something more than an ugly dream or a prudent game of skill for astute persons.

He departed now to the Austrian room, leaving me to follow with the book.

'Well, you know where to find me.'

I was grateful to him for his silence, for his acceptance, for his ceasing to jest. It was characteristic of him. Our bickerings were a thing of the past these days. We never touched on the controversial. He was human again, ate meat, had taken once more to smoking a pipe. I had never despised his austerities, I had only distrusted the direction in which they seemed to be leading him. Instinct, if we drive it underground, has a way of continuing the struggle invisibly, of waging a guerrilla war against us and perhaps defeating us in the end. Out of asceticism a man emerges a saint or a crank, and it had seemed to me that it was towards the second rather than the first that Mathews was heading. He was certainly a great deal pleasanter fellow now that his diet was no longer exclusively chopped roots. 'But you abandon smoking yourself for long periods,' Mathews might have said to me. 'Yes, but I abandon it simply because it depresses me and because the will seems stronger without it, the machine works more smoothly. I don't abandon it as part of a régime, as a way of striking a bargain with fate. Such bargains in the case of people of my temperament only lead to reaction.'

But we no longer discussed such matters.

We read de Régnier now in the Austrian room, undisturbed by the coming and going of those around us. Then about six o'clock I returned to the annexe for a bath. A hot bath was in the nature of an event. Anna had to be warned in advance, so that wood might be brought over and the stove lit and well-stoked. One gave notice, therefore, hours before. We liked Anna. Her eyes, grey-blue rather than hazel, with little lines at the corners of them, suddenly apparent when she smiled, were beautiful; and her forehead was beautiful too, the rounded brow of a madonna. Squat, slow-moving, clumsy in her movements, Botticelli might have painted her, if he had forgotten her body and remembered only those mild eyes and that round brow. She waited on us, endured the chronic disorder of our room, fetched us water, even darned for us, and all with that dumb devotion which one gives to children who know no better. And for reward she seemed satisfied with that slightly more human, less detached approach, which, compared with the average hotel visitor, we brought to our relationship with her. To us she was a person, not a chattel, but she seemed to expect to be looked on as a chattel and was surprised when she was not. She repaid us by mothering us, if only with the amazing benevolence of that smile. With Mathews she spoke German; with me she communicated chiefly by signs and by gestures of goodwill. I had bespoken my bath earlier in the afternoon, rattling the hot-water tap and miming the action of a person soaping his body. Anna had smiled, nodded her head to show that she had understood, and departed, wishing me the inevitable goodbye. She knew only two English words and one of these was 'goodbye,' which she used as an Austrian uses '*Grüss Gott*,' just as a word of greeting, so that she was perpetually bidding us farewell unnecessarily and without due cause. We were aware all too well of the brevity of our stay, but this innocent error of speech held it always before our eyes. Like monks who live every day in sight of their coffin, Anna's 'goodbye' was a perpetual reminder, not merely of the transitory nature of our visit, but of all things in life.

I took my bath, then read for a time on my bed. It was later than usual when I went across to dinner, filled with a latent sense of quiet contentment. And when the meal was over, contrary to almost invariable custom, instead of returning to my room I gravitated towards a table where Scrooge sat with two young Australians, one of them the youth who had fallen so badly on the Wiesenberg. I liked Scrooge. He had been nicknamed Scrooge by the two schoolboys over at the annexe on the strength of the rather strange headgear which he wore when ski-ing, a black woollen fisherman's cap, with a tassel, not unlike a nightcap. His whole ski-costume belonged approximately to the year 1913 – black trousers and puttees, and a tight, military-looking, black coat, with epauletted shoulders through which Scrooge thrust his gloves when he was not wearing them. It suggested Davos and the very early days of ski-ing. Scrooge was a cautious skier at all times, but a pleasant companion and conversationalist, thoughtful, sympathetic, sensitive. His complexion was dark, and his moustache jet black. Into his dark, rather foreign-looking eyes would come sometimes an expression self-defensive, slightly alarmed, as though steep snow-slopes were not the only problems life had to offer. He had contacts in the literary and publishing world, knew men whom I knew, and we had become good friends. We drifted now into a discussion on books, the reasons for their success or failure, and the part, if any, the critics play in determining their fate. Mathews, coming into the room, was soon drawn into the conversation.

The big double-dining room had been cleared, the tables pushed back from the centre of the room to the side; in a few minutes the carpenter, whose evening duty it was to furnish us with music, would put on the first record from the pile beside the gramophone in the little pantry. Thence the sound would be carried to the dining-room through a loud-speaker in the connecting hatchway, and the guests, who had been waiting for this, would begin to dance. This was the signal always for my nightly retreat, if it had not taken place already. The carpenter was later than usual to-night. Till he came it was very pleasant to discuss books and people and poetry. About nine o'clock I was surprised to see Scheiber bring in a party of strangers and conduct them past our table towards one on the far side of the room, whose occupants had left it when the meal was finished. Properly speaking, there were no strangers in that remote valley; everyone was either a guest, newly-arrived or of long stand-ing, an employee, or, very rarely, a personal friend of Scheiber's come up from some chalet towards Selrain. Once again I had for-gotten the Dortmünder and the fact that the guests there might choose to come up and dance here in the evening. Three girls and a tall dark youth of about eighteen followed Scheiber a little shyly as he led them between the tables. For an instant I failed to realise that the girl so much in my thoughts was one of them. Without the ski-cap, without her yellow jacket, and wearing a dark woollen dress with a touch of brightness about girdle and collar, it needed a lightning adaptation on my part to take in that it was she. Associated in my mind with a particular costume, she was a stranger without it. I was caught unprepared for this totally unexpected arrival. But only for an instant. Then, astonished as I was, I had just sufficient presence of mind to rise, move back my chair to let them pass, and greet her as she passed. I resumed my seat. I resumed the conversation. I saw them settle themselves at a table across the room. I saw the waitress come, take their order, and presently return with beer and coffee. I saw them talking quietly among themselves, as though not yet sure that they had been wise to leave the Dortmünder merely to listen to a chatter of foreign voices. Though I continued to talk to my friends, half my thoughts were elsewhere. I wondered would I have recognised her but for her eyes, those eyes, candid and fearless, which had looked into mine for an instant with the same honesty as on the first occasion when we met. It was by her eyes and her mouth that I had recognised her; but for them I might have imagined her a stranger.

Their sudden entry had disturbed my composure. My mind, that seemed to be, and indeed actually was, ardently occupied with the discussion of poetry, of obscurity, so-called and real, of how much the poet may ask of his reader, and how much the reader is entitled to resent as an unreasonable request and tax on his intelligence, was still more occupied with a single thought, 'She is there, only a few yards from you.' This thought, felt rather than formulated, embarrassed me, lest by its very insistence it should become evident to my companions. Lovers and madmen imagine that all eyes are focused on them, that it is impossible to conceal what is so insurgent in their thoughts. Mathews appeared to be giving the whole of his grave attention to the debate, but I thought that I caught the flicker of a smile on his face when he looked towards me, as though he knew why I remained. It was he who kept the conversation going, urging me to grope in memory for a sonnet of my own which neither of us could disinter.

> Contend then, since contention seems in blood.
> Into arena, both, Have-all, Seek-nought——

But the lines which followed refused to surrender except in isolated phrases, and presently we abandoned the attempt.

The carpenter had arrived. The radio-gramophone at last struck up. Chairs were drawn further back, so as to leave plenty of space for the dancers. I got up, went across to her table and asked her to dance.

379

In love the most significant moments are silent ones, moments of tacit admission which do not need speech. She nodded assent, rose to her feet, and we began to dance without a word. From the moment our hands touched something of wonder and reverence, something at the same time ardent and joyous and confident, beat in my pulse and made words superfluous. I seemed to have told her my thoughts. I seemed to have said to her, 'I am a little in love with you, and of course you know it.' The mere fact that she allowed me to hold her in my arms, not rigid and unresponsive, but with that warm and instant surrender of youth which is at once shy and yielding, argued that she understood. Even if this response on her part was largely imaginary, implying an awareness of my mood which she did not really possess, nevertheless to me it was real.

As we danced together I had leisure to remember my first impressions of her, and to compare them with those that I received now. It was strange in how many respects they differed. That original resemblance, which had so strongly affected me, seemed now – as though it had served its purpose – in large measure to have vanished. Instead, I began to detect dissimilarities. In the snow a likeness of colouring and complexion had stirred recollection, and to-night that remained, as well as a general kinship of expression. But that was all. There was not really any actual physical likeness. At the outset of love we form an impression, notice a particular aspect, and are then surprised at anything at variance with it, as though what the imagination first cherishes were something immutable, never to be changed, whereas really we have seen only a part, to be modified, perhaps even to be contradicted, by later impressions.

'What is your name?'

'Jopie – Jopie de Graaf.'

She pronounced it 'Yopie,' and I who, for want of any other name, had christened her after the heroine in the book I was reading, speaking about her to Mathews as though this really were her name, could rename her now. She spoke the embarrassed English of one still sensitive about making mistakes, slurring her words slightly, talking softly, just as she laughed softly, as though ashamed of attempting the foreign tongue at all. We exchanged an occasional remark, but for the most part we were silent. It was the first evening I had danced at Kühtai. Sometimes in the late afternoon after tea I would sit there, watching other couples dance, English girls with Austrian guides, all of them still in ski-clothes. There were good dancers, very good dancers, among them. I had never felt inclined to compete with such experts. But to-night was different. I made it my business to see that all the little group had partners. Alister was brought across and made dance. The Australian youth was roped in, too, despite his assertions, very quickly confirmed by performance, that he would make the world's worst partner. But a poor performer is better than none at all, and there were three girls in the Dutch party and only one youth, a pleasant, grave, good-looking boy with thoughtful brown eyes, brother of a blonde, rather beautiful girl named Sonia. I danced with Sonia, I danced with the 'duenna', friendly, homely, well-disposed, looking at me in quite kindly fashion through her rather heavily-lensed glasses, and completely belying the absurd rôle for which I had once cast her. And as well as with the members of the Dortmünder party, I felt obliged, lest my sudden complete break with habit should appear too conspicuous, to dance also with the one or two English girls in the *gasthof*, whom I had come to know, with the exuberant Peggy, and with a pleasant dark-haired girl called Mary.

'I thought you never danced!'

'Well, I do now. We're like that.'

My answer was blunt, almost defiant. She had only to notice the ratio of my dances with one person to those with anyone else to be aware of the reason for my dancing. Perhaps it was because she had already noticed it that she made her sly comment, to tease me.

Of every three dances, two were likely to be with Jopie. One air in particular seemed to make the dance mine by right. Again and again there would be a slight pause while the gramophone in the pantry was being rewound, and we would wait to see what was going to be played. It is curious how much love brings into our cognisance besides itself. Though the *gasthof* had a fair repertoire of records, there were one or two especial favourites which were always being chosen. For days now I had been listening to one tune at frequent intervals, and yet it is doubtful if it had even penetrated consciousness. It was already enormously popular, it had invaded two continents, the whole world was humming it, but I remained blissfully unaware even of its existence. I might have done so to the end of time, if I had not danced to it now. Because it was so popular, it was the first record which the carpenter put on that night. I danced to it with Jopie, and instantly it was endowed for me with an acute emotional significance. Its haunting, slightly sentimental, slightly cynical refrain was original in its way. Music can be utterly trite and yet delight us, establishing a hold over us which is largely associative. Some time was to elapse before I knew even the name of the tune, much less its words, but long before this had happened it had become indelibly impressed upon my brain, it had been given magic properties of evocation which a great composer might have envied for his work, and I was more conscious of every note, every bar, of this lilting, half-wistful, half-cynical refrain than the errand boys who had been whistling it for so long. For months afterwards I had only to hear it to be back in Kühtai.

Whenever this still nameless air was played – it was played a number of times in the course of the evening – I went across to Jopie and claimed the dance. There was another tune to which we danced also, which pleased me nearly as much. In this case the record had words, words in German, of which I could only distinguish a single one which sounded, appropriately enough, like *wundervoll*. Perhaps it was not that at all; perhaps it was something quite different. But what did it matter? For me it meant that. Wonderful. Yes, that was it. Wonderful. Wonderful to have fallen in love.

Dancing ceased when the carpenter seemed to think we had had enough music, and no one else could be troubled to provide it. The room was half empty. Many of those who had been watching at the beginning had now gone. I had danced with Jopie half the evening. Now our party joined a group of English visitors who had gathered round one of the best skiers in the place, Jacques, the schoolmaster whom I knew slightly. They were trying to persuade him to sing. Trim, well-groomed, altogether silent on most occasions, he seemed the least likely of troubadours. But, producing a mandolin, he sat down on one of the tables and began to twang it, and presently sang little impertinent songs with gay frivolity. He had a considerable repertoire, but when it had been exhausted, or when, tiring, he refused to play any more, we left the group and moved with our Dortmünder friends to the Austrian room.

'Who would have suspected Jacques of being a musician!'

'Yes, appearances are deceptive. Tell them about your experience, Monk.'

I told them about my Himalayan blunder, and they laughed at my discomfiture.

'It is the last time I'll ever ask anyone if they are tired after a long walk.'

I was tired myself now. Much seemed to have happened since awaking that morning and with the excuse that I must write a letter to catch the post, which left before half-past seven in the morning, I went out, to make my way up the trodden snowpath to the annexe. Above, in the still depths of the dark night, countless stars were glimmering. Now, as always, the valley seemed remote, nearer in spirit to those far stars than to the world itself. The edged ridges and peaks of the mountains towered up against the silent sky, and by their very indifference to all human concerns seemed to exercise a calming influence on the mind. A beast stirred, stamping on the cobbles beneath the dark covering of the stable roof that jutted black against the snow, then all was quiet again. Nothing disturbed the silence. The immensity of night, that whirling arc in which planets signified no more than the gleam of a glow worm, was mine to contemplate; and all things, even laughter, even love, seemed trivial by comparison.

Back in my room in the chalet, I could not sleep. All my thoughts, all that flood of emotion which for a moment the night sky had tranquillised, returned with redoubled vehemence. I longed to sleep, but could not. I lay awake, unable to check the constant flow of thoughts and images passing through my mind. What had happened to me? I had fallen in love. Well, was that such a crime? I had forgotten what it was to feel that a new face is of such paramount importance to us that we can only envisage the future in terms which include it. I had forgotten what it was to want to show kindness to and to make sacrifices for a stranger, which we might hesitate to make for a friend whom we had known for years. Philosophers, if they are surprised at such a sudden access of benevolence, only show that they have never been in love. I was conscious not so much of desire as of unrest, a vast unrest, soluble only in companionship. My thoughts were the typical thoughts of every lover who asks himself how the days that are coming can be made to concede the simple bounty of – for ever afterwards – granting frequent glimpses of the beloved, and who wonders how long he will be content with the mere largesse of chance, when everything argues that a lifetime is too short to satisfy that insistent hunger of the heart.

Mathews returned about midnight to tell me that he and the Australian had entertained the Dutch party to *Glühwein*, hot wine spiced with cinnamon and herbs, the most mellow and comforting of drinks, in the little Austrian room after I had gone.

'Why did you go, Monk? It was lovely. The waitress brought us a huge jug, from which the steam curled up, filling the air with a faint scent which we sniffed as one sniffs the scent of incense.'

He undressed and got into bed. Soon I was listening in the darkness to his slow, measured breathing in sleep. I resisted the temptation to get a book and read, lest the light should waken him. I was filled with that upsurge of creative energy which at another time would have found expression in art. Yet at the same time I was intensely weary. I had skied the greater part of the day, and I had danced now for two hours. Fatigue, if it passes a certain point, only makes us wakeful. The brain no longer desires to think, would like to cease thinking, its thoughts weary it to the verge of madness. But like a relentless driver who forces on a tired beast of burden Nature takes a terrible revenge for our excess. We refused the bounty which she offered earlier and, as punishment for our foolishness, she withholds it from us now. Like those who have nerved themselves to a task for so long that they feel unable to abandon it, the mind is left to go on mounting, mounting always the treadmill of its own thoughts.

I knew that treadmill well. Illness during the war had taught me all the successive phases of sleeplessness. First a wakeful excitement, an intense mental activity, in which we soon long vainly to discover some irrelevancy, some absurdity in our thought sequences, which will indicate that we are drifting into that easy half-world on the borderland of sleep. Then, following this mental activity, and when it has become completely distasteful to us, a single desire, the desire to forget, to let go, to abandon the torment of thought. Finally, absolute weariness, a terrible emptiness, a desert of exhaustion from which there seems no escape.

At last towards four in the morning I dropped off to sleep and slept for three or four hours.

'Tell Anna to bring me some breakfast over on a tray. I slept badly.'

'All right. Another message for Anna! "Aaanna, there's an air-lock in our radiator. Aaanna, the gentleman would like to break his fast!"'

He was used to giving them, for my ignorance of Anna's language made me dependent either on him, or on my ability to dramatise a situation in dumb-show. I could hear him now giving directions to her on the landing.

It was the first really sunny morning that we had had for several days. The weather had relented. With a great clattering of ski-boots, waxing of skis and careful packing of his rucksack, Mathews departed for the run, about which we had heard so much, on the north slopes at the back of the *gasthof*. Hitherto it had been regarded as unsafe, on account of fog, or from the threat of avalanches on the approaches to it.

'No, I shall not come with you. I may do a run this afternoon. Good luck. I hope you enjoy it.'

He returned in three hours' time triumphant, exultant, exclaiming, 'I shall remember that run in Heaven!'

I had thrown open the doors of the little veranda; from across the valley above the high wall of mountain the sun flooded the room where I lay in bed. I had intended to sleep, but, soon changing my mind, I had reached for the humble used envelope on which so many first inspirations are scribbled and had begun to shape a poem. The first draft was nearly complete when Mathews came in, but work on it was beginning to be a burden. The poem, as I would have it, was still recalcitrant. Wearier than ever for, though composition itself is a joy, the intense concentration which it entails is tiring, I got up, dressed and went across to eat my lunch in a kind of dream in which the people around me seemed separated from me as though by a curtain. The mind flagged. It asked only to rest. Would I ever learn moderation in anything, in ski-ing, in making verses, in love? I had been for runs on icy crust where one fell repeatedly – fell so often that the tired muscles cried out against what seemed a deliberate tyranny, fell till one felt less and less able to make the effort to rise to one's feet, fell till one had almost reached the point of weeping. Only as we grow older does experience convince us that all ardour must be paid for by the inevitable reaction, that if we drive mind or body too far we must be content to bear the cost.

That afternoon I was glad enough to get a short siesta and then to avail myself of the routine of the ski-class, to practise one turn over and over again on the same slope. It was something mechanical, something that did not need thought.

But next morning, after a night's sound sleep, melancholy had vanished. I felt refreshed. I wanted only to be alone. Even the tortured lines of my poem began to sort themselves out like the dead bones in the valley of the prophet, and I no longer viewed them with disgust. I got my skis and went down the Oetzthal valley. There I was little likely to encounter anyone. It was not so much a run as a walk on skis, for one must keep to the path most of the way, the trees on either side of the path and the gorge itself with its stream precluding any open running. It was these same trees which made it a fascinating change from where the *gasthof* stood, almost above the tree-line. Above that level there grew only a certain kind of small Siberian pine, and the little nameless shrub which, until the snow had well covered it, we skiers found so highly inconvenient. But the moment the path dipped towards the Oetzthal real trees began to show once more. The slopes on either side of the gorge were covered with them, large trees and small, little Christmas trees, completely rugged up in snow so that they looked like chessmen, great pines, heavily-laden firs, with a blanket of snow upon their layered branches. I felt myself back now in the scenery which I loved so well in Switzerland. Huge, broken tree-trunks brought down by some storm sprawled like giants on the ground, great masses of ice hanging about their twisted roots. There had been hard frosts for several nights. The stream down the centre of the gorge was partly frozen. Only a succession of the very hardest frosts can completely immobilise a mountain torrent, and, here and there, one could see the water creeping slowly forward under its coating of ice presently to break out in a small cascade, or to trickle slowly over some great mound of solid ice. The snow through which my skis pushed at the edge of the path was frozen into crystals, but not yet those huge crystals which are the size of halfpennies. If the frost held, that would be the next stage. The huge chaos of tumbled rock and tree-growth on either side added to the delight of my solitary walk; and the still-ness of the air, the resined smell of the fir trees, an occasional gush of water, and once the sudden faint chirp of a bird from a solitary tree in the centre of an open glade, were an indefinable reminder, impossible in Kühtai itself, that, though it was still months distant, there was such a season as spring.

At last I turned and, putting sealskins on my skis, began to mount back along the path. There was no hurry. One could pause from time to time, lean forward, holding the ski-sticks beneath one's armpits, and contemplate the view. When at last I reached the top of the gorge, and the dotted trees on the gentle slopes either side of the path began to grow fewer, it was nearly midday. I took the track which led up past the Dortmünder for it was the shorter of the two. On the path between it and the *gasthof* I met the Dutch girl with the spectacles, returning from a walk. I greeted her.

'Good morning. So you are not ski-ing. Where is your friend?'

'She is having her lesson' – and she nodded towards the slopes beyond the *gasthof*.

Two nights before, during the dance, we had said something about paying a visit one day to the Dortmünder. I told her now that we might come down that evening.

'After tea, about five-thirty.'

'We shall see you then.'

It was an encounter well timed. But I had only gone a few steps along the path after leaving her when I caught sight of the yellow jacket returning from the practice slopes. It was Jopie herself. I slackened my pace, dawdling deliberately, so that we should meet on the path a little way from the hotel.

'Well, Jopie?'

It was two days since I had seen her. At the dance I had seemed to lose a little of the original Jopie. But now I saw her again, fully as lovely as I had seen her first, vivid against the same background, a Primavera of the snows. She leaned forward on her ski-sticks, and looked at me with her candid, clear blue eyes, half laughing, as though she realised how much pleasure this meeting had given me.

'I have just seen your friend. I told her that we might come down to the Dortmünder after tea. Will you be there?'

'Yes. I shall be there.'

Nothing could have been more casual than the few words we had exchanged, or the manner in which we exchanged them. Mathews was scraping the snow from his skis in front of the *gasthof* when I joined him there. He must have seen us where we stood talking, for when I remarked that I had been down the valley he looked at me sardonically for a moment and then said with a smile:

'Yes, and in Paradise on the way back.'

His remark was wholly benevolent and without malice. Moreover, he was willing to come with me to the Dortmünder that evening. It is doubtful if he realised how intensely I looked forward to that visit. Even when we are in love we manage in some measure – like those physicians who attending royalty are expected at all costs to minimise the gravity of the situation – to disguise the extent of our overthrow. I was happy. He could see that. I was gravely and at the same time gloriously happy. Perhaps he could see that too. But he cannot have guessed, or it is at least most unlikely that he can have guessed, that fervour of enthusiasm which had taken possession of me, and which is like a reminder to us that we are, all of us, still living in a world of magic and have only to touch – quite by accident – the right spot, or to stretch up and let a finger contact the right leaf or the right folded bud on the magic tree, for the whole landscape to break instantly into a blaze of enchanted light.

When we love in this fashion we believe that it is possible for personality to transpire so completely in a face that we have no need to go in search of the individual for they have revealed themselves to us already in a flash through the intuition of our own heart. If we believe this, the magnitude of the implication – that swift recognition of soul by soul – is so vast that it might make even the most ardent physiognomist falter; yet we have no difficulty in accepting it, and it would seem to us absurd if anyone suggested that our knowledge of the beloved was not already fuller and much more complete than our knowledge is of many people with whom we have been acquainted for years.

It was nearly lunchtime. The wide path below the dining-room annexe was crowded with visitors removing their skis, adjusting a strap round them before carrying them into the basement, and stamping their nailed ski-boots to get their feet warm. Cheerful voices shouted to one another across intervening heads. The Anglo-Saxon race was in the ascendant; it had almost taken possession of the *gasthof*. There had been an amazing incident on the night of New Year's Eve, which had led to the sudden withdrawal of a number of foreigners. It was still referred to only in hushed tones and with bated breath. I myself knew of it solely by hearsay through Mathews, and he himself was not clear on all the details. After I had gone across to my room on New Year's Eve, he and the majority of the guests had remained on to see the New Year in. At midnight some students had risen suddenly in their seats and sung the Nazi song, to the huge indignation of a number of the other guests. The move apparently had been predetermined. It was only a few months since the murder of Dolfuss, and every Austrian present, who supported the Government, felt that he had been deliberately insulted. A fracas immediately started. A Frenchwoman, somewhat given to the melodramatic gesture – as Mathews and I had discovered one day, when we asked if we might borrow the mustard pot from her table, only to be refused it with a tremendous shrugging of shoulders – had shouted a protest, or perhaps an insult; and a blonde, bullet-headed man, who with his wife and sister-in-law and little boy shared the neighbouring table, had leaned over and struck her in the face. I had noticed this quartet when we first came, Teutonic-looking, stolid, and rather silent at meals. They had looked the last people to become protagonists in a dramatic incident, but the man was perhaps a political fanatic or else had drunk too much. The English guests had watched all this amazed. Most of them had no idea what the song was about.

Scheiber, the Manager, had moved about from table to table, trying to calm feeling down, begging people to forget politics and asking the singers to desist. An unsuccessful attempt was made to placate the Frenchwoman, who had become hysterical. Finally, it was whispered, the students had gone out and lit a swastika in the snow, boasting that the forbidden symbol, if seen nowhere else in Austria that night, would at least be seen in the highest inhabited spot of the Tyrol. Mathews could tell me no more. What he did tell me was all rather vague and had mostly come to him at secondhand, and the less the thing was talked about the better. He felt sorry for Scheiber. Next morning the Frenchwoman had appeared at breakfast with a large piece of sticking-plaster proudly flaunted over one eye, had ordered a sleigh and had announced her intention of going down to Innsbruck to complain about the incident. Immediately there were a number of hurried departures before the Frenchwoman should have carried her version of the affair to the authorities. Students left hastily and the trio with the little boy departed also the same day.

The Austrian room had suddenly emptied. But with the departure of the foreigners some of the English had taken to using it between meals, to write letters there, or for a game of chess, or as a quiet spot to which to retire with a book. Those who used it were of the less noisy sort, so that it retained its intimate character.

I used it a good deal myself, though I still took my meals in the big room. I had made my peace almost at once with Eltham, the mountaineer, acknowledging and laughing over my initial and highly inappropriate blunder. We had become good friends. Presently, at his own suggestion, he had joined me at my table. The shyest of men, never referring to his own exploits, always a little on the defensive against the world – or, rather, keeping as much of it at a distance as had power to irritate or enrage him – it was interesting to see how the barrier of shyness was not insurmountable. He would appear at breakfast with a small pot of raspberry jam of his own, and would push it across the table at me with a brusque, 'Here, have some of this.' It was almost as though it were an insult to offer it, and he was always considerably relieved if I accepted it without too much comment or protest. Though he had speedily got to know most of my tastes and interests, his own only transpired gradually and by accident. I learnt that he was a schoolmaster, that he was a naturalist, that he lived in the North of England. I learnt about his pets; and with each accession of knowledge I had the flattering sense of having triumphed over this reserve. If we genuinely like our fellow mortals, we are continually discovering in them not what is aggressive and contrary, but what is likeable and gentle; as though goodwill were the solvent which, by some process of spiritual chemistry, transmutes even dislike and suspicion, when it is given time. Like a centre of electrical force, the polarity of our being is perpetually attracting or repelling, and it amused me to think that though I had made such a bad start, the mere laughing admission that I had done so had been enough to establish a totally different current of feeling, so that, instead of eyeing one another with sour distrust, we were good friends.

It was pleasant to have his company at meals. But apart from meals, I had taken more and more, like Mathews, to using the Austrian room. It was there that I found him later in the afternoon, reading in a corner, and feigning reluctance to put down his book and accompany me to the Dortmünder.

'But you said that you would come.'

'I said that I would come, and I will, but don't fuss. Let me finish this chapter first.'

He pretended not to notice my impatience, and, feeling that it was useless to protest, I began to turn over the pages of a travel magazine that was lying on the table. I watched the clock anxiously for another quarter of an hour.

'Alister, haven't you finished your chocolate?'

'Yes, long ago. But why all this hurry?'

'I said that we would be down at half-past five, and it is nearly that now.'

'Very well, then. I suppose we must make a start.'

He put down his book, got up and we left the room.

He had brought a torch lamp with him, and by its light he led the way along the narrow path, stamping cautiously to feel if it was firm underfoot, for though the path was marked by occasional stakes, it was the easiest thing in the darkness to step off it and find oneself knee-deep in soft snow. We crossed the spot where the tiny stream was still running in the depths of its narrow crevasse. A few hundred yards more brought us to the Dortmünder, looming up a dark mass beside the first outposts of fir trees at the head of the gorge. The so-called Hütte was a large solid building of two stories and a basement, the lower story of stone, the upper of wood with ornamental wooden shutters and a fine tiled roof. We made our way round to the side entrance and knocked on a door in the basement over which an electric light was shining. An old man with a wide brown beard flecked with grey and wearing clothes of some heavy, green, felt-like material came to open it. He was the caretaker, but he might have been one of the huntsmen or foresters in the day when Maximilian had first built his hunting-lodge. Time stands still in these mountain retreats, and if Rip Van Winkle were to return after a hundred years' absence he would find the life much the same as it had been when he left it. The old man led us up a flight of stone stairs to the living-room above. What I noticed immediately, and what was so pleasant about the hut, was that, despite its up-to-dateness, it did not suggest any direct break with the past. There had merely been a new use of traditional methods and materials. The whole building was designed on modern but very simple and beautiful lines; the walls were panelled in a number of different and curiously grained woods. As we came through the doorway, Mathews uttered an exclamation of delight. But though I approved the room quite as fully as he did, my own first feeling was one of disappointment. There were not half a dozen people in the room, a few students talking in undertones at a table, two Italians playing chess, and a bearded youth unpacking his rucksack at a bench. Our friends were nowhere to be seen. We seemed at a loss, and, presently, the old man standing beside us realised that these were not the friends whom we had come to see, nor had our objective in coming been simply to drink a glass of beer in new surroundings. His heavy, nailed boots sounded on the wooden floor as he moved slowly across to a double door of beautifully-grained light-coloured wood, set in a wide semicircular arch of darker brown. He pushed it open and we saw that there was a second room beyond the first.

The Dutch girls were there and the tall dark boy with them, but to my disappointment there was no sign of Jopie. I had to come right into the room before I saw her. She was seated behind the door in the angle of the wall on the far side of a huge three-tiered stove of white tiles. She had put her feet up along the bench and was leaning back against the stove with a book upon her knees, while one of her friends, reading also, sat right behind the door with her feet up along the actual step of the stove.

They had waited for us. That is to say, no one had ordered anything until we should have arrived. Now they asked for chocolate. It was brought by the son of the caretaker, who, in the course of the evening, appeared periodically with an armful of great white split logs to stoke the stove. Mathews ordered wine, the Dutch youth and myself lager beer. We seated ourselves round the table, one of several tables of white wood, solid almost as slabs of marble, lovely to look at – tables truly superb.

I sat where I could see Jopie in her corner by the stove. Shyness suddenly descended upon the whole party, threatening it with catastrophe, and, contrary to precedent, I felt myself to be its first and worst victim. Nevertheless, I forced myself to talk, and Mathews, in his gentle, quiet way, made whatever conversational openings occurred to him.

The blonde girl, whose name was Sonia, and who was wearing a white ski-coat, told us that she and her brother Tom and a friend had arrived at Gries the same night that we did. She spoke English well, and had no difficulty in carrying on a conversation. The others were more diffident, but they had no need to feel anxious, for their mastery of the language was really extremely good. The momentary shyness which had seized on the party at the outset presently vanished, and we were soon chatting with animation.

We compared notes on the ardours of the walk up from Gries.

'We did not come up that night. We were too tired and there were no sleighs. We stayed the night at the inn and walked up next morning. We saw you and your wonderful coats. They were of great interest to us.'

'Our sheepskin coats?'

We told them how they had been bought seven years before in Jerusalem.

'I have been waiting all this time for a chance to wear mine. Alister is jealous now because it still looks so white, while his is soiled with travelling in all the third-class railway carriages in Europe.'

'I shall get it cleaned. I wear mine often. It is so wonderfully warm for travelling.'

'Yes, we were quite envious of them. We envied you the sleigh too.'

They were amused to hear how soon my seat in the sleigh had been vacated.

Periodically they would apologise for their pronunciation, and Mathews would assure them that they were perfectly right, or gravely give them the correct pronunciation, which they would try over several times until they had got it right. The girl by the door had been reading an English book when we arrived and spoke the best English of all. She was the only one of the party whom we had not met already. She had been here longer than the others, having come to the mountains for her health.

Of all the party, Jopie was the most silent. From her retreat in the corner by the stove, where she sat aloof and very upright, she listened to us, but made no effort to take much part in the general chatter. She must know that it was she who had occasioned our visit here to-night. Perhaps her friends had teased her about it, which would account for her shyness now.

Every time that I spoke to her or that she had to speak herself, the faint colour mounted slowly to her cheeks. The steady gaze of her eyes tried hard to repudiate this blush, the shy, defensive blush of someone ashamed and indignant with themselves for blushing at all.

As I looked at her across the diagonal breadth of the table between us, I had a feeling of guilt, as though I were a thief filching what I might have enjoyed without reserve had it been less precious to me.

> 'There was a battle in her face
> Between a lily and a rose,
> My love would have the lily win,
> And I the lily lose.'

But what may have been true for Davies was untrue for me now. I had no wish that the lily should lose. Rather, like her, I wished it to win. As long as she coloured every time I spoke to her, it seemed to me that I had no right to steal even a glance in her direction. Whenever I met those transparently blue eyes I imagined I saw in them a note of appeal as though they were saying, 'Be fair. Don't hurt me. Others may be sophisticated, but I am not.' They did not flinch; I admired what might almost be called the deliberate courage with which they met mine; but always that slight flush mounting to her cheeks betrayed the fact that she was doing something which she found it difficult to do.

Throughout the whole evening her attitude was one of self-depreciation, as though she distrusted herself among her more animated friends, with their more fluent command of English. And yet, if she felt at a disadvantage, her embarrassment was, in all likelihood, only increased by the realisation that I seemed to prefer the occasional word from her to all the chatter of her companions. Only when she laughed did constraint appear for a moment forgotten.

I picked up a book from the table. It was by the Dutchman, Fabricius.

'One of his books has been just been translated into English.'

'Which one?'

'*The Lions Starve in Naples.*'

'It is not one of his best,' they told me.

'One of the directors of the firm who published the translation is at the *gasthof* now. It was to him – the little man with the black moustache – that I was talking, the evening you all came up.'

Sonia told us that she had met a youth at the *gasthof* who wrote.

'Oh, what's his line?'

'Poetry, I think, and short stories. I'm not really sure.'

'What does he look like?'

She described him for us and we recognised him; a rather striking-looking youth, of about twenty-two, with high cheekbones and a faun-like expression, unpopular with Eltham because of his somewhat long hair and very assured manner.

'Do you know his name?'

'John Raines. He was at Cambridge. Then he was in Greece excavating there. Afterwards he came to Vienna, where he has had a severe illness. That is why he is on holiday now.'

'Kühtai is full of authors. There's a man called Paynton who writes novels, and Monk here has just published another book. He is waiting for reviews of it now.'

'Have you it with you?'

'Yes. I have one copy – an advance copy given me in London just before I left.'

'Anneke here reads more than any of us.'

We were only beginning to get their names straight. It was a little confusing until it was explained to us that there were two Annekes, this tall, animated girl who had been reading an English book when we arrived and Jopie's small friend with the spectacles. They came to be known to Mathews and myself as 'tall Anneke' and 'little Anneke.' Tall Anneke had moved from the step along the stove and was sitting hunched up on the far side of the table, hugging her knees. Lively, intelligent and amusing, she had no diffidence and never let the conversation flag.

'Every second book you see in a Dutch bookshop now is a translation.'

'Haven't you any authors of your own?'

'We have – a few.'

394

'But we don't seem to read them.'

'The Danes in Copenhagen make exactly the same complaint. There you see nothing but American stuff on the bookstalls.'

'Do the Dutch as a nation read much?'

'Don't you know what Voltaire said when he left Holland?' tall Anneke asked. ' "*Adieu canaux, canards, canailles.*" '

Everyone laughed, and Mathews said it was a libel on a great nation.

Sonia complained of being cold and Jopie moved from her place behind the stove to allow her to get warm. One of the girls mentioned that there was a magnificent wireless set at the Dortmünder.

'It's not really supposed to be used.'

'Why not?'

'For fear we should listen to Nazi propaganda.'

'It is used, even so.'

'The old man turns a deaf ear to any programme that is not political.'

'Sometimes very late at night we can even get New York.'

'That's pretty good.'

'Would you like to hear it now?'

'Yes. Can you get Ireland? Get Athlone. I would like to hear someone speaking from my own country.'

Sonia's brother Tom led the way into the larger room and a vain five minutes were spent turning knobs and trying to evoke an Irish voice for me. But the tale-bearing air refused to give up its secret, or the mountains, as sometimes happened, had hardened their hearts.

'What a pity. We get London quite often.'

Tom offered to show us the rest of the Hütte. He had shaken off his reserve and was taking more part in the conversation. He spoke slowly but well, and seemed to have all the worth and solidity of his race. It was not his first visit to Kühtai. He had been here before; indeed, the Dutch appeared to have discovered it before the English. Mathews and I followed him upstairs. The first dormitory contained beds, but the adjoining ones had tiers of bunks as on a ship. Like everything else in the Hütte, the work had been done extraordinarily well. Wood, beautifully polished, of different sorts and with different stains, had been used wherever possible. It was a complete illustration of the right use of local materials. A British or American modern room seemed gimcrack by comparison, anchored to no scheme or plan as this was anchored to local products, local traditions. Here was fine workmanship, comfort, extreme simplicity and solid serviceableness, every detail indicative of the good taste of whoever had planned the building and of the skill of the craftsmen who had carried it out.

We returned to the lower room. The two young Italians were still crouched over their game of chess. Fat, and somewhat indifferently shaved, neither was particularly attractive in appearance. Sonia had given a kind of shudder at the sight of them on our first entrance, as though to show her contempt. The wireless had been left on, and a violinist from Innsbruck or Vienna was playing some familiar, melancholy air. I knew it well, though I could not put a name to it. No other two instruments can affect us in quite the same way that the piano and the violin do. A piano can touch most of the emotions, can pause on a single note, as Chopin so often pauses, the melody suddenly and poignantly arrested, as though to give us time to sigh; but only the violin says plainly what life long ago made us suspect, that beauty and anguish, ecstasy and sorrow are children of the same parentage, and that if we accept one of them we must be willing to accept them all.

Mathews and Tom had re-entered the room beyond, but I lingered, held by this nostalgic melody until its last note had died away, lovely and wistful as only violin music can be.

When I rejoined them in the other room, Sonia was saying with venom:

'I hate Italians.'

She glanced towards the room beyond, as though she almost hoped her words would be overheard there, and instantly, despite my distaste for the two rather unattractive-looking young men next door, I felt a little sorry for them. Sonia's blonde, rather bold, type of beauty was just the kind to overwhelm an Italian. Perhaps they had even annoyed her by their attentions.

'I know why you hate them; because they stare at a girl if they think she is beautiful. Well, I do the same myself!'

I might. But assuredly I had not done much staring to-night. It was only a sort of defiant protest on behalf of the right to admire that had prompted my remark.

'No, it is not that. But I hate them,' and Sonia made a face.

Her expression, as she spoke, emphasised the whole wide gulf that exists between Nordic and Latin. It is an old complaint, this, against the Latin races. I had heard English girls, possibly secretly intrigued but more likely genuinely annoyed, complain that on the transcontinental trains an Italian will always plant himself in the corridor and linger there, if he thinks that he has seen a beautiful face, glancing from time to time at the newfound inamorata. Aphrodite, whom the Greeks spoke of as terrible, is still viewed with awe round the sea-board of the Mediterranean, or, according to Norman Douglas, it is at least the correct thing to pretend that she is taken seriously.

Douglas would have it that it really amounts to very little, that the Italian is ruthlessly realistic when it comes to actual match-making, and 'fundamentally sane in matters of the heart.' He makes unmerciful fun of what he calls the Italian game of gazing, which he maintains is a mere convention. He jeers at the passionate expression of love, and has even collected a number of letters to illustrate the lengths to which it can go, including one from a thirteen-year-old schoolgirl which begins: 'Idol of My Heart. Do not the stars call you when you look to Heaven? Does not the moon tell you, the blackcap on the willow when it says farewell to the sun? The birds of nature, the dreary country sadly covered by a few flowers that remain there? Once your look was passionate and pierced me like a sunny ray, now it seems the flame of a day. Does nothing tell you of imperishable love?

'I love you and love you as [illegible] loves its liberty, as the corn in the field loves the sun, as the sailor loves the sea, tranquil or stormy. To you I would give my felicity, my future; for one of your words I would spill my blood, drop by drop. . . . It is late at night and I am still awake, and at this hour my soul is sadder than ever in its great isolation [insolamende]. I look on my past love and your dear image. Too much I love you and [illegible] without your affection. . . .'

'Three further pages of this,' adds the cynical Douglas, who is convinced that only the very young and the hopelessly infatuated are capable of loving in this fashion, and that the Southerner even when he 'commits suicide', is generally shamming. If he gazes he does so because he thinks it looks manly. It is only 'part of a huge game.'

I wonder. A fellow countryman of Douglas three and a half centuries before wrote of love:

> 'It is engendered in the eyes,
> With gazing fed . . .'

And this letter from an unknown schoolgirl, with its bathos and its illegibilities, seems to me to contain quite as much of the material of poetry as many of the Celtic love songs and a good deal more sincerity than the much-vaunted letters of the Portuguese nun, a few pages of which were sufficient to convince me that they were spurious. It is nearer somehow to the heart of life than the vulgarity of American wisecrack flirtation, or the ponderous Wagnerian pomposity of love *à la* Tannhäuser, or the breezy unsentimentality of a certain type of Anglo-Saxon affection. When I was in Cyprus a youth knifed his sixteen-year-old sweetheart because he had found in her basket a little ballad sheet bought from a pedlar, which he suspected had been given her by another admirer. All day he followed her about among the orchards and olive groves near Famagusta waiting for an opportunity to plunge his knife between the shoulder-blades. Our host in Nicosia was Chief Justice of the island, and the discussion at dinner that night had been, not whether he should hang, but how soon he should hang. A dastardly crime, and yet I was foolish enough to be sorry for the embittered heart that had found hell for itself in a little ballad sheet hawked for sale by a travelling pedlar.

It was past seven o'clock, time for us to be returning to the *gasthof*. Mathews rose, saying that we must go. He had enjoyed the evening. I could see that he had enjoyed it. It was just the sort of gathering and the sort of conversation that he loved, untrammelled, full of zeal and enthusiasm, not political, not doctrinaire, but a symposium on life itself in all its aspects. When we had come, little more than an hour before, we had been strangers; now it seemed that we knew every one of these young people better than we knew any of our English friends at the *gasthof*. Only with the intensely reserved Eltham had I, for some surprising reason, established a corresponding degree of confidence in which we exchanged freely our true opinions and did not seem obliged to limit conversation to the superficial.

We walked back through the snow. Suddenly Mathews said to me:

'You must tell her.'

'Tell her what?'

'You must tell her that you are married.'

I KNEW that he was right.

Indeed it was I myself who had said to him the morning after the dance, 'Jopie must be told.'

But for some unknown reason he had pooh-poohed the idea completely then.

'You are a fool. She cares nothing for you. You mean absolutely nothing to her. You will spoil your chances of friendship with her altogether if you tell her now. Wait and tell her later. I tell you they think of us as the merest acquaintances.'

He had spoken sincerely. It would be an indication of vanity he implied, to show that I thought the information could be of the slightest interest to her one way or the other. Mephistopheles himself could not have put the case more forcibly. I had taken his advice and it was all the more astonishing to find him reversing it so completely now.

But back in our room in the annexe and getting ready for dinner, he reverted once more to the subject:

'You must tell her at once, Monk. Or else see the girl no more. Yes, you must tell her.'

Then he added, as if wishing to give me the key to his *volte-face*:

'She blushed every time you spoke to her to-night.'

It would have been easy to have told her when I first wanted to do so. It was not going to be by any means so easy now. Mathews' conscience had chosen an inconvenient moment to break into volcanic eruption.

'Don't you see, Alister, that by advising me to wait you have made a fatal mistake? It is becoming harder and harder to tell her now. By putting it off even a day I have made it doubly difficult. To tell her now is a confession. To have told her a few days ago would have been a casual revelation in the course of ordinary conversation. How am I to tell her? I can't say "Obviously, I admire you very much. I haven't made the faintest effort to conceal the fact. And now, lest such patent admiration should lead to the very faintest reciprocation of regard on your part, let me hasten to tell you that I am married." I shall seem not only a cad, but a prig.'

He remained adamant.

'You must tell her. Or not see her any more. You made a very good beginning to-night. You told them about your life in Ireland. You told them that you were a writer. That's a start. Now you can tell her more about yourself next time. But it must be done.'

His earnestness was so great that he did not smile, and I was ashamed to let him see that, with the misplaced sense of humour of those who are desperate, I was smiling myself.

'You forget that I asked you two days ago to tell her yourself. You could have mentioned casually that I was married and that I was a poet. That might have excused me in her eyes.

He had shown no desire to be my emissary then. Now it would be fatal for anyone to tell her but myself.

That I could joke ruefully in this fashion did not mean that I did not feel ashamed of myself. Never for an instant did I seriously think of rejecting Mathews' ultimatum. Indeed he was only saying what I myself had been the first to say. But undoubtedly each day, even those few hours this evening, had made the thing more difficult. I had let not only Jopie, but her friends, see how much I admired her. From the start I had been swept forward on a tide of emotion which I had made little or no effort to control. Everything since that first meeting in the snow had seemed marked with the inevitability of destiny, and I even told myself, and believed – with a shameless disregard for the facts – that I had not gone out to meet that destiny; but had, as it were, had it forced upon me. Nothing had been further from my thoughts when I came to Kühtai than even the mildest flirtation. And this very fact, paradoxically – by making what had happened to me all the more surprising and unpremeditated – had given a quite different colouring to the episode, and had almost justified it to me. I had used it to excuse myself in my own eyes and to bring in a verdict of not guilty on a far more serious charge than that of flirting. For to admire a person deeply may ultimately cause them graver hurt than to trifle light-heartedly with them. I was vaguely aware of this, but I preferred to forget it, lest consciousness should cloud the present by raising problems which belonged to the future. The very essence of lyric awareness is that 'now' receives a paramount emphasis.

Some such line of reason or unreason had kept me from analysing the situation too ruthlessly. But now conscience, reawakened by Mathews, told me that I had behaved badly in accepting only too willingly what had seemed like the decree of fate. By speaking, he had merely confirmed something which I felt myself. To remain silent was inexcusable. Even to speak now was a tardy concession to elementary honesty. The only choice was to tell Jopie, or not to see her again until just before I was leaving Kühtai. Next morning I awoke almost decided in my mind to accept the second alternative. Like the occupant of a boat which has been sailing quietly, or even drifting down-wind, and who suddenly notices that he is a good deal nearer a reef of rocks than he imagined, and that the only thing to do is to seize the tiller instantly and go about, so now it seemed to me perhaps the moment to draw back.

After all, I had been happy enough before this unexpected development. There was plenty to do in Kühtai besides falling in love. Down at the *gasthof* after breakfast there was the usual bustle and excitement. The ski-classes were assembling. The life of the place really centred round these classes. Without them the guests would soon have felt bored, whereas, with them, everyone felt that they were passing their time profitably and strenuously. The daily programme, fixed to a notice-board in the corridor, was studied in the same way that a recruit-officer studies the weekly programme of training when it is put up on Saturday morning in his regimental depot. Instead of seeing that I would attend a lecture on hay in stables, or that I would parade with my fellow officers for practice in 'ride and drive' (four horses attached to an army wagon), I would read that Trio would be taking Klasse I for a run on the Schwarz-moos at ten o'clock. 'Klassen II, III, Slope Weiss.' That meant that the rest of the ski-school would assemble for their usual practice in the usual place. The Slope Weiss was seldom without its two groups of faithful neophytes lined up like steps of stairs, to practise their stem and Christiania turns. On Saturday evening we had read on the board: 'Sunday. A day of rest (especially for instructors!).' But it was not to be. Perhaps Herr Scheiber dreaded even a single afternoon of idleness for his guests, and when lunch was over the classes had been got together after all.

Otto, the senior of the three instructors, was watching his pupils line up when I appeared now. He took the beginners, doubtless because of his patience and good humour. Kind-hearted, considerate, fond of children, he was adored by any youngsters who found themselves in his class. Like Trio, his face was scarred from duels at the University. The latest of these scars was only just healing, and on very cold days he wore his cap pulled well down over it, to prevent the cold getting into the wound.

Trio, hands in pockets, and looking chilled and inadequately clothed, as he always did at this hour, was stamping his feet impatiently and chaffing with Hans. I had grown fond of Trio. I forgave him that touch of malicious amusement with which he would ask us to attempt the impossible. Type of all debonair, imprudent youth, there was something lovable about Trio, and, as I discovered after a time, something considerate as well. He liked to play the buffoon. Hands in pockets, thrusting his lips out when he spoke and goggling with his eyes, he would pretend to be stupid, looking rather like a living version of Pinocchio. Actually, he was a handsome young man with fine brown eyes and a charming smile. Whereas Otto's scars were highly unbecoming, the slashed chin and cheeks of the good-looking Trio really suited him, adding a sort of devil-may-care grace to his face. On a day when it was inclined to snow Trio would appear shivering, in a white shirt and jacket open at the neck, and without gloves, his face blue with cold, cutting such a sorry figure that the whole class would implore him to accept the loan of coats, scarves, anything that would make him look warmer. But despite the fact that he appeared chilled to the marrow, he would refuse all such offers, would continue his instructions shivering, and would be dancing quite as gaily as anyone else at six o'clock that evening.

Trio could speak a little English, and if he got into difficulties he would turn for help to the tri-lingual Mathews, who would then translate his directions to some member of the class. His great expression when instructing, spoken in a slow, wheedling voice, was: 'Deeper. Deeper still,' meaning that the pupil must bend his knees and get down still lower before rising in the Christiania swing. He loved a little joke. Standing on the top of a mound, he would watch a pupil render some pathetic parody of the turn he had just been demonstrating, and would say in a tone of deep satisfaction:

'Yess' – thoughtfully. 'Yess.' Another slight pause. Then, as though clinching the matter: 'That is very bad indeed.'

Sometimes, very occasionally, he would mutter:

'Gut. Very gut.'

This was tremendous praise.

But his happiest moment was when a pupil would fail to lead with the correct foot in order to commence a required manœuvre. Then Trio – welcoming the opportunity of showing that he had an idiomatic knowledge of English and certain of his laugh – would call out,

'That is all wrong. You have your behind in front!' and the class would dissolve in instant laughter, as he had intended they should.

This morning Trio announced that he was going to join forces with Hans and the pupils of Klasse II for a joint run.

'We are going up the Langenthal gorge. It is really too easy a run for you people.'

It was no part of my ski-ing creed that, to be enjoyable, a run must be difficult. We went out past the Dortmünder and ran down through a small copse of pines towards the bed of the valley up which we would presently ascend. It was intensely cold, for we had dipped out of sunlight into a part of the gorge which the sun never reached in winter except in the very late afternoon. Here we halted to fumble with cold hands while we put on sealskins. Then we began to climb slowly in single file. The gradient was an easy one. Hands in pockets, trailing his long ski-sticks either side of him, Trio swung easily along, making the track in which the rest of us followed. The sun, cutting through a cleft in the mountains, shone on the slopes to our right, but not on us. Even with ski-sticks tucked under my arms, and hands thrust deep in my pockets, my fingers seemed on the point of freezing. The valley was without human habitation of any sort, without even a hay-hut. It seemed trespass on our part to invade it. It belonged rather to the wild creatures and to the ravens. I saw the tracks of a hare across the snow, and presently those of a group of chamois. Hans, who, with the second party, was following a little way behind, called out now that his class, if they went any further, would be too tired, and that he was going to stop. He withdrew with them to a mound on the right, where they could rest in the sun before returning. Trio waved him an airy farewell and pressed on. The ground steepened. The sides of the gorge closed in. On either side of us the mountain heights rose sheer, rock above, snow slopes, almost equally sheer, below. Down the face of one of these snow precipices, much as a mountain stream comes over a ledge to drop in a sheer tenuous fall absolutely straight, I could see the clear trace of a chamois dotted at intervals in the snow. It seemed as though only a winged creature, a Pegasus, could have made that track. The snow beneath our own feet was crisp and untrodden. It was nearly midday. At the head of the valley an offshoot from it opened up to our right. Climbing now in real earnest, we went up it, to halt on high ground near the top. There Trio helped his pupils to take off their sealskins and prepare for the descent. In the company of three middle-aged ladies, who seemed more ambitious and in better training than any of the men, I pressed on for another hundred yards to a cone-like mound just clear of the shadow. There, clearing the snow from a rock, we had the benefit of the sun, which five minutes before had risen above the mountain-top and was now casting shafts of light like spears from behind the fretted edges of rock.

Solon said that no man should call himself happy until the course of life was complete. He knew doubtless that, in the fickle mind, present distress will always outweigh past bliss, so that even Crœsus must wait for the last act of the drama before daring to boast. But I was happy now as I lay in the sun, looking down the long valley and catching a glimpse of the members of Hans' class as, one by one, moving as slowly as black-beetles across the snow, they began their retreat. The sun's rays warmed us; someone produced a packet of chocolate and passed it round. The stillness, the keen, sweet mountain air, made gentle now for the best part of an hour by this midday sunrise, the silence and beauty of this place, the nobility of the peaks which surrounded us – it would have been strange if all this had not brought content. I was happy as I basked there in the sun. I was happy as I buckled on my skis and ran down in un-tracked powder snow to rejoin Trio, and at his direction, to take the lead on the return journey. And I was happy as I re-entered the *gasthof* late for lunch, but triumphant after the morning's successful tour.

When one thing goes well with us, all seems to go well. In the afternoon, finding myself at a loose end, Trio's class being too tired after the morning run for any further exercise, I went out on the slope Weiss to practise straight running from the fence above the path. I had gadarened down this several times, and was standing halfway up the hill, turning over in my mind whether to make the whole ascent again, when I saw Jopie and Little Anneke, accom-panied by a guide from the Dortmünder and another man, come over the crest of the hill by the hay-chalet, returning, it would seem, from a run. This was unexpected, for they had hardly reached the stage yet when they were ready for a run. They had probably been up 'the Plum-pudding' and were returning. The guide led the way, running very slowly, taking an easy line; he turned at the bottom to watch the others descending. Anneke was ahead. She ran down the next dip to where the guide was waiting for her. The ground was in a series of waves, not too easy to negotiate, before the final descent to the level of the *gasthof*. Jopie; following a little way behind the others, paused at the top of the first wave. Then she advanced a little, dipped over the slope, and ran down, only to fall at the bottom.

When she got up she began to do something to the strap of the ski. I went towards her, for Anneke and the two men were by this time well in front. She looked pale, and was obviously tired after her run.

'Hullo, Jopie. Where have you been?'

She told me that they had been daring enough to venture a tour.

'That's pretty brave.'

'Yes. I have been falling all the time.'

'You know that Mathews promised to lend your friend, who reads so much, the life of Nijinsky. Has she got it yet?'

'Yes. He saw her at the hotel this morning and gave it to her.'

It was now or never.

'I am going to give you my own book – the one we were talking about the other night. It is prose, not poetry. Your English is quite good enough to read it. It is written very simply. It will tell you all about my life in Ireland, and about my wife and child[1] – about my wife and child, and the life we lead there, when we go there in the summer.'

It was done now. So easy once done, so hard in anticipation.

A man poised on a diving-board, waiting to take a plunge a little steeper than he is accustomed to, feels as I had felt a moment before. If I had confessed to a priest and received absolution for a hundred misdemeanours the sense of relief which rushed over me could hardly have been greater. I had nerved myself to the moment and I was glad. She knew. She must know. I had said 'my wife . . . my child' several times quite clearly. I was no longer a wolf in sheep's clothing – no, indeed, certainly not a wolf; at worst a sheep, one of the many sheep who look occasionally with mild, moist eyes over the fence which encloses them.

It was no joking matter. I had told her, not tongue in cheek, but with the flurried embarrassment of a schoolboy, and she could see from the manner of my telling that I was far from being the practised philanderer. Rather I was what Malwylda von Meysenberg fifty years before had described as a 'Don Juan of the ideal.'[2]

[1] Children, for there had been a second child since the writing of this book.

[2] Not such a flattering alternative, when I consult the passage in question. 'Just as the fleshly Don Juan looks for satisfaction of the senses in every beautiful form, so that intellectual Don Juan looks for the ideal in every beautiful soul with which his imagination is filled. He holds the reins which draw him towards this or that being for a lasting love, and yet a glance, a melody, a momentary sympathetic feeling suffices to lure his imagination elsewhere. He is surely the more dangerous of the two Don Juans because the wounds that he inflicts strike noble hearts and cannot be healed for it is the ideal in him that they have loved.'

From the moment Mathews had spoken to me – rather, from the moment Jopie had blushed – the full selfishness of my behaviour had been evident to me. No girl minds being admired, no girl objects to making an impression. But, to feel oneself appreciated, to be the subject of a compliment, is a quite different thing from the homage of love. It was my crime that when I admired, I admired extravagantly. Years before a sister had said to me: 'People like you and——'. – she named the man whom she was later to marry – 'cause far more unhappiness than the mere flirt, who never pretends to be serious. One knows where one is with the flirt, whereas with you——' Whereas with us it would have seemed absurd to offer anything less than serious homage. Beauty was too important. It either claimed complete allegiance or nothing at all. One was a scoundrel for the simple reason that one was an idealist; one might have been much better if one had been a little worse.

The confession which had cost me so much was received very calmly indeed. It is possible that I had told her something which she had surmised from the first. At any rate, she knew now. The guide, wondering at the delay, had turned back. He was already halfway towards us, remounting the slope. Jopie told me that she intended to stop at the *gasthof* on the way.

'There is something I want to get there.'

'Good. I will see you in a few minutes. I am just going to climb to the fence once more.'

She ran down the slope towards the guide and rejoined her companions. They all four resumed the descent. I climbed to the fence and stood there a minute wondering that the slopes below should be deserted so early, until I remembered that Hans' class too were probably recuperating after the ardours of their morning run. The valley seemed asleep in the stillness of early afternoon. A few figures climbed the opposite slope, holding the very end of their ski-sticks, thrusting forward their arms and feet alternately, and moving abruptly up the slope with a staccato step which gave them the similitude of puppets, or of figures in a dream. Once one of them called and the sound reached me in the clear air over the snow with an air of unreality, as though I listened too in a dream.

Down at the *gasthof* I found Jopie leaning over the front of the kiosk in the great corridor, choosing picture-postcards. The stall was usually locked, except immediately after meals. She had been lucky to get hold of the deaf attendant, who was seldom to be discovered when she was most wanted.

'Will you stay and have tea with me here?'

'Yes, if you like.'

She paid the girl for the postcards. I told her that I would go over to the annexe and fetch the book I had promised to give her.

'I'll only be a few minutes. I'll show you the room now where we have tea. It's just through here.'

Leading the way along the passage, I thought, 'Life is kind. Of course life is kind. How well things pan out if only one leaves them alone.' To worry or to contrive achieved nothing. To let the event come to one rather than to go in search of the event, that was wisdom. I had lingered talking to Scrooge that night, when they first came up from the Dortmünder, never dreaming that I should dance with Jopie before the evening ended, and now who could have foretold that I would be on the path at that particular spot at the one moment when the skiers returned over the ridge from their run?

The little Austrian room was empty. It was still early. I left Jopie, went across to the annexe, washed, drew out a suitcase from beneath my bed, flinging it open and searching hurriedly for the book I wanted; found it and thrust the case back in disorder. The annexe seemed deserted, but Anna met me at the foot of the stairs and gave me one of those smiles which typified to the full her capacity for acceptant happiness. She began to mount the wooden stairs with her slow, heavy step as I ran out of the door.

In the Austrian room I found Jopie tired probably by her run, sitting hunched up against the huge green glazed stove, with its little recessed 'windows' of old-fashioned globular glass, casting back to the time when the Emperor had sent his craftsmen from Innsbruck to adorn his hunting-lodge. The warm tiles of the porcelain stove could make a most comfortable support for one's back.

'You look as though you were shivering.'

She denied that she was as cold as that, and since the stove was very hot we moved away from it a little to the other table, by the small window, where Mathews took his meals. I produced the object of my hurried search at the annexe.

'Here is the book that I told you about.'

'Shall I be able to understand it?'

'Of course you will.'

She pursed her mouth in self-depreciation while I took out my pen, and examined critically the bottle of *gasthof* ink.

'Spell your name for me. I want to write it in the book.'

As she spelt it, I inscribed it, 'Jopie de Graaf, from the author. Kühtai,' and the date. Then I pushed it across to her.

'There. You can read it when you go back to Holland when you have more time.'

Tearing a page from a rough exercise book that happened to be lying on the table, I sliced it in half and wrote my address on one half.

'That is where I live in Dorset. Perhaps you will come to England one day and we shall see you.'

'Perhaps. I have been in England once already, but only for a few days.'

There was a chance that she might come again in the autumn to London, for some course of training that she could best take there. If she did come, she must pay us a visit. I told myself that she would come, she must come, that I would see her again — these are the sort of limitless overdrafts that one draws on the future, refusing to believe that life holds any partings. She told me that she had crossed with a Dutch team to play hockey at Ramsgate, and for some reason it seemed strange to think that she had had this one link with the country from which I had come. In just the same way, it had seemed strange to learn that before ever I met my wife in Taormina I must have heard her on a certain Armistice Day singing with the Bach Choir in the Sheldonian at Oxford. That discovery had given the occasion a romantic significance in my eyes which it had never possessed before. Everything which has happened to a person before we know them is in a sense romance, like something which has happened in a book. And in the same way it seemed strange now to think of Jopie and ten other Dutch girls exploring Ramsgate. She had never impressed me as a very athletic person, probably because she was still such a complete novice on skis; but, if she was good enough to go on a tour, I had obviously wronged her.

I pushed towards her the other lined half of the page torn from the exercise book.

'Write your address on that for me.'

She wrote her name and an address in The Hague, grumbling, rather gently, at the pen I had given her, whereas it was the cheap paper which was really at fault.

'You will not be able to read it, what I have written.'

'I can read it all right.'

The ink was dry and I put the slip of paper into my pocket. But the other half of the sheet must have been wet when it was thrust into the book, and we now discovered a huge blot, rather like a species of Chinese calligraphy, all down one side of my inscription.

'Bother. It is my fault. I did not notice that the ink was wet.'

She was full of contrition.

'I have a rubber. I'll get it right.'

'Can you?'

She watched me as I performed the operation.

It was four o'clock, not too soon to think about ordering our tea.

Jopie gave a shiver. It was I who had been brutal enough to move her away from the warm stove.

'Let's go back to the other table.'

'Yes, let's.'

We moved back. No maid had come as yet, but at that moment one happened to pass in the passage on her way to the pantry and I called to her. There was a little difficulty in explaining to her what we wanted. But just then Mathews appeared.

'Good, Alister. You can join us. Jopie is having tea with me. Now you can do the ordering.'

'Well, what do you both want?'

He showed no surprise at finding us together. I longed to say to him, 'It is done. I have told her. You need not worry.' But he seemed to realise the fact without being told. He could see the book on the table, and in any case my whole manner probably conveyed that my conscience was now clear and that he need no longer feel obliged to pour forth lava and hot ashes in a steady stream.

The maid stood waiting to take our order.

'Jopie, are you going to have tea, or coffee or chocolate? The chocolate is jolly good. It was Eltham who first made me try it.'

She elected for chocolate on my recommendation and the mountain climber's.

'Explain that we want "*thé complet*," Alister, with something to eat.'

Mathews gave the order, his own coffee, two chocolates and rolls.

'And honey. Don't forget the honey.'

'*Und drei Honig.*'

The girl departed. It would be some minutes before she returned. The service was good, but nothing was done against time in the *gasthof*, and there was a typically Austrian reluctance to appear to worry about a triviality like money. For drinks, or for extras in the afternoon like this one, you were never given a chit to sign. The maid carried the reckoning in her head and reminded you at the end of the day – or you reminded her – and she then collected the money from you. With such a large number of visitors and with several meals to remember, at which drinks might have been served, it seemed a haphazard arrangement, only too likely to work out to the advantage of the guest; but it was assumed that everyone was naturally honest and that no one would try to profit by it. This was typical. Alike in their honesty, their gaiety, their piety, and their charm, the Tyrolese are a unique people, and to study their virtues at firsthand and the creed, or conditions of life, which underlie and explain these virtues, is the sort of sociological experiment which doctrinaires never attempt, but which would be more enlightening than many that they do.

'Monk doesn't like that maid.'

'The one with the white-topped shoes?'

'Yes.'

'Why do you not like her?'

'Most of the maids are slow but pleasant, but that one is in my black books. I eat slowly, and if I put my knife and fork down for even a moment she snatches my plate away. However, I am not shy, and I insist on her bringing it back. She is the only stupid one of the lot. The rest are really very efficient.'

Jopie sat on the wooden bench with her back against the stove, one foot drawn up under her. I could look at her to my heart's content. She was wearing a woollen jacket or cardigan over a white flannel blouse with a low collar, and she had loosened her narrow, coloured, knitted scarf so that it hung across her shoulders like a stole. She had taken her cap off. Her hair, short at the back like a boy's, in a fashion that I detested, was fair, almost brown. In front it was longer, not cropped, but fastened back over the ear with a slide, long enough to make me forget completely, or at least to accept, the abhorred fashion. Her eyes were limpid, guileless and at the same time full of humour. Her face was not actually oval; the nose was friendly and attractive, and just missed being long; the mouth wide and mobile and slightly full-lipped, revealing when she laughed the whitest of teeth. But I noticed none of these things – that is to say, I noticed none of them in detail. Rather I was aware of a certain flushed and dreaming grace of expression, such as we discover in some of the drawings of da Vinci, and which delights us because it seems part of the very poetry of existence. Let us once discern beauty in a particular aspect, and every time we rediscover it, the same quality, which first impressed it on imagination, engraves it there more deeply still. I had no wish to analyse what Jopie's charm for me was. It would have been strange if I had. Instead, I was aware, vaguely, but oh how poignantly, of this face which might have leaned laughing from heaven; and I delighted in it because it seemed to me as natural as childhood, and as dreamy and lyrical and joyous as youth.

We told her how before we knew her real name and for want of a better one, we had called her after the heroine in the translation Mathews had lent me. She shook her head and made a little pout.

'I doan't like it.'

Mathews attempted to convince her that it was really a beautiful name.

'No, no. I doan't like it.'

Her voice gave a slightly slurred, burring sound to the 'No' and the 'don't,' an intonation characteristic of her, and then suddenly the light blue eyes, with the rather wide rim of white, kindled and she smiled in amusement; at us for giving her a nickname or at herself for being annoyed by it.

The maid came at last with Mathews' coffee and our chocolate. With them she brought rolls and butter and honey. But the thick golden run honey in its three flat glass dishes, which we regarded as such a luxury, was wasted on Jopie, who refused it, saying that it got into her teeth and made them ache.

'Perhaps you are right. This is not the place in which to get toothache. You would have to go to Innsbruck before anything could be done about it. We will eat your share.'

'Do.'

Sonia, looking her very smartest in her white ski jacket, came in with the English boy Raines, who had been very attentive to her now for several days. They crossed the room and sat down in the far corner, he rather moodily silent, more so than ever after she had reproved him for something he had just said. When their tea was brought he ordered some cakes and the sight of a plate laden with these suggested to me that I should do the same. More were brought, and Jopie, risking toothache, succumbed to a huge triangular piece of chocolate cake.

'How old are you, Jopie?'

'I am twenty.'

'Mathews guessed that you were nineteen.'

Just as the couple in the corner talked in undertones so our own

voices were lowered to a pitch sufficiently discreet not to seem to
monopolise the room.

'It's time for my French lesson. Jopie can share it.'

'Your what?'

'My French lesson.'

'Monk has a French lesson after tea every day. He speaks French
comme un canard Espagnol, but he loves it all the same. We are late for
breakfast in the mornings because he reads de Régnier aloud in bed
and I have to listen.'

Jopie looked at me questioningly and I nodded.

'What are you going to do, Monk? Make your mind up. If we are
going to read French you'll have to get the books.'

'All right. Presently. There's no hurry.'

The maid was clearing away the débris of our tea. Jopie's teeth
had survived the chocolate cake. The three honey dishes were empty.
She had unwound her scarf from her neck and laid it across the top
of the stove. She seemed rested and warmer at last. Mathews offered
her a cigarette, and she accepted it. I was not smoking myself and
I watched her enviously as she lit it, drew a long deep breath and
blew out the smoke through her nostrils with a quick impatience.
It was her one touch of sophistication, a little puzzling, since she was
not a frequent smoker, but I had noticed that another Dutch girl,
travelling with her mother, shyer and much more sheltered in
manner, smoked with just the same air of experience, and inhaled
deeply, as Jopie did now.

'Monk gave up smoking all the time he was finishing his book.'

'And now it seems stupid to start again.'

'Are you going to get the books? What are you going to bring?'

'Paul Fort.'

'And de Régnier?'

'Yes, and de Régnier.'

He had drunk his coffee at our table and seemed to enjoy our
companionship. He would entertain Jopie while I was away. As I
made my way across the snow, I thought to myself, 'Mathews is
sympathetic because he has been in love himself. It is quite untrue
to say that all the world loves a lover; how could they when half the
time the fellow is a nuisance to himself and everyone else? But it is
quite true to say that all the world is sorry for the poor devil.'
Alister had known both the heights and the depths of love; and I
remembered the poem which we had read a few mornings before,
'Le Miroir des Amants,' that mirror which the poet holds up to

lovers and in which they see *le variable Amour* offering to them either a poisoned chalice or a cup of ecstasy.

> *J'offre à votre visage, Amants et vous Amantes*
> *Ce Miroir, tour à tour morose et radieux.*

In the mirror the lovers, who see themselves reflected there, are of two sorts.

> *Les uns boivent en lui l'éternelle amertume*
> *Dont leur bouche à jamais gardera l'âcre pli*
> *Ou s'en vont, emportant en leur cœur qu'il consume*
> *Un feu sourd dont la cendre, hélas! est sans oubli,*
>
> *D'autres n'ont conservé de sa rencontre heureuse*
> *Que le frais souvenir des limpides ruisseaux*
> *Où leur mains doucement jointes en coupe creuse*
> *Ont puisé le bonheur qui chantait dans les eaux.*[1]

Mathews had seen both aspects in the mirror. He had known love as the freshness of a well-spring under a clear morning sky. His hands had been cupped to receive it. Even that act in itself is a ritual for which one should be grateful. But between the days of Dulcinea and now, he had passed through troubled waters. If he had not tasted Dead Sea fruit he had at least obtained a hint of its flavour. And listening to the measured lines of de Régnier on my friend's lips, when the poem was read, it had seemed to me that he had been lucky to escape the full bitterness which might have overtaken him, which had nearly overtaken him, when his sculptress changed her mind and decided to abandon him. She could never have made him happy; he would have become the puzzled satellite of a temperamental star, a star already finding the ascent of its particular heaven a difficult one. The poet was right, love was two-edged.

> *Amour, c'est toujours toi: Prince au double visage,*
> *Qui te mires par eux à ce miroir changeant!*

[1] Some drink therefrom an eternal bitterness
  From which their mouths will nevermore be free,
Depart, to carry in the heart's recess
  Slaked fires, whose ashes smart unceasingly.

Others bear naught away with them save joy,
  The morning memory of a limpid spring,
From which their hands, cupped in a joint employ,
  Have drawn such happiness as clear brooks sing.

Tapping my boots against the steps to knock the snow off, I re-entered the *gasthof*.

'Here are the books. Mind the paper cover of the Paul Fort. It's been coming off for a long time. That is why I have put elastic round it. It was given me by Werner in Château d'Œx. Do you remember him, Alister?'

'No.'

'He was pastor of one of the smaller Protestant groups. A good-looking man with a devoted wife and a rather beautiful child. I have never forgotten how I came back to Château d'Œx one winter and met him in the village street. I was rhapsodising about the joy of getting back to the mountains, to this veritable Arcady, when a look of scorn came into his face and he said with extreme bitterness, "This accursed place!" It was as though he were putting years of despair into those three words.'

'He probably felt smothered there. I suppose he was ambitious.'

'That spur which leaves all our flanks bleeding!'

'*Alors*. Now for the French lesson.'

Mathews suggested that we should begin with Paul Fort. I read a short poem, blundering over a word here and there, to be corrected by my tutor. Then I passed the book on. He found 'La Chaumière,' reading it rather deliberately and with a certain nervousness. It was my habit to take any liberties I liked with the language, even to the complete ignoring, in conversation, of such a trifling irrelevancy as gender. I had never had to talk French until I had found myself in my first billet in France, and then I had been demoralised by the willingness of the native to converse with me on a '*No bon!*' '*Me no compree*' basis. Grammar had seemed superfluous under such conditions.

The maid had cleared the table. We could spread our elbows. When it came to her turn, Jopie declared that her knowledge of the language was very little greater than her knowledge of English. But it was soon apparent that she was unduly modest, and that her accent was a great deal better than mine. She had moved round to the other side of the table away from the stove, which had been stoked with fresh logs and had become too hot. She sat now on my left, and Mathews, leaning back against the wall, was directly opposite me. He had his own book with him and presently abandoned de Régnier to us and began to read to himself, putting his feet along the bench and puffing at his pipe, with the air of a man who is well content. He was there to refer to if we needed him.

414

'Jopie, one has to be careful with de Régnier. He is a little luscious at times, a little "French." One never knows what is coming next.'

The series of sonnets associated with some journey the poet must have made in the Eastern Mediterranean seemed safe enough. I told Jopie how Mathews and I had wandered through Sicily living on oranges stolen from the groves, and on the cheese we had brought with us from Naples, how, coming to Girgenti, we had quarrelled furiously with a man who was savagely flogging a mule up a hill, and had finally, to his intense astonishment, pushed the cart up the steep hill ourselves, in a sea of mud; and how next morning we had watched the sun rise over temples that Æschylus may have seen. Then, thrusting the book across the table to her, I said, 'Now read us "Agrigentum." That was the old Greek name for Girgenti.'

She read the poem slowly and thoughtfully.

'Isn't it lovely?'

'Yes, it is lovely.'

We read a number of the poems together. The reader was given a minute to look over the poem before reading it aloud. Presently turning over the pages, to choose again, my eye caught the title 'La Beauté.' Here was all de Régnier's stately grace, that lovely, slow inevitability and resonance of language that delighted me. Jopie pulled the book a little towards her so that she could follow in the text.

> Ta divine présence éparse en chaque chose
> Se révèle parfois à nos yeux, Ô Beauté,
> Et tu es, tour à tour, en ta diversité
> Aussi bien ce fruit clos que cette étoile éclose:
>
> Tu es cette eau qui fuit et cette eau qui repose
> Entre les herbes d'or et le sable argenté,
> Cette senteur d'automme et ce parfum d'été,
> Et tu es cette aurore, et tu es cette rose.
>
> Le changeant univers est ta forme secrète;
> La nature en son jeu te reprend et te prête
> Les visages nombreux où je te reconnais.
>
> Mais jamais, ô Beauté, tu ne m'es apparue
> Plus belle que quand, grave et soudaine, tu fais
> D'une femme sans voile une Déesse nue.[1]

[1] Thy divine presence, latent in each thing
  Reveals itself, oh Beauty, to our eyes
And, always diverse, one by one, you bring
  Fruit, closed in bud, or star, disclosed in skies.

Our eyes, travelling together over the page a little ahead of the line that I was reading, caught the final one of the sonnet and met instantly in embarrassed laughter. She flushed crimson to the ears, and I slid my hand over the page half in jest, muttering, 'Well, we will take that for granted.'

'Now you know why I warned you, Jopie. I'll have to be more careful.'

She looked at me in amused confusion – confusion in which amusement prevailed despite her flushed cheeks. In this trivial incident we seemed to have moved a step further from the imputation of being mere chance acquaintances.

'We'd better stick to poems on places.'

I found the sonnet on Stamboul. Mathews, hearing Jopie ask if we had been there, laid down his book to tell her that he had preferred to visit Mount Athos.

'Monk had gone home. We had meant to go to Constantinople, but there was not time. He had the chance of a job and had to come back for an interview.'

Raines, the young Englishman with Sonia, called across from his corner of the room that he had been to Mount Athos, but that he thought the Peloponnese more beautiful. Mathews disagreed. He considered Mount Athos the most beautiful place he had visited. He told us how he had been rowed across from Salonica in a small fishing boat, the wind failing, and the fisherman, who had agreed to take him, having to row for twelve hours. Then when they arrived and saw the mountain with its cliff thousands of feet high descending sheer to the sea, the trees, the tropical growth clinging to the ledges, the fisherman had persuaded him to lie down at the bottom of the boat and sleep while he rowed on round the coast looking for a place to land.

Yes. It was good to travel; good, if only to have moments such as this to describe afterwards. We had been reading and talking for nearly

---

You are this lake, which sleeps unstirred between
  Gold reeds and silver sand; this stream which flows;
And you are autumn's breath, and summer seen
  In perfumed petals. You are dawn, and you are rose.

The changing universe is your secret mould.
Nature in her delight reshapes and lends
Countless fresh aspects to you. Each I hold

Sacred. But never, Beauty, do your ends
Seem surer, lovelier, than when – grave in your hands –
Woman, undraped, a naked goddess stands.

two hours. Jopie got up, saying that it was time for her to return.
'I'll come with you to the Dortmünder.'

She fetched the yellow wind-jacket from the hall, where she had left it hanging, put it on, and came with us to see the underground stable about which we had been telling her. But for a time the switch could not be found, Alister striking vesta after vesta, mere glims in Acheron, until at last someone's hand groped upon the switch in the darkness and the stable was lit up to reveal its sleepy fowl perched on barriers and its goats busily chewing the cud in the corner of their stall.

Mathews went across to the annexe, and I walked back to the Dortmünder with Jopie. We entered the ski-room downstairs and she turned to say goodbye to me. Colouring up, she thanked me once more for my gift of the book. Outside, above a cluster of dark pines, the stars glimmered, and, as he passed me with his heavy boots crunching the snow, a peasant carrying a milk pail wished me *'Grüss Gott.'*

Back in my room at the annexe, the first thing I did was to reach in my pocket for the slip on which Jopie had written her address. That half sheet of copy book paper had assumed crucial importance in my eyes. If I lost it, I would have lost the one means I had of communicating with her when we left Kühtai.

It will give the measure of its importance to me if I say that I was not content until I had pencilled a copy of the address into the back of my journal and then, placing the slip carefully elsewhere, reflected that I was at least now doubly covered, that it was not likely that my journal would be lost but that, even if it were, there was a good chance that the piece of paper would survive. The recollection of an action such as this can bring home to us after years the force of a particular emotion which might otherwise easily seem to have been ephemeral or fanciful. I hardly knew this Dutch girl. I was completely ignorant of her language and she was dependent upon a halting and perhaps too diffident use of mine. Nevertheless I had only to sit opposite her to feel convinced that fate was right and that in some way she must be made a part of whatever life held in store for me in the years to come. I was even mad enough at times to envisage a *ménage à trois* like the one envisaged by the guileless Shelley when he sent his famous – or, as some people think, infamous – invitation from France to Harriet, and so far from appearing fantastic my conviction at that moment seemed quite as real as any that had ever come to me.

Less than a week of our time in Kühtai remained. Next morning Trio announced that he would take his class on what the red-haired schoolboy in the annexe had named 'The Wizard Run'. It lay immediately at the back of the *gasthof*, where the ground rose precipitously, like a great snow cliff, concealing the fact that behind and above, out of sight, lay a plateau walled in on two sides by rocky heights. All that one saw from the valley floor was a towering snow wall. The angle of the slope was too steep to be very safe at any time, and during the week when snow had been falling even the experts had avoided it. But now after several nights' hard frost it was a different matter. We had already prospected a little way directly up its face, falling a good deal, all of us, on the subsequent descent. It was not necessary, however, to make this direct frontal assault. The usual route was to follow the sleigh path for a few hundred yards towards Gries, and then turn up a steep gully to the left, which led presently on to the plateau.

This was the way chosen to-day. Trio went slowly, a sure sign that a leader knows his business, and is thinking not of his own inclination, but of what will best suit the least experienced member of his expedition. His gloved hands, holding the ski-sticks just below the head, moved forward alternately, first one and then the other, in a controlled gesture like that of a signalman who pushes forward a lever firmly yet appears to be holding it back. The regularity of this movement corresponded to the rhythmic thrust of his long legs. He moved easily up the side of the gully. Nothing is more restful to the mind than this push of alternate skis over the snow. To climb thus is part of the joy of ski-ing and a joy which sophisticated skiers, for whom Mammon hastens to provide other modes of ascent, have never known, or have long ago forsaken.

The sun had just risen between the toothed edges of the mountains as we came out on the plateau. It laced the white plain, casting shafts of light across it, as though to rouse it out of sleep after the long, icy night. Everywhere the eye rested on an unbroken whiteness, except in those rare spots where a mound cast its mauve shadow across ground unreached by the sun. The plain must have been a mile long and not less than three-quarters of a mile wide. Ahead, and to the left, a precipitous barrier of grey granite rose, relentless, against the gentle blue of the sky. The snow stretched around us in all directions just as it had fallen, without the blemish of a single track. It would be our skis which would presently desecrate that whiteness. From the floor of the plateau rose one or two great hillocks, promising a little extra running to those energetic enough to climb them, and as I pushed forward over the snow I tasted, in an anticipatory thrill, the joy of that moment when the points of my skis would dip over the crest for the first steep plunge down.

Actually, however, the run, when it came, was a disappointment. Trio had told us not to take sandwiches, that we would be back at the *gasthof* in time for lunch. Perhaps this time factor worried him, or it may have been the slowness of some of his party, lagging far behind, which convinced him he had made a mistake in allowing them to come at all. At any rate, he halted soon by some rocks to wait for the stragglers to come up, and announced that we would start down from there when they were rested. Lying back in the sun, his hands joined together under his head on a rucksack, he surveyed infinity. A man and a woman, accompanied by a guide, overtook us and passed us with a greeting. They were going a good deal further; as far, in fact, as the enclosing walls would permit. Presently Klasse II appeared over the lip of the gully. They had brought their lunch with them, since they would need more time for the tour, and they were therefore in no hurry. In the company of two of them, I proceeded to climb a mound to the left so as to get a little extra running. By the time I returned to Trio, his party were ready for the descent. It was to prove *pénible* for most of his pupils. He admitted later that he had made a mistake, and had chosen too difficult a line, one which necessitated fast running on an undulating traverse. One sped furiously on, trying hard to keep the weight on the correct foot and to bend the knees sufficiently to act as shock-absorbers over the waves in the ground. The slope was far too steep for any skier of our status to attempt a downhill turn. The only thing to do was to wait until the necessity became acute, and then steer uphill until one came to a halt. After which there would follow the slow and elaborate ritual of a kick-turn. Trio shouted encouragement to the faint-hearted and after a time told me to go ahead, as they were only holding me back. Obviously a long apprenticeship to the kick-turn in Switzerland was standing me in good stead.

I ran down to the *gasthof* and had nearly finished lunch when the rest of the class appeared.

That afternoon, amusing myself on the practice slopes, I came suddenly on Little Anneke. She was alone.

'Hullo, Anneke. Where's Jopie?'

'She has gone with the guide up the Langenthal.'

'That's very daring of her. Tell her she's to come and have tea with me when she comes back.'

I had already sent another message to the same effect by Alister, when, earlier in the day, he had announced that he might go down to the Dortmünder for tea.

Anneke looked at me a little reproachfully.

'Oh, but you should come to us. She will be tired after getting back from her run.'

My thoughts went back to the time when I had viewed her with such suspicion as Jopie's dragon. She was a staunch friend, this Little Anneke, full of good works, doing a course in social welfare at Amsterdam, she had told us. I liked her by this time, and felt I enjoyed her goodwill. All the same, I shook my head.

'No. I won't come down to the Dortmünder. But will you and she both come and have tea with me to-morrow. In any case. Whether she comes or doesn't to-day. Is that all right? At half-past four?'

She thanked me, and I watched her as she did a cautious kick-turn prior to mounting the slope once more.

Jopie did not come, nor did I really expect her after what Anneke had said. The Langenthal was a longish expedition for a beginner. The run was easy enough, but even the easiest run, for those who have not yet mastered their turns, necessitates a lot of falling, and falling repeatedly in deep snow can be a shattering experience.

Mathews returned to the annexe at six and found me reading there.

'Did you go to the Dortmünder?'

'Yes. About four.'

'Was Jopie there?'

'Yes. And I gave her your message. She came back cold and dead-tired from a run. She said that she might or might not come. Did she?'

'No.'

'I could see that she was tired.'

'Little Anneke was on the Weiss slopes——'

'Monk, I wish you wouldn't call her "Arnika." It sounds like one of the labels in an apothecary's shop. She is Anneke, a friendly diminutive of Anna. She and the other girl pronounce themselves AHNEKE and AYNEKE to show the difference. AHNEKE is the tall one.'

'Well. I haven't your ear for foreign languages. It sounds like ARNIKA to me. Tell me about Jopie.'

'I have nothing to tell.'

A moment later he looked at me and added: 'You know, you are right. She is beautiful.'

Had he hitherto disagreed with me on the point? Once he had hinted that the impression she had made was largely the effect of the daffodil jacket against the snow. If he had really intended such heresy, this was recantation. It pleased me that he should say that he thought her beautiful. People in love, though they are certain themselves, are always delighted when another person endorses their verdict. Deep in their hearts there is the realisation that love, like every other mental impression, is partly subjective. It is reassuring to take counsel's opinion. 'Nay, but you who do not love her: Is she not pure gold, my mistress?' Browning's lines are every lover's wish that the beloved should be approved. Climbing in the Langenthal valley, I had heard an elderly man immediately behind me speaking to his companion of two girls at the Dortmünder, 'one of them with spectacles, and one very beautiful.' It may not have been Jopie at all. It may have been Sonia; but I was convinced from what he said that it was Jopie, and, listening with an impassive face, it had given me acute pleasure to hear her praised.

Mathews began to speak of his plans for the following day. He was anxious to attempt the tour on the far side of the valley. There was a risk of avalanches, but it was not a very serious one. The *gasthof* discouraged people setting off if conditions were really unsuitable.

But the project was to come to nothing after all. That evening after dinner he came to tell me that Scheiber had approached him in a great state. Trouble had been made at Innsbruck over the New Year's Eve incident. The Frenchwoman had kept her word and had given the authorities her version of the affair, a garbled and exaggerated version, full of such far-reaching political implications that the authorities were threatening to close the *gasthof* as a punishment to Scheiber for having allowed the incident to take place.

'Scheiber is beside himself. He came to me because I can speak German. Besides, he knows we like him. He has asked me to go down to Innsbruck to-morrow with Raines. We are to go to the British Consulate and try and get the British Consul to intercede for him, explaining that a mountain has been made out of a molehill.'

'And has it?'

'Yes. I should think so. Scheiber is sending us by sleigh to Selrain. We are to start early – at nine o'clock – and shall not get back till late. Someone else is coming to see the Dutch Consul.'

He left me, to make his preparations for the morning. I looked at my watch. It was nearly eight-thirty. The letters should soon be here. Often in the evening I would go out through the big double doors by the painted cupboard in the hall to watch the men un-loading the sleighs. The huge leather mail satchel was one of the first things to be taken off the leading sleigh. But it irritated the deaf girl if, in my anxiety to see if there was a letter for me, I followed her into the office and watched her opening the bag. There were never very many letters, but she preferred to sort them slowly and laboriously, and later place them on the board by the kiosk. And so, curbing my impatience with difficulty, I would often remain on the steps, as I did to-night, to watch the two sleighs unloaded – pro-visions for the *gasthof*, baggage for a new arrival, a pair of skis, a sack, a portmanteau. The bearded drivers went about their work, their heads swathed in cap-comforters, their breath ascending like smoke in the frosty night air, and icicles of frozen breath hanging raggedly from their moustaches. There were icicles too on the muzzle of the huge black mule, from whose heavy coat and still throbbing flanks rose a great cloud of steam. It was a magnificent beast, but it looked tired. The four hours' climb from Gries was arduous at any time, and still more so after a fresh fall of snow and before the track was trodden. Its heavy jet-black coat was rubbed grey over the shoulder blades where the leather breast-collar had chafed it. I slipped back into the corridor, as I sometimes did, to a table near the pantry, to take a stale roll from one of the wooden bread bowls cleared from dinner, and returned to give it to the mule, flattering myself that the beast seemed grateful. The sleighs had been drawn out of the way to one side of the track, and I followed the driver into the subterranean stable to watch him unharness. The smaller mule, waiting to be attended to, left its stall and began skating about on all four feet. The snow had formed in a ball under the hoofs, and until it melted it was almost impossible for the beast to stand upright on the stone paving. Slithering and slipping about, it threatened at every movement to fall, lurching finally into an adjoining stall already occupied by a cow. There was a volley of abuse from the driver. I could hear him cursing it and calling it '*Schweinhund.*' At last it was led back to its own stall at the far end beyond the goats, the harness taken off its still steaming body, and a double armful of hay brought to it. To-morrow it would start down immediately after breakfast on the same journey and return in the evening. It had twelve hours' respite, undisturbed by anything except the occasional grunt from a pig, or the nibbling of the goats nearby; twelve hours in a darkness scented by the dusty, heavy-smelling hay, and the warm breath of the cows, darkness so warm, so remote, so secure as to be almost as welcome to a man as to a mule.

Next morning, slapping his gloved hands together to keep his fingers warm, a rug over his knees and a rucksack at his feet, I saw Mathews installed in the narrow sleigh beside his fellow traveller Raines. A tall middle-aged Dutchman sat in the second sleigh, and they drove off to the music of mule-bells. Alister was sorry to lose a day's ski-ing, but I envied him the long drive down to Gries between pine trees, and the re-ascent in the evening by the narrow snow-path.

Scheiber had looked worried. I had heard him explaining his part to Mathews. We had grown to like this quiet little man, who, in his green ski-jacket with quilted black silk sleeves, sometimes appeared on the slopes in the afternoon to greet his guests and execute a faultless 'Christie' before departure. But he was generally too busy about his affairs to leave the guest-house often. By now most of his guests were English, and as he knew no English, an Austrian youth of sixteen, who also helped with the accounts, was his amanuensis and interpreter. The boy had only a hesitant command of the language, and was perpetually apologising for his deficiencies. We liked, too, Frau Scheiber, small, plump, homely, always with a friendly smile for Alister, and for me, because I was his friend. It struck me that perhaps I could be helpful in the matter as well as Mathews. I would draw up a petition which the guests would sign, explaining that Scheiber was in no way implicated, had in fact only tried to calm everyone down. We would send it to the British Embassy in Vienna, asking them to use their influence on his behalf. If the *gasthof* were to be closed at the height of the season it would be a serious blow, and Scheiber would almost certainly lose his job.

Scheiber approved the idea when I propounded it to him. It was easy enough to compose the petition and to copy it on to a sheet of foolscap, but it was a little harder to get all the English visitors to sign. It was ready on a table in the corridor when the classes assembled at ten o'clock, and it was not that they disapproved of the idea, but simply that they were in a hurry to get out on to the practice slopes. I went from class to class explaining the scheme, but there were a good many grumbles at the delay while people read the document before signing. Others, having got their skis out and on, were reluctant to take them off again.

'Oh, but you must. It would be such hard luck on Scheiber. Besides you don't want the place closed in the middle of your holiday.'

'I don't care. I'm going away in two days.'

The younger guests, Peggy and her contemporaries, were helpful enough. People like Scrooge cordially approved. But some of the older ones seemed to think it was none of their business. To me their insensitiveness seemed strange, this attitude so completely impersonal towards people who were doing everything to make their stay comfortable.

But I had had an even more glaring example of the same kind of insensitiveness a few evenings before.

Just before the New Year there had been a fresh influx of Britishers. Among these was a big Somerset man, red-faced, blue-jerseyed, a huge, cheery bull of a man, rejoining his wife, whom he was enormously delighted to see, and whom he obviously adored. She on her side took his affectionate advances very calmly, but in good part. These two sat with a group of friends at a round table near the door and the group made what was certainly their fair share of noise and laughter. Three little Austrian boys had come up to the hotel one night during dinner, probably from a chalet some distance down the valley. They were dressed up in fancy costume, with half-blackened faces, and were wearing peaked crowns while they carried wooden symbols on sticks in their hands. One carried a thing not unlike the toy with which English children imitate the sound of the corncrake; another carried a star. I imagine that they represented the Magi. We had watched them through the glass partition as they 'did their turn' in the larger room. They now came to the doorway of ours, and stopped near the table where the new arrivals were seated. Standing their ground stoutly, I could see them summoning up courage for what they had to do. The eldest stepped forward a pace or two and made a little set speech in German. Then they all three began to sing a chant or carol.

The little boy had delivered his rigmarole in a gruff, declamatory voice. He had obviously rehearsed it many times. At the table the group of Scots and English stopped talking for an instant, glanced with curiosity at the children who were standing directly beside them and obviously addressing them, and then – utterly indifferent to the little entertainment that was being staged for them and exactly as though nothing had happened – they turned away and resumed their talk, punctuated with laughter more raucous than ever. Never could the artist have received a more complete and absolute snub. Homer, who in his epic, is continually giving timely reminders of the dignity and importance of the bardic art, and of what is due to the bard himself, must have known at some time, what these children now knew, the bitterness of an audience equally indifferent.

The song, which had begun so bravely, was in danger of being spoilt. The elder boy's lip began to tremble, distressed by such complete unresponsiveness, and, thinking of the delight children feel in dressing up and in mime, my eyes suddenly filled, in anger or pity. I went across to Scrooge's table, and said indigantly,

'Those people . . . they infuriate me.'

He agreed that it showed a shocking lack of sensibility. The women of the party seemed the worst offenders, as though anything in a foreign language could lay no claim to their attention. But it was the big, jerseyed husband, looking generally like a burly sailor, but with jersey discarded on this occasion in favour of a dinner jacket, who formed the focus point of my wrath, until, in the days that followed, I discovered him to be a gentle, lamblike creature, probably quite incapable of deliberate unkindness.

I had appealed to Scrooge. I doubt if I should ever have appealed to Eltham. Scrooge was capable of being touched by an incident the significance of which would be altogether lost on the other. An owl with a broken leg would have been a different matter. Whereas to Scrooge an owl would have been just an owl. Life as we unfortunately know it flourishes on misunderstandings. Men are so different that they afford one another infinite opportunity for barbed criticism. I misunderstood the Somerset doctor. Eltham misunderstood Scrooge. Everyone is quick to put the worst construction on the action of others, and the Devil, with the aid of these misunderstandings and with a little help from the greed, and still more the fear, innate in man, gets his work done without any difficulty.

I could see that Eltham disliked Scrooge cordially, and that this antipathy was without actual cause, but rather basic in temperament. Presently Scrooge got a poisoned thumb, and two kind ladies from a neighbouring table used to attend to it after breakfast. A cup was filled with hot water and the thumb steeped in it. Eltham would glare at me and say bitterly, 'More pus for breakfast!' The first time he made this strange remark I imagined that it was an insulting reference to the food we were being given. Then it dawned on me that he was alluding to the ministrations across the room. His judgments on most of his fellow guests were harsh. 'That's an ugly piece of work,' he would say, looking at Raines across the room. And yet, despite these occasional jibes, I enjoyed my meals with the shy and caustic Eltham, who talked, not of Himalayan snows, but of the pet owls in his garden at home, of his schooldays, of birds and bird-watching, and of his distrust of all the formulæ with which men bolster up their confidence in life. Behind his bristling antipathies I had detected a capacity for friendliness and loyalty, something direct, simple, almost sentimental, absolutely dependable.

I cannot say what his reactions to the petition would have been, for he had departed on one of his solitary climbs before it was ready. Perhaps I was secretly relieved. The rest of the guests were rounded up. Some signed gladly enough, some a little unwillingly. The manifesto was taken along to the office, addressed, and handed over to the amanuensis to be sent off, and I hastened out to rejoin Klasse I at the side of the *gasthof*. Trio had told us to ask for a sandwich lunch, and we set off on the same expedition which we had made the day before. This morning, however, he had picked his party, more carefully, and by taking our food with us we should have more time for it.

There were only eight in the party, including a young woman who had lost her heart to Trio, and who seemed to have found favour in his eyes. Jaunty and self-assured, her flirtation had become serious enough to deprive her a little of her assurance. I could understand a girl losing her heart to the good-looking and gay Trio. He was charming and carefree and his scars only added to his good looks. One might have said of him what Dante said of another,

> *Biondo era, e bello e di gentile aspetto*
> *Ma l'un di eigli un colpo avea diviso.*

He was fair and beautiful and gentle of countenance,
Only a noble scar cut through one of his eyebrows.

To-day he surprised me by revealing a sudden streak of poetic appreciation which I had not suspected. We had climbed to the glistening white plateau and had advanced partly across it. Presently he halted by a rock to rest his party, near a great hillock of un-tracked snow. There we waited for the stragglers to come up.

Pointing with his stick to the precipice of granite beyond us, he said abruptly and with unusual feeling:

'I am seeing that many times, but, every time I see it I think it more wonderful.'

He had decided to take us on further, right up to the shoulder of the ridge immediately to our left. This would give us some excellent running back to the spot where we now were, and where we deposited our rucksacks in a heap. Climbing behind him, up a fold in the mountain, screened from the sun, I could wonder what view would be revealed to us when we reached the crest ahead. Behind, to the south, lay all the glory of the massed Alps towards Innsbruck, every peak and pinnacle picked out clearly in the morning air. Across the ridge one would look north towards the Oetzthal and Arlberg. But in actual fact only Trio himself was to see the view. The climbing grew steeper and steeper and presently, instead of a thick covering of powder snow, we found ourselves with only a thin layer of frozen snow immediately above rock. One by one the climbers decided to go no further, until only Trio and myself were left. We were traversing the slope carefully, but ten yards from the top I found myself digging the edges of my skis frantically into what was little more than rough ice and solid rock. They refused to grip. Trio had taken his off and was carrying them, but my boots had no nails and even by removing my skis I should have been little better off – not enough to get me over those last few yards. My heart failed me. A slip would mean a steep fall for some considerable distance. I watched him climb easily the few remaining yards, stand for a minute on the narrow ridge, his hand up, shading his eyes, looking out over the promised land about which, for the last half-hour, I had been speculating, and then turn. I envied him – Trio, to whom no feat on skis or in climbing seemed to present any difficulty.

I was already stooping to undo the strap of my ski, preparatory to edging cautiously down to a safer portion of the slope, when he rejoined me.

'It is cold up there. The wind gets you from the other side,' was all he said.

He made me lead the way down for a bit while he followed with the rest of his flock. Then, coming to the steep final pitch before the plateau, he passed me and, cutting a narrow track, plunged sheer down for nearly two hundred yards, to run out straight at the bottom. A good Schüss if ever there was one, and to run in his track would mean that I would go even faster. Could I hold it? But the track at least precluded all danger of hitting a concealed rock, and I plunged, compromising a little, however, when two-thirds of the way down, by getting one of my skis into heavier snow, with the result that I took a terrific toss when only a few feet from where he stood.

He looked at me severely.

'You should never run with one of your skis in a track and one out of it. It is the most dangerous thing you can do' was his reproof as I scrambled up after a somersault.

We lunched and rested once more by the rock where we had left our rucksacks, basking in the sun, amused to find that a member of the party who had deserted us, had left his lunch packet with us by mistake. It included cheese and chocolate which we devoured with relish. Trio's inamorata, Felicity – a little less felicitous, this being her last day in Kühtai – sat beside him propped against the rock, and no one seemed in any hurry to start down. The sun had moved round to the top of the Langenthal before at last we got under weigh, taking this time the route by the gully, taught by our previous experience. A long traverse along the gully side, where a great cornice of snow, hanging threateningly above one's head, like the sword of Damocles, made one hurry, brought me back to the sleigh-path more quickly than I had expected.

It had been a wonderful but tiring morning. That afternoon I found Jopie and little Anneke practising with their guide beyond the Weiss slopes.

'Don't forget that you are coming to tea with me to-day, Jopie.'

'No. I have not forr-gotten.'

I told them of Mathews' sudden departure to Innsbruck for the day.

'Jopie, you will have to take my French lesson instead.'

She shook her head slowly.

They left me and began to practise cautious stems on the gentler slopes immediately below the path. It was only a week – a week and a day, to be exact – since I had first noticed them there. All the inexplicable and inarticulate homage of the heart had been hers in that first instant, but it had been homage offered almost to an abstraction, to the principle of beauty and grace. Now she had become a living person, to whom I could speak, make smile, watch shake her head. In love it is this first step, the transition from mere admiration, which decides all the rest. There is always a moment when we can turn back, but if we do not turn back, then everything

428

follows with the inevitability of fate. What had made me take that first step, I asked myself. A twinge of conscience prompted such speculation. I would have been at less pains to analyse the cause of my subjection if I had not wondered sometimes whether I was not behaving selfishly, even where Jopie was concerned, and whether the homage I paid to her was not really being paid at Jopie's own expense. What was such admiration worth? A sterile tribute more likely to lead to unhappiness than anything else? If she had never set eyes on me, would her visit to Kühtai have been any the less interesting? She would have lost little, and she might have avoided a few moments of vague regret, the restlessness of all those to whom love has drawn near.

To me love was inspiration. It was vision. It was the moment of poetry. In the poem which I had written the day after the dance I had admitted that the scales were weighted unfairly, that love is never fruitless where the writer is concerned, because, even if it brings him nothing else, it brings him the gift of song. But I was aware that poetry is only the chance by-product of love, and that for others, when it leads to unhappiness, there is not this compensation. Why, it may be asked, did I worry at all? Surely I should know that a girl of twenty enjoys admiration, thrives on it, and need not be heartbroken if a man pays her a little attention. But the game of flirtation is only a good one provided it is played light-heartedly and everyone is obeying its rules. It was precisely this that worried me, for I knew that I was incapable of so playing it. Pretence love, merely to while away the time, had no meaning for me. I knew that it was unfair to let Jopie see that I really cared for her. I had seen the hell to which such devotions can lead. Recently in Dublin there had been a triple tragedy where a wife had shot herself in a taxi to leave the road clear for her rival; where the girl had died in hospital of blood-poisoning following an operation, and where the man who had made them both unhappy had soon after gassed himself. I was warned against such a hell. Tender-conscienced enough to see the danger, my conscience at the same time was not quite tender enough. It scorned trifling; it dreaded love; and so it tried to hold a middle and quite inconsistent course where love was inspiration and lyric delight and poetry to one person, while remaining less than a shadow to the other.

These were the admonitions conscience whispered to me in the night watches. But they were forgotten at other times. Amusing myself on the practice-slopes now, I looked forward to the moment

429

when we would meet at the *gasthof*. Encountering Anneke by the path about half-past four, I told her:

'Anneke, I will come as soon as I see you start back.'

Climbing to some new snow above the upper fence which would give me another hundred yards or so of running, I turned and looked back. They had already started. I could see them heading slowly across the flat ground at the foot of the hill. I ran down and overtook them just as they reached the *gasthof*.

They left their skis at the back of the building and we made our way to the Austrian room. Jopie seemed tired. Her lips were a deep red, so red, that for a moment, I wondered – mistakenly – whether she had departed from custom and used colour on them. I had never seen her do so before. Nor had she now; but the fact that normally her skin seemed to glow with a kind of inner transparent radiance, as though fire ran in her veins, explained now why they would seem so red when she was pale.

She was wearing a blue wind-jacket, tucked at the waist, lent her by tall Anneke.

'Why aren't you wearing your yellow jacket?'

'I don't like it. It hurts my shoulders,' and she shook her head.

I had grown familiar with the slurred syllables of her English accent. Her voice was not so much gruff as endowed with a resonant undertone, a slight burr, which made it different from most foreign accents. Her pale blue eyes, her most striking feature, large, innocent, humorous, had a wide edging of white to them, so that for some reason they always suggested Holland to me, the country of her origin. Without any hint of coquetry she looked at you as though to assess you, and then, discovering that her confidence was justified, laughed in the same moment. It was a laugh completely in keeping with the speaking voice of its owner, the deep gurgle of an amused child, a laugh shy, and at the same time so frank, that it seemed always to set the seal on our friendship.

Three jugs of chocolate had been brought. We were the only occupants of the room. Silence fell upon us. Only Anneke seemed inclined for conversation. Looking out of the window, I saw that daylight still lingered upon the snow, which continues to give back a reflection until all light in the sky is gone. Not only Jopie was tired; I was dead tired myself. Suddenly I wondered: was the thing wearing itself out? Was I already less in love with her than I was before? Was I about to see Jopie as one sees every individual except the beloved, not as part of the soul's history, but as part of the mere background and commonplace of life?

I had brought the French books, but they lay untouched on the table. Fatigue makes everything seem flat and unprofitable. Jopie told me that she had been reading my own book.

'But there are such hard words in it.'

'What words?'

'Well – cosmogony. What is cosmogony?'

I agreed that she could hardly be expected to know English words as hard as that.

'Don't worry. Very little of it is like that. All the rest of the book is quite easy.'

Looking across the table at her, I noticed now that we shared a mannerism, that like me she had the habit of raising one eyebrow and not the other. Could I excuse myself for having fallen in love with her by the fact that there must be some natural affinity between us? Were we born under the same star?

It was astonishing really how little I knew about her. She was a mystery to me in many ways. I knew nothing of the background of her life. She had none of the egoism of those who reveal themselves easily. It was as though two people in a forest had suddenly come into the same open, sunlit glade, and were to leave it again in an instant. I had an idea that her father was dead, that she must earn her own living. There was some talk of her learning to be a fashion artist. She and homely little Anneke, that tower of good sense and discretion, had rooms in the same hostel in Amsterdam. Jopie was from The Hague. She spoke little of herself, never seemed to boast, made no claims to artistic talent, and, beyond the fact that she was cultivated, as her French and English showed, and that she must have some athletic prowess to have been sent to England with a hockey team, her whole life was hidden from me. All I knew had come to me by accident or as a matter of inference. Her sense of humour was the one characteristic which transpired naturally and easily, as though she found in it the means of escaping from a shyness which would otherwise have been intolerable.

The gramophone began to play, and I heard again the tune that had stirred me so strangely. Leaving Anneke to the French books we went into the next room and began to dance. Both of us were still wearing our ski-boots, but it was the custom with all the guides and many of the visitors to dance in boots at this time of day, and sometimes even after dinner. Heavy and clumsy as it had seemed at first, I had soon grown accustomed to them, and enjoyed dancing in them, remembering how once before, returning from a night spent in a mountain hut, I had come upon the harvest celebrations of a high Alpine farm, and danced in boots upon a wooden platform to the hurdy-gurdy strains of three Swiss instrumentalists.

Trio was looking after the records, but he showed himself less quick in identifying my musical preferences than the carpenter with the stutter who waxed our skis. I had only to say, 'Vundervul' to the latter and he had instantly produced the German song record I wanted, the one which had pleased me the first night almost as much as the haunting melody which the whole world knew. But to Trio 'Vundervul' meant nothing. He professed to know no such tune. 'Can't you hum it for me?' 'No, I can't.' Suddenly, later in the evening, the air came back to me, and I hastened off to the pantry to tell Trio that I now remembered it. 'Listen, Trio, it's like this.' A mere bar or two was sufficient and he found it at once. Jopie and I danced to it.

'What does it mean, Jopie?'

'Oh, you girl-boy or something.' She made a face to imply that so far as the words went they were pretty good nonsense.

A foreigner and an English girl in black ski-trousers, dumpy and made-up, but clever enough, seized by some whim, took the floor and began to give an exhibition of a South American dance. There was much stamping of feet, raising of arms, and snapping of fingers. I enjoyed the music and I approved the perfect time they kept, but looking at Jopie beside me I saw her make a little pout of disgust.

'You don't like it?'

She shook her head.

We were sitting in a corner at a table pushed back like the rest to make room for the dancing. The room was hot and I leaned over to fling open the window behind us. The night was perfectly still; the moon had not yet risen, but the sky held thousands of stars. We could see the dark outline of the mountain heights which closed in the valley. Directly over one of the peaks three stars outstandingly bright rose upward in a straight line, part of a constellation familiar to me, though I could not name it for the moment.

We had deserted Anneke for some little time. Once she had strayed anxiously to the door and, peering short-sightedly across the room, had retreated again. Now she reappeared and came towards us. I felt ashamed of my rudeness.

'Anneke, will you dance with me?'

She was a better dancer than Jopie, but this was the only time I had danced with her to-day. At seven o'clock the maids came in to lay the tables. Slow, easy-going, good-humoured, they showed no impatience now or at any other time.

We stopped dancing. Going across to the annexe to fetch something, I noticed the white sheepskin coat lying across the foot of my bed, and, remembering how warm the room was in which she had been, and that Jopie had once expressed curiosity to see it, I caught it up and returned with it thrown over my arm.

'Here's the sheepskin coat, Jopie. You can wear it back to the Dortmünder if you like.'

She put it on. It was a little long for her, reaching almost to her ankles, and the shoulders were too high and sloping, as they always had been from the moment when the fleeces were cut and sewn in the bazaar at Jerusalem. Otherwise it fitted well, with its gold creamy fleece as lining, thick and curling; the outer sheepskin crudely patterned by the many joins of the separate skins.

'I can carry both lots of skis. Give them to me.'

With a pair on either shoulder, crossed so that they rested on one another, it was easy enough, and we set forth along the narrow path to the Dortmünder. Jopie walked slowly, with that slightly aloof and very straight carriage which I had grown to know so well. This and the transparently blue and virginal eyes with a note of almost mute appeal in them – as though she distrusted not so much you as herself – were a part of any mental picture I formed of her when she was not there. The moon had just risen, and there was enough light on the path to avoid that hesitation of step which in complete darkness makes one seem to be groping, or fumbling one's way rather than finding it. At the Dortmünder the bearded old caretaker, looking more like a mediæval forester than ever, was carrying an armful of wood up from the basement. He glanced curiously at Jopie's white-garbed figure, and watched her as she took it off.

'Tell him that the coat came from Jerusalem, Jopie.'

'*Yerusalem? Zo!*' and the old man's eyes gleamed for a moment with interest.

He reminded me of the pilgrims whom I had seen in the Holy City, listening to the bell-toned choir of male voices in the Russian church at midnight.

In the sitting-room Sonia was asleep by the big stove, covered with a rug. Tall Anneke told us that she had the sore throat that they all seemed to have got, and was out of humour, Raines having forgotten to send her a message that he had had to go to Innsbruck and could not come to tea.

'She is sorry for herself. We are all sorry for ourselves. I have the sore throat too,' and tall Anneke smiled wryly in spite of her misfortunes.

'Here is your coat. Thank you ver-ry much for it.'

The old man opened the heavy door for me, and let me out. I would be later than usual for dinner. As I drew nearer the *gasthof* I could hear the noise of sleigh-bells. The post must have come, and Mathews would have come up with it. There were the mules stretching out tired heads in front of the doorway. One of them shook itself so vigorously that it seemed as if it would shake its entire harness off, and the fur-capped driver, carrying a case up the steps, turned and shouted at it in anger.

Mathews had gone across to our room. He was cold and stiff after the long drive.

'Well, how did you like it?'

'I enjoyed the drive up from Gries by starlight.'

'Did you achieve anything in Innsbruck?'

'I don't know. I think so. The Consul will do the best he can. Scheiber seems grateful.'

'How did you like Raines?'

'Better as the day went on.'

'Our Himalayan friend refers to him as an ugly piece of work.'

'He would; they haven't much in common. He would have liked him even less if he had heard Raines confessing to me that he got drunk on New Year's Eve at the dance and kissed nearly every woman he danced with, including the poisonous Frenchwoman, who was the cause of all our trouble to-day.'

I laughed and made a face.

'I am glad I don't get ·drunk, if it leads to such catholicity of taste.'

There was a pause, then I said: 'Did he mention that he had forgotten to tell Sonia that he would not be taking tea with her?'

'No. We spoke of her, and then I said something about Jopie.'

'Oh – and what did Raines say?'

'He said, "Yes, she's very pretty too, but there's some other fellow admires her." '

Mathews chuckled. ' "Beauty is in the eye of the beholder." It's

434

what you are always telling me. You can't expect Raines to be too rhapsodical about Jopie. She's too simple, too natural. Besides, remember, to you Sonia is just a rather handsome, round-faced Dutch girl with fine eyes.'

We went across to dinner. When I came out, the post had been sorted, and among the letters on the board I noticed Scrooge's copy of the *Observer*. He had left the previous day.

'I'm sure he wouldn't mind if I opened it. He always used to lend it to me when he was here,' and I returned to the dining-room to read it.

Life occasionally springs a pleasant surprise on us, timing it at the moment when it will have the most force, just as an indulgent parent plans some delight for a child. Part of the art of living is to retain sufficient resilience to appreciate these moments, as the child does, when they come. Such a moment was in store for me now. As I opened the paper, my eye fell almost immediately on a full-length review of the book I had last published. I was not expecting any notice so soon, and here was one to please any author. My work had been lucky enough to fall into the hands of Basil de Selincourt, a critic completely in sympathy with the theme and its treatment, and he had praised the book as generously as critics can praise, when they really approve.

I read down the column in much the same mood that a man might read a letter from a lawyer in Australia informing him that he had been left a fortune. Mine now was to have had my book completely understood. Leigh Hunt called time to witness that Jenny had kissed him, and that this was to be recorded among the sweets that life had vouchsafed him. In the same way I record this moment – leaning over the dinner-table in the Alpengasthof and reading wholly generous praise, as amongst my life's sweets, and worthy to be remembered. The East has argued that since we are only happy when we cease to desire – that is, in the moment of attainment when, for the briefest instant, we possess – and therefore cease to wish to possess – the easiest and indeed the only road to happiness is never to desire anything, so retaining permanently that detachment, that release from volition, which achievement can only give for a second. But, though I admit that we tire soon of our toys, and that even achievement does not satisfy us for long, that we ignore past pleasures, see success only as vanity, and fame as a bauble, behaving generally like discontented children who can be wheedled into good humour, but fall to yelling again unless some new distraction is forthcoming – all of which points to the ephemeral nature of our ambitions – yet it seems to me that the reflection is rather on us, who tire so soon of our sweets, and grow ungrateful for them, than on the sweets themselves.

The moment that I have been describing was assuredly a good one, and I shall not shrug my shoulders at it now. I went to share my triumph with Mathews, and sat there at his table in the Austrian room, chatting with him a good deal later than was my custom. I was pleased, excited. About eleven o'clock I went across to our bedroom, leaving him to dance. The night, another of those silent starry nights that I had grown to expect in this place, was so beautiful that it seemed a crime to sleep yet. I flung open the door of the veranda, and drew out one of the folding chairs in which we basked in daytime. There, with my feet up, a rug and the sheepskin coat over my knees, I sat gazing at the mountains immediately opposite with their patterned effect of alternate dark and light patches of rock and snow. Those same three stars, which had brought themselves to my notice so vividly at dusk, had moved in the five-hour interval in an arc across the heavens so that, no longer vertical, they lay now a short distance above the horizon, like a fiery arrow on the point of vanishing into Switzerland. It was freezing hard, but the night had no harshness, it seemed only calm and lovely and amazingly still. I sat there for a long time, filled with a deep contentment. Life was good; it had its harsh moments, its terrible moments, but we would never revile it for these, if we remembered its grandeur and loveliness, its kindness in gentler moods. It was well-disposed; sooner or later, if one were steadfast, it relented; it had laughter as well as sorrow; as well as struggle, it held success.

Next morning, contrary to all custom, Mathews and I skied together. The classes had scattered, and, choosing 'the Wizard Run,' we mounted the gully and climbed slowly to the plateau above. The weather seemed about to change; there was less sun, and white fleecy clouds were gathering and massing to the south. But the snow itself remained perfect, crisp and powdered. We did not linger long on the plateau. Choosing as far as possible untracked snow, we ran swiftly down, taking a line right under the cornice, cutting one long hissing traverse the whole way as though riding a series of waves.

On our way back we arranged with some friends to do the 'Plum Pudding' run with them after lunch. It was an easy climb after the first ten minutes and did not take long.

As we got back to the *gasthof* we noticed a figure in a long grey chasseur's cloak gloomily pacing the pathway at the back.

'There's the inquisitor. I begin to feel quite sorry for him.'

The previous day an Austrian soldier had appeared at the *gasthof*. He had been sent up to investigate the events of New Year's Eve, and was to remain with us till further orders. Shunned by all, he spent his time wandering around, speaking to no one. He looked peculiarly stupid for the role chosen for him, and did not seem to be enjoying it. Since all the protagonists had fled, it was not going to be easy for him to collect evidence. Mathews told me that he had interrogated a number of the servants, but that their different versions conflicted.

'No one is telling the truth. They are all lying, afraid lest they should get Scheiber or themselves into trouble.'

The wretched man seemed to feel himself *de trop*. Prowling about the snow, taking a little exercise round the *gasthof* at midday, he looked almost as much out of place as a London policeman would have looked in the same setting. One longed to give him a pair of skis and tell him to enjoy himself. Everyone else was busily embarked on the search for pleasure. He alone, the stern slave of duty, had nothing to do.

We lunched and went across to the annexe. Once there, however, Mathews elected to remain reading on his bed, tired after a succession of late nights, when he would return to our room at one in the morning and go to bed by the light of an electric torch, waking me, generally, despite this act of consideration.

'Tell them I won't go. I'm dead beat.'

'All right. I don't think I'll go either,' and, shouting from the veranda to the friends, who were calling for us, that we had both changed our minds, I returned to my own book. Ten minutes later I flung it down.

'I think I will go after all.'

So little of our holiday remained that every moment on skis seemed doubly precious. We had decided to leave on Sunday and sleep one night at Innsbruck. It was Mathews' decision, and I had at first opposed it. A day in Innsbruck was a day wasted, but he insisted that, if we skied down to Gries, as we intended to do, we would be too tired to go on that night by train.

I set off in pursuit. My friends were slow climbers; it would be easy to overtake them. Only Mary and the indefatigable red-haired schoolboy from the annexe had gone in the end. It was Mary who had asked me, that first night, why I had suddenly taken it into my head to dance. I liked her, with her broad brow, her calm, steady brown eyes and her serene disposition. Indeed, I had grown to know and like all that party, who were by no means as superficial as my first, equally superficial, judgment of them had supposed. The group included Paynton, the writer, the irrepressible Peggy, and a young naval officer who showed as much interest in classical music as in things nautical. When I had got to know them better I had found them thoughtful and considerate, rather than noisy and self-assured. Peggy, gay, inconsequent, a little uncertain of herself, fundamentally good-natured, had won my heart by a single remark made one day when her companions were having a metaphysical discussion in the lounge after tea. I had listened to them for some time from a table nearby and eventually joined them. The air was full of contentions, bows drawn at a venture, such as: 'There can't be a God.' 'No, there is a God, but He's an Impersonal Force' – all the airy speculations in fact with which youth challenges the immensity of the unknown. Peggy had listened to it all in silence. Then, at last, she made her solitary contribution to the debate: 'Well, anyway, I believe in God, and I don't mind what anyone says.' 'So do I, Peggy, and say my prayers to Him every day of my life, even though He may be infinitely beyond personal interference in such petty details; though why – since consciousness is the highest thing we encounter here – we should think our Deity incapable of consciousness I don't know. Impersonality is an even greater limiting of godhead than personality; surely the "Impersonal" can contain the "Personal" as one of its aspects?'

Her companions might follow the line of my reasoning. She certainly did not. But I admired the courage which had made her suddenly and defiantly proclaim her faith. I had revised my opinion of her completely. Was it the serenity of life here amidst the snow that made it easier for us to overcome our prejudices?

I hastened after the two in front until I overtook them.

'I decided to come in the end, Mary. I believe it's going to snow; we'll have to hurry.'

The white clouds had moved lower down the mountain, and it was snowing already on the heights. It looked as though it might reach us at any moment. At the rocks we found a party of newcomers to the *gasthof* resting after their climb. I advised them not to delay; the moment the snow began it would be impossible to judge the gradient. We set off ourselves almost immediately. Less than ten minutes took us down what it had taken nearly an hour to climb; the light was bad, but the snow was perfect, and presently we dipped over the brow of the hill to see with relief the black fence in the valley below us.

It was not yet four o'clock; too soon to go in. Mathews had said he might go down to the Dortmünder to recover his copy of the life of Nijinsky from tall Anneke. I had given him a message for Jopie. Would she come up for tea? Now, as I pottered about on the slopes the far side of the *gasthof*, I thought I caught sight of her. A few yards further on and my surmise was proved correct. I had only to turn my skis downhill to join her. But I had miscalculated the ground and, running a little too far, found myself with my first ski safely across the deep, narrow crevasse in which the stream ran, and my second one stuck midway. Straddled across the stream, if was impossible for me to move without a very lively chance of falling in.

I called to Jopie: 'You must come to my rescue. I've no wish for an ice bath.'

She came.

'Don't laugh. I can't move. If I do move I shall fall in. I have undone the clip, but I can't get my foot out of the ski. Can you help me?'

She stooped down and presently managed to extricate my foot from the ski-binding, blushing a little and laughing not unkindly at my predicament.

'Well done. I was in that stream in another moment if you had not been there. Has Mathews given you my message? Will you come and have chocolate with me at five? We can change out of our ski-clothes before and dance afterwards.'

'I told your friend I would not come. We are all coming up after dinner and we will dance then. Won't that do?'

'I don't want to dance then. I shall be dead tired, and in any case I may have to pack.'

'But your packing cannot take you all that time. Will you eat so much dinner?'

It was the first that I had heard of their coming in the evening, and with the jealousy that preferred exclusive possession to sharing her with her friends, I wanted her now. We argued the point a little. Eventually she agreed that she would come. She would change, we would dance, and at the same time we could decide the evening programme. The other girls had said something about bringing up a round game and playing it.

'Come at five. I shall be packing, so I may be a minute or two late.'

Five had only just struck when I entered the Austrian room and looked round, hoping to see her. She was not there. Mathews was its only occupant. He looked up from his book.

'I saw Jopie and I was to tell you that she's not coming.'

'Yes, but I have seen her since then and she will come after all.'

The maid came and Mathews ordered his chocolate.

'Do you want me to order yours, Monk?'

'No. I'll wait.'

Sitting by the little window, I could see anyone who came to the door on that side of the *gasthof*. A dozen times as someone passed I looked up quickly from my book, but it was never Jopie. Mathews sipped his chocolate. Presently he consulted his watch.

'That clock is slow. Nearly ten minutes slow.'

The clock continued to tick noisily despite this exposure of its shortcomings, which had lessened still further the chance that Jopie might be coming at all. I moved over to the stove. I found it impossible to concentrate on my book. Every step outside drew my attention away from the page. The little window had fogged now from the heat of the room, and it was growing dark outside. The big, burly, mild-voiced Somerset doctor came in, sat down, took his spectacles from their case, put them on and began to write a letter. He wrote slowly like a child engaged on an imposition.

I continued to read moodily. Why had I been such a fool as to tell her that I might be late? It was an idiotic remark to have made, after urging her so tyrannically to come. Any girl would be annoyed at being treated so casually. Even so, Jopie was not the sort of person to take offence easily. There must be another reason. I decided it was little Anneke. Yes, without a doubt. She had probably said, 'He's too lazy to come down to the Dortmünder. Too lazy to dance after dinner. Don't go.' Jealousy breathes on the mirror and immediately distorts everything in it. I began to feel the impatient resentment of a child against the probably innocent Anneke, who had shown me nothing but kindness.

I looked at the clock a dozen times at least. I would deliberately wait what seemed to me a quarter of an hour at least, and then look up. Incredible, the hands had only advanced a few minutes. Once I rose, rubbed the window clear, looked out on the waste expanse of snow, saw that it was completely deserted, and returned to my seat.

440

'Aren't you going to have any chocolate?'

'No. I don't want any yet.'

Mathews smiled. It was part of my irritation that he should be the witness of my impatience.

It was now half-past five. She was not coming. Had something happened to her? I debated whether I should put my pride in my pocket, go down to the Dortmünder and find out. But to do so was – was what? – was to confess that I was even more in love than I admitted to myself, was to surrender completely to a mood that I imagined hitherto I had kept sternly in control. Only yesterday afternoon I had asked myself, was I on the road to being cured. Now my acute disappointment gave the clearest negative to that question. But to go to the Dortmünder in search of Jopie would be importunate. It would be almost abject abasement. After all, I would see her this evening; they were all coming up. I would have no tea, but I would stay and read. I settled sulkily to my book, though reading meant that I had to read every sentence twice over – sentences from which attention so easily wandered.

About a quarter to six I saw Mathews glance towards the door. For the fiftieth time – and without expectancy now – I looked quickly up. There was Jopie standing in the doorway. She had not changed; she was wearing her black ski-trousers and a bright green woollen cardigan of very soft wool, a contrast to her fair hair which was slightly ruffled. The miraculous had happened. She had come after all.

She must have seen the delight in my face as I jumped from the bench and greeted her. She offered no excuse, and I was too overjoyed at seeing her to have heard it if she had.

'There you are at last. I've waited for you. I'm absolutely starving. Alister has had his tea because he said you weren't coming. Come along and have something.'

She came to the table and sat down, loosened the scarf that she had round her neck, laid her gloves on the stove, and asked the maid, for whom I had rung hastily, if she could have a hot citron instead of the usual coffee or chocolate.

'It will do my throat good. You see, I have got the sore throat that they have all had.'

The hot lemonade was brought, and she began to drink it from the funnel-shaped glass. Presently she agreed to eat something.

'Cake? Yes, chocolate cake. Tell them chocolate cake, Mathews. It is the only kind she likes. Jopie, you are foolish. You say you have a sore throat and yet you haven't even changed out of your wet ski-boots. I am going over to our room to fetch you throat lozenges, the kind we gave the man in the next room when he was in bed for two days and coughed most of the night. He said they were splendid. And I shall bring you a pair of slippers and dry socks.'

'But I have changed my stockings. It is only my boots are a little wet.'

I went across to the annexe and returned quickly.

'Here you are, Jopie. Lozenges, de Régnier, and vapour rub. Rub your throat well with it to-night. You can give me back the jar to-morrow.'

'Jopie can keep yours, Monk. I have a jar of my own.'

'I would give Jopie almost anything in the world, but not my vapour rub. She can use some of it, but I won't give her the jar.'

'But I tell you I have some, Monk.'

Matthews was shocked at my niggardliness. Only a direct promise that his was henceforward to be mine could shake me.

Writing slowly at his table, the doctor must have heard our bickering, and been amused by it. He looked up from his letter now, and asked some patient question in his rather husky voice. Alister gave him the information he wanted, and then rose, saying he must go over to the annexe.

'Now, Jopie, you are in charge of his lesson. I must pack.'

The tea things were pushed away, and the book opened between us.

Now that she knew me better, Jopie had overcome her diffidence, and would venture an occasional correction of my pronunication. For some reason, I had got into the habit of pronouncing the word *soleil* as 'soyaye,' imagining the first 'l' to be mute, and this eccentricity always amused her. Since the word was a favourite with de Régnier, who is always referring to sunshine – the triumphant sunshine of an Athenian morning, or the wistful melancholy sunshine of late afternoon along the pathways of some château park – the correction had frequently to be made.

'Don't you like the poems, Jopie? Every word is grave and measured and deliberate.'

'Yes, but his music is too much the same. And it is always the same rhythm.'

'It is the same rhythm. But what a wonderful use he makes of it. It is as though one were being carried forward on a stream. The very pace of the words seems to evoke the mood he wants,' and I went on

442

to defend de Régnier on the grounds that in any case this was only one of his books.

'I can find you something quite different – even in this book.'

It was not so easy to find, but when I had found it I was rewarded by an enchanting smile. Though it added nothing to my feelings towards her and could add nothing, since the latter had sprung into existence completely mature, and fully armoured in the fashion that the myth has made Athene spring from the head of Zeus, nevertheless it pleased me – or I am mistaken and did I even trouble to be aware of it? – to discover that, despite her native diffidence, she was intelligent and understanding where the poems by the Frenchman were concerned, and at the same time that she had courage to express her own opinions. But even this, it must be confessed – the fact that her intelligence from time to time transpired easily and incidentally – was an irrelevance so far as I was concerned; for the truth is it could add nothing to an assessment already made, add nothing to it, and take nothing from it, for love determines its own evaluations according to a measure of its own. She was at her loveliest and most natural. Indeed, it could be said of her that she was always natural, and that part of her charm was her apparent unconsciousness of any reason why she should be thought charming. 'If I had said to her, 'Only Leonardo could have drawn you, Jopie, because only he knew how to make the beauty of a face seem something at once fugitive and eternal, as transitory as the shadows on a surface of a lake, and at the same time as absolute and certain as a law of nature,' she would have laughed and blushed crimson and I would have seen in her eyes an instant reproach not merely for having praised her extravagantly but for having spoken at all. A girl like Sonia lived conscious of admiration – it was inevitable that she should – but to Jopie it was just a pleasant surprise to be admired, one to be accepted and yet hardly admitted in so many words. Our whole friendship was based on this recognition of the necessity for silence. Little Anneke loved Jopie. I felt sure of that. There was something almost protective in her attitude towards her. If she had suspected me of laying deliberate siege to Jopie's heart for my own selfish amusement, she would have hated me. But she did not hate me, probably because she realised that the Jopie I loved was the same to whom she herself was devoted, and she forgave me because she could see enough reverence, enough reserve, in my attitude to justify her forgiveness.

443

And yet every moment was precious to me now as moments can only be precious to those who love. She had come, she was here beside me, she was mine to look at, and this commonplace so far from being a commonplace in my eyes seemed rather a miraculous dispensation of Providence. The very fact that I knew I possessed it made me loth to exercise it too often; so that I would keep my eyes on the book when I longed to look up and see the curve of that flushed cheek and catch a sudden expression of flower-like grace as she turned her face towards mine. It was not only the curve of the cheek that was lovely, but the glowing transparency of that flushed complexion, radiant as though youth and health and vitality had lifted it on to another plane of being, the plane on which we might all move if we had not lost some fundamental innocence intended for us. Leaning back against the stove, her head resting against the tiles, she seemed at once aware of my love, and, like myself, loth to admit it. The little room, its warmth a contrast to the fogged window pane and the snow outside, the book between us on the table, all added to the sense of intimacy so that, differently circumstanced, it might well have seemed the moment when, 'Lovers may sit together and say out all things are in their hearts.' Indeed, though I had said nothing I seemed to have said all, in just the same way that, when we had first danced together, I seemed, in the moment that her hand touched mine, by a direct intimation of sheer reverence and delight, to have admitted that I was in love with her.

We did not dance now. It was too late. The maids were already laying the tables in the other room and in any case neither of us seemed inclined to leave the comfort of the stove. Mathews rejoined us, cheerful with the consciousness of duty performed.

'I warn you, Monk, I am not going to do your packing for you. If you're not ready to-morrow after lunch I shall go without you.'

'I shall be ready. Don't worry.'

For the hundredth time, I noticed over the doorway the wooden board carved to resemble a scroll, with its four lines of brightly painted lettering. It was in the old-fashioned Gothic lettering, adorned with great wreathed capitals. For days I had looked across at it, wondering what the lines might mean. Now I asked Mathews. He read it aloud in German:

'Heute geh' ich, komm' ich wieder
Singen wir ganz andere Lieder –
Wo so viel sich hoffen lässt,
Ist der Abschied ja ein Fest.

'Do you know what it means, Jopie?'
She smiled and nodded her head.
'Alister, you must translate it.'

'To-day I go, I come again,
Let us sing quite different songs.
Where there is so much to be hoped for
Parting is really a joy.'

Where there was much to be hoped for parting was a joy? But if there was nothing to be hoped for – what was it, then?

It would be untrue to say that I felt at this time that there was absolutely nothing to be hoped for from the future. I had persuaded myself that in some way or other loyalties that seemed to threaten one another would be reconciled. I would not lose Jopie completely. She would come to England. My wife would invite her to Swanage. Just as Shelley assumed that his romantic love for Emilia Viviani in no sense endangered his love for Mary, and that nothing was easier to envisage than a state of ideal perfection in which three absolutely honest people would unite in a common devotion to one another – the whole of Epipsychidion being based on such an assumption – so, having once salved my conscience from the reproach of treachery or double dealing, I had allowed myself to dream that a situation, which I knew might invite disaster, could, if there were complete honesty on all sides, be solved.

But while one half of the mind comforted itself with this vague hopefulness, the other was fully aware that every moment spent in Jopie's company now was so much snatched from an inexorable foe. Parting held no promise for me. It was rather an unpleasantness to be forgotten so long as it was possible to forget. Time would have no more pity on me than on any other. I saw Mathews looking at me and doing his best not to smile. The ironic appropriateness of the words on the board over the doorway was obviously as plain to him as it was to me.

'How many of you are coming up from the Dortmünder this evening?'

'We are all coming. And they suggest we play games and do not dance all the time.'

'Yes, we might do that.'

Mathews got up from his bench.

'We'll have to move. They want to lay the tables here.'

I collected the French books while Jopie gathered her things together; her striped red-and-white woollen gloves from the top of the stove, where they had been drying, and her coat and scarf from the bench beside her.

'Jopie, leave your own coat here. I am going to lend you the sheepskin one. You can keep it and wear it back this evening when you come. It is warmer than your own.'

I had brought it with me when I had returned from the annexe. We went out into the corridor and I took it from its peg, and hung up her own in its place. I watched her as she put it on and turned up the high collar in front of a looking-glass, displaying for the first time since I had known her a touch of feminine vanity. It was excusable. When she turned away from the glass towards me, her eyes shining, she looked like the heroine of some German fairy tale. The very white coat, its collar forming almost a hood behind her head, showed her face framed against the golden curls of the fleece. Her flushed countenance, her fair hair, the vivid contrast of the brightly-coloured red scarf knotted about her neck and the red-and-white striped gloves made her look so lovely that it seemed to me that the coat had been bought in Jerusalem merely for this predestined moment.

We went out and down the steps. I walked with her as far as the little stream. There I turned back.

'Till this evening, Jopie. *A b' tôt*, as the Jerseyman says.'

I returned to my room and began to pack. The room was hot, the radiator covered with ski clothes and socks; sealskins hung across the door of the wardrobe; and, though Mathews had created order out of chaos where his own possessions were concerned, mine still littered the room and had to be sorted. Seated on one of the high, square wooden stools which took the place of chairs, I sorted papers, tore up some and packed others. When at last I had finished and looked at my watch I saw that it was long past eight o'clock. I went across to the *gasthof*. Most of the guests had finished dinner. The maid, slow in bringing me mine, looked at me with aggrieved disapproval, for she was the one with the white shoes for whom things were always wrong. Eltham had left. I was once more alone

446

at my table. The courses appeared one after the other, and I ate them in solitary abstraction, wondering whether the sleighs had yet come up and the post arrived. Mathews would have finished his meal long ago, would have put his feet up along the bench and would be deep in the book until the arrival of the Dortmünder party roused him from it.

But the sleighs were late. I went across to my room for something, and the first object to meet my gaze when I returned was the sheepskin coat hanging from one of the pegs in the great hall. In the Austrian room I found Alister, the two Annekes, Tom, Jopie, Sonia and Raines, gathered round a table in one corner, laughing a good deal and playing some game with dice.

'Isn't it rather like Ludo?'

'But it *is* Ludo!' they cried with one accord and more laughter.

They had found the board somewhere and were using chess pawns as pieces.

'We're having partners. You're playing with Jopie. Sit there. You take it in turn to shake the dice.'

Jopie had not wasted her time while waiting for my arrival. She had built a 'barrier,' which was holding the whole game up for the others.

'Well done. We shall keep them there indefinitely.'

But the barrier had presently to be broken. Swift vengeance followed, and our pieces were sent home by the very players we had kept waiting so long. Seated opposite us were Alister and little Anneke, who with a series of lucky sixes proceeded to win the game. Tiring of it someone suggested that we should play *vingt-et-un* instead.

'But we have no counters.'

The difficulty was solved by our collecting all the bundles of little wooden toothpicks from the tables in the dining-room, breaking them in half and using them as counters. Raines won the bank and we began to play.

But unless one is a born gambler *vingt-et-un* is a stupid game. There is no play, no skill, only chance and the instinct to take a risk. Even then the issue is so soon settled, the gamble so soon over, that it becomes monotonous. I longed for the moment when the gramophone would start. Never had it been so late. Was it because Trio's girl, Felicity, had left that morning and he was disconsolate? At last, about a quarter to ten, we saw him go into the office and heard the strains of music from next door.

'Jopie, will you dance this with me?'

We went into the next room and began to dance. The game of *vingt-et-un* continued. From time to time two of the party would leave it, but the game went on and we joined it or not as we liked. Alister had deserted it to dance with a tall dark Dutch girl who had come to the *gasthof* a day or two before with her mother, a new acquaintance in whom he had begun to show a certain interest. The room was less full than usual, the shaded lamps with their paper decorations threw the glow of their reflection upon our faces as we passed beneath them.

We danced silently. Jopie was wearing a brown knitted cardigan or blouse, with a bow of ribbon at the neck. All our dances were together, except one with little Anneke, a first-rate dancer, but nevertheless a 'duty dance' for me. About eleven o'clock the music ceased and we returned to the Austrian room to talk, laugh, eat crystallised fruits, discuss the Russian ballet, and chaff tall Anneke about her excellent English.

Through the little window between the Austrian room and the dining-room we beckoned to Alister to rejoin us. When he appeared bringing his partner with him there were protests that this made our numbers uneven, but I insisted that she must come, and we made room for her at the table. Alister and I ordered two litres of hot Glühwein. It was brought in glass jugs swathed in napkins, and we covered one while we poured out the other, a drink delicious and mellow, as characteristic of the mountains as the resinous smell of pines and larch trees.

'Jopie, it is nearly midnight. Am I going to see you back to the Dortmünder?'

She seemed to think that the others would be going soon and that she could accompany them. We went out into the big hall where the white coat was hanging. I helped her into it and turned up the hooded collar about her ears so that I could not see her head at all. It had been agreed that she should keep it again to-night, and that I should get it from her in the morning.

'Are you sure you don't want it?'

'No, a rug thrown over my feet will do as well.'

She felt in her bag and produced the jar of vapour rub.

'Thank you so much for this. I nearly forgot to give it to you.'

'No, you can keep it, Jopie. It's my Christmas present to you.'

She stooped down to fasten her brown snow-boots and I said, 'Let's have a look at the night.'

At the far end of the corridor towards the Dortmünder, a door opened on to the outer porch where a slatted wooden platform gave visitors an opportunity to knock the snow from their boots when they returned from ski-ing. We opened it and went out on to the platform. The night was absolutely still, but the sky had clouded and no stars pencilled its immense blackness. We stood there a minute. With very little encouragement, I should have kissed her. There are those to whom a kiss means nothing – and if it means nothing one is tempted to ask why trouble to give it? But let it mean anything, let it mean, as it would have meant in my case, all that the heart has held in trembling silence for days, and it becomes the Rubicon which, if we cross it, may change our whole fate. Perhaps her instinct told her this, all that was protective and wise and loyal to the moment, for she said quietly, 'I must see what the others are doing.' I followed her back to the little room, and she leant over the table, still in the white coat, to study with the rest of the party the map of some ski-tour. Putting my hand for a moment over the red-gloved hand on the table, I said,

'Good night, Jopie, I'll come down early in the morning and get the coat.'

I returned to the annexe. For another hour Alister remained talking to his new friend, but I had fallen into so deep a sleep by the time he returned that for the first time his advent did not awaken me.

I was up at seven o'clock. There was a great deal to be done. For, though we ourselves were not going to ski down to Gries until the afternoon, our luggage must go by sleigh that morning. We washed, shaved and then began to pack furiously. Anna of the mild grey-blue eyes and the calm rounded brow arrived to offer help and to urge us to be quick. One sleigh was going now, almost immediately, she told us, and it would take our suitcases. The other would leave at ten o'clock and all the rest of our kit must be ready by then. For the first time since our coming, her 'goodbye' would have been appropriate, but now she did not say it, lamenting instead to Mathews in German that we were departing, and insisting that we must come back again next year. She could do little to help us. Planted forlornly at the top of the stairs, she watched us through the doorway, looking at us with sad eyes, until our frenzied efforts to crush our possessions into some receptacle or other were too much for her, and she was forced to smile. It was pleasant to think that we had made real friends even in so short a time. Herr and Frau Scheiber seemed genuinely sorry that we were going. Scheiber had been down to Innsbruck the previous day and had returned in much better spirits. He seemed convinced that we had helped to save him from the wrath of the politicians. Frau Scheiber had made us a present of two large cans of the mountain berries which we used to eat at meals with our meat, and which had won our approval. They would serve to remind us of Kühtai when we were far away. Once again Alister's friendliness seemed to have established a more natural relationship between host and stranger than was customary, and, though in my case there was the bar of language, I had grown to feel the same myself.

'At ten! Do you hear what she says? The second sleigh goes at ten, and everything we have must go on it. We must have nothing but our skis this afternoon.'

Mathews had more or less finished, and had been across to the *gasthof* to have breakfast, but I was still packing frantically.

'What can I do to help you?'

'Nothing. I have practically finished. We shall need our sealskins this morning, so I am keeping mine out. My white coat is down at the Dortmünder. I'll leave my rucksack empty for it. Get these things down and don't let the sleigh go till I have returned.'

Looking out of the window on the landing, I saw that the day was still uncertain. In the half light of dawn the little chapel which stood on slightly higher ground at the back of the *gasthof*, separated from it by the pathway, looked quainter and lonelier than ever. Centuries old, as old probably as the hunting lodge itself, it seemed to confront the waste of snow about it with a stoic resolution and indifference. It was the smallest place of worship I had ever seen, no larger than the porch of an ordinary church, blunt at one end, wedge-shaped at the other, so that with its miniature wooden steeple rising from the centre of its pointed roof it looked not unlike a slice of Christmas cake with a sprig of holly stuck on top of it. Mass was celebrated here on Sunday, I believe, when some of the staff of the *gasthof*, or a peasant or two from down the valley towards St. Sigmund or Haggen, would attend; but I had never seen either priest or layman enter it. Only now, in the half light of the morning, I noticed Alister's friend, the tall, dark girl with the dark intense expression, leave it and cross the pathway back to the *gasthof*.

I had put on my steel knee-splint, which I should be wearing for the next twelve hours. It was nearly five to ten. I was still breakfastless, but that could wait. Packing at least was finished, and I ran down to the ski-room, put on my skis, and skied joyously down to the Dortmünder. It was terribly late. Propping my skis against the wall, I ran straight to the lower door which opened into the room where their skis were kept, and came face to face with Jopie who was just setting out to bring me my coat.

'You were so late. I thought I had better.'

'Splendid. Now you can come back and talk to me, while I have my breakfast. I haven't had any yet.'

I knelt down on the floor, and rolled the coat up quickly.

'You know your coat has a tear in it?'

'Yes, I know that. I did it yesterday. It caught on a nail.'

Looking up, I saw a smile of intense relief light up her face.

'Oh, I was afraid that I might have done it.'

She looked like a child that has nerved itself to make a confession, while at the same time fearing that its word may be doubted. She seemed too relieved to mind that she was blushing furiously, the colour mounting nearly to her temples.

'Have you your ski-jacket?' I asked her.

'Yes. I am just going to get it.'

When she returned wearing Anneke's dark blue jacket drawn in at the waist, the white coat was already in the rucksack and on my back. She had brought her skis and we went out to where mine were leaning against the wall. We kicked our toes into the toe-pieces and drew the clips tight. It had been cloudy and foggy the night before, when I went across to the annexe, looking still as though it might snow. But the morning had belied this and was improving all the time. A light covering of fleecy clouds was breaking up to show more and more blue sky. The air was frosty and bracing. Our luck had held, for to ski down to Gries in falling snow would have been no fun.

We returned along the path to the Alpengasthof. On the far side by the stable the sleighs were getting ready to start. Two of them held guests who, like ourselves, were leaving that day; while a third, made of flat rough boards, was piled high with luggage. Alister had seen our own tied on, and he seized my rucksack now and gave it to the driver. I had barely time to add the berry jam Frau Scheiber had given us, and cram it in on top of the coat.

'That's a load off my mind! At last I can breakfast with a clear conscience. Come along, Jopie.'

We went to the Austrian room, for they were already laying the tables for lunch in the other. Mathews came with us, sitting down at a table near by to write a letter, while Jopie, having refused the offer of a cup of coffee, leant back against the stove and watched me while I ate heartily.

'Alister, Jopie is coming with me to the foot of the Plum-pudding. I am going to leave her there in the sun. She would get too tired if she did the run. Even Mary, who is not a beginner, fell a lot yesterday afternoon. I can climb quickly and then return to her. Do you want to come too?'

He had spoken of sunbathing, but this seemed a better idea to him. The whole thing could be done in very little over an hour. The dark girl with whom he had danced so much the night before had joined us, wearing a high-throated yellow jersey, and he suggested that, like Jopie, she should come with us part of the way and then rest in the sun.

We went out on to the terrace. It was Sunday and there were no classes that day. In the afternoon there was to be a Slalom competition on the slopes immediately facing us: Scheiber himself, it was rumoured, would take part in it. A number of guests, among them Mary, in a great fur coat, had brought out chaises-longues and were basking in the sunlight.

We shouldered our skis and set off up the sleigh-path. The girl in the yellow polo jersey had gone on ahead, for although she had sealskins she was the slowest of the four. We did not overtake her till we had almost reached the hay barn, where the track levelled out before dropping down to Gries. We left the path and began to climb to the right up an easy gradient before tackling the steep flank of the hill itself.

The Plum-pudding run had been our first experience of ski-ing at Kühtai and it was now to be our swan-song. But whereas we had climbed that day with Trio, seeing practically nothing but dense white mist, and the snow, for a few yards in front of us, to-day the whole of the high mountain valley gleamed in sunlight, and, save for some grey, dove-coloured clouds at the back of the Langenthal Valley, the sky was one vast inverted bowl of blue above us.

For nearly five hundred years, since the days of the Emperor Maximilian, men had come to this spot in search of relaxation and pleasure, but had any of them in all those centuries tasted a keener exhilaration than ourselves now? The snow crystals flashed in the sunlight; and our skis, pushing through them and compressing them, made that slight crunching sound which is joy to the skier's heart. With every thrust forward we seemed to assert a godlike and carefree independence. We climbed in slanting sunlight, glad to escape the sharp, frosty nip of the air on the sleigh-path, while every minute the sun rose higher in the heaven.

'Jopie, if you come as far as that first mound you will have good untrodden snow in which to practise."

She had no sealskins and I took an easier angle across the face of the hill than I would have done if Mathews and I had been alone.

We climbed a little way, then halted, to look down the valley and across at the great jagged face of rock to our right. In front of the *gasthof*, which at this distance looked little larger than an ordinary chalet, were the shining snowfields, beyond them was the cleft in the ground where the river ran, beyond it the entrance to the steep gorge which led up to the lakes.

'Now we'll leave you. We shan't be long. Not more than an hour at the very most. Run down to the hay-barn and wait there in the sun if you get tired.'

We climbed straight and went quickly. It had been worth bringing skins. Soon we were at the corner where I had passed the party of skiers the day before, and a minute or two later we had come over the crest and were going along the almost level top of the Plum pudding before the final rise. The strap of one of Mathews' skis became unfastened, and, leaving him to deal with it, I went ahead until I reached the rocks which marked the summit. I thought of my first arrival there. Then it had been bitterly cold; dense white fog had surrounded us on every side and the imagination had created yawning precipices only a few yards from where one stood. Perhaps Trio's flippancy on that occasion had made me distrustful – quite unjustly – of his prudence; or the stories I had read of how easy it is to lose one's sense of direction on a mountain, or the drifting, clinging mist itself, had affected my imagination; for, had the fog lifted for an instant, I should have seen that we could not have been much safer had we been ski-ing on a feather-bed.

I took off my skis and sat down on a rock to wait for Mathews. Presently his head, with its knitted ear-cap, appeared over the edge of the hill, then the swinging shoulders, then the gloved hands holding the ends of the long ski-sticks.

'It's lovely here. But I think we should run down. We don't want to keep them waiting too long.'

He agreed. We undid our sealskins and tied them round our waists. This was the easiest way of carrying them, and, if one fell, it helped to prevent the snow getting up at the back of one's ski-jacket.

'Now for it.'

We took the whole of the first slope straight, a pitch steep enough to bring tears into one's eyes. There was nothing illusory in the exultation of that downward swoop now, in the sensation of flight as the snow slipped swiftly from beneath one's feet, in the tense muscles and indrawn breath.

At the bottom of the slope someone had fallen heavily a day or two before, and, failing to avoid the huge sitzmark that remained as evidence of the disaster, I crashed now. By the time I was up Mathews had drawn ahead, and though I once seemed about to overtake him his greater skill in turning told on the final stretch. By holding well to the right, I found unrun powder snow, and cut across its virgin smoothness, throwing up a little spout of white either side of my leading ski tip. Alister was down, but had fallen at the bottom of the last steep pitch. I followed, took it, as he had done, straight, and to my joy managed to avoid a similar fall.

Coming over the crest of the hill, I had looked instantly for Jopie. But no one was in sight. The slopes were deserted. Then I caught sight of the blue-jacketed figure at the side of the hay-barn. She had been basking in the sun, and had now risen to put on her skis and come and meet us.

'You have been quick. We did not expect you so soon.'

Alister looked at his watch, and told her that it had taken us thirty-five minutes to climb and less than seven to come down.

'Good going,' she said.

'*Alors*, let's go back to the *gasthof* and sit for a while in the sun.'

The other girl was practising on the slopes at the back of the haybarn. We called to her that we were returning, then set off, Jopie leading the way. I followed her. Alister dropped behind to wait for his friend. Jopie moved with a slow and almost clumsy deliberation, leaning heavily on her ski-sticks. On ski she always looked gauche and loosely jointed. Though much improved since that first day on the lower slope, she was still the beginner, and had not yet tasted the joy of birdlike movement. Suddenly a desire seized me to make plain to her for an instant what I had never made plain in words. Only my eyes may have told her the truth. Perhaps we are all more obvious than we realise. Perhaps she understood that the love she inspired was real in its own way and not sham; that, if she had not been here, it would not have been a case of my falling in love equally well with any one of half a dozen other people in Kühtai. But I told myself she had no proof. Once I had gone away any such intuition would mean less and less; in time she would come to doubt it. Now I longed to let the spoken word admit it; to save her, if she was disposed to wonder, all further speculation on the point. I owed her this much loyalty. But how was I to make the admission and, at the same time, make plain that this loyalty was not invalidating another and greater loyalty to which I remained steadfast? Since my marriage no other face had awakened suscepti-bility in the same way, a susceptibility of which I had been aware since childhood. And, anxious that she should realise that I was incapable – or that I hoped I was incapable – of treachery where love was concerned, and anxious at the same time to leave her with the assurance that what her heart told her was true, I said quietly:

'I've written to my wife, Jopie. I told her that there was a Dutch girl here with whom I had fallen quite a little in love. She'll under-stand.' Then I added lamely, 'It's the first time for seven years.'

She was a few steps in front of me on the pathway, and did not turn. She said nothing. But so clear was the air, and so silent our surroundings, that Mathews who was still waiting by the hay-barn heard every word distinctly, and was to tell me so later when we were alone.

We came over the rise and left the path.

'Now for your "run," Jopie. You must know it well by now.'

It scarcely deserved to be called a run, the four or five hundred yards back to the *gasthof*. We ran down, and at the bottom I asked her,

'Wouldn't you like to do it once again?'

'No, you are tired.'

'Only my ankles are tired after all that traversing.'

'And you have to go down to Gries this afternoon.'

It was nearly midday. My forebodings of the night before con-cerning the weather seemed likely to be fulfilled after all. The sky was clouding up. Light, fleecy grey clouds appeared from nowhere, and formed themselves into a semi-opaque mass. Only a few people remained on the terrace of the *gasthof*, feet up in their long chairs, loth to desert them once they were settled there, but beginning to feel cold despite their wraps.

We were warm ourselves and would soon become chilled if we remained there. We pushed open the door of the Austrian room, to discover three guides, Trio, Otto and Hans, seated near the green glazed stove, while another man played the violin. All four were singing romantic, sentimental, German songs, in deep, colourful basses. We sat down on the bench which ran round the stove, leant back our heads against the tiles, rested and dried ourselves.

'Don't put your gloves on top of the stove. They will only rot if you leave them there. At least, mine, which are mackintosh, do if I leave them on top of the radiator. Dry them here on the bench.'

We continued to sit there, saying nothing. Time had ceased to matter. The moment itself was good. To lean back against the stove, Jopie's head beside mine, to have been in the sun, to be conscious of a pleasant, warm lethargy after exercise, to be listening to our companions singing, that was enough, a contentment sufficient to ignore both past and future, as though we might command time to stand still and wait upon our pleasure.

Feeling rested, I reminded her that she promised to help me tie up two books.

'I meant to get them off by the post yesterday.'

'There are some letters for you on the board. Have you seen them?'

'No. There were none there last night. Well done, Jopie, to have noticed them.'

I went and fetched them. One was a card from my friend Kelly in Switzerland, who had been promised a copy of *The Seals*.

' "No seals have come up the Sarine as yet." The Sarine is the river in Château d'Œx. I promised to send him *The Seals*, but I have been waiting for copies to arrive.'

'You mention him in the book, don't you?'

'Yes, that's right. You have finished reading it, then?'

'Not quite. I've lent it to tall Anneke so that she can read it before we go.'

'Some copies have come now, and I must get them off before I leave. I want to send one to Kelly, and one to Rose Steger, who translated my prose-poems into German for *Der Bund*. Wait here while I get them. I'll bring paper and string.'

When I returned, Jopie was still by the stove, the four men, reassuringly indifferent to us, perhaps a little understanding, were no longer singing romantic songs, but something solemn and slow, more like a hymn, in which their voices blended even better than before.

We moved to the table, where it would be easier to tie up the parcels. Some young Austrian students, from the dormitory below our room, had settled at the other table and were eating sandwiches.

'Jopie, a tragedy nearly happened this morning. I thought I had lost my cheque-book. It was in an envelope and Anna had thrown it away with the rubbish.'

She opened her eyes very wide in amusement and horror.

'It was luck it hadn't been burnt. I have still to pay Scheiber.'

'Mathews would have come to your help.'

Both parcels were now tied up and addressed. Trio and his companions, grumbling at the ardours before them that afternoon in the *slalom*, had risen to their feet and departed. The three Austrian students remained eating their sandwiches and conversing in undertones.

Mathews came in to say that he was going to order his lunch.

'We must be on our way by two-thirty at the latest. Have you settled with Scheiber yet?'

'No. I am going to do it now.'

Jopie said that she would wait for me while I did so. I had told her I would walk back to the Dortmünder with her. She and her friends were doing a run down the lower valley that afternoon. They were only remaining another two days in Kühtai and wanted to make the most of the time.

I gathered up the débris of string from the table and went across to the office, found Scheiber and bade farewell to him and his wife. Generous, helpful, so little mercenary that one had to remind them of charges they might overlook, they managed to give the *gasthof*, large as it was, the feeling of one big family of friendly people. My heart warmed to Gomperz for having sent us here instead of to Obergurgl, where, according to Eltham, the wind blew cold off the glacier, and the guests shivered and cursed their luck.

Jopie went to retrieve her own dark coat, which she had left at the *gasthof* all night. It was on the peg by the mirror where she had hung it, but the black woollen earcap which I liked so much, and which she thought she had left with it, had gone, nor could we find it anywhere. We went back into the little room, looked on the bench, under the table, but it was nowhere to be seen.

'Do not bother. I will get it to-night. We are all coming up after supper.'

'All right. Give me your skis. I'll carry them for you.'

I laid them across my shoulder. They were remarkably light compared to mine, ash and not hickory, very thin and rather narrow – strange skis to give a beginner.

'Did you hire them?'

'Yes.'

'They are almost racing skis.'

We walked back cheerfully along the pathway of trodden snow.

Only a few minutes in her company remained. At such moments a defiant cheerfulness seizes those in love, and they seem to ignore time and fate, in the same way that Deirdre and Naisi ignored it over their game of chess. It is bravado, but effective bravado, convincing even to the actors themselves, sustaining the moment, saving it alike from sentiment and from melancholy. Perhaps it is misleading to speak in this way of my own cheerfulness if it implies that I accepted the finality of the occasion. My courage came partly from a refusal to see here the end of our friendship. I had the precious half-sheet of paper with the address at The Hague. I had her promise that she would write to me. There was the likelihood of her coming to London; of her visiting us in Swanage. So that the sky, so far from being overcast, was relatively cloudless, and every moment that remained to me in her company was still a pleasure. It was these roseate, if somewhat vague, hues of a friendship dawning rather than ending which upheld me and made farewell tolerable.

We had reached the Dortmünder, and I was about to take her skis through to the drying-room when, guided perhaps by the same instinctive caution which had come to her rescue the night before, she stopped me, asking for them to be propped against the wall.

'I shall be using them again. Leave them there.'

'Goodbye, Jopie. It has been lovely meeting you. Some day you must come and see us in England.'

'Goodbye.'

She gave me her gloved hand, a handshake at once friendly, honest and unsentimental. The clear, pale blue eyes looked at me frankly, and she went into the Dortmünder as I turned back to retrace my footsteps along the path.

An air of Sunday quiet seemed to have fallen upon Kühtai. I arrived back at the *gasthof* and went across to the annexe to wash my hands. Then, seized by a sudden impulse, I slipped for a moment into the little chapel to kneel there by the altar-rails and say a prayer of gratitude for these days in the sun. I had never entered it before. The cold, lonely little building seemed smaller than ever when one was inside; a priest and a congregation of half a dozen would almost fill it. Stark and bare and very chilly, its only adornment was an amazing painted and decorated screen behind the altar, in which some artist of the mountains had expressed his piety with peasant simplicity and at the same time zealot fervour.

Down at the *gasthof* I found that Mathews had almost finished his lunch.

'Where have you been? You must hurry. If we are to catch the bus for Innsbruck, we must be at Gries at the latest by five. And everyone tells me that the run down will be hard, iced over, where the path runs through the wood.'

He knew the value of an occasional admonition at such a time. But he had allowed a reasonably wide margin to get us to Gries. There was time to eat my lunch and to drink a cup of coffee with Paynton, who was to attend to any letter that might come from the British Embassy after we had gone. A hurried last look round our room revealed a bottle of Mathews' hair oil, discarded in a corner.

'Here, don't you want this?'

'No. I couldn't find room for it. I threw it away.'

I emptied the contents on to my head saying, 'It's a pity to waste it. I shan't be seeing anyone I love for the next twenty-four hours.'

There followed the donning of wind-jackets, the winding of seal-skins round our waists, much hand-shaking and cordiality of fare-well. Scheiber was asleep, resting before the *slalom*, but Trio, Hans and Otto were there. Anna had followed us over from the annexe, and a sprinkling of fellow guests, some of them strangers almost till this moment, came up, shook us by the hand and wished us luck. It was a last reminder of how friendly Kühtai had been. Once more and in quite good faith we vowed to Frau Scheiber that we would return. Kühtai would see us another year. We would come again to Carthage.

We set off up the sleigh path, Mathews with his skis over his shoulder, I with mine, one in either hand, suspended parallel to the sticks, the guard of the ski-stick hooked over the curved tip of the ski, and its handle under the strap of the binding, an easy if lazy way of carrying them. We were approaching the brow of the hill, that point where I had so often crashed across the path on that down-ward *schuss* which I so much favoured, when I saw two figures resting in the snow on the side of the path. They were Jopie and tall Anneke. They had taken off their skis and were resting on them, Jopie doubled up, with her feet slewed back under her, Anneke kneeling on the skis and sitting back on her heels. I was so little expecting to see them that for a moment and in the distance I wondered could I be mistaken. But there was no mistake, and at once I felt it was to the good nature of tall Anneke that I owed this last meeting. They told us that they had changed their plans. They were not going for a run after all, but were going to watch the *slalom*, like everyone else, and meanwhile had come here to practise.

459

On the slope across the valley we could see them now putting out the flags for the race.

'Goodbye, Anneke. Don't forget you are going to translate my book for me. Goodbye, Mary.'

The latter was ski-ing nearby and had come across to greet us.

'Walk with us to the top of the hill, Jopie.'

She agreed to do so.

We set off. Jopie reproached Alister with tearing us away from Kühtai a day earlier than need be.

'Why do you want a day in Innsbruck?'

It was said simply, half jestingly, a hint of reproach barely perceptible in the words.

He defended himself on the ground that it would be too tiring to do the run down to Gries and travel to Paris that same night. When we reached the crest of the hill by the hay-barn, she watched us as we stooped to put on our skis. Then for the second time that day I turned to say goodbye to her.

'Goodbye, Jopie.'

'Goodbye.'

She turned back. The points of my ski thrust forward into a track cut by some lone skier through the level snow at one side of the path, while Alister kept to the path itself, preferring it. Our farewell had been casual, banal almost. But that was not the measure of its significance for me. Nausicaa, parting from Odysseus, said to him, 'Farewell, stranger! See that thou rememberest me, on a day, in thine own country, for that to me first thou owest the price of life.' Jopie might have said, 'Farewell, stranger . . . remember me in thine own country, for to me you owe the recollection of what it is to suffer enchantment at the hands of love.'

And suddenly, though not for the first time, the whole folly of speaking of love where she was concerned and in relation to myself was brought home to me, and instead of that infinite world into which emotion allows us for a moment to pass I saw clearly that world of finite realities which, unless we are prepared to suffer, and to make others suffer, and perhaps even more so than ever then, forces itself upon our attention before long. It was absurd to speak of my loving – not of my being in love with, but of my loving – Jopie. The man who would love her, some young Dutchman – in whose eyes she would seem unique and infinitely precious, the predestined companion, the fit and only mother for his children – had still to appear upon the horizon of her life. He could claim her whole loyalty, for the simple reason that he was prepared to pledge his own. All efforts to steal from life, to take out of it more than we are prepared to put in, to trick it into showing special favour to us, when we are wholly unprepared and in no position to pay the price, all such efforts are doomed in the long run to failure. Sooner or later the bill will be presented to us, and since we cannot pay it our moral bankruptcy will transpire. We may blame life, blame conditions, blame social conventions, blame everything except ourselves, but that will only mean that we are still children where life's laws are concerned, greedy and petulant and somewhat unpleasant children. That inflexible spiritual justice which sees to it that the selfish and egotistical are scarcely ever happy, since they contain in themselves the seeds of their own discontent, will punish us with its retribution, which is really doubly severe if we are still blind to its origin. For the selfish and the stupid reap, not merely the reward of their faults, but the additional punishment – more poignant perhaps to the mind of a philosopher – that they are not even aware that they are suffering for those faults. They reproach Fate, whereas they should really reproach themselves.

I knew all this. I knew my own good fortune. I was happily married. I was in love with my wife. My marriage had been a romance, and was still one. My mind had always been aware that what was happening to me in Kühtai was happening, as it were, outside time; that it had no relation to reality – no relation, that is to say, to the future or to any event or circumstance that could be shaped by me. It was lyrical enthusiasm run mad, but it was all the more poignant for that very reason. Like an exile who, running a grave risk in doing so, revisits for a few hours a country from which he is banished, seeing once more all its familiar landmarks which he had not expected to see again, so had I crossed back into the enchanted territory of those who fall in love, and even now, as we set out for Gries, a part of my mind lingered there, as though unable to tear itself away.

The sun shone. We were on the summit of the watershed. Very soon the hill dipped and it was no longer necessary to push ourselves forward with our ski-sticks. The ground slipped gently away from beneath us, and, starting with that initially easy gradient, we began our descent of the series of steps which would take us eventually to Gries. It was varied running. One dipped, swooped, ran out, paused, dipped again. Once, turning back, I saw a huge pyramid wedge of mountain caught full in the sun, sunlight pooled all over its granite rock-faces and vast snow-covered flanks. It stood out with dramatic intensity against the blue of the sky, reminding me of the Golden Spear in my own country, and I called out to Mathews, who was a little ahead of me, to stop and look back at it. Then we pushed on again, dipped over another crest and lost the sunlight. The running became more difficult. It had been fairly open at first, track-running in the tracks of all those who had been down to Gries since the last fall of snow. But now it entered upon a wood-path phase, steeper and much harder. The snow on the path had been melted at midday, sometimes forming into little streams of water; now in the late afternoon it froze once more and became a skier's purgatory. One must be prepared to fall and fall again; if a turn went wrong; if the edges of the skis skidded, failing to grip the ice; if an obstacle suddenly presented itself. We congratulated ourselves that we had discarded our rucksacks, sending them down with the rest of the luggage on the sleigh. We were spared at least that added anguish. Deprived of the sunlight, the narrow valley was sombre, a little forbidding, its few barns dark and gloomy, its farm chalets poverty-stricken. I realised that Mathews had been right when he had viewed this run as an unsuitable prelude to all-night travelling. To avoid falling, to run under control and yet not to let the pace become too slow, kept every muscle occupied and the successive stages of the descent seemed endless. At last we began to pass children, toiling slowly upwards on their way home from school. A hay-luge was guided into the side of the track to allow us to get by, and an old woman murmured 'Grüss Gott' as we sped past in the fading light. Then when the light had almost gone, dipping suddenly through pines, I shot into Gries by the post-house, to find the main road frozen to solid ice.

Mathews had gone ahead towards the end, beating my time by about five minutes in the final outcome, and I found him seated in the café of the post-house, restoring himself with rum and hot milk.

'I recommend it, Monk. I recommend it.'

'No. I'll have coffee, I think, and rolls, and some of that chocolate cake you're eating.'

It was years since I had seen him, in Paris, betray all the ecstasy of the complete epicure over some species of bun which he used to purchase in a dingy little pastrycook's, near the Rue Gît-le-Cœur; and I could see that the chocolate cake now was giving him the same satisfaction.

We were both tired. The run down had been worth doing, but it had been even more fatiguing than we had expected. I took off my wind-jacket, spread it over the radiator to dry, and began to drink hot *café-au-lait* and get warm in the parlour of the inn.

Soon I felt rested. But I was filled with an intense loneliness – surprising even to myself – for Kühtai, for the life I had just left, for Jopie. There is a sort of nostalgia, indescribably melancholy, which everybody who has ever been in love must know. It was only a few hours since I had seen Jopie, and yet already she seemed immeasurably remote, lost to me, separated by a vast abyss.

I had nothing, absolutely nothing to remind me of her. It would have been easy to have asked Mathews to take a snapshot of her, but I had never done so, nor had I ever asked her for one myself. And this abstention had been deliberate. For love feeds on sentiment, and sentiment feeds upon whatever scraps of association it can find. It had seemed better to starve myself of any such possible token. This may seem to contradict what I have said already about my conviction that somehow, somewhere, I would see Jopie again, would share in some measure in her life. But surely, if we tell the truth about ourselves, it is just such contradictions that we will have to reveal, for the heart is contradictory. One half of my mind hoped to see her again; the other half impelled me to deny myself any slight reminder, any stimulus to memory which might artificially foster or prolong such a hope. But now, already, I had begun to regret my gesture of renunciation. I had nothing to remind me of her. She, at least, had my book, which she had still to finish. If she wished to be in my company, to share in my thoughts and actions for a few hours, she had only to read it. She could be with me, as it were, at one remove. But I had nothing, nothing to prevent me getting further and further from her at every minute – except the white coat with its fleece tinged with gold and brown, which she had once worn.

There seemed only one solvent for my loneliness. It could only be bridged if I were to speak to her on paper now. I thought to myself, 'I must write to her. I will write to her to-night. Why shouldn't I? She will be coming down to Innsbruck on Wednesday and may be foolish enough to attempt it on skis. She would be dead tired if she did. It would be folly to arrive at Gries tired out, and probably sit in the cold bus without a coat. It's my duty to write. I will write when I get to Innsbruck to-night.'

'We had better bring our things out. The people are getting into the bus.'

Mathews went out to make sure that all our luggage had been put on, and I gathered up my possessions. The bus filled rapidly; there were several people on it whom we knew by sight: the two Italians from the Dortmünder, the red-haired schoolboy, his sister and mother from the Alpengasthof. But their presence with us seemed only to emphasise further the impermanence of all things mortal, the nomadic nature of human life in which departures play so great a part. A pervasive melancholy, '*une mélancolie, vaste et tendre*' as Verlaine expresses it, took possession of me. Everything from birth to death was either an arrival or a going away, a greeting or a farewell. We were flotsam on the surface of a river whose current never ceased to flow.

'You're sure our kit is all on?'

'Yes, quite sure.'

The bus moved cautiously off, slowly, very slowly, more slowly even than when we had been coming up, because of the icy surface of the road, against whose dangers even the huge chains wound round the tyres did not seem to offer much assurance to the driver. The light was on the point of going altogether. Everywhere on the fences one could see huge wads of thick snow. Far below the road on one side ran a river, one looked down to it through scattered pines, while above on the other side rose a forest of firs, from the midst of which, suddenly and unexpectedly, like a moment in a Grimm's fairy tale, gleamed an occasional light. The snow had come with a vengeance since we arrived that evening from Innsbruck and the gravel had grated so harshly under the runners of our sleigh. The trees were blanketed, their branches were breaking under its weight.

We stopped at Selrain, and good staff work on Mathews' part secured us our letters. He had written ahead to tell them to keep our post for us. Diving into a café, he led the way to the kitchen, where we found a woman sitting in company with some nice children, wearing coloured pointed caps – elves' caps – and the elves looked at us with mild-eyed wonder as Mathews explained our sudden intrusion. A fat old man appeared and without any difficulty produced our letters, which we seized from him, thanking him and hurrying back to the bus.

It continued on its way. On the white road in front of us its headlights shed their slightly yellow radiance. Sweeping round corners, we would come on some pedestrian, a woman hurrying home, or a man muffled up to the ears, dragging with mittened hands a sledge behind him. Such rare encounters only made the road seem emptier. Alister was having a dispute with a drunk Austrian on the subject of another very drunk Austrian who had just left the bus. I could not tell what they were saying, but I could tell that it was heated, and presently I saw Mathews make that so characteristic gesture – what one might call his pooh-pooh gesture of ultimate remonstrance – in which he seemed to purse his lips, shake his head, shrug his shoulders and spread expostulatory hands, all in the same moment. It was the invariable sign that as a peaceable individual he did not wish to continue the argument further – but that he stuck to his point; a sort of smiling negation, rather like a duck ridding its feathers of water, which infuriated the Austrian, who continued to shout insults at him.

Lights appeared at the side of the road, at first the lights of single cottages; then the illuminated window of some tiny shop in which toys which had failed to find favour at Christmas still hung, surrounded by a medley of household provisions and knick knacks; finally, the well-lit roads of the suburbs with their arc-lamps.

'Where are we going, Alister?'

As usual, I had left it to him to decide. He was certain to have heard of somewhere a little quainter, a little more picturesque, than would be likely to fall to the lot of the casual traveller, who arrives in a place without previous enquiry. Not that I cared where we stayed. Innsbruck, which had been the gateway to adventure when we climbed into the bus outside the station a little over a fortnight before, was now merely the reminder that our holiday was over.

'To the Golden Rose. I'll phone there when we get to the station.'

'Whereabouts is it?'

'Not far from the station. It's very old, I'm told. About 1400. Montaigne stayed there once and complained of the shortness of the beds, and the fact that they were so high from the ground that you had to climb into them with a ladder.'

His phoning was successful. At the bus-stop an outside porter took charge of our luggage, pushing it on his barrow along the almost deserted, snow-covered street. The Herzog-Friedrich Strasse was quite near, and presently we came to the Lauben, with its line of high stone buildings, solid as a fortress, their upper windows, with slatted shutters, projecting flush with the street, while beneath them ran the pathway, along a dark arcade, almost like a tunnel or wine vault. Here the wrought-iron sign with its golden rose had been hanging out for no less than five centuries. Mathews entered an arched doorway in the arcade. I followed him.

'I think we're going to like it, Monk.'

A bearded Austrian, courteous and charming, and a connoisseur of art to judge by his walls, met us on the stairs and welcomed us. The porter carried up our luggage and we paid him. We were shown our bedrooms, dark, and with heavy, solid furniture, and after a wash a maid conducted us to the dining-room. Its atmosphere was at once hushed and friendly, influenced perhaps by the fact that it was Sunday evening. A party of fat, happy, middle-aged bourgeois were just completing their meal. The only other occupants of the room were a group of three men in a further corner, smoking and drinking coffee; and as we passed their table, to my surprise I recognised Hans Schneider, the founder of the Arlberg school, whom I used to view with awe at St. Anton, and who in little more than a year's time would be an exile from his country, banished by the invader as politically unsound.

'What are they giving us?'

'Bread soup, calves' head – and let's have beer.'

'Yes, let's have beer.'

We might have been back in one of those remote Swiss mountain inns, where, in the restaurant, guides converse at little tables in low undertones; or in a Paris brasserie, whither a whole family will come on Sunday to eat and talk with grave decorum.

Hungry after our journey, we ate with relish.

'Who was it told you about this place?'

'I forget. It may have been Scheiber, or perhaps Raines the day we drove down to Innsbruck.'

'One might be back in the time of Villon.'

'Yes, Monk, one might.'

In his few minutes' conversation with our courtly host, Mathews had collected quite a lot of information about the place. The first extant reference to the Golden Rose Inn was as early as 1452. Later the Emperor Maximilian had stayed here, and had ridden away with his train, leaving the accounts for his entourage still unpaid.

When we had finished eating, I asked the waitress if she would bring me writing paper and envelopes. They were brought, the notepaper with an emblazoned miniature of the signboard, a golden rose encirled by a wreath of laurel, a map on the back of the envelopes. If I wrote now, my letter would be in Kühtai by Tuesday. She would get it the day before she left.

'I am going to write to Jopie.'

'Monk!'

He looked at me with shocked amazement, as though by saying this I had furnished proof that I was harder hit than he imagined. His simple expostulatory 'Monk!' was so charged with disapproval that it was hardly necessary for him to follow it up by telling me he had overheard my words across the snow that morning.

'You tell the girl you are quite a little in love with her at midday, and you write to her the same evening. That's too serious altogether.'

I felt reproved, condemned, a little absurd even. His attitude all the time at Kühtai had varied from denunciatory disapproval to a mildly facetious but benevolent acceptance of the situation. Throughout he had displayed a curious vacillation of spirit. He had come with me that afternoon to the slopes by the Dortmünder to search for the yellow jacket, but, having been successful in our quest, he had refused night after night to come down to the hut itself. He had deprecated the idea that I ought to tell her I was married, and then, suddenly, he had insisted that either I must tell her or not see her again. He was shocked at the idea of my wanting to write to Jopie now, and yet a few days later he could say in a letter to me, 'You ought to write to The Hague within a week. Don't let too long elapse, not that I doubt Jopie's genuine interest in your friendship, but for *les jeunes filles en fleur* time is even longer than for us. . . .' What did it mean, all this blowing hot and cold? It was inexplicable, or, rather, it was only explicable in the light of Mathews' own character. He was a romantic, therefore he was on my side. But he had a sense of honour and responsibility, and periodically he probably asked himself whether he ought not to discourage a situation which looked as though it could end in infatuation. Presently, however, the romantic would reassert itself, and he would once more become sympathetic, almost encouraging. I had said to him one day, 'I thought I was getting too old for this to happen to me,' and he had replied instantly, 'Don't say that ever. When you are too old it will mean that I am nearly too old also.'

He might say this, but a day later he would go on the other foot and deprecate my impulsiveness. His tone of shocked horror now had been such that I decided I must be crazy. The note-paper remained on the table in front of me while we chatted about our run down to Gries.

Presently I said, 'I'm going to bed.'

'Yes. I am too.'

I had not written the letter. And I did not write it next morning.

I would write when I got back to England. Instead, as soon as I had had breakfast, I began to rummage in my case until I had found my journal, that journal in which I had not made a single entry the whole time that I was at Kühtai. Our character reveals itself on fairly consistent lines, and to look back hungrily on all that one thinks lovely has always been a part of mine. Just as in my last days in a place which I think beautiful, I gaze greedily at each detail of the landscape which I am about to leave, as though the eye could soak up beauty to be hoarded later in my journal, as a miser hoards up gold – a vain hope, of course – so now, when I realised that these days, of which I had noted nothing down were already slipping from me, it seemed to me that if I were to save anything of them, it must be saved instantly. Most of all I wanted some reminder of Jopie herself, some portrait of her, what she had looked like, her expression, her way of saying a thing, and it was just this that I found so hard, not simply to put in words but to envisage. I had lost it, because, like the scenes on which our eye rests and loves, it was fairy gold, not miser's, not to be carried away.

And so, though I had deliberately rejected the comfort Alister's camera might have brought me in my loneliness, still I thought it no crime to fine-comb memory now, for every detail, every little incident, every look, every glance, which it was still possible for me to remember and to record. I found the journal, and sat down at a table in my bedroom and began to write. Mathews left me, to explore the town and do some shopping. But I continued writing, writing, still writing. Every sentence was something salvaged from that utterly remorseless tide of time which would carry it away into nothingness if it was given the chance. I wrote furiously, and had my command of language equalled that of Montaigne it would have seemed barely adequate to my theme.

When Mathews returned some hours later he found me still writing. I slipped out for half an hour's shopping before lunch, but after lunch I was back at my table scribbling. I strove hard to set down how Jopie had actually looked, her expression, the charm of her calm forehead and of her eyes. But my attempts only maddened me by their ineffectuality. It was precisely this mental image which eluded me. I wrote, 'I am tormented by this inability to visualise completely.' I noted that her eyes 'seemed to give at once a challenge, a recognition and a reproach.' I tried to describe her leaning forward for a moment on her ski-sticks, propping herself with them as she spoke, but what I wrote was: 'I know that my heart leaps when I

468

see a yellow jersey on the snow slopes, even when it is the wrong one, and that when it is the right one and our paths eventually cross, meeting without either simulated surprise or disguised delight, and – leaning forward on her ski-sticks – she speaks to me for a moment, I know that she is all that is lovely, unspoilt and graceful in my eyes – not graceful on skis – but that her face has that quality of grace, of something deeper than mere attractiveness, a beauty of proportion, line and expression, which one finds in the drawings of Da Vinci. I can neither disguise my delight, nor can my delight perhaps be prevented from making her look all the more beautiful.' But this was not the description of a person at all, it was merely the description of an impression received. In other words, I found it far easier to describe my own emotion than to describe its cause. Still, little by little, as though recorded by its reflection in a mirror – that is to say the mirror of my own emotional reaction – I managed to put down some account of what had stirred me so much. The comparison with a Leonardo drawing was sound, for Jopie's face had the same dreamy quality, the same brooding serenity that there is in his St. Anne, a face made beautiful, not by any particular feature, but by an infused quality, a restfulness, a joy, which lifts it out of what might be commonplace into what actually is poetry, a poetry of line, of feeling, of expression.

It was four o'clock. Mathews was beginning to fuss.

'You will never be ready. You haven't done your packing yet.'

'No. And I have still to finish shopping.'

In the course of my sortie that morning, I had discovered a shop where I could buy Tyrolese costumes for my children; leather shorts, embroidered braces, and a green felt hat with a chamois beard in it for the little boy; white blouse, flowered skirt and black velvet bodice for his younger sister. In the window of another shop nearby a grey felt sports coat with silver buttons like acorns had pleased me, and I had asked a shop assistant of about my wife's height and build to put it on that I might see what likelihood there was of its fitting her. I had tasted extreme loneliness when leaving my family, as I always did, but now, making my purchases in Innsbruck, I began to experience something of the excitement of return. But none of these transactions had been completed. I must go to a bank and get money, and Mathews, as he saw me still writing at the table, got more and more worried.

'We will lose the train if you are not careful. If you will tell me what you have to pack——'

'Oh, throw everything into the suitcase – if it will go.'

But it would not go. That was just the trouble. My departure from the Golden Rose was a chaotic, nightmare affair in which the patience of Mathews showed up well. We collected my purchases at the shop. The shopkeeper who had never seen me till that morning accepted a cheque, and when the night train with its endless line of sleeping cars steamed in from Vienna and Budapest, we were actually on the platform awaiting it, even though my possessions had had to be brought piecemeal to the station.

The porter handed them up on to the steep running-board. We had third sleepers and a reasonable amount of room, for Mathews tipped the night-car attendant to avoid the addition of a stranger to the spare bunk. I repacked my possessions more tidily, undressed, and got into my berth. Soon I was listening to the steady beat of the wheels, and to the curiously muffled sound of occasional voices on the platform of some unknown station, or the tap-tap of an iron rod on the axle-shafts when we seemed to be halted indefinitely. Presently I fell asleep.

We were in Paris early next morning. Alister had booked a couple of rooms for us in a rather dingy little hotel near the Place Saint-Michel. We drove there, and when we had deposited our luggage, Alister went out in search of breakfast. But I remained behind. I had had coffee and a couple of *brioches* on the train. It seemed far more important that I should continue my journal than that I should breakfast. All the later part of our stay in Kühtai had still to be recorded; much could be gleaned if I allowed nothing to come between me and my purpose during these next few hours. And so, seated at a small, uncomfortable table in a little room with dirty lace curtains and a slot-machine on the wall for those who might feel disposed to purchase face-powder or cheap scent, I wrote, back once more amongst the snows of Austria. The only appropriate thing about my surroundings was the hotel's name – Hotel du Mont Blanc! Had some Genevan from the lakeside come here, years before, in the hope of making a good living amid the clatter of hoofs on cobble-stones and the dual-noted piping of taxis? I wrote steadily till lunchtime. Then I went out. Paris, for the first time in all the years that I had known her, seemed grey, dismal, joyless. I searched near the American Library – where I used once to see Joyce mouthing nervously over the great dictionaries, in which it was his habit to hunt for words – for a little restaurant where I had had many happy meals. But it had vanished; or else I had got my bearings completely wrong. There was nothing for it but to lunch nearby in a café almost as narrow as a coffin, and then depart speedily in search of a haircut near the Madeleine. Wandering into Brentano's bookshop, I was shown a copy of the *Spectator* with a display advertisement of my book. But even this could not dispel my melancholy, a melancholy for which I blamed the great city rather than myself. Something had happened to Paris; its gaiety, its vitality had gone. Was it the slump? Or was it me, after all? In economics a boom generally predicts a slump, and in the life of the emotions the same is probably true? Only on the Pont Alexandre III were the gigantic bronze children able to give me something of the delight which they always gave; but there followed instantly the melancholy reflection that such exuberance, such appreciation of the sheer vitality of childhood and of natural things, was possible in 1900, but had long since been deposed by the artists in favour of grim and joyless symbolism.

Next morning at the Gare St. Lazare, waiting for the gates to open on to the platform from which the train for Dieppe would start, I watched the early morning crowd which throngs a terminus at that hour of day, while Mathews went in search of a paper. Suddenly I looked up and saw at the far end of the platform over a great archway, through which people were pouring followed by porters with their luggage to another level of line, a huge enamelled notice, white lettering on a red background, '*Sortie Amsterdam*.' I looked at them, fascinated, as though they had been placed there expressly to catch my attention. They urged me to abandon all that was logical, to go through the archway and take a ticket for Holland. I thought, 'You have only to board a different train and you will be in Amsterdam to meet Jopie on Friday.' I had thought myself cut off irreparably from her. But now this trivial circumstance brought home to me that, of course, I could see her again if I wished. She was real. She was not even so far away. She existed. Holland, Amsterdam, The Hague. They also existed. There was a remedy for my loneliness. I need not even leave the station. I had only to walk a few yards to be already on my way to her.

And if she showed surprise? I would say to her, 'Just as you came to say goodbye to us a second time on the path above the *gasthof*, so I have come to see you now, to talk with you, and to say goodbye once more. Don't you know that in three days – no, in a single hour – one can taste the utmost depth of loneliness? Within a few minutes of parting from them, a man can be lonely for his children and for the woman who bore them, so that they seem immeasurably distant;

well, in the same way, it is possible for us to be lonely for our friends. I have come. I wanted to see you once again. That is all. Don't look so serious. Laugh. Admit that it is not a bad reason.'

She would laugh. And I would laugh too.

The idea was never seriously entertained for a moment, and yet the impulse was there, and it was genuine. It was one of those impulses which, like a still-born child, is perfect in every feature, and yet has never drawn breath.

I turned away. By one of those ironies which seem almost too pointed to be the outcome of chance, I saw over the opposite and corresponding archway at the other end of the station, in the same great letters, on the same red-enamelled background, another notice, the exact counterpart of the first: 'Sortie Rome.' It was ironic. Was it a parable? In every life, is there a *Sortie Amsterdam*, a *Sortie Rome*, to be taken or turned away from – to be rejected and remembered ever afterwards with a faint tinge of romantic regret – or to be accepted and perhaps remembered with a regret still more stinging?

Mathews had returned with the newspaper. I nudged his elbow and pointed to the two notices. He looked at them, puzzled for a moment. Then, as though the past had suddenly flooded back into his consciousness, his face cleared and he turned to me and smiled.

I had lamented in my journal my inability to envisage Jopie. But I was to see her once again after all. That night, just before going to sleep, at that moment, when, rarely – and never answering to any act of volition on our part, rather, if anything, banished instantly by something as definitely formulated as a wish – we sometimes see images of persons living or dead, projected in mental vision on the back of the eyelid, not vaguely or cloudily, but vividly and in astonishing detail, I suddenly saw the face of Jopie de Graaf. I had not been thinking of her at all at the time. But there she was, projected suddenly and with amazing clarity upon the screen of vision by this magic lantern of the mind. I had been striving for hours before, largely unsuccessfully, to remember what she looked like, to recollect distinctive features. But now Nature, in her mood of capricious indulgence, had taken the matter out of my hands, and I saw her absolutely clearly and vividly, as one sees a person in real life, or as one might see a person sunlit in a mirror. I saw the blue eyes, I saw the fair hair, I saw each feature, I saw the whole expression. In a flash she was there before me, although for twenty-four hours I had not been able to call up any image of her. And at once I thought, 'How simple! Why cannot we always do this? Why grope ineffectually for one's recollection of a person when one can recapture them with such complete realism upon the retina of "the inner eye."' There was nothing to explain why this should happen now, and not at any other time. Her appearance at this instant was as accidental and unforeseen as had been her first appearance that evening on the snow. The image vanished again almost as quickly as it had formed. But for an instant it had been there; she was there almost as though I could stretch out a finger and touch her; she had reappeared to me, and I looked on Jopie for the last time.

THE life of the emotions is like an underground stream which emerging sometimes into daylight becomes evident to all, but at others is hidden even from ourselves. We remain ignorant of how deeply a thing has touched us until some slight incident, some crucial event, tells us, or reminds us once more, what we were in danger of forgetting. Anything which has really touched the psyche, whether it be some trivial slight or humiliation, or some soul-stirring experience, is liable to rise up from the past in this fashion and suddenly confront us. But until it does – so long as it does not return to confront us, so long as it remains quiescent – we may be completely unaware of its strength.

Back in England I wrote to Jopie, and my wife wrote too, a friendly, warm-hearted note telling her that she must come and see us if she ever visited London. It is doubtful if I realised the generosity of spirit shown in this action: I was happy to be home again with those I loved, and already everything that had happened at Kühtai had begun to assume the aspect of a dream, an aspect not so much of unreality as of something finished and past. Jopie wrote back, thanking my wife *mille fois* for her suggestion, and giving me an amusing description of the descent to Gries, which they had made, after all, on skis, and in the course of which they had fallen so repeatedly and so painfully that, she said, they would have been glad to avail themselves of the ministrations of Alister's flask of cognac had he been there. She wrote from The Hague and her letter came just before my father's death, which was a great shock to me

473

and which created a still greater gulf in my life between all that had gone immediately before and all that followed. I went to Ireland and remained there some months, telling my wife, before I left, to write a line to Jopie explaining what had happened and that I was overwhelmed with family business. There the matter rested. There I was content that it should rest. I wished Jopie well. Sometimes in my thoughts I could see her, a young mother, lovely as before, holding up her child in some orchard in spring that it might touch the apple blossom, a face that Millet or Puvis de Chavannes would have loved to paint, with the serenity and calmness of still water, or the freshness and animation of a field of narcissi stirred by a morning breeze. That was her destiny surely, and it had no concern with me. The very fact that I wished her well prompted me to let her pass out of my life.

From the very first I had been conscious, alike in the poem written in the annexe that morning and in my thoughts, that I was behaving selfishly in allowing her to see how ardently I admired her. My own happiness was already secure. It was not threatened. But Jopie had yet to find the happiness which was hers by right. She had nothing to gain, I told myself, from any homage of mine. And this conviction, now that I was separated from her, naturally gained, rather than lost in strength, so that, when my own silence was followed by her silence, I felt that it was right, and that, whoever else might do so, I was the least likely person in the world to contribute to her real contentment.

But it is a testimony to the force with which that hidden stream of our emotions can re-emerge, though we have almost forgotten its existence, summoned, but oh so poignantly, out of forgetfulness, or, quite as often, out of the blind and casual insensitiveness of everyday acceptance, in which men see and know those whom they love without really seeing or knowing them at all – until death stabs them in a moment into sudden and acute awareness – it is a tribute to the force of that stream that, when a certain letter came nearly four years later and I opened it and read it, its effect on me was overwhelming. I felt numbed by it.

The letter bore a Dutch stamp and postmark. It was from no one I knew, nor from anyone who appeared to know me, though the fact that it was signed with the Christian name Anneke at first made me wonder whether it might not be from one of the two Dutch girls who had been at the Dortmünder. But it was plain that this was only a coincidence. The letter was from a stranger, and it was not a little strange that it should have reached me at all. It told me that Jopie was dead. Her parents were no longer living, and her friends could find no photograph of her in existence. Among her papers they had found a slip of paper with my name and address on it and, knowing that we had met in Austria, they thought that I might possibly have a snapshot taken at that time. It was obvious that they were confusing me with Mathews, for they referred to a literary friend who was my companion on the Kühtai visit. They apologised for troubling me, but if I had a snapshot of her then, and if I could send them a copy of it, not only the writer, but Jopie's own sister, would be most grateful for it.

All that morning, having returned to my work of raking seaweed from a heap to which it had been carted and spreading it thinly on the grass to dry in the sun, a portion of my mind kept repeating over and over again to itself. 'It isn't true. It isn't true,' as though by this reiterated denial I could change the course of events. It was a joke, I told myself, that Jopie herself, that her friends, were playing on me, to see how I would take the news. The mind is always reluctant to accept what is painful to it. All morning an inward voice continued to say, 'It isn't true. It isn't true.' But by afternoon this instinctive reflex of mental compensation had worn itself out. I was convinced that, despite the confusion of Mathews with myself – what could be easier, since they knew neither of us? – and the amazing fact that no photograph of Jopie should exist (amazing only to me who came of a family anxious to place every trivial occasion, every picnic and festival on record), the letter was and must be true. I sat down and wrote something of my dismay and grief, I asked for further news, explaining that it was my friend and not I who had possessed a Leica camera, and giving Alister's address in Grenoble, but saying that I feared it was most unlikely he had any photograph.

A week or two later an answer came, giving me a few further particulars. Jopie had died tragically. She had worried greatly when her sister was suddenly left a widow and very badly off, with a young child. She had felt the insecurity of their position and of her own. Some time afterwards she had gone to France. There she had been involved in a motor accident, and there had followed months of hospital, and, later still, the graver illness which was to kill her.

The friend who wrote had heard her speak often of Kühtai and of the fun it had been. But how much fun does life entitle us to, or how little? At Jopie's age I had suffered much, but even at that time I could count days and months of undeserved bliss, happiness already beyond deprivation. And, in the years that had followed war and illness, how much fun and how much contentment had been mine, mixed with occasional sorrow, occasional despair? It seemed to me that, in comparison with this girl, I had received full measure, pressed down and running over, and that I could never reproach life if I cared to count the hours of happiness which had been mine. But Jopie's twenty years of life before I had known her, and those few days in Kühtai, what had they been but a mere gathering of wild flowers in a moment of sunlight? If we love our children we may easily live to regret having spoiled them; but we will never regret having given them even a single hour of simple, unfeigned, innocent happiness; and every such hour is like a lodgement made to their account. But, if they were to die to-morrow, we would still feel – in spite of ourselves – that there was something tragically disproportionate in the showing made by all such lodgements. And it was so that I felt in regard to Jopie now. It was alien to my temperament to reproach Fate. Until we know more, we must be stoical in reverse, grateful in joy, and – within the limits of the shaping mind that helps to carve out destiny for us – acceptant always. But it seemed to me ironic that the slender store of happiness which Jopie had actually known should have been claimed so soon by Lethe, and, moreover, that no record of it existed, except perhaps the record made in my own brain. Like all other prodigalities of the natural world, it had been able to ask no repeal, no remission merely on the score that it was lovely. She was dead, and I, who had longed so greatly to see her again, then ceased to long, but in the vaguest fashion continued to imagine or expect that some day, in some way, I might meet her and speak to her again, could rule out for ever that expectation. I could say in the words in which Synge has rendered what Petrarch once said of Laura: 'But Death had his grudge against me, and he got up in the way, like an armed robber, with a pike in his hand.'

She had passed out of my life, but she remained perhaps nearer my thoughts than I imagined. One day in Dublin, some years later, I read in the paper that Andrew O'Connor had bequeathed a number of sculptures to the Municipal Gallery and that they were on view there. I went to see them, as much from a sense of civic obligation as anything else. The collection was interesting; but what made me return to the gallery more than once was a single piece, a girl's head in grey stone, 'La Vierge en Pierre. 1911.' This arrested my attention the moment I set eyes on it and gave me a unique pleasure. The block of pale grey stone was mounted on a black wooden square stand. The face emerged from the stone in the way that Rodin first made popular, but O'Connor had emphasised still further the possibilities of the method by leaving the roughly chiselled stone flush with the curve of the cheek on one side, while on the other he had cut back so as to show the whole depth of the head as far as the ear, and the hair drawn back over the ear. In the result he seems to be drawing our attention to beauty on two different planes; beauty of outline where the stone screens it; and beauty in depth with the full implication of the moulded chin and of the throat and neck deeply recessed and shadowed, revealing everything except the back of the head still sunk in the stone. I saw the face of a young girl, lovely, detached, a little wistful, emerging with an almost flower-like grace from the stone. The mouth is full, the chin rounded, the eyes brooding and distant, the eyebrows raised with a slightly nostalgic air, an expression which has just missed being tinged with momentary disdain. It is youth, but it is youth prepared for everything, prepared even for sorrow. The slight droop of the eyelids, and the hair drawn back austerely from the rounded forehead only help to emphasise a loveliness at once astonishingly young and a little sad. This stone head on its black wooden pillar drew me towards it again and again. The sculptor had reconciled the cold and intractable stone with the delicate and ineffable grace of a living countenance. I was entranced by it. I returned to the gallery simply that I might see it, and I was delighted when I discovered a French publication on O'Connor in which this head was reproduced. But I am doubtful if I was aware, immediately, or for some time to come, that what moved me so much was not merely the merits of a work of art but the fact that in this face I had partially rediscovered Jopie. It was she who looked back at me with fugitive grace from the roughly chiselled rock. All those qualities of spirit which her face had suggested to me, her grace, something at once human and elusive, something humorous, and, at the same time, capable of melancholy, were here, or potentially here.

Beauty and goodness are the two lodestars of life, for we flatter ourselves if we imagine that our apprehensions of truth can ever be more than partial and relative. It is better that beauty should move us too much than that it should fail to move us at all. There is nothing shameful in the fact that we should be stirred by it. It is only the blackness of our own hearts that makes the integrity of our motive suspect even to ourselves. If we loved disinterestedly we should not be ashamed to love, we should only be a little afraid. Faguet says: 'The romantic spirit consists in living beyond the horizon. It consists in being incapable of drawing from surrounding objects the savour, grace, charm and poetry which they always have. The romantic spirit consists in ignoring these things and believing that savour, grace, charm, poetry and happiness are always elsewhere than where we are.' This has some truth in it, but it is a little harsh. I would say rather that the romantic spirit consists in making time stand still, in stopping it at a particular point and letting it for ever after stand there. Like the hand which created the figures on Keats' Grecian Urn, it takes the moment and makes it 'for ever young'. It is mere dream stuff compared to the real texture of life. I think of love in its larger sense, of the loyalty I have found in it, the pledges given and taken, the patience and devotion shown, the lessons learned, the interests shared, the victories achieved. I have romantic memories there too; the Corso in Taormina; von Gloeden's garden and the thin, eager music of bamboo pipes; warm-hearted welcome on the platform of the little station at Ventnor West. The green shoot of love at first sight has grown and become a tree, and others have sheltered under it. This is a better thing than if it had been broken off, pressed in a book and left there to awaken tender memories. I feel the hand of Destiny here, too, and am grateful that such love has been mine. But that other, that 'imaginary' love with which a friend used to twit me, when he read my prose-poems, is a part of life too. It is not unreal, for our whole life is a mental life, an imaginative life, and the sharper the apprehensions of the imagination the more truly do we seem to live. It is only when men cease to admit this that they seem to be, not merely moving towards the grave, but already dead.